DE GAULLE

THE RULER

By the same author

DE GAULLE
THE REBEL 1890–1944

DE GAULLE

THE RULER
1945–1970

Jean Lacouture

*Translated from the French
by Alan Sheridan*

W·W·NORTON & COMPANY
New York   London

Copyright © 1991, 1986, 1985 by Jean Lacouture
Translation Copyright © 1991 HarperCollins Publishers Ltd.
First American Edition, 1992

Printed in the United States of America

Manufacturing by the Haddon Craftsmen.

ISBN 0-393-03084-9

W • W • Norton & Company, Inc., 500 Fifth Avenue, New York, N.Y. 10110
W • W • Norton & Company Ltd., 10 Coptic Street, London WC1A 1PU

1 2 3 4 5 6 7 8 9 0

Contents

V THE WORLD STAGE

VI THE STATE GENERAL

*PUBLISHER'S NOTE: Sources are given in the notes at the back of the book; footnotes are the author's unless supplied by the translator, when they are indicated thus: (trs.).

Preface

The abridgement of my biography of General de Gaulle into two volumes which, in its original French version had comprised three, caused me to formulate reservations which the present publisher had the elegance – may I say, "*le fair-play*"? – to publish as a preface at the beginning of the first volume.

I will not repeat it here. The excellence of the translation and presentation of the first volume has given me complete confidence in those who have taken on the responsibility of presenting the present volume to its British and American readers.

JEAN LACOUTURE
September, 1991

Acknowledgements

It is usual, on completing such a task, to thank those who have assisted the author, by meeting him or by corresponding with him, by answering this or that question, by providing this or that piece of information, by lending him this or that document. However, on this occasion, though I have already paid my, albeit modest, respects in the course of the book, I must abandon the usual courtesies: firstly because far too many people (some 350 in fact) have been so kind as to see me or write to me and, secondly, because some of them have asked to remain anonymous. My acknowledgements must then, for once, be collective. My gratitude, however, is nonetheless great for that.

But I must express my special gratitude to those who were willing to read my book, whole or in part, not, of course, that this implies the slightest responsibility for it: Paul Flamand, Jean-Claude Guillebaud, Georges Buis, Jean Laloy, Alfred Grosser, Jean-Marie Soutou and François Goguel. Their competence has spared me many errors. Those that remain are mine.

And how can I thank those who, once again, lavished their attentions on my manuscript, assisted with the notes and the bibliography? They include Marie-Christine Gerber, Catherine Grünblatt, Martine Tardieu, Dominique Miollan, Nicolas Aggiouri and, of course, Simonne Lacouture, my wife.

J.L.

The author and the publishers are grateful to the copyright holders for permission to reprint the following copyright material:

from *An Autobiography* by Abba Eban. Copyright © Abba Eban 1978. Reprinted by permission of Weidenfeld and Nicolson, London, and Scott Meredith Literary Agency, inc, 845 Third Avenue, New York, NY 10022

from *War Memoirs*, Vol. II, *Unity 1942-44* by Charles de Gaulle, translated from the French by Richard Howard. English translation © Simon and Schuster 1959. Reprinted by permission of Weidenfeld and Nicolson, London, and Simon and Schuster, New York

from *War Memoirs*, Vol. III, *Salvation 1944-46* by Charles de Gaulle, translated from the French by Richard Howard. English translation © Simon and Schuster 1960. Reprinted by permission of Weidenfeld and Nicolson, London, and Simon and Schuster, New York

from *Memoirs of Hope* by Charles de Gaulle, translated from the French by Terence Kilmartin. English translation © Weidenfeld and Nicolson 1971. Reprinted by permission of Weidenfeld and Nicolson, London

from *Churchill and De Gaulle* by Dr F. Kersaudy. Copyright © Dr F Kersaudy 1981. Reprinted by permission of HarperCollins Publishers Limited, London

from *The Troubled Partnership* by Henry Kissinger. Copyright © Henry Kissinger 1979. Reprinted by permission of McGraw Hill Publishing Co, New York

from *De Gaulle* by Bernard Ledwidge. Copyright © Bernard Ledwidge 1982. Reprinted by permission of Weidenfeld and Nicolson, London

from *Antimemoirs* by André Malraux, translated from the French by Terence Kilmartin. English translation copyright © Hamish Hamilton 1968. Reprinted by permission of Penguin Books, London

from *Leaders* by Richard M. Nixon. Copyright © Richard M Nixon, 1982. Reprinted by permission of Mcgraw Hill Publishing Co, New York

from *De Gaulle* by Alexander Werth. Copyright © Alexander Werth 1965. Reprinted by permission of Penguin Books, London, and Simon and Schuster, New York

I

POWER

CHAPTER ONE

"As God made me…"

The first shots were heard as the General's triumphant cortège, slowly parting the rejoicing crowd, entered the Place de la Concorde on its way from the Arc de Triomphe to Notre-Dame. It was nearly 4 p.m. on that "coronation" day, 26 August 1944.

The city was still swarming with enemies and well within reach of German artillery and aircraft. Was not "the man of 18 June" taking an almost insane risk in seeking, by such a demonstration of popular legitimation, to consolidate his heroic "legitimacy" of 1940 and thus forge "the unity of the nation"? Was the whole exercise to end in panic? Were the "political reefs" that he had felt under his feet as he walked the full length of the Champs-Elysées even sharper than he had suspected?

It took twenty minutes or so for the ill-assorted cortège of jeeps, "half-tracks", tanks and old Citroën *tractions avant* – led by the open car that de Gaulle had insisted on using – to reach Notre-Dame, after a brief stop-off in front of the Hôtel de Ville. In the meantime, those who were already being called the *tireurs de toit*, or roof marksmen, seemed to have given up any idea of upsetting the great celebration.

But the head of the provisional government had no sooner set foot on the cathedral square than the gunfire resumed louder than ever. He entered the nave through a mass of bodies that had thrown themselves to the ground in fear:

> It was immediately apparent to me that this was one of those contagious shooting matches which high feeling sometimes sets off in over-excited troops on the occasion of some fortuitous or provoked* incident. Nothing could be more important than for me not to yield to the panic of the crowd. I therefore went into the cathedral. Without electricity, the organ was silent, and the shots echoed inside the structure.[1]

As he took up position in front of the chair reserved for him, General Leclerc, waving his baton, stopped one of his soldiers firing in the direction of the vaults, while Claude Hettier de Boislambert snatched the pistol from a man who was pointing it at one of the stained-glass windows, convinced, he said, that someone was hiding behind it.[2] Nevertheless, bullets whistled through the air and pieces of stone flew off, wounding some people.

What the ceremony may have lacked in calm, it gained in eloquence: what a

*The word is highly significant. See below.

leader, people would say, to emerge intact from that new "murder in the cathedral"! Those who tried to disturb the "crowning" of the man who embodied Free France had nothing to show for their pains. If provocation was intended, it was certainly a miscalculation: everyone knew that Charles de Gaulle was always at his best when confronting danger.

In any case, however fervent his *Magnificat* may have been, the General still had his eyes peeled and his suspicions alerted. Who was responsible? Ten years later, when writing his *Mémoires de guerre*, he felt able to point the finger. Rejecting the hypothesis of "snipers on the roofs, German soldiers or members of the Vichy militia", Charles de Gaulle laid the blame squarely on "people who wanted to justify the maintenance of revolutionary power and the deployment of physical force". It seemed that "an attempt had been made to create the impression that threats still lurked in the shadows, that the resistance organizations must remain armed and vigilant, that COMAC,* the Parisian Liberation Committee (CPL) and the neighbourhood committees were still to take the responsibility for police action, justice and the purging of collaborators in order to protect the people against dangerous conspiracies."[3]

Communist tactics could hardly be described more clearly. Another witness, Alphonse Juin, declared that "there were certainly provocateurs", but refrained from going further. General Alain de Boissieu, Charles de Gaulle's son-in-law** and faithful interpreter, in a book published twenty-five years later, repeats the testimony of Charles Luizet. The day before, Luizet had taken up his post as prefect of police. Having, he says, "personally questioned the *tireurs de toit*" and convinced himself that their aim had been an attempt on the life of General de Gaulle, he concluded that they were "neither militiamen nor foreign agents", but "opponents of the CNR".***[4]

Most historians and witnesses are much more prudent. They refuse to give any explanation, not having found one. Adrien Dansette,† the best historian of the liberation of Paris, also dismisses any idea that it might have been extreme right-wing provocation, and nor does he allow one to believe it was the work of extreme left-wing activists, on the grounds that, if one were to accept it, one would have to "accept far more than I am prepared to do".[5]

Whatever version one adopts, the important thing is the meaning attributed to the affair by Charles de Gaulle. It sums up what was then his entire political strategy, a strategy to which, over the next quarter of a century, he hardly added anything: disordered acts can only be the work of people who can never realize their aims, or the work of evil-minded intriguers. Any disagreement with him can only be an affront to national unity. De Gaulle's insistence on a legitimacy based on the principle of unanimity is both contradicted and consoled, in any case complemented, by a constant dramatization: the man of the nation is perpetually at odds with the demons of division. He was all too well aware that the principle of

*Committee of Military Action of the National Council of the Resistance. (trs.)
**He married de Gaulle's daughter, Elisabeth. (trs.)
***Conseil national de la Résistance, in which there was a very ardent anti-Gaullist minority.
†Brother-in-law of one of General Leclerc's closest colleagues, and as such particularly well placed to obtain the most reliable information.

unanimity might decline into inertia if not enriched, if not given muscle, by some dramatic contradiction. So the first government of the new era would be one of "national unanimity" and each contact between the liberator and the masses would be described as if it were a sort of mystical immersion. Here is de Gaulle himself on the matter:

> "Here I am, as God made me!" is what I tried to communicate to those around me. "As you see, I am your brother, at home among the members of his family, but also a leader who cannot compromise with duty nor bend under his burden." Beneath the cheers and behind the stares, I saw the image of the people's soul. For the great majority, what mattered was the emotion provoked by this spectacle, exalted by this presence. In the heart of the multitude I was imbued with its joys and its cares. I felt especially close to those who, celebrating France's salvation but conscious that her inner demons had reawakened, suffered on her behalf the lucid anxiety of love![6]

Charles de Gaulle refused to declare a new republic and never ceased to affirm the continuity of the State. But it is clear that what the country was being given was very far from the Republic whose "survival" he was claiming to ensure. The power that he then seized, with the enthusiastic consent of a majority, was very different from the power that Lebrun, Daladier and Reynaud had exercised four years before.

At first he wanted to define his own role in accordance with the spirit of continuity. This was why he set up his government in the Ministry of War, 14 Rue Saint-Dominique, once the splendid townhouse of the Maréchal Duc de Richelieu. It had been acquired just before the Revolution by one of Louis XVI's last and most unpopular ministers, Loménie de Brienne. Later it became the home of "Madame Mère", Laetitia Bonaparte,* who, in her blue boudoir, often settled the conflicts between the various clans of her offspring. At the Restoration, Clarke, Duc de Feltre, moving from the service of the emperor to that of the Bourbons, made it the Ministry of War.

There, in November 1917, Georges Clemenceau chose to concentrate his governmental activities in a large grey office on the first floor – where, twenty-two years later, first Daladier, then Paul Reynaud, had tried to imitate him. It was on the other side of a huge waiting-room known as the billiard room, in the Hôtel de Brienne, that Under-Secretary of State Charles de Gaulle had hastily set up his office on 6 June 1940.

For someone intent on reviving and embodying the State, it was a splendid setting, inhabited by illustrious shades and precise memories, more stylish than the Elysée, nobler and more approachable than Matignon.** The choice, attentive as the General was to his own history – almost as much as to that of the nation – was judicious. By setting himself up in the Rue Saint-Dominique, de Gaulle wanted to be "at the centre". But, unlike many occupants of the place, it was not there that he was to live.

*Napoleon Bonaparte's mother. (trs.)
**The Elysée is the presidential palace, Matignon the home of the Prime Minister. (trs.)

Very soon a fine house was found for him on the edge of Paris at Neuilly. Yvonne de Gaulle remarked to Claude Mauriac that the place was "a degree above what I would have liked".[7] Charles de Gaulle, on the other hand, seems to have regarded it as quite natural that the State, in his person, should be accommodated in some style.

De Gaulle now had to confront the various power groups that had emerged out of the national uprising. He was all too aware of the aims of his allies and impatient to put a national seal on the victory. The image of the adored liberator – who was nevertheless still regarded by many and would continue to be regarded as a sort of regicide, a rebel, a usurper of the legitimate power of Marshal Pétain – was to re-emerge as crises arose and important decisions were made. For the time being, there was no prospect of a split between the man and his destiny. But already that tiny gap, which was to widen with the years, was beginning to appear. On 4 September, Claude Mauriac (who had been head of his private office for a week) notes a conversation between two of the General's closest colleagues, Geoffroy Chaudron de Courcel and Claude Guy, about what should be done should "the General feel obliged to withdraw tomorrow morning". Commenting thirty-three years later on this note, which he had rediscovered in his diaries, Mauriac regards it as "scarcely credible". De Gaulle was so conscious of his own legitimacy, so convinced that he had been incorporated into the very substance of France, that he regarded himself as invested with a limitless power of involvement and disengagement.

This de Gaulle, whom he referred to in the third person and regarded as outside himself, ahead of himself, like some column of fire that preceded him and inspired him, could not be tied down; and because the French could not be deprived of this guide for long, he had from time to time to drag himself away from the seat of power and take to the wilderness for his true stature and the sheer gap left by his absence to be perceived.

In that huge *Kriegspiel* that was Charles de Gaulle's life, what is the most constant, the most repetitive feature? For all the significant variations that his life underwent, from 1919 (when he thought of resigning from the army*) to 1969 (the statement of 28 April**), Charles de Gaulle, a rebel promoted sovereign by the decree of a very ancient history, seems always to have lived between two exiles: to be "the coming man", but also the man who could, at any moment, withdraw, freeing "de Gaulle" from the rabble and preserving "the symbol" for other times: this perhaps is the most important feature of that great nomad, settled at last, but not yet fenced in. This double nature, on the one hand symbolic, on the other active, was constantly to come into play within him and around him. It is one thing to be France; it is another to act on her behalf. At Vichy, the two functions had been separated and carried out by two men. Now, for the next seventeen months, a single man was to perform both functions. Until the German capitulation, in May

---

*See *De Gaulle: The Rebel 1890–1944*, p. 53. (trs.)
**De Gaulle's resignation as head of State; see below, p. 575.

1945, the stress was more usually placed on the symbolic aspect of the man of 18 June. With the advent of peace, it was to be the other function that emerged, until the contradiction between the two led him to retire.

In this de Gaulle one particular feature is worth mentioning, one that says a great deal about his hierarchy of values: the interest that he showed in men of letters and in their opinions. The degree to which, for him, the literary creator enjoyed more prestige than the politician, the economist or the soldier has often been remarked on. Only a few hours after his old house at Vémars* had been evacuated by its last occupant, François Mauriac was surprised to see a presidential car pull up in front of his door. His two sons had come to fetch him: the next day, 1 September 1944, the General was expecting him to lunch in the Rue Saint-Dominique. Twenty years later, in his *De Gaulle*, Mauriac describes how, when the General was announced, he had to "lean against the wall in order not to stumble", that he had "a new sense of what true greatness and true glory were".[8] But in his account of that meeting there is a suggestion of disappointment on Mauriac's part, due not to the man, but to the turn that their conversation took. Instead of taking Mauriac into his confidence on the subject of his strategic aims and his anxieties for the state of the world, the General chose to talk to him above all about a renovation of the Académie Française. What they talked about was not Roosevelt or Stalin, but André Gide and his moods.

Three days later, it was the turn of Paul Valéry to be received at the Rue Saint-Dominique. His notebooks give a delightful account of the meeting:

4 September 44: invited to dinner at the Ministry of War by de Gaulle, which I wasn't expecting. The General entered quietly. Remarkably tall. Two stars. Very strong nose. Brown-haired dolichocephal. Gaze fairly powerful and heavy. I found him much pleasanter than I expected. Does not seem any more informed about things than we are. Indeed very reserved about political questions. Doesn't seem to pay any attention to the arrests being carried out at the moment. As for the war, gives his impression of it several times: the ease of the Americans' advance is explained by an agreement between them and the Germans (perhaps, too, with Stalin, who isn't moving in the East), who would liquidate the Hitler–Himmler gang in order to make peace earlier (the fact is that the progress is scandalously rapid). I speak of Pétain.**

After dinner (which is good), sits me down on a sofa next to him and we talk. I still don't have a clear idea of the General, who seems fairly secretive. Difficult to carry out a chemical analysis that would separate the man, the soldier and the politician. It seems to me, however, that he has the concentration of a man who is playing one of the most complicated games. He holds a lot of cards in the game being played at the moment.[9]

*A town thirty miles from Paris. (trs.)
**Valéry was on very close terms with Pétain.

On 7 September, it was Georges Duhamel's turn:* in particular, he is keen to report that, on the subject of Pétain, it was de Gaulle's intention to give him a residence in the Midi, "where he would wait for death to come and take him".

Before long, Georges Bernanos** arrived. And then André Malraux, of course.*** As for Paul Claudel,† he remained confined at Brangues, in the Alps. But, on 19 September, the General replied to a message of congratulations from him in a very warm letter, followed, two months later, after receiving the celebrated "Ode to the General" (which de Gaulle insisted on placing at the head of all the documents concerning that period in the third volume of his *Mémoires de guerre*), a message in which he confided to the poet: "I believe that France is regaining her power. But what she needs now is serenity."[10]

Animosity with regard to the Allies, mistrust towards the Resistance, and confidence in the support of the masses were the three main elements in Gaullist thinking at the time of the Liberation. They are to be found again and again in the diary of his private secretary and in his own correspondence.

The fact that the liberation of Paris and his installation in power should have done so little to diminish Charles de Gaulle's prejudices against the "Anglo-Saxons" – the Americans and the British – may come as a surprise and a shock. But it should be remembered that it was not until 23 October 1944 that Washington and London formally recognized a government that so obviously represented the majority of its people.

With the Americans, the pretexts for quarrels were endless. After the ruffling of susceptibilities caused by General Gerow's insistence on wanting to remove the 2nd Armoured Division from the celebrations of the "coronation", a further disagreement arose. Had de Gaulle, Koenig or another French officer really asked for American reinforcements to keep order in Paris after Leclerc's troops had left for Strasbourg? In *Crusade in Europe*, General Eisenhower stated that this was the case, even displaying some amusement at the fact that a government, so touchy where independence was concerned, should have been capable of making such a request.

When *Crusade in Europe* appeared, de Gaulle denied that any such request had been made: "I was, of course, there to greet the American divisions passing through Paris on their way to further combat, but I had in no sense asked for them." In *Is Paris Burning?* Dominique Lapierre and Larry Collins declare that such support had certainly been requested by General Koenig (who, dining with Leclerc on 25 August, confided to his companions: "We have only just avoided a new Paris Commune"[11]).

Nevertheless, the head of the provisional government was not anxious to accommodate himself to his allies. At the first meal Claude Mauriac ever had with de

*Georges Duhamel (1884–1966), the novelist. (trs.)
**Georges Bernanos (1888–1948), the writer whose messages of support for the Free French had been broadcast from London. (trs.)
***André Malraux (1901–1976), the writer and Minister of Culture from 1959–69. (trs.)
†Paul Claudel (1868–1955), the writer and diplomat. (trs.)

Gaulle, on 31 August, de Gaulle exclaimed: "Make no mistake, they [the Americans and British] won't go until we kick them out." On 5 September, again to his private secretary, he remarked: "The Allies are betraying us, they're betraying Europe, the bastards. But they'll pay me for it. In fact, they're already beginning to pay for it, especially the British. Americans taking Brussels! What nerve . . . They'd have taken Paris if I hadn't been there".[12]

In the case of the Resistance organizations, the General's attitude was very similar to his mistrust of foreign powers. Before describing this struggle for the hegemony of the State, for the supremacy of structures over historical turmoil, it is worth noting at least one example of his vigilance. On 31 August, in the second letter he wrote to Yvonne de Gaulle after his installation in Paris, he said: "Things are settling down satisfactorily here. Of course, certain elements have tried to take advantage of the inevitable confusion and, if need be, to create it, to pull the blanket their way."[13]

After the dramatic day of the "coronation", those who judged, wrote about and claimed to form public opinion believed that it was on 12 September that he finally manifested himself as both the symbol and holder of political power. A sort of meeting had been organized at the Palais de Chaillot at which the head of the provisional government was to define, in the presence of the Resistance leaders and the senior officials of the new State, his plans for the short term as well as his philosophy of power. "I did so all the more sharply," he was to write in his *Mémoires de guerre*, "since, in an atmosphere where voices were already murmuring, I felt obliged to call things by their real names."[14]

For three days France had had a new government. Since the day before, the métro had been working. The day before that, François Mauriac had made a strong criticism of the excesses of political "justice". The body of the freed nation was still racked with pain. The General stood with his back against the red part of the enormous tricolour flag that had been set up as a background for the meeting (this could hardly have been an oversight on the part of the organizers of the ceremony) between Jules Jeanneney,* his new Minister of State, a symbol of the continuity of the Republic, and Georges Bidault,** who was there not so much as the new Foreign Minister, but as chairman of the CNR and whose speech was a sober homage to his dead comrades.

The speech was a summary of de Gaulle's thinking in the days immediately following the "coronation". The three chapter headings of his policy were stated in all their rigour: the authority of the central State could not tolerate any reservations or exceptions, civil or military; the victory over the Germans, and the growing part that she would have played in it, would give France the right to return to the front rank of nations; now freed, the French must, through a revival of production and a fairer distribution of wealth, recover the means of a decent life.

*Jules Jeanneney, the President of the Senate in 1940 who, more than any other, came to represent the democratic institutions of France during the war. See *De Gaulle: The Rebel 1890–1944*, p. 348. (trs.)

**Georges Bidault, the distinguished Resistance leader who was the first President of the Conseil national de la Résistance (CNR). See *De Gaulle: The Rebel 1890–1944*, p. 483. (trs.)

But however small the concessions he made to the organizers of the national uprising, he was well aware that many of these players in the Liberation were still restive.

Hearing the cheers and acclamations, I might have thought myself trans-ported back to the unanimous assemblies at the Albert Hall* and Brazzaville.** Yet something different in the tone of the enthusiasm, a certain restraint in the applause, the signs and winks exchanged among those present, the looks on their faces as they responded to what I said, gave me a strong sense that the "politicians", whether the old ones or the new ones, gave me only qualified approval...

More than ever, therefore, I had to find support among the people rather than among the élites – they would tend to come between the people and me. My popularity was like capital that would pay for the disappointments, inevitable in the midst of ruins.

But he was not alone. As he set about shaping a new State on the assumption that victory was assured, he was to form, under the fine ceilings of the Hôtel de Brienne, a trusted and stylish team of men with whom he would work. One of his faithful supporters, René Brouillet, points out one of the General's peculiarities in this regard:

The General made a very clear distinction between the men whom he had gathered around him, from whom he expected special devotion and absolute discretion, and those whom he had appointed to government posts – minis-ters, prefects, various administrators. The General expected the latter to embody in a decisive way the functions that they had been given, realizing that they were susceptible to many different forces and influences...

But, in the case of his personal staff, those known as the "entourage", he considered that he had made a very particular pact with them, which I can only call a "transparent commitment". It was not so much a complete crushing of self as a sort of Franciscan-type humility. He wanted to be surrounded by men doing their jobs properly, even if, on occasion, they expressed their own point of view.[15]

That first circle, made up of trusty and trusted men – his *maison* – was formed between late August and early October 1944. We have already glimpsed two or three of them – Gaston Palewski,*** Claude Guy, Claude Mauriac.

The grand vizier of this harem was Gaston Palewski, of course, the oldest companion – if one excepts Lucien Nachin, who at this time published the first book on de Gaulle,† but whom the General refrained from summoning.

Although Palewski ran this varied cohort from Clemenceau's office, the other depository of great secrets, Geoffroy de Courcel, who had no specific function,

*In London, where he addressed meetings, especially on 11 November 1942; see *De Gaulle: The Rebel 1890–1944*, p. 403.
**See *De Gaulle: The Rebel 1890–1944*, pp. 505–7. (trs.)
***Gaston Palewski: See *De Gaulle: The Rebel 1890–1944*, pp. 105, 240–60. (trs.)
†L. Nachin, *Charles de Gaulle, général de France* (Paris, Berger-Levrault, 1944).

was a diplomatic counsellor of sorts, entrusted with delicate missions to the Allies – and there was no shortage of these for the former second-in-command of the Free French, that impeccable and constant companion, to deal with.

Almost comparable was the influence of Claude Guy, a swaggering flying officer discovered by de Gaulle in Algiers, full of ideas, whose fervour and fruitful imagination appealed to the General. It was he who was to organize the de Gaulle–Malraux meeting, which was to have such important results. It was he who had the idea of calling in Claude Mauriac, a childhood friend, to whom the General immediately became attached, not only because the presence at his side of the son of one of the great French writers flattered his reverence for literature.

Alongside General de Rancourt, Etienne Burin des Roziers (a diplomatic counsellor soon to be entrusted with the highest responsibilities), Jean Donnedieu de Vabres (*auditeur* at the Conseil d'Etat), and Professor Desmouliez (a law professor), were three men who were soon to affirm their strong personalities: René Brouillet, Louis Vallon and Georges Pompidou.

The first, a graduate of the Ecole Normale Supérieure and a Catholic, was a long-time friend of Georges Bidault, with whom he had worked at the CNR. Louis Vallon, a graduate of the Ecole Polytechnique, a member of the Resistance from the outset, had been Chief of the non-military branch of the BCRA.* Close to the Socialist party, active in the Popular Front, Vallon was in charge of economic and financial affairs in the Rue Saint-Dominique. As for Pompidou, none of whose activities for the past four years particularly recommended him to de Gaulle's entourage, it has often been said that he owed his presence to the fact that the General once remarked that he needed a "*normalien* who could write".** Georges Pompidou's minutes and memos at least had the merit of reflecting reality and of acknowledging that the euphoria of the early days had given way to growing anxiety.

On 10 September, Georges Izard, one of the most infamous young left-wing leaders of this time, spoke to Claude Mauriac of "general anxiety". And on 30 September, Albert Camus, declaring that "we are emerging from euphoria", thought fit to add in *Combat*: "We are under no obligation to constantly approve of General de Gaulle." François Mauriac was much more explicit with his son, to whom he confided his anxiety on 11 September: "The General's entourage should at least make a show of confidence. For some days now, anxiety and doubt have been spreading."[16] And this just two weeks after the exalting day of 26 August!

Of course, those days also saw the first supplies of coal reaching Paris, the telephone lines being connected with Toulouse, the first trains leaving Paris for Rouen and Tours. But, although the blood was now flowing once again through the great, battered city, something bitter was already slipping into what above all was a revolt of the mind. Philippe Viannay, creator of Défense de la France, was soon to publish *Nous sommes les rebelles*[17] under the name of "Indomitus", a pamphlet expressing an extreme set of demands and deep dissatisfaction with the liberator. It was the first solemn public questioning, by a former colleague, of the power Charles de Gaulle had seized and of what he had done with it. Indomitus did not spare the Resistance. He expressed a major complaint of it:

*Bureau Central de Renseignement et d'Action Militaire (BCRA).
**Pompidou was not a particularly good writer, and said so himself.

It was the Resistance that brought de Gaulle to power. What has given de Gaulle the position to assume that power are his international contacts, his diplomatic successes, the extraordinary vigour with which he defends French interests. But the Resistance has brought him what he would never have been able to have without it: the sacrifice of hundreds of thousands of French men and women who immolated themselves for a cause.

What seems to have been the government's principal idea, as much before as after the Liberation, was to embrace and to unify the French nation through the work of the Resistance. One might say that it has looked for its support elsewhere than in what the Resistance had been able to offer, finding in the Resistance too many critical minds. Let it not be said that this government is based on the men of the Resistance. We shall say rather, without any perfidy, that an attempt has been made to associate the men of the Resistance with this government, I would almost go as far as to say to compromise some of them with it.[18]

No trace has survived of Charles de Gaulle's reaction to these words, which could not have escaped his attention. But, having noted the first rumblings of discontent that could be heard before the end of 1944, one should also remember Charles de Gaulle's feelings towards the Resistance and public opinion, here described today by Michel Debré:

General de Gaulle was astonished at how little public opinion realized that the Liberation and the resurrection of France as a State was little short of miraculous. The word came readily to his lips. And he considered the French to be very forgetful, very frivolous not to wonder at the fact that, despite their trials, their destitution, they were once again in the camp of the victors, living in a country that, though suffering from deprivation, had been restored in its unity, its integrity, and was now capable of resuming its eminent place in the concert of nations.[19]

CHAPTER TWO

The State

What was the most important task for the French government? To continue with the war? To ensure the survival of the French people? To guarantee public order, rebuild institutions, re-establish justice under the law? Where was one to begin? If it is true that governing is first of all a matter of establishing a hierarchy between various matters of urgency, no statesman was ever subjected to more various, more competing and more urgent demands than the head of the French provisional government in August 1944.

Everything that can be learnt about Charles de Gaulle shows that among the innumerable tasks facing him at the time when he took possession of power in a liberated Paris, he saw his supreme task as quite simply to restore the authority of the State. He believed that he had been called above all to unite it, to reconstruct it and to give it new impetus, for everything depended upon this.

One of the constant themes of those who write about the period immediately after the Liberation is the uncertainty as to whether it was really a "restoration of order" or a "revolution". Some are indignant that General de Gaulle, reappearing in the chaotic France of August 1944, did not become the Varlin of that Commune, or even the Vergniaud of that Convention.* This is to forget that the war was still going on, the American impact, the Communist challenge, the deep splits in the national community – and of course the temperament and outlook of de Gaulle himself. In any case, to believe that the man who, in June 1940, had unleashed not the Resistance (which was the work of many who were unaware of his initiative) but the questioning of Vichyism, is to ignore not only the history and personality of Charles de Gaulle, but that of the popular uprisings and their relation to the State in French history: whether white, blue or red, or blue-white-red, civil or military, secular or religious, the State has never taken long to absorb and control any movement rising from below.

When the balance sheet is drawn up regarding what was done between August 1944 and January 1946, it will be seen that the "revolutionary" elements did not play an inconsiderable part. Taking the first few months of the new regime, the period when the revolution supposedly failed, one is tempted to sum up the dilemma between regaining control and revolution with the formula "regaining control of a revolution". One can hardly deny the revolutionary character of the movement that swept away the apparatus of power that had been set up four years before at Vichy.

*Louis Varlin (1839–71), the Secretary of the French Section of the First International and the delegate in charge of finance under the Paris Commune of 1871. Pierre Vergniaud (1753–93), who, along with Mirabeau, was one of the French Revolution's most powerful orators. (trs.)

On 25 August, Charles de Gaulle refused to "proclaim the Republic" on the grounds that it had never ceased to exist. The day before, he had said to Philippe Viannay that France was not a country "that is beginning", but a country "that is carrying on". Was not the State, the object of all his cares, to be defined – unlike regimes, systems, dynasties and governments – by permanence and continuity?

If France was to "carry on", however, it could not perpetuate the Third Republic, still less Vichy. So the forces of the Liberation had to make it quite clear that it was the heir of neither; that its legitimacy had other sources than the inheritance of the old exiled Marshal or the institutional mechanisms that had seized up before the disaster of 1940. But it should be noted that although, in March 1942, Christian Pineau had had great difficulty in persuading de Gaulle not to reject the Third Republic and Vichy in equal measure,* in September 1944 de Gaulle made the man who embodied the republican spirit, Jules Jeanneney, his Minister of State and ignored the Marshal's final offer to make him, de Gaulle, the heir of Vichy. A week after his forced departure into exile, on 11 August, Philippe Pétain had given Admiral Auphan, his former Naval Minister, a secret mission to contact de Gaulle with a view to finding a formula for the transfer of power that would make it possible "to reconcile all French people of good faith" and "to avoid a civil war", on condition that "the principle of legitimacy" that he, Pétain, still claimed to embody was safeguarded. Auphan arrived in Paris on 12 August and, through General Giraud, sent General de Gaulle a "memorandum on the need for a legitimate transfer of power". This took place the day after the triumph in the Champs-Elysées. Auphan waited in vain. This is de Gaulle's own comment: "Without in any way doubting the importance for the moral future of the nation of the fact that in the end Pétain has fallen to de Gaulle, I can only respond to him with my silence."[1]

Was it conceivable, in the midst of the passions of that tumultuous summer, that Charles de Gaulle should deal, if only in formal terms, with a regime against which he had established his own legitimacy, which he had denounced at the very outset as disloyal to its word and treasonous to the Republic? It is surprising that a man as intelligent as Admiral Auphan could have been under such an illusion.

A fundamentally symbolic undertaking like that of the Free French, making claim above all to the "moral dimension" of the anti-Nazi war, was not open to compromise. With Giraud in 1943, a temporary and not always easy cooperation had been achieved on the theme of the struggle against the occupier. But with the Reich defeated or about to be, what common denominator could be found between those who were fleeing from Vichy and those entering Paris? Neither Charles de Gaulle nor the Resistance at home was ready to accept such a synthesis. For them, Vichy and collaboration were lies and betrayals.

Admiral Auphan's proposal was condemned above all by reality. At the end of 1944, it was clear to all that the Vichy regime was facing utter annihilation. Suddenly, this French State, which had aroused so much devotion and won over the majority of the élites of France, was sinking without trace. From one day to

*De Gaulle had been adamant in 1942 that the Third Republic was politically bankrupt; see *De Gaulle: The Rebel 1890–1944*, p. 382. (trs.)

another, it had no one to defend it, no prefect, no police... There was nothing left but individuals taking flight.

It is worth quoting here the observation of the American historian, Crane Brinton,* then a member of a commission sent to France by the OSS. In his cable to Washington he wrote: "Vichy has vanished, like Lewis Carroll's cat, – it hasn't even left a trace. I don't need to tell you that the question of whether the de Gaulle government is 'accepted' does not even arise!"

As for the hard-core collaborators, those who had worked with the occupying forces (often, in fact, against Vichy, against what they called the Marshal's lack of backbone), they had no other course but to move across the Rhine. They would be tracked down later. But in the case of the cadres of Vichy, which had embodied that very broad Anglophobic and anti-Gaullist, but also increasingly anti-German tendency, it was as if Vichy had never existed. In short, Charles de Gaulle did not come up against any opposition from his direct predecessors when he came to the task of restoring the State. The authority of the Marshal had vanished as soon as de Gaulle had set foot on French soil. Those who had run the system had merged into the mass of people who had switched sides – or were trying to do so. Despite terrible confrontations between Resistance forces and the Milice, between the autumn of 1943 and the summer of 1944, there was to be no French civil war.

So, to unify the State, de Gaulle did not have to contend with Vichy. Nor would he have had to operate it in terms of the Third Republic, which had long since disappeared. But by refusing to proclaim a new Republic and by installing himself in the Ministry of War offices where he had been Under-Secretary of State in 1940, he did seem to be trying desperately to blow on the old Republic's ashes.

A symbolic transference of powers was not unnecessary: de Gaulle gives due place to the visit, on 13 October 1944, of the former President, Lebrun, who had come to add "the approval of the sad ghost of the Third Republic to the chorus". Lebrun made his position quite clear: "It is true that I have not formally resigned. To whom could I have sent a resignation, since there is no longer a National Assembly qualified to replace me? But I want you to be certain that you can count absolutely on my support." It is difficult to resist quoting the General's comment on that visit of sympathy and offered investiture. "I shook his hand with compassion and cordiality," the General writes, adding: "As the leader of the State, he had lacked two essential things: he was not a leader, and there was no State."[2]

He did not even have to impose the State so that he might buttress his position with the Allies. Of course, Washington and London were still trying to discuss the question of power in France with him** despite the fact that everybody in France now recognized de Gaulle as head of State. But, by and large, the problems now faced by the Allies were only of a strategic kind. They would no longer take the form of a discussion about French sovereignty. Questions concerning the sources and realities of the provisional government's power were no longer to be asked by those who were fighting on French soil and achieving its liberation. For the

*Professor Crane Brinton, whom I met at Harvard in 1966, never tired of expressing the pleasure he had felt when he discovered, in 1944, the extent to which Washington's official information on France was contradicted.
**The Allies continued in these discussions until 23 October 1944.

American, British or Canadian General Staffs, there was no other power than the one exercised or delegated by the General in the Rue Saint-Dominique – and, in early September, a high-ranking diplomat, Jefferson Caffery, was sent to represent the interests of the United States in Paris.

In resurrecting the unitary and centralized State, which was General de Gaulle's prime objective, opposition came not from his enemies, or his predecessors, or even his suspicious allies, but from those who had done so much to bring it about: the activists of the Resistance at home, at the heart of the CNR, or the various Liberation Committees.

The debate that began, usually in disguised forms (interrupted by sudden outbursts), between the head of the provisional government, who was hoping to institutionalize his pre-eminence, and the organizers of the underground struggle, who had undermined the authority of Vichy and greatly contributed to expelling the occupiers, brought to the fore questions concerning the origins and exercise of power: the ambiguous relations between the State and the Nation, the difficult distinction between the provisional and the insurrectional, the confused relationship between the respect owed to liberty and the exercise of power. In a few months Charles de Gaulle was to show that in France the nation tends spontaneously to pour itself into the mould of the State, which has seniority over it.

In his *Mémoires* the General speaks of the Liberation Committees with a sometimes contemptuous coldness that gives little idea of their role in this period. Francis-Louis Closon, who, sent from London, carried out several important missions in France before becoming one of the founders of the new power and assuming heavy responsibilities for the region of the Nord, writes:

> The intervention of the Committees made possible the transition, at minimum cost, from the collapse of Vichy to the new authority. It had saved France from the terror of the void. The contribution of the Committees had been largely positive and made it possible to reassure a population that felt abandoned. For those who knew how to use them, they could be brakes on excessive energy as well as powerful means of action.[3]

Mention should be made here of some of the passages of arms between the various bodies emerging from the Resistance and the man of London, in which General de Gaulle's power was forged, but also in which his relations with competing forces, relations that led to the withdrawal of 20 January 1946, were established. To begin with, there was the meeting with the most powerful Resistance leader, Pierre Villon. He was one of the leaders of the Communist Party* and of the Front National, and one of the main organizers of COMAC, a man of determination and convictions, who, more than any other (apart from his comrade Charles Tillon, the commander-in-chief of the Franc-tireurs et partisans, the Resistance movement), had the support behind him to stand up to Charles de Gaulle. The General was quite aware of this.

In the morning of 28 August, two days after his "coronation", General de

*Parti communiste français (PCF). (trs.)

Gaulle summoned COMAC and the General Staff of the Free French Forces (FFIs) to the Rue Saint-Dominique. Villon's account is suggestive:

> Flying-Officer Guy asked the FFI officers to stand like a row of onions, in hierarchical order, with the members of COMAC standing apart. As he came in, de Gaulle declared: "There are a lot of colonels here!" He shook the officers' hands and asked each of them: "What is your job?" One of them said that he was a steel worker. "Well, you must go back to the steel works," he told him. Another was a teacher. "You must go back to school." In this way he implicitly announced his decision to dissolve the FFI.[4]

During the afternoon of the same day, de Gaulle received the members of the CNR. Jacques Debû-Bridel, who represented the moderates in the CNR, tells how Pierre Villon "pleaded...the cause of our shadow army, the need not to dilute it in the mass of the regular army, not to crush its enthusiasm," but without success.[5] That evening, COMAC held a press conference during which Villon made a "lively protest" against de Gaulle's decision.

The next day, de Gaulle received the leader of COMAC again, flanked this time by Georges Bidault, the chairman of the CNR: "Monsieur Villon, I know what role you have played. I am not unaware that you are not an ambitious man. However...[a pause, then] I would like to offer you an important ministerial post...[another pause]...but COMAC is finished!"

If we are to believe General Billotte, then appointed by de Gaulle to command the 10th Infantry Division, known as the "Paris division", 90 per cent of which consisted of the capital's FFI, these setbacks did not lead Pierre Villon to resign. No sooner had he been put at the head of this "problem" division than Billotte was summoned by General Koenig, Commander-in-Chief of the FFIs. "You will not be obeyed if you do not have the agreement of COMAC." No matter: Billotte, de Gaulle's former Chief of Staff, presented himself at Villon's Party headquarters, in the Rue de Varenne, a hundred yards from the Hôtel de Brienne.

Low walls, sandbags, barbed wire: it was like a film set of a fortress. The visitor was received by Villon: "I have come to tell you that I have been put in charge of the 10th Infantry Division." "Who appointed you?" "General de Gaulle, the head of government." "Never heard of him." Villon's irony was courteous, but heavy. There would be threats; above all, that integration would have to respect the personality of the *maquisards*. There would have to be regulations. But, in the end, Billotte was to have his regiment and they would get on well enough.[6]

And it was again Pierre Villon who appeared on the platform of the meeting of the Front National at the Mutualité on 29 September, launching the idea best calculated to arouse the General's mistrust: he invited the masses to "gather in patriotic assemblies and elect local committees to constitute the States General of the French Resistance". De Gaulle, in whose ears the words "States General" were not particularly welcome, let it be discreetly known to François Mauriac, through his son Claude, that he was "displeased" at his presence at the head of an organization of which he was to say, a month later, that it was "working against France".[7]

The debate on the unification of the military forces, the contradictions between the Gaullist centre and the periphery of the Resistance, were not the only obstacles to the reconstituting of the State. Until the country could be consulted – one tenth of it was still occupied and over two million prisoners and deportees would still have to wait ten months before being repatriated – it was important to create a government that not only governed, but also represented the full spectrum of public opinion.

When it sat at Algiers, the provisional government had already been enlarged to include the mainland resistance represented by Henri d'Astier and Henri Frenay, among others. But it was important, the General believed, to go much further. As long as he was in control, he could make up a team that was broadly open to the various tendencies, though he was aware that the entry of CNR leaders into his government would change the power ratios between that body and his own power. Calling on Socialists, Communists, Radicals, *modérés* and Christian Democrats, he claimed to be giving the country a cabinet of "national unanimity".

De Gaulle's Cabinet, formed on 8 September 1944 and presented to the public the next day, looked pretty impressive. It contained some of the men who had led the most dangerous combat against the occupiers, some of the most able of the Resistance leaders who had operated from outside the country, and several men who had in various ways taken up positions against Vichy and the occupation.

An attentive examination of the remarkable two-page document in which de Gaulle wrote the names and political allegiances of those whom he intended to summon, shows the extent to which the head of the provisional government was still feeling his way. The spellings are sometimes unsure and the choices hesitant. Although both lists are headed by the names of Jules Jeanneney, as Minister of State, and of Georges Bidault, who was to be given Foreign Affairs, one cannot but notice that the General had first chosen Alexandre Parodi for the Ministry of the Interior,* Thierry d'Argenlieu, an old Christian Democratic leader, for the Navy (which was eventually to go to Louis Jacquinot**); and that he had expected to create a Ministry of Armaments and a Ministry of Youth and Sports.

Two remarks might be made on the subject of ideological allegiances. First, there was a concern for carefully calculated balance. He under-represented the Communist Party in relation to other organizations (though it was over-represented in the higher echelons of the Resistance), but he took in two of its leaders. Secondly, he did well by the "Christian Democratic" tendency, offering it six portfolios. In this way the General was merely acknowledging, of course, the exceptional role played in the Resistance by such men as François de Menthon, Bidault and Pierre-Henri Teitgen.***

As for Communist participation, everything was settled on 6 September, two

*Alexandre Parodi, who had become de Gaulle's delegate-general in France in April 1944. See *De Gaulle: The Rebel 1890–1944*, p. 533. (trs.)

**Louis Jacquinot, a conservative deputy from Lorraine, well known in the years of the Third Republic. (trs.)

***See *De Gaulle: The Rebel 1890–1944*, pp. 379–81. (trs.)

days before the final formation of the government, during a visit to the Rue Saint-Dominique by Jacques Duclos.* Tillon** and Billoux*** were chosen.

But who, in fact, had chosen Tillon? De Gaulle or Duclos? It may be thought that de Gaulle had wanted to call on the services of the first of the Communists to stand up against the occupiers, but Philippe Robrieux, who knows as much as anyone about the mechanisms of the Party, suggests that it was Duclos who chose Tillon, "because it was a devious, effective, if not elegant way of removing from the Party the most prestigious leader of the Resistance".[8] The fact remains that the PCF was content in the end with a portion of the government similar to those of the Christian Democrats and Socialists. Shyness was not in its nature. Some, such as Benoît Frachon and above all Auguste Lecoeur, who, like Tillon, had struggled against the occupiers before the USSR entered the war, protested against this treatment, demanding that, given the ratio of forces, "the Party can ask for more".[9]

The order went out from Maurice Thorez, the General Secretary of the PCF, that there was to be no immediate conflict with de Gaulle. For Stalin was haunted by the hypothesis of a reversal of alliances, whereby the Anglo-Saxons would join up with the forces of the Reich and move eastwards. They must not, therefore, be given the pretext of a political victory of the "Reds" in France. The PCF would therefore go along with de Gaulle until the time was ripe for Thorez's return from Moscow. Indeed, at his meeting with Duclos, on 6 September, de Gaulle promised to study the Thorez file with the greatest urgency.[10]

Something should also be said about the General's two most symbolic choices: that of Georges Bidault for Foreign Affairs and that of Jules Jeanneney for Minister of State. By giving the Quai d'Orsay to the chairman of the CNR, de Gaulle was killing three birds with one stone: he was honouring the CNR by giving its leader that most highly prized of the portfolios; he was expressing a sense of continuity by giving the greatest diplomatic responsibility to a history teacher and journalist who, long before joining the Resistance, had been a strong opponent in 1938 of the Munich Pact; and he was robbing the CNR of its figurehead while, at the same time, tying him up in an area in which he, de Gaulle, intended to be the master. The choice of Jules Jeanneney as Minister of State, as the Prime Minister's right-hand man, was also very significant. Indeed, Clemenceau's former colleague had rejected any compromise with Vichy; and when he was consulted by the London Committee in 1942, he gave a reply that was to serve, in a way, as the legal basis of the regime that was being set up.

The new government met for the first time in the late morning of 9 September at the Hôtel Matignon. The offices of its Cabinet Secretary, Louis Joxe, had already been set up there. Almost on his first day, Joxe was given a ticking-off. Coming from the Rue Saint-Dominique, the General saw a tricolour flag bearing the Cross of Lorraine floating over the building in the Rue de Varenne: "I have told you time and time again, the national flag is made up of three colours and no additional emblem!"[11] The Resistance and Free France had to give way to France.

*Jacques Duclos, who had led the PCF in metropolitan France. (trs.)
**Charles Tillon, leader of the FTP. (trs.)
***François Billoux, one of the communists whom de Gaulle had included in the CFLN. See *De Gaulle: The Rebel 1890–1944*, p. 512. (trs.)

General de Gaulle opened the session himself: "The government of the Republic, somewhat altered in its makeup, is resuming its work."

Pierre-Henri Teitgen has recounted how, won over after a few minutes by the authority, the ease, and the breadth of vision that de Gaulle displayed before his twenty ministers, he slipped a note to Bidault who was sitting next to him, bearing these four words: "This man is extraordinary." The piece of paper came back at once bearing the following question: "Was not Lucifer the most beautiful of the angels?"[12]

Neither de Gaulle's misfortunes nor his triumph seemed to have smoothed the roughness of a character that then seemed, to most people, to be unbearable. His talent had blossomed, his political experience seemed timeless, his vision and authority were dazzling. And, no sooner had he shown some signs of human tenderness, of which he was, like everybody else, capable, than some incident would occur, giving him a pretext to take a grip on himself, to close in on himself: it might be a communiqué from Eisenhower that had been published without his being previously informed, a Liberation Committee that had expressed an opinion without reference to the State, or some working-class organization getting its revenge. He would then thunder, threaten and close in on himself.

As President of the Council (as Prime Minister in other words), he would let his ministers speak, sometimes even going so far as to praise a particular line of argument, then present his own point of view, take the trouble to explain it, and deliver his verdict. "He was a good Prime Minister," Louis Joxe insists.[13] Neither conciliatory nor despotic, he presented himself as an arbiter between two theses or two methods, which he took up and refashioned to suit himself, and between which he made his decision. In this way he never gave in, because the eventual solution became his.* Everything was conducted with the greatest style, and usually with the clearest sense of the long-term interests of the State – which was not always the same thing as the short-term interests of the majority of citizens.

Mention should also be made of the General's rather dry sense of humour. Pierre Mendès France recounts how his colleague Pleven once suggested that some Alsatian banker, adversely affected by a measure that had been taken in the general interest, might receive some distinction or other by way of compensation. "Is the Minister of Finance suggesting that when we shut the brothels, we should hand out the Légion d'honneur to the pimps?" the General snapped.[14]

But how far did this government of "national unanimity" extend its authority? Louis Joxe, a former history teacher, declared:

> The government's authority was progressing, of course, but France was no longer anything more than an archipelago and the royal domain, that of the first Capetians. As far as Montlhéry and later as far as the Loire, communications seemed efficient enough, but what was happening beyond that? I can't say how moved I was when, in late September, the Matignon telephonist told me: "There's a call for you from Toulouse," and I heard the voice of an old friend, the Commissioner for the Republic, Pierre Bertaux, who indeed seemed as surprised as I was.[15]

*See Chapter 5.

If we are to have any idea of what was involved in reviving the State, some account must be given of the situation, as seen from the government's point of view. Not one of the country's ports was in use.* Not a single bridge was left to cross the Loire from Nevers to Saint-Nazaire, or to cross the Rhône between Lyon and the sea, or to cross the Seine to the west of Mantes. Less than a quarter of the available trucks were roadworthy, there was no telephone, no radio, no properly working airport. Lacking the means of transport and communications, the government could act only, during the first few months, by fits and starts.[16] Worse still, the barriers between the various geographical and social elements in the nation led to an extraordinary ignorance on the part of French citizens of one another.

Although they had some reason to know what collaboration was, the French, according to Michel Debré,[17] were almost entirely ignorant of what part the Resistance had played. Only a minority had actively taken part in it. Many had lent a hand. Many more had expressed some sympathy for it. But that great anonymous body had, of its nature, escaped social awareness: and its upsurge came as a surprise, especially as it was swollen to quite incredible proportions by impostors. What and who was to be believed, in that uncontrollable emergence? At this time France was living through a great tragic game in which fantasies took the place of opinion, rumour of memory, imputations of reputations.

This is how Charles de Gaulle described the situation in the provinces at the time when he undertook to take the country firmly in hand:

> The news that reached us from a vast majority of the departments showed them to be in tremendous confusion. No doubt the commissioners of the Republic and the prefects appointed in advance were fulfilling their functions. But they had the greatest difficulty restoring matters and men to theirs. Too much outrage, accumulated over four years, was fermenting under the lid to avoid an explosion. Many resistance units were proceeding with punishments and purges on their own. Naturally, political calculation, professional rivalry and personal reprisals took advantage of the circumstances, so that irregular arrests, arbitrary fines and summary executions added confusion to the chaos resulting from general destitution. The risk would have been a limited one if the Communist Party's policy had not been to exploit these disturbances in order to seize power in the provinces as it had tried to do in Paris.

I quote that last sentence even though it may reflect the state of mind of the writer of the *Mémoires de guerre* in 1954, not that of the head of the provisional government in 1944, because it sums up at least one of his "working hypotheses" of the time. But at least four of the Commissioners of the Republic whom I have asked the question, Michel Debré (Angers), Henry Ingrand (Clermont-Ferrand), Pierre Boursicot (Limoges) and Raymond Aubrac (Marseille), doubt whether the PCF seriously intended to use the political and military weapons at its disposal in autumn 1944 to seize power in Paris and the provinces.

*Bordeaux, the only port capable of working, was unable to function as the Germans still controlled the Gironde river.

In what was said forty years later by those who were the rebuilders of the State in the twenty great provincial centres at the time, problems of communication, supplies and justice were more pressing than any challenge to their authority by some Communist plot. In a letter sent to me in May 1984, Gaston Cusin, who was Commissioner of the Republic for the Aquitaine, explained the tasks facing his colleagues and himself at that time:

> The primary aim was *order*, the foundation of the State, the outcome of the Resistance, the condition of victory.
>
> Our main concern was the re-establishment of *transportation*, in order to recover economic, political and military unity.
>
> Our main problem was *supplies*, making sure that local resources would be where they should be, without the help of the government or any other regions.
>
> Apart from a few romantic maquis leaders who were cut off from one of the centres of the PCF (Moscow, London, Algiers, then Paris), I never believed that the Communists were planning a seizure of power in 1944 or 1945.[18]

De Gaulle, when reviewing the FFI battalions on 15 September, was touched "to see them attempting to look like regular units despite their disparities". He found that the inhabitants of Lyon "had no intention of overthrowing national life" and what they wanted above all was "order". Pleased with the welcome given him by this city, well known for its stand-offishness, he left it "convinced that the Government, provided it truly governed, would surmount all obstacles here, and that order would prevail since the State was reappearing at the nation's head".[19]

At Marseille, on 15 September, he found the atmosphere "ominous" on account of the destruction wrought on city and harbour, the "destitution" in which the population vegetated, and the "anonymous dictatorship" of the Communist Party, which the public authorities had not, in his view, opposed with sufficient vigour. So he instructed the Minister of War to send a regiment from Algeria to Marseille "to facilitate matters" at once.

> In this great city [de Gaulle wrote], chaotic and stricken as it was, I felt better than anywhere else that only the resistance movement could determine France's recovery, but that this supreme hope would certainly founder if liberation were confused with disorder. It must be said that the appearance of General de Gaulle speaking to the crowds aroused a wave of popular enthusiasm which made every problem seem simpler. Probably they became so, in fact, as soon as they seemed so.[20]

After a quick flight to Toulon, where he noted that after so many disasters, defections and suicides, the navy had "swallowed its disappointments and recovered its hopes", he set out for the south-west. "On 16 September," he writes, "I went to Toulouse, a considerably disturbed city." This is his own form of litotes. In fact, on arriving at Toulouse, it seemed as if he were confronting a revolution on the march. Not only because "dissensions had always torn the southwestern departments", but because many of the Spaniards who had joined the maquis in the region were now leaving it, thinking of returning under arms to their own country, which was still under Franco, and because the Communists, advantageously placed and well organized, stirred up these sparks in order to take matters in hand. His prejudices, the impression he had that the Commissioner of the Republic, Pierre Bertaux, was "grappling with the encroachments of certain leaders of the Forces of the Interior", made him sometimes behave like a lion-tamer in a cage of wild animals, sometimes like a sergeant-major on a barracks square.

The most notorious episodes of this Toulouse trip brought him up against an individual who, like Pierre Villon in Paris, was of a size to stand up to him: Serge Asher, known as "Ravanel", a twenty-six-year-old graduate of the Ecole Polytechnique, a sub-lieutenant in 1939 who, a few months before, had been given command of the FFIs of the region by COMAC and the rank of colonel by General Koenig. This is how de Gaulle describes him:

> Around Ravanel, leaders of the armed units constituted something like a soviet. The members of this council claimed to carry out the necessary purges with their own men, while the *gendarmerie* and the *garde mobile* were confined to remote barracks. A Spanish "division" was forming in the region with the loudly publicized purpose of marching on Barcelona. To top it all, an English general known as "Colonel Hilary" held several units under his command which only took orders from London.[21]

The International! In fact Hilary (who was promptly put on a plane by de Gaulle) had given the maquis in the region enormous help, of which André Malraux, who had worked with him, was to give abundant evidence to the General. One should also read his account of the parade under arms at Toulouse to realize how far he could carry a certain type of condescension.

At Bordeaux, things were to be less dramatic. There, too, the visitor found "the atmosphere strained". He rightly saw the main reason for this in the fact that the war was still near at hand or threatening: strong, well-armed German contingents were still holding the mouth of the Gironde. "Bordeaux tempered its joy at being free with its fear of ceasing to be so." Furthermore, collaboration had been embodied in a particularly important individual, the mayor Adrien Marquet, a close friend of Pierre Laval's, while the Resistance had been divided against itself by the defection of one of its leading organizers.

Nor can one ignore the bitter memories that Charles de Gaulle could not fail to recall: this was the city that he had had to flee four years and three months before in the midst of France's collapse.

On the whole, that tour of the France of the *sans culottes* would leave the head of the provisional government with a rather lukewarm memory. What his private secretary wrote the day after de Gaulle's return to Paris on 18 September is very telling. "The trial of strength has already begun. It isn't going to be easy. As soon as the government has some troops at its disposal, the problem will be solved." There was still a problem: that of the "patriotic militias", a more or less direct emanation of the CNR, which had created them in March 1944 with a view to "maintaining order" after the Liberation.

These organizations lent themselves less easily to integration than the FFIs: they were not forces that regarded themselves as military and were therefore called upon to congregate within the framework of the army, under the authority of the High Command. In this way order could be maintained, but above all an enthusiasm for the Resistance, which was officially the inspiration of the new power, could be sustained.

Charles de Gaulle did not stop at such distinctions. Military or civil, the authority of the State, of its police, and legal system, could not be divided. Those militias assumed too many rights of requisition, interfered in too many things – in matters concerning public order, in particular – which were the sole responsibility of the State. He was waiting for an opportunity and grasped the first suitable one to appear. On 23 October, he learnt that at Maubeuge two collaborators who had been condemned to death and pardoned by him had been executed by the "patriotic militias". The next day, Adrien Tixier, the Minister of the Interior, whom he had summoned and reprimanded in the middle of the night, read out at a meeting of the Council of Ministers the order dissolving the militias (it was to be published five days later) accompanied by this single comment: "The insurrectional period is over."

The following day, Claude Mauriac heard de Gaulle soliloquize thus:

"They've had it with their militias! Yes! If they resist, we'll shoot in the air. But they won't resist. And if a poor policeman gets killed, I shall feel sorry for him, but he will at least have put the police on the right side once and for all and made the others look pretty odious." And he went on, erect, raising his voice: "In the middle of a meeting of the Council of Ministers, I told them ... 'Billoux! Tillon!, that's what the government has to do. Now, if you don't agree ...' But they didn't turn a hair. They stayed, and from then on, from the moment that two Communists had assumed responsibility for the thing, the game was won." His face lit up with malign pleasure. That triumphant face, that tall, erect body was the embodiment of self-control and strength. De Gaulle concluded, "You see, the Communists aren't dangerous. You don't have a revolution without revolutionaries. And there's only one revolutionary in France and that's me!"[22]

So power was established – single, central, personalized. The State was restored, without compromise, the national insurrection crushed, though squealing all the way. In describing the situation in which, as a result of its own actions, the Resistance then found itself, de Gaulle writes:

It was in the nation's interest that the men who had led the struggle against the invader should participate equally in the work of recovery ... As the enemy withdrew and Vichy disappeared, they had been tempted, like Goethe's Faust, to say to the moment: "Stay, you are so splendid!" The Liberation, in fact, deprived the Resistance of its principal point. Nostalgia came upon them. Especially since these brave and adventurous men had experienced the sombre attractions of the dangerous clandestine struggle, which they would not renounce.[23]

The republican State was not only a government, with its prefects and an army: it was also a representation of the nation, capable of controlling the executive, providing it with suggestions and criticisms, until such time as it was able to legislate and give the country its new institutions.

Because over two million French people were still being held in Germany, as prisoners, deportees or work exiles, and because war was still being fought in seven departments, no electoral consultation worthy of the name was yet possible. There was no other possible assembly but the consultative one that had sat at Algiers,* even if enlarged to take in representatives of the Resistance who had been unable to reach Algiers.

In his *Mémoires* de Gaulle does not stress that this was an essential act of the new power: what he says reveals perhaps even more condescension to the parliamentarians who had been summoned to form an assembly than to the maquisards trying, in front of him, to pass themselves off as soldiers.

The majority of the politicians, whether they had always been or recently become so, were eager to see the revival of public life. They aspired to an arena where they could make themselves heard and gain access to posts of command. Not that I gave such a body the capacity to act. I was well aware of the fact that Assemblies, despite their fine speeches, are ruled by the fear of action. Besides, I knew of the rivalries which already divided the men of the resistance; therefore I had no expectation that the representatives would effectively support a resolved policy. But I did hope that they would support a mystique of recovery which would inspire the French people. In any case, I thought it wise to offer a sop to their seething spirits.[24]

On 12 October, the Consultative Assembly was set up by decree. It consisted of 248 delegates, including the 19 members of the CNR (Georges Bidault, its chairman, being a member of the government). With 174 representatives, the Resistance seemed to have the lion's share, former parliamentarians being given only 60 seats and the overseas general councils 12 (including one Muslim Algerian, one Senegalese and an Indian). But, meeting for the first time in the Palais du Luxembourg on 7 November (the Palais-Bourbon would receive the elected assembly), the enlarged Consultative Assembly refrained from adopting as its President the Resistance candidate, Pascal Copeau, the leader of Libération-Sud and the dominant personality in the CNR, who was very close to the Communists. It chose instead the Socialist parliamentarian, Félix Gouin, who had already presided over it in Algeria, but who could hardly be said to embody renewal.

*See *De Gaulle: The Rebel 1890–1944*, pp. 493–500. (trs.)

Two days later, de Gaulle was invited by the Assembly to define the aims of the government and the relations that it expected to have with the body meeting at the Palais du Luxembourg. In Algiers he had always been able to make it quite clear that the opinions of such an assembly were not expected to impede his majestic progress. On 9 November his thinking was much the same.

> From among the lessons to be learnt from the unprecedented trials that France is undergoing, one that stands out in the most striking way is the link, of an almost organic kind, between disaster and tyranny and between success and the Republic! It is as if, for the French nation, there were a natural contract between greatness and liberty.

A few days earlier, on 25 October, he summoned a press conference, of a type for which he was to become well known, but which was not yet familiar (he had held two in London, one in Algiers and one, three months before, in Washington). When questioned on the "morale" of France, he replied: "The French people wish to decide the form of their institutions for themselves, and they are determined not to accept a dictatorship of any sort. France will step forth on the road of new democracy without any trouble, because it is the will of the people."

And when one journalist then asked him what he meant by "new democracy", he hesitated slightly before replying: "I believe ... Oh! You are going to start me on a long speech, and I have already explained what France thinks on this subject. I believe that the form of democracy that France wants is a political system whereby, as far as is possible – for men remain men – the abuses of the old parliamentary regime will be abolished."[25]

Hardly a revolutionary statement, of course, even a rather backward-looking one. Indeed it would seem that at this time the General was rather inclined to favour a return to institutions close to those of the Third Republic, minus the "abuses". And choosing Jules Jeanneney as mentor of his government hardly signified that he was planning an institutional upheaval – except by introducing recourse to the referendum. The theme was always the same: France is a country that is carrying on – without repeating herself.

Many of those who were hoping to make the spirit of the Resistance the yeast of a political renewal without overthrowing the established order, dreamt of forming a great "Labour Party", drawing its inspiration from recent struggles, rejecting both capitalism and Marxism, attracting the youngest tendencies of the Section Française de l'Internationale Ouvrière (the old Socialist Party), the more dynamic of the Christian Democratic elements and the more innovatory nationalist ones: it was, in short, the movement of which Pierre Brossolette, in London, had made himself the prophet.

Men like Georges Izard, Léo Hamon, P.-O. Lapie or Philippe Viannay, part of the *Combat* editorial team, perhaps André Malraux, were waiting for the General to encourage the formation of such a party: it did not come. Why? De Gaulle was, let it not be forgotten, entirely devoted to the restoration of the State. Any confusion between the centre and a political movement, however open, however unanimist it might be, seemed to him to be dangerous. Did he not run the risk of being compromised by such a movement, identified with it? And he could hardly forget the sinister precedent of the fascist States and State-parties.

Although he did nothing to encourage the project of a great "Labour Party" as in Britain de Gaulle did not refrain from lending a hand in the foundation of what was to be called the Mouvement Républicain Populaire (MRP), which aimed at offering Catholics (primarily, but not exclusively) a political structure inspired by the spirit of the Resistance.

There are many reasons why Charles de Gaulle took an interest in this initiative. The first was his old sympathy for that current of opinion that had led him, six or seven years before, to form an alliance with the organizers of Jeune République, and to join the "Friends of *Temps présent*".* The second was that, among the creators of the new movement, there were men, like Maurice Schumann, whom he could trust. Lastly, he thought that, by coming together on a Christian theme, those young, enthusiastic men, the Bidaults and the Teitgens, would inevitably move away from that *résistancialisme* that was beginning to get on his nerves.

The MRP held its constituent conference on 26 November, declaring from the outset that it was the "party of fidelity" – to the General, of course, but also to commitments of earlier years. The names of its leaders read like a history of the Resistance: foremost among them was the former chairman of the CNR, now Foreign Minister, Georges Bidault. It had a respected newspaper, *L'Aube*, whose columnist was Maurice Schumann. It had the wind in its sails, and the blessing of the General went with it.

The government was governing, an assembly was deliberating, the prefects – and judges – were in place. Some, of course, were already tempted to draw up a balance sheet of failure, not of the reborn State, but of the Resistance, which seemed to them to have been immolated on the altar of *raison d'état*. But if we are to assess what had been accomplished since the Normandy landing, three essential achievements must be borne in mind.

To begin with, France had a French government. Secondly, attempts to transmit power from Vichy to Paris had been strangled at birth. Thirdly, civil war had been avoided. Who could say on the eve of the assault of June 1944 that these three points were achieved in advance?

On 6 June, at dawn, the text issued by General Eisenhower was still imbued with the spirit of AMGOT,** the administration of France by a foreign military bureaucracy, against which Anthony Eden had strongly, but in vain, warned his American partners. By resolutely ignoring these plans, by swiftly occupying the space left vacant and without a serious crisis with the Americans and British, de Gaulle cut short those disastrous plans, which might well have led to a new resistance, this time against France's allies.

But up to the end of August, with the more or less avowed patronage of Washington and its agents in Europe, manoeuvres had been set in train with a view

*See *De Gaulle: The Rebel 1890–1944*, pp. 168–9, 240. (trs.)
**Allied Military Government for Occupied Territory; see *De Gaulle: The Rebel 1890–1944*, pp. 502–3, 524–35. (trs.)

to "capping" the Liberation with the ruins of the Vichyite administration, of which Admiral Auphan's attempts were the final manifestation. Such a short-circuit could not fail to cause a fire. That, too, had been ignored and avoided.

Lastly, the civil war, with which an ideologically riven France had been pregnant – even at the heart of her resistance movements, a France in which the absence of authority went hand in hand with the upsurge of innumerable petty war chiefs and the terrifying proliferation of weapons throughout the country – had also been prevented.

By de Gaulle's formidable demonstration of authority? Yes. But also because the Communists, aware of the ratio of forces at home and abroad, chose not to utilize their politico-military advantages in an attempted seizure of power, even a partial one, preferring, when all was said and done, to go along with the General rather than against him. This, in a way, could also be credited to the head of the provisional government.

CHAPTER THREE

The National Territory

"You talk of liberty, honour, purification. And what are you doing about the victory? What I see, above everything else, is France victorious."[1] This was what General de Gaulle said to his secretary, Claude Mauriac, who had come to get him to sign a text that referred to a "purified" France on 10 October 1944.

Indeed, victory was no longer in the forefront of most people's minds. Everybody could see that the liberation of Paris had taken place. The only people who seemed concerned at the time about removing the enemy from the six departments still occupied were the populations themselves, the combatants entrusted with the task of liberating them – and the man who, on 18 June 1940, had chosen to call on the French people to remain in the war, in order to share in the victory. The French regarded the struggle as being over and were now only concerned about survival. Almost all the combatants at this time, from General de Lattre to Leclerc's humblest mechanic, had a strong sense that the country had forgotten or ignored them.

As we know, de Gaulle had never doubted that the Third Reich would be defeated: he announced as much to his London companions as they arrived on British soil during that disastrous summer in 1940. And he had never ceased for a moment to give the impression that, as he saw it, the only question of any importance was the part that France would play in the collapse of the Nazis and the place that would be given to her in the reconstruction of Europe and the world.

Of course, he was not taken in by the word victory. But he had to keep his people on the alert, even if it meant manipulating reality to some extent. A few years later, the man who was then Leclerc's Chief of General Staff was to hear de Gaulle say:

> We bluffed you, didn't we, Guillebon! But what did you expect? We had to whip up the mass of our compatriots from the resignation into which they had fallen, interest them in our fights, make them believe that they were taking part in the victory. We had to make our Allies see our successes, intervene almost everywhere at once, make ourselves felt, kick up a lot of dust![2]

He certainly intended to do that, either by excess or by default. The closer victory came, the more necessary was the bluff: soon they would have to put their trump cards on the table. Who had fewer than he? But who talked loudest of them? And who laid them on the table more suddenly?

After all, not everything had been said. The expert on motorized units that he had become over the last ten years was perfectly well aware that the sudden slowing down of the allied offensive in October 1944 was largely due to excessive wear and tear, and even more to inadequate supplies of petrol. Nevertheless, he thought fit to add to these technical problems an anxiety based on his experience over four years of relations between the Allies.

What worried him was not so much the rivalries between the British and American generals but rather the intentions that he attributed to the American command.

His confidants (Guy, Mauriac, Joxe, Juin) often echoed such preoccupations. Why did Eisenhower impede the progress of his British partners on his left and the French on his right? Were Bradley's American troops to enter Germany alone and thus be in a position to impose a solution coming from Washington? And this might be an agreement with one of the Führer's lieutenants who happened to be a little less compromised than the others in the regime's atrocities and willing to be associated with a general volte-face against the Soviets, or a direct agreement with Stalin excluding all other partners.

Sometimes, too, de Gaulle was thinking of the use by the Reich of the new absolute weapons, as they were then called, on which all the German laboratories were working flat out: V2s even more powerful than those that were ravaging London, bacteriological weapons, jet-propelled planes, nuclear bombs. He knew that if Hitler's power was not crushed at its source the liberty of Europe would remain in doubt. Echoes of these various preoccupations are to be found in Claude Mauriac's journal.[3]

Although he had delegated responsibility for operations to a group of colleagues led by Alphonse Juin – Chief of Staff at the Ministry of National Defence, a breezy, methodical organizer and a patient mediator between the American General Staff and himself, between de Lattre and Leclerc, between Leclerc, de Lattre and their American superiors, Bradley, Hodges, Patton, Devers or Patch – de Gaulle remained responsible for the strategic direction of French troops. Indeed, his decisions on these matters were formulated in an exchange of letters between Eisenhower and himself, on 13 and 21 September.

The American Commander-in-Chief informed him of the responsibilities assigned to the great French units, mainly consisting of liberating southern Alsace (Mulhouse, Colmar). De Gaulle replied, acknowledging the fact that the French were thereby being given an autonomous zone of action with some satisfaction. But he went further: he demanded for the 1st Army a much wider field of responsibility and for the 2nd Armoured Division the specific mission of liberating Strasbourg, an idea that Eisenhower did not seem to be hostile to. Louis Joxe pays homage to this "good will shown in almost all circumstances by the American Commander-in-Chief in trying to accommodate our susceptibilities and to restore to France her true place, to recognize what was due to de Gaulle. Only he could make de Gaulle accept the inevitable and spare him the intolerable. The preservation of the friendship between the two countries owes a lot to Eisenhower."[4]

From the military point of view, the battle so far had consisted of three contrasting phases. Between 5 June and 30 July the landing at Arromanches, and the setting up and widening of the "bridgehead" round Bayeux, Caen and Saint-Lô had been achieved. Yet the Wehrmacht was holding firm.

The second act began with the sudden tearing open of the German front at Avranches on 31 July. Patton and his 3rd Army plunged into the gap and drove towards the Ile-de-France, circumventing Paris by the south, aiming for the Meuse, leaving Leclerc's 2nd Armoured Division, following the same route, to aim for Paris itself. Meanwhile, the British and Canadians, under Montgomery, were moving from the Seine to Flanders. Everywhere FFI units had opened up the way, surprising the allied chiefs of staff by their efficiency.

On 15 August, however, General de Lattre's B Army, now part of the forces of Generals Devers and Patch, rushed from the Mediterranean towards the Rhine: although Patton had only taken six weeks to bring his tanks from Avranches to Nancy (liberated on 15 September), de Lattre took only a month to bring his from Marseille to Belfort. On 12 September, the vanguards of the 1st Army (coming from Provence) and of the 2nd Armoured Division (coming from Normandy) met at Montbard, in Burgundy. Thus, at the end of September 1944, enemy forces had retreated as far as the Vosges, apart from a few pockets still held by the Germans.

Suddenly, on 30 September, these breaking waves seemed to freeze, like those of the Arctic in winter. The third act of the Liberation was to be one of stagnation. Patton's and Montgomery's tanks were short of fuel. Hitler, stunned by the attempt on his life of 20 July, had recovered and, taking advantage of a pause in the Soviet advance on East Prussia, put new life into his troops on the Rhine, the Meuse and the Vosges. The end of the war, anticipated in September for the end of the year, was now postponed by several months. De Gaulle's commentary on this postponement of hopes is remarkable:

> That the war was to continue was certainly tragic from the point of view of the losses, damage and expense which the French would still have to endure. But, from the viewpoint of France's higher interests – which is something quite different from the immediate advantage of the French population – I did not regret it. With the war dragging on, our help would be needed in the battle of the Rhine and of the Danube. Our position in the world and, still more, the opinion our own people would have of themselves for many generations to come depended on this fact. Lastly, what an opportunity this supreme phase offered for national unity, for now every Frenchman would be subjected to the same trials, no longer divided, as they had been yesterday, but henceforth living in identical conditions and governed by a single power![5]

Once again we are at the heart of de Gaulle's thought and of the debate that constantly brought him into conflict with his American allies, even with Eisenhower, for whom the war was measured in miles, tons, troop numbers, human losses, and had to be governed by such notions as the shortest time, the best and most productive deal.

De Gaulle did not see war in terms of equations. Of all the circumstances in which a great talent could find expression, war was the one in which moral unity was best achieved and in which the authority of the State was most clearly demonstrated. For de Gaulle, war was a forge. Not that he took any pleasure in it: he left the glory of battle to others. But although it is true that he liked storms, the storms of peace served his genius no less.

But to fight on, France needed weapons. And the France of 1944 had no more than that of 1794. The main problem was not finding men, but arming them with equipment capable of opposing that of the Wehrmacht, which was still a first-class army and was still to prove it.

It was a long story, which began with the Churchill–de Gaulle accords of 7 August 1940, continued in 1942 with the extension to Free France of the lend-lease agreements made between Washington and London, and ended with Henri Giraud's trip to the United States in July 1943. Behind all these negotiations was the tireless and efficient work of Jean Monnet, the inspiration and driving force of the American Victory Program, which was to contribute in a decisive way to the arming of eleven French divisions, three of them armoured.

For de Gaulle and his colleagues, this was only a starting point, a minimum. For the Americans, it was a maximum. As de Lattre writes in his *Histoire de la 1ʳᵉ armée française*, the American General Staff understood "that the French army would be made up *a* to *z* in North Africa, according to the rules that it had laid down". This seemed to exclude recourse to a mass uprising and even to the gradual integration of "the popular forces" as the Allied armies moved across national territory, if they wanted to go on receiving American supplies and equipment.

Throughout October 1944, French requests came up against obstinate refusals from the American combined chiefs of staff. On 13 October de Gaulle wrote an urgent note to Eisenhower and, on the 15th, Juin was in contact with General Marshall. The American Chief of Staff did not mince his words: Washington had no intention of allowing the creation of new large French units, only a few battalions.[6] In the National Defence Committee, de Gaulle declared that he would have to ignore this order: the time of American supervision was over. Weapons would have to be obtained and the National Defence Committee would decide where they went. This was made all the easier by the fact that Churchill had cabled from London declaring that he was inclined to deliver the equipment to France, uncertain as he was of how long American forces would be stationed in Europe.*

Then, on 25 October 1944, during a press conference, de Gaulle chose to bring the problem out into the open: "I can tell you that since the beginning of the battle of France, we have not received from our allies what is required to arm a single major French unit."

From then on, French pressure continued to increase. On 18 November, General Juin made his government's intentions quite plain to his colleague Bedell Smith, Eisenhower's Chief of Staff:

> The reconstitution of the French army has a moral aspect. France, an imperial power, cannot end the war with eight divisions in line. So the government has decided to build up eight new divisions, together with the

*A suggestion that was not to be verified during the Prime Minister's visit to Paris, on 11 and 12 November.

ancillary services to go with them. Whether or not the Allies provide the equipment required, the forces will be set up with whatever means France has at its disposal; it is above all a matter of will.[7]

Finally, on 3 January, the combined chiefs of staff declared that they were ready to accept the French plan known as the 30 November 1944 plan, which advocated the formation of eight new divisions, including one armoured division, and a rapid expansion of the airforce. But although the American General Staff now seemed to be ready to cooperate, in Washington the President opposed such plans. In a letter to General de Gaulle dated 25 January 1945, he continued to describe the acceleration of French rearmament as "unreasonable". SHAEF* justified its reluctance by explaining that post-war French rearmament was not its responsibility and that it had to deal only with the operational question. Indeed, rearmed French units would not be ready in time to take part in battle.

Clearly, neither the enormous success won by those in charge of "Overlord" nor the Liberation of Paris was enough to smooth relations between General de Gaulle and his American allies. Franklin D. Roosevelt's personal animosity towards the Free French and its leader was gradually being replaced by straight-forward disharmony between Charles de Gaulle's political, symbolic view of things and the essentially technological, practical view that continued to dominate the actions and decisions of the Allied Commander-in-Chief.

For de Gaulle and his generals, French territory was where fifteen centuries of national history had to be restored: for Eisenhower or Omar Bradley, it was just one sector in the battle for Europe, the end of which lay not with the resurrection of this or that nation, but with the crushing of Nazism, the protection of the West and, potentially, American leadership.

Hence a constant gap between analyses and projects causing disharmony, hurt feelings and sharp exchanges, culminating in the celebrated Strasbourg affair, a psychodrama in which the incompatibility of the French and the Americans was played out.

On 23 September de Gaulle extracted from Eisenhower the decision to order Leclerc to forge ahead to Strasbourg. It was a mission that de Gaulle regarded as of the utmost importance. First, because the commander of the 2nd Armoured Division and his men were the embodiment of de Gaulle's own thinking – modern technology applied to military strategy, on the one hand, and, on the other, the intransigence of the Free French spirit. Secondly, fourteen months earlier, on the evening of the taking of Koufra, Leclerc had sworn to raise his flag on the spire of Strasbourg cathedral. It was important for the Gaullist legend that this promise should be kept.

An expert in the dramatization and manipulation of symbols, de Gaulle could not let slip such an opportunity of recalling the epic and prophetic character of the undertaking begun in June 1940. Landing in France on 1 August, Leclerc had declared that he was ready "to surmount any obstacle, even in the face of the reasonable principles of the art of war".[8] A maverick, Leclerc was also an excellent

*Supreme Headquarters of Allied European Force.

staff officer. His progress from Utah Beach to Strasbourg was "faultless": that superb thrust constantly benefited from his sense of daring.

The offensive on Strasbourg began on 18 November. The crossing of the Vosges, transformed into a bastion by the Wehrmacht, presented seemingly insoluble problems for a unit designed for speed and clear breakthroughs. Leclerc chose the least practicable routes, the ones, therefore, least defended by a methodical enemy. He emerged into the Alsatian plain on 22 September and a day later, at 10.30 a.m., the entire division was able to hear the message, "Material is in iodine": Colonel Rouvillois' tanks were in the heart of the city.

Two hours later, sitting in the great reception room of the Kaiserspalast, Leclerc remarked to Colonel Dio, his oldest companion: "Now we can croak!" At precisely that moment, the building was struck by an enemy shell, and the great chandelier was smashed, showering Leclerc with a hail of glass from which he emerged booming with laughter.[9]

Meeting that afternoon at the Palais du Luxembourg, the Consultative Assembly heard General de Gaulle announce in a highly emotional voice the happy conclusion "of one of the most brilliant episodes in our military history" and one that had also won the admiration of the Allies.

This dazzling operation did not, however, settle the fate of Alsace or of the national territory. The forces of the Reich reorganized solidly around Metz and particularly around Colmar. From then on, as we know, the battle for the liberation of France was to drag on till the spring of 1945. But very few people believed that the Third Reich was still capable of a major offensive – though Churchill, on his way to Quebec in September, did refer his colleagues to Ludendorff's formidable onslaught in July 1918 and suggested that a parallel offensive was not impossible.

Meanwhile, among the commanders, arguments raged between Montgomery, an advocate of a direct thrust on Berlin enabling the Allies to get there before the Russians, and Eisenhower, who favoured an advance on a broad front. Hanson Baldwin, a reporter on the *New York Times*, wrote in an article published on 16 December that at that date Hitler still had a hundred divisions on the western front, at a time when Eisenhower could only put sixty into battle (though, it is true, they were equipped with seven times more tanks and fifteen times more planes).

On the same day the Führer launched what his principal military adviser, General Jodl, called "an act of despair, the emergence from a fortress threatened with hunger". That offensive through the Ardennes, with the intention of repeating the stroke of genius of May 1940 that had brought France to its knees, was aimed at Charleroi, Liège and Antwerp, thereby cutting off Montgomery and his 21st Army group from the rest of the Allied forces.

For ten days, von Manteuffel's and Sepp Dietrich's 5th and 6th Armoured Armies battered the American and British forces, opening up a fifty-mile breach as far as Bastogne, which Eisenhower was only able to hold by deploying his crack paratroops.* It was an unexpected onslaught that threw the Allied General Staff

---

*They were to be joined by the French paratroops of the 2nd Régiment de chasseurs parachutistes (RCP).

into disarray. Montgomery proposed a retreat to south of the Meuse, only to be accused of cowardice by Bradley and Patton.

Might the dark days of May and June 1940 return? In his journal, Claude Mauriac describes those "terrifying hours", "the panic of the commentators", the "dramatic imprecision of the news". "A lot of people were already contemplating the re-taking of Paris. I was very concerned myself, though I did take it on myself to 'raise the spirits' of those around me, in the family, of course, where morale was very low, but also in the General's office."[10]

Suddenly everything changed: from 26 December, Luxembourg and Belgium were no longer threatened by Hitler. Instead the Nazi leader chose Alsace and Strasbourg as his principal targets, placing Himmler and the former *Gauleiter* of Alsace, Wagner, personally in charge of the operation. Leclerc, who had been visited by de Gaulle at Erstein on 24 December, was able to gather on-the-spot information about the so-called "North Wind" operation.[11]

De Gaulle, busy exploiting the first dividends of his recent Moscow visit, became once again the intransigent spokesman of French integrity. Who would dare to lay a finger on that Gaullist masterpiece, the Liberation of Strasbourg, the recovery of the most symbolic fragment of national territory, the realization of the most daring, and therefore most significant, oath of Free France?

During his visit to Alsace on 24 and 25 December, de Gaulle resumed contact with the commanding officers of the 1st Army, immobilized outside Colmar, and with their closest American companions. From a military point of view, he found de Lattre and his men bitter and shocked by a "malaise, whose deep cause lies in the nation's non-participation in the war". From the political and moral point of view, de Gaulle saw Alsace as "loyal, but anxious". From the strategic point of view, he sensed that if the German offensive were broken on the difficult terrain of the Ardennes, it might find a new dynamism by turning on Strasbourg, which the Nazi ideology, like French patriotism, had turned into a symbol.

"At precisely this moment," de Gaulle writes in his *Mémoires*, "a regrettable incident occurred after the German breakthrough in the Ardennes: the Allied Command decided to evacuate Alsace, withdrawing Patch's and de Lattre's armies to the Vosges." He went on to comment on a decision that

> appeared logical from the Allied point of view, but to France it was not acceptable. That the French Army should abandon one of our provinces, and this province in particular, without even engaging in a battle to defend it; that the German troops, followed by Himmler and his Gestapo, should return in triumph to Strasbourg, to Mulhouse and to Selestat, would be a terrible wound inflicted on the honour of our country and its soldiers, a terrible reason for the Alsatians to despair of France, a profound blow to the nation's confidence in de Gaulle. Naturally, I did not agree to it. If the French government entrusted its forces to the command of a foreign leader, it was on the formal condition that the use made of those forces accord with the nation's interest. If not, the French Government was obliged to resume command of its forces. This is what I determined to do, with all the less

scruple since Allied headquarters had not even deigned to inform me of a matter which touched France to the quick.[12]

A great deal of homage has been paid to the spirit of understanding and loyalty that Eisenhower usually showed towards his French allies. An exception has to be made here, however. This man of methodical reason was so surprised by the Führer's offensive that he lost his legendary sang-froid and thought fit, in his account of the affair, to write that "the Strasbourg question was to plague me throughout the duration of the Ardennes battle".[13]

News of the decision to withdraw had been given to General de Lattre in an instruction from Devers on 29 December. It was written in English of course, which de Lattre interpreted wrongly, seeing it only as proposing withdrawal as a hypothesis.[14] However one judges de Lattre, who did not convey this disturbing instruction to de Gaulle, the treatment that he himself received is particularly shocking. Colonel de Souzy, placed in charge of liaison between de Lattre and Devers, was kept in ignorance of Eisenhower's real intentions for thirty hours! "The secret of our withdrawal was kept even from our liaison mission," de Lattre was to write to de Gaulle on 3 January. This secret was less well kept in Paris, where, on 28 December, Juin, visiting Eisenhower's headquarters, got wind of the plan and informed de Gaulle of it: he needed nothing more to be on his guard. He realized that Eisenhower wanted to present him with a *fait accompli* and prepared his response. In the collection of writings by Jean de Lattre entitled *Ne pas subir*,[15] André Kaspi writes that de Lattre decided "to take charge of the defence of Strasbourg" (by immediately sending there the 1st Free French Division, the 3rd Allied Infantry Division and Malraux's Alsace-Lorraine Brigade) without waiting for de Gaulle's message, which only arrived "shortly afterwards".

De Gaulle's instructions to the commander of the 1st Army are contained in two documents. The first, dated 1 January, was written "in the event that the Allied forces withdraw from their present positions" and instructed de Lattre "to take on the defence of Strasbourg". The second, of 2 January, which is simply a telegram from Juin to de Lattre, written when Eisenhower's decision had reached Paris,* stated: "General de Gaulle confirms the orders given you in his letter of yesterday."

De Lattre wrote to Devers that although "the 1st Army is not at present capable of defending Strasbourg directly, it has decided to do everything in its power to cover the city on the south". And de Lattre placed particular stress on the fate that the Allies' withdrawal would bring the Alsatians, "who had welcomed the liberating allies with open arms", "the most savage reprisals of an inhuman enemy". Much the same point of view was expressed by George Patton, who noted in his diary on 25 December that such a measure would amount to "condemning to death or slavery all the inhabitants of Alsace and Lorraine" and that if he were ordered to retreat he would ask to be "relieved".[16]

In his *Mémoires de guerre* de Gaulle presents the affair as if his reactions had

---

*General du Vigier, the new military governor of Strasbourg, supplied de Lattre with this information.

constantly anticipated the initiatives of the American Commander-in-Chief. Whether as a result of his liking for Eisenhower or of self-esteem, he did not want it to appear that he was so close to being outmanoeuvred by the Commander-in-Chief. In fact, Eisenhower showed a surprising degree of duplicity by trying to present the French with no alternative, and it required Churchill's intervention, the formidable pugnacity of de Gaulle and a lucky combination of circumstances to prevent honest "Ike" from handing Strasbourg over to the Nazis and thus committing what might be called a war crime by default.

The most Gaullist statement made during this crisis came, curiously enough, from Alphonse Juin. On 2 January, as soon as de Gaulle and he were warned of the terrible decision, he rushed to Bedell Smith, Eisenhower's Chief of Staff. "General de Gaulle," Juin announced, "has ordered de Lattre to take on the defence of Strasbourg."

"In that case, which amounts quite simply to disobedience," Bedell Smith retorted, "the French 1st Army will not have a single bullet or litre of petrol."

"Very well. Then General de Gaulle will forbid American forces to use French railways and communications."

That same evening, de Gaulle sent a cable to Roosevelt saying that "this retreat would be deplorable", and asked him "in confidence to intervene in this affair, which runs the risk of having serious consequences in every respect". He sent the same message to Churchill, adding this sentence: "I am asking you to support me in this grave affair."

The only response he received from Roosevelt was a rebuff, typical of the President's unchanging attitude towards him, whether de Gaulle was head of the Free French or of the French provisional government, recognized or not. Through his Ambassador, Jefferson Caffery, Roosevelt replied that, since this was a purely military affair, he would leave the matter to Eisenhower.[17]

A "purely military" affair? Were the reprisals that the Nazis would take on the Strasbourg population simply a matter for the General Staff? What would have been the reaction of the American press and world opinion if such a possibility had come about? Let us not forget that the Yalta Conference was only a month away. What a weakening of Western positions, vis-à-vis Stalin, would the handing back of Alsace to Hitler have represented!

Churchill's reaction was quite different. He had no sooner received the telegram from Paris than he jumped into a plane. He quite obviously intended to lend a hand to the French. He knew what Alsace meant to them. By 3 January he was in Versailles, where, at the Trianon Palace, the Allied headquarters, a conference was taking place that would apparently decide the fate of Strasbourg.

Jacques Nobécourt has ingeniously combined the three main accounts of the conference: "I happened to be there," Churchill writes amusingly. Eisenhower, even more comically, maintains that "Mr Churchill happened to be at headquarters just as I was receiving de Gaulle." De Gaulle himself is scarcely less playful: "Mr Churchill thought that he should come, probably willing to use his good offices."[18]

Equally strange is the parallel between the various accounts of the conference. De Gaulle devotes two pages to it,[19] in which he plays, as we might expect, the principal role; Eisenhower sums it up in a few sentences. Churchill even goes so far as to pass it over in silence, assured that his presence alone, backing the French, settled the matter. General Juin writes that "there was not even any discussion".[20]

In fact, a third element played what may have been a crucial role. Just as the meeting was about to begin, Eisenhower learnt that the German offensive in the north had been broken. The operation in Alsace, however hard it may be, now appeared to be no more than a desperate attempt to create a diversion. A retreat was no longer necessary.

So "Ike" tried to counter with excellent strategic arguments the humiliation that de Gaulle and Churchill had inflicted on him by forcing him to cancel immediately the evacuation orders that had been given to Devers and Patch.

As for Charles de Gaulle, he once again employed his genius for generously pardoning those whom he had affronted. No sooner had he got Eisenhower to agree to send Bedell Smith to Devers with the counter-order concerning Strasbourg, than he "agreed with Eisenhower that Juin should accompany Bedell Smith, which would be an additional guarantee for me". He then goes on to describe Eisenhower and himself "taking tea together after this friendly discussion". Eisenhower went on to complain of Montgomery as "a general of great ability, but a bitter critic and a mistrustful subordinate". "We parted good friends," de Gaulle concludes.[21]

Did he do all that he might have done for things to go similarly well with Churchill? It is quite clear that the British Prime Minister had played an important role in the triumph of the French position. As they were leaving Versailles, Juin remarked to de Gaulle that Churchill deserved some thanks from him. "'Bah!' he exclaimed and sank back with a gloomy look into his meditations."[22]

It can be said that de Gaulle showed even less understanding for de Lattre. That same morning, the head of the 1st Army had sent him a telegram from Montbéliard in which he begged de Gaulle to act in such a way "that I may reconcile my duty as a French general to my country, to the honour of my army and to you, my political and military chief – a duty that I shall place before everything – with my duty as a soldier, my disciplinary duty towards the Supreme Command of the Allied forces".[23] Charles de Gaulle replied to this moving and highly honourable appeal with these few cutting words: "I am not very pleased with your last despatches in which you seem to feel that the mission to defend Strasbourg, which was entrusted to your army in my letter of 1 January, is dependent on agreement by the Allied High Command."[24] Two days later, de Lattre expressed "surprise" at this dressing-down, but declared his "total submission to the government, that is to say, to you" – words that must have cost that proud man a great deal and which de Gaulle might have been better advised not to force from him.

The whole affair had been kept secret. A simple communiqué from the office of the head of the provisional government indicated, on 4 January, that an inter-Allied military conference had taken place the day before at Versailles, with no mention of its purpose. The same day, during the daily signing of correspondence, the General could not refrain from remarking to Claude Mauriac: "Did you know that the Americans wanted to evacuate Strasbourg?" "Have they got to that point?" "They have got to that point. They are quite simply terrified. Yesterday, at Versailles, in Churchill's presence, I had a lot of trouble convincing Eisenhower." In any case, the episode coloured the General's thinking for some time. Claude Mauriac cites him as saying some months later: "And what would I do if the Americans abandoned us: would I have to form an alliance with Germany?"

But Hitler had not given up the idea of seizing Alsace. The battle was to last for three weeks, showing that Eisenhower's prudence, though unbearable from the French point of view, and the consequences of which would have been terrible in terms both of human life and of diplomacy, did not stem from faint-heartedness. The Wehrmacht was still a formidable war machine. Strasbourg and Alsace were still prime targets for the Reich. Having cleverly helped to avoid a retreat without cutting himself off from his American allies, de Lattre handled the affair skilfully and energetically, using to the best possible advantage such diverse forces as the 2nd Armoured Division and the "Alsace-Lorraine brigade", into which André Malraux breathed an emotional inspiration that turned that disparate unit into a sort of waking dream of Gaullism.

What gives the Strasbourg affair its exemplary character, according to de Gaulle, was of course the fate of the Alsatians and the questioning of the French victory. What de Gaulle found so intolerable about the Strasbourg affair, was not only that this province, which above all others possessed symbolic significance, was to be handed over to the enemy purely on grounds of military strategy; it was also that a part of national territory was being disposed of without France, in the person of de Gaulle, being consulted.

Why, one may ask, stress here the differences between General Eisenhower and General de Gaulle? Because here, it was not a question, as so often, between Roosevelt and de Gaulle: it was much more profoundly a matter of different conceptions, based on different missions and historical cultures.

On the Strasbourg crisis one reads in Eisenhower's memoirs: "de Gaulle's argument seemed to be based on political considerations, that is to say, on sentiment, founded more on emotion than on logic and commonsense."[25] One wonders what Charles de Gaulle's reaction was when he read those words? One can see him raise his eyebrows, his eyes widen. Ah, those Americans!

Rather than allowing him the privilege here of the final word, it seems just to give it to one of the liberators of Strasbourg, who was also one of the first members of the Free French movement, Colonel de Guillebon: "For General de Gaulle, the political weight of weapons was always far more important than their use in combat. I am not preferring combat to politics, but I am saying that, for him, however important, however decisive combat may have been, he always gave priority to political action."[26]

CHAPTER FOUR

Rank

One chapter in Charles de Gaulle's *Mémoires* begins with this sentence, a genuine piece of self-parody: "Every State turned its eyes upon liberated France."[1] Scarcely risen from the depths into which she had sunk four years before, France could not afford to ignore any recognition of her resurrection. That humiliated country had seen too much and had received or given herself too many wounds, felt too much shame not to be thirsty for revenge, for precedence and theatrical restorations. In this sense, Charles de Gaulle expresses well the mandate that his people had tacitly given him to carry out.

On 25 October 1944, Charles de Gaulle received the international press at the Rue Saint-Dominique. Having declared in a preamble that "France has come home", he said that he was ready to answer questions. One of the journalists, who asked him to "comment" on the recognition of the French government two days before by the Allies, received this brief reply: "I can tell you that the government is satisfied that people are willing to call it by its name." Clearly, de Gaulle was not overcome with gratitude. And, on this point, it is easy to understand why.

Indeed, right to the end, the recognition of a French government had been marked by President Roosevelt's ill-will and Winston Churchill's moodiness. Here now was a government acclaimed by the masses, borne up by a popular enthusiasm evidenced by thousands of foreign observers, especially by the innumerable American and British correspondents who had been combing France over the last three months. But although in September, Washington and London had recognized the Italian Cabinet of Signor Bonomi, head of a government still technically at war with the Allies and which had not been given any authority by popular vote, they still refused to grant the same "favour" to their brother-in-arms Charles de Gaulle, three months after the liberation of Paris. The British Parliament saw this as one of the "farces" of the period and the American press denounced the State Department's inconsistencies in vain.

Suddenly, in late October, everything began to move. Roosevelt agreed at last to change his mind, so suddenly that Churchill and Eden had the impression that he wanted to "double-cross" them. Why? His motives were essentially electoral. The presidential elections were a week away. Advisers in the White House suggested that by ignoring de Gaulle, whose trip to New York three months before had evidently been a success and who had since been received in triumph in his own capital, Roosevelt would lose too many votes. So he invented the notion that Eisenhower had "transferred his powers" to de Gaulle. The recognition of the French provisional government was given on 23 October, in Paris, by the two Western capitals, joined by Moscow, which had been warned at the last minute.

Was the curt answer that de Gaulle gave two days before at his press conference enough to describe his reactions at this time? There are the accounts of two conflicting eyewitnesses. The British Ambassador, Alfred Duff Cooper, whom de Gaulle received on 23 October for dinner, accompanied by Anthony Eden's wife, speaks of "an excessively cool, gloomy evening" and notes that the General made no reference to the fact that his government had been recognized by the three great powers in the course of the afternoon. And when the diplomat asked him if he were not pleased at seeing "this question settled at last", he replied, "It will never be settled." But, that same day, Claude Mauriac had seen a de Gaulle, "whose face was as if transfigured by an ill-concealed joy (that 'recognition' had been won at last)".

Two weeks later, de Gaulle, the head of a recognized French provisional government, sent Franklin Roosevelt, who had just been re-elected for a fourth term, his "warmest congratulations" and wished him well, he stressed, in the "great tasks that await you after those that you have so splendidly carried out". Again, it was as head of the French provisional government that de Gaulle issued an invitation to Winston Churchill and Anthony Eden, as well as to Franklin Roosevelt and his Secretary of State, Cordell Hull, to come to Paris at the beginning of November. The Americans, however, refused. In a telegram, dated 17 November 1944, a French official in Washington said, "when questioned about his answer to the French government's invitation, the President replied that he hoped to be able to go to France one day, but that he regarded it as more important to meet the British and Russian leaders first". "More important"? Of course, but did he have to put it quite like that?[2] The British, on the other hand, said that they would be delighted to accept the invitation of the head of the French government. The visit, however, did not pass off without setbacks.

In the autumn of 1944, relations between the French and British were not smooth. This was not only because Churchill had supported Roosevelt over recognition of the provisional government, but because London was no more favourable than Washington to equipping major French units at this time, and above all because in the Levant the interminable quarrel between Sir Edward Spears and his French neighbours had flared up again.* Furthermore, Churchill continued to treat French sovereignty with glorious disdain: on 14 August, he had landed in Corsica, without warning any French officials.

Then, in late October, General de Gaulle learnt that old Winston was about to land in Paris, without anyone being warned. The following peremptory telegram was sent to the Quai d'Orsay, the War Ministry, the General Staff, the prefect of the Seine and the prefect of police: "If Mr Churchill happens to pass through Paris, no arrangements, no demonstrations, no presence of any kind must be organized on the French side without my agreement. Inform everybody that I attach the greatest possible importance to this."[3]

On both sides, however, the Ambassadors did all they could to organize the planned official visit. Bidault suggested the date of 11 November (Armistice Day of the First World War), which irritated de Gaulle: it was not too exclusively a

*See *De Gaulle: The Rebel 1890–1944*, p. 496. (trs.)

French festival. The Quai d'Orsay held firm: very little would be done to sweeten Churchill's mood. According to the best expert in French affairs at the British Foreign Office, Oliver Harvey, the "PM still violently anti-de Gaulle. De Gaulle believed to be in a nasty and clamorous mood. We all tremble for the result."[4]

On 10 November, however, Winston Churchill, accompanied by his wife, his daughter Mary and Anthony Eden, landed at Orly, where he was received by General de Gaulle, Georges Bidault and a strong government delegation. "We gave them the best possible reception," de Gaulle wrote. "Paris cheered them heartily." There was no discordant note, quite the contrary, in Churchill's version. Installed with his party in the Quai d'Orsay, he found the "organization and service sumptuous" and was even delighted to use the gold bath that Goering had had installed during one of his Paris trips (while Eden had to be satisfied with a silver one).

On 11 November, Armistice Day, the "coronation" of 26 August was now to be matched, on the same Champs-Elysées, by the sanctification of the great wartime alliance. The two heads of government ascended the avenue to the Arc de Triomphe, standing in an open car, cheered by a huge crowd: "I've never seen anything so fantastic," Duff Cooper wrote. "I've never heard more sustained, thunderous cheering than that which greeted their arrival," General Ismay remarked.[5]

De Gaulle and Churchill (who was wearing an Air Chief Marshal's blue uniform) descended the avenue on foot, causing even greater enthusiasm. Louis Joxe has left a description of the old gentleman at these moments of exaltation: "The waves of the multitude carried him on to the Place de la Concorde, but he came with his sea legs. Overcome, he moved forward, a smile on his lips, his baby face reflecting feelings of child-like simplicity."[6]

When they arrived at the statue of Clemenceau, de Gaulle, who ordered the cortège to stop, asked for the song *Le Père la Victoire** to be sung. De Gaulle, as he wrote in his *Mémoires de guerre*, said "'For you!' I said to him in English. And it was only his due. Then I reminded him that at Chequers, on the evening of a black day, he had sung me our old Paulus song word perfect."[7]

They stopped off at the Invalides, in front of Foch's grave. Then, de Gaulle in his *Mémoires* goes on, "the distinguished Englishman bent for a long time over Napoleon's tomb. 'In all the world,' he said to me, 'there is nothing greater!'" These words suggest that Winston Churchill had a more Gaullist idea of greatness than de Gaulle himself!

For the occasion of his reception at the Rue Saint-Dominique, where the lunch and political discussions were to take place, Gaston Palewski had turned the Hôtel de Brienne into a "fairy-tale palace". The reception room was dominated by a bust of Marlborough, the visitor's ancestor. Visibly startled, Churchill paused on the doorstep and murmured to himself: "It's too much."[8]

De Gaulle's speech after the meal was not calculated to cool the listener's enthusiasm: "In a thousand years France, which has had some experience of combat, travail and suffering, will not have forgotten what was accomplished in this

*A refrain composed in 1918 by the *chansonnier* Paulus in honour of the "Tiger" (Clemenceau).

war through combat, travail and suffering, by the noble people whom the very honourable Winston Churchill is taking with him to the summits of one of the greatest glories of the world." To which Churchill replied, evoking shared memories of the war: "General de Gaulle and I have known one another in every kind of weather. I mean in every temperature."[9]

It was now time for the political talks. "This time," the General writes, "it was a matter of business, not sentiment, so we found our interlocutors more reticent." An attentive reading of the minutes of the conference* does not give the impression of "reticence", but rather, on the part of the English visitor, of prudence based on relations with de Gaulle, whose ambiguousness was no secret to him. Neither on the rearmament of France, nor on Germany, nor on the Far East were the British then free to commit themselves. As for the Levant, three years of tumultuous experience had taught them to be reserved.

De Gaulle opened fire by demanding weapons. His guests pointed out that everything depended on the duration of the war: if it were over in three months, the Allies would have to concentrate their resources on the existing units; if it lasted for six months (which is what happened, in the event), then they would have to call for new French forces. In any case, Churchill went on, the rebirth of a great French army is one of the bases of British policy: "Without the French army, there can be no secure European settlement." At which point Bidault intervened to stress the crucial psychological importance of an active participation of the French in the victory, for "they have to revenge themselves on the past".

The discussion continued well. De Gaulle saw it as an opportunity to pose the problem of zones of occupation in Germany. Eden suggested that Great Britain was ready to hand over part of hers to the French, as had been agreed in common with Washington and Moscow, and Churchill went further, declaring that "at six o'clock this evening your entry into the London Consultative Commission,** in which your thesis will be discussed, will be announced". Of course, the French leaders were aware that this had already been achieved: but this solemn confirmation certainly gave the talks a positive character.

It was on Germany and Poland that de Gaulle began to sense some disappointment. The British did not seem ready to recognize France's specific rights to the Saar or the Ruhr, only the right to benefit from reparations deriving from them. As for the Poles, Eden did not hide the fact that if they were to be allowed to extend westwards to the Oder, their government in London would be more or less forced to come to an understanding with the Lublin Committee, which enjoyed the mighty support of the Soviets. And when de Gaulle, alerted, spoke of the risks of Russian hegemonism and of the need to preserve Polish independence, Churchill scarcely reassured him by saying that he had received, from Stalin himself, "formal assurances on this subject".

What had come of the "basic" plans for a United Nations, which Roosevelt had mentioned to de Gaulle in July at the White House? The General had wanted to get further details out of his visitors. Were they not interested? Was not Singapore,

---

*As they were written up in General de Gaulle's *cabinet* and published in the *Mémoires de guerre* (III, pp. 350–9).
**The European Consultative Commission, the main body of Inter-Allied coordination.

as well as Dakar, in question? Churchill remained evasive, as he also was on the future of Indo-China – but not on the subject of the Italian colonies, on which London regarded Rome's "rights" as foreclosed. And what of the Levant? The General declared unambiguously that he wanted "the real independence" of Syria and the Lebanon but that the maintenance of order there ought to remain in French hands until the end of hostilities. Eden challenged this, somewhat sourly, while Bidault declared in passionate terms that the Levant, where many French had died, represented "a sacred patrimony" for France.

There was still some distance between the two points of view, and almost everything became a pretext, on one side or the other, for heated exchanges. When Churchill suggested that "colonies were no longer a guarantee of happiness or a sign of power" and that "modern squadrons counted more than overseas territories", he drew this response from Charles de Gaulle: "You're right. But you wouldn't exchange Singapore for squadrons!"

Curiously enough, it is not in the official account of the meeting that the most important confidence made by Churchill to de Gaulle is to be found. It is in the body of his *Mémoires* that the General refers to the celebrated meeting a month before in Moscow during which, armed with coloured crayons, Stalin and Churchill had divided up Eastern Europe into zones of influence with indecent merriment. "'In Romania,' Churchill said, 'the Russians will have 90 per cent, the British 10 per cent. In Bulgaria, they will have 75 per cent and we 25 per cent. But in Greece we will have 90 per cent, they 10 per cent. And in Hungary and Yugoslavia, our influence will be equal.'"*

This staggering admission, rather than the way talks between Eden and Bidault proceeded, gives some foundation to de Gaulle's bitter reflection immediately following his description of the Franco-British talks. "It was evident that they considered themselves players of a game to which we were not admitted. Our remarks left Churchill in no doubt that the only situation we found acceptable was that of full partner. The French people deserved to settle their own affairs without outside intervention."

Describing this conversation ten years later, the General makes it sound rather bitter. It would not seem that at the time he was so alarmed. Claude Mauriac describes him, after meeting Churchill on the steps of the Hôtel de Brienne, "radiant and so pleased that he came over to shake my hand".[10]

The next day, tears streaming down his cheeks, Churchill was made an honorary citizen of the city of Paris at the Hôtel de Ville. He insisted on meeting the members of the National Council of the Resistance and of the Parisian Liberation Committee, "and many combatants of the preceding August", de Gaulle adds. What Churchill wanted, he says, was "to see the men behind the insurrection"! In de Gaulle's *Mémoires de guerre* he thought fit to add: "Perhaps, too, he cherished the hope of finding adversaries of de Gaulle among them." Churchill's comment on this meeting is nevertheless amusing: "I expected to find myself surrounded by noisy and undisciplined insurgents. Your revolutionaries look like Labour Members! This is fine for law and order, but not very picturesque."[11]

*One should read the account of this astonishing scene in Churchill's *The Second World War* (London, Cassell, 1949, Vol. VI, pp. 134–5).

The final talk between the two leaders brought out once again the divergence between their two points of view. De Gaulle's version is telling: when the General suggested to his guests that the two old European nations should come to an agreement that would enable them to "shape the peace together", a "third way", rather than allow it to be imposed upon them by Washington and Moscow, for "public opinion instinctively shies away from giants", Churchill replied that "in politics as in strategy, it is better to persuade the stronger than to pit yourself against him". What the Prime Minister was trying to do was to enlighten the Americans, who "do not always use [their immense resources] to the best advantage", and to moderate the appetites of Russia, "a great beast which has been starved for a long time".

In terms of grand design, the talks were a failure, but de Gaulle did derive some advantages from the picturesque visit of the old British champion. He observed that it was clear that "England favoured France's political resurgence, that she would continue to do so for reasons of equilibrium, tradition and security, that she desired a formal alliance with us, but would not consent to link her strategy with ours, believing herself in a position to function independently between Moscow and Washington."[12]

So Winston Churchill was not to be a fellow traveller along the "third way". De Gaulle was to try to travel along it alone. This would take him first to Moscow, where, as soon as the British visitors had gone home, Stalin asked him to come on a week's visit in early December.

Charles de Gaulle did not undertake the journey without revealing his game to the French and to the world. On 22 November, he reminded the Consultative Assembly that, following his talks with Churchill and prior to his visit to Stalin, "we were beginning to possess means of diplomatic action worthy of France" so that France might once again play her role as "one of the greatest States". Consequently, he was going to ensure that France became a member of the Security Council of the future United Nations.

Declaring unambiguously that France would not consider herself committed to any arrangement – especially concerning Germany – "in which we have not deliberated under the same conditions as those who adopted them", he called for the laying of "the foundations for that valuable edifice: the future unity of Europe", based on specific acts binding its three poles: Moscow, London and Paris. And his conclusion is no more modest than the projects proposed:

> a country is offered a destiny great in proportion to the gravity of its ordeal. But we cannot uphold our rights nor accomplish our duties if we forgo power itself. Despite our losses and our woes, despite human weariness, we must reinstate the power of France! This, henceforth, is our great cause![13]

Having declared his ambitions and laid down the direction to be followed, he now had to begin the most classical of all diplomatic manoeuvres, the one that had been attempted by all the great French strategists from Francis I to Poincaré: the great alliance in the East, thereby outflanking the Germans.

There were two central premises that de Gaulle took to Moscow. The first was that any *rapprochement* between Paris and Moscow would strengthen his position and give him more room for manoeuvre *vis-à-vis* the Americans and the British. The second was that, inflamed with hatred against Germany and concerned above all to ensure his position in Eastern Europe and the Balkans, Stalin would support his main ambition: to guarantee the French control over the left bank of the Rhine.

Visionary that he was, he did not see that Washington and London had already forged such strong links with Stalin and done so many deals with him that what the French had to offer seemed dated and derisory by comparison. Nor did he understand that Stalin, though eager to satisfy French appetites over the question of the Rhine and Germany in general, was still too bound up with his great Western allies to engage in a manoeuvre that might upset them on a terrain that he regarded as their hunting ground.

The third mistake was that de Gaulle, aware of the extra value given to French diplomacy by his personal talents, did not realize that the splendour of his vision and style could not conceal his country's extreme weakness, at a time when everything was a question of groups of armies and thousands of tanks. And no man in the world was less capable of thinking otherwise than the Soviet Marshal, who is credited with the famous remark: "The pope? How many divisions?"

De Gaulle set off assured that, having forced Roosevelt to change his mind and to recognize the French provisional government,* so forcing open the door of the Allied Commission in London for the French, he was to find in Stalin a partner ready to dismember Germany and to give the Americans something to think about. He was to find a host incapable of concealing his heavy condescension towards this weak visitor, a host who expected only one thing of him: his complicity, as representative of a country that still enjoyed historical prestige in Warsaw, in enslaving Poland. Because he was able to resist the temptation to win Stalin's support at such a price,** all he brought back from Moscow was a face-saving pact – and a few splendid pages of his *Mémoires de guerre*.***

It was a long trip. De Gaulle and his party (Bidault, Juin, Palewski, Maurice Dejean,† Girard Charbonnières,†† Jean Laloy, Burin des Roziers, Guy) left Paris on 24 November and did not arrive in Moscow until 2 December, stopping off at Cairo (where de Gaulle found King Farouk "prudent, well-informed, of an agile mind"), Teheran (where he encouraged the Shah to resist London and Washington, as well as Moscow), Baku and Stalingrad – which the General had insisted on visiting to pay homage to the victors of the "decisive" battle of the war.

At Stalingrad the visitors were very struck by the contrast between the terrible

*Roosevelt had now been re-elected and no longer needed to accommodate him.
**A rejection that he would nevertheless have to qualify: see later, p. 52.
***However one may admire him, one could not be content with this account. I have used the memories of Jean Laloy (who was, as it happened, the General's interpreter), reproduced in an article in the *Revue des études slaves* (Mélanges Pierre Pascal, 1982), complemented and commented upon orally during an interview in 1984; those of Ambassador Garreau; those of Alexander Werth, who was then present at Moscow and who, in his *De Gaulle* (London, Penguin Books, 1965), cites the official Soviet sources; and fragments of the Russian archives communicated to the author by Professor Georges Mond.
†He was political director at the Quai d'Orsay.
††Bidault's *directeur de cabinet*.

ruins and miserable condition of the population, on the one hand, and the rebuild-
ing, already completed, of the huge tank factory, on the other. Legend has it that,
viewing the battlefield, de Gaulle remarked to Molotov: "What a great people!
The Germans, I mean." Jean Laloy, who was constantly at his side, denies that de
Gaulle said any such thing: "Molotov wasn't at Stalingrad at the time and, anyway,
General de Gaulle would not have been so irresponsible."[14] But the day before, at
Vosdock, the diplomat adds, the General had expressed, in front of his French
party, his admiration for the "great people" that had driven its war effort so far and
valiantly continued its struggle against Eisenhower's forces.

The visitor asked the authorities in Stalingrad to gather the workers together so
that he might convey to them "the greetings of the French workers". Laloy,
translating his brief speech, noticed "the unresponsive, hostile look" of their
audience. That evening the General remarked to Laloy: "It isn't a popular regime.
There is no enthusiasm in those masses. On 11 November, in Paris,* it was quite
different, it was a free people."[15]

It was on the morning of Saturday 2 December that de Gaulle's train entered
the station in Moscow, where Molotov and a cohort of officials were waiting. In the
Mémoires de guerre Charles de Gaulle refers to the presence of "a considerable
crowd . . . from which arose a hum of sympathetic voices". Alexander Werth challenges this point. "De Gaulle stared at the crowd," he writes, "and the crowd
stared back, scarcely knowing who he was; there was certainly no 'hum' of any
kind. Bidault later, indeed, told me that he and de Gaulle had been greatly
perplexed by the total indifference shown them by the Soviet crowds."[16]

The first day saw the first incident. De Gaulle had been invited to stay at the
House of the Guests of the USSR, in Spiridonovska Street. Suddenly, without
consulting anyone, he decided that he would stay with Palewski and Guy at the
Embassy – which, having been damaged by a German bomb, was highly uncom-
fortable and badly heated. "It's camp life," de Gaulle commented, undismayed.
Ambassador Garreau tried to reason with him: "Be careful! The Russians will be
outraged. Stalin is very touchy!" The General wouldn't give in. The Russians
were mortified: they did not realize what had happened until the evening when,
receiving de Gaulle at the Kremlin for the first time, Stalin, as Roger Garreau
recounts, "gave him a frosty welcome that did not augur well".[17] In his *Mémoires de
guerre* de Gaulle gives an account of this first contact, from which it emerges that
Stalin, his eyes lowered as he drew hieroglyphics on a sheet of paper, made it quite
clear that de Gaulle was not to depend on him for his great German plan, and that,
in any case, where the Ruhr and the Saar were concerned, nothing would be
decided without consultation with Roosevelt and Churchill: thus the visitor's
hopes were shattered at one blow. On the other hand, Stalin informed him that, to
the west, Poland should extend to the Oder and the Neisse.

In other words, Stalin was demanding what interested him and was offering
nothing in return – except the signature of an agreement between Moscow and
Paris to warn of any new German aggression. De Gaulle, furious, could not resist
mentioning the pact that had been signed in that very place, a little under ten years

*During Churchill's visit.

before, by Pierre Laval. Having given himself the pleasure of "pricking" his greedy hosts, he thought fit to add: "I am not Pierre Laval."[18] This gives a fairly good idea of the tone of the conversations.

According to a Soviet document, the discussion was above all about Germany and her western and eastern frontiers:

> Stalin asked what prevented France from becoming once again a great country. De Gaulle replied that it was above all the Germans, who still have to be conquered. The French know what Soviet Russia has done for them, they know that Soviet Russia played a crucial role in their liberation. [Stalin stressed the need for an alliance and] de Gaulle said that, apart from Germany, only Russia and France had a continental geographical position in Europe. Those two countries were Germany's neighbours and, consequently, were under its threat. De Gaulle said that it would be a good decision if the Rhineland were detached from Germany and given back to France. Perhaps in the case of its northern part, that is to say, the Ruhr basin, he would agree to setting up a regime that was not French, but international. As for the Rhineland, it ought to be detached from Germany and rejoined to French territory. Marshal Stalin said that he did not think problems would be solved by frontiers alone. He is right. But in spite of everything, the question of frontiers really does exist. The question is important, not only in relation to Germany's western frontiers, but also in relation to her eastern frontiers. De Gaulle said that he did not think that France would make serious objections to the transfer of East Prussia to the Poles. That province had always been a pernicious element in German policy.[19]

The next day, a Sunday, after the mass that the General wanted to attend at St-Louis-des-Français (the only Catholic church open in the USSR) where he would meet most of the tiny French colony in Moscow, came the first official meal. Stalin seemed in a better mood.

The portrait that de Gaulle draws of Stalin in his *Mémoires de guerre* is even more famous than those he left of Churchill and Roosevelt: "As a Communist disguised as a Marshal, a dictator preferring the tactics of guile, a conqueror with an affable smile, he was a past master of deception. But so fierce was his passion that it often gleamed through this armour and gave him a certain sinister charm."[20] For Jean Laloy, Stalin was

> a short man, wearing uniform and black boots, with a rolling gait, his eyes crinkling in a smile of profound insincerity. But where was the block of granite, the monolithic man represented in official portraits? What we had here was a sultan who stayed inside, in his seraglio, far from daylight and crowds, shut up in his calculations, his plottings, his mistrust. The complexion was yellowish, pale, the cheeks drawn, the eyes shining, but with rings under them, the silvery, diaphanous hair cut very short, the moustache carefully trimmed, grey, the voice light, very light, scarcely audible.[21]

De Gaulle greeted the little man pleasantly enough. "You celebrated a victory yesterday, Marshal." "Oh! A few towns in Hungary, a few towns. What we need is Vienna. That's where we're going."* They took their seats. Molotov raised his glass "to our alliance". The word hit the bull's-eye. And Laloy strained his ears, for, between two sips of vodka, he heard the old sultan add: "And not a pact à la Laval, but a real alliance!"[22]

A little later, the quiet voice was raised again: "It must be very difficult to govern a country like France, where everyone is so restless!" "Yes," the General answered. "And I cannot imitate your example, as you are inimitable."

Stalin mentioned Thorez. This was met by an irritated silence on de Gaulle's part. "Don't take offence at my indiscretion!" Stalin went on. "Let me only say that I know Thorez and that in my opinion he is a good Frenchman. If I were in your place, I would not put him in prison. At least, not right away!"[23]

Next day, a lunch was given at the French Embassy for Soviet writers. The most celebrated guest, Ilya Ehrenburg, presented the General with a copy of his most "French" novel, *The Fall of Paris*, in which the collapse of 1940 is mercilessly described. Laloy recounts that, in the train home, the General commented on his reading of it: "If we had had 8000 kilometres behind us, we could now write *The Fall of Moscow*. We must not let them annoy us."

But they did. It was not so much Molotov's underlings' rewording of the draft pact written by Bidault; but, at their next meeting, on 6 December, Stalin, confronting the main subject of Poland head on, did so in a manner in which neither "friendship" nor cunning played any part. De Gaulle describes him as "snarling, snapping and eloquent": it was quite clear that "the Polish question was the principal object of his passion and the centre of his policy".**

The General argued that it was up to the Poles to decide on their own government. Until a new regime was in place, France could see no reason to break with the government that had taken refuge in London in favour of the Lublin Committee set up by Moscow. Stalin replied harshly, denouncing the London Poles, those "anti-Russians", those "reactionaries", whom he had the temerity to blame for setting off the Warsaw Uprising quite arbitrarily and without consulting the Soviet command. (The truth was, of course, that Stalin had cynically allowed the Germans to crush it without intervening himself.) He went on to urge de Gaulle, if he had any influence over the Polish people, to abandon the position of the Americans and British and to support the men of Lublin.

Once again the visitor took refuge behind the decision of the Polish people expressed by universal suffrage, fully expecting his host to respond even more angrily. Instead his manner softened: "Bah! We'll understand each other anyway." De Gaulle concludes: "It was apparent that Stalin was going to try to sell us the pact in exchange for our public approbation of his Polish operation."[24]

The affair became more complicated when Churchill, according to de Gaulle, intervened and proposed a three-sided pact – the Soviet Union, France and Britain. According to Werth's account, "Stalin kept up communications with Churchill throughout de Gaulle's visit", to cover himself and also to catch de

*It was to take the Red Army another four months to reach Vienna, on 13 April 1945.
**Poland had obsessed him for so long that it had been the subject of his first dispute with Lenin.

Gaulle unawares. This proposal did not please de Gaulle, as his *Mémoires* reveal. Why had Churchill spoken to Stalin alone without warning him? As for content, Russia and France were the powers neighbouring Germany. They had specific reasons for coming to an agreement on German policy, and those reasons would naturally be different from those of Great Britain. In fact, he saw this pact as further evidence of the "junior partner" role into which he had been forced, a mere wagon tacked on to the train assembled in 1942 when the Anglo-Soviet pact had been signed.[25] He summed up the position in which he found himself to one of his diplomatic advisers: "One cannot assimilate the relations between France and Russia, between which no difference exists, with the relations between France and Britain, which are still divided by certain questions of interest."[26] This was a provocative statement, but it says a great deal about the question. For de Gaulle knew perfectly well that he was trying to ensure that he left Moscow with firm assurances from Stalin over the question of the Rhine, none of which would have met with British approval.

The General said to Stalin that he had decided to leave Moscow on the 10th, whether or not there was any agreement. Stalin took this well enough. Announcing that he had given up the project of a tripartite pact ("Churchill will be offended, of course. Once again . . . "), he presented this gesture as an important concession made to his guest. And, to show that he was in favour of the agreement, he invited the General to a great farewell dinner.

Meanwhile, de Gaulle was to reject Molotov's attempts to get him to agree, by means of a common communiqué, to exchange "official representatives" with Lublin, to receive representatives of the said committee, and to talk with representatives of the United States (Averell Harriman) and of Great Britain (John Balfour), thereby suggesting that their governments should do the same with him. And it was not without anxiety that he heard Harriman declare: "For our part, we Americans have decided to behave to the Russians as if we trusted them."[27] After Yalta, he was not to forget these words. In his *Mémoires*, de Gaulle maintained that he "did not agree" to recognizing the Lublin "government" because "all things are possible, even the fact that an action that accords with honour and honesty ultimately appeared to be a prudent political investment".[28]

Some, including Alexander Werth, have doubted whether this refusal would have been maintained if Stalin had approved of the General's plans for the Rhine. They cite a Moscow document from which it emerges that Bidault replied to an argument put forward by Molotov: "I don't think the Franco-Soviet pact has recognition of Lublin as a pre-condition. But don't forget that we, too, have problems that require urgent solutions, particularly on the Rhine."[29] Does this *rapprochement* imply that de Gaulle and his team were ready to carry bargaining to the limit? The Ruhr against Poland? It is hardly believable, if only for this reason: de Gaulle did not have the means to deliver it. Why would Stalin have made such a concession – this time running the risk of really annoying his great allies – in exchange for a French concession that was really of minor importance?

In short, it was with a sense of resignation, that "the business has failed",[30] that the French delegation was shown in to the Catherine Hall of the Kremlin, where they found about forty Soviet dignitaries waiting for them. The Marshal sat down between de Gaulle and Harriman in the middle of a table that "sparkled with inconceivable luxury". Josef Visarionovich, de Gaulle observes, "assumed the manners of a peasant of rudimentary culture, applying to the most immense of problems the judgements of rough good sense". He ate heavily during each course and helped himself copiously to the bottles of Crimean wine which were placed in front of him. Laloy observes that he spoke much more with Harriman, on his left, than with de Gaulle, on his right, and "began to cheer up".

Then began the celebrated scene, that of the toasts made by Stalin. Thirty times, de Gaulle reports, the dictator raised his glass to salute first his French, American and British guests, then his ministers, his generals, his engineers, mingling praises with threats.

> Each time [Laloy recounts] little Stalin waddled up to them. When he reached Air Marshal Novikov he praised his talents, then suddenly said: "And if he doesn't do a good job, we'll have him strung up!" I noticed his eyes narrow interrogatively: "Do those French devils understand? Or do they think we can't have a little laugh?"* It was like watching the grand prince sitting at table with his *druzina* in Kiev, mother of the Russian cities. There was a strange crudity and bitterness about it all. No trace of sincerity, enthusiasm or revolutionary passion.[31]

Toasting the Poles, Stalin suddenly turned to Gaston Palewski and said "for one never stops being Polish, does one, M. Palewski?"

De Gaulle wrote a fine page on the banquet:

> This tragi-comic scene could have no other purpose than to impress the French by displaying Soviet might and the domination of the man at its head. Having witnessed it, I was still less inclined to support the sacrifice of Poland. Therefore it was with cool aloofness, in the *salon* after dinner, that I observed, sitting around Stalin and myself, the obstinate chorus of diplomats.[32]

Stalin, too, pretended to be bored. "Ah, those diplomats! How boring they are! Why do they have to talk like that? A machine-gun, that's what we need! Turn a machine-gun on them. They'd shut up soon enough . . . " Again and again he came back to this theme of the machine-gun, without apparently noticing the General's coolness. He called Bulganin over: "Fetch me a machine-gun and load it. Those diplomats! What a race!" "I stopped translating," Laloy adds. "I had no wish to anger the great guest, who looked anxious and gloomy."[33]

Stalin then invited his guests to accompany him into a neighbouring room to see a film made in 1938, showing the coming conflict with Germany. The Red Army triumphs, of course, and revolution breaks out in Berlin. "I fear that M. de Gaulle doesn't care for the end of the story," the Marshal remarked. "I replied, somewhat annoyed: 'Your victory, in any case, pleases me, especially as at the beginning of

*Alexander Werth reports how, the next day, one of the French diplomats confided to him: "He seemed to be making fun of us" (*De Gaulle*, p. 186).

the real war things between you and the Germans were quite different from the way they are shown in that film.'"[34] The film ended. The lights came up. The General suddenly look his leave. Stalin was disappointed: "But there's another film, an amusing one." But de Gaulle was already moving away. Stalin sat down again, apparently finding this quite natural. The delegation was horrified, but was led away by the General – leaving Bidault, Garreau and Dejean to try to salvage negotiations with Molotov.

The General took his leave. They were up late at the Embassy. Two hours later, Dejean telephoned Palewski: "The text is ready. If the General agrees with it, we'll sign." On the matter of the key question, that of the Lublin Committee, a compromise had been reached: there would be an exchange of unofficial representatives* concerned with material questions and particularly French prisoners.

At 5 a.m. everybody met again (including Stalin) in Molotov's office in the House of People's Commissars. The Marshal muttered in Molotov's ear: "Bidault had you, eh, he had you, didn't he?"[35] And to de Gaulle he said: "You played your hand well! Well done! I like dealing with someone who knows what he wants, even if he doesn't share my views."[36] He spoke of Hitler as "a poor wretch who won't escape from this one", and de Gaulle heard the famous remark: "After all, only death wins."** And when the General invited him to come to Paris, the little Marshal replied: "Yes, I'll come, yes, if I'm not dead. I'll be dead soon. I'm weak, weak, a poor old man."[37]

There were more toasts. The "poor old man" stood up, his legs slightly apart: "I want to drink to the pact, to the alliance. France must be strong... France now has leaders, uncompromising, unyielding leaders... I am glad for her. It's what France needs..." Then he came to the central subject, advocating an independent, democratic Poland. "The tsars had a bad policy of trying to dominate the other Slav peoples. We have a new policy. Let Slavs everywhere be independent and free! Poland used to be an embarrassment in Franco-Russian relations: all that's finished with now." And Laloy, translating him word for word, said to himself under his breath: "Has he lost his senses? How else can he say such a thing?"

Everyone drank to Franco-Polish-Soviet friendship. Stalin turned to de Gaulle: "What do you think of that, M. de Gaulle?" "I am in complete agreement with what Marshal Stalin has *said****... I shall repeat it in Paris and everyone will hear it." Stalin, glass in hand, shook his head slightly, as if to call us to witness: "He's against it, he's against it, I can see perfectly well that he's against it." The General did not reply.

Stalin so arranged matters that the farewells became "effusive", to use de Gaulle's word. "You can count on me!" he declared to his guests. "If France needed us, we would share what we had with you down to our last crumb!" These generous words did not stop him suddenly snapping at his interpreter: "You know

*On the French side, this was to be Christian Fouchet, who joined the delegation at Moscow and who was to reach Lublin three weeks later.
**Which Laloy does not quote. This would suggest that it is apocryphal.
***In Laloy's version, the word is underlined.

too much! I'd better send you to Siberia." De Gaulle took his leave. As he left the room, he turned round: "I saw Stalin sitting, alone, at the table. He had started eating again." Suddenly, in the corridor, Laloy heard someone running behind him. He caught the humble interpreter by the arm. It was Stalin: "Well, did you forget to say goodbye to me?"[38]

Next day, in the train crossing the steppes, General de Gaulle was talking with Laloy: "It isn't a popular regime. It's against man's nature..." There was a moment of silence, followed by this explosion: "We've got those people on our hands for the next hundred years!"[39]

Was it the sense of an inhuman regime, spreading its power over Europe, that he brought back from the USSR? Once again, he had confused the respect paid to the French on account of his formidable personal presence with his country's real power. To face up to a man who was then throwing some two hundred divisions across central Europe did not mean that his ten divisions allowed him to realize his ideas for the Rhineland – though his failure in Moscow did not make him give them up.

Apparently, he had made only a few small concessions: the sending of an unofficial representative to Lublin did not imply that the French government had abandoned the Poles in London. All the same, since the promises made to Stalin by Churchill in October, it was the first such step made by a non-Communist country. The General said to Christian Fouchet on the morning of 10 December, before catching the train for Paris: "You will be France for all the Poles and France for all our liberated soldiers. You will tell me as soon as possible what is happening and how you see things. For the rest, you will have to manage as best you can!"[40]

What had he received from his greedy hosts in exchange for this gesture? A pact in which nothing is said that was not already self-evident: that the two countries would fight to ultimate victory, that they would not sign a separate peace, that they would cooperate within the United Nations Organization.

As for Stalin, although he showered praise on "M. de Gaulle", once his back was turned it was clear that Stalin had a very low opinion of him. To Harriman, the American Ambassador, he declared a few days later that he had found de Gaulle "difficult and stubborn".[41] And to Roosevelt, at Yalta, who asked him how he had got on with the General during the Moscow visit, Stalin replied that he found him "unsubtle and devoid of realism in his judgement of the contribution made by France to victory".[42]

Overall, it seemed that the Moscow visit had confused, rather than clarified, relations between Stalin and de Gaulle. Independently of the innumerable cultural and historical incompatibilities separating them and of the thorny Polish affair, they were also profoundly opposed in their political views and strategy. For Stalin, everything could be measured: machinery, men, steel, blood and sweat. For de Gaulle, the world was led by imponderables, ideas, myths and words.

French public opinion perceived the trip to the USSR and the face-to-face meeting between de Gaulle and Stalin as expressions of national revival. So classic, so traditional an operation, one so directly in line with diplomatic history running from Richelieu to Poincaré, could not fail to seduce a people desperate for nostalgia – not to mention the praise of that quarter of the French population that then supported the Communist Party and saw the Soviet allies as builders of a new world.

For the PCF, the pact was all the more of a victory in that it coincided with the return to France on 27 November of "Maurice", that same Thorez who had been the subject of one of the most significant clashes between the Marshal and the General.*

Reporting on his trip and commenting on the pact before the Consultative Assembly, on 21 December, de Gaulle won an unqualified success. But although the Moscow pact made the French dream of past glories and helped them to believe that they were once again a Great Power, the immediate outcome of the meeting was to qualify that optimism. Hardly had the deadly threat to Strasbourg been lifted, in early January, than the American and British press revealed that a conference would take place soon of the American, British and Russian leaders with a view to taking measures that would hasten the end of the war, to draw up plans for regulating the peace and to work out the organization of the United Nations. There was no question of French involvement.

Charles de Gaulle's reaction was strong: not only had he not been invited, he had not even been informed. He put his complaint in a note handed to his three "Allies" on 15 January. Nothing came of it. Describing the Allies' plans for Europe in the House of Commons, on 18 January, Winston Churchill did not even mention France. What did this omission mean? The French ambassador in London, René Massigli, tried to explain the Prime Minister's silence to Georges Bidault:

> If he had spoken of France, he would have been forced to mention the question of French participation in the coming conference of heads of government. Now although the British government, according to the information that I have received, is favourable to this, it is not yet aware of the reactions of Moscow and Washington to the note that you handed to the ambassadors of the three countries on 15 January. Faithful to the method that had always been his, the British Prime Minister was unwilling to make a declaration on so delicate a subject without first being informed of the American and Soviet positions.[43]

We now know that Churchill was perfectly aware of the positions of his two partners, each as negative as the other. Stalin, who had eyes only for Poland, had just noted that de Gaulle was even more hostile to his designs on that country than Roosevelt or even Churchill. In July, Roosevelt, who had thoughts only for the United Nations Organization, was able to appreciate the reservations of de Gaulle towards anything that concerned his grandiose world order supported by bases "borrowed" from the old empires. Only Churchill could regard – given the community of their outlooks on many points – de Gaulle's presence as useful. Hence the following telegram from Massigli, dated 22 January:

*See De Gaulle: The Rebel 1890–1944, pp. 469–71. (trs.)

The British position seems to be the following: they are favourable in principle to French participation in the coming conference.

They recognize that most of the questions on the agenda are of direct interest to us and that no decision could be taken without our expressing our views, in one way or another.

As I have already informed the Department, Mr Eden did not wait for us to take steps before making it clear twice, in Washington and Moscow, that France must be associated at least with any decision concerning Germany. But it certainly seems that this position has not been followed by a response from the other two allies.[44]

Three days later, General de Gaulle summoned the international press. The first question he was asked concerned the Yalta Conference of which he knew nothing. Had France been invited or not? De Gaulle replied smoothly.

"You may be assured that we have heard that there is, indeed, to be a meeting of several heads of government or heads of State of the United Nations. France has not been invited to take part in that meeting."

"Have any steps been taken by the French government?"

"You know that we are on good diplomatic relations with the governments we are talking about. Those relations are close enough for those governments to be in no doubt of France's wish to participate with them in the great discussions planned."[45]

In fact, although Eden tried to persuade his Prime Minister to get de Gaulle invited at least for the discussions concerning Germany,[46] Churchill was hostile to the General's taking part in the talks because he regarded him as unbearable, and because he had himself decided to be the spokesman of French interests – a task that, supported by Eden, he carried out with admirable eloquence. The old Francophile took particular pleasure in presenting himself as the spokesman of France, thus embodying both the dreams of the Plantagenets and the project for union of June 1940.

Although the British wanted to do without de Gaulle, Washington did not want the General's exclusion from the Conference to revive a quarrel that had already lasted too long. So on 27 January Roosevelt delegated his close adviser and intimate friend, Harry Hopkins, as his special envoy to Paris, in the hope of dissipating old clouds and anticipating others.

"Harry Hopkins," de Gaulle writes, "was supposed to 'sugar-coat' the pill. But since he was a high-minded as well as a skilful man, he approached the matter from its most significant aspect and asked to discuss the fundamental question of Franco-American relations." What is the cause of the "discomfort", the "unfortunate state of relations" between the two nations? the General asked his visitor. "The cause," Hopkins replied,

is above all the stupefying disappointment we suffered when we saw France collapse and surrender in the disaster of 1940. Our traditional concept of her value and her energy was overthrown in an instant. Add to this the fact that those French military or political leaders in whom we successively placed our trust because they seemed to symbolize the France we had believed in did not show themselves – and this is the least that can be said – worthy of our hopes.

According to Charles de Gaulle's version, Roosevelt's representative then seems to have made an admission that provides a key to the affair: "It is true that you yourself, General de Gaulle, then became the living proof of our mistake. We have not favoured you up to the present, but we acknowledge what you have accomplished." Hopkins did not refrain from adding that "knowing the political inconstancy that riddles your country", your allies are "justified in being circumspect".[47]

De Gaulle did not want to let the arguments about "the stupefying disappointment" pass without reminding his visitor that in her misfortune, in June 1940, France had waited in vain for some sign of encouragement from Washington, even a secret one, that would have encouraged Paul Reynaud to continue the fight. Recognizing that without the "colossal war effort" made by the United States the Liberation of France "would not have been possible", he concludes by deploring that the United States could "undertake to settle Europe's future in France's absence", thus giving the French "the impression that you no longer consider the greatness of France necessary to the world and to yourselves. This is responsible for the coolness you feel in our country and even in this office."

Harry Hopkins (who was already undermined by the cancer that was to kill him six months later, shortly after the death of Roosevelt) complained that de Gaulle had not had a word of sympathy for a guest who had come, as he had done, with outstretched hand. However, this did not prevent him, at Yalta, from exercising his considerable influence on behalf of French interests, acting on Roosevelt in the same way that Eden was acting on Churchill.

This is not the place for a detailed account of Yalta. For the French provisional government, it will be enough to quote a few extracts from *Roosevelt and Hopkins* by Robert Sherwood, taking into account the care with which its author stresses the services rendered by Hopkins to the cause of peace.

According to Sherwood, Stalin proved very hostile to France's participation in the administration of Germany and, for almost the entire conference, Roosevelt shared his opinion. But "Winston and Anthony [Eden] fought like lions in the cause of France," Hopkins, from his sickbed, giving them constant support. To persuade Stalin to accept France's participation in the Control Commission in Germany, Churchill maintained that, without France's support, Great Britain could not be responsible alone for containing Germany on the continent. Roosevelt then declared that he agreed to granting France an occupation zone, but he considered, like Stalin, that she should not sit on the supervisory body. During a final session, Churchill, pleading for an increase in the role of France, declared that he did not wish that she should belong, for the moment at least, to the club of the Great Powers. "A club in which one enters only with five million soldiers," said Stalin. "Three million," Churchill, who knew his arithmetic, corrected him.

However, he added that, in his opinion, if the French were allowed to take part in the Control Commission, "they would keep quiet for a time". And, in the end, Hopkins persuaded Roosevelt to agree with Churchill. France could not be given a zone to administer in Germany if she were not part of the Control Commission. He thought that relations with the French would be easier if they were part of the Commission.[48]

The question that a biographer of Charles de Gaulle cannot fail to ask on the subject of Yalta is two-fold: had France any right to be asked to be there? Would the General's presence in the Crimea have made the outcome any different? The answer to the first question seems to be simple: no. The answer to the second requires greater boldness, but, again, one is tempted to say no.

In so far as Yalta was a war conference, following on from that of Teheran, and situated at a time when victory seemed assured even if most of German territory had yet to be conquered and when the gigantic efforts of the Allied armies came before any other consideration, there was a certain reality brought out by the joke of the "club of five million soldiers": France had only ten divisions in the field, less than a quarter of what a General Zhukov or General Koniev had under their separate commands, or a Montgomery or a Bradley.

This was enough to weaken General de Gaulle's arguments for French participation in discussions dealing with the reconstitution of Europe or the creation of a world organization. Of course, de Gaulle felt impelled to make his views known on such subjects as German frontiers or collective security. But so did the leaders of other countries that, like France, "did not carry such weight". The sacrifices and successes of Free France were still not enough, in 1945, to efface the shame of June 1940, Vichy and collaboration.

There can also be no doubt that de Gaulle was now paying for the methods that he had used to rise from the abyss. Could he have revived France without mistreating his allies? Too weak to bow before others in 1940, the General was not strong enough to impose his will in 1945. But from the point of view of the higher interests of the country, this irritating exclusion does not seem to have cost very much.

At Yalta, Charles de Gaulle would certainly have sided with Churchill, thus stressing the complicity between Roosevelt and Stalin. It would have been harder for Roosevelt to shift positions in favour of French arguments.

Of course, General de Gaulle would certainly have contributed to the resistance put up by the Americans and British to Stalin's manoeuvres regarding Poland, but given his Moscow decisions – self-determination of the Poles, an exchange of unofficial representatives with the Lublin Committee, which had meanwhile become the "Warsaw provisional government" – how could he have altered the outcome of the conference?

According to the conclusions of the Crimea Conference, France: (a) was given an occupation zone in Germany; (b) became a member of the Allied Control Commission, that is to say, of the military government of Germany that was to be set up in Berlin; and (c) was made a full member of the Security Council of the United Nations, whose inaugural conference was to take place at San Francisco.

What French statesman could then have hoped for more? For a man like de

Gaulle, to receive is not the same thing as to conquer. What he would have brought back from Crimea as so many trophies of glory he saw as having been given him from afar. What a trick his allies had played on him!

But he was big enough to receive a present as haughtily as a wound. In the *Mémoires de guerre* we read that these arrangements were "in no way offensive" and "gave us important satisfactions".[49] It is said that, between de Gaulle and his great allies, the lull in the storm was never to last long. No sooner had the General been informed of his "presents", on 12 February, than the American Ambassador handed him an invitation from Roosevelt to meet him during his return trip, at Algiers. And the crisis flared up once again: for this invitation, de Gaulle writes in his *Mémoires*, seemed "an affront". So he declined the invitation, unleashing new storms and setting off against himself, this time, not only the American and British press, but, for the first time, a large section of French observers and politicians.

This was the heart of the matter: France's "rank" was in jeopardy. So we have to try to see the situation clearly, beyond the polemics unleashed. This time, de Gaulle's behaviour seemed indefensible: the rejection of an opportunity to put relations between Paris and Washington on a fresh footing seemed all the more unfortunate in that the President died two months later. This was to add a negative touch to the brutality of the political rejection: to refuse to be reconciled with a man on the verge of death.

Let us sum up the broad outlines of the affair. During his stay in Paris, on 27 January, Harry Hopkins suggested to Georges Bidault that a Roosevelt–de Gaulle meeting might be arranged for the day after the Yalta Conference. According to the *Mémoires de guerre*, the French Foreign Minister advised the visitor against giving such an invitation, since the General would not care to be linked with decisions made at Yalta that had not included him.[50] But Hopkins's papers[51] show that the day after the Yalta talks ended, he received a message from Bidault to the effect that the General had no wish to take part in the last stage of the negotiations, as Hopkins had proposed, but made it clear that de Gaulle "would be delighted to meet Roosevelt during his journey home".

Did the minister misinterpret his leader's wishes? Did he think that he could force de Gaulle's hand? When the American ambassador Jefferson Caffery, disturbed at having to pass on to Roosevelt de Gaulle's refusal, told Bidault how indignant he was at this change of position, the French minister could find no better excuse than the General's moods.

It would seem that three reasons governed Charles de Gaulle's mind. The first was what Bidault had anticipated – the refusal to approve measures adopted privately in a conference from which France had been excluded.

Secondly, Roosevelt had invited, "on board his battleship... Arab kings and heads of State of eastern countries, including the presidents of republics under French mandate". To be received in the same conditions struck de Gaulle as "an affront, whatever the present relationship of forces". And he ends this passage with the following significant words: "The sovereignty, the dignity of a great nation must be inviolable. I was responsible for that of France."[52]

Thirdly, and most important, Roosevelt had invited de Gaulle to Algiers: "Why should the American President invite the French President* to visit him in France? Perhaps for Franklin Roosevelt Algiers was not France, but all the more reason to remind him of the fact."[53]

How could FDR's advisers allow him to make such a blunder? Were they unaware that, legally, Algiers was still French territory? At best, they could not have forgotten that Algiers was a thorn in the side of French–US relations. At the level of *Realpolitik* (one on which de Gaulle found himself particularly at home), the refusal to meet Franklin Roosevelt, at a time when the President's prejudices were beginning to crumble under the blows of Hopkins and Cordell Hull's successor, Edward Stettinius, and when the Yalta triumvirate were finally prepared to receive France, if not as a war comrade, at least as a partner in the peace, was a costly one. That, at least, was how the press and public opinion considered it: within the government, de Gaulle won the approval of a majority of his colleagues, but not that of his Foreign Minister, Georges Bidault, who, dining with Claude Mauriac at the same time as the General was receiving Jefferson Caffery to inform him of his decision, declared gloomily: "Those three** are putting themselves into a situation to receive the worst slaps in the face from the General." There was a silence, then he went on: "Events seem to be proving de Gaulle right, but I am less in agreement than ever. I think he's mad."[54]

But this madness was to change the course of events no more than France's absence at Yalta. The important decisions had already been taken. France had recovered most of her responsibilities within an alliance whose members were to follow the same road for some time yet.

We cannot leave the subject of Yalta without observing the extent to which General de Gaulle helped to exaggerate the significance of the meeting from which he had been excluded. The idea of a hastily worked out "carving up of the world" in the Crimea between Stalin and a dying Roosevelt, abandoning half of Europe to the first so that the second could be left free to reign over the seas and outlying areas, came from him.

In fact, however fierce he turned out to be in various episodes of the negotiations, Stalin gained nothing at Yalta that he did not already have or that he would soon make sure he would have. If a carve-up did take place, it was three months later in Moscow between Churchill and Stalin, when the latter, with a few pencil marks, put in his pocket several million Hungarians and Romanians. This did not happen at Yalta.

Yalta was not a tragedy, but the photograph of a tragedy. The Soviet superpower won from it only the ratification of its military conquests – and if some corrective was brought to the war map and to the ratio of forces it was the reintegration of France with the conquerors. General de Gaulle won few victories that were as unambiguous as that one, the result of a battle that he had not apparently fought – except in four years of previous struggles during which he had persuaded Winston Churchill and Anthony Eden to act, in the Crimea, as the good advocates of a recovering France.

*   *   *

*The term was an audacious one, to say the least, at this time.
**The three present at Yalta.

In late April 1945, the Third Reich was on its last legs. Russians and Americans had joined up on the Elbe, Hamburg had fallen into the hands of the British, the Red Army was entering Berlin, the French 1st Army was heading for the Danube. On 30 April, in the bunker surrounded by the Russian vanguard, Hitler killed himself – but not before expelling from the Nazi Party his two appointed successors, Goering and Himmler, for having tried in turn, *in extremis*, to negotiate with the Western powers with a view to turning them round, supported by what was left of the Reich, against the USSR. SS Reichsführer Heinrich Himmler, a Nazi of Nazis, the executioner-in-chief, the engineer of genocide, sent a message to de Gaulle in which he urged him not to put himself in the hands of either the Anglo-Saxons, who "will treat him as a satellite", or of the Soviets, who "will liquidate" him, but to choose

> an "entente" with defeated Germany. Proclaim it at once! Lose no time in entering into relations with those men in the Reich who still possess *de facto* power and are willing to lead their country in a new direction. They're ready to do so. They invite you to command them. If you overcome the spirit of vengeance, if you seize the opportunity history offers you today, you will be the greatest man of all time.[55]

In his *Mémoires de guerre*, de Gaulle makes an odd comment on that insane document: he found "an element of truth in the picture it sketched". *Truth?* This way of presenting Himmler as a precursor of Adenauer is shocking, to say the least. In any case, the SS leader got no answer. Admiral Doenitz had no alternative but to resign himself to the unconditional surrender that the Allies demanded.

On 3 May, de Gaulle informed the Allies that he had appointed General de Lattre to represent France at the signing in Berlin of the cease-fire – and, four days later, informed the commander of the 1st Army that, if called upon to sign as a "witness", he must "demand conditions equivalent to those given the British representative, unless the latter signs on Eisenhower's behalf".

Meanwhile, the surrender of the German armies was signed at the Allied headquarters in Reims, on 7 May at 1 a.m., by General Jodl (Hitler's Chief of Staff) and Bedell Smith (Eisenhower's Chief of Staff), with General Susloparov, representing the Red Army, and Sevez, Deputy Chief of Staff of the French army, as the witnesses.

But the symmetrical and much more solemn ceremony organized by the Soviets two days later in Berlin, in which Marshal Zhukov, the victor of the last battles, was to receive the surrender of Field Marshal Keitel (the very same who, with the Führer at his side, imposed a humiliating surrender on the defeated French on 22 June 1940) did not pass altogether smoothly. For, where the requirements of rank were concerned, de Lattre was at least the equal of his master.

To begin with, de Lattre had to get himself recognized by Zhukov, who had not been informed that a French representative was coming; a tricolour then had to be hastily put together out of three bits of cloth; he then had to get accepted as a "witness" authorized to sign the Surrender in the same way as the US Air Force General Spaatz and the British Air Marshal Tedder; he then had to resist a counter-attack from Vishinsky, Zhukov's political adviser, who declared that these "witnesses" were doing double duty with Eisenhower's representatives; lastly, they had to sit round the signing table before which, at midnight, Keitel appeared. De Lattre describes the scene:

> He clicked his heels and saluted, haughtily, with his field marshal's baton. No one stood up. At first Keitel looked straight in front of him and, the baton still raised, looked from left to right, slowly, until his eye caught the tricolour flag. "Ach!" he muttered, "the French are here too! That's all we needed!"

On the afternoon of 8 May, Charles de Gaulle was able to declare on the radio: "The war has been won! Victory is here! It is the victory of the United Nations and the victory of France. The French commander was present and took part in the signing of the surrender document..."[56] In his *Mémoires de guerre*, de Gaulle writes: "The mission to which I was prompted by France's distress was now accomplished."[57]

Was it that prodigious achievement that freed him and led him to sketch out, before the Consultative Assembly on 15 May, an almost detached, if not critical analysis of the type of authority that he had exercised? It contains this curious plea in the form of an examination of conscience:

> A single sword, a single territory, a single justice, a single law. I do not doubt that this obstinately centralizing rigour seemed heavy to this or that group. This or that ally may have taken offence at this inflexibility of independence and sovereignty. But if France was to remain indivisible our effort had to be undivided at all costs.[58]

Indivisible? For the time being, it was the battle for rank that de Gaulle was to continue to fight, a battle that now took place in the United States. On 25 April, the inaugural conference of the United Nations opened at San Francisco. Roosevelt had died thirteen days before the opening of what was to be the culmination of his enormous efforts.

The French delegation was led by Georges Bidault, supported by Paul Boncour, an old-timer of the League of Nations and once close to de Gaulle in the Thirties. They had with them a remarkable set of instructions* handed to Bidault on the eve of his departure for the United States. The main idea that emerges from this text shows that Charles de Gaulle, who was to show so much hostility to the United Nations Organization (UNO), saw it at first as a useful instrument of collective security.

Although France had just been admitted as a permanent member of the Security Council, de Gaulle did not want to limit his possibilities by being bound by the Council's decision alone. He reminded his representatives, of course, that France must affirm herself as a Great Power; but he recommended that they do everything possible to strengthen the General Assembly in relation to the Council

---

*Lettres, Notes et Carnets (V, pp. 417–25) reveals these instructions as the work of Charles de Gaulle.

– on the grounds that the Assembly brought together the small and middle-sized powers on whom the diplomatic influence of France could most naturally be exerted, as well as ensuring that the organization was as democratic as it could be.

But the most significant instruction is this: "The most concrete result that we may derive from this conference is to link the United States to the security of the European continent, with a view to the necessary balance of forces in Europe." Thus General de Gaulle declares himself to be, even before the end of the hostilities with the Reich, a pioneer of the Atlantic Alliance.

So concerns with rank did not always deflect Charles de Gaulle's attention from realities: if it is true that France, at San Francisco, was put back in the first rank, as one of the Big Five possessing the right of veto, she must not shut herself up in that fortress. She must realize that it may be as beneficial to her to assume the role of the greatest of the small as to play that of the smallest of the great.

Although the strategy of rank could be accommodated in General de Gaulle with the clearest awareness of realities, it did not bring him only success. From the recognition of the French provisional government by the Big Three on 23 October 1944, to Churchill's visit to Paris, from the trip to Moscow to the Yalta decisions, and then to France's entry into the United Nations Security Council, de Gaulle had certainly made progress where rank was concerned, whether taking it by force or receiving it from other hands. But this apparently irresistible rise reached a setback in late July 1945, when the Big Three decided to meet again – this time at Potsdam, and again without de Gaulle.

In his *Mémoires*, Charles de Gaulle is keen to say that he did not regret his exclusion. Of course, he admits that he did feel at the time "renewed irritation". But was it not preferable to remain outside "superfluous" discussions?

> Naturally I regretted that I had not been present at Teheran. There, as a matter of fact, I would have defended the equilibrium of Europe while there would still have been some point in doing so. Subsequently I was sorry not to have been allowed to take part in the Yalta Conference, since there were still some chances of preventing the iron curtain from cutting Europe in two. Now everything had been arranged – what could I have done at Potsdam?[59]

And he adds that the conference appeared to have ended in "uproar". The word is certainly excessive. Harry Truman, the new President of the United States, had already given proof to Stalin of the pugnacity for which he was to be noted. Although Churchill seemed to have aged and, according to his old colleague Cadogan, said "quite a few silly things", he, too, faced up to the Georgian with unimpaired vitality – as witness this exchange:

> *Churchill*: And how are the reparations to be paid?
> *Stalin*: There's still quite a lot of fat on Germany.
> *Churchill*: I shall never agree to a situation that would condemn the inhabitants of the Ruhr to die of hunger simply because the Poles occupy all the cereal-producing lands in the East.
> *Stalin*: I'm not in the habit of complaining. We have lost five million men

during this war. We are terribly short of coal, and of many other things. If I described our situation and our needs, I would make even the Prime Minister weep.[60]

On the eve of the conference, rumour had it that Stalin had had cardiac trouble. His partners saw no sign of this. Harry Truman held firm. But on 25 July, Churchill learnt that the British electors had just replaced him by the Labour leader, Clement Attlee. This removal of his toughest opponent, a new demonstration in his eyes of the fragility of the democracies, could not but increase Stalin's ferocious appetite.

The fall of Churchill in the middle of the negotiations, the man who for five years de Gaulle had constantly consorted with, affronted, defied, wheedled, bullied and curiously admired, inspired the General to a meditation worthy of the subject. Having expressed his "sadness" (which probably concealed secret relief), he recalled that "this great politician had always been convinced that France was necessary to the free world", that "this exceptional artist was certainly conscious of the dramatic character of my mission", but once he saw de Gaulle as the representative of "an ambitious State apparently eager to recover her power in Europe and the world, Churchill had quite naturally felt something of Pitt's spirit in his soul". But what remained "ineffaceable", was, de Gaulle concluded, that "without him my efforts would have been futile from the start" and that "by lending me a strong and willing hand when he did, Churchill had vitally aided the cause of France".[61]

Charles de Gaulle did not resign himself, however, to what had been decided at Potsdam, where he saw not only the "uproar" of the western powers confronting Stalin, but the beginning of a process that was leading to the reunification of Germany. On 28 August 1945, a French memorandum handed to the Allies denounced the Potsdam decisions as seeming "to take for granted the reconstitution of a single German state. In the French government's view a division of Germany into several states, if it came about not as an imposed solution, but as the consequence of a natural development, would be favourable to the maintenance of security in Europe." And a few days later, this even more outspoken text was issued:

> There can be no question this time of a temporary occupation of the Rhineland. The security of France and of Europe requires that certain western regions of the Reich be permanently removed from German sovereignty. For such a policy to succeed the populations must be given *the sense of permanence, the certainty that they will no longer have anything to fear from a return of things.*[62]

As we shall see, these arguments were to bring de Gaulle some rough treatment from his allies and few results.

* * *

Charles de Gaulle finally recovered France's status as a Great Power with the ceremonial State visit to a victorious Washington after the San Francisco conference. The opportunity missed with Roosevelt at the beginning of the year was offered once again: Harry Truman welcomed de Gaulle to the White House on 22 August, and the General came to realize in the course of three interviews with Roosevelt's successor that his hosts were well disposed to France, at least in two domains. As for coal supplies, the new American leader gave a favourable reception to the plan to attach the Saar economically to France; on that of overseas territories, de Gaulle spoke of leading the French colonies towards independence, and Truman indicated, on the subject of Indo-China, that his administration "would not oppose a return to French authority and the French army in that country". This was a considerable change in the positions formerly held by Roosevelt.

The face-to-face meeting between Truman and de Gaulle was fruitful. The General's reception from the American public, always kindly disposed to champions, giants, performers, was even more so. At New York, Mayor Fiorello La Guardia gave him a reception worthy of Lindbergh; de Gaulle was to take obvious pleasure in remembering the shouts of "Hello, Charlie!" that punctuated the "indescribable storm" of the New York crowd. In that "explosion of enthusiasm" de Gaulle thought that he could detect "the extent of the city's extraordinary love of France".[63]

A few hours later, he was in Chicago, which was to be no less exuberant. Hervé Alphand recounts[64] how the plane arrived an hour late at the airport; their hosts, having drunk rather liberally in the meantime, were to give the General a reception that resounded with animal cries.

But however warm the popular welcome was, however understanding President Truman and his Secretary of State, James Byrnes, tried to be, there was at least one point on which the two sides could not agree: the German question, from which the whole of the General's strategy flowed. Truman, a positive thinker if ever there was one, could not understand that a country whose material annihilation he had observed in Berlin would now be capable of threatening anybody, whereas Stalin, whom he had just faced in Potsdam, seemed to him to embody the sole peril now facing the West. Did not a harsh policy towards the defeated run the risk of throwing Germany towards Communism?

As we have seen, de Gaulle saw things quite differently. Although he was quite willing to see Germany prosper and come closer to her victors, he demanded guarantees: an end of the centralized Reich, the autonomy of the left bank of the Rhine, an international regime in the Ruhr. Truman had "some reservations" and these continued to affect relations between the two governments.

It is clear that, from General de Gaulle's point of view, Harry Truman's replacement of Franklin Roosevelt at the White House was an improvement. He would now be appreciated in terms of what he did, not in terms of some strange, historical and impassioned quarrel. He had simply become an awkward partner – a very awkward partner. The archives of the Quai d'Orsay bear traces of misunderstandings that were, on account of the German question, to mark relations between Washington and Paris.

In an interview in *The Times* on 10 September 1945, General de Gaulle produced the best argument in favour of the French position: by holding Germany with a firm hand, one would help to reassure the countries of central Europe, thus avoiding a situation in which they would have to appeal to Moscow for protection against her. This would help to loosen the Russian hold on eastern Europe.

This argument was not enough to convince the American diplomats. On 2 October 1945, the American Secretary of State, James Byrnes, confided to his French colleague, Georges Bidault, that he "did not really understand the French position". He could not see what interest France could have in having beside her an unhappy neighbour, with too little space and unable to satisfy its needs. Nor could he see how the dismemberment of western Germany could be justified.

The mutual incomprehension was to last until the end of the year. In early December 1945, General Lucius Clay, United States representative on the Berlin Four-Power Commission (the military government of Germany), which France had been allowed to join despite Soviet opposition, declared to one of his French colleagues:

> If the USSR agrees, as Great Britain already does in principle, you will be excluded from the government of Germany within a few days.* You have not understood that Germany had to be governed from Berlin and not from Paris and that the general interest of Europe goes beyond the defence of French interests and petty questions of restitution. So much the worse for you.[65]

Charles de Gaulle himself was led to question whether his policy of punishing and dismembering Germany was well founded. Raymond Aron, in the weekly *Points de vue*, wrote at this time: "Punish Germany? Hitler took it upon himself to do that. We are still obsessed with the German question, as if the world were continuing to gravitate round Europe. To go back to the division of Germany is to go back three centuries."[66]

It is a fine thing to get one's rank back, and no one was better fitted to fight that battle than Charles de Gaulle – and he did it with grandiose determination. But, on the subject of the Rhine, his crusade began to look ridiculous. In times of misfortune excess is required. But did France, now back in place and peace restored, have to persist in pursuing such a controversial course?

At all events, France was independent. And, for the French, humiliation was at an end.

---

*A threat that was not carried out.

CHAPTER FIVE

The Superintendent of Penury

"L'intendance suivra"* is one of those overused historical sayings, one of those key formulae that though belonging to myth are no less (or more) significant for being so. It is one of those sayings that the great man did not even need to say, so appropriate it would have been if it had emanated from him. One has only to read the second and third chapters of Volume III of the *Mémoires de guerre* to realize that de Gaulle did not always isolate himself in the clouds of high strategy and world diplomacy and was quite capable of devoting long pages to what he calls "the human condition", that is to say, the everyday experience of French people and the values that were supposed to inspire them. Those who were his closest colleagues at this time – Palewski, Brouillet, Joxe – attest to the fact that, in meetings of the Council of Ministers or in the work of his private office, he in no way ignored *intendance* business. This is what Brouillet has to say: "General de Gaulle has acquired the reputation of attending only to foreign affairs. I can attest to the contrary. Those of us who, like Vallon and myself, were concerned with the economic, the political and the social had access to him just as often as the others."[1]

The material situation of France, or rather of the French people, was tragic. I cannot refrain from evoking here my own memories of the children of that time, so pale that they looked as if they had been dug out of the cellars in which they had so often sought refuge; of the skeleton-like old men, who, waiting for the return of men from the army or concentration camps, seemed to be stuck forever in queues, while the women worked for the whole family; of those vague crowds wandering, from an improbable train to an impossible bus, from Périgueux to Metz, from Avignon to Cherbourg.

France was a country haunted by hunger and cold, concerned with food tickets, food obtained "on the side", deals with the shopkeepers who dominated the market; and a country on which weighed, in Jean Cassou's words, "the only inheritance from Vichy, the mystique of the black market".

For some weeks the exaltation of Liberation swept away all before it and acted as a drug on public opinion. But as soon as the cold grew worse and the burden of the ongoing war grew heavier, poverty became a national obsession. The countryside, so often the main victim in wars, suffered this time less than the urban centres; despite requisitions, it only handed over what it did not need itself. The

*Which may be translated as "the administrators will follow". The "intendance" was, in French history, the administration of the provinces, but it is also the Quartermaster General's Department or service corps in an army. Clearly the words convey a high-minded military man's contempt for the most "civilian" section of an army. (trs.)

ever-increasing gap between the anger of the exhausted people and the great national ambition to which de Gaulle was calling it, was made the object of innumerable jokes. In the satirical magazine *Le Canard enchaîné*, Claude Garnier published a cartoon in which he showed the "government train". From the first carriage, reserved to "foreign affairs", emerges an enormous de Gaulle, behind whom a tiny Bidault tries to sit.* Then, from carriage to carriage, from justice to public works and finance, the carriages sink deeper into the mud, until, at the end, the carriage marked "supplies" is almost submerged.

That cartoon dates from January 1945. Three months later, the situation was even worse: the rations distributed to those having a right to them had sunk from 1000 calories to scarcely 900: nearly three times that was needed for normal work. It amounted to under 100 grams of bread a day, first 90, then 60 grams of meat a week. There was deep anger, especially in the worst-off regions, Provence and the Nord. Describing a visit to Lille by General de Gaulle, whom his native city welcomed enthusiastically, the Commissioner of the Republic tells how, as soon as the visitor had left, life resumed, "constricted, belts tightened, food tickets unhonoured, unrest skilfully maintained by opponents on both sides, demands for summary executions on the public square, rumours about the inability of the government to do better than when the Germans were here."[2]

"The greater the confusion, the greater the necessity of governing."[3] The General applied this eminently Gaullist axiom as much as his missions abroad allowed. "I attempted to make my aims equal to the demands and the dimensions of the subject. To govern by bold and arduous efforts and despite all disadvantages. This was my programme."[4] This is a new version of the strategy of circumstances which he had expounded in the Thirties.

It was in Lille, on 1 October, that he defined the broad lines of his economic strategy, the first lineaments of which had been traced out three weeks before in the speech at the Palais de Chaillot:**

> What we want, then, is to harness in common all that we possess on this earth and, to do this, there is no other way than what is called the planned economy. We want the State to plan the economic effort of the entire nation to the benefit of all and to do so in such a way as to improve the life of every Frenchman and Frenchwoman.
>
> At the point at which we find ourselves, it is no longer possible to accept those concentrations of interest that are called in the world trusts. The collectivity, that is to say, the State, must take direction of the great sources of the common wealth and supervise certain other activities without, of course, excluding those great levers in human activity, initiative and fair profit.[5]

Had he said anything different for a quarter of a century? Initiative on the part of the State, nationalization, planning, participation – there we have in a few lines a compendium of Gaullist thinking.

*When shown the cartoon, the minister remarked: "The front carriage is rather full..."
**See above, Chapter 1, pp. 9–10.

Two fundamental choices confronted Charles de Gaulle and the provisional government: one concerning governmental reform, the other administration. Should they, as the CNR, the left of the Resistance and a strong tendency within the government and Consultative Assembly advocated, take advantage of the profound mutation brought about by the collapse of Vichy, the crushing of Nazism, and the emergence of Free France, to give the country a new socio-economic apparatus, implying different relations of production and radically questioning the capitalism whose leaders in France had so often been compromised with the occupiers?

Should tomorrow be played off against today, the long term against the short term, the country kept corsetted in the rigour of the economic war following the war itself, in order to increase its chances of winning the battles against inflation and for production? Or should it be allowed at last to breathe, by gradually relaxing constraints, rationing, regimentation and by giving free play to initiative, even if that meant overlooking illegal and anti-patriotic profiteering?

The two types of choice were not automatically linked. One could choose economic rigour in the context of a timid reformism and let inflation rip while introducing a "revolution" of structures. Politically, the divisions were extremely complex. Although, from a historical viewpoint, one is tempted to place rigour and revolution "on the left", it has to be admitted that power over the economic domain belonged to the "right". Maurice Thorez, the Communist Party General Secretary, declared to André Philip: "We are for revolution tomorrow. Meanwhile, we want the capitalist system to function according to its own laws. We are not going to help the capitalist system to improve."[6]

The advocates of a policy of austerity had a leader: Pierre Mendès France, supported by a fairly large section of the SFIO* and above all by an influential and brilliant team of technocrats that he had gathered round him in Algiers or met up with again in Paris (Ardant, Riquebourg, Goetze, Guindey, Largentaye, Bloch-Lainé). Also there was Georges Boris, a friend of Mendès France, who had been in turn an adviser to Léon Blum and an associate of Charles de Gaulle, a convinced socialist who, "in the absence of revolutionary surgery", called for the system to be subjected to "rigorous orthopaedics".

In Algiers, Mendès France had been the minister responsible for economic and financial affairs as a whole. On his return to Paris, he found that he was in charge only of the Economy – a mere "fragment" of the ministry, "the least important in the General's thinking", he confided to me later. "He regarded my views as healthy, my concern for social equity, my single 'long-term' concerns justified. But he was rather mistrustful. By confining me to economic affairs, he was turning me into a social experimenter."[7]

The General had entrusted financial affairs, on René Pleven's advice, to a professional banker, Aimé Lepercq, a man from the North, a very brave member of the Resistance and organizer of the Paris uprising. He was not a conservative and his relations with Mendès France were to be excellent, with Jean Riquebourg acting as liaison agent: but his professional prejudices were to play against the innovation.

*Section française de l'Internationale Ouvrière – the French Socialist Party. (trs.)

The mechanisms of the liberal economy were already in place when the new minister was killed in an accident, in December. After thinking of allowing Mendès France to take up all his former responsibilities,[8] the General chose to call on René Pleven, who was rather unwilling to assume these crushing responsibilities, but who was now, more than anyone else, de Gaulle's confidant. Thus were put in place the protagonists of the most important of the debates that, in this domain, the "superintendent" would have to settle.

The question that arose first was the extent to which the socio-economic system was to be reformed. Was the productive apparatus to be completely changed or was it to be adjusted at the least cost? On this question, Raymond Aron relates a highly suggestive statement by Charles de Gaulle. Five years later, the sociologist was arguing, in his presence, that the French make a revolution from time to time, but never reforms. The General corrected him: "They only make reforms after the revolution."[9] Regarding himself as "the only revolutionary" in France, as we have seen, and confronted by a latent revolution, General de Gaulle put himself forward as the leader of the advocates of the most radical reforms.

Nothing could be more Gaullist than this text by Pierre Lefaucheux,* published in April 1945 in the *Cahiers politiques*: "The failure of capitalism had not been clearly understood despite the economic difficulties of the period 1919–35. It appeared with overwhelming clarity when a whole section of the employer class of 1940 rushed towards collaboration."[10] Was capitalism condemned, not for what it was, but for the diversion that an accident of history had led it into?

In his *Mémoires de guerre*, de Gaulle is concerned to remember that the great reform movement of 1944–45 was not a hasty improvisation:

> The programme had long since been determined. For I had prepared the realization of my original intentions, while the resistance fighters, of whatever tendency, were merely unanimous in their intentions. The study committees working clandestinely in France or openly in London and in Africa, had prepared drafts. In the course of one year, decrees and laws passed on my responsibility involved changes of enormous significance for the structure of the French economy and the condition of the workers, changes which pre-war governments had discussed fruitlessly for more than half a century.[11]

The "socialization" of the French economy carried out by de Gaulle was essentially expressed in five orders and laws, various in their origins, motivations and arrangements. They concerned the coal industry, the Renault and Gnome-et-Rhône factories, air transport and credit.

It was the nationalization of credit, a basic article in the CNR programme, that was the crowning of the Gaullist State control of the economy. Only the Bank of France, which had been put under State control in 1936, and the four greatest

---

*Lefaucheux was one of the organizers of the CGE (Comité général d'études) of the Resistance, who was put in charge of the Régie Renault.

banks (Crédit Lyonnais, Société Générale, Crédit Foncier and BNP*) were nationalized – though they were left with a large degree of managerial autonomy. The business banks, such as Rothschild and Paribas, escaped the net. But over half of French banking activity was now under government control.

In matters of structural reform, de Gaulle acted as a leader, unhesitatingly directing an operation that satisfied at one and the same time the Jacobin impatient to give the State new, powerful tools, and the puritan disinclined to accommodate the power of money, which had always been anathema to him.

But, in the matter of choosing the form of control that those responsible for the French economy should operate, we find him hesitant, driven back to the role of arbiter, which never came easily to him. In this area, the intransigent leader hesitated.

The party of rigour had lost the first round, and perhaps even the first two. As early as March 1944, in Algiers, Pierre Mendès France wrote to Georges Boris that his attempts to reduce inflation by freezing prices and wages and by tapping monetary surpluses was opposed by the Minister of Social Affairs, Adrien Tixier, who, under the influence of the CGT** and the PCF, insisted on rapid and large wage rises. He added that most of the members of the government – including General de Gaulle – were "terrified. No one wanted to run the risk of unpopularity."[12] And in August, again in Algiers, he published a note on the absolute priority to be given to saving the currency. "It will be necessary, at each stage, to resist the inevitable temptation of easy solutions."[13] The minister had no sooner arrived in Paris than he learnt of the decision taken by his colleagues, who had got there before him, on 28 August: a 40 per cent rise in wages, which, added to a 50 per cent increase in family allowances, set off an immediate, dramatic rise in inflation.

The government still decided against Mendès France's advice to launch a great "Liberation Loan". The fact that in this affair, in the fundamental choice between rigour à la Mendès and the convenience of high wages and borrowing, the General should have supported the latter against the former – he, the man who had declared that it was necessary "to govern despite all disadvantages" – is one of the puzzles of this life of contrasts.

There were two opposing views. The rigourists, who were inspired by Mendès France, demanded drastic monetary restrictions with a view to adjusting them to the shortage of goods available and striking at the illegal profits made during the war. Then there was the view represented by Pleven, who thought that the French had suffered too much already over the past five years to have new restrictions, especially monetary ones, inflicted on them. Here is Bloch-Lainé:

> It is too simple to say that Mendès was quite right and Pleven quite wrong. The counter-indications to the Mendès plan for severe devaluation were not negligible, especially this one: because the Americans did not recognize Free France, they had refused until October to print our banknotes (whereas

*Banque Nationale Populaire. (trs.)
**Confédération générale de travail, the largest and most Communist-dominated of the three trade union confederations. (trs.)

they had done so for the Belgians). We were therefore short of substitute money.[14]

The debate had begun within the government in December 1944. It appeared that Mendès France and Boris were supported only by two Socialist ministers, Laurent and Tixier. The Communists were hostile to Mendès's plan. The General refused to give an opinion. Then, on 18 January, the Minister of the National Economy handed the General his resignation, in one of the most critical letters that de Gaulle had ever received from an associate, and which he nevertheless published in an appendix of Volume III of the *Mémoires de guerre*:

> *Mon général*, I appeal to you, to your clear-sightedness, to your inflexibility, to all that has made the French nation have confidence in you, to take steps for the public health. I decline the responsibility for the heavy decisions against which I have striven in vain; I cannot accept measures which I think unworthy. I ask you therefore to give me my liberty.[15]

De Gaulle refused to accept the resignation and summoned the two antagonists, Pleven and Mendès France, to spend the following Sunday with him at his Bois de Boulogne home. Pleven spoke for twenty minutes, Mendès for over two hours. The General's first conclusion, according to Louis Vallon, was: "I shall never again allow anyone to talk to me for three hours on end about economics."[16]

René Pleven made a few concessions by accepting the free exchange of banknotes, which he had wanted to hold back until the summer. As a result, Mendès agreed to stay in the government. But, realizing that his policy had been finally abandoned, he confirmed his resignation on 5 April.

> As was to be expected, Pierre Mendès France resigned from the Government, at his own request. He did so with dignity, and I kept all my admiration for a colleague of such exceptional merit. Furthermore, if I did not adopt the policy he advocated, neither did I adopt an attitude preventing me from doing so eventually, should circumstances change. For Mendès France to be in a position to apply it eventually, however, he must remain faithful to his doctrine. For this reason his resignation was really a service to the State.[17]

There is no doubt that Charles de Gaulle held Pierre Mendès France in great esteem. The documents quoted above testify to this. Their convergences of character and of views as to the future of France welded them together for ever. But René Pleven, who was so different from Charles de Gaulle, had been his most useful colleague in time of war, the man in whom, more than in any other, he had placed his trust (so much so that he arranged never to take the same plane as he). Thus that flexible friend of the Americans and British had in fact become de Gaulle's right-hand man. Such factors counted at the time of the economic debate in 1945.

The policy that Mendès France was proposing was courageous, austere, burdened with "inconveniences"; it was a matter of climbing slowly and painfully upwards. For such an operation to succeed, the General had to place his name, his authority, his glory behind it. But this discussion began at the time of his trip to Moscow, continued during the tragedy of Strasbourg and culminated during the Yalta Conference. He was dealing with Stalin, Eisenhower and Roosevelt: he was in the grip of the very thing that concerned him most passionately – national greatness.

In de Gaulle's balance sheet, one may try to put on the positive side the nationalizations, for all their ambiguities, their partial failures and their relative flexibility. The inflation involved in the choice of April 1945 and the sacrifice of his most determined opponents were certainly, and for a long time to come, to be placed on the negative side. Then there is the question of economic planning.

The broad outlines had been laid down in Algiers by Pierre Mendès France and his colleagues, notably Jean de Largentaye. It was only after Jean Monnet's return from the United States in early 1946 – after de Gaulle's departure – that economic planning really came into force, in the very flexible form given it by the pure pragmatist that the author of the Victory Program was.

In his *Mémoires*, de Gaulle stresses three reforms that he is right to regard as essential: the extension of social insurance to cover all salaried workers automatically, a measure that did much more than all the wage rises to remove people from the horror of the working-class (or peasant) condition; the revision of the status of farm tenancy, which stabilized farmers on the land and paved the way for most of them to become owners of their land; and the setting up of factory committees, which tended to free the workers from "the role of instruments to which they had hitherto been confined"[18] and marked the first steps towards the association of capital, labour and technology that he saw as "the human structure of tomorrow's economy".

Can one compare the socio-economic balance-sheet of that government, which contained Socialists and Communists, with that of its immediate predecessor, the Cabinet of the Popular Front? In 1936, a Socialist was at the helm, but the Communists were kept to one side (indeed they were already hostile to nationalization in a reformist context). The international environment in which Blum acted – the imminence of war – was even more constricting than the one confronting de Gaulle after victory. But the economic tools at the disposal of the men of 1936 were not comparable with the ruined, fragmented economy left to the men of the Liberation.

Taking these differences into account, the two "performances" may be regarded as comparable: rehabilitation of working-class conditions, efforts to increase capital investment, a general prejudice in favour of planning, the thrust of inflation. It was not to be one of the least ironies of the history of that time that it placed in parallel the gentle disciple of Jaurès and the imperious restorer of French greatness, in a competition in which one tried to carry out his ideological vocation, while the other, with irritated benevolence, presided over a world that had moved away from his genius.

CHAPTER SIX

A Merciless Past

On 23 August 1944, a young doctor had just taken over the Ministry of Health, where he had been appointed by his "boss", Pasteur Vallery-Radot. His name was Paul Milliez. During the war, he had led the main resistance movement of the medical profession. On the desk of the Vichy minister's *chef-de-cabinet*, he found, conspicuously on view, a bundle of letters denouncing Jewish doctors to the Germans: it was a time bomb "left" by the fleeing Vichy officials, anxious to show that there were no exceptions to their baseness. Milliez, almost vomiting, hesitated, then set light to that parcel of filth.

Charles de Gaulle could not ignore what had been done in France or in France's name by all those who had held power from 17 June 1940 to 25 August 1944. War-time Gaullism mobilized groups and people round themes borrowed from both Joan of Arc and the Jacobins. On the one side were the "patriots", on the other the "traitors". Take, for instance, the speech made by General de Gaulle at Casablanca on 8 August 1943, a year before he had to confront the problems of the Liberation. Echoing Clemenceau's famous words – "the country will know that it is defended!" – de Gaulle declared: "One day, the country will have to know that it has been avenged!" And he went on: "There is only one word to say, 'treason', only one thing to do, 'justice'!"[1]

In 1944, de Gaulle was no more free than his Belgian or Dutch neighbours to decide between clemency and strictness. He could only try to channel people's feelings and orientate their unleashed lust for revenge (which often took hideous forms) in the direction of a *minimum* respect for the law.

When he did confront this painful subject in his *Mémoires*, five years after the event, in full possession of the figures drawn up by investigators, Charles de Gaulle could rightly recall the crime for which revenge was taken:

> 60 000 persons had been executed and more than 200 000 deported of whom a bare 50 000 survived. Furthermore, 35 000 men and women had been condemned by Vichy tribunals; 15 000 officers degraded under suspicion of being in the Resistance.* Now resentment was beyond control. The Government's duty was to keep a cool head, but to pass the sponge over so many crimes and abuses would have meant leaving a monstrous abscess to infect the country for ever. Justice must be done.

*Not to mention those who, like him, had been condemned to death.

He thought it right to add: "Justice was meted out as impartially as was humanly possible, considering the passions awakened. Those judgements which later proved to be ill-founded were extremely rare." We shall come back, of course, to the approval so generously granted de Gaulle by the General. Acquitted by himself, the General was not so acquitted by the victims of "impartial" justice. Before calling the counsel for the defence to the bar, we shall allow the prosecution to speak, as is only right.

There was Maurice Bardèche, the brother-in-law of the writer, Robert Brasillach, victim of one of those acts of "justice" of which the Liberators probably felt least proud. For Bardèche there was no "liberation" of Paris, only an "evacuation". In 1947, "France is occupied by the resisters", while General de Gaulle's policies, "far from placing us in an advantageous position at the negotiating table...have kept us out".

> It has been established, I believe, that 180 000 French citizens were shot by the Germans or died during deportation. Are you sure that the Resistance does not bear the responsibility for a good many of those 180 000 dead? If the historians who will come after us are capable one day of establishing statistics, two of them will be instructive. The first is that of the German officers and men murdered on French territory. The second is that of French citizens shot. I would be very surprised if the two graphs were not parallel.[2]

For Maurice Bardèche, the guilty men were not the executioners of Châteaubriant, but the hostages; they had all done something against the Wehrmacht. And who was responsible for throwing women and children into the furnace of Oradour, if not the *maquisards* who had dared to attack the SS on their way to the Normandy front?

We now come to two members of the Resistance, the writers Jean Paulhan and François Mauriac. In his *Lettre aux directeurs de la Résistance*,[3] Paulhan declares that, taking families into account, the victims of the Liberation must be estimated at 1 500 000 and indeed stresses the abuses of this "justice". He does not maintain that the occupiers were not the "enemy". He points out that – the laws being what they were in France in 1944 – none of those who appeared before the various liberation courts were "judged",[4] since neither article 75 nor article 83 of the Penal Code applied, in his view, either to Pétain, Laval, Brasillach or any of the others. Thus the "purge" was merely a tissue of denials of justice and judicious errors.

But he, too, weakens his case by provocative counter-truths. What is one to think of an author who writes that at Vichy, in July 1940, "M. Paul Reynaud and M. Vincent Auriol, and the following day Léon Blum, Jules Moch, Herriot, proposed handing over all State powers to Marshal Pétain – whom they begged to negotiate, to come to an agreement with, in short to collaborate with Germany." Why does the defence of noble causes lead a man of Paulhan's stature to offer such indecent calumnies?

The punishment of collaborators was ill-founded, badly carried out and badly supervised. Contrary to the order given by de Gaulle on 25 August 1944, it went on far longer than necessary, leading to quite evident denials of justice. Tried in January 1945, Robert Brasillach was condemned to death. Two years later, he would have received a five-year prison sentence and would quite likely be sitting in the Académie Française today. Angeli, the Prefect of the Rhône, was tried at Lyon and condemned to death. Since the Appeal Court reversed the sentence, he was retried, this time in Paris: he was given a four-year prison sentence.

No one has spoken more eloquently of these abuses than François Mauriac, who opposed them from the outset. Ten years later, in a letter to a correspondent who is not named, but was probably his fellow-Academician Jacques de Lacretelle, he makes this overall judgement:

> The purge was the result of a lie and flagrant injustice. The lie consisted in denying the evident legality (I am not saying legitimacy) of Vichy. Those who followed its political orders ought all therefore (traitors, denouncers and torturers apart) to benefit at the very least from mitigating circumstances.
>
> The injustice lay in the emergency courts. It was a useless injustice since hostilities were still continuing and courts martial would have been sufficient to the task. It was a stupid injustice because it played the Communists' game and provided them with a weapon that they used in an appalling way. At that time, in masterly fashion, whatever one says, General de Gaulle deprived them of all the others, but he left them that one.[5]

But can one denounce the errors, abuses, excesses of the purge without remembering that the repression of 1944–45 was only one of the later phases of a tragic process that had been preceded by the "order" enforced by Vichy and the Nazi occupiers? Between June 1944 and May 1945 almost all the violence occurred while the battle was still raging against an invader whose status may have been ambiguous (as a result of the armistice and of Montoire) until June 1944. From the Normandy landing onwards, for the overwhelming majority of the population whatever the standing of the Germans had been they were now the "enemy": an enemy that, from Sainte-Mère-l'Eglise to Oradour, from Asq to Tulle and Mont-Valérien, left in its wake thousands of French men and women, hanged, shot or burnt alive.

This "justice" meted out by the Liberation had a double source. The first, based on an essentially political logic, may be seen from two points of view. First, Vichy had been the seat only of a "pseudo-government", so fallacious that General de Gaulle did not even have to proclaim a new Republic, because the old one had never ceased to exist. Everything that had been done in the name of that usurping system was therefore illegal. Second, since the Armistice of 26 June 1940 had not, by definition, put an end to the state of war, the occupiers remained legally, until peace was signed, enemies.

Although it is difficult to challenge the second point – the Armistice did not bring the state of war to an end – it is obviously much more difficult to argue the fundamental illegality of the Vichy government. From 17 June to 10 July 1940, whatever one may think of it, the Cabinet presided over by Marshal Pétain, regularly summoned by the head of State and plebiscited by the nation, was obviously legal. It was as such that it signed the Armistice with Hitler.

The second source of this "justice" was of a revolutionary, or spontaneous nature. If this or that individual were prosecuted at that time, it was also in terms of a politico-social dialectic that had served as a background to national history for the past five years – or for the past seventy-five years. During the great debates of the mid-1930s, the nation had been divided against itself. But some of the debates went back even further. When, during his trial, Charles Maurras shouted out, "It's revenge for the Dreyfus affair!", he was partly right, but he might also have said: "It's the victory of the Popular Front."

In such circumstances, one cannot in any case speak of equity. It was the time when, criticizing the "indulgence" shown by a court called upon to try a leading Vichy politician, Jacques Duclos declared: "One must judge with a sacred hate!" And during the trial of Jacques Benoist-Méchin, one of his Communist comrades called out: "We had deaths to avenge!"

One cannot offer a simple balance sheet of the purges without recalling that there were few figures more violently and constantly argued over in contemporary polemics. A series of investigations, carried out by the police in 1948, by the Ministry of the Interior in 1951–52, and again by the police in 1958; by the American historian Peter Novick and the French historian Charles-Louis Foulon; and finally by the History Committee on the History of the Second World War in the 1970s have made it possible to establish what look like serious figures. I shall refer above all to those of Marcel Baudot, a former Inspector-General of the Archives de France, whose competence and good faith are above question.

A number of kinds of distinction have to be made. Who? When? In what circumstances? To begin with, as we have seen, we have to define the authors of executions and reprisals, which may seem elementary but has not always been done: Marcel Baudot notes that the 680 victims of the massacre of Oradour were for a long time counted in the statistics for the "terror" of 1945, and Charles-Louis Foulon shows how the newspaper *Spécial-Dernière*, having published the photograph of a "traitor" tortured and executed by the FFIs, had to apologize a week later: the man in question was a *maquisard* who had been hanged by the Germans. On the other hand, victims of the summary purges were, especially in the Midi, presented as martyrs of the Resistance.

There is another useful distinction: that between victims before and after 6 June 1944 (the date of the landing and of General de Gaulle's call for the "national insurrection"), and those who were reported after 26 August 1944 (the point at which Charles de Gaulle took up his responsibilities, established courts and assumed control of the civil service).

Lastly, there is the distinction between the summary executions, which were often mere murders, and the decisions of the criminal and civil courts.

If one takes the figures examined by Baudot (and with him such serious historians as J.-P. Rioux or C.-L. Foulon) it has to be admitted that close on 10 000 French citizens were executed or killed by what might be called the forces of the Liberation – including 767 executions of legal sentences.

To examine the action of the courts alone, one has to turn to the figures arrived at by Peter Novick: of the 163 077 cases tried, 73 501 were dismissed or the accused was acquitted (45 per cent); and there were 40 249 sentences involving the loss of civil rights, 26 649 sentences to gaol, 10 434 sentences to hard labour for a time, 2777 of hard labour in perpetuity, 7037 sentences to death, including 4397 in absentia – and, taking presidential pardons into account, 767 executions.

Peter Novick shows that, contrary to legend, justice was less severe in France than in the other West European countries occupied by the Nazis: in percentage terms of the population, three times more people were executed in Belgium, twice as many in Holland and Denmark. If justice acted more quickly in those countries, the percentage of persons imprisoned was 0.94 per 1000 in France, 3.74 per 1000 in Denmark, 4.19 in the Netherlands, 5.96 in Belgium and 6.33 in Norway; furthermore, the suspended prison sentences, the releases on bail, the dismissals of cases, the refusals to suspend civil rights were more rapid and more numerous in France than elsewhere.[6]

But the important thing here is obviously the action taken by General de Gaulle, head of the provisional government and interim head of State, on the course of this justice – by his statements, his part in drawing up or implementing laws concerning capital crimes (those that set up the emergency courts, on 26 June, 26 August and 28 November 1944) and by the exercise of the right of pardon.

In any case, when he seized the centre of legal power, on 25 August 1945, Charles de Gaulle did have a record on the matter. Seventeen months earlier, he had had Pierre Pucheu executed, after being condemned to death by the military court in Algiers. He wrote to General Giraud, "the government is the sole qualified judge".[7] This decision and the tone in which it was expressed might have led one to foresee a policy of massive repression.

But, in the speech that he gave two weeks later, on 4 April 1944, he took care to distinguish between the "punishment" of collaborators, the "sanctions" against those who had merely obeyed orders and the humiliation incurred by fools, thus seeming to reserve the full might of justice to those who had taken initiatives in favour of the occupiers or acted in open collaboration with them.

To be more precise, Michel Debré (who, as Commissioner of the Republic in Angers, had to take over the responsibilities for both the law and the police) states that the authorities emanating from the Resistance had decided to distinguish quite clearly between the activities of collaboration with the occupiers, which fell under the repressive jurisdiction, and mere obedience to the Vichy authorities, which came under the administrative courts.[8] It was everyday practice and popular pressure that overcame plans that were certainly less strict than the purgings that took place between August 1944 and the end of 1945.

It is clear that, when confronted by the problem of purging, Charles de Gaulle had his hands free with regard to Yalta or the United Nations. So let us consider the context in which he took his decisions and the pressures on him to do so.

The context is that of a provisional government in which the militant Resistance and the Socialist and Communist leaders hold about half of the portfolios and are at least bound by the demands expressed by those they represent in favour of a severe policy of repression, coupled with the insistent clamour from the Consultative Assembly – the less power a parliament has, the more demanding it is on matters of "principle".

Within the government, the relevant minister was the Christian Democrat, François de Menthon, a law professor, certainly an honest man and far removed from anything to do with sectarianism, violence and the exercise of terror. He was to be succeeded during the summer* by his colleague Pierre-Henri Teitgen, also a lawyer by profession, who, like him, had been in the Resistance and was in fact the celebrated "Tristan".

Can one speak of popular pressure? Yes and no. No, because an analysis of General de Gaulle's correspondence shows that he was driven to exercise clemency. Yes, because studies of the public opinion of the time, especially those coming from the provincial *commissaires*, indicate that a disturbed, disorientated, hungry population was looking for scapegoats and naturally found them among the defeated.

Nowadays one can imagine a government suddenly deciding that the ministers in the Pétain government, the prefects of the Vichy police, the members of the French Gestapo and of the Waffen SS had done no more than obey Marshal Pétain and that he alone ought to be put on trial (this was the thesis proposed by Maurice Bardèche) and that since the single individual responsible was living abroad (in accordance with General de Gaulle's wishes), there was nothing the legal system could do about it. Anyone who knew the France of 1944 knows very well that such a course was impossible.

And whoever seriously suggests that the cessation of hostilities, on 8 May 1945, should have suddenly ended all acts of revenge and opened the way for an amnesty must not forget that this was also the date when the deportees began to return, when people began to learn of the full horror that they and their fellow prisoners had suffered. When thousands and thousands of ghosts in striped jackets bore witness to Auschwitz, who could dissociate that immeasurable and unnameable crime from those who, from near or far, had helped to preserve, to serve, to praise, to supply the executioners?

May 1945, which might have been the moment for clemency, was, on the contrary, that of indignation. How can one assess the shock caused to General de Gaulle by the return of four members of his family who had worn convicts' clothes – above all his niece, Geneviève, of whom he was particularly fond? De Gaulle's attitude to the purges has to be considered from a position that was so clearly his own: that of the right to pardon. He regarded this right in the highest light and he exercised it widely, saving from death two-thirds of those whose files he had examined, especially women, minors and almost all the "scapegoats". It might even be said that the use he made of this prerogative of heads of State was one of the essential elements in Charles de Gaulle's exercise of power between 1944 and 1946.

In late January 1945, realizing that this task was one more burden on the General, René Brouillet and the Garde de Sceaux, François de Menthon, suggested transferring the right of pardon to the Minister of State, Jules Jeanneney, a

---

*When de Menthon's services were required at the Nuremberg Trials.

good lawyer and a man of honour. With Jeanneney having given his agreement, though not without disquiet, Brouillet put his plan to the General. "Out of the question, Brouillet. It is the royal prerogative *par excellence*, the highest responsibility of a head of State, the only one that he cannot delegate. For that, and for nothing else, do I have to account only to God."[9]

In that trial of trials of the Liberation, account must be taken of the role played by Mauriac, father and son, of the tireless campaign waged by François Mauriac, columnist of *Le Figaro*, in favour of indulgence and of the presence at de Gaulle's side of Claude Mauriac, who did not cease to plead for a minimum of justice to be accorded to Charles Maurras or Robert Brasillach. And what of Henri Béraud? The death sentence passed on this right-wing polemicist in December 1944 was one of the worst scandals of judicial purging. In his well-known column, between 1940 and 1944, he constantly abused an England that he detested. But then his plebeian xenophobia was also directed at the Germans. If he had shown a lack of intelligence towards the friend, where was the association with the enemy that alone would warrant the death sentence to be executed? To send such a man to his death was a sheer denial of justice. On 4 January 1945, Mauriac published in *Le Figaro* a violent attack on the "inequity" of the death sentence that had been passed the day before. Late in the night of 6 January, the General received Henri Béraud's defenders, including Maître Albert Naud,* who found him "impenetrable". When the barrister tried to hand him his client's file, the General cut him short: "Useless!" Naud left very worried. Next day, Henri Béraud was pardoned.

A week later, de Gaulle asked Claude Mauriac:

"What did your father think when he learnt that I had pardoned Béraud?"

"You know, he never considered the problem from the political angle as you must do, but only from a sentimental point of view..."

Charles Maurras, the founder of *Action française*, was the leader and symbol of the antisemitic extreme right. He had been the bard of the Vichy regime. During his imprisonment at Lyon, Claude Mauriac had handed the General, on behalf of his father, a letter from David Eccles, an English university teacher specializing in France, warning that the condemning to death of that great French writer would be taken very badly indeed throughout the world. The General's secretary dotted the "i"s:

"If Maurras were condemned to death and executed, an irremediable ditch would be dug between a whole category of French people and you."

"But where is he?"

"At Lyon..."

"You really think that he doesn't risk the guillotine."

"But he does risk death, *mon Général*. You know how things are in the provinces at the moment and anything could be done before you hear of it."

De Gaulle telephoned the Minister of Justice:

"I'm ringing about Maurras. It is of the utmost importance that he is not judged in some corner: the country would not understand. It's a *political* trial.

---

*He was Pierre Laval's defence counsel the following year.

We are dealing with the promoter of National Revolution. At Lyon he couldn't explain himself. *He must be allowed to explain himself.* It's a matter for the High Court, don't you think ... There's no question about it: the High Court will judge him. It will be the trial of the National Revolution."[10]

As he concluded, he turned to Claude Mauriac: "We can count on the High Court not to hurt him. High Courts are used to showing mercy."[11] In fact, Maurras was tried at Lyon – which shows the limits of the power then exercised by de Gaulle and his minister. But the founder of *Action française* (whose denunciation of a Jewish family in February 1944 had led to the death of one of the sons of that family) was saved.

Robert Brasillach, his disciple, was a brilliant writer, fascinated by Nazism. Of all those who advocated an alliance with the Nazis within the "New Europe", he was probably, with Drieu la Rochelle, the man whose writings weighed most heavily. He pursued François Mauriac with vigilant hatred, denouncing him as the embodiment of "enJewished" and treasonable Christianity, who had supported the "Reds" in Spain and the "terrorist" maquis. He spared Mauriac no sarcasm, no insult, no imputation – relating not only to his work, but also to his private life.

Brasillach gave himself up on 14 September. Taken into custody, he was to go before the courts early in 1945: everybody knew, including himself, that he ran the risk of losing his head. On 19 January at 1 p.m. Robert Brasillach appeared before the court. At 6 p.m. he was condemned to death. Rejecting appearances by witnesses for the defence, he had pleaded on his writings alone, on his words alone – some of which were quite simply unspeakable.

The condemned man might be pardoned. An appeal for clemency was set up, with François Mauriac as its ardent spokesman. A petition – signed by sixty-three writers, supporters as well as opponents of the Resistance – was inspired by Mauriac's attempts to influence the man who held the pardon in his hands.

On Saturday 3 February, François Mauriac was received at the Rue Saint-Dominique by the General. What struck him about de Gaulle was "his prodigious capacity for contempt", his "aristocratic officer side; full of pride and awareness of his superiority" and also his relative scepticism about the "apparent legitimacy of Vichy" and of the "Pétain myth".

Speaking of the Brasillach case, François Mauriac felt that "de Gaulle is favourably disposed: 'Brasillach is a matter of public opinion. I don't think he'll be shot.'"

"I have the very clear impression," François Mauriac adds to his son, "that the *political* question did not arise for him when it was a matter of giving or refusing pardon. It's a point that contradicts the General's apparent inhumanity. I must add that he spoke to me of the purges with a great deal of tact and sensitivity."[12] Brasillach's barrister, who saw the General the following night, did not get the same impression. De Gaulle refused any exchange, asked no questions, seemed little moved by the list of signatories of the petition in favour of the condemned man. On Monday 5 February, it was learnt that General de Gaulle, having meanwhile studied the file, which Claude Mauriac declared to be "damning", refused a pardon. Robert Brasillach was shot the following morning, 6 February.

The intransigents (PCF, CNR, etc.), having failed to obtain the heads either of Béraud or of Maurras, insisted on that of Brasillach, the only leading collaborationist intellectual – in the absence of Drieu la Rochelle, who was in hiding, and Céline, who had taken refuge in Germany – available for them to vent their anger on.

Louis Vallon, one of the General's old London companions, has recounted how, in Brasillach's file, it was a photograph of the writer wearing German uniform* that had removed any doubts from the mind of de Gaulle.[13] What more eloquent testimony could "intelligence with the enemy" have? The same argument was advanced by de Gaulle during a conversation with the great actor Louis Jouvet, who, two years later, asked him why he had decided not to pardon Brasillach.

A few weeks later, Claude Mauriac could not mention the writer's end without regret. Charles de Gaulle replied: "What of it! He was shot, like a soldier!" A singular homage to the responsibility of intellectuals.

It was Philippe Pétain who presented the biggest problem. Immediately after the Liberation, de Gaulle declared to anybody who would listen that he wanted the Marshal to end his days in peace either in Switzerland or "in the Midi, where he would wait for death to come and take him".[14] Taken from Vichy on 20 August 1944 by a platoon of the Wehrmacht, the Marshal was driven to Sigmaringen, a small, aristocratic town near Württemberg, where he was joined by a few of his faithful followers. On 20 September, the Marshal asked to return to France, knowing that he would be put on trial.

Philippe Pétain, who was exasperated by the divisions among what was left of his supporters at Sigmaringen** and who noted the progress of the French army through Baden-Württemberg, wrote to Hitler on 5 April demanding to be allowed to return to France, for it would be "to forfeit my honour" to "seek refuge abroad" in order to avoid his responsibilities. But he was not obeyed: Pétain was taken to Switzerland, where, on 23 April, after various deals with de Gaulle, the Federal Council discreetly allowed him to remain – if he so wished. But the Marshal thought only of returning to France: on 26 April, he turned up at the frontier, where he was put in the care of General Koenig.

The train taking him to Paris was stopped on several occasions by a hostile crowd: at Pontarlier, the windows of the carriage were stoned by a crowd shouting insults. Mme Pétain asked their guard: "Is it here that we are to be assassinated?"

The Marshal was imprisoned in the fortress of Montrouge, where, on 30 April, his interrogation began. There were few volunteers to take on his defence: on 15 May, Maître Isorni took over the direction of the French team. The trial opened on 26 July, in the small hall of the first courtroom of the Palais de Justice in Paris, where the High Court sat. Surprisingly enough, almost nothing emerges, either in private or in public, of the General's thoughts on the matter. When writing his *Mémoires de guerre*, he is keen to record that neither his government nor he himself intervened in the investigation carried out by the High Court – except to recommend that they reach their conclusions as soon as possible.

---

*Brasillach's sister has denied that her brother ever wore that uniform. (trs.)
**On this episode, one should of course read Céline's story, *D'un château l'autre*.

The trial of Pierre Laval did not allow him to be quite so circumspect, on account of the extravagant behaviour that marked that pretence of justice, in which the former prime minister's misdeeds seemed constantly to balance those with which he was charged. Of the twenty-five examinations of witnesses planned by the examining magistrate, only twelve took place. The jury consisted of twelve members of the Resistance and twelve parliamentarians, all antagonistic towards him, all desperate for revenge or compensation: on more than one occasion one of them would stand up in the middle of the proceedings and promise the accused that he would get twelve bullets in his body! Most of the witnesses were absent and the judge, Mongibeaux, adopted an openly accusing attitude: it was not a trial, it was a settling of accounts.

In his *Mémoires de guerre*, de Gaulle gives a strange version of the trial, asserting that Laval "attempted to surround his trial with an aura of irregularity so that justice would either have recourse to some new trial or commute the sentence of capital punishment". It was as if the former Prime Minister deprived the lawyers of certain means of defence and formed a jury bent on revenge. By saying or getting others to say that the trial had to be over before the elections (an interview with Claude Mauriac reflects this haste), the General directly assumed part of the responsibility for the chaotic proceedings.

On 8 October, after three days of incoherent exchanges, two of which took place without the presence of the accused and his defenders, Pierre Laval asked to return to the court. P.-H. Teitgen, the Garde des Sceaux, advised this course on his lawyers: the court usher went and discreetly conveyed this offer to the judge, who interrupted him angrily: "He can go to hell. We've got to bring it to an end."[15]

Next day, 9 October, the Marshal's right-hand man was condemned to death. His lawyers immediately requested an audience with General de Gaulle, urging Reynaud, Blum and Mauriac to support their requests. The first published an article condemning the conduct of the trial, the second gave permission to the lawyers to declare that he deplored that Laval had not been properly tried, the third wrote to Teitgen demanding "proper justice".

On 12 October, at 7 p.m., General de Gaulle received the condemned man's lawyers in the Rue Saint-Dominique. The reception was courteous, but cold. To British journalists, the General had declared a few hours before that there would "certainly not" be another trial. Unmoved, he listened to the pleas of Maître Naud and his colleagues.

On the evening of 14 October, Laval's lawyers were warned by the authorities that their client would be executed the following morning, against the view of the Minister of Justice that the execution should be postponed. Here, again, violent political pressure has often been deduced. The decisive elections of 21 October 1945 were only a week away.

On 15 October, as the magistrates and defence counsel were about to enter the condemned man's cell to inform him that he would soon be executed, Pierre Laval swallowed a cyanide tablet. However, after over an hour's treatment he was brought round. The procurator, Mornet, then decreed: "The execution may now proceed." But the condemned man continued to vomit. Can one execute a dying man? The prefect of police, Luizet, preferred to obtain the opinion of the head of government. He rushed over to the Rue Saint-Dominique. General de Gaulle listened to him, eyes half closed: "Pierre Laval no longer belongs to us. Let the officer commanding the platoon do his duty."[16]

CHAPTER SEVEN

The Centrifugal "Empire"

Charles de Gaulle was fully aware that decolonization was inevitable. It is all said in his *Mémoires de guerre*:

> If overseas territories were to cut themselves off from Metropolitan France, or if our forces were to be engaged in those territories, what would our position be in Europe? Conversely, if those territories remained associated with us, we would have every opportunity for action on the continent! The age-old destiny of France! Yet after what had happened on the soil of our African and Asian possessions, any attempt to maintain our Empire there as it had been would be perilous, particularly when new nationalist movements were springing up all over the world with Russia and America competing for their adherence. If the peoples for whom we were responsible were to remain with France tomorrow, we had to take the initiative and transform a relation which at present was merely one of dependency for them. On condition, of course, that we remained firm, like a nation that knows what it wants, not going back on its word, but insisting on loyalty to the word given it as well.[1]

De Gaulle was not only the man of "circumstances": he was also the man who had "a certain idea of France". He was a realist, but he also had a powerful sense of national unity and sovereignty. This conflict between a dominating temperament nourished on a history of conquest and an intelligence alert to contemporary realities was constantly to give a tragic character to de Gaulle's treatment of the crises and convulsions that now beset the Empire from the Far East to West Africa, not forgetting the Levant, which, for four years, was the focus of some of his worst trials and tribulations.

Of Indo-China, de Gaulle knew only two things: that by defining it as a "balcony over the Pacific", his friend Paul Reynaud had eloquently indicated its strategic interest, and that his "hostile ally" Roosevelt seemed determined to expel the exploiting French, who, in any case, were incapable of guaranteeing its protection.* Military imperatives and anti-American defiance were to help to lock in a policy which, though illuminated by that dazzling intelligence, seemed animated only by a concern to restore to the French nation an inheritance that was all the more precious in that it was far away and symbolized the world-wide character of the collection of lands and peoples grouped under the tricolour flag.

On entering the Rue Saint-Dominique in 1944, de Gaulle already had an Indo-

---

*In fact, according to the American historian Bernard Seilsheimer, FDR's ideas on this subject were evolving in 1944.

Chinese past. By the time of the appeal of June 1940, he had in a sense put Indo-China in brackets – as he suggests in the *Mémoires de guerre*: "To me, sailing a very small boat on the ocean of war, Indo-China then seemed to me like a big disabled ship that I could not help until at last I had gathered together all the means of rescue. Seeing it disappear in the mist, I swore to myself to bring it back one day."[2]

The "means of rescue" soon appeared. They were men. At Chungking, where Chiang Kai-shek had moved his government, while continuing to fight the Japanese, a small Free French mission had been set up, consisting of Dr Béchamp and the explorer Guibaut, who was soon to be relieved by Professor Escarra; at Calcutta, the French Governor kept up contact with the British authorities. A rubber manufacturer, François de Langlade, had made contact with two planters from Malaysia, Mario Bogret and William Bazé, hostile to the Vichy government. In Chinese Yunnan, two information officers, Major Tuttenges and Captain Milon, set up one of the best networks in the region, while the diplomatic counsellor of the pro-Vichy Governor-General Decoux, Claude de Boisanger, sent an emissary called François to de Gaulle. Thus, little by little, the foundations were laid for a concerted effort.

From summer 1943, then, de Gaulle was able to draw up an Indo-Chinese strategy. The principles of this strategy were expressed in a declaration to the peoples of Indo-China, delivered in Algiers on 8 December 1943, which, while reaffirming the principle of French sovereignty in the peninsula, opened up prospects of collective development, in the form of a "free and close association between France and the Indo-Chinese peoples".

The military means were beginning to be brought together in India, under the direction of General Blaizot, head of the "expeditionary corps", whose task it now was to bring Indo-China back to the Free French side. Then, in August 1944, de Gaulle sent a close confidant to Indo-China, François de Langlade, whose mission was to contact Admiral Decoux, the High Commissioner appointed by Pétain. But, when the Free French envoy proposed that Indo-China should be brought over to the side of the Allies, Decoux replied that if Indo-China were to be brought back into the French orbit it would be better employed improving their relations with Japan, which had no hostile intentions and hoped in the long term to use the French to negotiate with the Americans and British.

By trying to come to an agreement with Decoux, the General was in fact breaking with what had seemed to be an article of faith with him: the men of Vichy were all the same, they would pay any price to keep their jobs. For once, he tried to compromise – and failed pitifully.

On 9 March 1945, in the late afternoon, an event occurred that de Gaulle had foreseen, but which nevertheless upset his military and political plans: the Japanese took over all forms of power in the Indo-Chinese peninsula, interning French civil servants and soldiers and massacring all those who tried to resist. The French presence in Indo-China being thus reduced to nothing, the Japanese set up in the various capitals (Hue, Phnom Penh, Luang Prabang) governments declared to be "independent" – and which were, in fact, more so than has often been said.

The Japanese action might have had the beneficial effect of bringing the Americans closer to a France now implicated in the merciless struggle against Tokyo. Nothing of the kind took place. The Americans, led by General Wedemeyer, continued to follow the line of evicting the French to the benefit of the Chinese.

Did the activities of the anti-Japanese resistance, which de Gaulle had set in train since 1943, lead to the Japanese take-over in March 1945? And if he had followed Admiral Decoux's advice ("Leave the Japanese alone!"*), would it have made any difference? Most historians, military and civil, tend to doubt it. These activities were not important enough to affect the major decisions of the Tokyo General Staff. It was the loss of the Philippines, six months earlier, that forced the Japanese strategists to alter their plans.

Although he had foreseen it, Charles de Gaulle was nevertheless "caught on the wrong foot" by the operation of 9 March. Indeed, he was preparing to publish a declaration of political intentions, which would provide the political foundations necessary for the great enterprise that he was planning of returning to Indo-China. This document transformed the Indo-Chinese colony into a federal State, bringing together the five Indo-Chinese countries (Annam, Tonkin, Cochin China, Cambodia, Laos) under the authority of a Governor-General appointed by Paris, the whole State being part of the "French Union". Read today, this document seems to be well behind the realities of the time. But it did open up certain prospects: the problem was that it was not published until 24 March 1945, two weeks after the Japanese seizure, when the "independence" of those countries had been proclaimed and French authority abolished. What good could be said of this promise of federal autonomy to countries that had already been offered independence by a Japan that everyone regarded as being on its last legs?

Furthermore, the declaration of 24 March had a major defect: it placed on the same level Indo-Chinese "countries" as different in "culture, race and tradition" as Cambodia and Laos, and the three "ky"** that made up what was not yet called Vietnam. It was not the timid character of this federalism "within the French Union" which the political groups of Hanoi and Saigon found so unacceptable; it was that the three Vietnamese "ky" were still divided, and this only reflected the old aims of the colonizers, rather than current political realities.

Rejected by its supposed beneficiaries even before it had been implemented, the declaration of 24 March was to serve, unfortunately, as a charter of General de Gaulle's policies in Indo-China. And it was to make the question of Cochin China the main obstacle to any agreement with Hanoi (by trusted colleagues of the same de Gaulle) which might end the war and ensure that the Vietnamese revolution might become bound up with the "new France".

The Japanese takeover of March was not likely to shift a man like de Gaulle towards liberalism. What had just been taken from "him", he was immediately less anxious to consider handing over, if even in a gradual and limited form. For him, the "recovery" of Vietnam could not but take on new urgency and vigour, especially as three events were to occur that aggravated French "dispossession": the explosion at Hiroshima, which certainly brought the invaders to their knees but

---

*Admiral Decoux, *A la barre de l'Indochine* (Paris, Plon, 1949).
**Of the south (Cochinchina), the centre (Annam) and the north (Tonkin).

further increased the power of American hegemony over the Far East; the decision at the Potsdam conference to divide Indo-China into two parts: in the north, as far as the 16th parallel, the Chungking Chinese were given the task of eliminating what remained of the Japanese army, while, in the south, the British were given the same task; lastly, the Vietnamese revolution of August was punctuated, on 2 September, at Hanoi, by a declaration of independence that was given authentification by the abdication of Emperor Bao-Dai.

Where, in all this, can one find the slightest trace of a French presence or French authority? It was certainly in this spirit that de Gaulle, already familiar with this kind of situation, sent General Leclerc out to Asia in August 1945, as Commander of the Expeditionary Force, and Thierry d'Argenlieu, High-Commissioner in Indo-China. After a stop-off at Kandy (Ceylon), Leclerc landed at Saigon on 5 October, preceded a month before by a light strike unit, the 5th RIC, which, on 23 September, had reoccupied the administrative buildings and thus begun the "reconquest".

But a week after his arrival Leclerc cabled to de Gaulle: "It will be a complete mistake to negotiate in a serious way with the representatives of the Vietminh before giving them a show of our strength." To which de Gaulle replied at once: "My dear friend, we have nothing to say to the locals as long as we have no strength. Up till then, we may, prudently and depending on the opportunity, make certain contacts, but that is all."

Admiral d'Argenlieu, appointed High Commissioner to Saigon on 15 August, the day of Japan's capitulation, flew out to Asia on 5 September. He received this message from General de Gaulle before he left: "Dear Admiral. There's a big piece left for us to take back, a great game to play. It's up to you! Off you go. Be assured of my profound friendship. C. de Gaulle."

At Chandernagor, Thierry d'Argenlieu received Jean Sainteny, Commissioner for Northern Indo-China, who had come from Hanoi, where he was in contact with the leaders of the revolution, and an emissary of General Leclerc, Paul Mus, who advised him not to go to Saigon until order was better re-established there. It did not need any more than this to make d'Argenlieu jump into the first plane, though not before sending a message to Leclerc in Indo-China urging him "to show the greatest possible force", but avoiding "compromising the future by bloodshed between Frenchmen and Annamites".[3]

While at Hanoi, Sainteny and his team increased contacts with Ho Chi Minh and his followers, while Leclerc took a few weeks to subjugate Cochin China, and while in Paris, as we shall see, de Gaulle was bringing to fruition a "secret plan", d'Argenlieu considered the Commissioner's ideas about the future of the three "ky".

"How can we misunderstand or underestimate the almost world-wide current that is carrying mankind towards political or social forms which call for the end of colonialism? The objection is that once the word independence is out, our partners will abuse it. Take care lest, by making the gesture too late, you lose the benefit of it."[4] And, to conclude, he proposed a system in which French sovereignty would play a similar role to that of the British Crown in the Commonwealth.

Yet d'Argenlieu was to assume a more conservative posture over the next few months. Why? Although we cannot discount a personal reaction on the part of the superior refusing to be "overtaken" by his subordinate Leclerc, who from February on presented himself as a determined advocate of an agreement with the Vietminh that might lead to independence, there was something even more important. On 20 January 1946, de Gaulle had announced that he was to relinquish power. According to d'Argenlieu's thinking, the presence of General de Gaulle at the head of the French State permitted concessions that would not be permitted after he had gone. Once de Gaulle had left, the greatness and skill of the French might be transformed into abandonment and weakness.

One might add that from 21 January 1946, d'Argenlieu saw himself, in relation to Indo-China, as de Gaulle, in 1940, saw himself in relation to the Empire. He regarded the General's retirement as a temporary one, his return as guaranteed, and the legitimacy of the State as more or less suspended. Until de Gaulle returned, he considered that his role was purely conservatory. He said as much quite clearly to Philippe Devillers on 3 August 1946, at Dalat: "I am here to maintain and hold. Before long General de Gaulle will return to government. I am maintaining things until he comes back."[5] This seems to me to be the key to the reversal of the "liberal" of the last days of 1945 into the saboteur of the peace invented in March 1946 by Sainteny, Ho Chi Minh and Leclerc.*

Who had suggested to de Gaulle the idea of basing the solution to the Vietnamese problem in the person of Vinh San, the former emperor Duy Tan? De Gaulle was quite capable of inventing his own ideas. In his *Mémoires* he refers to a "secret plan".[6] The fact is that on 25 March 1945, two weeks after Japan's seizure of Indo-China, he began to make contact with the former sovereign, who, from the beginning of the war, had shown great sympathy for Free France.

Before his discussions with de Gaulle about the process of restoration, Vinh San wanted to compose a "political" testament. In it, he was to demand reunification of the three Vietnamese "ky", which in due course would be given independence within an Indo-Chinese federation of Vietnam, Laos and Cambodia. "When I presented Vinh San's 'testament' to the General," Alain de Boissieu relates, "I was rather worried what his reaction would be. He took it very well, asked me if the author was a man of worth and, obtaining a positive reply, confirmed that he would see him."[7]

It was on 14 December 1945 that prince Vinh San had talks with the General. In his *Mémoires*, de Gaulle recalls that he discussed with him, "as one man to another", what they might do together. "Whoever the persons my Government was obliged to deal with, I intended to go to Indo-China myself to settle matters in due form when the time came."[8] As for Vinh San, he summed up the situation thus: "It's done, it's decided, the French government will put me back on the throne of Annam. De Gaulle will accompany me when I go back there. He has in mind early March."[9]

In a letter, the former sovereign wrote to M. Thébault, his adviser: "So I shall go back to Indo-China perhaps to get blown up by a bomb or stabbed. It's the destiny of princes. I face the prospect without fear. I would have done this because I am a prince, but I shall not slip away."

---

*Leclerc, as a result of this, was to be subjected to de Gaulle's thunder.

Ten days after his meeting with General de Gaulle, Vinh San set off for Réunion, anxious to see his family again before taking the road for Indo-China. The plane stopped off at Algiers, then at Fort-Lamy. Between the capital of Chad and Bangui, it disappeared without trace. Informing the General of the news the following day, Palewski heard him mutter to himself: "What bad luck France has." De Gaulle refused to regard this example of France's misfortune as an accident, seeing it as the work of the British secret service.[10]

The subject of Indo-China supposedly reveals de Gaulle's prejudices against British policy, though these allegations are constantly contradicted by the facts. The Levant, however, was a different question: his Anglophobia was much more prominent here.

Two violent crises in the East had brought relations between Charles de Gaulle and Winston Churchill to boiling point: during the summer of 1941, after the Armistice signed at Saint-Jean-d'Acre and, a year later, when the Madagascar affair poisoned the quarrel over the Levant.* The crisis that was to break out in the spring of 1945 was to go well beyond them in intensity. It was on this occasion that the General actually used the word "war" (against the British Empire!), and this had never crossed his lips before.

It has been said often enough that the Near East was the least likely place in the world for good relations to be established between France and Great Britain in war-time. Of course, in early May 1945, the war was coming to a close, ending certain difficulties. But this was to give place to other fevers – above all the awakening of an Arab nationalism that had been repressed for too long and far too harshly not to explode violently.

In the versions of the crisis offered by General de Gaulle, whether in his speeches and press conferences or in his *Mémoires*, this factor is systematically erased. Refusing to admit that Syrians and Lebanese would enthusiastically reject the sequellae of French tutelage, de Gaulle preferred to incriminate the British. It suited him better to be the victim of the voracity of a great power than to meet the demands for freedom coming from people "protected" by France.

Although a study of all the texts of the period** shows that nothing like a plot to replace the tricolour flag with the Union Jack was being cooked up in London, it is true that those carrying out British policy in the Levant were animated by violent anti-French feelings. It is true that the BBC's Arabic Service, which was widely listened to in the Levant, did not spare the French officials.

Faced with the rise of Arab nationalism from the Nile to the Euphrates, London tried not only to be in the forefront of efforts to create an Arab League in Alexandria in March 1945, but also tried to deflect Arab anger and frustration towards a weaker and at the time unpopular ally. But it would not seem that this minor manipulation was planned by the British government, as General de Gaulle believed and declared.

*See *De Gaulle: The Rebel 1890–1944*, pp. 352–67. (trs.)
**At least until all the French archives can be consulted.

In his *Churchill and De Gaulle*, François Kersaudy produces a very enlightening document: a letter from Winston Churchill to Edward Spears dated 12 December 1943, in which the Prime Minister warns his old friend against an actively anti-French Arab strategy: "All arguments and means of pressure used by the Levant people against the French might one day be turned against us; we should discourage the throwing of stones since we have greenhouses of our own. It should be our endeavour to damp down the whole issue in order not to raise very great difficulties for ourselves; there is no question of our trying to take the place of the French in the Levant."[11] It was largely because he refused to obey these directives that Spears was removed from Beirut six months later and replaced by a civil servant more attentive to the directives of his government.

Public disturbances had begun at Damascus and Beirut in January 1945. The Arab masses were well aware that the world that was being shaped by Washington and Moscow was susceptible to the realization of their own aspirations. In Syria and in the Lebanon a profound discontent was building up against the French notion of "independence" proclaimed in 1941 by General Catroux and authenticated on several occasions by General de Gaulle.

On the grounds that until treaties were signed, they were responsible for maintaining order, the French authorities maintained a system of military occupation that was usually meddlesome and sometimes brutal. Catroux's successors had never shown his skill and tact: for example, in November 1943 the imprisoning of the President of the Lebanese Republic unleashed a storm of outrage. In the aftermath, practically all links with Syrians and the Lebanese had reached an *impasse*. The situation was smouldering.

Convinced that at Yalta Stalin and Roosevelt had left Churchill "a free hand" in the Levant to act against the French as he pleased, General de Gaulle could not be other than suspicious of the British. Alerted by Beynet's pessimistic reports, and impatient to demonstrate that France would not be pushed out by "Anglo-Saxon intrigues", he decided in mid-April to send reinforcements to Beirut.

There were only three battalions, and they had to be transported on two cruisers, the *Montcalm* and the *Jeanne d'Arc*, but this was enough to appear intimidating to the press in Baghdad and Cairo – not to mention the press in London and Washington.

On 30 April the British Ambassador, Duff Cooper, turned up at the Rue Saint-Dominique with a warning: General Paget, British Commander-in-Chief in the Middle East, strongly advised against sending troops; it might provoke disturbances. De Gaulle was furious: by what right did this British officer take the liberty of interfering in French affairs? The Ambassador pointed out in vain that the British General Staff had "higher" responsibilities over the Arab Middle East; de Gaulle replied that these arrangements were valid only during military operations, that France remained responsible for maintaining order in the states of the Levant and that she would not tolerate this attempt to "remove" her – at which Duff Cooper withdrew after warning that "complications" might ensue.

On 5 May 1945, before the House of Commons, Winston Churchill reaffirmed that Great Britain had no intention of usurping France's position in the Middle East, but, on the other hand, he did not regard it as a British responsibility to defend the "privileges" enjoyed by Paris in that region; and he concluded this ambiguous intervention by asking General de Gaulle, in the strongest terms, to give up sending any reinforcements into that extremely sensitive area. At the same time, a division of the British 9th Army was on its way to the same area.

Three days later, as Europe was celebrating the Armistice signed the previous night at Reims, disturbances broke out in Syria, where the local police led anti-French demonstrations. The Druze jebel blew up a few days later. On 27 May, the fever reached Damascus. In his *Mémoires de guerre*, de Gaulle speaks of violent riots during which "British machine-guns and grenades" were used. In any case, on 29 May, French citizens, civilians and soldiers, were threatened and abused. Then, on the evening of that same 29 May, about 8 p.m., General Oliva-Roget* ordered his troops to open fire on the crowd and the parliament building in Damascus. General de Gaulle points out that only Syrians, Senegalese, two cannon and one plane were used during the repression. The fact is that two days later there were over a thousand dead (including several British citizens).

In London, in the afternoon of 30 May, the French Ambassador, René Massigli, was summoned by Churchill: the British authorities, he was told, could not "remain passive" if the disturbances continued. One can imagine the effect produced by this message on General de Gaulle. Opening the *Mémoires de guerre*, we read: "I was obliged to recognize that our men, simultaneously attacked by British troops and Syrian insurgents, would be in an untenable position... Whatever my indignation, I decided I must agree to a cease-fire".[12]

This was done that evening, at 11 p.m., London being informed immediately. But calm did not return. Street fighting continued throughout the 31st. According to the British representative, T. Shone,[13] the forces of General Oliva-Roget continued their intervention after the "cease-fire", firing on civilians, an American school and even a British Red Cross train.

On 31 May, at 4 p.m., Anthony Eden read to the Commons a message from Winston Churchill to General de Gaulle, warning him that to his "profound regret" he had to "order the [British] Commander-in-Chief to intervene with a view to preventing further bloodshed". To avoid any "collision" between British and French forces, the French government was invited "immediately" to order a cease-fire and to withdraw its forces to their quarters.

De Gaulle and his representatives in the Levant had acted clumsily, provocatively and brutally. And was not London taking advantage of the fact to inflict a cruel snub on French policy? This undisguised ultimatum was all the more cruel in being delivered from the benches of the British Parliament without de Gaulle's even being warned.**

On 1 June, while Charles de Gaulle was holding a meeting of the Council of Ministers in order to keep them informed of the development of the crisis and his "sadness and irritation" at seeing London "undermining the foundations of the

---

*General Catroux told me twenty years later that the choice of this unstable leader to take on such responsibilities had been particularly unfortunate.

**In *The Second World War*, Winston Churchill writes that the French were not kept informed only because of an "error of transmission", not because of any "disobliging intention" (Vol. VI, p. 222).

alliance", General Paget arrived at Beirut from Cairo to hand his French neighbour, General Beynet, an ultimatum laying down the terms of Churchill's
ultimatum to De Gaulle – to which de Gaulle replied by instructing General
Beynet not to take account of the British intervention.

On 2 June, de Gaulle held a press conference to try to stir up public opinion.
Naturally presenting his version of the affair, the General rejected the offer of
"tripartite" negotiations made by Churchill (Britain, France and the Middle East)
and suggested the organization of a conference of the interested powers "with a
view to international cooperation". This amounted to drawing the USA and
USSR into the region in order to embarrass the British.

Having risked himself on this perilous terrain, de Gaulle had the good sense to
add that neither France nor he himself felt "the slightest anger, the least rancour
towards the British people", for which the French had "the highest consideration,
the greatest possible esteem". And he concluded: "Interests must be reconciled."*

But this sang-froid was not to last. We have evidence of the anger that overtook
him when he met his uncharitable allies. Indeed, on 4 June, he summoned Sir
Alfred Duff Cooper, and said: "'We are not, I admit, in a position to open
hostilities against you at the present time. But you have insulted France and
betrayed the West. This cannot be forgotten.' Duff Cooper stood up and walked
out."[14] The Ambassador's version is rather less dramatic. Referring to a "stormy
interview", he declares that the General "could not have been more stiff if he had
been declaring war on us". Sir Alfred adds: "We got rather heated. It was a very
unpleasant half-hour."[15]

A few years later, Charles de Gaulle was to draw this conclusion from the
quarrel over the Levant in the spring of 1945:

> The day would soon come when a functioning United Nations would
> assume the responsibility the League of Nations had previously entrusted to
> France in Syria and Lebanon. We would then be justified in removing the
> last vestiges of our authority from the Levant, without having abandoned this
> area to any other power. I did not doubt that the agitation supported in the
> Levant by our former allies would spread throughout the entire Middle East
> to the detriment of these sorcerer's apprentices, and that eventually the
> British and the Americans would pay dearly for the enterprise they had
> launched against France.[16]

On 14 August 1944, just prior to leaving Algiers for Paris, Charles de Gaulle had
sent this significant directive to General Martin, Commander of the Army Corps
at Algiers: "We mustn't let North Africa slip between our fingers as we are

---

*For his part, Churchill cabled General Paget that day: "As soon as you are master of the
situation, you have to show the greatest consideration to the French. Your greatest triumph will
be to establish a peace without rancour." To the Syrian President, Choukry Kouatly, he cabled
this message: "Now that we have come to your aid, I hope you will not make the task more
difficult by acts of violence and exaggerations. The French have as much right as you to fair
treatment."

liberating France."[17] This, then, was a man who would not be found wanting. He would leave to others idle illusions, the myth of good North Africa welded for ever to France and with no other aspirations than to be identified with the "motherland". He had seen Juin's and Montsabert's Muslim soldiers fight in Italy – and, in a few days, they were about to set foot in France between Nice and Marseille. He had made the link between blood shed and rights acquired and he knew very well, as a patriot himself, that the aspirations of a proud people tended to nationalism.

When Charles de Gaulle was meditating on the future of the three North African countries, they had been in crisis for ten years. In Tunisia, the nationalist movement had sprung into action in March 1934 with the creation of the Néo-Destour party by Habib Bourguiba. At the same time the Committee of Moroccan Action was created, while, in Algiers, the Oulema movement presented an Algerian nation as the aim of true believers – two years later, Messali Hadj inspired the masses to demand independence.

The victory of the signatories of the Atlantic Pact might have been, as in 1918, only that of one imperial system over another. But it so happened that two of the victors in 1945, the USA and the USSR, made the destruction of the colonial system one of their articles of faith, while the United Kingdom tried to play the card of Arab nationalism in order to save part of its empire. Thus the spring of 1945 was marked by two conferences that were to have enormous repercussions throughout North Africa: the first, which took place in March, near Cairo, led to the creation of the Arab League; the second, at San Francisco, laid the foundations for the United Nations Organization.

The Tunisian and Moroccan protectorates had moved first. In Bourguiba's absence – the Tunisian leader had been imprisoned in 1938 and, on being released in 1942 by the Axis authorities, had settled in Italy, but without collaborating with the enemies of France – Bey Moncef created a government that was fuelled by nationalist feelings. General Giraud thought fit in May 1943 to depose the sovereign and exile him to Pau, thus turning him into a national hero. But it was Bourguiba who, benefiting from the overt benevolence of the American authorities, revived the liberation movement by claiming, in October 1944, "the internal autonomy of the Tunisian nation together with a constitutional monarchy".

The response from Paris was so negative that Habib Bourguiba left his country in March 1945 for Egypt, just at the time that the Arab League, which was to disillusion him even more than the French protectors, was being set up.

General de Gaulle invited Bey Moncef's successor to Paris for the Quatorze Juillet celebrations in 1945. Sidi Lamine was not averse to presenting himself as the spokesman of Tunisian claims. In his *Mémoires*, de Gaulle describes how the Bey of Tunis expressed "the aspirations of his people" in accordance with "the demands of the time". De Gaulle refrained from contradicting him in any way and envisaged the opening of "talks": the response was probably positive enough to be received "with great friendliness".[18]

Two months earlier, the Moroccan sovereign, Mohammed Ben Youssef, had been received in Paris in similar fashion. And yet problems were even deeper in the case of Morocco. In January 1944, riots broke out at Rabat and Fez and were harshly put down: there was talk of twenty deaths in the capital, forty at Fez, and the courts condemned over a thousand "ringleaders" to harsh sentences.

The de Gaulle–Ben Youssef talks were not without substance. According to Charles de Gaulle, the sultan would have admitted that the protectorate had brought a great deal to his country, but that it was merely a "transition between the Morocco of former times and a free, modern state", adding, "I believe the moment has come to make a concerted move in that direction."

Thus, in the case of both protectorates, both their sovereigns and the spokesmen of French "historical legitimacy" had laid the foundations for a renewal intended to transform relations of a colonial type into a negotiated association.

The Algeria that was emerging from the war was bubbling over with impatience, without having a recognized interpreter, at least in Paris. Of course, since the publication of the *Manifesto of the Algerian People* on 12 February 1943, Ferhât Abbâs had been accepted as the spokesman of the urban, politicized bourgeoisie. Sheikh Brahimi, leader of the Oulemas, expressed the views of those who saw Islam as the essential framework of collective life. Above all, there was Messali, who led the most radical and consequently most popular tendency, whose slogan was quite simply the independence of an Arab, Muslim Algeria.

Messali's party, the Parti du Peuple Algérien (PPA), had been dissolved. But when Ferhât Abbâs had set up the association of the Friends of the Manifesto and of Liberty, Messali had the intelligence to penetrate it with his own followers and at the same time with those of Sheikh Brahimi. So much so that Abbas' moderate programme – an "autonomous" Algerian republic federated to a "renewed" French republic – was to be rapidly reorientated by the more stirring slogans of the populist leader: "An Algeria federated to France, no. To the Arab world, yes!" Such propaganda was all the more successful in stirring up Algeria in the spring of 1945 in that poverty in Algeria was then at its worst.

While Paris was getting ready to celebrate victory, apparently concerned only about the Levant, Algeria quietly smouldered with anger. Young Algerians had got themselves killed overseas for the common cause and their country had to be content with the order of 7 March 1944 granting French citizenship to a few tens of thousands of Muslims – a measure that the spokesmen of Algerian Islam condemned, denouncing those who benefited from it as infidels, converts, apostates. On 1 May, violent demonstrations took place in Algiers and Oran. The police opened fire: there were four dead.[19] A week earlier, Messali was deported to Brazzaville. With Abbâs sick and overworked, and Messali out of the way, the movement could only exploit popular passion, and this was to explode in the triangle formed by Sétif, Guelma and Bougie, the most sensitive region in Algeria, the region of the Kabylia of the Babors, "the chosen land of revolts for seventeen centuries", it has been said.[20]

In an atmosphere made more unstable by the deportation of Messali and the clashes of 1 May, demonstrations were being organized for the victory celebrations on 8 May. At Sétif, it was also market day. The demonstrators were shouting: "Free Messali: independent Algeria". "On both sides," writes Germaine Tillion, who has researched the whole affair at length, "people came into the town armed, gripped with intense fear. There is nothing more dangerous than fear. It was fear that triggered off the massacre here."[21]

Groups of armed *fellahs* seized Europeans. Twenty-seven of them were murdered in the evening of 8 May. Then the movement spread to the surrounding *douars*, and seventy-five French colonists were murdered during the following day.

The repression was appalling. Henri Bénazet, a reputedly conservative journalist, described it as "inhuman". General Duval, commanding the region of Constantine, provided the artillery, while the airforce razed to the ground villages around Sétif, Guelma and Kerrata, and units of troops killed and pillaged for forty-eight hours.

The balance sheet of these massacres has since given rise to as much controversy as the origin and nature of the uprising. The civil authorities spoke of 400 dead, then of 1500. The army advanced the figures of 6000 to 8000. On the Algerian side, there was soon talk of 15 000, then of 30 000 victims, and the propaganda of the FLN* eventually declared that this "genocide" had accounted for "over 45 000 dead". In an issue of *El Moudjahid*, published on 8 May 1985, even the figure of 80 000 victims was advanced.

Historians, Algerian as well as French, dispute the nature of the repression movement. Mohammed Harbi, denying that the uprising was organized, speaks of "riots", but adds that from 11 May delegates of the PPA encouraged the regional organizations "to broaden the insurrection" and that a general uprising had been planned for the night of 22 May.** Hocine Aït Ahmed, who, from that day, went underground to become one of the nine "historical leaders" of the revolution of 1954–62, saw the movement of 1945 as inevitably leading to failure: it was an uprising without organization or aims.

All the official reports cited by C.-R. Ageron show clearly that both the civilian and the military sides were aware of the increasing dangers. The director of political affairs in Algiers, Augustin Berque, and the boss of the 2nd Bureau at Army Headquarters, Colonel Schoën, were cautious and opposed to force.

And what of the Governor-General, Yves Chataigneau, a peaceable man if ever there was one, whom the Europeans in Algeria had nicknamed Mohammed to show what they thought of him? One of his closest colleagues, Laurent Preziosi, has told me that, since Chataigneau was in Paris on the day the uprising broke out, it was the Governor-General's Secretary-General, M. Gazagne, who took the first decisions, and in a very different spirit from that of his superior. On his return, Chataigneau called to his office the three generals commanding the French forces in Algiers, Oran and Constantine. According to M. Preziosi, the third, General Duval, had insisted on "the widespread nature of the rebellion" and the need to bring in the armed forces. His two colleagues said that they had announced preventative measures, but the Governor-General ordered them to await his orders before carrying them out, and added that Algeria would return to calm only if it was given a new status.[22] Hence the difficulty in locating responsibility for the crushing repression. De Gaulle, who, as head of government, must be credited

*Front de libération nationale.
**It was cancelled, at the last minute, by this order: "Don't cut the bull's throat!"

with the decisions taken,* gives only three lines to the episode.[23] "In Algeria, an insurrection begun in the Constantinois and synchronized with the Syrian riots in May, was put down by Governor General Chataigneau."

What part was played by General Duval, commander of French forces in the Constantinois? When later appointed to Morocco he confessed to a man who is no longer alive either and whose confidences one therefore hesitates to cite here. But everything seems to suggest that all the orders in fact came from Constantine.

It is difficult to find any trace of the affair among de Gaulle's former colleagues. It is worth noting, however, that the Chief of General Staff at the time was Alphonse Juin, who had no doubts about the "maintenance of order" in Algeria. The Air Minister, Charles Tillon, has assured me that he knew nothing of the role played by the dozen or so pieces of equipment used to shoot down the *mechtas* until after the event.[24] Neither the General's *Notes et Carnets* nor Claude Mauriac's *Journal* mention the dramatic events. We know from Charles-André Julien that the "Tubert Commission" (named after its chairman, the head of the Gendarmerie in Algiers, who was very close to the Communists) was told very quickly to break off its investigation on the orders of the head of government, without even being able to draw up figures for the human losses involved in the uprising and its repression.

Was this an attempt at camouflage? The fact is that, during the affair as a whole, de Gaulle, through the general instructions given nine months earlier to the army commander in Algeria, then on 12 May to the Governor-General and by the discretion with which he surrounded the affair, seems to have been a causal element rather than an obstacle to the terrible repression.

---

*And who, according to the Algerian historian, Mahfoud Kaddache, telegrammed the governor-general on 12 May "to take all necessary measures to suppress the anti-French activities of a minority of agitators".

CHAPTER EIGHT

"Oui, Oui, mon Général"

More a law-maker, perhaps, than an interpreter of the law, General de Gaulle clearly preferred to promulgate laws than to carry them out – even his own. He approached the drawing up and discussion of the two Constitutions of the Fourth and Fifth Republics – the first made against him, the second by and for him – not simply with application, but with a sort of passion. But however fascinated he may have been by this politico-juridical exercise, Charles de Gaulle was not naturally at ease with the subject.

A strong executive and a shift towards direct democracy at the expense of the elected assemblies were ideas that de Gaulle often referred to, but there had been Vichy and its senile absolutism, the pack of defeated generals and dry-land admirals who, failing to defeat the Third Reich, had made prisoners of Blum, Reynaud, Mandel. There had also been the polemics about the General's authoritarianism in London, his "iron contempt". The most faithful of all the General's faithful followers, Claude Hettier de Boislambert, assures us that people underestimated the horror that his leader had felt when compared with Bonaparte. The attacks of Muselier, Raymond Aron and Kérillis affected him much more than anybody believed.[1] De Gaulle had a very low opinion of parliamentarians and parties, but he regarded democracy as an essential part of the heritage that he took on in June 1940, together with territorial integrity, rank, Empire and the sword.

> Save in periods of public danger, there can be no such thing as a lasting dictatorship, unless a single faction, resolved to overpower the rest, supports it against all comers. Only the Army could give me the means of controlling the country by constraining the recalcitrant elements. But this military omnipotence, established by force in peacetime, would soon appear unjustified to adherents of every tendency. Public safety was now assured, and I had no desire to maintain the momentary dictatorship which I had exercised in the course of the storm and which I would not fail to prolong or resume if the nation were in danger.[2]

He had observed how the Anglo-Saxon democracies had triumphed over the totalitarian states without abandoning their principles or their traditions of government. Nevertheless, he came back to the old caesarian idea of the incompatibility between respect for liberty and the struggle for national salvation. (It should be noted, moreover, that this passage was written in the middle of the cold war, at a time when the imminence of the next world conflict was regarded as certain.)

* * *

In the institutional domain, de Gaulle fully embodied the conflict between a powerfully dominating nature and a culture based on the balance of powers.

The team that he had gathered round him in 1945 was a good expression of that culture. Few heads of State, I imagine, were ever surrounded by so many colleagues with knowledge of legal problems. The man who governed France from the Rue Saint-Dominique gathered round him not only law professors and *conseillers d'Etat*, men like Cassin and de Menthon, Capitant and Teitgen, Pierre Laroque, Pierre Tissier, Donnedieu de Vabres, Alfred Coste-Floret and Desmouliez, but also politicians particularly attuned to the law: Jules Jeanneney, Michel Debré and Alexandre Parodi. If he was to begin addressing institutional questions somewhat tentatively, he was soon to gain confidence: and as soon as he had carried out his initial administrative duties, in early 1946, he was to put institutional questions to the forefront of his tasks.

In 1945, the General and his team did not set about reviving the institutions of French government without recourse to certain texts. At Algiers on 21 April 1944, de Gaulle had signed an order which, in the absence of anything better, laid down two rules. First, the French people would elect "a constituent assembly" after the victory. Second, this election would take place at the latest one year after the complete liberation of national territory – which was achieved only in May 1945. Thus, just when he was embarking on his great work, de Gaulle was bound by two prescriptions emanating from his own authority: to call elections not later than May 1946 and to organize the election of "a constituent assembly".

Having laid down these two rules, the General began to question how they were to be applied. He had no intention of delaying the election (which would be preceded by municipal and cantonal elections): on the contrary, he would organize elections six months before the latest date they could be called. But the nature of parliamentary representation and exactly what system would be used were to give rise to highly diverse arguments.

It was about this time that two men were freed from camps in Germany who had embodied the Third Republic: Edouard Herriot and Léon Blum. The General clearly took the opinions of both men into account, especially those of Blum, who, from his prison cell, had boldly intervened in his favour with Roosevelt and Churchill. But the impact of their arguments was blunted by their rejection of the General's offer that they should both be made Ministers of State, along with Jules Jeanneney.

When the government met on 31 May 1945 to work out the broad outlines of its institutional policy, the General announced that he would consult the country before the end of the year. In fact he was careful not to reveal his ideas. We read in the *Mémoires* that, even at this time, he had arrived at a clear idea of "what the ideal institutions would be". "As I saw it, the State must have a head, that is, a leader in whom the nation could see beyond its own fluctuations, a man in charge of essential matters and the guarantor of its fate. It was also necessary that this executive must not originate in parliament."[3]

What he is defining here is a presidential regime – the one that Blum had just outlined in *A l'échelle humaine* (*On the Human Scale* – the publication of which had a profound effect on public opinion), and which de Gaulle was not himself to propose until a year later, when he no longer possessed the means to implement it. But why was something that seemed so clear at Bayeux in 1946, and again while writing the *Mémoires*, drowned in 1945 in so many marches and counter-marches, orders and counter-orders? On 2 June, Charles de Gaulle summoned the international press and informed it of the dramatic development in the Franco-British crisis in the Near East. As François Mauriac was leaving, he suggested to the General that he should "talk of something other than Syria". Seizing the opportunity, de Gaulle threw light on his plans concerning the theme and modalities of the future popular consultation.

> Some consider that the Constitution of 1875 is still valid and that, consequently, we must elect a Chamber of Deputies and a Senate [which would then meet] as a National Assembly. Others say that this constitution is dead and that, consequently, it is necessary to proceed to elections for a Constituent Assembly. Finally, others think that since the slate has effectively been wiped clean, we must consult the country on the terms that would serve as a basis for its Constitution. I do not consider that it is the right moment for me to divulge my own feelings on the matter.[4]

Consulting the country? What did that mean? Does not "consulting", apart from an actual election, amount to creating a direct link between the leader and the masses? To speak of the "country" rather than of the "people", is this not to use the language of the right? The PCF denounced the "plebiscite" immediately, to be followed rather less categorically by the SFIO and even the MRP.

But was he not committed, by the order of April 1944, to consult "the French people" with a view to electing a "constituent assembly"? Those words are certainly part of the Algiers text.

On 26 June, a rumour that the Socialist and Communist ministers were to leave the government grew. In the Rue Saint-Dominique, René Brouillet observed that de Gaulle ought either to resign or to present himself before the people as a candidate of the right: Palewski objected because in the case of de Gaulle, political loyalties were split. That evening, Charles de Gaulle met Léon Blum, who, lunching the following day with François Mauriac, declared that, if de Gaulle insisted on having elected assemblies like those of the Third Republic, the left would withdraw its cooperation. The Socialist leader added that he had the impression "that the General was looking for a way of leaving office".[5]

Suddenly, General de Gaulle disappeared. This time, he did not go far. He shut himself up at Neuilly. For three days, from Wednesday 4 July to Saturday 7 July, de Gaulle pondered his decision. He then summoned in rapid succession two cabinet meetings, on the 7th and 9th. On Saturday 7 July, de Gaulle came out unambiguously in favour of the election of a Constituent Assembly. But, having studied its implementation with the man who was sitting on his right, Jules Jeanneney, he indicated that a procedure subject to referendum would limit the powers of the Constituent Assembly. And, before taking leave of his ministers, he summoned them for Monday, the 9th. Before going back to Neuilly, he dropped off at the Rue Saint-Dominique to sign letters, which he had neglected for three days. Claude Mauriac adds that "for the first time for a long time, I was able to get my correspondence signed. The General had never seemed more at peace; he had never given me the impression of greater mastery. Seeing the name of Mme Halna du Fretay, at the bottom of a letter that I had handed him, his finger swooped down on the paper, marking it with the nail. 'It was at her house at Arras that I met Pétain!'"

The cabinet meeting of 9 July was to be one of the liveliest of that time, and it lasted for six hours. Jeanneney proposed that several questions be put to the electors (whether they wished to abandon the Constitution of 1875; whether they wanted to elect a Constituent Assembly with limited powers; whether they wanted this fundamental law to be itself subjected to a referendum). But the General won a majority for his idea. He supported a project put forward by Capitant: a referendum involving a single question, concerning a text broadly outlining the law. But, very soon, this restriction on the free choice of the citizens revived the storm: the following day the press spoke only of "personal power", "the day of the dupes".

In the morning of the 12th, the little "Soviet" of the Rue Saint-Dominique met around Gaston Palewski, *directeur de cabinet*. Brouillet, Vallon, Burin des Roziers and Claude Mauriac urged Palewski to oppose the rigid project that the General was planning to present to the French electors in favour of a more flexible formula that would make it easier to shape public opinion. What they proposed was two questions: do you want the assembly that is to be elected to be a constituent assembly? If so, must it be given only limited powers? And eventually they managed to persuade de Gaulle to agree to ask the electors two questions instead of one.

The broadcast made by de Gaulle on the evening of 12 July, with emendations proposed by the "plotters", remained fairly vague. Carefully balanced, it paid tribute to the achievements of the Third Republic, but recalled its failures. In any case the General pointed out that the French would not have to answer only one question, but would also be asked about the change of republic and the breadth of the powers given to a possible Constituent Assembly. And the General added that he would give his own opinion at a later date. The next day, a third Council of Ministers approved this new change of direction and, as he left Matignon, the General whispered to Jules Jeanneney: "You were right. It will be more loyal."

All that remained was to confront the Consultative Assembly. The press set the tone: for two weeks, references to the 18 Brumaire of Louis Bonaparte were constantly cited. The sittings of 27 and 28 July 1945 bristled with personal and ideological attacks on de Gaulle. They amounted to no more than aggressive warnings as to his intentions. The word "plebiscite" came constantly to the lips of left-wing speakers.

On 29 July, the General replied to questions, taking care to control a mood that might otherwise have led to a deterioration in the debate. To the Radical Marcel Plaisant, who referred to Louis-Napoleon's coup d'état of 1851, he retorted: "The Republic? I picked up its flag, its laws and even its name!" But he recovered his sang-froid:

After so many successive regimes, our country runs the risk of treating institutions with scepticism. In order to give the people back its faith in a constitution, without which democracy would be profoundly doomed, it is right that it should be associated in a direct way with the new constitution, not only by ratifying it, but also by seizing the foundation trowel. To have any chance of arousing in the nation this faith in the constitution, without which all that will be written will be texts without virtue, it is indispensable that the very procedure to be applied to the working out of a constitution be adapted to the psychology of the country. Now I am convinced that this psychology is one of renewal.[6]

Two intelligent men, Vincent Auriol and Claude Bourdet, understood that the Assembly and the General were involved in a head-on struggle that could have no satisfactory outcome, and threw out a life-belt: an amendment signed by them that made it clear that the government would be responsible to the Assembly, but could only be overthrown by a censure motion passed by an absolute majority and that it would share with the Chamber the preparation of laws. This judicious compromise was rejected – by a very small majority, 108 to 101 – by an Assembly that wanted to demonstrate its abstract power, in a last negative fling. But it did not stop there: led by the Communists, it demanded full powers for the Constituent Assembly that would be elected in October, knowing that the country would then have to choose between the General and the Assembly. It was a vain defiance of de Gaulle.

The Communists had a clear objective: they aimed at replacing the General's authority with a power based on parliament, which in turn would be passed on by their mass organizations. This strategy for the conquest of power had two axes: universal suffrage and pressure from the streets. With the General out of the way and the MRP excluded from the majority, the PCF would be left with the SFIO, which would no longer be an insurmountable obstacle to the establishment of a people's democracy.[7]

In Charles de Gaulle's decision to go it alone, some have chosen to see nothing but machiavellianism. One may prefer the light shed on this almost unique retraction in Charles de Gaulle's career by the confidant of the years to come, Olivier Guichard, in his book, *Mon Général*.

I believe that the General was genuinely uncertain as to what to do with the enormous fish that History had stuck on the end of his line: an elected assembly. The General manoeuvred brilliantly to impose his will, but without knowing exactly what he wanted to do. Thus his changes gave the impression that he was machiavellian – which hardened opposition. He remained master in the game, but it was the game itself that eluded him.[8]

On 8 September, de Gaulle confided in Claude Mauriac: "The French *must* vote yes-yes. They must. Or I shall . . . " Was he really thinking, as Blum suspected in late June, of retiring? There is no great man who, when circumvented, challenged, harassed by lesser men, does not reveal, from time to time, his lassitude or disgust. It is both a temptation to make a clean sweep and an act of blackmail that he would do so: this theme recurred three or four times between London and Algiers.

There are a number of things that were said by him or those around him that support the idea that he might resign. One of the members of his private office reported to Robert de Saint-Jean that the General had said: "I prefer my legend to power." And speaking to Roger Stéphane, another of the General's colleagues remarked: "He does not cling to power, but he cannot conceive of a limited power. He's an absolutist."[9]

The electoral prospects were becoming clearer. On 13 August, the SFIO held a congress that was above all a celebration of the great leader who had survived the death camps, Léon Blum. The old man seized this opportunity to launch an operation of renewal in the Socialist Party. Without putting Marxism into question, he tried to replace the theme of the "class struggle" with that of "class action", which would be less anathema to his neighbours in the Centre, and would give primacy to Jean Jaurès, not Marx, as the inspiration of the French working-class movement. Was this a strategy for shifting the party to the centre? This is certainly how the left of the party interpreted Léon Blum's statements. Was he really initiating a break with the Stalinists? No: the powerful left-wing current, which in 1946 was to bring Guy Mollet to the post of Secretary-General, remained attached to the slogan of "Unity of action" with the PCF. But the SFIO was to take a different position from that of the Communists on the referendum.

General de Gaulle had no doubt about the hostility of the PCF. In his campaign in favour of the double "yes", the Communists issued a slogan urging people to say "yes" to the first question (the election of a Constituent Assembly) and "no" to the second (the limitation of its powers). The SFIO, for its part, ended up, after a good deal of hesitation, on the side of Blum and Auriol, in favour of a double "yes", as also did the MRP and the UDSR (Union démocratique et socialiste de la Résistance), led by René Pleven, Jacques Soustelle and François Mitterrand. As for the Radicals, who were the only ones to reject the idea of a Constituent Assembly, their response would be a double "no".

As the referendum approached – it would coincide with the elections to the Assembly, which everything seemed to suggest would be a Constituent Assembly – the prefects produced a mass of information on public opinion. The archives of the Ministry of the Interior hold several fascinating documents. For example, in one dated 11 September 1945, the prefecture of the Nord (where the General was supposed to enjoy exceptional support, which had been confirmed during his trip there in September–October 1944), Communist propaganda denounced him as a candidate for "personal power" and "the agent of international capitalism".

A report by the prefect of the Tarn sounded more favourable. The prefects of the Hérault and the Gard even dared to predict a majority of "yes" votes to the two questions posed at the referendum, while in Charente-Maritime the authorities at La Rochelle referred to a meeting in the course of which a Communist declared that "de Gaulle prefers the trust of the trusts to that of the people". In the Moselle a mayor had ordered the portrait of General de Gaulle and the Croix de Lorraine on the flags to be removed from the town hall.

The head of government did not want to intervene in the electoral campaign in too obvious a way. But on 17 October, he could no longer contain himself. Four days before the referendum, he seized the microphone once more to proclaim:

> I am preparing to hand back to national representation the exceptional powers that I have exercised since 18 June 1940, in the name of the Republic, for the salvation of the State, and the service of the fatherland. This time again, I see it as my duty to let each of you know what seems to me to be the national interest. As for the referendum, I wish from the bottom of my heart that you will answer "yes" to the first and "yes" to the second question.[10]

On 21 October, 96 per cent of the electors said yes to the first question, 66 per cent to the second. Thus having been warned against the first proposition only by the old guard of the Radical party, the electorate gave the General triumphal approval. The vigorous intervention of the PCF deprived him of a comparable success for the second proposition. A third of the French electorate came out in favour of the idea of the "omnipotence of the parties", to use the General's phrase.

Was he entirely satisfied with the triumph of the first "yes", when it was the second that was most important to him? It was on the second "yes" that his own future and the extent of the obstacles that the new Chamber might set up against his progress depended. That two-thirds success on the second question must have concerned him as much as the results of the votes cast in the elections for the Assembly on the same day.*

So de Gaulle had endowed the nation with a new constitutional apparatus, while preventing the sovereignty of that Assembly being absolute. The Communists declared that they would accept this expression of popular will. But the future of the Assembly would depend not so much on its juridical nature as on its political composition. More than the referendum, it was the elections of 21 October that were to give the regime its style and lay down its destiny.

It was a special date in the political history of France: for the first time (and the last until 1981) Communists and Socialists together had an absolute majority of the seats. With 303 deputies out of 586, they were in a position to govern. "France," writes Jacques Fauvet (who was rapidly becoming the best political

---

*Elections to the Constituent Assembly, 21 October 1945**

	VOTES	%	SEATS
PCF	5 011 000	26.1	160
MRP	4 937 000	25.6	152
SFIO	4 711 000	24.6	142
Modérés (conservatives)	2 785 000	14.4	61
Radicals	1 725 000	9.3	29

The so-called "unclassified" deputies, belonging to small groups, are not listed in this table.

observer of the Fourth Republic), "seemed at this time to be ready for a Popular Front, perhaps even ready to become a people's democracy. Only the presence of one man – de Gaulle – and with him, and after him, that of one party – the MRP – were to save her from that fate."[11]

Could de Gaulle have anticipated this outcome? Was it the inevitable culmination of the national uprising of which he had been the herald?

De Gaulle soon came to realize that institutions are made of men and that in a democracy ideas and legal constructions depend on majorities. He had fought to avoid parliamentary "omnipotence". He refused to fight for what was the most important thing: good institutions that only a "good" majority could give him – whether or not he led it.

He was not to make the same mistake again.

CHAPTER NINE

The One and the Others

We must not confuse the de Gaulle of 1945 with the polished de Gaulle of 1958 and after. At the end of the war, he was able to hoist himself into the camp of the victors, dragging France along with him. But what a state France was in! It was made quite clear to him that he was regarded as a parvenu. And a poor parvenu at that! And the French, rather bewildered, blamed him a little for the worldwide responsibilities that he was imposing on them.

Immediately after the war de Gaulle was full of creative power, of inspired aggressiveness; he went forward, armed from head to toe, ready for the cut and thrust, burdened by history, implacable and assured of a prophetic legitimacy. He was intolerant, tending readily to sarcasm, in the thrall of bitter trials and immense projects. In five years, he had been through everything, isolation, condemnations, defeats, betrayals and humiliations. He had overcome every disaster: he had descended the Champs-Elysées to the acclamation of the crowd only to ascend it – alone.

But history is there, and it always repeats itself. When, in 1943, Charles de Gaulle decided to mobilize the political parties for his cause, he contracted a debt. In time of war, they were all reverent, happy to be guarantors to make up the numbers. In time of peace, they rediscovered their pride. The services that they had rendered during the conflict would be remembered and added up.

Olivier Guichard has subtly summed up the relationship that was established between de Gaulle and the parties in 1944–45: in the name of unity, the General's strategy had, during the war, "caught the parties and movements in a trap. And they found it hard to accept as a leader the man whom they wished above all to see as the Symbol. But, once the war was over, the trap reversed its mechanism: the parties were in a position to entrap the General."[1]

Did de Gaulle want, therefore, a radical reshaping of the representative system, smashing those old structures and putting in their place a debate between movements that had sprung from the Resistance? There is nothing to suggest that he encouraged the formation, on the one hand, of a great "Labourist" movement, inspired by the British Labour Party, and, on the other hand, a no less wide Christian regrouping, of a liberal and moderate type, like the German Zentrum. On the contrary, everything suggests that he rejected this schema, considering the old mechanisms more appropriate in time of war to guarantee democratic legitimacy, and when peace came, easier to manoeuvre.

The Mouvement de libération nationale emerged from the Resistance as a political expression of the MURs (Unified Movements of the Resistance) in

October 1942, in London, under the protection of General de Gaulle and Jean Moulin. It brought together those who, in the post-Resistance turmoil, had not joined a Front National patronized by the PCF. But – whether out of hesitation or on the advice of the leaders – many of the sympathizers of the PCF or even members of the Party had remained in the MLN until early 1945.

The main theme of the congress then summoned by that body was to decide whether the movement was or was not to merge with the Front National – which would have guaranteed the PCF's grip on the whole of the Resistance and upset the balance of forces in the higher echelons of the state. It was no accident that one of the advocates of the merger, Pascal Copeau, who was then very close to the Communist party, declared: "In order to gain the respect of General de Gaulle's government the forces of the Resistance must unite."

But Copeau, d'Astier and their Communist friends came up against strong opposition from a far from ordinary speaker. André Malraux, wearing his colonel's uniform as commander of the Alsace-Lorraine brigade, which was then in combat between Strasbourg and Colmar, leaped on to the platform and declared: "General de Gaulle's government* is not only the government of France, but the government of the Liberation and of the Resistance. It is therefore not up to us to question it." The response of the Communists was best expressed not at the meeting, but by Pierre Hervé in *Action*: "Are we talking about a new party that, uniting the ideology of planning with a tendency to authority, would begin as neo-socialist, only to end in neo-fascism with a view to ushering in the reign of the Saviour?"

The opponents of the merger (Malraux, Philip, Frenay) won by 250 votes to 119. It was a victory that led nowhere. A veto had been recorded against the power of the PCF, but no structure was to emerge from this rear-guard combat.

If, after its "no to the PCF" congress, the MLN disappeared, as if that veto had exhausted all its possibilities, it was because no signal of understanding or encouragement came from the Rue Saint-Dominique. Malraux and his comrades, retiring again from the barricades where they had been struggling to prevent a merger with the Communists, aimed at giving the Resistance an organization capable of winning General de Gaulle's respect, did not receive the slightest sign of support. They had gone off to get themselves killed for a man who did not even seem to notice their existence.

If General de Gaulle's ostentatious refusal to participate in party struggles allowed of one kind of exception, in this period, it was in favour of the Mouvement républicain populaire (MRP). By baptizing this new version of Christian democracy thus, Maurice Schumann was aware that he was providing an eloquent summary of the thinking of the movement, its attachment to the republic and a concern for popular support.

But the links between the General and this enterprise were not just a semantic matter. On several occasions the deep, long-standing relations between Charles de Gaulle and Christian democracy has been noted from the days of the congress of the Jeune République and the struggles for the armoured divisions, at the side of

---

*Malraux was not yet in any direct contact with de Gaulle's government.

Philippe Serre. Before the creation of the MRP, the first Cabinet formed in Paris by the General was dominated by men like Bidault, Menthon, and Teitgen, who were essentially of the same persuasion. And the choice of Maurice Schumann, one of his London colleagues, as President of the Movement, at the Constitutive Congress of 25 and 26 November 1944, could not but increase Charles de Gaulle's sympathy for the emergent MRP.

The fact that, eleven months after its creation, the Movement was in a position equal to that of the Communists and larger than that of the Socialists certainly gave the General some encouragement. In fact, this movement, which emerged with unexpected success in the public life of liberated France, was soon to distance itself from the General, for reasons that were excellently expressed in a speech made on 4 February 1982 by Pierre-Henri Teitgen.

> The MRP was not at all what the General would have liked it to be. On three or four occasions in 1945, he explained to me, in one of those phrases of which he alone had the secret, that the misfortune of France was that "the right is outside the Nation while the left is against the State", that in order to bring the right back into the Nation it would be necessary, therefore, to transform the MRP into an "intelligent conservative party" capable of bringing together and organizing the right which had lost its direction in face of the socialist left. But, in 1945, the leaders and membership of the MRP felt closer to a "humanist socialism" than to an "intelligent conservatism". They wanted, within a centre-left "labourism", to agree on a programme of government with the Socialists. In fact, the heart of the MRP beat on the left, athough its electoral support was largely on the right.
>
> By way of justifying our mistrust and refusal we should add the contempt that the General had for all political parties. They had no place in his plebiscitory system of direct democracy. Like all the others, the MRP was in the end, for him, just "a little party that made its own little soup in its own little corner".[2]

To these various misunderstandings was added the role played by certain men, beginning with Georges Bidault. Although the former President of the CNR was, within the MRP, one of those who orientated the tendencies in the rather conservative direction desired by the General, he was an anti-Gaullist in all other areas, and this in the end set up a profound antipathy between the two men. As Bidault wrote hmself: "There are two things that exasperate de Gaulle, two things that he cannot bear: the Allies and the Resistance." And he added, in Claude Mauriac's presence, and after calling the head of the government "mad": "That's where ambition leads, to despair... or rather – for despair is not quite the right word – to desolation and loss of hope."[3]

In order truly to be "the party of fidelity", as de Gaulle hoped it would be, what did the MRP have to become? To begin with, it had to cease to be a party and become a wakeful convergence, a constant convocation of individuals polarized towards him. The only groups with which he felt at ease were bound together by discipline, or by circumstances likely to encourage political evolution. For de Gaulle politics was an activity that is codified by institutions, as a succession of "moments" creating their own requirements and temporary regroupings: everything ordered by that single factor, a certain idea of France.

With the SFIO, de Gaulle's relations were to be even more strange. The decisive role played, in London, by the emissaries of this party and by communications from Léon Blum has already been remarked on. The services rendered in London by André Philip and Félix Gouin, the quality, which very soon became recognized, of ministers like Robert Lacoste, Jules Moch or Christian Pineau, showed him that the SFIO was a good source of servants of the state. And as soon as he had returned from deportation, Léon Blum was to emerge as the great socialist personality of Western Europe.

Until the opening of the Constituent Assembly, relations between the Socialists and Charles de Gaulle remained good, even if the General had resigned himself to the pre-eminence that many of them gave their party. There was, for example, the audience that he gave to five of the leaders of the SFIO, a few days after the first Socialist congress, which coincided with the opening session of the Consultative Assembly. The delegation at the Rue Saint-Dominique consisted of Vincent Auriol, Daniel Mayer, André Philip, Edouard Depreux and Jules Moch. Vincent Auriol conveyed to him "the affectionate fellow-feeling" of the Socialist congress. De Gaulle replied that he was "touched" and went on: "The overwhelming majority of the French people is socialist inclined, though it is not communist. France is on the left. She is social or socialist. She is profoundly democratic, perhaps more democratic than parliamentarian."

The souring of relations between the General and the Socialists took place in three stages. The first was bound up with the return of Léon Blum after two years' deportation. The General offered Blum a post as his Minister of State, but he refused it. De Gaulle was not used to such treatment: nothing could subsequently overcome his bitter resentment. The second stage came when the "parties of the left" threatened to leave the government at the end of June 1945. The third, more serious, stage occurred in November 1945, a few days after the elections and the relative failure of the SFIO: the party of Léon Blum came only third in the Constituent Assembly, after the PCF and the MRP. De Gaulle did not care for losers.

The concerns of the Communist Party, in the months after the Liberation, were embodied in a single man: Maurice Thorez. The first aim of the Party after the war was to see its Secretary-General brought back from his enforced exile in the USSR and to restore to him the leadership of the party. As soon as Thorez was back in France, the entire efforts of the PCF went into the creation of a sovereign assembly, thereby establishing at the summit of the State the power of a popular assembly favourably disposed to the Communists. Having partly failed in this,

Thorez and his friends were to make sure that they had dominant, or at least impregnable, positions in the government.

As to the return to France of Maurice Thorez, condemned in 1939 for desertion,* there are two legends. According to the first, the fate of the Communist leader was negotiated in Moscow between de Gaulle and Stalin, the former agreeing to take the Secretary-General of the PCF into a high governmental office in exchange for an assurance of cooperation by the Communists in the economic recovery and the rearmament of France. In fact, Thorez had already left for Paris when de Gaulle arrived in Moscow. The second legend, whereby Thorez "paid" for his return by ordering the dissolution of the patriotic militias, the secular arm of the Communist party, does not stand up to examination either.

But it should not be thought that the operation of Thorez's return proceeded without a hitch. However non-conformist he may have been, however much given to the extravagances of history, Charles de Gaulle was a soldier through and through. He did not care at all for the word "desertion". The return of Thorez nevertheless presented him with problems that were not all of a legal kind. Quite obviously, the decision cost him something, though it gave him some satisfaction. This emerges from a few sentences in the *Mémoires de guerre*:

> Taking former circumstances into account, I considered that the return of Maurice Thorez as head of the Communist Party would involve more advantages than drawbacks at the time. Thorez, while making every effort to advance the interests of Communism, was to serve the public interest on several occasions. On the day after his return to France, he brought an end to the last vestiges of the "patriotic militias" which certain of his people insisted on maintaining in a new clandestine situation.[4]

De Gaulle was satisfied that the Communists obtained no more than 26 per cent of the votes in the elections of 1945, which was nevertheless a huge percentage and gave them 160 seats in the Assembly. But he sensed that Thorez's return to the helm of the party was a victory of the State over revolution. If the PCF had passed into the hands of certain Resistance leaders, the resulting confrontation might have presented a challenge to the General's authority. Excited by their victory, assured of strong popular support, still possessing secret arms and funds, these men and their troops would not have given up so quickly what they had gained during the insurrectional period; they would have made more of their relative superiority and strength. None of them was naive enough to consider a seizure of power, given the presence of the Allied armies in France. But from the Leninist point of view, their return to legality might be accompanied by even more bitter conflicts with de Gaulle and the maintenance of various forces of "popular dissuasion".

Thorez posed the problem in a quite different way, as the General realized at

*On 25 November 1939, the military court at Amiens passed a sentence of six years' imprisonment on him for going abroad in time of war – a sentence whose moderation suggests that the judges, even in the atmosphere then reigning, were aware of the complexity of the case involving the party leader.

once. For him, de Gaulle's France was the ally of the USSR, the socialist father-land. The battle fought by the Resistance was for him only a subsidiary operation to ensure that nothing was done to weaken Stalin's allies. The strength of the French State came before serving the masses. Unity, production, independence of the English-speaking allies, even the temporary maintenance of the Empire – in these aims, which Thorez imposed on his party, the Communist leader was in agreement with de Gaulle.

To play the "Thorez card" was, for de Gaulle (given that Thorez was playing the "de Gaulle card"), not only to avail himself of a shield against the militants. It was also the expression of a wish to temper the type of parliamentary vehemence embodied by Jacques Duclos. On this terrain, in which the operation was to be much less fruitful, no one did more than Jacques Duclos, one of the most effective speakers in the Constituent Assembly, to turn the PCF against the General. The memoirs of the deputy from the Hautes-Pyrénées are, as far as this period goes, little more than a long attack on the man whom, in private, Duclos called "Badinguet".* He had even been known to criticize de Gaulle, in the Assembly, for lacking greatness!

The Constituent Assembly held its inaugural session at the Palais-Bourbon, in the presence of Charles de Gaulle. "Sitting in a lower row in the arena, I sensed converging upon me the weary stares of six hundred parliamentarians and felt, almost physically, the weight of general uneasiness."[5]

The reunion of the Liberator and the Assembly took place in bitterness and suspicion. These mutual feelings were never to be overcome. The election as president of the Assembly on 8 November of Félix Gouin, a companion in London and Algiers, was not enough to sweeten the atmosphere: already the SFIO, of which Gouin was a faithful servant, was embarked on a guerrilla war against the General. The parties to whom he had appealed from London turned the tables and the General had to submit to their dominance in Paris. Likewise, having fought all summer to reduce the power of the Assembly, he was to see that same Assembly rise up against the powers of the executive. With a view to placing maximum constraints on the General's future action, the Communists proposed that he should sign a so-called "imperative" order before being elected as president of the Council of Ministers – Prime Minister.

The session of 13 November looked very like Charles de Gaulle's second "coronation". After the crowd in the Champs-Elysées, he received the plebiscite of the nation's elected representatives: a motion declaring that "Charles de Gaulle deserves the admiration of the nation!" was passed, and, by 555 votes out of 555 voting deputies, he was elected head of government.

Nothing is as disturbing as such a triumph. De Gaulle was not taken in. To a friend, he confided: "We are moving toward the decisive trial of the representative regime."[6] In fact, the unanimity would not last for twelve hours. Indeed, the aim of

*The pseudonym of Napoleon III. The name came from the workman whose clothes and identity Napoleon borrowed to escape from Ham Fortress.

the Communist Party, having failed to get its candidate nominated, was strong enough to ensure that it received one of the "important" ministries – Interior, Defence or Foreign Affairs.

Maurice Thorez made his demands, which de Gaulle immediately rejected. He was forming the government, not the Communist Party. He had been elected to do so. He had the highest esteem for the abilities of the Communist leaders and their fitness to occupy responsible positions, but he could not give them any of these essential levers of power.

Thorez protested and withdrew. Scarcely was he back in the Party's head-quarters in the Carrefour de Châteaudun, than he wrote a letter denouncing the General's remarks, which questioned "the national character of our party and its policy" and hurt a party that had had "75 000 of its members shot".* To which de Gaulle replied, also by letter, that his argument did not involve the least "outrage to the memory of any Frenchman who died for France". And he confirmed that he was asking the PCF "to participate in the government". Thorez and his friends kept to their demands.

Opening Claude Mauriac's notebook, we read:

> The possibility of General de Gaulle's departure is becoming a probability. I learnt from the newspaper headlines that the handing in of de Gaulle's letter of resignation was imminent. Palewski still has the letter of resignation, but the delivery has been postponed. He leaves Neuilly; arrives at the office of the President of the Chamber; hands in the letter to Gouin... Will it be made public? No doubt. The General is giving up.[7]

It was not, in fact, a resignation. De Gaulle merely "handed back his mandate" to Félix Gouin, who could always give it back to him. Meanwhile, he decided to address the country, and it was in that broadcast, which went out on 17 November, that Charles de Gaulle made one of his most famous statements about the PCF:

> Much as I was disposed to associate the men of the party in question broadly in the economic and social work of the government, I did not believe it possible to entrust them with any of the three levers controlling foreign policy, namely: the diplomacy that expresses it, the army that sustains it and the police that protects it.

To conclude, the General said that he was ready to leave power "without bitter-ness", but willing, if the Assembly "confirmed" him in his "burden", to "take it up again in the best interests and honour of France". Lastly, on Sunday 18 November, in a letter to the Constituent Assembly, he asked it whether or not it was "withdrawing" his mandate. In Paris the atmosphere was tense. The Palais-Bourbon was surrounded by a cordon of troops. There were police blocks more or less everywhere. There were troops posted near the Pont de la Concorde. The

---

*Most historians would now reduce this figure to about 12 500, which is nevertheless a huge figure.

Palais-Bourbon was full, while a few hundred yards away the team in the Rue Saint-Dominique tried to keep up its spirits. The General had received Léon Blum during the night; he came in "with the face of a man who would not be persuaded, he left shaken, perhaps convinced".[8]

At the end of the debate, the success of the pro-Gaullists (MRP and most of the SFIO) was larger than expected. But before the vote took place André Philip declared at the rostrum that the passing of the Socialist motion involved, for the head of government, an "imperative mandate". This is François Mauriac's comment:

> Let us do justice to M. André Philip, a companion of the earliest hour: the cock has not yet crowed for him. He had not denied his leader, but already he is giving him an imperative mandate. The Assembly, today, has taken precautions. It is well aware what a wave of stupor would overcome this exhausted and saddened country if that man went. But the important thing for the deputies is to be able to say: "He wanted to go; we did not chase him away."
>
> So it was to be the hour of Pilate. So we would find ourselves again among people of the same stature. He would no longer be on our horizon, standing at his lookout post, that strange character who is of the stature of nobody else, that individual whose "greatness" we had finally grown tired of.

That evening, De Gaulle was thinking again of leaving. The parties that he had forced into following him were now imposing this "mandate" on him, this halter, something which, as everybody knew, he could not abide. He was widely regarded as indispensable and unbearable. It looked as if things might turn out badly. Remembering his thoughts on that evening, he confided a few years later to Maurice Schumann that, if he had decided nevertheless to try his luck, it was because he had taken "pity on this country".[9]

On the crucial matter of the "decisive portfolio" demanded by the Communists, and which would certainly be that of National Defence, various compromises were proposed. Were there not three armed forces – army, navy and airforce? In the end, the General adopted the most ingenious solution, suggested by Etienne Burin des Roziers. The ministry would be subdivided into its elements: the essentially economic aspect of armaments was given to the Communist Charles Tillon; its strictly military section, the armed forces, was entrusted to the deportee Edmond Michelet, a member of the Resistance since June 1940 and a leading figure in the MRP – both, of course, under the General's supervision.

The Communists were also given one Ministry of State, which was entrusted to Maurice Thorez, and three of the economic ministries; to the MRP went the great departments of Foreign Affairs and Justice, in addition to the one running the armed forces; the SFIO were given the Ministry of the Interior with Tixier; and several of the important posts went to pure Gaullists – Pleven, Soustelle, Malraux.

The severest test for the alliance between de Gaulle and the parties lay in the Constitutional Commission, presided over by André Philip – that honest man, who on arrival in London had warned his new leader that once Nazism was overcome they would go their own ways. "You will fight for the grandeur of France, I for a socialist Europe..."

Reading now the list of decisions taken by that Commission, one has the impression that it was not so much a commission as a tribunal, a High Court. In three weeks, the Philip Commission had decided: (a) that the President would be elected only by the Assembly, (b) that de Gaulle would no longer chair the Council of Ministers, (c) that he would not even chair the meetings of the Committee of National Defence, and (d) that he would no longer enjoy the right to grant pardon (and one can imagine the crucial importance attached by the General to this most "regal" of rights). The Commission even discussed the question as to whether the "head of State" should be allowed to appoint the President of the Council of Ministers!

Reading these projects, one wonders what went through the heads of intelligent men who, knowing that de Gaulle would be instated as President of the Republic, tried to force him into a uniform that would have been too tight for a local mayor. It was inevitable that the General should hear something of what was being said in the Commission. He asked, not its chairman, with whom relations were decidedly difficult, but his colleague François de Menthon, the Garde des Sceaux in the Liberation Cabinet, to inform him of the work of the Commission. This senior member of the MRP replied that, not being "elected by the people", it was not up to him (de Gaulle) to "meddle" in the affairs of the Commission.

There was no debate, strike, parliamentary session or discussion in the Council of Ministers that did not lead General de Gaulle to this observation: "One cannot serve both France and one's party."[10] It was at this time that he arrived at the conclusion that he summed up some years later in his *Mémoires*: "At this point in my journey, the support the nation offered me was growing slight and uncertain. The current of popular enthusiasm which had been poured so generously on me was now channelled in various directions. The nation no longer delegated anything but parties around me. France had recovered her integrity, her status, her equilibrium and her overseas territories." Here was substance to nourish for a while the strategies of party politicians, their desire to control the State, their opinion that the "man of the storm" had now played his part and must step aside. "For myself, having summed up the possibilities, I had decided on my conduct. I should in any case be able to withdraw from events before they withdrew from me."[11]

And, two pages later, de Gaulle adds this crucial observation: "To France and the French, I owed something further — to leave as a man morally intact."[12]

CHAPTER TEN

The Art of Retreat

As in the case of his decision of June 1940, we must try to discover and explain the reasons why de Gaulle left in January 1946. It is not a question of equating the two. But when twelve years of history – from 1946 to 1958 – see one republic languish, another conceived and another de Gaulle emerge, the process has to be described.

Just as one has detected in de Gaulle a rebel by predestination whose outrageous act of 1940 was merely the culmination of a career consistently marked by rejections and acts of defiance, so we find here a general who has remembered that one of the fundamental laws of war is the strategic retreat. Temperamentally, de Gaulle was of an "offensive" type, but he had retained from the art of war a taste for the austere grandeur of the strategic retreat. Everything drove him forward. But, when progress was blocked, he knew that there was no point in persisting and retreated. For his nature was one not so much of attack as of movement, or rather manoeuvre: that is the keyword of *Vers l'armée de métier*, that key book.

The impasse had become clear ever since the parties, legitimated by the elections of 21 October, had become masters of the terrain. The Socialists considered that they had now paid their debt to him. The MRP, now that Léon Blum's SFIO had decided to work with them more closely, and not with the Communists, saw de Gaulle as less indispensable.

Harassed by the Assembly, which thought only of ridding itself of the muzzle imposed upon it by the second "yes" of the October referendum, trampled underfoot by the Constitutional Commission, General de Gaulle did not have a much easier life as head of government. Jules Moch has described some of the confrontations that occurred between him and Georges Bidault, of all the ministers the one with whom his personal relations were, in fact, most tense and with whom he had most conflicts of jurisdiction.

On the subject of an agreement signed in London by Ambassador René Massigli, with a view to "regrouping" the forces of Britain and France in the Levant – an operation that allowed the British to gain new advantages – General de Gaulle interrupted his Foreign Minister's exposition:

> London's bad faith is, once again, indisputable. The British are trying to install themselves in the Lebanon in the same proportion as in Syria – four to one. So I have decided to recall our negotiator, General de Larminat. We shall accept neither the *diktat* of the British nor the occupation of the Lebanon by them. We must not make room for them. We must hold firm, resume negotiations, or say to them: "Bugger off!"

Bidault: They have the strength. Twice as many men as us.

De Gaulle: Very well! I shall send more!

Bidault: The mood out there is very bad. We're getting kicked out!

De Gaulle: There will be no question of that! Let us be determined to defend ourselves! We mustn't start negotiating with the British again. This perpetual begging attitude can only lose us feathers!

Bidault: We haven't lost any feathers, while I've been here.

De Gaulle: But the problem is quite simple: it's a question of regrouping the French in the Lebanon, not the British!

Bidault: There is no question of anything else!

De Gaulle: Then let's stick to it![1]

Even the debate on social issues became acrimonious. The threat of a general strike by all public employees put not only public order in question, but also the cohesion of the government and the personal authority of two men, de Gaulle and Thorez: the first because he was the head of government and constantly preached respect for the State; the second because, as Minister of State, he was in charge of the public sector. Moreover, the public employees' unions, which pointed out that the upgrading of salaries did not compensate for the 60 per cent increase in the cost of living over the past year, were supported by the SFIO, but not by the PCF. In his *Mémoires*, de Gaulle pretends to be surprised that in such circumstances it was "Communist support" that "by a curious complication" made it possible to overcome a "major crisis".[2]

This support stemmed both from the responsibilities of the ministers and from electoral sociology. In 1945, the SFIO represented the aspirations of most office workers and middle management. So when the SFIO and the CGT announced a big protest meeting, Maurice Thorez's friends felt just as much defied as did Charles de Gaulle. During this meeting it was a Communist speaker who declared: "To go on strike would be a crime against the nation!"

The affair of the public employees turned out to be only a warning shot. The real test of strength between de Gaulle and the Assembly, and the real test of the General's ability to survive the war of attrition, was the debate on the budget – and more particularly the military budget.

The debate threatened to be so lively, so acrimonious, that for the session of 31 December, when military expenditure would be discussed, the Assembly president, Gouin, had the picturesque notion of stopping the clocks at midnight, so that all outstanding business might be completed, as the government had requested, by 1 January.

As the night of 31 December–1 January came to an end, an obscure Socialist deputy, Jean Capdeville, demanded a 20 per cent reduction in military expenditure, because of the "wastage" of which the army was guilty. Very soon, André Philip and Jacques Duclos supported and broadened the attack.

The debate was turning in such a direction that on the morning of 1 January the telephone rang at the General's home at Neuilly. It was Pierre-Henri Teitgen calling de Gaulle: his presence was becoming indispensable. The General, who valued his sleep, refused at first, but then allowed himself to be persuaded. But when Teitgen told him that the offensive was being led by André Philip, de Gaulle decided to call Philip himself:

> "If you don't withdraw your amendment, I shall ask for a vote of confidence!"
>
> "That will be the third time in a week you've threatened us with it. It's too serious a question to be decided in bed, before one has shaved and without consulting any member of the government!" The only response Philip heard was a click. De Gaulle had hung up.[3]

The debate had certainly reached boiling-point. The Socialist deputies seemed possessed, as if by denouncing de Gaulle they were determined to make him pay for some offence or betrayal. A forewarned witness, Major de Boissieu (who, three days later, was to become General de Gaulle's son-in-law) took his place in seats reserved for members of the head of government's private office, where one could "perfectly assess the atmosphere reigning in the semi-circle. It was quite simply horrible. One really had the impression that a circle of hate was closing round General de Gaulle."[4]

André Philip and Albert Gazier declared that they did not wish to overthrow the government and that their sole aim was to force it "to bend to the parliamentary will". Everything was leading to an explosion. It was not just de Gaulle's nerve that snapped, it was his character that exploded. "What a strange view M. André Philip has of the government of the Republic! Yes, there are two views. Does one want a government that governs or does one want an all-powerful Assembly, instructing a government to carry out its wishes?" And he went on to defend his view of "a government constituted in such a way that it alone – I say alone – bears entire responsibility for the executive power. And if the Assembly refuses it all or part of the means it considers necessary to carry out the responsibility of the executive power, then that government resigns and another government appears . . . "[5]

It was during that same session that Charles de Gaulle pronounced the decisive words:

> I repeat that I am speaking for the future. We have begun the reconstruction of the Republic. You will continue with the work. However you do it, I think I can tell you in all conscience and it will no doubt be the last time that I shall speak here, I think I can tell you in all conscience that if you do it without taking into account the lessons of our political history over the last fifty years and in particular what took place in 1940, if you fail to take account of the absolute need for authority, dignity and responsibility in Government, you will find yourselves in a situation in which, sooner or later, I am warning you, you will bitterly regret taking the course that you will have taken.[6]

In his *Mémoires*, Charles de Gaulle recounts how "that evening, probing hearts and hopes, I realized that the matter was already decided, that it would be vain and even unworthy to presume to govern. I must now prepare my own departure from the scene."[7]

But he could still take some time off for reflection, away from the feverish activity of Paris. Just such an opportunity arose with the marriage of his daughter Elisabeth to Major de Boissieu, one of Leclerc's men, which, taking place on 3 January, allowed him to escape from the closed circle of political passions.

Although it is not usual for the parents to go away, on the night of a wedding, General and Mme de Gaulle, soon joined by their respective brothers, Pierre (the youngest of the de Gaulles) and Jacques (the eldest of the Vendroux), took the train on 5 January for the Cap d'Antibes.*

The villa "Sous le vent" where de Gaulle stayed is very beautiful, isolated in the midst of pine trees. Here, he reread Retz and Saint-Simon, and the outings delighted him, especially those by car to Biot, Vence or La Turbie. His brother-in-law describes him as "very sensitive to the charm of that coast". But press photographers – and the merely curious – often made him flee.

Between two walks among the rocks and under the pines, smoking like a steam engine, Charles de Gaulle pursued a monologue addressed to his brother-in-law: "I have come here so that the French can be in no doubt that, if I give up 'business', it will not be on sudden impulse after some incident in which the parties try to obstruct me, but after mature reflection."[8]

Charles de Gaulle was still undecided when, on 13 January 1946, after a final run round the Cap d'Antibes, the General's big Cadillac** took everybody to the station of Golfe Juan where the presidential carriage was waiting.

After dinner, Charles de Gaulle, his brother and his brother-in-law were left alone to talk. The General asked each of them what he thought of the prospect of his retirement.

Pierre de Gaulle spoke first, showing that one did not have to be a great politician or someone who had long haunted the corridors of power to give a great man good advice. In the present circumstances, he pointed out to his brother, a departure would be "misunderstood" by a public that had by and large remained "favourable" to him. By resigning, he would run the risk of being blamed for difficulties that could only get worse. Pierre de Gaulle considered that "the Constituent Assembly ought to be forced to present within two months a constitution that would strengthen the authority of the executive power". There would then be new elections and the General could then, depending on the results, "either resign or accept a new presidential mandate". Jacques Vendroux expressed another opinion. He had recently immersed himself in the atmosphere of the Palais-Bourbon; for him, the "ill humour and impatience" of the parliamentarians were such that they were capable of "every betrayal". He suggested, therefore, "providing the gap was not too long", letting "the parties try out an experiment that would condemn them to impotence and confusion, and wait for the people to force them to call the General back to lead the country once more". Jacques Vendroux adds that although "Charles is sensitive to some of his brother's arguments", he felt that "he had already decided, deep down in himself, to go".[9]

* * *

*Elisabeth and Alain de Boissieu left for Morocco.
**Given by the United States administration after the Liberation.

Jules Moch, the Minister of Public Works and Transport, knew that traditionally the minister in charge of transport welcomed the head of government on his arrival in one of the capital's railway stations. He therefore arranged for his convoy to leave a quarter of an hour before the General arrived.

He learnt that only Charles de Gaulle's travelling companions were expected at the Gare de Lyon, he himself having decided to get off the train discreetly at Maisons-Alfort. What did that strange decision mean? Jules Moch rushed off and arrived in time to see the head of government get out of his carriage via a step-ladder held by the prefect Luizet and a railway worker... De Gaulle noticed the minister standing at the end of the platform. "Oh, kind of you to come," he said. De Gaulle had enough sense of the State to appreciate a diligent minister: "Since you came, come and join me in my car and tell your chauffeur to follow us to the Rue Saint-Dominique." And, no sooner were they settled, than the General turned to his companion and told him that he was about to reveal something important to him, which he asked him to keep secret:

> I don't feel that I am made for this kind of fight. I don't want to be attacked, criticized, challenged every day by men who have no other distinction than the fact that they got themselves elected in some little place in France. At Antibes, I took time off to reflect. The result: I can't resign myself to enduring the criticisms of parties and irresponsible men, to seeing my decisions challenged, my ministers criticized, myself attacked, my prestige diminished. Since I cannot govern as I wish, that is to say fully, rather than see my power dismembered, *I'm going!*

"You have no right to leave," Moch objected. "You joined the parliamentary game, you must go on playing it."

The General listened to this lesson "with rare patience", Moch notes. Just as they were arriving at the Rue Saint-Dominique, he said slowly, as if lost in thought: "Maybe you're right. It is difficult to imagine Joan of Arc married, a mother, and who knows what else? An unfaithful husband..."[10]

A week passed and de Gaulle informed a few initiates, the Ministers of the Interior, Justice and War, of his decision, as well as his Minister of Information, André Malraux. On 18 January, the General chaired a meeting at the Rue Saint-Dominique of the Commissioners of the Republic. Alain Savary, who worked at Angers, was one of them. How could he forget the words the General then addressed to his faithful followers: "Hurry back to your posts! I'm going: look out."? From the few things that the General then said, the future Minister of Education got a clear impression that de Gaulle was expecting to be called back to office by public opinion.[11]

On 10 January a debate took place in the Assembly in which an exasperated Charles de Gaulle clashed with Edouard Herriot. It concerned the regularization, in the *Journal officiel*, of the crosses of the Légion d'honneur given by General Giraud to combatants killed in November 1942 during the landings in North Africa, in combat against the American forces. Using all his considerable vocal powers, Edouard Herriot, who had sent to Vichy his own cross of the Legion of

Honour, declared indignantly: "Our national order must be respected, or abolished!" The left applauded, mixing applause with jeers.

De Gaulle stood up, livid, and could not resist, in passing, giving a lesson to the Radical leader: brandishing the cross of the Legion of Honour, he pointed out to him that, according to the Code, one cannot resign from the Légion d'honneur, one can only refuse it or be excluded from it. But this debating victory is unimportant compared with what such an incident reveals, as summed up in the *Mémoires de guerre*: "Such an attack, on such a subject, was naturally disagreeable to me. But the reception given to it, in my presence, by an Assembly the majority of whose members have but lately answered my call to honour, filled me, I must admit, with disgust."[12]

It was on 16 January that de Gaulle seems to have given his decision an irrevocable character. On the evening of the 18th, Francisque Gay, Minister of State temporarily in charge of Foreign Affairs while Georges Bidault represented France at the session of the United Nations taking place in London, was talking to de Gaulle about the internal crisis in the Levant – which, as we know, always set the General's nerves on edge. So Gay had to listen to an anti-British diatribe. Then suddenly the General said: "I've had enough, next Sunday I'll summon you at midday to tell you that I'm going."

And as if to set aside an objection that he expected his visitor to make on the subject of personal power, the General went on: "I am generally attributed with one quality: intelligence. So how can people suppose that I am so unintelligent as to think that I want to carry out a *coup d'état* as certain people claim. The time for *coups d'état* is over; it's an anachronism and in no way suits my temperament."

According to the account that Gay made to Georgette Elgey shortly before his death in 1963, the dialogue went as follows:

> "*Mon général*, there is only one word to describe your departure and I cannot, being a mere civilian, say it in front of a soldier like yourself."
> De Gaulle understood that I was describing his departure as desertion. He said nothing.* I went on:
> "But, after you, *mon général?*"
> De Gaulle interrupted me in a condescending tone of voice that showed quite clearly that I had understood nothing:
> "Come now, before a week is up, they'll be sending a delegation asking me to come back. But, on that occasion, I shall come back on my conditions."[13]

On the evening of 19 January, messengers on motorbikes went all over Paris delivering to ministers a summons to a meeting of the Council in the Salle des Armures in the Rue Saint-Dominique.

General de Gaulle arrived shortly after noon, in uniform, looking, according to Jules Moch, "stiff and drawn". As to his behaviour, the character of the meeting, even what was said at it, there are several contradictory versions. Given the importance, uniqueness and interest of the event and the number of eloquent

*Which seems unlikely.

witnesses, this is hardly surprising. Even Jules Moch, who had reason to be the least surprised, is content in *Une si longue vie*, to reproduce, apart from a few small details, the version given in the *Mémoires de guerre*. To begin with, let us do likewise:

> I came in, shook hands all round and before anyone sat down, spoke these words: "The exclusive regime of parties has reappeared. I disapprove of it. But apart from establishing a dictatorship by force, which I do not desire and which would certainly end in disaster, I have no means of preventing this happening. I must therefore withdraw. Today, in fact, I shall send the President of the National Assembly a letter informing him of the Government's resignation. I sincerely thank each of you for the support you have given me and urge you to remain at your posts in order to assure the conduct of business until your successors are appointed." The ministers impressed me as being more grieved than astonished.[14]

The General adds that none of them said anything asking him to reconsider his decision or even regretting it. How could any of them have done either? All those who were there agree on this point at least: he left "as always, in a gust of wind," says Louis Joxe.

The most credible version, it seems to me, is that remembered, with the help of notes, by Tanguy-Prigent, the Socialist Minister of Agriculture, well known for his lack of self-interest and his simple loyalty. I reproduce it here as it was given me by his daughter, Mireille:

> At noon we arrived at the Rue Saint-Dominique and went to the Salle des Armures. De Gaulle arrived and declared: "Gentlemen, I asked you to come here in order to tell you that I have decided to resign. I consider that my mission is ended. France is free: she took part in the final victory. France is on the Rhine, her Empire is free and defended; we are going back to Indo-China. At home there are regular elections, so democracy has been re-established; I considered that my role was over on 21 October 1945. I already wanted to go then, but, since there was unanimity behind my name in the Constituent Assembly, I stayed. The three parties continue to attack one another and are preoccupied with the forthcoming elections – it is my view that this is a misfortune for France – and I have no intention of taking part in these party struggles. I have no wish to declare my preference for one over another. I shall ask M. Vincent Auriol to take over my responsibilities until such a time as the National Constituent Assembly has appointed my successor and, in order to prevent any demonstrations whatsoever about my person, I am leaving for the country." And he left immediately.
>
> After which, Jules Moch said: "I think we can hold a little meeting. M. Francisque Gay, who is the oldest of us, will chair that meeting. The situation is very serious," he added, "the three parties must commit themselves to maintaining the present formula so that all this does not degenerate into a long crisis."

Teitgen: "For us in the MRP, General de Gaulle's departure makes our participation in the government more difficult. We shall certainly have some difficulty with our own comrades, but, if there is a Socialist-Communist government, we shall form a constructive opposition and, when we are not in agreement on certain things, we shall be loyal."

Thorez: "De Gaulle's leaving. Why is he leaving? Because he considers that the experiment hasn't succeeded? We would go so far as to say: will a formula that has not succeeded with de Gaulle succeed without de Gaulle? Let's be reasonable. I agree that this government is resigning, but I am and we are in favour of a government of union. Of course, in the two working-class parties, Communist and Socialist, there will be thought of a two-party govenment, but we shall have to explain to them why, for reasons of international, financial, and economic policy, what we need is a three-party* government."

Tanguy-Prigent's account concludes with this reflection: "General de Gaulle's departure and his attitude look like, firstly, an abandonment of post, given the state in which France is at present, and, secondly, an anti-parliamentarian manoeuvre. It's an anti-democratic manoeuvre."

Hastily rejoining his MRP colleagues, to whom Teitgen gave a brief account of the meeting in the Hall of Armour, Georges Bidault denounced the General's "thoughtless lack of civic spirit",[15] while Vincent Auriol wrote the General a letter, which was handed to him that evening at Neuilly. The Minister of State urged the General to give up the idea of delivering a "farewell to the people of France": "You will run the risk of dividing the country. The road that will lead France to the recovery that you have undertaken so courageously after liberating her is long and hard. I beg you, do not set up any obstacle on that road, above all between you and the republicans."[16] In his *Mémoires* Charles de Gaulle refers to the letter from Vincent Auriol.

I calmed the Minister of State's fears. As a matter of fact, had I chosen to explain the reasons for my retirement, I would not have failed to do so, and this explanation, given to a sovereign people, would not have been contrary to democratic principles. But I considered that my silence would weigh more heavily than anything else, that thoughtful minds would understand why I had left, and that the rest would sooner or later be informed by events themselves.[17]

So General de Gaulle's resignation was accompanied only by his letter to the President of the National Assembly of 20 January:

I considered that my task would end when the representatives of the nation met and the political parties were in a position to assume their responsibilities.

*With the MRP.

If I agreed to remain at the head of the government after 13 November 1945, it was both to respond to the unanimous appeal that the Constituent National Assembly had sent me and to ensure a necessary transition. That transition has now been achieved.

Furthermore, after terrible ordeals, France is no longer in a state of emergency. Certainly many sufferings still weigh upon our people, and grave problems remain. But the very life of the French people is, in all essential respects, assured. Our economic activity is staging a recovery, our territories are once again in our own hands. We have re-established ourselves in Indo-China. Public order is not threatened. Abroad, despite the anxieties that persist, our independence is assured. We are holding the Rhine. We are participating, in the first rank, in the new international organization, and it is in Paris that the first peace conference is to be held this coming spring.

As I retire, I would express my profoundly sincere wish that the government that will follow the one that I have had the honour to lead may succeed in the task that is still to be carried out.

How can we not agree that André Malraux was right when, a few days later, he confided to Claude Mauriac: "The trouble is not so much his departure, as the letter that accompanied it, or at least the regrettable last paragraph."

In his *Mémoires de guerre* de Gaulle agrees that Félix Gouin sent him an "extremely gratifying" reply. Praising the General's "dignity" and "disinterestedness" and bowing before "the imperative reasons" that dictated his decision, the President of the Assembly expressed on behalf of his colleagues a regret "that they will no longer see the destiny of their country controlled by the man who has always enjoyed their confidence" and assured him "of their gratitude and of that of the entire French nation".

All the witnesses (especially Jules Moch) have described the unhappy Gouin, whom his colleagues immediately entrusted with the succession,* bursting into tears and saying "Follow de Gaulle, I? Impossible!" Received at Neuilly by the General on the evening of 20 January, he tried desperately to dissuade him from his decision. De Gaulle resisted every assault, and concluded by saying: "France always needs a man in reserve."[18] Yet, in the Socialist daily, *Le Populaire*, on 24 January, Léon Blum paid noble homage to the man who "contrary to his personal temperament" has enabled France "to recover her democratic institutions".

But what of the MRP, the "party of fidelity"? During the meeting that followed the General's departure, Gay, Michelet and Teitgen suggested that "three-party" government would continue, without de Gaulle. That same evening, Georges Bidault, declaring "This is the best day in my life!", immediately supported this decision. But the movement also included members who were more ardently supporters of the General, beginning with its chairman, Maurice Schumann.

Schumann let it be known[19] that support for "a three-party government without de Gaulle" had been imposed on him by a letter from General Billotte (himself an

---

*The Communists having vetoed the appointment of Vincent Auriol, who had been proposed by the General.

ardent Gaullist) dated 22 January. In that message, Billotte, then Assistant Chief of General Staff in the army, told Schumann that the departure of the MRP would create an imbalance in favour of the Marxist parties within the government that the American and British military leaders would react against.

According to Pierre Billotte, who learnt that a narrow majority of the MRP leaders tended to be in favour of leaving the government, he hastily scribbled a note to Schumann, his friend from London days, telling him that: (a) the army would not accept a Thorez government, (b) the Empire would gradually secede, and (c) the retaliatory measures taken by Washington would be unbearable: he was in daily contact with the American General Staff and was well aware of the mood prevailing in it.[20]

Why did de Gaulle choose to break a contract made two months previously with an apparently unanimous Assembly and why did he do it in January 1946? The answers are to be found in statements made by the General in public and in private since 1 January.

Though he was an orator and was better than anyone at silencing an opponent with a word, Charles de Gaulle could not accustom himself to this type of confrontation. Was it a matter of disdain for "mediocrity"? It was actually something quite different, for the two conflicts that did more than any others to throw him out of the arena were ones in which he opposed two men of culture and talents, two intellectuals like himself – Philip and Auriol. What he found intolerable was just how confined the Palais-Bourbon was. Nothing "moved" there; there was nothing but turmoil.

But there was more. Charles de Gaulle would not have been the man of London if foreign affairs had not dominated his personal interests. In January 1946, he noted that in three areas which were of fundamental importance – Germany, the Levant, Indo-China – misfortune was being showered upon him. His plans for controlling the left bank of the Rhine were meeting increasing opposition from his Anglo-Saxon allies and indifference from Moscow. In the Middle East, London was claiming to impose upon him a common evacuation of the Levant, which would leave the British flag floating alone from Cairo to Baghdad. In Indo-China, the Vinh San solution had just collapsed with the tragic death of the pretender to the throne. Everything that he had set his heart on seemed to have been struck by a sort of fatality.

And we must not forget the chances of another war. From October 1945, de Gaulle foresaw a great conflict between the West and the USSR. Nothing could have driven him more to resume his freedom than his awareness that he might once again have to play the role of a focus of national unity against a new invasion. Better to be called back as a saviour when the time came.

Lastly, one must not forget the exhaustion that had overcome this man as a result of the storms that he had had to face for over five years. It is significant that this man of steel considered it right to spend a few days on the Côte d'Azur before even making his decision. I am not saying, of course, that de Gaulle's attention was diverted from power by the charms of the south of France, but, combined with his old obsession of escape (I'll leave them in the lurch! They'll see what it's like without de Gaulle!), a sort of historical lassitude played its part.

This brings us to the second question. In the "they'll see", there is the beginning of the inevitable recall of the exceptional man. So we must look carefully at the tactical dimension of the resignation of 20 January 1946. For some, it is clear: it was merely a tactical step back, in order to make the recall inevitable. For others, the departure is part of long-term plans for his own life: having ended the heroic period, having married off his daughter and begun the rebuilding of his house at Colombey, which had been sacked by the occupiers, the great man had to withdraw from active life, write his *Mémoires* and hold himself ready to serve his country once again in the years that lay ahead.

The advocates of the thesis of a tactical and temporary retreat base their arguments particularly on what the General had said to Francisque Gay on 18 January: "Before a week is up they'll be sending a delegation asking me to come back..." I myself have heard two of the General's close colleagues, Rémy Roure, who was a fellow-prisoner at Ingolstadt, in 1917, and later became a columnist on *Le Monde*, and Edmond Michelet, who in 1946 was his Army Minister, say how General de Gaulle then spoke of a mere "mishap", by which he meant that his followers should be convinced of this, behave accordingly and be "ready" to resume their burdens. Louis Vallon reported that, according to de Gaulle, that retreat was "a six-month affair". Once again, it is Claude Mauriac who finds the most accurate turn of phrase: "*As far as the immediate future is concerned*, the decision is irrevocable."[21]

We shall see the General's thinking evolve, from the idea of a tactical retreat to that of arranging another kind of life for himself, from the ideal of the retired hero to that of the saviour responding to the calls of the multitude. At an early stage, it was the idea of break that dominated, the idea of being on the periphery, at a distance.

> At first I thought of travelling to some distant region where I could wait* in peace. But the tide of insult and invective launched against me by political headquarters and the majority of newspapers determined me to remain in Metropolitan France so that no one could suppose that such attacks upset me. I therefore rented the Pavillon de Marly** from the Service des Beaux-Arts, and lived there until May.[22]

But the most negative judgement on this episode comes from the General. To his nephew, Michel Cailliau, he remarked a few years later: "I have made at least one political mistake in my life: my departure in January 1946. I thought the French would recall me very quickly. Because they didn't do so, France wasted several years."

---

*The word "wait" is clearly used advisedly.
**The house is traditionally reserved for official figures.

II

EXILE

CHAPTER ELEVEN

An Impatient Hermit

"A king in exile." This was how one of his teachers at his military academy described him in 1924. It was also how he found himself after his "abdication" of 20 January 1946. He was still more a king than exiled, perhaps. What sovereign, once deposed, does not dream of his return and prepare for it? As a head of government he had remained in many respects a rebel. In his retirement, he was already, in thought, the sovereign. His *Mémoires de guerre* brilliantly defined the situation:

> While the regime gave itself up to the euphoria of old habits regained, the mass of the French people, on the contrary, sank back into distress. Gone was that atmosphere of exaltation, that hope of success, that ambition for France which supported the national soul. Every Frenchman, whatever his tendency, had the troubling suspicion that with the General had vanished something primordial, permanent and necessary which he incarnated in history and which the regime of parties could not represent.[1]

When Jacques Vendroux, Mme de Gaulle's brother, but also an MRP deputy, was received at Marly Pavillon, he was struck by its smallness: it had the air of a place where the inmate was under "house arrest". He writes: "Although he claimed to want peace and quiet, Charles de Gaulle was too dynamic to adapt himself for long to total inaction. He thought about things and began to draw up the plan of the *Mémoires* to which he now devoted most of his time."[2]

On 16 February, François Mauriac was received for over an hour. Later, he described what the flamboyant retired leader had said:

> De Gaulle says he had to go because the parties were making government impossible. He knew this and made up his mind long ago. The actual timing did not matter, give or take a week.
>
> It's a fact that it is impossible to govern with the parties. It's also a fact that an assembly, of whatever kind, has never governed in France – that power has always eluded parliament, whatever form it took. What the country needs is a leader. He then explained how he saw the Constitution and, I'm telling you, if he had his way, the President would have a lot of power!
>
> According to him there are three possibilities for the immediate future: "Either we'll stay in the present mess and mediocrity for quite a long time; or the Communists will seize power – in which case there'll be a major war,

because the Russians would set up in France, which the Americans and British could in no way accept; or I come back."[3]

The situation of Charles de Gaulle, mythically a general to all eternity, but legally a retired colonel, was odd enough to be posing the government certain problems, including some of a bureaucratic type. It was Edmond Michelet, the most faithful of all his followers, who was "his minister" in charge of the armed forces. He asked de Gaulle how they were to settle the General's "situation in the army", a situation that, according to the minister, "President Gouin naturally wants to be as high as possible". Marshal of France, a title so closely associated with Pétain, and his inferiors? Four days later, Michelet received one of the most implacable, if stinging, letters ever written by the General.

> My dear Minister,
> . . . Since 18 June 1940 – the date on which I gave up my responsibilities and set out in a rather unusual direction – the events that have taken place have been of such a nature and of such a dimension that it would be impossible to "regularize" a situation absolutely without precedent.
>
> Indeed, there has been no need whatever to change anything in that situation during the five years, seven months and three days of a very great trial. Any "administrative solution" that one might try to apply to it today would, therefore, take on a strange, even ridiculous character.
>
> The only course that measures up to the situation is to leave things as they are. One day, death will take it upon itself to smooth over the difficulty, if there still is one.[4]

The General seemed to display to his visitors at Marly a growing optimism for himself and a pessimism about the affairs of the world. In his eyes, the collapse of the parties was imminent and could only lead to a revival that would have to take the form of his return. But on what conditions? His answer was categorical and he repeated it many times to Claude Mauriac: unconditional surrender of the party system.

But although he believed that the French people could be brought back to life, he also believed in the inevitability of a conflict between the West and Communism. It was the time when Churchill was prophesying the same. But contrary to what he said to Colonel Passy on 7 December 1941, at the time of Pearl Harbor, de Gaulle no longer believed in a Russian military victory. Meanwhile, it is true, there had been the dropping of the atom bomb on Hiroshima on 6 August 1945. He also spoke of Soviet "bluff", maintaining that the Russians were not inclined to wage "a war that they would certainly lose" – recalling that between 1941 and 1945 the USSR, deprived of the support of the West, was "beaten by a people of 70 million inhabitants, which is no great achievement".[5]

But the great affair of the moment was the referendum that would decide on the future of the institutions of the new republic. Detached though he wanted to be, or as he wanted people to believe he was, he took a passionate interest in this battle in which, through that of his country, his own future was in play.

Six weeks before the referendum, planned for 5 May, he told Claude Mauriac: "One must vote *against* the Constitution of course! Against that trick of the parties, that 'deal' that the stupid Constitution they have worked out represents for them. It would be an appreciable result if the country showed that it wants nothing to do with it."[6]

Two weeks later, the MRP rejected the Socialists' constitution. And on 5 May, the electorate voted against the proposed constitution presented by the Communists and the SFIO: 53 per cent voted "no", over a million more votes than those voting "yes".*

De Gaulle saw this as a sign of the need for a "return" and decided to launch his manifesto at Bayeux, a city that symbolized the Allied landing of 1944.** The timing was particularly appropriate in that on Sunday 2 June, the electors gave the left another slap in the face in voting for the second Constituent Assembly. The MRP emerged as the winners, moving up from 24 per cent to over 28 per cent of the votes cast, whereas the Communists and the SFIO lost ground.

The General, who, at the end of May, had returned to his restored house at Colombey, confided these words to his secretary: "The Communists have failed in their tactics and will not recover. They are now on the defensive and have been dropped – or are about to be – by innumerable scheming swine! Now, believe me, it is too late for them."[7]

"If only Napoleon had been able to take a year off, his whole fate would have been different," de Gaulle observed in June 1946. A year? That may have been true for Napoleon, who had the memory of Waterloo to wipe out. But de Gaulle did not have a disaster to expiate. It was not even six years since he had launched his crusade. He surely had no intention of retiring, only retreating, prior to a counter-attack.

On 16 June, he was at Bayeux, being welcomed by the prefect, surrounded by his old war companions. Under driving rain, Charles de Gaulle, standing on a podium erected as on 14 June 1944 in front of Bayeux castle, in uniform and sporting only the insignia of Free France, addressed the French people, recalling past disappointments and triumphs, and outlining a possible future.

The Bayeux speech, which the General took two months to write, twenty-seven minutes to deliver, twelve years to think over and ten years to put into practice, is worth careful analysis. It contains both a penetrating rereading of the history of Free France and a fascinating projection of what was to be the whole history of Gaullism. It was the founding monument of the second Gaullism, just as the June appeal was the charter of the first. As always with de Gaulle the historian, the past was invoked as the basis for a future project. He presents an elegant opposition between "the initial disaster of France and the Allies" and "the final victory of the Allies and France": a distributive justice and an historical balance that were to cost it dear. Free France, de Gaulle said, had "a sense of its moral superiority, the

*10 600 000 Against: 9 500 000 For.
**See *De Gaulle: The Rebel 1890–1944*, pp. 530–1.

awareness that it was carrying out a sort of priestly ministry of sacrifice and example, a passion for risk and enterprise, a sovereign trust in the strength and cunning of its powerful exorcism. Such was the psychology of that elite that came from nothing." A fine attack on dictatorship follows:

> First it takes on an appearance of dynamism, contrasting with the anarchy that had preceded it. But the risks, the efforts gradually become excessive. In the end, the spring snaps. The grandiose edifice crumbles in misery and blood. The nation finds itself broken in two, in a worse state than it had been before the adventure began.

Lastly come the General's institutional prescriptions, inspired both by the principles of Montesquieu, a liberal monarchist, and the ideas of Michel Debré, a convinced republican. They would not have caused such a commotion if he had not provided this flamboyant description of how he saw the mission of the head of state:

> It is from the head of State, placed above the parties, elected by a college including the parliament, but much wider and made up in such a way as to make him the President of the French Union as well as of the Republic, that the executive power must proceed. It is the task of the head of State to reconcile the general interest, where appointments are concerned, with the direction that emerges from the parliament. It will be his job to appoint ministers and, first of all, of course, the prime minister. It is the job of the head of State to promulgate laws and issue decrees. He presides over the Councils of the Government. He serves as an arbiter above political contingencies. It is his duty, if the nation is in danger, to guarantee national independence.

The Bayeux speech caused "strong reactions". The most interesting was that of Léon Blum in *Le Populaire* of 21 June. Blum, who was always fair, declares that "between the General and democracy, one notes something like an incompatibility of temperament". But what democracy has he in mind? The democracy described in *A l'échelle humaine* or that dreamt of by Guy Mollet and André Philip, reducing the head of State to a powerless figurehead?

Rereading the text today, it is with some surprise that one remembers the reception that was then given it: the word "Bonapartism" was on many people's lips.* The text says nothing of the kind. But there is the man. Whether or not there was an "incompatibility of temperament", the personal relations of de Gaulle with democracy were quite clearly ambiguous.

The Bayeux speech could have no emotional impact on true republicans. The problem was not so much the manifesto as the General's character. It was because they refused to go back under his domination that many pretended to discover, in what he said, the whiff of a Bonapartism that one looks for in vain. The Bayeux manifesto does not contravene the rules of a democracy as it had been fashioned

*On those of the author of this book, among others.

by its founding fathers, from Walpole to Montesquieu and from Jefferson to Masaryk. Charles de Gaulle claimed to be opening up the way for the future. Who he was was what prevented people hearing what he was saying, and what he was saying was too strong to be accepted. This master of "circumstances" now found them hostile to his proposals. It is not enough to say what is true and necessary. It also has to be said at the right time and in such a way that the listener can take it in. In 1934, *Vers l'armée de métier* was a manifesto of truth. It was not listened to, not only because those to whom it was addressed were deaf or obstinate, but because the author had dressed up his admonition with a provocative title and a haughty style.

So the Bayeux speech, that appeal to republican effectiveness, was to be received, on account of its grandiose style and the climate of the time, as a threatening order and a challenge to democracy. Misunderstood once more, de Gaulle saw himself thrown back to a position where he was automatically sarcastic to democrats – if not to democracy itself.

However pressing they may have been, constitutional problems were not the only ones to occupy his mind. On 1 July at Colombey, he spoke to a visitor about the atom bomb that had just been exploded on Bikini ("the only question of any real importance"), of the international supervision that should now be set up, and of the "European federation" that should be created round France and Britain.

The de Gaulle of summer 1946 was angered by the necessary (but inadequate) concessions made in Indo-China by his friends Leclerc and Sainteny. He believed that a third world war was imminent. He was too much a writer and orator not to use speeches as an outlet for an upsurge of anger that might otherwise drive him to extremes of action. So he shut himself up in his study at Colombey and wrote the speech that he was to deliver at Bar-le-Duc on 29 July 1946. In it he warned Europe against the reconstitution of the Reich, advocating the rebirth of a confederation of German states situated between the Rhine and the Oder. Then, on 28 August, he went off to the Ile de Sein to speak to those fishermen who, one June day in 1940, "were all that was left of France".*

On 26 August, on the way to the Ile de Sein, the General met Paul Coste-Floret in Paris, who proudly presented him with a draft constitution in which the powers of the head of State took on a certain consistency (so much so that the Communists denounced the text as "Bonapartist", while Pascal Copeau, who was close to the PCF, declared that it was "moving in the direction of Bayeux"). De Gaulle retorted that these modifications were not enough to make the draft satisfactory and that he would oppose it.

In the MRP, however, there were many who refused to resign themselves to failure. Above all there was Maurice Schumann, who informed the General (through his brother-in-law, Jacques Vendroux, an MRP deputy) that the new draft constitution would respect at least the most important thing, the separation of powers. If an agreement was not reached on this text, the parties of the left would gang up together to impose "even more demagogic institutions".

---

*All able-bodied men of this Breton island set sail to rejoin their compatriots in London – at a time when Free French forces were no more than a handful.

Schumann got P.-H. Teitgen (he had become the real leader of the MRP) to go to Colombey to persuade the General to support the Coste-Floret text. He was received by de Gaulle, in the presence of Jacques Vendroux, but got no more than a new warning. That evening, trying to present this reaction as a semi-approval to the MRP group, he was quickly challenged by Charles de Gaulle's brother-in-law:

> I pointed out that I myself had just come from Colombey, where I had followed Pierre-Henri Teitgen into my brother-in-law's study, and that I had been instructed to confirm that he was totally opposed to the draft law and determined to declare his view publicly. Needless to say, I was throwing a terribly cold water over the gathering. The leaders were dismayed and my colleagues confused. I said to Alfred* Coste-Floret, who seemed annoyed, that it was now up to him, if he wanted to, to rewrite the draft for the second reading. I did not conceal that I thought it would all have to start again from scratch and that I did not think such an operation could possibly be successful.[8]

In an attempt to prevent a resignation that would symbolize the "physical" break between the MRP and the General, Maurice Schumann addressed a moving entreaty to Vendroux: "All who are Gaullists at heart – read Mauriac's article in yesterday's *Figaro* or Rémy Roure's article in this evening's *Le Monde* – will say 'yes and revision'. Are you going to let the General be a prisoner of those who hate him? No, my dear friend! Save him from himself!" Maurice Schumann tried to avoid a break between the General and the MRP, and begged him to approve the draft law, pending the necessary revisions.

Charles de Gaulle's answer came on 29 September, in a speech given at Epinal, where the municipality had invited him to celebrate the second anniversary of the liberation of the town. A few hours after the Constituent Assembly had adopted (by 440 votes to 106) Coste-Floret's draft constitution, which was to be put for approval to the electorate on 13 October, the General delivered, on the Place du Maréchal Foch, a vehement attack on it:

> We who believe that nothing is more important for France than to restore as soon as possible the efficiency and authority of the republican State, consider that [the draft constitution] cannot be approved because it does not correspond to the necessary conditions. Such a compromise does not seem to us to provide a framework worthy of the Republic. In this harsh and dangerous world, in which the ambitious grouping of the Slavs, under a boundless power, rises up against a young America, overflowing with resources, we shall solve the vast problems of the present and future only under the direction of a just and strong State.[9]

The draft constitution was nevertheless approved on 13 October by 35 per cent of the registered voters (a little over nine million votes), with 33 per cent against and

---

*It is actually Alfred's twin brother, Paul Coste-Floret, who is referred to here.

32 per cent abstentions. It was a failure for the General, which was made worse on 10 November 1946: the elections that gave France her first legislative assembly in the framework of the new Constitution made the Communists the largest party in France with 183 deputies (30 more than in June), while the MRP, though impeded in its progress (it moved from 166 to 173 deputies), showed that its break with de Gaulle had hardly weakened it. The Gaullist Union, set up by René Capitant (with the General's approval), received only 3 per cent of the votes and was represented in the Assembly by only 5 (later 6) deputies.

Was Charles de Gaulle deeply affected by this? Claude Mauriac's notebooks show him above all irritated by a question that nobody was asking: why does de Gaulle not accept the supreme office of President? "But, Mauriac, how can you explain that after all I have said to them about this unacceptable Constitution, they should be so stupid, so base, as to believe that I would be capable of such baseness, such stupidity, as to offer myself as a candidate for the presidency of the Republic?"[10] He was pretending to forget that the faithful friend to whom he was speaking had tried, with many other faithful friends, to plead for that "stupidity": if the danger was as great as he said it was and if the country would need to be saved, he would be better placed to do it at the Elysée than at Colombey.

Nevertheless the rumour was persistent enough, in those last days of 1946, for General de Gaulle to consider it necessary, on 28 December, to issue a communiqué in which he declared: "So, in all conscience, I do not believe that I would be serving the country by claiming to become the guarantor of a constitution that consecrates this regime and to preside, without power, over a powerless State."

So the President that the new parliament was to elect, at a special session in Versailles on 16 January, was not to be Charles de Gaulle. And yet, that evening, seeing the presidential car enter the Place de l'Etoile from the Avenue Foch, some of us looked hard to see who, in the black limousine, was sitting at the back, to the right of Léon Blum, the ephemeral head of government. Of course, it was M. Vincent Auriol, who had been elected at the Versailles session, by a comfortable majority, against Champetier de Ribes, Gasser and Michel Clemenceau.*

At first relations between de Gaulle and the new President were not lacking in cordiality. Immediately after being elected, Vincent Auriol sent the General a warm, skilfully elegant message in which he assured de Gaulle that despite his "apprehensions" democracy would triumph. On 20 January 1947, the General replied that he was "very touched" by the president's reference to "the work of the Resistance". He, too, was convinced that democracy would overcome all obstacles "since one day the State, through its institutions and its men, will dominate divisions and fulfil its object, which is to serve only the common interest".

Without any bitterness against the new president, Charles de Gaulle was to comment, with unexpected benevolence, on the new State's first steps. On 2 February 1947, his visitors at Colombey heard him comment on the difficulties then facing the country. "De Gaulle would not have done any better. It is in the power of no man to raise France up when the means of doing so are missing. But I amused the French with flags. I amused them with the Rhine."

*The candidates of the MRP, the Radicals and the Right.

And when Claude Mauriac went back, with some insistence, to the sufferings of the French people, who were no longer to be "amused by the Rhine", he replied: "I suffer deeply, constantly, to see France in this situation." He then let slip the great news: "I'm going to try a *Rassemblement*. It's the only hope."

Why did he join battle in April 1947? No answer to this question is to be found in any of Charles de Gaulle's writings or correspondence. But in that spring of 1947, "circumstances" scarcely drove a man like him to inaction. Both on the international stage and in France itself, the dangers were increasing and becoming more specific. There were the first skirmishes of the Cold War, the premonitory signs of a coming civil war with the exclusion of the Communists from the government, the great insurrectional strikes called by the CGT, and the deterioration of the Indo-Chinese expedition into a true war. The man of storms felt that the climate was returning in which his true stature would once again be recognized. On 17 July 1947 he confided to Claude Mauriac: "Of course, there'll be a war!"[11]

A group of former members of France Libre, founded in October 1946, were preparing, in secret, a political movement that would allow de Gaulle to return to power. André Malraux was its leader, flanked by Jacques Foccart, Jacques Soustelle, Jacques Baumel, Alain Bozel, Pierre Lefranc, Brigitte Friang, Diomède Catroux and a few rank-and-file members also uncertain of the future. "We had the impression that the spirit of the Resistance was returning. It was almost as if we believed that we were going back underground," writes Brigitte Friang.

The General was not a man to allow his hand to be forced, but this group did express his own impatience. It was to be one of the elements in his decision which, it seems, he took in September 1946. About the same time de Gaulle took into his confidence a man who could not be kept out of it: Gaston Palewski.[12] And Malraux was now brought into the picture. Jacques Soustelle's apartment, in the Avenue Henri-Martin, was another centre of activity for the "new Resistance": Foccart, Baumel, Gilbert Renault (alias Rémy) and Guillain de Bénouville often met there, and General de Gaulle also had at his disposal a private office set up in "Napoleon's sadlery", on the Quai Branly.

De Gaulle now set about recruiting supporters for his *Rassemblement*. Only those who had collaborated during the war were to be excluded from joining. And even this impediment was to become more flexible in time.

To begin with, the General was thinking of his wartime companions. There was René Pleven, for so long his right-hand man, but he was "shocked that the great memory of Free France, decorated with the Croix de Lorraine, should be invoked in a debate concerning French internal politics".[13] Pierre Mendès France resisted for the same reasons; likewise René Mayer, whose refusal irritated de Gaulle greatly; and he waited in vain for Joxe, Passy and Parodi to join him.

But the die was cast. De Gaulle could no longer contain his impatience. On 4 March, a meeting held in the suite that he occupied in the Hôtel La Pérouse, in the presence of his brother-in-law, Jacques Vendroux, Rémy and Soustelle, the movement was baptized: de Gaulle chose the name "Rassemblement du peuple français" (RPF).

And although many of those who had been called had reservations or had actually warned him against it, the General could depend on the enthusiastic approval of some of those whom he regarded as "the best", because they had shown proof of lucidity and courage at the time of greatest danger: Palewski, Jacques Chaban-Delmas, Pasteur Vallery-Radot, Guillain de Bénouville, Debré, Vallon, Yves Morandat and Jacques Baumel.

The operation was to be broken down into three stages: on 30 March at Bruneval, the General would give evidence to rumour and refer to the imminence of an important decision; on 7 April at Strasbourg, he would proclaim the birth of the organization; on 14 April, in Paris, a communiqué would make it official. It was a clever series of moves, no less cleverly placed when the Chamber was on holiday and when the government headed by the Socialist Ramadier was in debate and seemed to be breaking up under pressure from the Communists. Between the parliamentary void and government storms, would not the new Rassemblement seem a miraculous appearance of hope?

In 1941 Bruneval, a cliff in Normandy, had been made a radar station by the Germans. On 27 February 1942, British and Canadian commandos (containing some thirty or so Free French) had destroyed those installations. It was this deed of arms that de Gaulle had chosen to celebrate, standing beside the British and Canadian Ambassadors (his friends Alfred Duff Cooper and General Vanier), a representative from the American Embassy and two British generals – together with Admiral d'Argenlieu and General de Larminat. A few leading politicians – Maurice Schumann, Jacques Soustelle, Edmond Michelet – had joined the party.

"Will he talk politics?" Duff Cooper asked Rémy, before agreeing to join the expedition as Her Majesty's representative. To which the former secret agent replied that de Gaulle had never talked of anything else, but that the British nation had never had occasion to regret it.

The crowd was enormous. Fifty thousand people had gathered on that deserted cliff. Were they all supporters or were many of them simply sightseers? Rémy, the organizer of the festivities, had to declare that a few thousand were wartime comrades: "It is the most splendid meeting of the networks that has ever been seen, or will ever be seen." The special reporter from *Le Monde*, Raymond Millet, described the "chaos of the bottle-necks on the muddy roads, from which the cars, after the ceremony, tried in vain to escape". But everywhere, he goes on, one could hear the General's voice, which, "thanks to the loudspeakers, swamped the British or French fighters and bombers, and the breaking of the waves".

Ah! Comrades, it is true that after so many trials, the voices of division, that is to say, of decadence, have been able for a time to drown that of the national interest. The tide rises and falls. Perhaps it is in the nature of things that obscure gropings should follow a clear, great effort. But the times are too difficult, life is too uncertain, the world is too harsh, for one to be able to vegetate in the shadows. Our people bears grave wounds, but one has only to listen to the beatings of its unhappy heart to know that it intends to live, to be cured, to grow. The day will come when, rejecting sterile games and reforming the ill-built structure in which the nation has lost its way and the State has lost all authority, the great mass of French people shall gather together upon France.

There then rose up the cry of "de Gaulle au pouvoir!"

Although the commentators present remained prudent, the reactions of the Paris press the following day, 31 March, were largely anxious or hostile. Léon Blum set the tone, writing in *Le Populaire*: "Although I am in no sense inclined to exaggerate the gravity of the situation, I have to say that a struggle has now begun." In *Libération*, J.-R. Tournoux spoke of a "crusade", but, in *Combat*, Raymond Aron assured his readers that the country had a "majority of democrats" (he was not only excluding de Gaulle, but also the Communists).

Claude Mauriac commented: "Speech at Bruneval. Great excitement, anxiety and joy. My father mistrustful. This time is the Rubicon. I shall go with de Gaulle to the end. Fidelity is the only faith left to me."[14]

The government acted quickly. Paul Ramadier, the Prime Minister, set out for Colombey in the late afternoon of 31 March. He arrived at half-past nine and de Gaulle was getting ready to go to bed. "There is a gentleman at the door asking to see you, *mon Général*." "Who is he?" "He says he's the head of the government." Just the kind of words to delight de Gaulle.

The decision taken at the end of the nocturnal meeting – the authorities would be at the General's side on commemorative festivals and would be absent only at the political demonstrations of the opposition – was reasonable enough. At Strasbourg, the General's visit was to take place over two days; the first, Easter Sunday, was to pay homage to the Americans who had died in the liberation of Alsace, the second to an affirmation of political Gaullism. The choice of the Alsatian capital was a good one, not only because that town was a symbol of French patriotism, but also because the mayor, Charles Frey, was a sympathizer, as was the prefect of the Bas-Rhin, Bernard Cornut-Gentille, and the general commanding the French forces there, Paul de Langlade, one of Leclerc's former lieutenants.

Charles de Gaulle, flanked by the American Ambassador, Jefferson Caffery, Generals de Lattre and Koenig, and Admiral d'Argenlieu, walked through an excited crowd from which arose innumerable cries of "de Gaulle au pouvoir!"

Whenever, in the world, justice is wounded, a faint alarm bell rings in French and American consciences. Our two democracies have always found the same powerful resonance when they have had to defend threatened liberty.

If, by some misfortune, a new tyranny were to arise that would threaten all or part of the world, we are certain in advance that the United States and France would agree to oppose it. May that firm certainty give strength everywhere to the hearts and minds of free men and may it always be so!

It was the following day, 7 April, at the Hôtel de Ville, on the Place Broglie, that de Gaulle crossed at least an internal Rubicon – a return to responsibilities through the quest for power. Before announcing the creation of the Rassemblement, de

Gaulle was anxious to draw up a balance sheet of the state of the country when he began the great undertaking of national renewal. As in June 1940, he had to convey his own stature by the hyperbolic denunciation of others – here described as abasing the State and liquidating the Empire:

The Republic, which we have brought out of the tomb in which national despair had first plunged it, the Republic that we dreamt of as we fought for her, the Republic that must now be identified with our renewal, will be efficiency, concord and liberty, or it will be only impotence and dissolution as we see it disappear, from infiltration to infiltration, under a certain dictatorship, or lose, in anarchy, even the independence of France. It is time that French men and women who think and feel like this, as I am sure the overwhelming mass of our people do, came together to prove it. It is time for the Rassemblement of the French People to be formed and organized, so that, within the framework of the law, over and above differences of opinion, the great effort of common salvation and the profound reform of the State may be begun and triumph.

And with the crowd he sang the *Marseillaise* – which had been composed a few hundred yards from that spot. Around de Gaulle, the men who already formed his General Staff – Malraux, Soustelle, Palewski, Baumel, Rémy, Diethelm, Guy, Giacobbi, Claude Mauriac – looked like conquerors. And many other friends – Jacques Chaban-Delmas, Edmond Michelet, René Capitant, Mme Eboué, Louis Vallon, Antoine Avinin, Pasteur Vallery-Radot, Raulin-Laboureur, Albert Ollivier, Paul Kalb (known as "Jacques Dalsace") – came to show their approval.

In Paris, the press reactions were negative, but more qualified than after the Bruneval speech. On the left, *L'Humanité* began shouting about "personal power" and *Franc-Tireur* spoke of "antiquated thinking"; in *Le Populaire*, on 8 April, Léon Blum argued that if the theses defended by the General "distance him ineluctably from the Republic, at the same time, he denies with the same tenacity any categorical break with republican doctrines, traditions or vocabulary". In the highest reaches of the State, there was no attempt to minimize the implications of the General's moves. Lunching at the Elysée on 8 April, Léon Blum said that he saw de Gaulle as "a prisoner of his illusions", doomed to be "swamped by elements of a totalitarian mentality" and, whereas he could have sensibly become the head of a "great social republican party", he would, as an "absolute autocrat", throw "a shadow over his glory, which should have remained pure".

The actual founding of the Rassemblement was to be 14 April. It was on that day that a document written for de Gaulle by Malraux was published.

In the present situation, the future of the country and the destiny of each one of us is at stake. The nation must be guided by a coherent, orderly, concentrated state, capable of choosing and applying the measures required by public safety. The present system, in which rigid, opposed parties divide up power among themselves, must therefore be replaced by another, in which the executive power proceeds from the country and not from the parties, and in which each insoluble conflict is settled by the people itself. Today the Rassemblement du peuple français is created. I am assuming its leadership.

I invite all Frenchmen and Frenchwomen who wish to unite for the common good, as they did so for the liberation and victory of France, to join me in the Rassemblement.

Vive la France! Vive la République!

                                                    Charles de Gaulle

Highly irritated by press reactions, de Gaulle decided to give a press conference on Thursday 24 April at the Maison de la Résistance, in the Rue François-Ier. For two hours, a packed gathering of French and foreign journalists bombarded him with questions. Wearing a navy blue suit and looking considerably rejuvenated, the General defended himself.

"Will the RPF take part in elections?"

"That is not its aim," de Gaulle replied, "but it will do so."

"To what extent and in what form?"

"Since we have neither a radio station nor newspapers of our own, the Rassemblement might well retain its mystery more than it would like."

"Will the RPF tend to become the single party?"

"Experience, yesterday and today, has shown that the single party is nothing more than a dictatorship. We shall not be returning to such follies, which are contrary to our very ideal."

"I have read André de Kérillis' book, *De Gaulle dictateur...*" one journalist began.

"I haven't," de Gaulle interrupted.

"The fact that you have never presented yourself at any election gives the impression that your democratic feelings are rather weak."

"Does one have to be a candidate in order to be a republican?"

When someone referred to Bonaparte, the General responded, this time with some enthusiasm: "Yes, I have returned from Egypt, and even from Italy, and from Libya, the Rhine and the Danube as well. I have entered Paris, Lyon, Marseille in the steps of our victorious troops. Have I strangled the Republic?"

In this period opinion polls were fairly rare. However, one was carried out in late May 1947 by the French Institute of Public Opinion (IFOP). If they had to choose between General de Gaulle and his opponents, 40 per cent of those questioned would opt for the first, 33 per cent for the others – which would give de Gaulle a small majority of voters. But when the questions became more precise, only 26 per cent of those questioned came out in favour of the Rassemblement.[15] A vaguely sympathetic majority did not yet constitute active support. De Gaulle, yes. The RPF? Hmmm...

In June, at Lille, his native city, the General vaguely sketched out an economic and social programme of "association" intended to supersede the class struggle, defended what he had done at the time of the Liberation and delivered a harsh attack on the power that threatened Europe from the East. According to the *France-Soir* reporter, the "delirious crowd" that morning in Lille was reminiscent of "the first days of the Liberation"; but in the afternoon, for the political speech at the Croisé-Laroche, there were scarcely more than 20 000 spectators. It was a good enough turnout, but seems to indicate that the historical character of the Liberator of 1944 was more important, even in his own city, than the founder of the Rassemblement.

Indeed that summer of 1947 saw the beginnings of the Cold War. After the breakdown in April of the great East–West negotiations on Germany and the exclusion of the Communist ministers from French and Italian governments, the dislocation of the "great war-time alliance" became quite evident. The offer of American aid, on the one hand, and the apparent permanence of the Russian occupation of Eastern Europe on the other, emphasized the "great schism". In what was already becoming a world conflict, de Gaulle took sides, and the RPF, created initially with a view to reforming institutions at home, was suddenly to change emphasis and become a movement that was above all anti-Bolshevik.

On 26 and 27 July, Charles de Gaulle toured Brittany, from Auray to Pontivy and from Loudéac to Saint-Marcel, referring everywhere to the Resistance and its victories of summer 1944. On the Sunday, the municipal council of Rennes having indicated that it had no wish to welcome the President of the RPF, it was at the headquarters of the Red Cross, outside the town, that he delivered his speech. It was an unprecedently violent attack on "a group of men who . . . place the service of a foreign State above all else".

What a challenge! To appreciate the effect that such an attack would produce at this time, one has to try to work oneself back into the atmosphere of the France of 1947, in which the PCF was a citadel radiating prestige and power and controlling large sectors of intellectual life:

> . . . In our midst, on our soil, are men who have vowed obedience to the orders of a foreign enterprise of domination, directed by the masters of a great Slav power. Their aim is to attain dictatorship in our country, as men like them have been able to do elsewhere with the support of that power . . . That bloc of close on 400 000 000 men now borders Sweden, Turkey, Greece, Italy! Its frontier is separated from ours only by 500 kilometres, in other words, scarcely the distance of two stages in the Tour de France bicycle race! . . . We, who have never toyed with men's freedom or with the independence of France, we say that this state of things runs the risk, sooner or later, of putting both in the worst danger.

Everywhere the reaction was one of stupefaction. He had actually dared to say it! The speech, which was of unprecedented clarity, was entirely centred on the "separatists" of the PCF and Soviet power; it was to do much more for the growth of the RPF than all the institutional analyses and constructions that had hitherto been the subject of the General's interventions.

How better to give unity to a body than by turning it against an external enemy, even one that had put down deep roots at home? By carefully avoiding the word "Communists", which had been integrated into the national sensibility through the struggles of the Resistance, and by substituting for it the dismissive term "separatists", by relaunching the theme of the "fifth column", of treason at home bound up with foreign invasions, that is to say, by resuscitating the atmosphere of 1940, de Gaulle mobilized his troops far better than against "the parties" – which represented more or less everybody.

CHAPTER TWELVE

To the Threshold of Power?

In late June 1947, at the Rue de Solférino, de Gaulle chaired a meeting of the Executive Committee of the Rassemblement du peuple français. He was sitting in the middle of the long table, between Malraux and Palewski. Opposite them, Soustelle was reporting on the membership campaign: "We shall soon have a million companions." The Secretary-General had no sooner finished speaking than the General declared, as if it were self-evident: "We'll put up candidates at the local elections in October."[1]

So from the very beginning the double nature of the RPF, anti-parliamentary at heart and legalistic in its head, was clear. It was a contradiction that was to bedevil it, under the General's arbitration, throughout its existence.

Anyway, the RPF did opt to participate in the local elections expected in October. It was the General himself who made the decision public on 24 August, in a tone that was in no way that of a challenge:

An opportunity is about to be offered to every Frenchman and every French-woman to make his or her will known. The Rassemblement will present lists of candidates throughout France. The lists to be made up will include men and women of various tendencies who have come together to work for the common task of the public weal without in any way denying any of their convictions.

On 25 September, the day before the opening of the first campaign in which he had joined forces with his followers, the General confided to Claude Mauriac:

I'm told old Auriol will be calling for me one of these mornings ... Personally, I'm sure he won't and, anyway, he knows perfectly well that I won't accept his – or their – conditions. In France, at the present time, energy and enthusiasm are to be found only in two sectors: the Communist Party and the RPF. And even the energy of the Communist Party is declining. This time, things are moving, you know: the RPF is taking off.[2]

And what of membership? The most fantastic figures circulated. There was soon talk of the RPF's half a million membership. *L'Etincelle* reported 750 000 in June and 1 500 000 in October, though these reports were exaggerated and it would be closer to the truth to say that the RPF had a membership of 400 000 by the time of the October elections – which was twenty per cent below the membership of the PCF, but higher than those of the SFIO and MRP put together.

Jean Charlot, who has made a very subtle social analysis of this first wave of members,[3] observes that in its earliest stages the RPF "recruited mainly from the mass of uncommitted French citizens". They included only 3 per cent of active members of the Resistance, but 5 per cent of soldiers and police, 20 per cent of public employees, and more ex-servicemen of the First World War than of the Second – which was hard to explain. It was largely a middle-aged, lower-middle-class movement, whose geographical roots were almost all north of the Loire (Departments of the Nord, Brittany, Alsace, Lorraine and Champagne), with the sole exception of the Gironde.

Although, in terms of mass membership, the movement seemed to be rooted above all in formerly unpoliticized social strata, recruitment for the RPF did pose problems. In 1947, France had forty-five million inhabitants and an electorate of just under twenty-five million. But how many were capable of taking on political responsibilities, of canvassing for votes? Very few. And most of those were already involved in the MRP, the SFIO or the PCF, to take only the mass-membership parties.

The RPF could only develop, therefore, at the expense of existing political groups, or by superimposing itself here and there on one of them. Since the PCF was declared the main enemy at the outset and as the SFIO rejected the type of ideology implicit in the General's programme – nationalism and a strong State – this left only the MRP. There were three kinds of response. The first was that of Maurice Schumann, who was deeply hurt: in late June 1947, he made it clear to de Gaulle that the RPF, by forming a "screen" between the people and him, removed the MRP from the very power that he might claim would be theirs by the end of the year.[4] The second, one of indignant rejection, was that particularly of Pierre-Henri Teitgen, who insisted from late April that there could be no "double membership". The third, positive, was embodied by Edmond Michelet.

The campaign launched by General de Gaulle on 27 August was dominated by one theme: anti-Communism, or, to use his own terminology, anti-separatism. It was a crusade. On 1 August, a circular signed by Soustelle stressed "the enormous effect" that the Rennes speech had had and declared that "for the first time since the Liberation, a voice has dared to denounce the Communist peril, just as a voice denounced the capitulation of 1940".[5]

Circumstances helped: the Cold War had begun. Moscow was exerting pressure on the Czech government to forgo the benefits of the Marshall Plan; there was the trial and hanging of Nikolai Petkov in Bulgaria; and the reconstruction of the International as the Cominform furthered the threatening character of Stalinism.

The RPF campaign culminated on 5 October at Vincennes, where "the population of Paris, the Seine, the Seine-et-Oise and the Seine-et-Marne" was summoned. At the racetrack a huge white platform had been set up opposite the grandstand over which fluttered the tricolour flag and blue banners bearing the Cross of Lorraine. A crowd estimated (by the RPF) at over 500 000 had gathered. A band was playing military marches.

The speaker, who seemed even more gigantic and imposing than ever by being perched on a platform, waved his long arms as if to ward off – or to raise – the storm. In his growling voice, made even more impressive by the microphones, he recalled the achievements of his government of 1944–46 and "the abyss" into which the parties had since thrown France, then went on to attack the "separatists", to greet the power of the United States, "the counterweight to the worldwide ambitions of the Soviets". And he launched the appeal of the RPF for the forthcoming elections and let fly at the detested parties, describing each of them "cooking its own little soup, on its own little fire, in its own little corner". On the vast space of Vincennes, the laughter became a groundswell, starting off half a million laughers.

Certainly Vincennes showed the social convergence, the ideological pluralism, the political symbiosis to which the RPF veered: when Louis Vallon, the organizer of the rally and the only speaker to precede the General, went up to the speaker's rostrum, he looked out on a crowd not very different from those in which he had mingled eight years before, as an active member of the Popular Front.[6]

The results of the votes cast in the local elections of 19 October 1947 went beyond all hopes. Next day, the front page of *Le Monde* bore the headline "40 per cent of the votes to the RPF", followed by a smaller headline pointing out that the Gaullist movement "had robbed the MRP of over half of its constituency". It was a triumph, a landslide.

The day after the elections, André Malraux stated that the General "will accept power only after a referendum and a formal mandate from the people, even if the President of the Republic were to offer him power with the assent of the parties and workers' organizations".

De Gaulle's own statement reflects a conquering mood: "The present National Assembly must be dissolved as soon as possible, though not before it has set up an electoral system which will provide the future parliament with a coherent majority. It will then be up to the nation to mandate its representatives with a view to changing bad institutions without delay."[7]

The RPF won in thirteen of the twenty-five cities (Paris, Marseille, Lille, Algiers, Strasbourg, Bordeaux, Nancy, Le Mans, Grenoble, Sainte-Etienne, Reims, Angers, Caen), thus guaranteeing power over the French urban landscape, that is to say, the most modern, the most productive part of the country. No party had ever obtained, in a democratic vote, such a triumph.

Curiously enough, if we read Vincent Auriol's diary for 27 October, we see that he is astonishingly unaffected by the event. The victory was a crushing rejection of the politicians elected in 1946 and of the institutions then being denounced by de Gaulle, but Auriol, the head of State, simply noted: "One can already see one movement of public opinion that is very clear. The Communists are losing. The only immediate problem: supplies."[8]

There are few periods in Charles de Gaulle's life that are harder to understand than those months of late 1947 and early 1948, when he sat back on those municipal laurels that he had wanted to conquer as a means and which he suddenly seemed to regard as an end. One might have expected new initiatives, bold manoeuvres, vast public meetings from that great imaginative theoretician of the offensive. But no. All one got was the constant reminder of well-honed arguments.

"If we had had the slightest notion of how to negotiate," a close colleague of the General's later confided, "we would have been in power in a fortnight." But, according to several witnesses, de Gaulle and Soustelle were so certain of the collapse of the "parties" that they regarded it as ridiculous even to negotiate a "timetable".

Some, particularly those around Malraux, thought differently. This is what Brigitte Friang suggests: "If the idea of the *coup* ever crossed our minds, it was on the evening of 26 October 1947."[9] Even the General must have considered the possibility, since, a few years later, he confided to Louis Terrenoire: "Koenig, who was commanding the armies of occupation, wouldn't have gone along with it. And, anyway, I saw soon enough that revolutionary Paris wasn't shifting. We'd have had the supporters of Frédéric-Dupont."*[10]

De Gaulle had not wanted to force destiny. Those who saw him at this time remarked that he was not so much impatient to seize power as keen to analyse the crisis that was still shaking France: since June – a month after the divorce between the Communists and the governing parties – strikes had spread like a typhoon throughout the country. In November, they assumed an insurrectional character: some town halls taken over by the RPF were attacked and broken into: at Marseille, the Gaullist mayor, Maître Carlini, was actually thrown from the window of the Hôtel de Ville.

The atmosphere everywhere was frightful. Civil war stalked the streets – dead were found at Arras, Valence, Saint-Omer – while the daily ration of bread was brought back to 200 grams. Remembering those months from the summer of 1947 to the autumn of 1948, Jacques Fauvet spoke of a "terrible year".

The threat of civil war emanating from the PCF meant that Jules Moch was forced to confront it with such resolution and determination that de Gaulle was almost pushed out of the limelight. The battle then raging found this leader powerless. He could do no more than observe and comment. Very soon – and this, eventually, was to be the condemnation of the RPF – a frightened public opinion noted that Moch, the iron Socialist in the Ministry of the Interior, was the man for the crisis.

Two other explanations for de Gaulle's apparent hesitation might be added. On 28 November 1947, the war leader who had embodied the spirit and energy of the Free French with the greatest intensity and panache, Philippe Leclerc de Hauteclocque, recently appointed Inspector-General of French forces in North Africa, was killed in a plane crash. It has been said that the sandstorm that threw Leclerc's plane onto a railway embankment was not the only cause of his death, though no public or private inquiry has been able to establish the slightest proof of criminal intent.

To Leclerc's widow, de Gaulle immediately wrote a letter that expresses his "immense pain" and goes on: "I loved your husband: he was not only the companion of the worst and greatest days, but a dependable friend, incapable of any

*A politician of the extreme right. (trs.)

feeling, any action, any gesture, any word that betrayed the slightest mediocrity." As we have seen, Charles de Gaulle was sometimes capable of expressing his feelings. Did he ever do so better than here, where private grief was coupled with an awareness of an irreparable loss, which seems to have deeply upset him for a long time?

On the occasion of the death of Anne de Gaulle, on 6 February 1948, he expressed his grief with even greater simplicity. The little disabled girl had reached her twentieth year, but her life was continually under threat: she eventually died of bronchial pneumonia. Two days after Anne's death, the General wrote to his daughter Elisabeth:

> Anne grew weaker and weaker, finding it more and more difficult to breathe. Then she went. She died in my arms, with Maman, and Mme Michigau* beside her, while the doctor gave her an injection *in extremis*. The parish priest rushed here to bless her. She is a freed soul. But the disappearance of our poor sick child, our little hopeless girl, has caused us immense pain. I know that it has meant the same for you. May little Anne protect us from the heights of heaven and protect, above all you yourself, my beloved daughter Elisabeth.[11]

The Charles de Gaulle after the birth of Anne was no longer quite the same as before. The Charles de Gaulle deprived of his dear daughter would also be transformed – and, initially at least, go through a period of deep depression.

Meanwhile, on 12 November 1947, in the Maison de la Résistance, Rue François-Ier, de Gaulle had held a press conference before three hundred journalists, at which his verve does not seem to have been blunted either by victory or by the abandonment of old colleagues:

> It did not require great prescience on my part to predict, six months ago, what was going to happen and I do not claim any in predicting to you today that the Rassemblement will grow until it embraces the entire nation, with the exception of course of the separatists and certain sad, wild, isolated individuals. The waves are getting up. I assure you that they will swell and break. Those who refuse to understand will be swept aside. If they stand on the shore, spouting nonsense to no purpose, their curses will be so much spitting into the sea.[12]

It is clear that, though he seems to have excluded a seizure of power, he is nevertheless no more in favour of negotiation. Victory had not diminished his demands. This was to become apparent a few weeks later when, on 4 January 1948, at Saint-Etienne, he launched his manifesto for "association", against "exploitation" and "the class struggle", and the tasks offered to a "renewed trade unionism": for, he declared, if France was capable of surviving the trial of war, it

---

*The sick girl's governess.

was "because the working class showed that it could eventually get a grip on itself".[13]

That demonstration, very working-class in style, very militant (there were more shouts of "de Gaulle to power!") gathered an enormous crowd: "Over 100 000 people, at Saint-Etienne, it was unhoped for", Lucien Neuwirth, who was there as one of the organizers, later told me. "On that day, even more than the day after the local elections, I really thought that the General was about to seize power."[14] What, then, would have been the point of a conference organized in Paris, a few weeks later, in a setting that the General's brother, leader of the municipal council, could place at the RPF's disposal? Why did the General Staff at the Rue de Solférino reject this audacious move, which would not have put it outside the law, but preferred to hold its first conference at Marseille?

What the General wanted was an enormous mass demonstration, an appeal to the "real" people, to demonstrate the originality, the power and the effectiveness of the RPF and his own charisma. This was how the leader of Free France wanted to extend the decisive electoral victory of 1947. The first national conference of the RPF was to be an opportunity of doing this. And all the leaders of the movement were mobilized, early in 1948, with a view to the enormous demonstration to take place at Marseille that April, though Rémy and those responsible for law and order were fully aware of the risks: defeated at the local elections, the strong local Communist Party considered that it was in a position to forbid de Gaulle to appear there.

The General's supporters remember the Marseille "conference" as a magical moment. For Brigitte Friang, it was "the greatest moment of the RPF, the heights, the moment when everything seemed possible. When Malraux gave his magnificent speech, I handed out the text to the press: I saw foreign journalists weeping!"[15] Malraux, as delegate in charge of propaganda, spoke before de Gaulle. The night before, the General asked him: "What are you going to say?" Malraux replied: "I'll talk to them about chivalry!" The leader of the RPF looked dubious: "Try." Then came the great incantatory speech that no one who was there has forgotten:

> O French faces, which I see around me and on which I see again those Gothic faces beside me in captivity, on which I see again the simple faces of the cavalry men of Verdun, those faces that are the faces of France – let the Stalinist journalists laugh! An immense honour is given to you: this great body of France, groping in the shadows, watched by a world so often fascinated by it, it is given to you to raise it up with your perishable hands. France is like those great iron statues buried after ancient conquerors pass by and which suddenly, in times of cataclysms, are unearthed by a flash of lightning. That body has been tragically unearthed.

De Gaulle chose a more prosaic style:

> I repeat that it is by general elections that the nation must be given at the earliest opportunity the means of sealing its own union in itself and showing

the world that it has done so. Only then will it be possible to reform the political system, to govern, to renew and, if necessary, to face the storms.[16]

On 12 November 1950, the eve of his sixtieth birthday, de Gaulle received the good wishes of his colleagues at the Rue de Solférino, the RPF headquarters. They stressed the great hours they had lived through, ten years before, rather than the enterprise that they had embarked on over the past three years.

Five months earlier, the forces of North Korea had advanced southwards, thus defying the entire West. Since then, under the command of Douglas MacArthur, the so-called United Nations forces tried painfully to overcome their initial reverses. The President of the RPF paid as much anxious attention to the operation as if he were personally engaged in the conflict: a battalion of French engineers was fighting under the tricolour flag and commanded by the oldest surviving officer of Free France, Monclare.

On 19 August, at the height of the retreat of the United Nations troops, Charles de Gaulle summoned the press to convey his thoughts on this Asian confrontation. His pessimism could hardly have been more explicit: for him, the Korean war was merely the prelude to an infinitely wider conflict. If he did not speak of a Third World War, what he said implied it.

Two months later, the dangers were still rising: at Tonkin in Vietnam, French forces were collapsing under the thrust of the Vietminh, now supported by People's China. It was a débâcle, especially at Caobang. On 14 November 1950, de Gaulle confided to Georges Pompidou, an implacable listener: "The war is spreading and will not stop. France will not recover in time, will be invaded, bombed." And he predicted that, this time, those responsible would be "strung up", for "the Communists are tough and the people will have suffered. There'll be atomic attacks, hunger, deportation. The Americans, too, are brutes."[17] It was this idea of inevitable, if not imminent, war that haunted him and dominated any other concern at this time. It was only when MacArthur got the upper hand, moving back towards the 38th parallel, that de Gaulle returned to the affairs of the RPF.

When, exactly, did the tide begin to turn? With the legislative elections in 1951? Charles Pasqua, who lived through those upheavals as a local RPF organizer in Provence, places the turning-point much earlier:

Things began to go wrong in September 1948. Where? At Grenoble. It was there that, on the occasion of an RPF demonstration, we fell into a trap laid for us by Jules Moch. One man was killed, the first such incident caused by an RPF demonstration: he was a Communist and his death was exploited to the full by the press and radio to present us as factious murderers. The operation succeeded and it cost us very dear. Until then only the Communists really frightened people. From that day on we lost a lot of sympathy. Nothing was ever the same again.[18]

As Minister of the Interior, and therefore the privileged adversary of the RPF, Jules Moch did not fail to turn the spotlight on to the "shootings" attributable to the Gaullists. In a directive to the prefects, the Socialist minister made the point very plain.

> (a) *The Government draws a distinction between the liberator of the national territory and the head of a political movement.* As the second, General de Gaulle has a right to the protection due to any citizen on national territory, but not to various marks of honour.
>
> (b) *Rigorous searches must be carried out for weapons.* At Grenoble, RPF elements were armed. I would also point out that the Paris police, having been instructed to search those going to a large RPF demonstration, and the Communist counter-demonstration, arrested twenty-six people for carrying weapons 22 of whom were members of the RPF and 4 Communists.

Summoning the press three days later, the General declared:

> It was I who re-established the right of assembly. I observe that we are losing it. When the French people hold public meetings, they are often disturbed by separatists. It is quite natural on their part. But it so happens that public order is not maintained by those whose task it is to maintain it. And above all it would seem that those in charge of the present regime wish to use these incidents for the interests of what they call "their politics". We are entering a very serious area here.

All the more serious in that a few days later, according to André Astoux, "the companions of the RPF took their revenge at La Seyne, a working-class housing estate near Toulon. The meeting took place on the harbour side. When the Communists tried to prevent it, the marines arrived on one side, the sailors on the other, and the Communists were forced into the sea, together with their two deputies."[19]

Where would such an intervention by the armed forces in support of the RPF and against the elected representatives of the people leave the country? The left-wing press demanded the "dissolution of the RPF's civil war gangs". But no serious investigation seems to have been carried out. Was the Minister of the Interior really in a position to allow the services of order to do their worst? On the eve of the elections to the Council of the Republic, the affair could not fail to alter the public image of the RPF.

The great forthcoming battle, of course, was that of the legislative elections of 1951. The government led by René Pleven, then by Henri Queuille, fixed the date for 17 June, though not without taking precautions against the double pressure exerted on it by the PCF and the RPF, by inventing an electoral law that was more ingenious than honest.

The so-called system of "alliances" has been vilified in every way, arousing the most varied anathemas from the Communists as well as the Gaullists, each taking the other as their target. On the one hand, it was seen as "the most cynical challenge to the representative system" and, on the other, "the most unjust electoral law in our history". It was really a very artificial system: when one of the coalition won an absolute majority in one of the 183 constituencies, it took all the seats. It is to Malraux that we owe the best caricature of the system: "Take an archbishop, add some venerable member of a masonic lodge, remove a plumber, multiply by a sub-mistress of a brothel and shake: you will have an 'alliance' deputy!"[20]

Was this a swindle? The General several times declared that it was. It was, in any case, a specious manipulation of universal suffrage. But, as *Le Monde* reminded him, every electoral law is "merely a more or less distorting prism interposed between public opinion and its representation".[21] The leaders of the MRP, the SFIO, the Radicals and *Modérés* (conservatives) had considered that, without this law, the RPF and PCF would have won enough seats (180 each?) to allow them to block the exercise of power: they had taken steps to prevent such an outcome.

"There will be no alliance," declared de Gaulle. For him, the RPF must stand in splendid isolation, at the centre, as an absolute reference. Could the French people be "assembled" or could it not? It was not a matter of winning, but of being above the others, a force for synthesis.

Every attempt to make him alter his decision, even when coming from such faithful and reputedly sagacious "companions" as Roger Frey, Jacques Foccart, Olivier Guichard, Michel Debré and Jacques Chaban-Delmas, were met by a contemptuous refusal. He would allow himself to give in only in a few special cases, in order to elect a few men whom he particularly wanted to get into parliament – Léon Noël, Pierre Billotte and Guillain de Bénouville; and, on 23 May 1951, the Management Council of the RPF declared itself solemnly against alliances.

When questioned now on the subject, most of the General's companions consider that his decision was unfortunate: having chosen to achieve power through legality and the electoral process, it was not reasonable to reject the electoral system. But the General was supported by the dispenser of symbols, Malraux, as well as by the manager of realities, Soustelle. When the supreme triumvirate was in agreement in this way, no other point of view could prevail.

Another, more secretive, debate was taking place in the top echelons of the RPF prior to the great electoral debate: should the General be a candidate? A sentence here and there vaguely suggested that he might throw himself into the battle in order the better to assume his collective responsibilities – especially as, when he tried to persuade some of his most faithful colleagues to throw themselves into the adventure, one of them, André Malraux, could not resist pointing out that his arguments would carry more weight if he himself set the example. Malraux, persisting in his refusal, received a note from the General: "Brutus always wins over Caesar." But one day he assured me that if de Gaulle had himself entered the arena, he would have followed him.[22]

Was the idea that de Gaulle might stand – at Lille, for example, where he was sure to get 75 per cent of the votes – ever plausible? When this was suggested to him, his response was reported by Jacques Soustelle thus: "Can you see me putting on my little cap in my little cupboard in the cloakroom of the Palais-

Bourbon?" Soustelle's acidic comment is: "The argument does not strike me as unanswerable. Many a blighted hope was to spring from the President of the RPF's repugnance for parliamentary life."[23]

Georges Pompidou, also urging him to present himself, received this reply: "It is my card never to have subjected myself to the common law. I'm not going to start now. And, anyway, I am presenting myself throughout the whole of France!"

De Gaulle had declared in his broadcast: "On 18 June, yes! on 18 June, everyone will see that France has won!" On that morning, it was the government that could feel confident: the government coalition would win. The PCF and RPF topped the list in terms of votes cast, but, given the system of "alliances", it was the third force that was to control the Assembly.

120 deputies... a half-victory? No, it was a failure. The first evidence of the General's reaction comes from Jean Chauveau, editor of the *Rassemblement*, who recounts: "One had only to take a look at the General to realize that he already knew that the game was up."[24]

At a press conference on 22 June, de Gaulle looked in good form as he listed his opponents' losses (the "separatists", who lost 450 000 votes, the MRP more than half of its votes), whereas the RPF, with 4 150 000 votes, was close on the heels of the PCF. Was that as far as his ambition went? To come a brilliant second to Maurice Thorez! In October 1947, the Rassemblement had won 40 per cent of the votes. In June 1951, here it was with 22 per cent.

In fact, the system of alliances, directed against the Communists even more clearly than against the Gaullists, had achieved its first aim, the second slightly less so: with 26 per cent of the votes, the PCF won only 16 per cent of the seats, whereas the Rassemblement won 19 per cent with 22 per cent of the votes cast. Were it not for these sorry distortions, the PCF would have won 175 seats, the RPF 160. This would have been enough to block the parliamentary machinery. What use would the General have made of such a formidable means of pressure?

The General defined his strategy: an offer to assume direction of "affairs", a refusal to "participate" in it with others, a rejection of any "obstruction", the choice of a "constructive opposition" and above all an intense effort to develop the movement throughout the country; these were his public projects in the days following one of the most severe reverses in his career. He betrayed no sign of defeat. It was an attitude worthy of him and of his past. But de Gaulle knew that his undertaking had now failed. From now on, writes Jacques Soustelle, who was to live through this drama more intensely than anybody else, the RPF "not having won everything, could lose everything. A terribly difficult game had been embarked on: that of parliamentary Gaullism."[25]

CHAPTER THIRTEEN

Return to the Desert

From 18 June 1951, the RPF, as a great national ambition and as a coherent force in the General's hands, was finished. The elected deputies were in the Assembly. The electoral battle of 1951 was to be no more than a storm. But there was a heavy sense of nostalgia, which, linked to the hatred for the Republic, seemed to be dragging the country down. De Gaulle was to fight his way in vain through the contradiction of his contempt for a seizure of power and his contempt for parliament. By opting for the latter, which seemed to him to be the lesser evil, by choosing the less harmful route, in any case the less costly to his glory, he had become trapped and doomed his enterprise first to dissociation, then to corruption.

On the day after the elections of June 1951, the leader of the RPF must have had severe doubts as to the future of the movement, and even about its necessity. On 8 July he confided to his *chef de cabinet*: "No one can get anywhere in the parliament and through the parliament. It can neither do anything nor get anywhere." And Pompidou made this rather harsh comment: "Well? Of course, he wants to make an effort in the country. But what exactly does he want to do? Destroy the system from the outside? I suppose he has given that up. Then what? Keep the RPF going for ever with the idea that something may turn up some day?"[1] The experience of parliamentary Gaullism was to be the occasion of a break between the President of the RPF and its former Secretary-General Jacques Soustelle.

Thirty years later, after the inexpiable conflicts that brought the two men into violent opposition over the Algeria question, who can say what de Gaulle really thought of Soustelle? What is clear, in any case, is that in June 1951, the General regarded the RPF's Secretary-General as a loyal and competent lieutenant.

The first great parliamentary test came in the summer of 1951 and it was this that led to the split between de Gaulle and Soustelle. The two men were on good terms at the RPF headquarters, sharing the same spirit of rigour and regarding institutions and men from a common point of view. A mutual friend, sensing de Gaulle's growing irritation with Soustelle's approaches to the Elysée, vouched for the fidelity of the deputy for Lyon. "Emotionally, he is faithful to me," the General replied. "But, politically, he is betraying me." No one who belongs to an institution can avoid the grip it has over him and it leaves its mark on him. Uncompromising by temperament, Soustelle was to become a negotiator. From the Salle des Quatre Colonnes at the Palais-Bourbon to the office of Vincent Auriol at the Elysée, he was gradually to imbibe those "poisons" of the Fourth Republic, so often denounced by the leader of the RPF – and by himself.

But who wanted that? If he had not wanted his "companions" to catch the parliamentary fever, he did not have to throw them into the furnace. Soustelle, Chaban and Fouchet were not Nazis in the Reichstag, totalitarians barricaded up in their hatred, but republicans in the grip of a democratic institution *par excellence*. This led to the implacable decline in relations between the General and his "right-hand man".

On 9 January 1952 Auriol, the President of the Republic, called on Jacques Soustelle to try to form a government. By "parliamentizing" the RPF, he was dreaming of isolating de Gaulle in his intransigence. Soustelle, who wanted to emerge from the ghetto in which the Assembly confined his group, was inclined to accept. He would not do so, of course, without referring to de Gaulle. But the very fact that he had been tempted by the offer raised first suspicion, then distrust at Colombey.

But the RPF, however damaged its leadership now was, had suffered only a slight dent from the Elysée. It was only at the beginning of May 1952 that the internal discord started to manifest itself publicly. Charles de Gaulle had confronted Churchill and Roosevelt, Stalin and Eisenhower, Blum and Thorez without flinching: now he was faced with M. Pinay, mayor of Saint-Chamond and a former supporter of Vichy, who put himself forward for the Premiership. What more average Frenchman could there be? What more effective adversary could there be to oppose de Gaulle than this harmless looking nonentity? Although de Gaulle had ordered the RPF deputies to vote against him on 6 March, twenty-seven of them voted for Antoine Pinay. And so the great turning-point began, leading to the schism within the RPF, and the regrouping of the right – the beginnings of Vichy's revenge.

On 10 March, at a press conference held at the Palais d'Orsay, de Gaulle launched a few rockets: the Rassemblement du peuple français, which he had founded and directed "with qualified companions", went well beyond the winning of elections. "It enters more or less into the minds of everybody, even of those who vote against it. It is what was already known, during the war, as 'Gaullism'." And he launched the famous formulation: "Every Frenchman was, is or will be a 'Gaullist'. I would not swear that at some moment, unfortunately too late!, even Marshal Pétain was not won over to some extent." For the time being, it seemed that the RPF was obviously Gaullist, though less so than it had been: at the party conference, which took place in the Paris suburb of Saint-Maur on 5 July, a split emerged. The General remained in the majority, but the haemorrhage was there for all to see. De Gaulle considered giving up parliamentary action, and perhaps more besides. He confided to Jacques Bruneau, RPF delegate for Brittany: "I'm going back to Colombey and shelving the RPF." And when the visitor hinted at the possibility of a return to power in the near future, de Gaulle shook his head: "No, Bruneau, never. Unless we find ourselves losing Algeria."[2]

Disillusioned by the "parliamentary voice", did Charles de Gaulle now dream of a *coup d'état*? Olivier Guichard relates what the General said in July 1954 to departmental delegates of the RPF: "A coup, as in Guatemala, leads to nothing. It simply replaces one sergeant-major with another. It does absolutely nothing for the country. Unless there is at its root general consent. Then it immediately becomes the national operation by which a country rids itself of a regime and puts another in its place."[3]

General de Gaulle's thoughts on this fundamental question seem to have been summed up in a meeting with Dominique Ponchardier* in December 1953; the latter maintained that without an "operation", the RPF would sink into "demobilization", then into a "rout". The General replied: "I try to get him to accept that the show of force ought to be no more than an extra push, based on 'events'."[4]

On 6 May 1953, de Gaulle published the declaration that seemed to put an end to a great adventure. The tone was that neither of a defeated, nor even of an angry man. It was that of a man who has lost a battle, but has not lost the war.

> The efforts that I have put in since the war, surrounded by resolute Frenchmen, have not so far succeeded. I do not deny it. This is, it must be feared, to the detriment of France. Things being what they are, what is the Rassemblement to do? It remains an ardent, convinced instrument. Above all, it must distance itself from a regime that is sterile and which cannot, for the moment, change. Companions will be able quite legitimately to present themselves at this or that election, but they will do so individually and not in its name. Nor in parliament will they take part, as a body and as such, in the series of combinations, deals, votes of confidence, investitures that are the games, poisons and delights of the system.
>
> On the other hand, it is more than ever in the public interest that the Rassemblement, freed from the electoral and parliamentary impasse, should organize itself and extend throughout the country to carry out its mission, which is to serve as a vanguard for the social and national regrouping of the people with a view to changing the new regime.
>
> The collapse of illusions is at hand. We must prepare the remedy.[5]

Was it a failure? Most historians of the RPF use the word. But Olivier Guichard objects that if the RPF may have been a mistake in the short term, it was a success in the long term. "If, in 1958, we were able to set up the UNR in three months and provide the electors with candidates and candidates with active supporters, it was because the RPF had succeeded in depth and had been more than a flash in the pan."[6] So was the RPF a sketch for the Fifth Republic, a building site temporarily abandoned on which the contractors of 1958 erected their fortress? Pierre Lefranc proposes this ingenious commentary:

> It was during those years of travelling through France, of endless tours, of visits to ordinary people, of nights spent in their homes, that de Gaulle learnt to know the French. We know the idea that he had of France. But what idea did he have of the French? A few official visits in the aftermath of the liberation, a few appearances before huge crowds. In the RPF, he acquired a familiarity with the people that is the key to his behaviour after 1948, of his

*He was for a long time in charge of the RPF's *service d'ordre*.

art of finding the right tone of voice, the striking arguments, a simple way of
talking, the art of persuading. For de Gaulle the RPF had been his discovery
of the French.[7]

In fact, there were two RPFs, at any rate two ages of the Rassemblement.

The first, from April 1947 to June 1951, was that of the conquest of power
through electoral means. The General had thought that he would be able to obtain
the 180–200 seats that would enable him to influence and obtain, as Louis Vallon
put it, the "legal surrender" of the established power, leaving room for a
reconstruction, a strengthening of the Republic.

The second was opened up by the great electoral disappointments of June 1951.
Permanent (verbal) aggression was levelled at the "system" that had proved unable
to tolerate the Gaullist graft. It is summed up by these words of the General, in late
July 1953: "Of course, de Gaulle isn't in power, but we have killed off the
regime."[8] But nevertheless this period remained marked, on the part of the
Gaullists, by something equivocal, the fascinated waiting for the cataclysm. Was it
waiting or wishing?

And that was the nub of the matter. The RPF was, despite a few stray impulses
noted on the way, neither an insurrectional movement nor a pre-fascist organization. It was legalistic in the main and the General was able to keep those who
entertained other dreams to heel – if sometimes in an equivocal way, as, it would
seem, with Ponchardier.

But from the triumphalism of 1947 to the gloom of 1953, a negative shadow
floated over this ambiguous undertaking. Charles de Gaulle was too sensitive to
the role of myths in history not to be aware of the essentially negative impact of
the RPF: and that was why he despatched it with such speed in his *Mémoires
d'espoir*,* devoting only fifteen lines to an undertaking that had taken up five years
of his life.

The RPF was technically useful, as a first draft or building-site of the Fifth
Republic, and François Mauriac, an impassioned adversary of the enterprise,
admits as much in his book on de Gaulle.[9] But what a price was paid for this
"usefulness"! It had a lasting and damaging effect on the de Gaulle myth, creating
a caricature of the man of 18 June that was to weigh heavily on relations between
the General and very broad sectors of public opinion.

"The crossing of the desert," said Edmond Michelet. He was thinking of Moses,
wandering for forty years through Sinai before pointing out to his people, from the
top of Mount Nebo, the land of Canaan, when he described the life of Charles de
Gaulle from his dismissal of the RPF in December 1955 to his return to power in
the spring of 1958.

In the *Mémoires d'espoir* de Gaulle describes this period in his life thus:

*According to General de Boissieu, 'Charles de Gaulle intended, in the last chapter of this
unfinished book, to return to the subject, aware that he had not paid sufficient tribute to his
companions in the RPF (interview of May 1984).

I was living at the time in complete retirement at La Boisserie, at home to nobody but my family and people from the village, and going only very occasionally to Paris where I received a mere handful of visitors. For the next six years, from 1952 to 1958, I was to devote myself to writing my War Memoirs without intervening in public affairs.[10]

The legend of withdrawal thus forged conformed, of course, to the more or less prophetic, if not mystical, myth that the hero wished to sustain. But, as we shall see, this solitude was filled with people, this withdrawal was rich in public activities, and this "hermit" did not ignore the affairs of the world.

In the hexagonal tower (hexagonal like France itself: was the symbolic significance intended?) to which he retired to write his *Mémoires*, Charles de Gaulle was not this time, as in 1946, the hero too great for everyday little men: he was the voiceless prophet who had not been heard. In this sense, the withdrawal of 1952 was more painful than that of 1946, if only on account of the state in which France was then suffering.

Colombey-les-Deux-Eglises is a village of some five or six hundred souls that has two churches only in name. It is in the Haute-Marne, an austere department, little visited by tourists, twenty kilometres from Chaumont, a township whose military past is more considerable than its economic present. It takes over three hours to get to Paris, people say. The neighbours were discreetly respectful, as were the municipal councillors. The parish priest sometimes went for lunch. La Boisserie, restored after the Liberation, is a public man's retirement home – comfortable (central heating was installed there in 1948) and suitable as both retreat and retirement home, for work and reflection.

Entry is through a gate surmounted by two greenish bronze horses' heads. An avenue winding its way through a fairly large garden leads to the grey house, which was fairly elegant until the General added the corner tower, which jars and makes it rather *nouveau riche*. It was there that he set up his study. The dining-room has heavy oak furniture, the drawing room is hung with green linen, semi-rustic, semi-antique in style: the atmosphere is that of a provincial bourgeois family. The furniture is late Louis XV to early Napoléon III and Regency – a combination due to the chance of inheritance, wedding presents and the needs of garrison life. The dining-room and the small sitting-room were where everyday life took place. The children, Mme de Gaulle or guests were only very rarely allowed into the General's tower.

The walls of the study, which was organized round the big dark mahogany Empire desk, flanked by a file in which, the General declared, Louis XIV kept the despatches from his ambassadors, were covered with books – Michelet, Thiers, Voltaire, Bergson – and decorated with a few signed photographs: of Roosevelt, Chiang Kai-shek, Thierry d'Argenlieu.

Conversation during or after meals was an art that Charles de Gaulle practised here with moderation, as if he had no need to throw two violent waves of history over his serene asylum – except when Malraux or Vallon provoked him. Then the host would give himself up to it, but not excessively; he was so impatient to get back to his Empire desk.

The climate is harsh. During a visit in December 1947, before the central heating was installed, Jean Marin was seized by the arm and planted in front of the French windows, which were receiving the full brunt of the wind and rain. General de Gaulle then opened both doors wide and, turning round triumphantly to the perplexed visitor, declared: "Ah! Ils parlent de la douce France! La voilà, la douce France. Elle est terrible, la France!"[11]

Yet he felt at home in the austere atmosphere of Colombey. In winter, treading the snow and braving the squalls, he would roam through the Forêt des Dhuits like a wolf at the time of Charles the Bold.

With or without radiators, the house was difficult to heat. The General made a habit of tending the fire, throwing on logs, poking it. He liked those gestures, just as he walked in the park religiously three times a day, in the morning, after lunch and before dinner.

His life was meticulously regulated, from the breakfast at 7.30 – tea with a few *biscottes* – to the long sessions in the study, when he wrote his letters and *Mémoires*, to the very early meals, to the walks, to the games of patience, which he played more and more, as if to turn the word into a rule of life. There he would sit, his right thumb between his teeth, slightly bent over the card-table in the small sitting-room.

He did not care to spend long at meals, expediting them like "current business", even though he enjoyed a good appetite and was quite capable, on occasion, of giving in to greed – he was fond of what the de Gaulles called the *plats canaille*, such "vulgar" dishes as *miroton* (hash of beef with onions), *boeuf bourguignon*, stewed rabbit with prunes. If Soustelle, an occasional guest, is to be believed, the cheer was "robust" and more than adequately "washed down", the General taking care never to leave glasses empty. This did not spare him a celebrated retort from Louis Vallon. The General, who was fond enough of Vallon to allow himself to make personal remarks on occasion, remarked between two mouthfuls: "They tell me you've taken to drink, Vallon?" "Not in your house, in any case, *Mon Général*!" Vallon shot back.

Colombey was above all the domain of Yvonne de Gaulle. She liked to see her husband at peace. She was pleased that he had turned away at last from the storms of public life, from the whirlpools of politics. Claude Guy, after a visit to Colombey in July 1953, just after the RPF had been "put on the shelf", confided to Louis Terrenoire that he had been "struck" by the attitude of Mme de Gaulle, who seemed to him to be possessed now by "the assurance, so longed for, that she would preserve her husband for History, but for History only".[12]

Then, in May 1954, the Secretary-General of the RPF made this note, which went much further: "After taking leave of the General, I thought that 'Aunt Yvonne' was winning. Whenever I have gone alone to La Boisserie she has always referred, increasingly, but in measured terms, to the damage that the commitments of a public life in the last days of the Rassemblement were causing to the historical figure of the Liberator."[13]

The de Gaulles had no fortune; that of the Vendrouxs had disappeared. The General had only a colonel's pension and it was not until 1955 that the royalties from the *Mémoires de guerre* began to come in, but they were passed on to the

Fondation Anne-de-Gaulle, a charity for handicapped children. Furthermore, Charles de Gaulle had little notion of money, handing out cheques to his children and relations, as his correspondence discreetly confirms. So the end of a month was always a difficult time. Pierre Galante recounts how the General, noticing one day that one of his finest pieces of family silver had disappeared, pointed it out to his wife, who replied: "And what do you think we're living on, *mon ami?*"[14]

The General's health was robust. But, in late 1952, his sight began to deteriorate so much that he had to have an operation for a cataract, the sequellae of which were often painful. "I wouldn't have my worst enemy suffer what I am suffering," he said to J.-R. Terrenoire – a surprising remark from such a stoic.

He now had to wear, first dark glasses, then glasses with very thick lenses, which irritated him enormously and undermined his morale. He confided, among others, in his son-in-law, Alain de Boissieu, who notes: "This cataract operation has tired him. He thinks he'll have to wear spectacles all the time: 'Can you see de Gaulle reviewing troops with thick spectacles on his nose. No, it isn't possible. One has to know when to turn the page!'"[15]

However much he may have wanted to shut himself away at La Boisserie, General de Gaulle's "life in the desert" was much less that of a recluse than might be thought. Of course, from 1952, he had been able to devote most of his time to writing his *Mémoires*. But his life remained open to the outside world, first because he undertook four great trips between 1953 and 1957 to Africa and round the world, but also because politics itself, in the widest sense, and independently of any electoral campaign, needed him and kept him at the forefront of the stage: three press conferences, four important speeches, a dozen declarations, a demonstration in the Place de l'Etoile, did not, in those years prior to 1958, add up to a retirement from the world. It was a desert that was populated, active and, in the final analysis, fertile.

His opposition to all the governments of the Fourth Republic spared only one, that of Pierre Mendès France. He had wanted to get Mendès France invested, with the votes of the Gaullist group, but he did not hide from him that, given the situation and the constitutional regime, he did not believe that he could succeed in governing.

The new head of government, having won the vote of confidence at dawn on 18 June 1954, immediately sent de Gaulle this warm telegram: "On this anniversary, which is also the day that I assume heavy responsibilities, I am reliving the noble lessons of patriotism and devotion to the public good that your trust has allowed me to receive from you." The General replied with a communiqué on 22 June, in which he declares that "whatever men's intentions, the present regime can produce nothing but illusions and caprices".

This did not stop de Gaulle, a month later, admitting that Mendès "could not have got more" out of the Geneva conference on Indo-China. It was a rare compliment coming from his lips. And although, at first, he criticized the concessions made by Mendès France to Tunisia, he came round, before the end of the year, to approve of them on the whole. On 13 October 1954, he even agreed to receive Mendès France at the Hôtel La Perouse. It was a friendly meeting, during which de Gaulle remarked to his visitor: "The regime may allow you to liquidate

Indo-China, to liquidate the EDC, to liquidate Tunisia, to accept German rearmament or to increase wages, that is to say, to relieve it of its burdens, but the regime does not allow you to carry out a constructive policy, a French policy. People may wave their hats as you pass, because you are new and likeable, but when you have rid the regime of what bothered it, then the regime will get rid of you." In fact, nothing positive emerged from that exceptional meeting. But Mendès France did not hide how pleased and moved he was by the homage paid him by de Gaulle. Addressing his "companions", who had met for a "national day", the General had praised "the ardour, the valour, the vigour of the present President of the Council". What man of the regime had ever received such encouragement?

Between 1952 and 1958, the life of Charles de Gaulle was dominated by the reading and publication of the first two volumes of his *Mémoires de guerre*. If Xenophon valued his *Anabasis* higher than the retreat that had inspired it and T. E. Lawrence expected posterity to praise his *Seven Pillars of Wisdom* rather than the Arab revolt, Charles de Gaulle attached more importance to the great leap of 1940 and to the invention of Free France than to his account of it. But, let there be no mistake: those memoirs are a great deal more than the personal plea of a highly controversial statesman or the compensatory reflection of a celebrated man in retirement. For their author, they embodied his very deeds and projected a huge task. They represented a stage in his history and therefore, for him, in the history of France. They were also, for him as for many others, a work of art.

Charles de Gaulle wrote with difficulty, painfully even, and crossed out a great deal; the manuscripts, as they piled up on the Empire desk, could only be deciphered by someone very familiar with them. This task fell to his daughter, Elisabeth de Boissieu, which had the advantage of reducing any risk of mistakes or indiscretions to a minimum.

As his work advanced, General de Gaulle tried out what he had written on a growing number of friends and specialists – Malraux, Raymond Aron, Michelet, Vendroux. The reading always ended with a "What do you think of it?" Others were asked "Does it suit you?" Or "Can it be published?"

In early February 1954, Charles de Gaulle informed his close friends: "Well, that's it. I've finished it!" The six hundred or so pages typed by his daughter lay on his desk, and his publishers, Charles Orengo, Maurice Bourdel and Marcel Jullian, could now come and collect them on behalf of the publishing house of Plon. He had chosen that firm himself for its seriousness, its traditions and because it had already published his *La France et son armée* in 1938.

By mid-October the first copies were sent out to La Boisserie. The first four were sent to the pope, the Comte de Paris, the President of the Republic and the Queen of England. The press was enthusiastic from the outset, and 100 000 copies were sold in five weeks. Who would say that this triumph did not help to arouse new hopes in this man constantly in the grip of dejection?

* * *

Between 1953 and 1957, Charles de Gaulle left Colombey four times on long trips overseas. In March 1953, he went back to Africa, to those parts at least where the French flag still flew (Senegal, Sudan, Niger), with a short detour to the Belgian Congo. Six months later, he visited Madagascar, the Comoro Islands, Djibouti, calling on his old friend, Emperor Haile Selassie of Ethiopia, on the way. Three years later, in August and September 1956, he set out on an even bolder expedition from the West Indies to Tahiti and through New Caledonia. There, at Noumea, he was to open new perspectives, proposing that these "French lands" should evolve towards a freer status within "a great political whole", for which France would be responsible: ideas that were to be taken up again by Socialist governments in the 1980s, in opposition to those then being advocated by de Gaulle. The General's fourth journey, between 10 and 18 March 1957, took him to the Sahara, from Colomb-Béchar to Tamanrasset and Ghardaïa. While the Algerian war was at its height, oil flowed at Edjelé and Hassi-Messaoud. This source of energy, suddenly appearing, visible, eloquent, helped to regenerate him. The charms of the Sahara, even the dazzling charms of Mzab, left him cold.

In early June 1955, he decided to summon the press to the Hôtel Continental. The two hundred or so journalists who answered his call were not disappointed: "I am happy to see you. It is over a year since we met. Everything suggests that a long time will elapse before we see each other again." But, he prophesied, "the country, deep down, is rediscovering its vitality. The shock will come that will be the signal of recovery." It was the situation in North Africa that seemed to him to be crucial. This is how he describes his favoured solution between France and her North African colonies: "I say that no other policy but one aimed at substituting association for domination in French North Africa ... would be either valid or worthy of France, since association could take the form of a federal-type link between states, for example between Morocco or Tunisia and France, or that of the integration of a territory possessing its own character, for example, Algeria, in a wider community than France."[16] All the words of the future are there. He then declared himself to be "disinterested".

In early 1956, the horizon of political Gaullism seemed dark indeed. The man of 18 June had, to all appearances, been embalmed alive. But a series of contacts, ceremonies, declarations, throughout the years 1956 and 1957, suggest that de Gaulle was still very much alive and present in French public life.

On 1 May 1956, at the request of Pierre Mendès France, he received the former head of government, now Minister of State in the Guy Mollet government. The two companions of Algiers days noted that there were divergences between them, de Gaulle stressing the reform of institutions, Mendès peace in Algeria. There was certainly a meeting of minds, but one that amply showed the leader of the Left that it was still with de Gaulle that the essential dialogue had to take place.

On 20 June 1957, L'Express, which could hardly be regarded as a Gaullist propaganda sheet, published an interview with Habib Bourguiba in which the Tunisian leader clearly expressed the wish that Charles de Gaulle would resume responsibility for the government in order to make France accept the changes and sacrifices necessary if peace were to return to Algeria.

It was a very precise, very well argued statement, which was a positive sign.

Moreover, it appeared in a paper whose owner was a close friend of Mendès France, and it was the latter who had wanted these questions to be posed to the Tunisian President in order to get this sort of answer.

De Gaulle was being brought to the centre of the debate. Whoever was concerned at this time with the Algerian question came sooner or later to solicit his opinion. Thus, on leaving Paris for New York, where he was to argue France's difficult case before the United Nations, Christian Pineau asked to be received by the General, who did not conceal from him that in his view independence was, sooner or later, unavoidable. Pineau recounts: "My stomach heaved and I said to him at once: 'But, *mon Général*, say so: that will clarify the situation at last!' 'It's too soon. There can be no question of my saying anything before I have the means to act!'"[17] But the rumour began to run round Paris: de Gaulle seems to be in favour of recognizing Algerian independence sooner or later. Those in his confidence – Guichard and Foccart – denied it. But speculation followed its course, fed on truncated quotations and supposed allegations. De Gaulle considered it useful to fall silent. Then, on 12 September 1957, the General's office published the following communiqué:

> Statements sometimes attributed in the press to General de Gaulle by certain of his visitors, following occasional and fragmentary conversations, commit only those who attribute them to him.
>
> When General de Gaulle believes it to be useful to inform public opinion of his thoughts, he will do so himself, and publicly.
>
> This applies, in particular, to the subject of Algeria.[18]

In October 1957, a new government was formed by Félix Gaillard, a Radical. On 5 November, Edmond Michelet notes in his diary: "I'm against Chaban-Delmas's participating in that ridiculous Gaillard ministry."[19] The mayor of Bordeaux justified his entry into that ministry, in which he was in charge of National Defence, on the grounds that he wanted to pursue the atomic weapons programme begun under the Mendès France and Edgar Faure governments.

But Chaban's participation in the Gaillard Cabinet was to have a far more direct effect than that on General de Gaulle's future: he created in Algiers a network made up of faithful friends, to inform the Defence Minister of the real situation in Algeria. This was a praiseworthy concern, but the real aim of this body was to expand and become an important part of the huge machinery that, from one crisis to the next, was to bring de Gaulle back to power.

The "boss" of this network was Léon Delbecque, a man whom Chaban had not chosen by chance. If any man in France could claim at this time to be a "shock" Gaullist it was this Lillois (for seven years he had run the activities of the RPF in the North of France). At his side was another provincial RPF organizer, Lucien Neuwirth, who was responsible for the dynamism of the Gaullist movement in the region round Saint-Etienne. The third man, Guy Ribeaud, was also very active in the RPF and a personal friend of Jacques Soustelle. But the network would not have had its rapidly acquired prestige if it had not had as its army representative one of the most popular paratroop officers in the army, Major Jean Poujet. Having spent a terrible captivity in the prisons of the Vietminh, he then became one of the most prestigious "centurions" in the African Army. To Delbecque, Neuwirth and Ribeaud, he was the essential, sacrosanct officer.

Such was the team of Gaullists who, at the centre of the action, were to play an incomparable role over the next few months.

In early February 1958, the General received a man from whom he had been separated by political choices since 1946, but who remained, deep down, a faithful follower: Maurice Schumann, MRP deputy for the Nord, a member of several governments of the Fourth Republic. When Schumann said that the settling of the Algerian affair might sooner or later require the intervention of de Gaulle, he suddenly heard to his astonishment, the outline of a plan prepared in unexpected detail:

> What I then heard was already the speech of 16 September 1959. In front of me, the General unveiled his plan of self-determination, eighteen months in advance. The three options were absorption by France, association and secession! Ever since, when I have heard the men of *Algérie française* claiming allegiance to the General,* I have told myself that History advances masked.[20]

At the very moment when de Gaulle was detailing to Schumann his views on Algeria, on 8 February 1958, the Tunisian village of Sakhiet-Sidi-Youssef was bombed by the French airforce. In that frontier area, where the Algerian FLN had taken up position and set up not only a hospital, but combat posts, shots were fired at a French plane flying over the frontier. "Legitimate defence!" the French General Staff argued in Algiers and ordered a reprisal operation: it resulted in 78 dead and almost 100 wounded, and hit a lorry of the international Red Cross in which Swiss and Swedish civil servants were killed. The Defence Minister in Paris had not even been consulted, before the action was taken, by the authorities in Algiers. It certainly gave some indication of how little the armed forces respected the central government.

The reaction of Habib Bourguiba, the Tunisian head of State, is well known: denouncing this act of "piracy" immediately and appealing to the United Nations, he recalled his Ambassador in Paris, Mohammed Masmoudi, whose political connections were innumerable and influential. That evening, indeed, the Tunisian diplomat dined at the home of Roger Stéphane, a writer whose militant anti-colonialism had taken on a Gaullist form, with Olivier Guichard. The idea immediately took root in the fertile mind of Charles de Gaulle's *chef de cabinet* to have the unhappy diplomat received at Colombey. The General agreed at once. The ambassador's departure for Tunis had been arranged for 10 February: it was at 6 p.m. on the 9th that he was received at La Boisserie, which he left two hours later, to all appearances transfigured. De Gaulle ended the meeting by asking the Tunisians to restrain their anger "in order not to insult the future",[21] to which the ambassador declared that he had felt it his duty, on leaving his post, "to meet the man who embodied the true conscience of France".[22]

*The *Algérie française* wanted Algeria to be ruled by Frenchmen.

It was a conviction that was soon shared by Habib Bourguiba, who did not need this drama to think so, as we have seen, any more than did the King of Morocco and his son, Prince Hassan, who had been received at the Rue de Solférino a few months before.

On 10 February the office in the Rue de Solférino published a communiqué that may be regarded as the General's political "return".

> General de Gaulle has listened to what the Ambassador thought that he should tell him about recent incidents on the Franco-Tunisian frontier and the views of his government concerning the settlement of problems in North Africa, in so far as these concern the Tunisian Republic. The General replied to M. Masmoudi that he hoped that, on the Tunisian side, present difficulties would not be allowed to compromise the future as far as the association of France and Tunisia was concerned.[23]

That episode of February 1958 was decisive. Things were never to be the same again. It gave François Mauriac an opportunity of reviving his Gaullist hope: "The country knew that it could have recourse to him when everything seemed lost. Well, that hour has come. We are in the last act of *Don Juan*."

A number of politicians who were particularly concerned about a solution in Algeria decided to take stock. On 3 March 1958, in a restaurant in the Rue des Pyramides, Jean-Jacques Servan-Schreiber, the proprietor of *L'Express*, brought together Pierre Mendès France, François Mitterrand, Robert Buron, a former MRP minister with an anti-colonialist reputation, Alain Savary, the Socialist minister who had resigned from Guy Mollet's cabinet after the seizure of Ben Bella's* plane, and Maurice Duverger, a law professor whose editorials in *Le Monde* were highly influential.

This brains-trust of the liberal left agreed, with more or less satisfaction, that the solution of the terrible Algerian problem was one that only de Gaulle could carry through, but that the same de Gaulle could not win enough support in parliament. How could these two propositions be reconciled?

One of the diners in the Rue des Pyramides decided to bring his calculations to the knowledge of a wider public: the day after this meeting, Maurice Duverger had an article published in *Le Monde*. Under the heading "When?", Duverger wrote in a hundred lines the history of the next six months. Declaring that it was no longer a question whether de Gaulle would come back, that much was evident. "The real question," he went on, was "*when* will de Gaulle's second government begin? Either it will be before everything is irreparably lost – in which case he will settle the Algerian question...open up the possibilities of the Franco-African community...perhaps even lay the foundations for a new foreign policy, and make possible a reform in depth of our political institutions – or our politicians will call on de Gaulle when it is too late, when failure is imminent, so that he could go some way in masking their failure and take on some of the blame that should be theirs."

*The chief "external" leader of the FLN, who, travelling with four companions on board a Moroccan plane bound for Tunis, had been "intercepted" over the Mediterranean by fighters operating from Algiers.

On 15 April the Gaillard cabinet was overturned after a brilliant attack from Jacques Soustelle, who, in the best Gaullist traditions, denounced the involvement of the French government in the procedure of Anglo-American "good offices" (whose representatives were Robert Murphy and Harold Beeley) between France and Tunisia, which could only lead to the internationalization of the Algerian affair.

It was at his request that Generals Salan and Jouhaud handed Gaillard a memorandum on 26 April demanding of the government that it commit itself to never tolerating a situation in which Algeria "would cease to be an integral part of France". Thus the army, supposedly the instrument of the government, was invited by the government to impose its views on it.

For General de Gaulle, this was heresy, scandal, the world turned upside down! What he thought of the military leaders in Algiers, in any case, we know from an account of a meeting between him and André Philip, in late March, in the Rue de Solférino:

> *De Gaulle*:   Only if Algeria becomes independent can we get ourselves out of this mess.
> *André Philip*:   Yes, but I'm worried about it. Over there an army revolt is being planned, under your name, in favour of *Algérie française*.
> *De Gaulle*: If there were a government, it would govern, and the army would obey. The army only rebels when it is frustrated of its natural instinct to obey. If there is no government, the army will seize power in Algiers. And, seeing that there is no longer a State, I shall seize power in Paris, in order to save the Republic.
> *André Philip*:   But then you will never be able to declare the independence of Algeria!
> *De Gaulle*:   Come now, Philip, don't be naïve. You've lived in Algeria as I have. You know them. All they do is shout their heads off. So all we have to do is to let them shout! As for the soldiers, I shall do nothing until their leaders have devoured one another.[24]

On 27 April 1958, Léon Delbecque, head of the Gaullist network in Algiers, entered the General's office on the first floor of the Rue de Solférino. The day before, a violent demonstration had triggered off the fever smouldering in Algiers. What could Charles de Gaulle expect of those who, in Algeria, were trying to open the way for him? Delbecque wanted to involve the General in a gesture, a statement, a promise that would bind him. "Well, *mon Général*, what will you do if . . ." The answer was long in coming, but come it did: "Delbecque, I will know how to assume my responsibilities."

CHAPTER FOURTEEN

The 17th Brumaire

In his quest to embrace the whole of France, Charles de Gaulle seems to have set about re-inventing in turn, from Clovis to Clemenceau, our founding heroes. Only one of them never seems to have inspired his references: Bonaparte, whose cynicism and excess he was all too ready to denounce. But in the spring of 1958 it did not require much for the General to walk in the footsteps of the man of Brumaire.*

The explosion of May 1958 did not shake a France slumbering after an over-indulgent meal, as was the case in May 1968. But nor was it a cry of social or economic anger. It brought upheaval to a France that was economically expanding, in which the standard of living had been rising regularly for five or six years, as also had the birth rate; a France of guaranteed full employment, in which the crises that did occur were crises of growth: a country that, under a weak and incoherent regime, had won the post-war battle.[1] The upheaval that brought France to the edge of civil war had nothing to do with social bitterness or the anger of the deprived. It was essentially a political crisis.

Three factors led to it in an almost irresistible way: the powerlessness of the political institutions, the threat to territorial integrity brought about by the Algerian insurrection, the low standing of the French nation in the order of world powers. It is clear that these three elements were closely related. But the third was not simply a consequence of the other two: the decline of France dated quite obviously from June 1940, if not from the great blood-lettings of 1914–18. What was new was the awareness of the decline, especially after the abortive Suez adventure.** Since 1956, the French had lived in a state of bitter frustration, blaming their unfortunate governors.

It was clear that the general decline could not last: the gap between the overwhelming urgency of the problem posed in Algeria and the means at the disposal of the regime to solve it was striking, even scandalous. There was no less absurd a gap between the inability of the men in power to confront the historic challenges of decolonization and the dislocation of the state, and the internal exile in which the man who seemed most capable of saving them was confined.

Was there a plot? This notion cannot be dissociated from organization and secrecy, and both were certainly what was most missing in that seditious effervescence in the spring of 1958. There was a whirlwind of intrigues but the

*Napoleon Bonaparte, who assumed power as First Consul on 9 November (18 Brumaire) 1799.(trs.)
**Organized in concert by London, Paris and Jerusalem against Colonel Nasser's Egypt, after the nationalization of the Canal Company, in July 1956, by the Egyptian government.

only "plot" to which the word might justly be applied was that which claimed allegiance, rightly or wrongly, to General de Gaulle.

Gaullism "in action", confronting the agony of the Fourth Republic, in search of a government in early May 1958, was a pyramid. At the summit was the General. He floated from Colombey to the Rue de Solférino, detached from intrigues, but not from news, releasing three successive statements: de Gaulle will not come back; in any case, de Gaulle will not come back as a result of a *coup d'état*; de Gaulle will be the hostage of nobody and will make up his mind only when he is in possession of the means to act. He was free, therefore, but concerned, and closely so.

Immediately under him was a small General Staff which both informed and protected him, possessed of innumerable ears and capable of discreet initiatives: the key figures here were Guichard, the confidant who operated from the office and whose task it was to deal with the mass media and politicians, and Foccart, whose antennae stretched overseas and whose contacts and acts were on the border of legality. Then came three men: Debré, Soustelle and Chaban-Delmas. Senator Michel Debré, *rapporteur* of the Council of State, lived and acted at this time on the frontiers of sedition. His paper, the *Courrier de la colère*, was constantly calling for a sacred insurrection. Did he believe that he had returned to the times of the Resistance? Comparing the end of French Algeria to the War, he spoke, wrote, acted in a state of epic indignation, apparently unaware that this regime, unlike that of the Germans, left him free to express his beliefs. Jacques Soustelle was of a legalistic turn of mind, though he was not always able to control the Union for the Salvation and Renewal of French Algeria (USRAF), which he had founded. Impassioned, impulsive, but disciplined, Soustelle would find himself in the end at the outposts and even carried shoulder-high. But he was too rational and ultimately too legalistic to break the taboos. Jacques Chaban-Delmas operated inside the system. From midnight on 13 May, he was no longer Defence Minister, but until then he would have succeeded in making the Delbecque network the Trojan Horse of Gaullism in Algeria. Without Chaban, and therefore without Delbecque, where would the operation of 13 May have been?

If, for de Gaulle and his followers, the debate had begun between those who gave priority to keeping Algeria French and those who saw this crisis as above all a focus for energies that might bring de Gaulle back to power, no such discussion arose among the soldiers. For most of the generals, the honour and prestige of the army were committed to keeping Algeria in French hands. Having been defeated in Indo-China through the mistakes of its generals, frustrated by the Suez escapade and confined to humiliatingly small areas in Tunisia and Morocco, the army was desperate for "its" victory in Algeria. This victory was so passionately believed in that, in order to achieve it, the government had committed the army to a horrible, humiliating mission: police repression. Only a victorious conclusion could justify such actions, even the use of torture, or at least melt them into a positive balance sheet. For de Gaulle there was something absurd in investing (sinking?) the whole of France's military force in tracking down a few thousand guerrillas overseas. But the army could not abandon what it saw as its military objective, without feeling shame or humiliation. Between de

Gaulle and the army there was not only an incompatibility of mood, but also one of attitude.

In early May 1958, the civil and military authorities in Algiers felt that the power of the French State was beginning to question the prodigious effort that France had so far accepted in order to keep Algeria: for although it had 450 000 men to fight 25 000 rebels and felt sure that it would defeat them within a few years, Salan denounced as treason the slightest reduction in the military presence. As government succeeded government, the men of French Algeria perceived, with each month that passed, less and less resolve in the State whose authority they were supposed to be upholding. However ambiguous he might be, de Gaulle, all the same, would be a State, a force that could be convinced or circumvented.

The war itself, in any case, was thought to be going their way. In Kabylia, of course, Amirouche still held the mountains. The Bibans were ablaze, as was the Collo peninsula. But in the east the forces of General Gilles, an energetic paratrooper, had just inflicted terrible losses on the Army of National Liberation (ALN). In the west, where the Ouarsenis was unsettled, Wilaya V (the fifth province in Algeria according to the FLN) had been shifted. The battle of Algiers in 1957 had ended with the crushing of the rebels, all of whose "historic leaders" (except one) were now in prison or dead. The balance sheet that Salan presented to Lacoste and Chaban, however rigged it may have been (and from which it emerges that more "rebels" were killed than weapons were seized), was telling: victory was within reach. Who would dare to rob the army of it?

Three dates mark the beginning of this semi-revolution that was to lead to the foundation of the Fifth Republic. On 26 April there was an enormous demonstration in Algiers with a view to preventing the formation in Paris of a "treasonable" government. It was a demonstration that everybody presents as the dress rehearsal of the great day planned for the beginning of May during which the army and the people of Algiers would force Paris to hand over power to a government of "public safety". From then on, Algiers was at boiling point.

On 5 May, General Ganeval, who was in charge of the military side at the Elysée, met Olivier Guichard, on behalf of M. Coty, who thought an explosion was imminent, and to sound out General de Gaulle's intentions, with a view to paving the way for his legal return to power. On 8 May, in Algiers, the Minister for Algeria told the officers in charge that the army must be on its guard against what was happening in Paris.

The next day, the most surprising move occurred in this surprising sequence: Generals Salan, Allard, Jouhaud and Massu and Admiral Auboyneau handed to Robert Lacoste – who was about to leave Algiers for Paris – a message to transmit through General Ely, Chief of General Staff, to the President of the Republic. It was a sort of ultimatum to the head of State:

> The army in Algeria is disturbed by the sense of its responsibility for the men who are fighting on behalf of the French population inland and who feel abandoned, and of the Muslim French who have renewed their trust in France. The army, to a man, would regard any abandonment of this national heritage as an outrage. We could not predict its desperate reaction.

It was a move of unprecedented seriousness. René Rémond notes pertinently that "it was the first time (in contemporary history) that the army had become threatening and took the liberty to dictate to the authorities of the Republic what their conduct should be".[2]

Confusing as it may seem, the bid for power of 13 May had been meticulously planned. A general strike began at 1 p.m., a meeting of 100 000 people at the war memorial in the Plateau des Clières, a vast esplanade divided by steps that led to the seat of the General Government of Algeria (the GG) before which stretched the Forum: the singing of the *Marseillaise* in honour of the French prisoners executed by the FLN, cries of "l'armée au pouvoir!"; everything followed the official scenario. But the real ringleaders wanted to put the seal of a popular uprising on that day. When the ceremony at the war memorial ended, at 6.30 p.m., Pierre Lagaillarde, President of the students and wearing a paratrooper's uniform, cried: "To the GG!" and ordered an assault on the building that symbolized the State. Colonel Vaudrey, in charge of security, ordered his men to retreat behind the railings, while the paratroops of the 3rd RPC, under the command of Colonel Trinquier, flanked the excited crowd in friendly fashion and obligingly gave the mutineers a truck to batter down first the outer gates then the doors of the building. A few minutes later, Lagaillarde appeared at the top of the huge edifice, while the crowd swarmed into the building, vandalizing the offices, ransacking the files, throwing documents and typewriters out of the window. The street had won, with the complicity of a few army officers.

Half an hour later a furious Massu appeared. "Get them to stop this racket!" But he was seized and carried away by the crowd – and he agreed to assume the head of this yelling Commune: he would be chairman of a "Committee of Public Safety", consisting of rioters led by Lagaillarde, and three colonels, Thomazo, Duchasse and Trinquier, the officer whose troops had assisted the riot. When Salan arrived at about 8 p.m., it was all over. When the Commander-in-Chief appeared on the balcony of the GG and tried to launch an appeal for calm to the tens of thousands of Algérois massed on the Forum, he was booed. The crowd yelled at him "Massu, Massu!"

The new "chairman" then appeared, in "para" uniform and began in his deep voice to declare his aims: "I, General Massu, have just formed a Committee of Public Safety, so that a government of Public Safety under General de Gaulle may be formed in France!" The name was out. At 9.30 p.m., having forbidden him to use any weapons against the crowd, Gaillard – as head of government for a few hours – gave General Salan, who could not even leave his office, general powers for "the maintenance of order". Addressing those in charge, Gaillard sighed down the telephone that "only de Gaulle can get us out of this".[3] At midnight, in the Palais-Bourbon, as the indignation caused by the act of sedition had gradually built up a majority in favour of a Pflimlin government, Félix Gaillard's office took its last decision, to break off all communications, either by telephone, telegram or radio, with Algiers. Three hours later, Pierre Pflimlin was sworn in as head of government.

But what precisely was de Gaulle doing while that crowd had set out to win the golden fleece for him, in the African night? He has described his thoughts in the

Mémoires d'espoir – written, it is true, ten years later, by an old sovereign inclined to mythologize and ennoble events.

> It was clear that the country was heading straight for subversion, the sudden arrival in Paris of an airborne vanguard, and the establishment of a military dictatorship based on a state of siege analogous to that which now existed in Algiers, which would inevitably provoke in retaliation more and more extended strikes, widespread obstruction, and active resistance on a growing scale. In short, the prospect was one of chaos, culminating in civil war, unless a national authority could immediately rally opinion, take over power and restore the State. And that authority could be none other than mine.
>
> I had to choose the moment when, closing the shadow-theatre, I would release the *deux ex machina*, in other words make my entrance. Should I wait until, events becoming violent, collective fear would guarantee me a general and prolonged ascent [or] should I intervene without delay in order to nip the nascent disaster in the bud, at the risk of being subsequently challenged and thwarted by people who had recovered their equanimity?[4]

He chose the second method – but not to give the country some temporary release of pressure. He needed, he was to write, to seize that "historic opportunity" to stabilize the State, to resolve "the vital problem of decolonization" and to re-establish the independence of the country. "Notwithstanding the doubts which I felt about myself owing to my age – sixty-seven years – the gaps in my knowledge and my limited abilities," he had decided to assume the risk of personifying "this great national ambition".

On the morning of 14 May, Algiers and Paris awoke, uncertain of what the day might hold. In Algiers the GG had been taken and Paris had been forced to hand over local powers to the army. But in Paris a government had been formed, thus challenging Algiers, though not without losing ultimate control over it. Although the President of the Republic ordered the generals to return to the fold, there were innumerable signs that in Algiers things were only just beginning; and the first communiqué of the Committee of Public Safety, published that day, called once again for the formation of a government of public safety led by de Gaulle.

Next day Raoul Salan displayed a decisiveness that many of those who had observed him over the past few days thought that he lacked: appearing on the balcony of the GG at noon, he harangued a crowd of some ten thousand Algérois. "Vive l'Algérie française!" he cried. Just as he was about to move back, he was caught by Delbecque who muttered to him harshly: "Shout *Vive de Gaulle*!" Then, he faced the crowd once more and shouted his "Vive de Gaulle!"

Thus the official depository of the powers of the Republic in Algeria had declared in favour of de Gaulle. The strategy of the various "networks" operating on both sides of the Mediterranean in de Gaulle's name was working. But de Gaulle had not waited to be crowned by Salan. The day before, he had written a text, handed to Guichard on the morning of 15 May and communicated by the

AFP around 6 p.m., which was to be crucial. It was his May appeal, the manifesto of the future regime.

It consists of less than a hundred words. It is de Gaulle at his best:

> The degradation of the State inevitably brings with it the distancing of the associated peoples, disturbance in the fighting forces, national dislocation, loss of independence. For twelve years, France, in the grip of problems too severe to be solved by the regime of the parties, has embarked on this disastrous process.
>
> Not so long ago the country, in its depths, trusted me to lead it in its entirety to its salvation.
>
> Today, with the trials that face it once again, let it know that I am ready to assume the powers of the Republic.

There was not a word about Algeria, even if it did mention the "associated peoples" – which certainly seemed to include it, but from a very different point of view from that of the masters of Algiers. The whole great debate to come is already encapsulated in these brief sentences. Nevertheless, these words were also to consolidate the rebels. As René Rémond writes: "13 May had shattered legal power. General de Gaulle's intervention attacked its legitimacy."[6] But was this one of de Gaulle's aims?

At the National Assembly, the Socialist Guy Mollet, the new Vice-President of the Council, declared that "if we are to keep the enormous respect, the profound admiration that is in our hearts, the General must complete his declaration by stating that, if asked to form a government, he would be prepared to appear before the National Assembly with a programme and, if defeated, to withdraw".[7]

On 16 May, at the Forum in Algiers, a surprising demonstration took place in which a crowd of Muslims was seen fraternizing warmly with Europeans. They could not all have been put there by the secret service: they expressed something that seemed authentic. Jacques Soustelle gave the slip to the guard placed in front of his house and reached Switzerland, then Algiers, where the crowd greeted him, but where Salan threatened to expel him and, after appearing beside him on the balcony overlooking the Forum, sent him off inland. The same day, a new tornado shook the army: General Ely, Chief of General Staff, regarded as the conscience of his comrades, resigned.

On 19 May, at the Hotel du Palais d'Orsay, General de Gaulle summoned the press. At 3 p.m., he made his entrance in the old, gilt reception room, and sat down behind a small, green-covered table. He was wearing civilian clothes. The man seemed to us to have put on weight during his three years of isolation. The face, with its blotchy complexion, had filled out, he looked swollen round the eyes, he held his spectacles in his hand most of the time.

Then Maurice Duverger, who had predicted his return in an article in *Le Monde* two months earlier, asked him if the power that he was claiming did not run the risk of endangering public liberties. It was a sight to behold: de Gaulle, making full use of his presence, his head brandished as if for an armoured attack, his arms opening as if to fly off and the voice mixing thunder and tremulous irritation, said:

"Have I done so? On the contrary, it was I who re-established liberties when they had disappeared. Does anyone think that at sixty-seven I'm going to start a career as a dictator?"

Refusing to define his policy for Algeria and recalling that his aim was to "arbitrate", he withdrew on a pleasantly private note: "I'm going to retire to my village and I shall be at the country's disposal."

In the press and in the Assembly, reactions were moderate. Pierre Mendès France deplored that no condemnation of the sedition in Algiers had been made. Pflimlin reserved judgement: he feared the worst. But Algiers was won over. On the evening of 20 May, General Salan paid him this homage: "*Mon Général*, your words have brought hope to our heart."

The General's moment certainly seemed to be at hand. His walks in the grounds of Colombey were getting more impatient every day. He let it be known that he wanted to meet the head of government, Pierre Pflimlin, at the earliest possible moment. He even decided where the meeting was to take place: the park of the Château Saint-Cloud.

Pierre Pflimlin agreed to the General's wishes. It was too late for face-saving or haggling over details. About 10 p.m. on 26 May, he slipped out of the Hôtel Matignon, which was besieged by the press, and made his way to Saint-Cloud, where he found a friendly de Gaulle already there. Pflimlin did not exclude the possibility that he might withdraw, so long as de Gaulle condemned the sedition in Algiers. Things were left vague. Almost immediately on returning to La Boisserie, Charles de Gaulle wrote a statement that was to be issued shortly after noon by his private office and which was nothing short of bewildering:

> Yesterday I set in motion the regular procedure necessary for the establish-ment of a republican government capable of ensuring the unity and independence of the country.
>
> I expect this process to continue and the country to show, by its calm and dignity, that it wishes to see it succeed.
>
> In these conditions any action that threatens public order, from whatever quarter it may come, will run the risk of serious consequences. While taking the circumstances into account, I could not countenance it.
>
> I expect the land, sea and air forces in Algeria to observe exemplary discipline under the orders of their commanders: General Salan, Admiral Auboyneau, and General Jouhaud.
>
> I put my trust in those commanders and intend to make contact with them.

One can imagine the astonishment of the Prime Minister on reading this state-ment. But, as Emmanuel d'Astier was to write a few months later, "M. Pflimlin does not have the stature to call the Great Visionary a liar."* President Coty begged Pflimlin not to react hastily, for what really interested him were the last two paragraphs of the General's communiqué: de Gaulle had declared his veto on the

---

*M. Pflimlin has always refused to give his version of the conversation at Saint-Cloud. In particular, he refused to give it to me in January 1985.

coup d'état, which everyone in Paris believed to be imminent. This coup, so feared by the head of State, went by the code name "Resurrection". General Massu, who had conceived it, defined it thus:

> To raise up the people of Paris during a march converging on the Champs-Elysées and the Palais-Bourbon, of elements transported by air, landing at Le Bourget and Villacoublay. To obtain, by means of a mass demonstration, the fall of the present government and the setting up of a republican government of Public Safety under the leadership of General de Gaulle. Lastly, it is imperative that the operation should preserve the essential character that marked the events of 13 May in Algiers.
> It is not a military *coup d'état*.
> It is not a rebellion.[8]

General Jouhaud has described how the operation was planned:

> Two regiments of paratroops from Algeria and two formations of paratroops stationed in the South-West of mainland France were to be assembled at intervals of a few hours in the Paris region. With the complicity or passivity of the police and CRS,* the paratroops were to occupy the Hôtel de Ville, the prefecture of police, the regional centre of the postal service, the Eiffel Tower, the studios of French radio and television, the National Assembly, the Foreign Ministry, the offices of the President of the Council.[9]

Responsibility for the transportation of troops lay with General de Rancourt, an old Free French officer, who had commanded the Lorraine Group during the war (a bomber squadron in which Pierre Mendès France had served), and had later been General de Gaulle's military *chef de cabinet*. Contacted by Major Vitasse, Massu's emissary, Rancourt immediately asked for advice from de Gaulle's office: he would do nothing without specific agreement from Colombey. According to General Jouhaud, he met Michel Debré at the Rue de Solférino, and obtained from the General's closest colleagues "complete agreement" and "concluded from this that de Gaulle was favourable to 'Resurrection'".[10]

According to his *Journal de marche*, Major Vitasse arrived in Paris on 21 May and was seen at 10 a.m. in the Rue de Solférino by Foccart and Lefranc, obtaining "complete agreement" to carry out the plan. But this is challenged by Pierre Lefranc. In *Avec qui vous savez*, the General's faithful colleague states that it was on 24 May, with Jacques Foccart, and in an apartment near the Val-de-Grâce, that he met "Major Vitasse, who had been sent by the General Staff in Algiers to put the final touches on Operation 'Resurrection', that is to say, the landing on Paris of a few battalions of paratroops. We had great difficulty in making him understand that the operation seemed to us to be useless and harmful. He left us sickened and convinced that he had met saboteurs."[11]

Vitasse's *Journal de marche* nevertheless describes three other meetings with

---

*The Compagnie républicaine de sécurité (CRS) – the State Security Police. (trs.)

intimates of the General: on 25 May and twice on 27 May, at 10 a.m. with "Messrs Debré, Foccart, Guichard, Lefranc, La Malène, General Nicot" and in the afternoon "at Debré's", with General de Beaufort.*[12]

But what did Charles de Gaulle think of all this? In Algiers, General Salan was lost in conjecture. On 28 May, he sent his Chief of General Staff, General Dulac, to Colombey. Dulac flew at night from Algiers to Villacoublay and arrived at La Boisserie just before 10 a.m. The visitors were welcomed "cordially" by de Gaulle, who, taking Dulac into his office, asked about the situation of the Commander-in-Chief in Algiers: "Is he really in charge? Is he really obeyed?" He was clearly trying to find out whether someone else was not pulling the strings, someone whom he could not control. (Soustelle? Sérigny? The extreme right?) Dulac reassured his host, guaranteeing that at most Salan was navigating between the Committees of Public Safety and "a few paratroops involved more or less consciously in neo-fascism".

The General then went to the heart of the question: "The Socialists don't want de Gaulle.** Then what do you do?" One could hardly be more direct – or crude. Dulac, rather taken aback, then tried to explain to his host, in the greatest possible detail, what the "Resurrection" plan consisted of.

> The forces initially intended for the operation struck him as too light. He then asked me when – according to the plan – General Salan would be arriving. I told him that General Salan, with General Massu, would arrive with the first wave. He then explained to me his own thoughts: "I don't want to appear at once. It mustn't look as if I have come back solely as a result of this operation. After a few days I want to be called in as an arbiter, by everyone, to take charge of the country in order to spare her useless divisions. I must be seen as the man of reconciliation and not as the champion of one of the factions confronting one another." And de Gaulle concluded solemnly: "It would have been immensely more preferable if my return to affairs had followed the usual procedure. We've got to save the outfit as best we can! You will tell General Salan that what he has done and what he will do is for the good of France."

And Dulac concluded from the meeting that "General Salan had the green light to set the operation in motion – or not."[13]

This account has been challenged by Gaullist historiography, which tends to stress the mysterious ambiguity of de Gaulle's language and the General's black humour, which only a few privileged persons were capable of decoding accurately. If de Gaulle had wanted to stand surety for the military operation intended to bring Paris to heel, would he have set about it any differently?

So what had gone wrong after the extraordinary act of bluff seemed to have put the regime back on its feet the day before? The Socialist group in the Assembly reacted very badly to the communiqué about the "usual procedure". In the even-

*General de Gaulle's future special Chief of General Staff.
**The SFIO group had just voted by a very large majority against the "de Gaulle solution".

ing of the 27th, by 117 votes to 3, it declared itself hostile to the "candidature" of General de Gaulle, which struck it as "a defiance of republican legality". The parliamentary veto then seemed irreversible, Guy Mollet's indirect approaches doomed to failure. It was after reading this statement that an irritated de Gaulle asked to see an emissary from Algiers – and this was Dulac. So everyone was running round in circles, while in Algeria and at Mont-de-Marsan the "paras" were getting ready. With a parliament locked into rejection and an army ready to jump, the country had never been more in need of an arbiter.

On 28 May, the regime did spring temporarily to life: Pflimlin got the Chamber (by 408 votes to 166) to adopt a bill for constitutional reform strengthening the powers of the executive. He then summoned a Cabinet meeting which was dominated by a dramatic intervention by Pleven, denouncing the vanity of that powerless body, Pflimlin obviously drawing similar conclusions as he then went off to hand in his resignation to René Coty.

That afternoon a demonstration of "republican defence", consisting of between 150 000 and 200 000, marched behind a single member of the government, Albert Gazier, Socialist Minister of Information, flanked by Pierre Mendès France, François Mitterrand, Edouard Daladier, André Philip and the Communist leader, Waldeck Rochet, following the traditional left-wing route from the Place de la Nation to the Place de la République.

On the night of 28 May, de Gaulle met the second and third figures in the hierarchy of the State, Gaston Monnerville, President of the Council of the Republic, and André Le Troquer, President of the National Assembly, who spoke of dictatorship. He drew this pitiless reply from de Gaulle: "Well, if parliament follows you, I shall have no alternative but to let you have it out with the paratroops, while I go back into retirement and shut myself up with my grief."[14]

On the morning of 29 May 1958, one of the most dramatic meetings of this dramatic period was taking place in the Rue de Solférino – at least according to the account sent by one of the protagonists, General Nicot, of the airforce general staff, to General Jouhaud. Nicot describes how, having been sent by the military leaders to find out whether de Gaulle agreed to the launching of "Resurrection", he was received on 29 May at 11 a.m. in the Rue de Solférino by Messrs Foccart, Debré, Lefranc, Guichard and others:

These gentlemen repeated to me the General's green light: "You can start the operation." I then insisted that a telephone call be made, in my presence, to Colombey, because I could not rely on the assertion of a highly excited group. It was not until 11.30, or noon, that we got through to La Boisserie. Lefranc, I think it was, expounded the scruples of the chiefs of staff of the three armed forces, which were ready to launch the operation, though they were not willing to take such a decision without a formal, explicit, go-ahead from the General. I did not, of course, hear what was being said at the other end of the line, but at the end of the conversation, Lefranc said: "Yes, General, very well, General, my respects, General" and, turning to me and the others, who were standing around us, said that "the General gives his complete agreement for the operation to be launched without delay".

General Jouhaud goes on:

> General Nicot rushed to the Air Ministry to convey de Gaulle's decision to
> General Gelée, the Airforce Chief of General Staff. He telephoned me
> shortly before 3 p.m. in Algiers, to keep me informed of the situation and of
> the decision of the Chiefs of General Staff to implement "Resurrection".
> Unfortunately, we could not hear one another clearly and the conversation
> was interrupted. A telegram was therefore sent to me. "To General Jou-
> haud: Confirmation interrupted conversation on telephone with General
> Jouhaud. Tell General Commander-in-Chief and General Massu that
> General de Gaulle in complete agreement. We expect your arrival in echelon
> from 02.30 hours 30 May 1958. In metropolitan France means in place
> before you. No change to be made. Confirm your agreement without delay to
> General Puget.* Grandfather."
> Meanwhile, General Gelée gave the order to General de Rancourt for the
> transport planes to take off for the South-West. The order was carried out
> and, about 15.30 hours, six Dakotas were in the air. *Operation "Resurrection"
> had begun*.
> However, the Chiefs of General Staff were to postpone the operation
> when they learnt that President Coty was to receive General de Gaulle later
> that evening, to confer full powers on him. I received a second telegram:
> "For General Jouhaud – President of the Republic receiving Grand Charles,
> operation planned to be postponed."[15]

Is General Nicot's account a construction, too hastily put together by a wounded
man like Edmond Jouhaud, who had good reasons to grasp at anything that might
affect Charles de Gaulle's prestige? Pierre Lefranc, without questioning General
Nicot's sincerity, declares that the telephone call described by that officer "did
not take place". This denial, expressed in a letter to *Le Monde* published by that
newspaper on 18 June 1984, gave rise to a "counter-denial" by General Nicot.
Pierre Lefranc was later to tell me that none of the men present during those
excited hours whom he had since questioned (Debré, Guichard, Foccart and
Bonneville) had the slightest memory of that telephone call. "On 29 May,"
Lefranc insists, "everything was in play. It would take more than M. Le
Troquer's bad temper to stop the 'procedure' begun on the 27th. On that day, de
Gaulle had made public his decision, often expressed to us, to have nothing to do
with a military intervention. This does not mean that there were not some advocates of a recourse to action among us, with whom we sometimes had violent
arguments."[16]

By receiving de Gaulle, René Coty opened the way to a more pacific
"Resurrection".

From the late morning of 29 May, while the dialogue was taking place between
the Rue de Solférino and La Boisserie, whose conclusion General Nicot witnessed
(or thought he had witnessed), the head of State announced that he would be

*Assistant Chief of Airforce General Staff.

sending a "message to the Chambers" at 3 p.m. What did M. Coty say? That the country was "on the edge of civil war" and that he had therefore turned to "the most illustrious of Frenchmen, the man who, in the darkest years of our history, was our leader in the reconquest of liberty and who had rejected dictatorship in order to establish the Republic". The President proposed, therefore, that he and General de Gaulle should confer with a view to forming a "government of national safety", entrusted with the task of "a major reform of our institutions". And the President of the Republic concluded that in the event of failure he would have no alternative but to resign.

Charles de Gaulle "welcomed" this message. He left Colombey and, at 7.30 p.m., entered the Elysée.

> René Coty greeted me on the threshold, bubbling over with emotion. Alone in his study, we reached an understanding at once. He concurred in my plan. I agreed to be sworn in by the National Assembly on June 1, when I would read a brief declaration without taking part in the debate. We took leave of each other amid a throng of frantic journalists and enthusiastic onlookers who had invaded the park.[17]

They certainly reached an understanding quickly. But de Gaulle had compromised on two points: full powers for six months and not for one year, and the appearance before the Assembly. That evening he announced his aims. "The events that press upon us may, from one day to another, become tragic. It is of the utmost urgency to recreate national unity, to re-establish order in the State and to raise the public powers to the level of their duties."

Was it, in actual fact, a *coup d'état*? General Salan was very close to "doing the necessary, for the good of France". The orders to abandon "Resurrection" on 29 May got there in time, of course, but only just. And several of the best-informed army chiefs – Dulac, Nicot, Jouhaud, Salan, Trinquier – claim that in many of the discussions at the time about the intervention of the "paras", the Gaullists were the keenest on resorting to direct action: Delbecque in Algiers, Debré in Paris.

French law does not recognize hypothetical crime. It condemns only actions. The paratroops did not land on Paris and the Fourth Republic was liquidated without a shot being fired. The political class did not capitulate under the blows of the centurions, but gave in to a combination of threats and pressure. There is more than just a shade of truth in Pierre Mendès France's remark that "It's because parliament went to bed that there was no *coup d'état*."

Charles de Gaulle did not return "in Massu's pocket". Yes, he did follow the "regular process", or almost. But that great man, as if intoxicated by the proximity of power and as if detached from all laws by the country's misfortune, played so many cards at once that some of them have to be doubted. For, in the end, three inevitable questions have to be asked:

– Did the Fourth Republic die of its own accord, General de Gaulle doing no more than filling a political and institutional vacuum?

– If military pressure was exerted to hasten the end of the dying Republic, was General de Gaulle aware of it?

– If he was aware of it, did the General lend a hand to the process whereby the Republic was "killed off"?

To the first question, the answer is no. Interventions did hasten the end. To the second, the answer is yes. The General was kept informed of "Resurrection". To the third question, the answer is very likely yes.

Are we, then, to assimilate 13 May 1958 with Bonaparte's 18 Brumaire?* To a journalist who had objected to the dubious procedure indulged in during the last days of May, one of the General's closest colleagues replied: "Look at the composition of de Gaulle's government: Mollet, Pinay, Pflimlin, Jacquinot. Those are the factious men promoted by that *coup d'état!*" A few weeks before his death, Gaston Palewski said to me:

> Suppose de Gaulle had disappeared before May 1958, or had barricaded himself up at La Boisserie. The uprising in Algiers against the Pflimlin government would not have been contained in Algeria. Neither Jules Moch, nor Pflimlin would have protected Paris from "Resurrection". You had a choice between the Soustelle–Bidault–Duchet–Morice quartet and the Salan–Massu–Trinquier trio.[18]

And although there were many democrats, like Pierre Mendès France and François Mitterrand, who refused to rally to de Gaulle's government, most of those who had tried up till 28 May to stem the movement in the name of republican legality – Pierre Pflimlin and Jules Moch above all – were among those who voted for the investiture of de Gaulle.

Let us conclude with two attempts at synthesis. There is that of Henri Guillemin, hardly a Gaullist: "The Gaullist strategy consisted of allowing the political class to see the threat of violence and therefore to side with him, and to let the soldiers believe that he was their man."[19] Then there is that of Jean Chauvel, the former Ambassador in London: "All liberties being in danger, de Gaulle offered the only possibility of saving some of them."[20] Both views are more or less true.

The government formed by de Gaulle, between 13 May and 1 June 1958, looks like homage paid to the defeated Republic. The Ministers of State were Pierre Pflimlin, the man who had raised the white flag, Guy Mollet, the great mediator,

---

*The most disturbing document produced against General de Gaulle in May 1958 is perhaps a letter addressed to his son and published in June 1985 in Vol. 7 of the *Lettres, Notes et Carnets* (June 1951–May 1958).

In that letter, dated 29 May 1958 (p. 365), de Gaulle writes: "According to my information, action would be imminent from the south, northwards." And the General adds: "Yesterday I received Le Troquet and Monnerville, sent to me by President Coty, to work out with me under what conditions I could form a government under the present regime. But it is infinitely probable that nothing more will be done under the regime, which is not even capable any longer of wanting anything." From this one does not have to go very far to conclude that "action from the south, northwards", was inevitable.

Houphouët-Boigny, the African, and Louis Jacquinot, for whom it must have been his tenth government (and who had already been de Gaulle's Minister of State in 1944–45). Antoine Pinay was at Finance, the Radical Jean Berthoin at Education, the MRP Paul Bacon at Labour. Only three totally committed Gaullists – Michel Debré at Justice, André Malraux at Information and Edmond Michelet at Veterans – joined the combination, from which Jacques Soustelle was excluded. It was a government rather more of continuity than of break.

And these names do not say all. The General offered important posts – the budget and energy – to men close to Pierre Mendès France: François Bloch-Lainé and Etienne Hirsch. And when he received Maurice Couve de Murville, then Ambassador in Bonn, to offer him the Quai d'Orsay, half the discussion concerned Algeria.

The big day, 1 June 1958, when the General met the National Assembly, arrived. It was a Sunday. It was 11.20 p.m. As a terrible storm raged overhead, the Palais-Bourbon welcomed Charles de Gaulle, who had not set foot in it since 6 January 1946.

Had he won in advance? On two of the three questions asked, yes. The Assembly would scarcely have any problem granting de Gaulle the "special powers" that had been given to Guy Mollet (even by the Communist members) two years before. And there was agreement on parliament's being dismissed for six months. But there remained the "constituent powers" – with whatever guarantees de Gaulle's project surrounded the profound reform proposed. How could the Assembly not suffer from what might be called the "complex of July 1940"? However fundamental the differences between the two situations and the two projects, the handing over of such powers to the providential man could not fail to move a democrat.

In his *Mémoires d'espoir*, de Gaulle assures us that he then felt the Chamber to be "bubbling over with an intense and on the whole sympathetic curiosity towards me". *Le Monde* reported that "There was an impressive silence from the extreme right to the extreme left. Finding himself back in a place that he had never cared for, and in which he had never felt at ease, the Prime Minister-designate was in a hurry to deliver his message. He was moved, very moved." What did he say to obtain the investiture?

At this time, when so many opportunities in so many areas are open to France, she finds herself threatened by dislocation and perhaps civil war. It is in these circumstances that I have offered to try once more to lead the country, the State, the Republic, and so, at the request of the head of State, I have come to ask the National Assembly to invest me with a heavy duty.

If I am to assume it, I need first and foremost your trust. Then, without any delay – for events do not allow us any – the Parliament must vote for the bills that will be put before it. This being done, the Assemblies will retire until the date agreed for the opening of their next ordinary session. Thus the government of the Republic, invested by the national representation and possessed in extreme urgency of the means of action, will be able to respond to the unity, integrity and independence of France.

The Assembly reacted rather coolly to this not very original reminder of the Gaullist theses. Seventeen speakers followed one another at the tribune. Most attention was given to Pierre Mendès France, who was gripped by such emotion that he stumbled over several words.

> A year ago, six months ago, even three weeks ago, I thought that de Gaulle was France's great opportunity. I have often said to friends that he might be the salvation of the country. But a certain event, the sedition in Algiers, has taken place. The General has clearly stood surety for it, whether he intended to or not. I feel torn in two. Whatever my personal feelings for General de Gaulle, I shall not vote for his investiture. I cannot accept a vote under the threat of an insurrection and a military uprising. The decision that is about to be taken will not be a free one: it has been dictated. I'm not referring to individual threats, but to the blackmail of civil war and the threat of an uprising against the people's representatives. If de Gaulle guarantees us the safeguard of liberties, respect for the rights of man, the re-establishment of a renewed popular representation, contained by the separation of powers, we shall have the assurances that we have a right and duty to demand.

No less ambiguous was François Mitterrand:

> When the most illustrious of Frenchmen presents himself for our votes, I cannot forget that he is first and foremost presented and supported by an undisciplined army. In law, he will derive his power from the national representations; in fact, he already holds it by a bid for power [loud applause on the extreme left and on many of the left benches]. You will come round in time, I have been told. If General de Gaulle is a founder of a new form of democracy, the liberator of the African peoples, the maintainer of the French presence everywhere beyond the seas, the restorer of national unity, if he gives France the continuity and authority that she needs, I shall rally to him.

The result of the vote: Number of votes cast, 553; For, 329; Against, 224 – a comfortable majority.

Charles de Gaulle, invested as head of government, returned the following day to the Palais-Bourbon to obtain the full powers required to reform the constitution. In *Mémoires d'espoir*, he wrote that he wanted "to add a touch of affability to the last moments of the last assembly of the regime". But there is always an intruder to upset the gentlest ceremonies. Maître Tixier-Vignancourt, an old supporter of Marshal Pétain, appeared, declaring, in his bell-like tones, that he had voted for the full powers – de Gaulle looked overwhelmed: he raised his hands to heaven in a gesture of powerlessness – but that he could not approve of the delegation of "constituent powers", for "I would never have thought that I would be asked to delegate my constituent power twice in my life and that the man who was asking me to do so for the second time was he who had punished me* for having done so the first."

*After the war this barrister, a leading light of Vichy, was for a long time ineligible to practise at the bar.

Nobody took the trouble – least of all Charles de Gaulle – to reply to this provocation by informing the deputy from Orthez that in 1958 no foreign army was occupying national territory and that if some of his colleagues had denounced pressure and threats, they had not come, as in July 1940, from Nazi forces camped eighty kilometres from Vichy. The General took the opportunity to make a profession of republican faith:

> What will be done, not by me alone, but by the government with the collaboration of the consultative committee, will be the coronation of the republic, a continuation of what exists, for what I am doing is of course to enable the Republic to continue [loud, prolonged applause]. Will there be a main Assembly, elected by universal suffrage? Of course! The best proof of that is the pleasure and honour that I feel at being among you this evening [laughter and applause]. The government will be responsible to Parliament, there cannot be a presidential regime, the functions of the President of the Council cannot be confused with those of the President of the Republic.

The time had come for the peroration, as if that whole session had been merely a ceremony leading to this moment when, as in every ritual involving authority, it is given the real power to express itself through the magic of words:

> Before a vote is taken that will be crucial for the future of the Republic, I would like to say this: the entire question is whether the Republic will reform itself or whether it will enter into I know not what subversion. I would draw your attention to the fact that we need at least three-fifths of the vote. If that majority is not attained, we shall be forced, by the constitution, to proceed to a referendum with the shortest possible delay.
>
> At the present time, such an operation, preceded by an electoral campaign, would be harmful. It would not change the final result, but would create agitation in people's minds on a difficult subject. I would add that, if the vote amounts to a vote of confidence in the government to promote and obtain by universal suffrage the necessary change in our institutions, the man who is now speaking to you will bear it as an honour all his life [loud, prolonged applause in the centre, right, extreme right and on many benches of the left].

The vote took place. As the votes were being counted, Paul Reynaud came to greet Charles de Gaulle, who suddenly got up to shake his hand.

André Le Troquer announced that the bill had been passed by 350 votes to 161, the three-fifths majority required on a constitutional matter.* Its main provisions were as follows:

– Universal suffrage is the source of the legislative and executive powers;

– Both powers must be effectively separated so that government and parliament assume, each in its own way, and under its own responsibility, full use of its powers;

– Government must be responsible before parliament;

*A few hours later, the Council of the Republic adopted it in turn, by 236 votes to 30.

– Judicial authority must remain independent in order to guarantee respect for the essential liberties as defined by the preamble of the Constitution of 1946 and by the Declaration of Human Rights;

– The Constitution must allow the relations between the Republic and the peoples associated with it to be organized;

– In order to establish the bill, the government seeks the advice of a Consultative Committee, on which will sit members of the parliament appointed by the competent committees of the National Assembly and of the Council of the Republic;

– The bill prepared by the Council of Ministers, after taking advice from the Council of State, will be submitted to referendum.

The Fourth Republic was buried without many prayers. Jacques Fauvet, a journalist, delivered this bitter obituary to the dead regime.

> The State has collapsed first in Algeria, then in Corsica. The administrative surface has cracked at the first rather rough shock. Everything leads one to think that the same would have taken place in metropolitan France. In the last few days nobody has been sure of anybody. But if there are men who have ill served [the Fourth Republic] there are those who have betrayed it. For two and a half years above all, democracy reigned. It did not govern. Neither in the parties, in which minorities were confined. Nor in the country, where opposition, non-conformity even, were regarded as treason. Several of those who said not a word nor made a gesture against the abdication of governments, have suddenly found their voices again to protest and vote against the man who has taken cognizance of their inadequacy. But not all these belated defenders of the Republic have refused to give their confidence to General de Gaulle. At least one last tradition of the system has been respected: those responsible for the collapse are following the liquidator.[21]

The reactions of France's allies were reserved. The *New York Times* made this comment: "The French National Assembly, by giving General de Gaulle the right to govern by decree for the next six months, is providing him with an opportunity to drag his country out of the mess into which it has sunk and prevent it from sinking into civil war."[22] Joseph Alsop of the *New York Herald Tribune* predicted that, as a result of the seizure of power by de Gaulle, the "old relations between France and her allies are at an end".[23] In London, preference was given to memories of the war-time alliance rather than to reminders of the clashes between de Gaulle and Churchill. Strong reservations were nevertheless made, especially in the Labour Party, about the powers handed to the new government.

And how did de Gaulle see this extraordinary change in fortune? Here again we must turn to the *Mémoires d'espoir*:

> A feeling of immense relief swept over the country. For my return gave the impression that things were back to normal. Instantly the storm clouds vanished from the national horizon. Now that the Captain was at the helm of

the ship of State, there was a sense that the harsh problems with which the nation had for so long been faced would at last be resolved. And here I was, committed by the contract which the France of the past, the present and the future had thrust upon me eighteen years before in order to avoid disaster; here I was, still bound by the exceptional trust which the French people reposed in me; here I was, obliged as always to be the same de Gaulle who was held personally responsible for everything that happened at home or abroad, whose every word and every gesture, even when they were wrongly imputed to him, became subjects of universal discussion, and who could not appear anywhere without exciting ardent acclamation. The high dignity of the leader combined with the heavy chains of the servant![24]

On 2 June, the General moved into the Hôtel Matignon, the seat of the head of government, M. Coty remaining head of State. A team of followers immediately appeared: Georges Pompidou was *directeur de cabinet*, Olivier Guichard was his assistant, Pierre Lefranc and Jacques Foccart were entrusted with special responsibilities. It was like old times at the Rue de Solférino. The most urgent problem was Algeria. De Gaulle let it be known that he would be going there immediately. But before he left he had to settle the great operation of the Ides of May. At Matignon on 3 June Léon Delbecque heard the General, who was not given to compliments, remark to him: "You haven't made a single mistake! That's very good. But you must admit that I, too, have played my cards well!" That same evening, the new President of the Council, before moving into Matignon, retired for the last time to the Hôtel La Pérouse. The night porter was waiting for him and accompanied him, respectfully, in the lift. The General tapped him on the back and chuckled: "Albert, I've won!"

III

THE RETURN

CHAPTER FIFTEEN

Algeria, the Motive Force of the Explosion

In his *Mémoires d'espoir* de Gaulle wrote that in June 1958, "whatever I myself had undoubtedly hoped for at other times, there was in my view no longer any alternative for Algeria but self-determination".[1]

Questioning the General on this point in April 1970, Bernard Tricot, who between 1958 and 1963 was the architect of his Algerian policy, was given this reply: "Well, yes! I had long thought that Algeria would become independent one day. Ask any of the men who knew me before that date and you'll see what they say." I questioned those men, in particular Geoffroy de Courcel, the longest-standing colleague and Secretary-General at the Elysée between 1959 and 1962.

> In 1955 I was one of the three French representatives in the negotiations for the autonomy of Tunisia and I went to see the General. We were both convinced that sooner or later it would become independent. And I thought that it was still possible to find a solution for Algeria in the form of a federation with France: "Listen, Courcel," de Gaulle said, "we must be under no illusions, one day Algeria will be independent." So, from 1955, General de Gaulle regarded independence as unavoidable, but he had hoped that it would be the culmination of a gradual evolution carried out in harmony with France.[2]

On the eve of General de Gaulle's departure for Algiers, a highly significant examination of his intentions appeared in the *New York Herald Tribune*.

> During recent meetings with important visitors, General de Gaulle has declared that he is favourable to a solution for Algeria that would involve a definite timetable for the granting of independence. But since Algeria is here and now bound geographically and economically with France, it would be associated with the French Union. This implies a negotiated rather than a military solution of the North African rebellion. The great question is whether the General will be able to implement his views.[3]

General de Gaulle's Caravelle landed at Maison-Blanche at 11.35 a.m. on 4 June. Among those waiting to receive him were General Salan, the government's delegate since 13 May, Jacques Soustelle and Léon Delbecque, General Massu and an innumerable cohort of individuals in highly decorated uniforms.

The new Prime Minister was accompanied by three ministers (Louis Jacquinot and Max Lejeune, former ministers of the Fourth Republic, whose arrival greatly angered the men of Algiers, and Pierre Guillaumat, who was responsible for the armed forces), General Ely, who, the day before, had been reinstated as Chief of General Staff, René Brouillet, Secretary-General of Algerian Affairs, and Olivier Guichard, Jacques Foccart and Philippe Ragueneau, the press secretary.

De Gaulle, wearing a sand-coloured uniform, seemed to be in a good mood. He warmly shook the hands of Salan, Soustelle and even Massu, who then introduced him to the Committee of Public Safety. He then took to the road for the Summer Palace in Algiers, sitting beside Raoul Salan.

Charles de Gaulle was given a reception by the Algiers crowd that the special correspondents of *Le Monde* described as "delirious", adding that "the spectacle resembled both an American-style triumph and the Tour de France". The drive from the airport to the city was like a crazy obstacle race, watched by a joyful, noisy crowd. The Rue Michelet was drowned in confetti, streamers and torn-up newspapers. The whole European population acclaimed de Gaulle without the slightest reservation, its joy unbounded. Though they had little support in Algiers itself, there were important groups of Muslims who had joined the cheering crowd, like them, waving flags and shouting slogans. General de Gaulle seemed moved by this show of feeling.

In the afternoon on board the cruiser *De Grasse*, de Gaulle greeted that "great French city" of Algiers and expressed the wish that the movement of "renewal" might "from here embrace the whole of France".[4] It was certainly a step forward towards his hosts. He was to make a few more. Now came the great meeting at the Forum with thousands of Algérois. It was an extraordinary encounter between Charles de Gaulle and that passionate, mixed, demanding and generous people, which expected everything and whose excitable enthusiasm could so easily turn to furious dismissal. Speaker followed speaker on the balcony. M. Denis, a member of the Committee of Public Safety, yelled into the microphone: "We must have done with the system, we must have done with all those bastards!" which brought him a noisy ovation.

General de Gaulle arrived at the GG (Gouvernement Général) at 7 p.m. His party made its way to the huge balcony that was being used as a platform. The giant then appeared, a column between the columns of the balcony, made even taller by his two arms, raised like masts; there was an extraordinary burst of applause, interjected by shouts of "Algérie française", "Soustelle", "Vive l'armée". On either side of the extraordinary figure stood Salan and Soustelle, each of whom said a few words ending in "Vive l'Algérie française!" before standing back.

De Gaulle approached the microphone, breathed in, like a diver before his brief effort, and declared, in two stages, separated by a slight pause: "Je vous ai [three words that were inaudible] compris!"* There was stupefied silence for two or three seconds, followed by a yell of collective joy. De Gaulle held them. In all his

*Literally, "I have understood you". The French might be more idiomatically rendered as "I understand". (trs.)

career as a public speaker, he had never known, he would never know, a second like that one. Those words, "seemingly spontaneous but in reality carefully calculated, which I hope would fire their enthusiasm without committing me further than I was willing to go" were his tour de force. Thus he launched the two rockets that would light up the paths to the various alternatives he could already see: first, that of the "single college", the political solution in which the Algerian people, through their elected representatives, would decide; then, the appeal to the fighting enemies whose "courage" was praised. Who would not have been ruined by speaking such words a few months before?

> I know what has happened here. I see what you have wanted to do. I see that the road that you have opened up in Algeria is the road to renewal and brotherhood.
>
> Well! I take cognizance of all that in the name of France and I declare that from this day France considers that throughout Algeria there is only one category of inhabitant: there are only French citizens, wholly and entirely French, with the same rights and the same duties. On this land the French army has been the leaven, the witness, and it is the guarantee of the movement that has developed here. It has been able to stem the tide and tap its energy. I pay homage to it. I express my confidence in it. I count on it today and tomorrow.
>
> French wholly and entirely, in a single college, and in less than three months time all the French, including the ten million French citizens of Algeria, will have an opportunity to decide their own destiny.
>
> Ah! If only they could all take part in this huge demonstration, all those in your towns, your douars, your plains, your jebels!
>
> If only even those could take part who, out of despair, believed that they had a duty to wage a struggle on this land, which I personally recognize is courageous – for there is no shortage of courage in the land of Algeria – but is nonetheless cruel and fratricidal.
>
> I, de Gaulle, open the doors of reconciliation to those men.
>
> Never more than here and never more than on this night, have I understood how great, how generous France is.
>
> *Vive la République! Vive la France!*

The frenzied cheering, the collective delirium did not stop all those who were there from reflecting. In fact, what had he said? He had committed himself to equality of rights between Europeans and Muslims, and this did not necessarily mean a "French Algeria".

Even before commentators favourable to the Algerian FLN, such as Jean Amrouche (in *Le Monde* of 6 June), proclaimed that the "single college" was the opening up at last to the emancipation of Algeria, some of Charles de Gaulle's most faithful followers were anxiously wondering why he had made no reference to "integration" or to *Algérie française*. De Gaulle went back to the Summer Palace, where he was joined immediately by his son-in-law, Colonel Alain de Boissieu. It was so warm that Boissieu suggested that his father-in-law take off his tunic and put on a dressing-gown. This the General did, before sinking into an armchair and, to the amazement of this man who knew him so well, asking for a whisky.

After swallowing the first mouthful, he asked:

"What do *you* think?* Haven't I committed myself too far?"

"We would have wished you to take up a position on the celebrated *Algérie française*."

"I didn't do that on purpose, because the *Algérie française* of the colonist isn't the *Algérie française* of the army, still less that of the Muslims. I'm going to try to find the most French solution to put an end to this drama, though it's already very late. I'm ten years too old."

And then he asked, "To bring this affair to a satisfactory end, I require the obedience of the army. Will your comrades be obedient?"

The army mustn't try to outflank me in this business, to impose a solution. It will have to follow me in what I do. Make sure you tell your comrades that above all we have got to win the battle on the ground, then they must let me get on with it. I shall try to find, as I say, the most French solution. The fact that we are going to grant the single college transforms the problem. Tell your comrades that if they disobey me, if they outflank me, if they resist me during negotiations, I shall simply strengthen my hand.[5]

On 5 June, it was Constantine's turn to welcome de Gaulle. It was a city soaked in the atmosphere of war, a city that was still overwhelmingly Arab. "The welcome was different from that of Algiers, less tense, but more profoundly warm. It was a joyful crowd."[6]

There remained the Oranie, the western coast of Algeria, where the European population was more dominant, more intransigent and sure of its rights. The day before the General's arrival, the Committee for Public Safety in Oran had got rid of the Gaullist mayor, M. Fouques-Duparc, on the pretext that he had been "installed by the system", that is to say, elected prior to 1958. This explains the rather rough reception of de Gaulle on 6 June.

To begin with, a lively incident brought him up against the crowd in Oran stadium, where he was delivering his speech. Clearly manipulated by the organizers, groups close to the rostrum chanted "Vive Soustelle!" De Gaulle lost his temper and, this time, could not hold back an Olympian "Oh! Do shut up!", which was broadcast to the entire crowd by the microphone. De Gaulle's former right-hand man looked, this time, like a troublemaker. He went off and confided his grievances to Colonel de Boissieu: "What does the General want? Does he want me to put a bullet in my head?"[7]

In the afternoon, de Gaulle visited Mostaganem, the prosperous centre of a rich agricultural region. It was here that the most controversial episode of this campaign to ensure the primacy of the central State took place. This is how Jacques Soustelle, whose account reflects an irresistible sincerity, describes it:

The enormous crowd, almost entirely Muslims, pressed into the streets and

*Meaning "You, the officers".

public square in front of the town hall. A wave of almost unsustainable emotion swept over those human masses that we looked down upon from the town hall balcony. The crowd went delirious when de Gaulle spoke: "From this sorely tried and tested land a fresh air has risen that has spread over the whole of France, reminding her of her true vocation. To what you have done for her, she must respond by doing here what is her duty, that is to say, to consider that she has, from one end of Algeria to another, in every category, in every community that peoples this land, only one kind of child. Mostaganem, I thank you. I thank you from the bottom of my heart, the heart of a man who knows what it is to carry one of the heaviest responsibilities in history. *Vive Mostaganem! Vive l'Algérie française! Vive la France!*"[8]

So he had said it at last. Charles de Gaulle, who for three days had been so careful not to allow himself to be trapped in any slogan, had just shouted, between "Vive Mostaganem!" and "Vive la République!", that "Vive l'Algérie française!" that the generals, Soustelle and the Committees of Public Safety had been waiting for since his arrival at Algiers. Those four words, spoken just prior to his departure for Paris, have given rise to as many tireless glosses as his "Je vous ai compris!"

During such trips, carried out in a stifling atmosphere, we must allow for psychological pressure, a sort of thralldom. That moving and moved crowd described by Soustelle, with its immense emotional pressure, must have played its role. And like a great actor in the fifth act, Charles de Gaulle did "crack" just a little.

He was a man of sixty-seven, swept up by events of historical importance and projected in a few days from the shadows of Colombey to the sun-baked square in Mostaganem, before a hallucinated crowd. At Montreal, nine years later, he refrained from using the words *Québec libre*. At Mostaganem, he let out the words that he had decided, until those final moments of trial, to hold back.

On returning to Paris on the evening of 6 June, General de Gaulle could draw at least three important conclusions from his trip: the extremists had been marginalized; the army was, by and large, following him; and the Muslim population was hesitating, seeming to see the FLN as the defeated party in the great game that had been played out since mid-May.

As a man of circumstances, General de Gaulle could not fail to be swept up, transported by that Algeria in which a powerful brotherhood of warriors had given rise to a movement that had France as its aim and hope. The machiavellian politician in him refused to believe in the lasting nature of that upsurge. But he also had "a certain idea of France" which was not incompatible with that rallying of masses in search first of peace, then of a nation. And what if it were true? What if those enthusiasms were not due solely to clever colonels able to manipulate crowds, train groups and wash brains? From Algiers to Bône, he had seen what he had not expected, something enormous and ungraspable. Ten million citizens offering themselves to the Republic.

The ineluctable character of Algerian independence seemed to him to be so clear only because France was so weak. But had not everything changed since he had been at the helm? De Gaulle the historian was certainly still convinced that

Algeria would one day be independent, but the statesman confronted by the popular crescendo that he had just witnessed could certainly ask himself questions.

Did he go back to Paris a changed man? De Gaulle's fundamental clarity of thought must never be underestimated. Pierre Lefranc tells how he heard de Gaulle tell him as they drove from the airport to the Hôtel Matignon:

> They're dreaming. They're forgetting that there are nine million Muslims to one million Europeans. Integration would mean eighty Muslim deputies in the National Assembly. It would be they who would lay down the law. What is the army after all? And the French over there? The big ones have understood nothing, they're clinging on; the little ones are terrified.

The next day, the General returned to the subject over lunch.

> We can't keep Algeria. I'm the first to regret it, believe me, but the proportion of Europeans is too low. Morocco and Tunisia have already got their independence. Even if one closes frontiers, ideas get through. We have to find a form of cooperation in which the interests of France will be protected.[9]

So the celebrated "sunstroke", which had spared none of those who had plunged into the frothy Algeria of those years for any length of time, had spared de Gaulle.

"He hadn't changed," Guichard wrote. Twelve years of exile had filled him out. A month of crisis and defiance had reforged him. The de Gaulles had moved into the Hôtel Matignon. The apartment reserved to the President of the Council (which he had hardly ever used during his earlier residence) was no more than a four-room pied-à-terre. The de Gaulles made the best of it, regretting the space and fresh air of Colombey. So the small drawing-room, the only "living-room" available in the apartment, was Madame de Gaulle's domain; the General almost always received guests in the large office, where he chaired the working meetings in which the new Constitution was being prepared and in which the Ministers of State, Georges Pompidou and Raymond Janot, the expert given special responsibility for this task, resided.

The de Gaulle government was made up in haste, with Georges Pompidou, whom he had put in charge of his private office, Olivier Guichard, Pierre Lefranc and Michel Debré forming the initial kernel. "We drew up the list of names and telephoned round to the four corners of France, munching sandwiches on the bed of the small room next to the General's," Pierre Lefranc recounts.

The General set out from a principle. In order to govern, he had to surround himself by three kinds of men: representatives of public opinion (that is to say, of the existing parties), senior civil servants and, of course, Gaullists.

De Gaulle wanted to give the key ministries to eminent technocrats: for Foreign Affairs, his preference lay in the direction of Joxe or Alphand, both former members of the Free French movement, but in the end his choice fell on Maurice

Couve de Murville, whom he had known and thought highly of at Algiers, then in Italy and who had been Ambassador at Bonn. The Interior Ministry was to go to Emile Pelletier, prefect of the department of the Seine. Pierre Guillaumat, son of one of the very few French generals whom Captain de Gaulle had admired,* was put in charge of the Armed Forces: as the former head of atomic research in France, he would orientate the French army in that direction. De Gaulle thought of giving Finance to one of the best experts of the younger generation, François Bloch-Lainé, whom he had known as an administrator of the funds of the Resistance. Bloch-Lainé declined the offer and suggested Antoine Pinay, who was duly appointed. He called on the services of three of the most faithful Gaullists: Michel Debré, André Malraux** and Edmond Michelet. The first was to be in charge of Justice, the second Information, the third of the Veterans. But de Gaulle confirmed to his friend Léon Noël: "It was not the ministry I'd like to have formed."

A government is all very well, but for a man like de Gaulle, trained with army disciplines, a good, cohesive private office, consisting of men he could depend on, was hardly less important. In this ambiguous and powerful role that was now his, that of President of a Council of Ministers endowed with full powers, not only to govern, but to restructure the institutions of the Republic and to rethink the nature of the Empire, the team brought together at Matignon, the one and only source of power, assumed an unprecedented importance.

It is not absurd to regard those twenty men as the true government of the country, acting as a miniature parliament. Whatever the composition of the government (and whatever significance may be attached to the maintenance of M. Coty at the Elysée), decision-making came from the Hôtel Matignon, where, in an office overlooking the inner courtyard, sat the next most powerful man after General de Gaulle himself: Georges Pompidou. A former French teacher, who had been a member of the General's private office at the Liberation, then rapporteur at the Council of State, then head of the private office of the chairman of the RPF, then managing director of the Rothschild Bank, he was, at this time, forty-four and at the height of his abilities.

For the General, in the middle of the May crisis, to call on Pompidou, who had been so openly sceptical of his chances of being brought back to power, and who a few years before had preferred the management of private wealth to the service of the state, he must have recognized in Pompidou abilities that were available nowhere else. As head of the Prime Minister's office, Georges Pompidou was to be a brilliant success, taking in hand two of the four essential policy areas – not Algeria or the restoration of diplomatic independence, but constitutional revision and financial recovery – using his tremendous competence and skill at handling people.

Responsibility for relations with the press – which were at first quite tense – was

*General Louis Guillaumat (1863–1940) had distinguished himself at Verdun in 1916, the battle at which de Gaulle had been taken prisoner. (trs.)
**Who was soon to be followed by Soustelle, the writer becoming Minister of Culture. (trs.) De Gaulle himself assumed responsibility for National Defence.

given to Simonne Servais, a young, attractive and competent woman who had run NATO's information office, and to Philippe Ragueneau, who had been one of the organizers of the Free French press office.

The Matignon team was not content just to inspire the administration: it was also involved in politics. Olivier Guichard was put in charge of relations with the various political parties and organizations as in Rue de Solférino days, flanked by Pierre Lefranc and Jacques Foccart. It was in their offices that was to be founded the new "General's party", the Union pour la nouvelle République (UNR). To deal with Algerian affairs a "secretariat general" was formed, led by the diplomat René Brouillet, assisted by Bernard Tricot.

So General de Gaulle's government was being put in place. A *cabinet*, or private office, which functioned as a concentrated government, a government that behaved like a miniature parliament – while, at the Elysée, President Coty was content to chair the meetings of the Council of Ministers, which in fact merely rubber-stamped what had been decided at Matignon. Much has been made of the success of Georges Pompidou, but we must also recognize the part played by General de Gaulle himself. The brilliance of his first moves, the novelty of his statements, the audacity of his initiatives, helped to satisfy the French people's hunger for change.

What most of those who were involved in this episode remember is an impression of freedom, of non-conformity, the rejection of all protocol. What struck them was the memory of work that was burdened only by concern for efficiency.[10]

Later, protocol, hierarchies and the unchangeable rules of the game returned. The General was to dress for great State occasions, ministers were to concentrate on their own departments and the Matignon spring was no longer to be the epicentre of government.

The summer and autumn of 1958 saw the blossoming in de Gaulle of qualities that were never perhaps to be combined so fruitfully: from the manipulative eloquence of the "Je vous ai compris!" speech to the boldness of the plan for stabilizing the currency, from the imagination deployed in Africa to the speed with which he came to a decision on constitutional matters, one sees this sixty-seven-year-old man casting over this somewhat degraded French landscape an eye of merciless lucidity and exercising a jubilant authority over it.

In short, this "resurrected" Charles de Gaulle certainly displayed, in political matters, the combination of talents of which the May operation had tended to reveal only the more sulphurous aspects. Returning to history as if he had left it only to give himself a little time to reflect, his gait somewhat heavier, like that of a prince of the church, he resumed possession of the kingdom with sovereign calm.

CHAPTER SIXTEEN

The Constitution Made Man

There was scarcely any piece of writing of which de Gaulle was more proud than the speech delivered at Bayeux on 14 June 1946, in which he described the "institutions that France needs". Later, those who were working with him on the 1958 constitution (Raymond Janot, François Goguel, François Luchaire and others) testify that he argued with keenness and competence, though revealing on occasion the reflexes of a temperament more inclined to decision than to comment.

But we know that the "Bayeux constitution", without infringing any aspect of essential liberties, did not win the support of all republicans. The fact that the executive was no longer drawn from the "national representation", but rooted in popular suffrage,* therefore independent, seemed anathema to many and there were cries of Bonapartism. De Gaulle held firm and in June 1958 brought out his project once again. "On this subject, which was all-important," he writes in the *Mémoires d'espoir*, "I had laid down the basic essentials twelve years before."[1] For him, as for his colleagues, the new institutions could not but be inspired by the text of June 1946. This time, France was not emerging from a war, lost or won. She was in the middle of fighting one. The General had just restored State authority to Algeria, but this great conspiracy born out of the agony of the Fourth Republic remained in a state of suspension. A fever was shaking the country, in which dozens of "Committees of Public Safety" were springing up, vanishing and being reborn.

In an article in *Le Monde* of 27 June 1958, Jacques Fauvet, who in principle was not a Gaullist, expressed the latent fears that kept such intrigues flourishing:

> Between the Republic and fascism, there is only one barrier at present: the very person of General de Gaulle. He alone can stop Paris becoming Algiers. He alone can re-establish the separation of powers that is essential to the republican regime: that of the civil and military powers. But when the enemies of liberty believe that time is no longer working in their favour, will they wait for the end of the year?

Indeed, the day before, de Gaulle had declared on television that provided the people gave him their approval in the forthcoming referendum, he guaranteed that "before the end of the year, public powers capable of bearing their responsibilities will be normally in place."

*In a prophetic article, Blum declared that the Bayeux Constitution tended to turn the Head of State into an individual elected by universal suffrage.

For the law of 3 June 1958 to be carried out in full, the bill for the constitution drawn up by the government had to be submitted to a referendum. It called on the assistance of a "Consultative Committee" consisting largely of members of the relevant committees in both Chambers. Until such time as this body was set up, the government set about its work on two levels.

At the Hôtel Matignon, de Gaulle formed and chaired a study group consisting of the four Ministers of State (Mollet, Pflimlin, Houphouët and Jacquinot), his old friend René Cassin, one of his earliest companions in London and since then vice-president of the Council of State, Raymond Janot and Georges Pompidou.

The General may have inspired and chaired the meetings at Matignon, but he was very far from agreeing with all his ministers' ideas. For them, the main aim was to purge and restore parliamentarianism. The General also wanted to restore parliament: but his main concern was the consolidation of the executive, the power of a head of State to whom the exercise of sovereignty would be transferred. What is clear is that the Matignon group (with the General at its head) was concerned to stress the parliamentary character of the new system by specifying from the outset that the head of government would be responsible to the National Assembly and that a motion of censure from it would interrupt his mandate.

It is no less clear that the team at the Ministry of Justice in the Place Vendôme stressed the vigour of the powers of the executive and more specifically the role of the head of State as a "guide": a word that, like the previous one, was to give rise to endless comment. And while the first group suggested a collaboration of carefully distinguished powers, the second stressed rather their strict separation.

There was no divergence between the proposals of the ancients on the left bank, at Matignon, and those of the moderns working on the right bank, at the Place Vendôme, on the strengthening of the role of the Senate. Michel Debré, having had a long and brilliant career there, was deeply attached to the assembly that met at the Palais du Luxembourg, and de Gaulle had always opposed a single-chamber parliament. Of course, the General had thought of radically transforming the composition and the function and significance of the upper chamber. In the plane, on his return from his first trip to Algiers, he spoke to François Luchaire and described to him the broad outlines of "his" constitution, indicating that, in his view, the Senate ought now to be made up of three elements: one-third politicians, one-third professionals and one-third representatives from the overseas territories. Luchaire argued firmly against such an idea.[2] The Council of the Republic, which was to be given back its old title of Senate, was to see its functions preserved, all the more so in that its President was to be consulted at length.

The parallel work of the two groups was to end five weeks later with the hasty writing of what was called the *cahier rouge*, a forty-two-page document bound in scarlet and submitted to the Consultative Committee, as laid down by the law of 3 June. But the principles now being laid down seemed hard to grasp: there was the supremacy of a two-headed executive, the President and the prime minister; the second had responsibility before the National Assembly, which the president, on the other hand, had the right to dissolve; a two-chamber parliament; full powers recognized to the head of State in cases of national crisis; the supervision of legislative activity by the setting up of a Constitutional Council; and the right of the executive to call for a referendum.

The Constitutional Consultative Committee (CCC) came into being on 29 July. It sat in the west wing of the Palais-Royal, next to the Council of State. It consisted of sixteen members of the National Assembly, ten of the Council of the Republic and thirteen appointed by the government; it was chaired by Paul Reynaud.

There was little discussion in the CCC, it seems, about the duration of the presidential mandate. The parliamentarians were used to the seven-year term. But there was a great deal of debate about the college whose task it would be to elect the head of State, which would consist of 60 000 or 80 000 electors, depending on whether or not municipal councillors were included. There was no debate as to whether the head of State should be elected by universal suffrage.[3]

The most lively discussion concerned article 14 (which was to become the celebrated article 16), which gave the head of state, in the event of a grave national crisis, the right to take "whatever measures are required by the circumstances". Nobody objected in principle to this sort of temporary, legal abandonment of legality, but questions were asked as to what those "circumstances" and "measures required" might be. And what would then become of the parliament? On 8 August, the consultants at the Palais-Royal saw the smiling, self-confident de Gaulle appear to answer the questions, particularly about the balance of the different powers. They found him, the Le Monde journalist observed, "accessible as he had never been before". He declared that the head of State was an arbiter "above the powers and conflicts of powers". But he added that according to the bill, the President of the Council, now to be called Prime Minister, was not responsible to the President of the Republic, but to parliament, and alone would direct government policy.

General de Gaulle, clearly anxious to ensure the right of the head of State to resort to exceptional powers, referred to the "events" of May. "If they had got worse, who would have responded for the legitimacy of the State?" he demanded. He even went so far as to say that "it was by anticipating Article 16, that President Coty had avoided civil war when he called on parliament to abandon its opposition to the return of General de Gaulle".[4] Since the General had taken such care to stress the exceptional character of this procedure, even agreeing that the text could be modified to give the Constitutional Council the power to judge whether the institutions "really were threatened in a serious and immediate way", nobody objected to it in principle.

All that remained was to get the broad outlines of the draft Constitution approved by referendum on 28 September. Before that Charles de Gaulle would address the citizens of mainland France on 4 September, the anniversary of the declaration of the Third Republic. No historical reference was missed: the Place de la République was chosen as the site of the demonstration, at André Malraux's request.

Access to the Place de la République was difficult: metal barriers obstructed anybody but those with invitations and veterans carrying their cards. From 4.30 p.m., 3000 helmeted riot troops of the CRS contained the crowd on the Boulevards de Magenta, du Tempe and Saint-Martin, and on the Avenue de la

République. On the platform there were various notables of the regime, a bench on which were sitting a few dozen workers that their respective ministers would decorate and, surrounded by Republican Guards, the podium from which three speakers, including the General, would address the crowd. Huge streamers and "V" signs represented both the Fifth Republic and victory.

La voix de la France, a little-known Gaullist paper that called for a "yes vote" on 28 September, was being distributed. But, before the demonstration began, the sound of another crowd, in the distance, in the direction of the Rue de Turbigo, could be heard: posters could be seen displaying the word "no" in capital letters. Balloons floated up carrying streamers bearing the same "no". The counter-demonstration was beginning. Cries of "No to dictatorship!" "Fascism will not pass!" were answered by others: "Thorez to Moscow!" and "De Gaulle! De Gaulle!"

Then Malraux appeared, his Napoleonic forelock of dark hair covering his pale forehead.

> In 1941, the head of the Free French declared: "We say: liberty, equality, fraternity, because it is our determination to remain faithful to the democratic principles that our ancestors have derived from the genius of our race and it is those principles that are at stake in this war for life or death." There are still many of you who heard, night after night: "This is London. The French are speaking to the French. Honour and Nation. You are about to hear General de Gaulle."

De Gaulle climbed the steps up to the platform, wearing civilian clothes and without a hat. He was thinner and seemed in prime form. Facing the microphones, he opened his arms to form a "V". He then outlined his plans like a good teacher:

> This draft constitution has been drawn up for the people that we are, in the century and the world in which we live, so that the country may be effectively led by those whom it mandates and accord them the confidence inspired by legitimacy. That there may exist, above political struggles, a national arbiter, elected by citizens holding a public mandate, entrusted with the task of ensuring the proper functioning of institutions, having the right to resort to the judgement of the sovereign people, responding, in cases of extreme danger, to the independence, honour, integrity of France and of the salvation of the Republic. That there should exist a government made to govern, given the time and ability to do so, which will not be diverted from its task by anything else and which, therefore, will merit the support of the country. That there should exist a parliament destined to represent the political will of the nation, to pass laws, to supervise the executive, without claiming to exceed its proper role. That government and parliament should collaborate, but remain separate as far as their responsibilities are concerned and that no member of one may, at the same time, be a member of the other. Such is the balanced structure that power must assume. The rest will depend upon people. That, French men and women, is what the Constitution that will be

submitted for your approval on 28 September consists of. With all my heart, in the name of France, I ask you to reply "yes".

The cheering was very loud and the shouts of "oui!" spread through the crowd. The "merci" that the General muttered almost under his breath was picked up and magnified by the microphones. But there were hostile shouts, too, and pamphlets bearing the word "non!" fluttered over the crowd.

Although there was no serious confrontation between supporters of the "yes" and of the "no", the counter-demonstrators clashed with the forces of order. In the Rue de Turbigo, people carrying hostile placards were driven back by police charges. In the Rue de Bretagne, men fell under CRS truncheons. Bloodstains were seen in the Rue Beaubourg. When they did occur, clashes were violent, as in the Rue Réaumur, near the Boulevard de Sebastopol, where the police set off tear gas. The demonstrators dispersed only to reassemble in the streets nearby. According to *Le Monde*, ten of the wounded demonstrators were taken to hospital, as were six policemen. The campaign for the referendum had begun. Criticism of the new constitution came from Raymond Aron, who spoke of a "parliamentary Empire", and François Mitterrand, who wrote that the new Constitution combined the vices "both of Louis-Philippe and Louis-Napoléon", a hegemony of notables and arbitrary recourse to the previously conditioned masses. Pierre Mendès France expressed strong disapproval of this "elective monarchy" and Jean-Paul Sartre, in an article in *Les Temps modernes*, rather than taking de Gaulle to task, railed mercilessly at the French people, "those frogs who are asking for a king".

It is not an easy task to go back to the prevailing atmosphere of 1958 and to establish what a reasonably well-informed citizen might make of the recent ups and downs in public life and decide whether or not to support the inventors of the new system. French electors could not fail to be struck by the most striking arrangements of the new constitution. There had been a bold shift of power from the legislative to the executive, whether embodied by the head of State or by the Prime Minister. French citizens were being asked to approve a system that ensured not only the separation of powers, but the primacy of an "executive" now finding its source in popular sovereignty, endowed with the role of permanent arbiter.

This executive was two-headed, the Prime Minister not appearing as the mere executant of the decisions issued by the head of State. Of course, the character of General de Gaulle himself, who nobody doubted would be the head of State by the end of the year, tended to concentrate interest on him and on his view of the future exercise of power. But although the head of State must be the "arbiter", it was the government that "determined" and "carried out" the nation's policies. We should not pause overlong perhaps on the various meanings of the word "arbiter", but ask rather what "government" means here: the best analysts of the 1958 Constitution have noted that the government is the organ that sits in the Council of Ministers under the chairmanship of the head of State, who is, therefore, certainly part, and a preponderant part, of the government's decision-making process.

In the minds of the parliamentarians of 1958, the supremacy of the President over the Prime Minister was not self-evident. Pierre Pflimlin tells how he had suggested to General de Gaulle that he should stay at Matignon as prime minister, where he had held the levers of the machine so successfully, rather than go to the Elysée and play the role of the nation's father. The General retorted: "It isn't a job suited to a man of my age. I'm no longer capable of assuming such responsibilities." This amounts to saying that, in his view, the "arbiter" of the Elysée would leave most governmental responsibility to the man in the Matignon.

In any case, the weight of the executive was so heavy that this republic has tended to place itself at the frontiers of the democratic world. When the powers of decision and action are elevated to this degree above the organs of deliberation and supervision, can one still speak of an "executive", which is supposed to "execute" orders and policies coming from elsewhere. Should one not rather speak of an "initiating", "creative", or simply "active" power? It then becomes tempting to distinguish within that formidable "executive" a "decision-making" power at the Elysée and an "executant" power at Matignon.

To go still further in pursuit of the thinking of the founders of the Fifth Republic, one might quote this brief exchange between Michel Debré and a lawyer who asked him whether the creation of the Constitutional Council meant that "for the 'sacralization' of the law (which was the dominant feature of our French public law from 1789 to 1958) the 1958 texts had substituted the 'sacralization' of the constitution". Debré's reply was: "The Constitutional Council is not at all a marginal, but an essential legal body. What is true is that, under the Third and Fourth Republics, the law was sacrosanct; under the Fifth Republic, the Constitution is sacrosanct."[5] And this brings us to the heart of the second Gaullism. The constitution was "sacrosanct" in that it brought all individuals together into a collective person, by which the French merge together to form that ideal whole that is called France.

Power had come back to Charles de Gaulle through Africa. It was from Africa again that the pressures, demands and ultimatums of the colonialists in Algiers reached him.

Africa was certainly part of his visual field. In 1958, the French-speaking part of the continent belonged to a French Union that seemed like a nebulous entity on the verge of dissolution. While the North African peoples obtained their independence or fought to achieve it, those of sub-Saharan Africa were moving, from congress to parliamentary pressure, but not without setbacks, towards the slow recognition of their political personality.

France's relationship with its colonies had been shaped by the so-called Outline Law of 1956. Prepared by a group of intelligent and enterprising Ministers for France Overseas (Buron, Pflimlin, Mitterrand and Defferre), the Bill stressed the need for internal autonomy, each territory being endowed with a Council of Government whose President was originally the French governor and the vice-president a native citizen. But the second had soon supplanted the first.

Aspiration for independence gave vigour to the leaders of this Africa in movement, who did not fail to see in the terrible Anglo-French fiasco of Suez the sign of the collapse of the colonial system and welcomed the independence of the British

Gold Coast, Ghana, as the opening of a new age. The principal political organization of "French Africa", the Rassemblement Démocratique Africain (RDA), presided over by the leader of the Ivory Coast, Félix Houphouët-Boigny, had come out in favour of an immediate recognition of the "right to independence". He was supported by the Guinean, Sékou Touré, who laid particular stress on the problem of regrouping territories into a huge totality that, once independence had been recognized, would negotiate a status of association with France. The RDA's rival party, the Parti du Regroupement Africain (PRA), which the Senegalese Léopold Senghor inspired with his prestige and talent, tended to stress the unification of the various territories that had been "Balkanized" by colonization, as well as political emancipation. Challenging the federal formula advocated by the RDA, the PRA pleaded for a confederation within which the African states could avail themselves of their independence.

Thus as de Gaulle assumed power, he was confronted by a continent impatient for its demands to be met. He may have decided that a break between Algeria and France was inevitable, but he had by no means reached the same conclusion with respect to France's other African territories.

As head of the provisional government between 1944 and 1946, he had treated the Empire roughly at times, willing to take any steps in May 1945 to avoid North Africa "slipping between our fingers", risking serious conflicts with Great Britain to impede the emancipation of the Levantine states and, in Indo-China, supporting the advocates of reconquest against those of negotiation. Nevertheless, because at Brazzaville in 1944 he had spoken of emancipation, Africa expected a great deal from General de Gaulle in 1958. Too much, perhaps, for he was a federalist. That is to say, he considered that in the institutional set-up that should be proposed to the Africans a single State structure, a single national sovereignty, should emerge: that of France. For him, none of the partners of France to the south or west of the Sahara was a nation and therefore had no calling to be a State, with the possible exception of Madagascar. And he had not forgotten Algeria either. In short, what he originally favoured was a highly structured whole, much closer to the French Union than to the British Commonwealth, over which the French State and its head, who would be President both of the Republic and the Community, would hold sway.

On the occasion of the festivities of 14 July, the majority of the African leaders whom de Gaulle received at the Hôtel Matignon declared that they were in agreement with the first projects that had been presented to them. Though the inspiration of the most separatist tendencies, Sékou Touré himself came out in favour of "the rapid constitution with the French Republic of a great federation of autonomous, fraternal and interdependent states that, on the international plane, would be a force for peace and progress".[6]

Ten days later, the African leaders received the constitutional draft bill. It gave rise to a wave of bitterness. It was laid down quite clearly that the members of the Federation would be merely "autonomous". It was not much more than had been offered two years before by the Defferre Outline Law. Instead of representation in the National Assembly the Africans were being offered a few seats in the Senate, and no formal recognition of the right to independence. Léopold Senghor spoke of "unequivocal withdrawal" and announced that such a bill could not be defended by such friends of France as himself.

The PRA congress, then being held at Cotonou (Dahomey*), came to an end on 1 August 1958, unanimously approving a call for immediate independence in which the idea of a Franco-African community disappeared entirely. What the representatives at the Congress wanted was "immediate independence". If there were still any question of federation, it would no longer be with France, but among the various African territories, which were called upon to form a "United States of Africa" which would negotiate with France, on the basis of independence, "a multinational confederation of free and equal peoples".[7]

Charles de Gaulle was not a man to ignore the warnings. On 8 August, at the Constitutional Consultative Committee, he declared that he accepted the introduction of the term "self-determination" in the constitution, although he considered it to be "inelegant from a linguistic point of view". So the right of the Africans to independence was now recognized.

One more word emerged from the debates of the Constitutional Consultative Committee: Community. It was not totally new. De Gaulle had used it in several speeches, as had the Africans, especially the members of the RDA. But when the new body was being planned, the names "union" and "association" had been rejected. Raymond Janot then whispered in the ear of the future President of Madagascar, Philibert Tsiranana, the word "community", which, when launched by the Madagascan leader, won general support.

At the time when he was speaking before the CCC, making crucial changes not only to the form, but to the very substance of the contract proposed to Africa, de Gaulle was also planning a tour of the continent in the second half of August. Two planes left Paris on 20 August. In the first were Charles de Gaulle and two ministers, Pierre Pflimlin and Bernard Cornut-Gentille; in the second were the security services and the international press.** As a result, observers saw very little of the head of government and there were scarcely any opportunities of gauging his intentions and impressions.

On the afternoon of Thursday 21 August, the General was welcomed at Tananarive, Madagascar, by Tsiranana and an extremely warm crowd. The speeches given before the Territorial Assembly at the Mahasima stadium on 22 August were variations on his decision of 8 August. "In five weeks the choice will be given to Madagascar, as to all the other territories, and in the same conditions, to establish the community of which I speak, or to separate its fate from France and the other territories. Tomorrow you will be once again a State."

The General's speech was applauded, but there were those who argued against it. The Madagascan "Independence Congress", like the PRA, demanded recognition of sovereignty as a prior condition to any negotiations. But the commentary given to me at the time by Philibert Tsiranana sums up the opinion of the majority: "The extremists, by asking for the moon, have still got nowhere. I, by accepting the outline-law to begin with, then this autonomy, am leading the Malagasies three-

*Since renamed Bénin.
**Among them was the author, as the special correspondent for Le Monde, whose reports have been used in this chapter.

quarters of the way. After we've joined the Community, we'll soon leave it, when we are mature, perhaps in a year, perhaps in a century, but I think before very long."

Warmly welcomed at Tananarive, de Gaulle was enthusiastically cheered at Brazzaville, the capital of the Congo. It was there that he showed more clearly than he had at Tananarive the right of French-speaking Africa to decide freely on its own fate and in whatever peaceful form it chose. The speech that he delivered on Sunday 24 August was to appear henceforth as the charter of Franco-African relations:

> People say: "We have a right to independence." Of course they have! A territory will be able to take it as soon as it votes "no" at the referendum of 28 September. And that will mean that it does not wish to take part in the community proposed and that in fact it is seceding. This will mean that it wishes to pursue its own course, alone, at its own risk and peril. Mainland France will draw the consequences of this and I guarantee that it will not oppose it.
>
>   Better still, if, within that Community, any territory, as the days pass, feels capable of bearing all the burdens, of carrying out all the duties of independence, well! it will be up to that territory to decide the matter by its elected Assembly and, if necessary, by a referendum of its inhabitants. The Community would then take the necessary steps and an agreement would govern the conditions of transfer between this territory, which would assume its independence and follow its own road, and the Community itself.

"After such a speech, there is no longer a Franco-African problem. Who could vote against de Gaulle?" declared an astonished Gabriel d'Arboussier, President of the Grand Council of French West Africa at Abidjan airport, where General de Gaulle was welcomed by shouts of "Oui, oui".

On to Conakry where he was to meet Sékou Touré. The General's plane landed at 4 p.m. His first contact with Sékou Touré (whom he had actually seen two weeks before at Matignon) was warm. The Guinean leader joined the visitor in his car. The welcome at Conakry was no less enthusiastic than the visitors had received in the three principal cities where they had stopped on the way. Here at Conakry was a political celebration, organized by a Minister of the Interior called Keita Fobeba,* who happened to be one of the great masters of contemporary folk ballet. This theatrical triumph that he had organized had, for Sékou Touré, only one aim: to show de Gaulle that *he* was Guinea.

Sékou Touré's speech at the Territorial Assembly was a diatribe against colonialism, an appeal for the formation of two great African states, whose capitals would be at Dakar and Brazzaville, and a paeon for pan-Africanism: "Guinea is merely one sensitive, trembling fragment of the Africa that is being reborn." Repeating such phrases as "We prefer poverty in freedom to wealth without dignity", Sékou Touré triggered off frenzied cheering of the crowd massed at the

---

*Liquidated a few years later by Sékou Touré.

end of the hall. But he went on to say: "We are African citizens, members of the Franco-African community. We intend to exercise our sovereign right to independence, but we intend to remain bound to France. In that association with France, we will become a free, proud and sovereign people."

Beside him, pale with fatigue, General de Gaulle seemed less affected by the sentences coming from the platform than by the bursts of applause that rose from the audience. Was this young Africa rejecting him? And France with him?

When de Gaulle rose to reply, he seemed tired and over-wrought. But what he said that Monday evening was more moving than the fine lessons that he had given on earlier days of his African tour. And we, French witnesses not exactly known for our Gaullist conformism, were even more touched.

We heard a man already old, bowed down with experience, invincibly proud of his country's past but lucid enough to recognize the aspirations of deprived peoples. We heard the old world, rich in experience, ready with its recipes, reluctant to bow out, conscious of the end of a period.

> I have listened, listened well, with the greatest attention, to what has been said here. We believed, and I have proved it when necessary, that the African peoples are being called upon to determine their own fate. I now believe that this was only a stage, that they will continue their evolution and neither I nor France will ever challenge it. There has been talk of independence. I say here more loudly still than elsewhere that independence is at the disposal of Guinea. She may take it on 28 September by saying "no" to the proposition that is being made to her, and in that case I guarantee that mainland France will not set any obstacle in her path. She will of course have to suffer the consequences, but there will be no obstacles, and your territory will be able, as it wishes, and in whatever conditions it wishes, to follow whatever road it wishes. I break off now, awaiting the opportunity to come to see you in a few months when things have been settled and we shall demonstrate together publicly... the foundation of our community. And if I am not to see you again, know that the memory that I keep of my stay in this great, beautiful and noble city, this hard-working city, this city of the future, that memory I shall never lose.

In the car that took him back to the Governor's office, Sékou Touré sat next to him again. What did they say to one another? During the evening at the Governor's residence I managed to get a word with Sékou Touré: "Was it an aggressive yes, or a no?"

"What we want is a true marriage. A marriage between equals involves the right to divorce. But that right does not mean one wishes to break it off."

"The General recognized that right at Brazzaville."

"The text of the Constitution speaks only of a penal secession. We want freedom, not talk of punishment."

During the evening at Dakar, under the auspices of the High Commissioner, M. Messmer, attempts were made at reconciliation by several African leaders. But the two antagonists kept to their positions – Sékou Touré deciding that he would be voting "No" by issuing, with his Nigerian colleague Bakary Djibo, a violent communiqué denouncing "a constitution that is an affront to the dignity, the freedom and the unity of Africa, and would keep us in the complex of the colonial regime". On the Place Protet, where de Gaulle went to harangue the crowd, placards demanded immediate independence and African unity, while extreme left-wing activists of the Parti Africain de l'Indépendance (PAI) waved red flags at the back of the square. The General got up and yelled out:

> You gentlemen carrying placards, if you want independence, you can have it! People shout: "De Gaulle! De Gaulle!" I also note that when he is here and speaks, things are clear and no one is bored. I would have preferred, of course, that this be done in a more complete silence. I don't blame anybody. I am keen to repeat to the Africa that I love the expression of my friendship, the expression of France's confidence and I am sure that, despite systematic agitations and organized misunderstandings, the answer of the Senegalese and of Africa to the question that I ask of them, in the name of France, will be "yes, yes, yes".

In the plane that brought him back to Paris, via Algiers, General de Gaulle could conclude that his African tour had been reasonably successful. He had won three battles out of five, gathering up on his way the adhesion of most of the territories concerned, and he had learnt a lot – if only by assessing on the spot the power of the nationalist tendencies and the almost magical character of the word "independence".

If de Gaulle had set out for Africa having launched the idea of a right to immediate secession, during the journey he had come to accept the possibility of amicable separation.

Between the General's return to Paris and his speech at the Place de la République, five days later, the architects of the constitutional bill could do no more than implement the changes necessitated by the traveller's innovations. In the speech of 4 September 1958, the word "independence" did not reappear. But the General certainly specified that each "territory" would become a "self-governing state". As a result, most of the objections made from Tananarive to Dakar disappeared or were concealed.

In an article in *La Nef*, François Mitterrand voiced the contradiction which he faced: should the French left agree to exchange the democratic advance that the creation of the Community could guarantee Africa for the decline in democracy that the Constitution would, in his opinion, bring about in mainland France?[8]

The attachment of de Gaulle to the idea of the referendum is one of the innovations Gaullist politics brought to France, in an anti-parliamentarianism that is every now and again contradicted by the republican reasoning of a man who is perfectly well aware that democracy cannot operate without parties and parliament.

De Gaulle had had the idea of appealing to the French without passing through their parliamentary representatives as early as 1945. The Armistice was no sooner signed than he took the decision "to consult the country on the terms that will serve as a basis for the Constitution". In fact, the procedure implemented under the vigilant supervision of so perfect a republican as Jules Jeanneney functioned quite well and in June 1946 Charles de Gaulle made the referendum an essential element in his "Bayeux Constitution".

It was not Charles de Gaulle, but Georges Pompidou who declared to the Chamber, in October 1962, that "the referendum is the most perfect form of democracy". But it was certainly de Gaulle who insisted on specifying in the 1958 Constitution that "national sovereignty belongs to the people, which exercises it through its representatives and by means of referendum".

To say that reason objects to the principle of this referendum, whereby the long constitutional document is submitted to a simple answer of "yes" or "no", by men and women from Majunga to Valenciennes, is perhaps to question universal suffrage itself. But what was shocking, in the case of the constitutional referendum of 1958, was that the question asked could not have had the same meaning in mainland France as it had in Algeria, or in the French Union as a whole.

On 5 September Le Journal Officiel published the Constitution that was to be submitted for the approval of French citizens at home and overseas. What did to vote "Yes" mean? "It meant," de Gaulle writes in Mémoires d'espoir, "answering 'yes' to de Gaulle, and investing in him their trust because the future of France was at stake."[9] But it is possible to examine the question a little more closely than that. Was to vote "Yes" no more than to authenticate the movement of May? Was it reasonable to recognize such formidable powers in de Gaulle? Was this Constitution essentially regressive?

At one and the same time, it was democracy, the Empire and the alliances of the country that were in question and that were, in one word, to be lost or saved, when, in September 1958, one voted in the referendum.

It should also be observed that the referendum would act upon the parties like a dissolvent. For thirteen years Charles de Gaulle had dreamt of breaking up the parties, smashing their alliances, setting them against one another, humiliating their feudal pride. They were now confused and shamefaced, except for the party that had once been his, the MRP, which was now united in saying "yes", and the PCF, which was united in saying "no". All the parties, except these two, had now been divided by the hero's reign. Thus one of de Gaulle's major aims had been achieved. He certainly wanted political groupings to survive, because he was not a totalitarian, because he hated dictatorship, but he preferred them to be subordinated, deferential and toothless.

In an article forming part of a collection entitled Elections Abroad, two British academics, well-known specialists in French politics, Philip Williams and Martin Harrison, presented a superbly sarcastic description of this campaign:[10] it began by evoking the inaugural ceremony on 4 September during which "foreign journalists were already being treated for bruises inflicted on them by over-zealous members of the 'forces of order'".[11] This certainly stresses an incident that I personally cannot remember, though I would not challenge its veracity. Throughout their study, carried out on the spot and conscientiously (in a spirit clearly favourable to the opposition), the two British academics stress the formidable inequality of means at the disposal of the two camps in the competition, and above all the official character assumed by the "yes" campaign.

The "no" campaign was timid, not to say resigned. Not only did the referendum strike everybody as unequal, but at the back of everybody's mind was the decisive objection of the advocates of the "yes": without Charles de Gaulle, it would be the colonels... Many of those who voted "no" did so without really wanting their camp to win, but, as Maurice Duverger wrote at the time in a *Le Monde* editorial, so that the General's victory should not be a "crushing" one.

And what of the press? In Paris the only dailies clearly campaigning for the "no" were *L'Humanité* and its "fellow-traveller", *Libération*. *Le Monde*, as usual, behaved in its own way. It published, alternately, articles favourable to the "yes" and to the "no" votes. But, on the day before the referendum, the editor, Hubert Beuve-Méry, after carefully listing the reasons for saying "no", concluded with a "yes", which did not fail to arouse consternation among the editorial staff. Among the weeklies, *France-Observateur*, run by Claude Bourdet and Gilles Martinet, the organizers of the Union de la Gauche Socialiste (UGS), campaigned for the "no" vote as did *L'Express* (whose most famous contributor, François Mauriac, ardently advocated a "yes" in his own column). One can sum up the whole battle fought out in the press (in Paris and in the provinces) by suggesting that 30 per cent of the titles came out unequivocally for the "yes" vote, 40 per cent were more or less favourable to it, 20 per cent remained undecided and 10 per cent called for a "no" vote.

What of radio and the ever-increasing presence of television? From August, a very lively argument had been conducted between Jacques Soustelle and a group of the parliamentary opposition denouncing the government's grip on the audio-visual mass media. Quite obviously, the official filter did not exclude opposition spokesmen (who had the right to normal air time – an opportunity that they made poor use of), but it gave such prominence to the PCF that it seemed to the public that the only true "no" vote was that offered by the Communists. Only the party of Maurice Thorez carried out an active, coherent campaign; but in so complex a debate, and one that engaged individual conscience to such a degree, arguments other than those of the Communists might have shifted the undecided to the "no" side. Hence the relevance and effectiveness of Soustelle's selective strategy.

De Gaulle himself intervened, of course, in the debate: who could challenge his right to plead for his own work, his own plans and his own person? His arguments are well summed up in the radio and television broadcast that he recorded on Friday 26 July, the day before the referendum, at the Hôtel Matignon.

The percentage that must be obtained by the "yes" vote will be of enormous importance. Who, then, would wish to abstain? By asking you to choose the State and national unity, I think I am expressing what so many generations who built the nation in the course of the centuries have also desired. I believe that I am saying out loud what, deep down, all French men and women desire for their country today, including those who, for particular reasons or passions, will give in to the negative side.[12]

One paragraph of this appeal was given particular attention: it was the one dealing with Algeria. "By virtue of the fact that Algerian men and women of the various Communities will take part in the great consultation, all together for the first time in complete equality, it will be established that in the midst of their trials and tribulations they place their trust in France and, if I may say so, in me."

There is no mention of "French", but "Algerian" men and women. There is no longer any question at all of treating votes emanating from Algeria as the same as those from Provence or Normandy: it was a matter of establishing that the Algerians would "place their trust in France" and in de Gaulle. France was not them, it was an external entity. However, this did not prevent General Salan, the government's Delegate-General, from turning the campaign for the referendum in Algeria into a straightforward propaganda campaign for *Algérie française*.

The Algerians voted well – even very well. Eighty per cent of the registered voters went to the ballot boxes, and over 96 per cent of them answered "yes", 118 000 brave souls voting "no". It was a failure for the FLN, which had advised its followers to boycott the consultation.

On the evening of 28 September 1958 de Gaulle could congratulate himself on a triumph. Over 79 per cent had voted "yes", with under 15 per cent of abstentions. It was a historical phenomenon. As a vote that had remained free, it was an unprecedented landslide in modern France that amazed historians and political scientists. The "yes" vote won in every department, including those south of the Loire where Gaullism was far less strong than the extreme left. The "no" vote won only 4 600 000 electors, whereas two and a half years before the PCF alone had won a million more votes: 5 555 000.

But what did this prodigious victory mean? An article in *Le Monde* on 30 September, by Hubert Beuve-Méry – who, let us recall, had come out two days before in favour of the "yes" votes – marks both the enormous success and its ambiguity: "This blank cheque that General de Gaulle received from parliament four months ago has just been renewed to a degree that he himself no doubt hardly hoped for. The legitimacy of the new power is thus founded in brilliant fashion and the extent of that power has temporarily no other limit than the wisdom of one man."

On 3 October, less than a week after the referendum, the General left France for Algeria to present a five-year plan for the development of the country. In order to give some advantages to the advocates of integration, the Matignon team had taken out a research project prepared two years before by Robert Lacoste's colleagues. The project may not have been new, but at least it was bold: equalization of wages between Algeria and mainland France, a commitment to reserve one-tenth of public-sector jobs to young Algerians, the development and redistribution to Muslims of 250 000 hectares of arable land, and an intensive educational programme for young Algerians. All this meant a considerable investment of effort and money. Did one improve in this way something that one was planning to abandon? Addressing the people of Constantine, de Gaulle summed up his plan thus:

What will be the political consequences of such a development, involving as it does such a wide-ranging and long-standing effort? It seems to me that it would serve no purpose to fix in advance what the undertaking will gradually fashion of its own accord. In any case, because it is in the nature of things, the destiny of Algeria will be based both on its own personality and on a close interdependence with mainland France.

So, turning to those who are prolonging a fratricidal struggle, I say to them: why kill? The important thing is to keep people alive. Why hate? We must cooperate! Cease therefore this absurd combat! The prisons will then open at once. A future, too, will open, great enough for everybody, especially for you.

It was two speeches in one, each expressing a particular policy: an "interdependence" bordering on integration, even though words cannot fix the realities that only the "undertaking" will shape; an opening towards those fighting on the other side, to whom is offered a "future" great enough for all, "particularly" for them.

How did poor Salan, who had declared a few hours earlier that his men were confronting "not warriors, but murderers",[13] see things? The effect produced in Salan's team was such that even Charles de Gaulle's son-in-law, Colonel Alain de Boissieu, complained of the General's refusal to support "the people out there in Algiers". There was, General Dulac writes, "the detestable resurgence of the attitudes of Power" that would turn "everybody's anxiety into some people's anger".[14]

Neither Salan nor his supporters were at the end of their troubles: on 13 October, indeed, the Delegate-General received a letter from de Gaulle informing him that "the time has come when soldiers must cease to belong to all organizations bearing a political character. As from now there is no justification for their belonging to such groups. I order them to withdraw from them without delay."[15]

De Gaulle could not have been clearer: by ordering officers to withdraw from the Committees of Public Safety (CSP), he was disavowing "our action on 13 May", Salan writes. How would the army react? This is how Salan describes the situation: "I summoned Massu, chairman of the Algeria-Sahara CSP, and told him of the decision. He looked at me, utterly downcast. I tried to console him. We had to obey, of course, whatever it cost us." Next day, on 14 October, Raoul Salan was in Paris, facing de Gaulle.

"Well, Salan, what about the Committees of Public Safety?"

"I am rather apprehensive, *mon Général*. Just as I was about to get on the plane, Massu came to warn me that he feared there would be disturbances in Algiers."

"Well, it's up to you, Massu and Godard, that nothing of the kind takes place. You have the population in hand, and above all, on the electoral posters, no adjective ending in 'ist'!"*

*Obviously directed at the words "Gaullist".

That evening, the Delegate-General was back in Algiers with Massu and Godard, who showed him a pamphlet: "Algerian men and women, we have been betrayed. Everybody go to the Forum on 16 October at 3 p.m. to demonstrate against the political parties that want to liquidate French Algeria, to demand the return of the soldiers to the CSPs." Furthermore, the CSP had called for a general strike. In a broadcast Salan had made it clear that he opposed it: "One doesn't have two '13 Mays' in five months!"[16] The plan fizzled out, but this new attack of fever gave some idea of the collapse of discipline even among those in responsible positions.

During the summer of 1958, French intelligence services got hold of reports written by some of the most prestigious FLN leaders (Ouamrane, Belkacem Krim, Lakhdar Ben Tobbal) that referred to "the losses in competent, politically trained cadres", the "disgust and discouragement that have overcome the best", the growth of "embourgeoisement, bureaucracy and careerism", the greater efficacity of the "Morice line" (the electrified barrier isolating Algeria from Tunisia) and, lastly, "the exhaustion of the combatants" after four years spent in the underground.

Furthermore, the Algerian underground forces had been weakened by the "purges" that had been carried out by several of their leaders – especially the celebrated Wilaya III, operating in Kabylia, under the command of the best military leader to have emerged out of the conflict, Colonel Amirouche, a former jeweller from Azazga.

This relative weakening of the FLN's combative power was, it is true, compensated for by the successes in the area of propaganda and influence won by its spokesmen in the United Nations, in Africa and in Asia – even in many Western countries. Every military setback was counterbalanced by a diplomatic advance that was, of course, beyond the reach of the French forces. In 1958 the FLN was still an enemy to be feared, without which the future of Algeria could not be defined.

Should one speak of one or of several FLNs? In 1958 it had (at least) two heads. One, known as the Comité de coordination et d'exécution (CCE), was based in Algiers, Tunis and Cairo, without being able to impose its authority as the central body of the movement, while the Conseil national de la révolution algérienne (CNRA) was too large to meet regularly. The other was the group formed by four of the movement's founders, Ben Bella, Boudiaf, Khider and Aït Ahmed who had been imprisoned in 1956 and who were thought to be mistrustful of anything decided without their approval.

On 19 September, in Cairo, a provisional government of the Algerian Republic (GPRA) under the chairmanship of Ferhât Abbâs was launched. The moment was well chosen. Ferhât Abbâs was a naturally moderate leader, of bourgeois background and essentially French education (and married to a woman from Alsace). It was difficult to estimate his personal influence and room for manoeuvre in an organization dominated by combatants who regarded him as a timid bourgeois. But he could not fail to be seen as a "valuable interlocutor" as soon as he enjoyed the collective support of his organization.

That the formation of a rebel Algerian "government" was anathema to many French people was obvious enough. But what was de Gaulle to make of this?

Wasn't there a parallel with his own "rebel government" of 18 June 1940? There is no evidence as to the General's initial reaction to the formation of the GPRA. De Gaulle's second, longer-term, reaction could only be realistic: there was now someone he could talk to. He had one more advantage (on top of all the others): "politicians", not soldiers or terrorists, whom he could talk to. He therefore decided to hold a press conference on 23 October 1958, organized for the first and last time at the Hôtel Matignon. He would make known his intentions concerning contacts with the enemy. The prospects were all the more favourable in that the day before this meeting with the press Ferhât Abbâs had given an interview on British television in which he praised the General and expressed his hope for a political solution to the conflict.

In fact, this episode was to be the first step on the long road that, three and a half years later, was to lead to the Franco-Algerian agreements at Evian, a first step due to a misunderstanding: whereas the FLN leaders thought that General de Gaulle awaited them in Paris for political talks on the future of Algeria, the head of the French government thought that, because the insurrection was in a state of profound lassitude, its leaders wanted above all an end to armed conflict. In short, when General de Gaulle appeared on Thursday 23 October, before three hundred journalists summoned to the reception room of the Hôtel Matignon, many of them thought that a conclusion to the Algerian war was in sight and that what was going to be said would be the opening of a political phase. De Gaulle declared:

> The men of the insurrection have fought courageously. Let the peace of the brave come and I am sure that the hatreds will gradually fade. I said "the peace of the brave". What does that mean? Simply this: that those who have opened fire cease to do so and return, without humiliation, to their families and their work.
>
> Martial wisdom has used for centuries the white flag of the parliamentarians when one wants weapons to fall silent. And I reply, that in that case the combatants would be treated and received honourably. If delegates were appointed to come and settle with authority the end of hostilities, they would have only to address themselves to the Ambassador of France at Tunis or Rabat.[17]

As to the fundamental problem, the form that a new Algeria would take, he described it thus: "Future solutions would be based on the courageous personality of Algeria and its close association with mainland France." The value of a text is affected by the atmosphere surrounding it and the spirit in which it is received. Like J.-J. Servan-Schreiber, I remember the statement as a positive act and hope. According to Pierre Mendès France, there was "this time a chance, a serious opportunity".[18] The left-wing press followed suit, the right-wing press fumed.

The General's entourage were so sure of success that M. Pompidou had decided to set out next day for Tunis with a view to organizing the movement of "delegates", and three rooms had been booked for them at the Hôtel Crillon. But while the advocates of negotiation were beginning to feel hopeful, Jacques Soustelle, the Minister of Information, gave an extremely guarded interpretation of the General's words, while *L'Echo d'Alger* and the pamphlets distributed by the army spoke only of the General's invitation to the rebels to surrender.

It was not until the afternoon of Saturday 25 October that we learnt that, in the eyes of the men of the GPRA, de Gaulle's declaration amounted to a rejection of negotiations, "but that the FLN remained ready to appoint representatives with a view to negotiating a true overall solution of the Algerian problem".[19]

Dumbfounded, the General's colleagues telephoned Colombey on the Saturday evening, fully expecting to trigger off a tornado. They heard a good-humoured voice say: "Right. That isn't very serious. A slight setback on the path to an important negotiation. But they're wrong. In the eyes of the world, they'll look like bloody nuisances."

Negotiations having been aborted, Algeria now found herself faced with legislative elections, on 23 November. What could be expected at a time when insurrection no longer took the form of bloody attacks, but posed enough of a threat to harden the repressive atmosphere?

The aim, as defined by de Gaulle, was a noble one: to bring forward a political class with which it would be possible to work out the future status of Algeria. But was this not to forget that the élite that they were hoping to bring forward already existed? The large majority of it, men like Abbâs or Yazid, had passed over to the FLN, or, like Abderahmane Farès, were holding themselves in reserve. Was de Gaulle pretending to ignore this fact? Did he believe that the FLN was merely a bunch of thugs, Egyptian agents and arms dealers? In instructions given to General Salan, de Gaulle excluded as candidates only those who "participate in terrorist action" and were by that fact "acting illegally", and made it clear that he wanted the spirit of association with France to be expressed.

On 30 November, the elections came and went like a well-oiled military exercise. The FLN made scarcely any attempt to disturb them. Only the advocates of *Algérie française* were elected, from Pierre Lagaillarde to the Bachaga Boualem. Raoul Salan's comment, in his inimitable tone, was: "We are very relaxed and aware that things have settled down after the troubles of 1956 and early 1957." They were to be his last official words as supreme representative of the French government in Algeria.*

In this affair, one might feel more sympathy for the unfortunate General Salan, who had to deal with the perfectly understandable anxiety of the French in Algeria and a disorientated army, if he had not so foolishly overestimated his stature and role. He had navigated through the storm with prudent skill, but having fulfilled his task, he had suddenly begun to see himself as what events had made him appear.

---

*He was replaced in Algiers by two officials: one civilian, Paul Delouvrier, a well-known economist, and one military, General Maurice Challe, an officer of great experience and ability.

CHAPTER SEVENTEEN

Greatness in Perspective

The philosophy inspiring Charles de Gaulle's diplomatic words and actions is simple and strong: all human activity is ordered round the nation, which in turn is shaped by history and geography, armed by the State, held together by common interests, animated by culture and led by a hero. Ideologies, for de Gaulle, were meaningless: forms of professional diplomacy hardly counted at all. Who "negotiated" less and signed fewer treaties than de Gaulle? His foreign policy was merely a long march in which France would be dragged back to the position it once could claim in the pantheon of nations.

The history of Free France had taught de Gaulle that the diplomatic debate was inspired not so much by the ratio of strength as by the ratio of vulnerabilities. The weak could contain the strong, or even force them to reflect, by their potential "nuisance" value. He had certainly shown that he knew how to use this ratio when the opportunity arose: the whole history of relations between de Gaulle and the Americans on the one hand and the Russians on the other rests on it.

But this visionary was a good observer of reality. He had shown himself capable of denouncing the state of the French forces in 1939, calculating realistically the terrible destitution of 1940, and had been vocal in his dealings with Churchill and Roosevelt during the war. He had learnt his lessons the hard way.

These "keys to Gaullist diplomacy" would not be complete if one did not add something that is its essential dimension: the use of public opinion. Secretive in the extreme, de Gaulle could also be intensely public. One reads in the *Mémoires d'espoir*: "As was my wont, I saw fit to apprise the public of my plans." It was a tactic that he was to use often.

At the time he returned to power in 1958, Charles de Gaulle was a man without illusions. He was aware of the poor showing of French industry and the sorry state of its scientific research; he had a very precise idea of the divided, unstable condition of the State that he was setting out to strengthen and restore.

And yet he had decided to put France back in the first class of nations. What did such an ambition rest on? What foundation did he have for his project? The French, perhaps. But there were others to take into account. In the idea that he still had of France, there was a belief that his country was endowed with very specific gifts of which the world could not fail to take account. He was gambling on a whole set of experiences, talents, relations, formulas, which enabled him to "dope" a country weakened by frequent and long trials, and the lack of resources and space that make for greatness today.

Furthermore, not being given to false modesty or excessive self-criticism, when he considered the advantages at France's disposal as she entered the lists, de

Gaulle regarded himself as outstandingly important. He had taken the measure of most of the men of his time. Roosevelt and Stalin had gone; Churchill had been replaced by Eden, then Macmillan, whom he wrongly saw as a pale imitation of the great man, and Eisenhower was leading a quiet life at the White House. Of course, he was yet to discover Adenauer, Khrushchev and Mao. He looked forward to it, but saw nothing to intimidate him. "In this poor world," he wrote in his *Mémoires d'espoir*, "which deserves to be handled gently, we had to advance step by step, acting as circumstances demanded and respecting the susceptibilities of war. I myself had struck many a blow in my time, but never at the pride of a people nor at the dignity of its leaders."[1] This is apparent in one of the first acts of the de Gaulle–Couve–Joxe team: the accords concluded with Hassan II and Habib Bourguiba on 14 and 17 June, which had no other aim than the evacuation of French military forces from Morocco and from Tunisia (except for Bizerte). And, at one stroke, the extremely troubled relations between France and these two countries since their independence in 1956 were made much more healthy. So it was by significant concessions that Charles de Gaulle inaugurated his diplomatic action.

His second significant foreign policy decision was made on 15 June 1958. The Félix Gaillard Cabinet, in March 1958, had signed agreements with the governments of West Germany and Italy whereby these two countries would now have a right to the exchange of information with regard to nuclear research. Whether or not this information might be used for military purposes it was becoming increasingly apparent that this exchange of information could not go ahead without the Soviet Union's agreement. So the French government warned the two friendly capitals that it would have to rescind the March decisions. On 23 June, Paul-Henri Spaak, the NATO Secretary-General, was summoned by de Gaulle. Certainly, the Belgian diplomat was among those most profoundly alarmed by General de Gaulle's return to power: one of the most ardent advocates of European unity, he had not forgotten the furious campaigns led by de Gaulle and his friends against the Common Market. As Secretary-General of the Atlantic Pact, he regarded de Gaulle as a critic of American power and of a defence organization which was essentially under Washington's leadership. What was the old nationalist troublemaker up to now?

At the end of this meeting, Spaak wrote a memorandum in which he noted that de Gaulle had told him that NATO remained essential to the defence of the free world but that the Anglo-Saxon influence was too great and that France did not play the part in it that she should. As for the Common Market, the General declared that if it proved its economic efficiency Paris would be a loyal member of it and that he was in no way against the building up of a united Europe.

On 29 June it was the turn of the British Prime Minister, Harold Macmillan, to climb the stairs of the Hôtel Matignon. De Gaulle had known him for a long time: few men in the world had done more for him than Her Majesty's representative in North Africa in 1943–44. But this meeting did not go entirely smoothly.

1. 1 October 1944: the "Marseillaise" in Normandy. On de Gaulle's left, Pierre Mendès France, Economics Minister, and André Diethelm, War Minister. On the steps, people in regional costume.

2. Strasbourg, December 1944.
From left to right: General de
Lattre, commander of the First
Army, de Gaulle, Churchill.

3. In the Kremlin, the night of
9-10 December 1944. Molotov
signs the Franco-Soviet pact.
Behind Molotov, from left to
right: Stalin, Jean Laloy, diplomat
and interpreter, de Gaulle and
Georges Bidault, Foreign
Minister.

4. De Gaulle's cabinet, 13 November 1945. From left to right: Georges Bidault, Jules Moch, Maurice Thorez, Edmond Michelet, Paul Giaccobi, Vincent Auriol (future President, 1947-54), René Pleven, de Gaulle, Tangu Prigent, Eugène Thomas, Pierre-Henri Teitgen, Francisque Gay, Charles Tillon, François Billoux, Marcel-Paul, Adrien Tixier, Louis Jacquinot, Jacques Soustelle.

5. Leclerc welcomes d'Argenlieu to Saigon, 1 November 1946. From left to right: Philippe Leclerc, Georges Thierry d'Argenlieu, General Gracey.

6. Ho Chi Minh and Jean Sainteny on board a seaplane, within sight of the *Emile-Bertin*, the cruiser on which Admiral d'Argenlieu awaited them in Along Bay, 24 March 1946.

7. La Boisserie, after the building of the hexagonal tower in which de Gaulle wrote his *Mémoires de Guerre*.

8. Eve of his retreat to the Cap d'Antibes, January 1946: de Gaulle, Mme de Gaulle and Pierre de Gaulle, Charles's brother.

9. André Philip, Finance Minister.
10. Jules Moch, Interior Minister.
11. Pierre-Henri Teitgen, Information Minister.
12. Jacques Duclos, co-leader (with Maurice Thorez) of the French Communist Party.

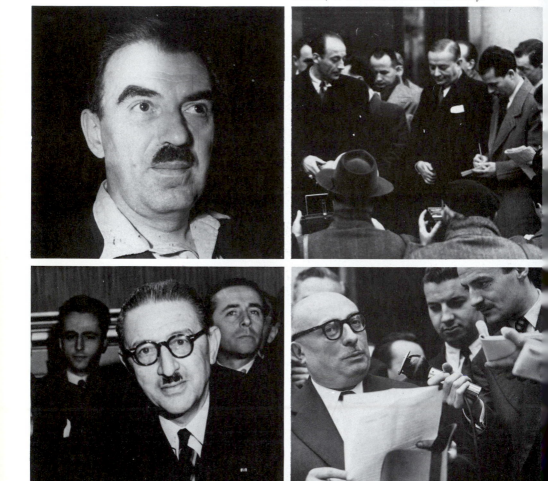

13. René Pleven, de Gaulle's right-hand man in London, became Finance Minister and Prime Minister; Vincent Auriol became Minister of State and President of the Republic.

14. To de Gaulle's right: Charles Tillon, head of the Communist resistance organization, later Air Minister (1945). Behind: Robert Lacoste, Labour Minister, Charles Luizet, prefect of police, Gaston Palewski, de Gaulle's *directeur de cabinet*, General Emile Béthouart, de Gaulle's Chief of General Staff, Captain Claude Guy, aide de camp.

15. The Bayeux speech, 16 June 1946.

16. "Migration of the Storks" by Jean Effel (with Prime Minister Paul Ramadier as a Republican cockerel).

LES BEAUX JOURS

Migration
des
échassiers

(Copyright by France-Soir
and J. Effel)

17. Charles de Gaulle and the American Ambassador Jefferson Caffery in Strasbourg, 6 April 1947, on the eve of the speech announcing the formation of the RPF.

18. RPF rallies: the Vincennes speech

The men of the RPF

19. André Malraux, the RPF head of propaganda.

20. Jacques Soustelle, secretary.

21. Pierre Lefranc was in charge of de Gaulle's journeys through France.

22. Olivier Guichard, *chef de cabinet*.

23. Colonel "Rémy" (Gilbert Renault), a famous Resistance leader.

24. Michel Debré, later Prime Minister during the Fifth Republic.

25. Gaston Palewski, later Minister for Scientific Research during the Fifth Republic.

26. Jacques Chaban-Delmas, several times minister under the Fourth Republic, later Prime Minister during the Fifth Republic (1969-71).

27. De Gaulle at Brazzaville, 25 August 1958. In civilian clothes: Roger Barberot, officer of the Free French Naval Forces, later head of the *"commando noir"* in Algeria, then Ambassador to Uruguay.

28. In Algiers, confronting the centurions. On de Gaulle's right and left, General Edmond Jouhaud, chief of the Air Force in Algeria, and General Raoul Salan, chief of the French Army. Behind them, between de Gaulle and Salon, René Brouillet, de Gaulle's *directeur de cabinet*.

29. Place de la République, 4 September 1958:
a new constitution, but the initials remain the same.

30. On the steps of the Elysée, 8 January 1959.
The Fourth Republic, in morning dress, receives the Fifth, in morning dress.

In the midst of our friendly discussions which touched upon a great many topics, [Macmillan] suddenly declared with great feeling: "The Common Market is the Continental System all over again. Britain cannot accept it. I beg you to give it up. Otherwise, we shall be embarking on a war which will doubtless be economic at first but which runs the risk of gradually spreading into other fields."[2]

I have reproduced the version of what Macmillan said as recorded by de Gaulle in the *Mémoires d'espoir*. It is indeed breathtaking, but nobody denied it.

Questions have often been asked about de Gaulle's sudden conversion to the Common Market. With him, the principle of contradiction explains many things. It is not an exaggeration to suggest that this attempt by the British to exert pressure, the many attempts then being made by the British to drown the European Community in a European Free Trade Association (EFTA) thought up by Reginald Maudling, did much to reconcile de Gaulle with the Europe of the Common Market: if his British neighbours were so very much alarmed by it, it must be of benefit to the Continent.

In any case it was when he was confronted by a campaign launched by London against the Community that the General "broke the spell", as he himself wrote, and made it quite clear that he would accept only an organization with a common external trade agreement and agricultural policy. Unity is never achieved without threat or pressure: this was the signal service paid to the European cause by the excellent Harold Macmillan.

Hardly a day passed, then, without de Gaulle taking some crucial decision in the area of French diplomacy: on 1 July, he wrote to Nikita Khrushchev, who two years earlier had called for a summit to discuss the cessation of nuclear testing. De Gaulle wrote saying that he was in agreement: there should be a summit but it should be restricted to the "four main powers" – France, Britain, the USSR and the USA.[3] This would be a good opportunity for de Gaulle to reappear at the summit of world politics, to take the measure of the new protagonists and to demonstrate his tact, competence and authority, thirteen years after the Yalta Conference from which he had been excluded.

Before this "return" to the world scene materialized de Gaulle received a visit from the American Secretary of State, John Foster Dulles. It was a deeply interesting meeting, because it was the first real Franco-American dialogue since General de Gaulle's return to power.

M. Couve de Murville, who had been the French Ambassador to Washington, knew Dulles and informed the General of the Secretary of State's "legalistic puritanism" and his Manichaeanism, tending to see the world as doomed to a conflict between the powers of "evil" (the Communists) and of "good" (the Americans and their allies). An account of this meeting is offered by André Malraux in his *Antimemoirs*. "I remembered seeing John Foster Dulles, the American Secretary of State, drive through the gates of the Hôtel Matignon in an enormous car, like a Roman proconsul entering some city of the east. The following day, the General said to me: 'Either there is a West, with a common policy towards the rest of the world or else ... But there will be no West.'"[4] The puritan crusader and the machiavellian Catholic were face to face. This is the account of Hervé Alphand, who, as French Ambassador in Washington, took part in the meeting:

> It was an important meeting and Dulles talked to me about it on several different occasions. He had told de Gaulle that the world was divided into two blocs, the good Western liberals and the wicked Communists. He was astonished when de Gaulle replied that he was quite mistaken, that the ideas of nationhood were pre-eminent and that they counted much more than the ideological contradictions between Marxism-Leninism and capitalism. It was the first time that I had heard so fundamental a confrontation of those two theses, with all that they were to involve in the future in our relations with the Soviet Union and China.[5]

Next day, Dulles confided to Spaak: "We shall have a rough time." The account written up by the American party and published by Bernard Ledwidge in *De Gaulle and the Americans*,[6] shows that it was highly interesting on at least three points: nuclear policy, the organization of Western defence and the Middle East.

The contradiction was a deep one. In fact, it was little short of an indictment, drawn up by the General, that touched on almost all the problems that were to form the "trans-Atlantic misunderstandings", to use Henry Kissinger's term. What de Gaulle was raising here was the independence of Europe (even its existence as a diplomatic and military entity), without gaining the slightest approval. However, beyond the very harsh claims that he was making, de Gaulle did express the sympathy that he felt for the United States. This man never forgot that American power was necessary to the freedom of the West and that, however enormous their responsibilities, the Americans assumed them with wisdom and dignity.

If he criticized the ways in which decisions and the organization of the Alliance were reached, de Gaulle never questioned the fundamental interdependence between France and her great allies, whose "strength and liberal spirit" he admired – and hoped to see survive. And he observed that each nation has "its day" and that in 1958 the day belonged to the United States (and the Russians). There was more nostalgia than bitterness in his observation – determined as he was that he would see the return of France's "day" in the future.

Ten days after the confrontation at Matignon, the feverish situation in the Lebanon suddenly spread to the whole of the Middle East: on 14 July 1958, a military junta overthrew a monarchy in Baghdad that was openly pro-Western. It was certainly something for the West to be alarmed about: the event had occurred six months after the setting up of the "United Arab Republic", which had turned Syria into the northern province of Egypt. Was Nasser conquering the whole of the Middle East?

Washington thought so and decided to act by sending 10 000 men to Beirut, while London sent 3000 paratroops to the support of her ally, King Hussein of Jordan: General de Gaulle had not even been warned – though, on 5 July, he had warned Dulles against any initiative of this type, but assured him that France would take part in any necessary action. He could do little more than try to save face by sending the cruiser *De Grasse* to anchor off Beirut. In a meeting of the Council of Ministers, de Gaulle was quick to point out just how far France was being kept out of the decision-making process.

In early August, Chinese Communist artillery bombed the islands of Quemoy and Matsu, which were held by the forces of Chiang Kai-shek. It was an "almost ritual"[7] operation at this time – but one that Washington now took badly enough for Dulles to speak of a military action against continental China: the Seventh Fleet cast anchor in the straits of Formosa, quite close to Quemoy. Were the Nationalists to succeed in involving the United States in an attempt to reconquer Maoist China? It was conceivable, but once again de Gaulle was kept in ignorance of decisions that might lead to a wider conflict.

Certainly that had to be changed: in early September, the General asked his Foreign Minister to draft a note warning the Americans against such practices in the Alliance. However, before committing himself to the questioning of US policy the General had to be sure of his relations with his European counterparts and above all to take the measure of France's relations with the German Federal Republic. No one was unaware, he least of all, that German opinion had reacted unfavourably to his return to power, an event that brought back into the front rank a man whose name was bound up with the defeat of 1945. Konrad Adenauer, the head of the German government, does not seem to have thought differently: though the Chancellor was as suspicious of the Germanophobia attributed to the General as of the reservations that his new neighbour was supposed to entertain with regard to Europe and especially of his supposed anti-Americanism. With a view to clarifying relations between Bonn and Paris, de Gaulle decided to send an invitation to Adenauer to come to France. Better still, he would invite him to his home at Colombey, an honour that had been paid to no other foreign politician.

And so the old Chancellor arrived on the steps of La Boisserie, where, according to François Seydoux, the French Ambassador to Bonn, he arrived "with some emotion. He wanted the General to see him as he was."[8] The account of the conversations on 14 and 15 September provided by General de Gaulle is convincing. He could wish neither to demean a visitor who had won his esteem from the outset, nor build himself up at his expense. And everything that his prodigious memory retained of the exchange reflects very well the personalities, viewpoints and relations of the two men.

To begin with, the Chancellor expressed regret that what had already been achieved between Bonn and Paris still seemed to be of a temporary nature, as if marked by such passing circumstances as "Germany's defeat and France's exhaustion" and that they should now build up "something more durable". The General replied that France was ready to do so – on four conditions: "Acceptance of existing frontiers, good will in relations with the Middle East, complete renunciation of atomic armaments, and unremitting patience as regards reunification".[9]

Where differences of viewpoint arose – on Britain and Europe, on the common agricultural policy, on the functioning of the Atlantic pact – de Gaulle does indicate them. And he quotes some of his visitor's fine and highly significant words: "I am glad to see France resume her rightful place in the world. Allow me to say, however, that the German people, although their spirit is different from that of the French, have a similar need for dignity. Having seen you and listened to you, I feel confident that you are willing to help Germany recover that dignity."[10]

The dinner that followed, to which Mme de Gaulle had invited ministers and ambassadors, is described by François Seydoux: "A strangely peaceful family sort of atmosphere. De Gaulle and Adenauer are friends from a long way back. They like one another; they are pleased, each with the other and each with himself."[11] According to eyewitnesses, Adenauer returned to Bonn "radiant": what he declared to the German press was what he was later to write in his *Memoirs*:

> De Gaulle corresponded in no way to the idea that the press had given of him in recent months: he looked young and his nationalism was much less virulent than is usually thought. He was well informed about world affairs and particularly aware of the great importance of Franco-German relations, not only for the whole of Europe and, therefore, for the rest of the world. My idea of de Gaulle had been quite different from the man I discovered. I was agreeably surprised by his simplicity and naturalness.[12]

From 15 September 1958 onwards, right up to the brilliantly successful visit paid by Adenauer and de Gaulle to one another in 1962, relations between the French and the Germans became ever closer.

The meeting at Colombey was Charles de Gaulle's first great diplomatic success. For a long time, it was to be his only one. But he won it on the crucial ground of Franco-German relations. Can it be thought that this success seemed to him all the greater as it would limit the ability of the British to influence the government in Bonn? He knew perfectly well that he had obtained nothing from Adenauer that would not be at the expense of British wishes. This did not exactly displease him.

But de Gaulle was not a man to wallow in triumph. He had not only put his historical seal on the Franco-German *rapprochement*, but had set off a sort of guerrilla war against American hegemony and the exclusion of France from the atomic club.

On 17 September 1958, two days after Chancellor Adenauer left Colombey, de Gaulle sent the following memorandum to President Eisenhower and to Prime Minister Macmillan.

> Recent events in the Middle East and in the Straits of Formosa* have helped to show that the present organization of the Western alliance no longer fulfills the conditions necessary for security in the free world. The inter-dependence demanded by the risks incurred is not matched by cooperation in decision-making and in the delegation of responsibilities. The French government has been led to draw certain conclusions and to make the following proposals.
>
> 1. The Atlantic Alliance was conceived and its implementation prepared with a view to a possible zone of action that no longer corresponds to current events. With the world being what it is, one can no longer see an organization such as NATO as properly equipped to deal with the tasks in hand,

*The bombing of Quemoy and Matsu and the movements of the American Seventh Fleet.

limited as it is to the security of the North Atlantic, as if everything that occurs, for example, in the Middle East or in Africa were of no immediate and direct interest to Europe, and as if the responsibilities of France did not extend to Africa, the Indian Ocean and to the Pacific, in exactly the same way as those of Great Britain and the United States. Furthermore, the range of action of ships, planes and other weapons makes so narrow a system militarily outdated. It is true that it was originally accepted that atomic armaments would remain the monopoly of the United States for some time, and this might justify Washington's power in making decisions of global importance. But, on this point, too, one must recognize that circumstances have changed and need to be accepted.

2. France can no longer regard NATO, in its present form, therefore, as satisfying the conditions of the security of the free world and, in particular, of her own. It seems necessary to France that a world-wide organization should be created and that it should include the United States, Britain and France. This organization would have, on the one hand, to take common decisions in political questions affecting world security and, on the other hand, to draw up and, if necessary, to implement plans of strategic action, particularly where the use of nuclear weapons is concerned.

3. The French government regards such a security organization as indispensable. As from now it subordinates to it any further development of its present participation in NATO and proposes, if it seemed necessary to achieve this, to invoke the revision procedure of the North Atlantic Treaty in accordance with Article 12.

4. The French government suggests that the questions raised in this note should as soon as possible be made the object of consultations between the United States, Great Britain and France. It proposes that these consultations should take place in Washington and, to begin with, through ambassadors and the permanent representatives.[13]

"I was raising the standard" was how de Gaulle summed up the operation in *Mémoires d'espoir*. Did he really believe that he had been successful, even partially so, after confronting the solid, impenetrable figure of John Foster Dulles?

"No," Maurice Couve de Murville now says. "He acted in this way in order to mark an epoch and to lay the foundations for a long-term reconstruction of the Alliance. But he was under no illusions."[14]

It has often been said or written that the "memorandum" met with no significant answer, and General de Gaulle himself wrote that the recipients answered him "evasively". This is not quite true. An answer was sent to de Gaulle by Eisenhower, a month later, on 20 October. Whatever one may think of the affair, the letter from the American President is both clear and dignified:

A significant development has occurred in NATO over the last two years. In that organization, consultations have gone beyond the limits of the European zone. We have tried to use the NATO Council to inform or consult with our allies on the threat facing the free world in the Far and Middle East. We have also tried to use the Council to develop a common policy with regard to the Soviet bloc. We think that this habit of consultation between the nations belonging to NATO must be extended, but it cannot be made compulsory. I do not think that we can allow ourselves to lose the good relations that are developing between the members of NATO or the bonds that are being forged between them.

We cannot allow ourselves to adopt a system that would give our other allies, or other countries in the free world, the impression that crucial decisions, touching their vital interests, are taken without their participation. As far as NATO is concerned, I must say in all frankness that I foresee very serious problems, both inside and outside that organization, if any attempt is made to alter the North Atlantic Treaty, with a view to extending its range beyond the regions covered by it at present. I recognize that, if it is to live, an association must constantly evolve and find ways of making itself useful, in the face of changing circumstances. I am quite ready to study this aspect of the problem in the appropriate way.

In his book on French diplomacy, Couve de Murville recognizes the difficulty that the Americans probably felt in getting their other allies to accept the idea of NATO. He adds that discussions then took place between France, the United States and Great Britain, continued until the end of Eisenhower's presidency and were resumed when Kennedy took over.[15]

Chancellor Adenauer, who might quite rightly have been alarmed at his new friend's initiative, did not bring the subject up when the General visited his residence at Bad-Kreuznach on 26 November. In Eastern Europe the situation was grave: on 10 November, Khrushchev announced that the USSR was going to question the status of Berlin and, because it regarded the presence of the three Western powers in the former German capital to be without foundation, was going to transfer to the German Democratic Republic all the powers still being exercised there by the Soviet Union. Here they were on the edge of a conflict about essentials: the East–West balance in Europe. In case the Soviet leaders were unclear of the West's position, Dulles and Eisenhower reminded them. Nevertheless, they carried the matter further, on 27 November, by sending a note to the Western powers announcing that Moscow was abrogating the 1945 agreements on Berlin, which ought to become a free, demilitarized city. Offering to open up negotiations on this theme, the Kremlin made it known that, if no agreement had been reached within six months, the USSR and the GDR would settle the matter between themselves.

It was with the Memorandum of 17 September in mind that the talks between the West German and French leaders at Bad-Kreuznach and Dulles's second visit to Paris took place: de Gaulle may have been an awkward partner in time of peace, but he was an ally who could be relied upon in time of danger. This was certainly the prevailing tone of the German press at the time: confronted by the threat from the Kremlin, which would sink West Berlin in the Soviet ocean, it was clear that at least one Westerner would not give in and would refuse unreservedly "to negotiate under threat of an ultimatum".

* * *

So 1958 drew to a close with profound international anxiety for the year to come. As Charles de Gaulle was preparing to enter the Elysée,* the diplomatic record of those first months of Gaullist diplomacy would have been positive – clarification of relations with Washington, strengthening of the links with Bonn, support for the European project, relaxation of tension with several Arab states without putting Franco-Israeli friendship in danger. But then there was the deterioration of Franco-British relations.

The British Prime Minister, Harold Macmillan, had outlined Britain's reluctance to accept continental unification which, according to the eternal precepts of British diplomacy, could only be directed against the United Kingdom. All the efforts of the London government would tend, therefore, if not to destroy that body, at least to try to water it down in a wider entity that could be supervised by the Foreign Office, namely, the European Free Trade Association. London had hoped that de Gaulle's long-standing antipathy to the European Community would play in its favour. But the General had only to glimpse such a manoeuvre on the part of the British Foreign Office to rediscover what a good, strong European he was: and he would be all the more of a European because that particular Europe would be animated by ideas coming from Paris.

Given these underhand attempts at mutual encirclement, the time had come when each side would put its cards on the table. A meeting was arranged in London on 6 November between Reginald Maudling and Selwyn Lloyd on one side, and Couve de Murville on the other. Taking up a clear position against the idea of a free trade area and for a common market, the French minister realized that "We are about to reach the most critical stage in Franco-British relations since June 1940."[16]

Things grew even worse on 15 December, during a final attempt at conciliation at Brussels. The British, who had hoped to bring France round to their idea, with German support, were amazed to see the Germans declare that they were against the Free Trade Area. Macmillan, who had misjudged the importance and depth of the Colombey agreement between de Gaulle and Adenauer, was to write in his diary that Adenauer had betrayed him. This was not so, but de Gaulle did carry more weight, at Bonn, than his predecessors and even, for a time, than Macmillan.

Having become the midwife of this Europe that he had for so long and so bitterly vilified, could de Gaulle have brought about that salubrious operation without cruelly affecting Franco-British relations? However strong the memory of the war may have been and even if one gave more importance to the immense services given to defeated France by the British nation than to the intrigues fomented by the Foreign Office against the position of the old rival, one has to admit that he could not. The European idea of Adenauer and Maudling's more limited idea of union were inevitably going to lead to confrontation, and, since it was the continent that was in question, it was quite normal that the views of the continentals should prevail. Paris triumphed – and showed no mercy.

*Elected President of the Republic on 21 December 1958, he was to be installed at the Elysée on 8 January 1959. (See Chap. 9.)

And yet, even while these negotiations were taking place, Charles de Gaulle was decorating Winston Churchill with the Cross of the Liberation at the Hôtel Matignon. A witness like Pierre Sudreau remembers the brotherly gaze with which the old man was greeted by his wartime companion as he walked towards him. Others thought they saw in it a gleam of commiseration.

CHAPTER EIGHTEEN

A Parliament, a Currency, a Throne...

"I don't have anything to do with electoral matters": he repeated this remark a score of times at this period and, although he had been very active in the campaign for the referendum of September, he was, in October and November, withdrawn and mistrustful. When his supporters created the UNR Guichard remembers how de Gaulle had taken no part in it, yet Guichard adds: "Nevertheless I kept him informed about the details of the operation."[1]

The campaign for the legislative elections was rather dull, and was dominated, just as the referendum had been, by the presence of General de Gaulle. The most common type of slogan was: "A vote for Dupont is a vote for de Gaulle." The polls of 23 and 30 November 1958 were to begin with a cruel defeat of the left – 10 Communist deputies re-elected out of 138,* 44 SFIO out of 88, 23 Radicals out of 56. It was a victory for the right, with the conservatives winning 132 seats, as against their former 95, and the UNR winning no fewer than 196 seats.

And what names there were among those who had lost their seats! Six former Presidents of the Council, including Pierre Mendès France and Edgar Faure; François Mitterrand; the Socialists Defferre, Jules Moch, Pineau; the Communist Duclos; the MRP P.-H. Teitgen; the former President of the National Assembly, Le Troquer. It was nothing short of a massacre. "With 37.5 per cent of the votes," Maurice Duverger wrote at the time, "the right-wing coalition – conservatives and UNR – has won 66 per cent of the seats in mainland France; with a higher figure (38.7 per cent) the centre coalition – SFIO, MRP, Radicals – has attained only 28.8 per cent of the seats. It is rare for elections to distort the national representation to this degree. With his official candidatures, Napoleon III obtained scarcely more effective results."[2]

Despite this marriage of convenience with the old conservatives, whom he hated and whose betrayal in May 1952 he had not forgotten, it was above all a success for Charles de Gaulle. The referendum had turned into a plebiscite: the elections had turned into a referendum. It was not so much men who had been sent to the parliament as 350 "yes" votes echoing the 80 per cent of 28 September. But the General welcomed this victory with mixed feelings: the art of manoeuvre, of which he was the master, is practised more easily on various small groups than on large, coherent parties.

The Republic now had an Assembly; it was now waiting to know who its President and Prime Minister would be. With the presidency, the General kept his intentions shrouded at first, but his decision was announced in a communiqué on

*It has been calculated that in November 1958, the UNR won one seat for 20 000 votes, the MRP one for 40 000, the Socialists one for 50 000, and the Communists one for 360 000.

2 December. Did he ever hesitate as to the choice of post he would take on? The constitutional text makes it quite clear that the government was entrusted with the task of "leading and laying down the policy of the nation" (which is certainly what de Gaulle intended to do) and defines the role of head of State, the President, more vaguely as that of an "arbiter" and "guarantor". Did Charles de Gaulle never think of staying at Matignon, where the day-to-day work was to be done, and leaving a Coty or several of them to idle away their days at the Elysée? The simple answer is "No".

As for the Prime Minister, the head of government, he was to be no longer "President of the Council", but first of the President of the Republic's ministers, and the position was not to remain unoccupied for long. Everything led Charles de Gaulle to promote the Garde des Sceaux, Michel Debré, on account of his untarnished fidelity, his capacity for work, the role that he had played in drawing up the Constitution, his parliamentary experience, his strong position in the UNR and his favourable relations with the army in Algeria. Michel Debré is not a man to criticize the General today, nor to denounce the encroachment of the Elysée on Matignon through the implementation of the President's special powers. But when, referring to his own experience and to later presidencies, it was suggested to him in 1985 that the man in Matignon was, of necessity, an executant above all and rather, to use General de Gaulle's own words, the "head of the administration" than the "head of government", he objected strongly: "The role of Prime Minister was and must be, in the spirit of the constitution, essentially political."[3]

On the responsibilities of the head of state, Article 5 of the Constitution, which Debré took care to write himself, is eloquent: "The President of the Republic watches over the Constitution. He ensures, by his arbitration, the regular functioning of the public powers and the continuity of the State. He is the guarantor of national independence, of the integrity of the territory, of respect for agreements, for the Community and for treaties."

The Prime Minister has to live under the aegis of this figure watching over, arbitrating, guaranteeing. He is not the executive: he is the executor of that decisive power. It is an elusive, delicate relationship, made up of constant improvisation and endless compromises – to the detriment, always, of Matignon.

A perhaps apocryphal, but amusing, story sums up this type of relationship. Soon after he became Prime Minister, Michel Debré was received by the General and set about outlining how he thought the system should work: "*Mon Général*, decisions at a national level are your responsibility. The Prime Minister is in charge of everyday business – the fixing of the price of milk, for example." The General said nothing. Debré went home. The next day, on the radio, he learnt that the price of milk had just been increased.

Whatever their relationship may have been, the General pays unqualified homage to Michel Debré in his *Mémoires d'espoir*. Speaking of the Prime Minister's responsibilities, he writes:

> Michel Debré was the first to assume this cardinal and virtually limitless role under the Fifth Republic. He set his stamp upon it, and it was a powerful and enduring one. Convinced that France needed greatness, and that it was

through the State that greatness was won or lost, he had dedicated himself to public life in the service of the State and France. In this cause, his mind was open to every idea, his feelings were aroused, and often wounded, by every occurrence, his will was equal to every task. Always tense with eagerness to activate, to reform, to put right, he fought without sparing himself and endured without losing heart.[4]

The legend of a de Gaulle disdaining the affairs of everyday government does not stand up to examination. It is true that his gaze rested more naturally upon distant hilltops than on the footpaths in front of him. But he was more in touch with realities than people often believed: no one knew better than he, for example, how much the fierce attachment of the French to their monthly incomes nourished their dreams. In 1945, it is true, his Economics Minister lost an opportunity to smash the inflationary spiral that was to bring the country to ruin over the next thirteen years. But by closely observing the agony of the Fourth Republic, he had come to realize that it had been deeply affected by institutional debility and financial haemorrhages.

When he regained power at the end of May 1958, it was not Capitant, Joxe or Terrenoire whom he asked to become his chief of staff at Matignon, but Georges Pompidou, who had become one of the shrewdest observers of the country's financial crises. Potentially rich, the French economy suffered from two apparently incurable ills: it was undermined by inflation and remained inefficient because of protectionism. In 1958, the budgetary imbalance was disastrous. When de Gaulle's government moved into Matignon, on 3 June 1958, questions were being asked whether the State would be able to pay its bills on 30 June.

The doctor officially appointed to cure the country's ills was the Minister of Finance, Antoine Pinay. General de Gaulle did not think particularly highly of Pinay, who, for him, embodied the failings of the Fourth Republic. But in order to rally the support of the world of money, without which monetary and financial recovery was impossible, no one could serve the purpose better than the man who embodied savers' confidence in the franc.

What could be expected of M. Pinay in the first instance if not the launching of a loan, as he had so successfully done in 1952? He could hardly confound expectations, and the General gave his agreement for the operation, which, linking the two most confidence-boosting names for those with money (de Gaulle and Pinay), could hardly fail, especially since it involved, like the one put through by M. Pinay six years before, considerable tax advantages. The sum of 320 milliard francs was raised in five weeks. It was a great success: the treasury now had sufficient funds for its needs. The State was solvent.

But for the General it was not just a matter of filling gaps. The important thing was to effect a reversal of current trends and to set in train a long-term recovery. De Gaulle wanted an overall plan, with long-term aims, imbued with bold hopes. In financial affairs what he needed was the equivalent of what he was undertaking in institutions, decolonization and international relations. It was not the prudent Pinay, but the radical-thinking liberal economist, Jacques Rueff, who presented the General with the hoped-for "master plan".

His argument was a strong one. The French evil was inflation. In order to rebalance the accounts, inflation had to be brought under control. To do this, an attack had to be made on its two major sources: public finances (by limiting the finance available to the Treasury to money that could be raised on the financial market) and the money supply (by limiting the preferential discount given by the Bank of France on medium-term loans to industry and housing). Rueff concluded: "The key to this policy is the restoration of the franc."[5] And he set about this task at the head of a team of experts that brought together economists of the most conservative views, such as C.-J. Gignoux, and the most *dirigiste* (interventionist) views, such as Jean-Marcel Jeanneney* and Raoul de Vitry, chairman of Péchiney and the archetype of the big French industrialist.

On 8 November, de Gaulle, flanked by Georges Pompidou, received Rueff, in the presence of Pinay and the Governor of the Bank of France. Pinay raised strong objections to the drastic nature of the project: he demanded modifications both in the fiscal and the monetary fields. But de Gaulle, who considered that one should not "recoil before any measure, however unpopular it may be, in order to balance the public finances",[6] obviously declared in favour of the plan. "It was the coherence and fervour of the plan as well as its daring and ambition that won me over."[7]

In the Rueff Plan (which was later to be associated, quite wrongly, with the name of M. Pinay**), three decisions were crucial: heavy devaluation of the franc, an increase in taxation, and the liberalization of imports and exports. The devaluation, by 17.45 per cent, was complemented by a measure intended to catch people's imagination. It was entirely Gaullist in style: the establishment of a "heavy franc", the equivalent of 100 1958 francs, "whose losses," de Gaulle writes in *Mémoires d'espoir*, "were a reflection of our national ordeals". Thus, according to de Gaulle, "the venerable French franc" would win back "something of its former substance".[8] Side by side with this, a set of measures was proposed to remedy the disordered state of the public finances.

The second aspect of the plan concerned taxation. One of the main aims was to reduce the budgetary deficit in a radical way. Rueff had proposed that it should be reduced from 1200 to 488 milliard francs. Since de Gaulle had himself approved, on 20 November, a steep increase in military expenditure, as a result of the war in Algeria and the cost of nuclear research, a compromise figure of 587 milliard had to be agreed. Nevertheless, it was a considerable effort, which required 300 milliard francs from new taxes and close on 400 milliard francs in expenditure cuts. Hence the abolition of many social and agricultural grants and the raising of taxes (on wine, spirits and tobacco), and of certain utilities (gas, electricity, transport, coal, postal services). Every departmental budget was affected, except those for housing, education, and, of course, the armed forces.

But it was the third aspect of the plan that was perhaps the most important and the one in which Jacques Rueff's, and Charles de Gaulle's, boldness is shown to best effect: the liberalization of imports and exports that was to enable France to

---

*Friend and future minister of Michel Debré, then of Couve de Murville.
**Who, in the event of failure, would have been held responsible for it.

keep her word concerning the Common Market. (The Pflimlin government had let it be known to its European partners, in May, that France would not be ready to enter into competition on 1 January 1959, as laid down by the treaty.)

The decision of December 1958 made France, for so long restricted by protectionism, subject to the healthy laws of international competition. This involved nothing less than the freeing of 90 per cent of currency transactions in the EEC zone and the immediate reduction by close on 10 per cent of customs tariffs with the five partners of the Treaty of Rome.

The liberalization adopted on the recommendation of the Rueff Committee would goad French producers into action. Thus the 1958 plan brought together three bodies of thought that twelve years of history had made to look contradictory or discordant: those of Jean Monnet, Jacques Rueff and Charles de Gaulle.

The plan did, like all plans, create losers, above all the wage-earners and small farmers. During one of the many exchanges of views that he had about this time with the General, Roger Goetze, financial adviser to the head of government,* once remarked to the General: "The French will squeal." "So what?" de Gaulle retorted.[9]

It was a striking reversal of roles thirteen years after the debates of 1945 about the Mendès France plan, of which Goetze had been one of the promoters. At that time the General had recoiled before inflicting new ordeals on a French people that had just emerged from war, whereas in 1958 he considered that the rise in the standard of living made a certain dose of austerity bearable.

The Socialists, five of whom were members of the government, followed the example of their leader, Guy Mollet, and announced their resignation. De Gaulle reacted with the following letter:

My dear Guy Mollet,

One question is above everything: to put the Republic back in place. It will be done on 8 January,** in liberty, in democracy, with the overwhelming approval of the people.

You entered my government in order to form it with me. You cannot, you must not, leave me, just as we are about to reach our goal. It is a matter of principle. The budget is a matter of circumstance. On 8 January, with the parliamentary regime established, you will of course be free.

Guy Mollet was a man of duty as well as a man of party. He remained in the Council, flanked by his friends.***

In the evening of Sunday 28 December, General de Gaulle put the final touches to the operation that had made him the central figure of a great economic battle. He appeared on the television screens for the first time as the elected holder of the supreme office, "as France's guide and as head of the Republican State", commit-

---

*And himself an ardent advocate of the plan. (trs.)
**The day on which de Gaulle, having been elected Head of State on 21 December, would be installed at the Elysée.
***Apart from André Boulloche, who preferred to stand down. (trs.)

ting himself, profoundly and solemnly, as solely responsible for the rigorous measures that had just been decided on:

> Our country will feel itself sorely tried, but the reconstruction aimed at is such that it will compensate for all else. Without this effort and these sacrifices, we would remain a country in the rearguard, perpetually oscillating between crisis and mediocrity. On the other hand, if we succeed, what a leap forward on the road that leads to the heights![10]

The statement that opened up to Charles de Gaulle the gates of the Elysée was published on 2 December. The election would take place on 21 December 1958. In his *Mémoires*, the General stresses how unusual this situation was for him: "Full though my public career had been, this was the first time that I had stood for election."[11]

In the summer, the members of the Constituent Assembly had chosen (Article 6 of the Constitution) to form an electoral college comprised of members of the Parliament, the general councils and the assemblies of the overseas territories, and the elected representatives of municipal councils and of overseas administrative bodies – in all, some 80 000 previously elected individuals. What did they represent? Certainly more rural societies than urban groups, which was to lead Georges Vedel to write wittily that the new President would be "elected by rye and chestnut".*

In any case, the Fifth Republic avoided the misfortune of a single candidature. No one was in any doubt as to the outcome of the ballot. Nevertheless, the opposition from the left did offer a challenge. The Communists wanted to enter the competition by putting up Georges Marrane, a senator for the Seine, a former member of the Resistance, who had welcomed General de Gaulle to the Hôtel de Ville on 25 August 1944 in the name of the capital's Liberation Committee. The non-Communist left (the Union des forces démocratiques, founded by Daniel Mayer) chose, after a good deal of hesitation, to be represented by Albert Chatelet.

Curiously enough, confronted by these two quite uncharismatic left-wing candidates, the two truly anti-Gaullist tendencies, on the right, declined to present a candidate. The Vichyist tendency, which did not lack support in the electoral body and whose strength had just been demonstrated by the success of a large number of Independents (the conservatives) on 30 November, did not try their luck. The Algiers extremists, who, since the removal of Salan, no longer had any illusions as to the General's intentions, did not believe that it was the right moment to express their indignation.

From the historical point of view, three tendencies in the Resistance were represented in the Presidential elections, and from the point of view of the crucial political question of the time the election was between three advocates of Algerian emancipation. On 21 December 1958 General de Gaulle was elected with 78.5 per cent of the votes cast** – which confirmed the results of the referendum three

---

*Two typical products of the poorer regions. (trs.)
**The Communist receiving 13 per cent and Albert Chatelet 8.5 per cent.

months earlier. For seven whole days de Gaulle said nothing. And when he did speak it was not so much to thank the French people for the mandate that it had given him as to announce and comment upon the "Rueff Plan". Clearly de Gaulle felt so legitimately in power, so deeply involved with the work to be done, that the verdict of 21 December seemed little more than a confirmation.

A few sentences, all the same, are significant:

> The national task that has devolved on me for the last eighteen years has just been endorsed by this result. As France's guide and as head of the Republican State, I shall exercise supreme authority in all the breadth it now carries and in the new spirit that has invested me with it. The call that has been addressed to me by the French people expresses their instinct for survival. They have entrusted me with their leadership because they want to be shown the path, not indeed towards idle comfort but towards endeavour and renewal.[12]

The time had come for observers, specialists, political commentators to ask themselves about the nature of this regime that had sprung up the previous spring. And since the French can only try to see a situation clearly by examining history and can only offer a retrospective definition, it will be as well to quote some of those historical references.

In an article published in November 1958 in the magazine *Preuves*, Raymond Aron, who had aroused the General's irritation fifteen years before in London by comparing him in the review *France Libre* with the Bonapartes, commented on the results of the referendum by declaring that de Gaulle had ensured for himself a Roman-style dictatorship, "a power both absolute and limited". Returning to his earlier reflections, Aron wrote:

> The beneficiary of the Bonapartist context (the climate of national crisis, the discredit of the parliament, the popularity of one man), whether he is called Louis-Napoléon, Boulanger, Pétain or de Gaulle, whether he be an adventurer, a trifler, an old man or an authentically great man, must possess a particular virtue: he must be able to transcend the quarrels of the French people, be both on the right and on the left, unite the France of before 1789 with the France of after 1789.[13]

What do Louis-Napoléon, Boulanger, Pétain and Charles de Gaulle have in common? What have December 1851 and May 1958, the France of June 1940 and that of September 1958 in common? The best way of understanding the system adopted by the French in 1958 is to see it in this historical light, but to see its radical, almost savage originality.

A personal sovereign, respectful of collective sovereignty, de Gaulle had to create a system in which there would be no compulsion, no fetters and, in short, no intermediaries. Was this authoritarianism? His knowledge of politics, his familiarity with Montesquieu, the closely related aberrations that lay at the origin of his prodigious personal career compelled him to employ self-limitation, to replace traditional constraints ("power stops power") with a "restraint" that would find few exceptions.

Thus, as supreme guide, freed of intermediaries and other feudalities (those of money, trade unionism, the press and the parties), Charles de Gaulle gave himself the mission to release France from the constraints that still dogged her steps and impeded her resurrection. He would be free to act in order to make France free. The proud mission lay before him. This is the essence of Gaullism.

But what was Charles de Gaulle? Who was this man, in relation to the author of *Le Fil de l'épée*, to "Colonel Motor", to the rebel of 1940, to the intransigent visitor of Roosevelt and Stalin, to the man of "iron contempt" in late 1946 and even to the moody chairman of the RPF?

All those who were close to him in 1958 say that he was a changed man. He was no longer the man who had shut himself up at Marly in January 1946 and then at Colombey in 1955. I might sum up the convergent evidence in these words of François Goguel: "Distance from power had transformed his character. All his former aggressive defensiveness had given way to an open sociability." More rounded, more convivial, and more anxious to be informed than before, more tolerant of objections, in search of opinion and expertise, more in tune with the times, less in a hurry to make up his mind, accessible to the exchange of ideas, seeking not only to shine, but also to find illumination, this man seemed in 1958 to have joined the human race.

There were a few more gestures to perform. On 8 January 1959, at noon, on the steps of the Elysée between a double row of guards wearing copper helmets, two men faced each other. Coming down the steps was an old gentleman with a tired smile: René Coty. Mounting them, very straight, another gentleman, hand outstretched: Charles de Gaulle. There they met in the presence of René Cassin, an old companion from London, now Vice-President of the Council of State, who declared the results of the ballot of 21 December, not without allowing himself to give a little, very discreet advice:

> A true democracy requires not only that those who hold authority accept comparable responsibilities, but also that the primacy of law be placed in the safe keeping of justice ... Those who know how in the most crucial moments you have performed the boldest actions, while respecting both institutions and promises given, have confidence that under your seven-year term the Republic will not be content to continue and to prosper with dynamism and rejuvenated structures, but that it will retain France's human face, haloed with a noble prestige that has won it the affection of peoples and especially of that of our brother member states of the Community.[14]

De Gaulle, his face waxier than ever, wearing round his neck the solemn collar of Grand Master of the Order of the Légion d'honneur, with which he had been decorated by the Chancellor of the Order, his old friend Georges Catroux, received this unfurling of honours with stoical jubilation.

René Coty said only a few, but well chosen words: "The first of the French is now the first in France."[15] De Gaulle was less laconic: "The national interest in the Nation, the common interest in the Community, that is what I have the duty to represent now as yesterday, in any case to make it prevail and even, if public safety requires it, to impose it."[16]

At 2.30 p.m., the two "presidents" ascended a tricolour-decorated Champs-Elysée side by side and, under the Arc de Triomphe, paid homage to the Unknown Soldier.

Protocol dictated that after the laying of the sheaf of corn, a few salutes and the *Marseillaise*, the new President would lead the old one to his car, and that Coty would then drive back down the Champs-Elysées alone. But the rites were no sooner carried out, under the eyes of the republican guards and eminent citizens, than General de Gaulle plunged into the crowd calling out, "Au revoir, Monsieur Coty!", which the former President regarded as somewhat curt, if not cavalier. Was this a premeditated gesture on the part of the General, who wanted to show, however harsh it may have seemed, that he had no predecessor and had received from M. Coty no "power", for, since May, the former President had possessed none?[17] It would seem to be the most logical interpretation.

This time Charles de Gaulle did not descend the Champs-Elysées on foot. Protocol forbade it. A car awaited him. Custom had it that the head of State was flanked by his principal colleague. And who was that to be? Debré was not to be officially appointed Prime Minister until the next day. Then Chaban-Delmas, President of the Chamber? Or Monnerville, President of the Senate, officially the second figure in the State and who, in May, had certainly helped René Coty avoid the worst? Or de Courcel, the earliest companion? No: the General made a sign to Georges Pompidou, who got in and sat beside him, for the few minutes of the journey from the Etoile to the Elysée. Yet Pompidou was no longer anything more than his former cabinet secretary at Matignon, who had refused to follow him to the Elysée and had already joined the Rothschild Bank.

Why this surprising gesture? It was a reward for services rendered. For six months, the former French literature teacher had been an incomparable chief of general staff to the head of government, coordinating the work on the constitution, bringing vigour to the administration, directing the great operation of financial recovery and convincing the General of its need. In short, he had been irreplaceable – and he was to become so again.

And so, at 5 p.m. on 8 January 1959, the General was at the Elysée:

I heard all the doors of the palace closing behind me. But at the same time I saw the prospect of a great undertaking open up before me. True, by contrast with the task which had fallen to me eighteen years earlier, my mission would be devoid of the stirring imperatives of an heroic period. The peoples of the world, and ours more than most, no longer felt the need to rise above themselves which danger enjoined upon them. In short, it was in a time which on all sides was drawn towards mediocrity that I must bid for greatness.[18]

IV

THE BREAK

CHAPTER NINETEEN

The "King's House"

Although haunted by his age, it was as a sovereign in full command of his powers that de Gaulle entered the Elysée in January 1959.

Was there ever a place so ill-fitting to the style of man who now resided there? This man, who had always chosen the "noble" spaces of the Left Bank bound by the Invalides, the Ecole Militaire, Saint-François-Xavier and the Val-de-Grâce – those districts of pen and sword where his family had brought him up, where he had studied, practised his profession, haunted places sanctified by history, exercised power, from the Rue Saint-Dominique to the Rue de Varenne; that heroic, abstract Paris where people write, administer, pray, draw up war plans, bury national heroes and where, when victory came, he had set up house – this man was now thrown into the district of jewellers, tailors and restaurants.

Were it not for the incurably bourgeois appearance of his immediate environment, General de Gaulle, who took little note of such things, would have got used to it. It has been said that he was unaffected by bad weather, rather indifferent to interior decor, unconcerned about his comfort, ignorant of the various styles of objets d'art and antique furniture, and was attached only to memories – provided they were associated with dear or admired people, or his own history.

But he took great care in choosing his own office. His colleagues had suggested that he take the huge corner room known as the *chambre du roi* which looked out on to the rose garden and the Rue de l'Elysée, and from which there was direct access to the private apartments – the largest and most comfortable.* He regarded as more solemn, and therefore more suitable to its function, the central room, known as the *Salon Doré*, which, in his *Mémoires*, he calls the *pièce capitale*.

The Louis XV style blended fairly well with those of the First and Second Empires. On the ceiling, nymphs from the Pompadour period capered about, and over the fireplace were scantily dressed muses of the Eugénie period. On one wall, there was a scene depicting Don Quixote, which one might say was the only thing to accord with the style of the occupant were it not that a model of a monument by Bourdelle, dedicated to the Liberation, and a globe given the General by his closest colleagues, had been placed next to it. It was a fine, if rather conventional room, hesitating between the frivolous and the pompous, lacking true grandeur or elegance, but well lit by the three windows looking out over the gardens.

The door in front of the President's desk led to a room occupied by the aides-de-camp, through which passed all visitors, including, on Wednesday mornings,

*Where Valéry Giscard d'Estaing chose to work, whereas Georges Pompidou and François Mitterrand decided to occupy the same room as de Gaulle.

the ministers expected in the Council Chamber, which was next to it. On the other side of the President's office was that of the Secretary-General and then that of the *directeur de cabinet* which the head of State could reach only through a narrow passage-way in which there was no room for two people to pass: visitors to Geoffroy de Courcel and René Brouillet, faced with the giant feeling his way through the half-light, sometimes had to beat a retreat.

In that Elysée, caught between the shops of the Rue du Faubourg and the Champs-Elysées and where a third of the space was devoted to receptions, from the *Salon d'Argent* to the *Salon Murat* and the *Salle des Fêtes*, there was not enough space left for the colleagues of a head of State who had also taken over the central responsibilities of government. The staff consisted of forty-five individuals, as opposed to the twelve that had previously worked for Presidents Auriol and Coty. As a result, the intensity of their activities and responsibilities grew, on those premises, in inverse ratio to the space occupied.

First to be there were the most senior of "Gaullists", Geoffroy de Courcel, promoted Secretary-General, René Brouillet, *directeur de cabinet*, and the technical advisers, Guichard, Lefranc, Foccart: a sort of academy of Free France, the Resistance and the RPF. And, gradually, one was to see the substitution of a team derived half from Carlton Gardens, and half from the Rue de Solférino, with a General Staff trained, like those of most French public men, by the Council of State, the Ecole Normale Supérieure, the Cour des Comptes, and the Quai d'Orsay. Administration was gaining ground over history.

The General expected three things of the men he asked to join him: that they were "national" (a term he never defined, but which apparently excluded any adhesion to notions such as European or Atlantic supranationality and any allegiance to a "foreign party", a reference to the PCF); that they were capable of "transparency" (that is to say they were unlikely to be indiscreet or to make pronouncements in public that differed from the General's views); lastly, that they be of good will. But, however "transparent" and unreservedly devoted to public service thus conceived, the President's men nevertheless left their individual mark, whether their responsibilities lay, in the General's words, with the "State" or with the "nation": a distinction drawn between the Secretariat-General, the hinge linking de Gaulle with the government and the civil service as a whole, and the Cabinet (private office), which was entrusted with relations with the political parties, the trade unions, the press and public opinion.

Geoffroy de Courcel was called to head the Secretariat-General in early 1959, not so much because Georges Pompidou had turned down the offer but because de Gaulle had benefited from de Courcel's competence and legendary discretion for over twenty years. From January 1959 to February 1962, when he retired for reasons of health, de Courcel's mission was almost constantly focused on the settlement of the Algerian question and the General had shared his views on the subject with him since 1955.

The team that de Courcel gathered round him consisted of four advisers. For diplomatic affairs, J.-M. Boegner, who had held similar responsibilities at Matignon since June 1958 and was soon to give way to Pierre Maillard; for economic and financial matters, André de Lattre; for questions of education and science, Pierre Lelong; for legal matters, Bernard Tricot, who had previously been René Brouillet's assistant in charge of Algerian affairs.

René Brouillet became *directeur de cabinet*. Since autumn 1945, he had been close to the General, even though he had kept his distance from the RPF. Although he could not claim Geoffroy de Courcel's length of service, he possessed the ability to handle men with tact, not the least quality required in pursuing the affairs of the often inconsiderate sovereign. Thanks to this, the iron fist of Gaullism was frequently concealed beneath his velvet glove.

Brouillet was assisted notably by Pierre Lefranc, who for many long years had been given many different, often unrewarding, tasks at the General's side. Among other things, he was put in charge of relations with political organizations and the audio-visual media, in parallel with Olivier Guichard, who joined the Secretariat-General. Xavier de Beaulaincourt was an unchanging private secretary; Raymond Labelle assisted M. Brouillet, as did Xavier de Lignac; Jean Chauveau was put in charge of press relations, soon to be followed by two diplomats of great worth, Gilbert Pérol and Pierre-Louis Blanc. The first devoted a remarkable article to the question in the review *Espoir*, where he wrote: "For the General, I did not exist as a press officer. I was just one of the elements of that gigantic misunderstanding that, as long as he was in power, and perhaps throughout his life, the General's relations with the press represented. Those relations were fundamentally bad, based as they were on mutual misunderstanding and irritation." But, Pérol adds, "nothing was more important to him than reading the newspapers and magazines – the French press, from Paris and the provinces, but also certain foreign papers, British, American, German – and above all, the mark of the press man, dailies. He loved the smell of fresh ink and paper, and hated anonymous press summaries, which watered everything down."[1]

The General read *Le Monde* from beginning to end. But he did not care for that newspaper, to say the least, regarding it as not "national". Gilbert Pérol found him one day correcting an article on the front page of *Le Monde*, leaving a zig-zag of corrections: those people were not even capable of writing correct French![2]

There were three other essential structures in de Gaulle's Elysée: the Secretariat-General for African and Madagascan Affairs, which was first held by Raymond Janot, the artisan of the 1958 Constitution and, after his departure for television, Jacques Foccart – who enlarged his responsibilities to include certain aspects of "information"; the head of State's private General Staff, headed first by General Guy de Beaufort, then by his colleague Jean Olié; and the Aides-de-Camp (representing army, navy and airforce), from Bonneval to Flohic and from d'Escrienne to Desgrées du Loû, the "ultimate guards".

It was outside the Elysée, during outings and trips, that the four celebrated "gorillas", Comiti, Tessier, Djouder and Auvray, originally appointed by Dominique Ponchardier to defend the President, came into play. Lefranc persuaded the official security services to allow this iron guard to be gradually integrated into an official security framework. It was well known, he writes, "that none of them would hesitate to throw himself on a grenade or put himself between any weapon and the General".[3]

General de Gaulle usually got up at about 7.30 a.m. After a very light breakfast of tea and *biscottes* (a kind of rusk), he spent about an hour reading the daily newspapers. He got to his office at about 9.30, where, on the right-hand side of his desk, he found a summary of the morning's press, diplomatic telegrams, documents relating to the next Council of Ministers, notes on his next visitors. All these things would soon bear comments in his hand for the eyes of the Prime Minister and Secretary-General.

Apart from Wednesdays, when the Council of Ministers met, he received the Prime Minister twice a week in the late morning, the Foreign Minister and the Minister for the Armed Forces at least once and sometimes twice a week, and the Finance Minister almost as often. Most weeks he chaired an inter-ministerial meeting, often devoted to Algeria.

At 1 p.m., three times a week, he received guests. His formula, as to the number of places round the table, was "the more Graces, the fewer Muses". Six or seven, not including the hosts, was a number that made it possible, without having to raise one's voice, to have a single conversation, which the General kept up with a pleasant banality, occasionally slipping in a thread of biting humour.

Two afternoons a week were devoted to solitary work: the study of files or the writing of speeches. Another two were spent giving audiences, carefully vetted by his private office. Every day, from 6 p.m., the General received in turn the four key men of his "household" – the Secretary-General, the *directeur de cabinet*, the Secretary-General of African and Madagascan Affairs, and the head of his private staff. Shortly before 8 o'clock, through the narrow passageway skirting the former *chambre du roi*, he hurried to the *salon jaune* where the television and the newspapers awaited him, a daily event which he missed only on days when he was receiving visitors.

He himself has suggested how his evenings were spent better than anyone else could describe them: "The time – all too short – not taken up by the exercise of my functions I spent quietly alone with my wife. In the evenings, television and occasionally the cinema brought our contemporaries before our eyes instead of the other way round."[4] He was very fond of television. With unflagging interest he would watch the same Western two or three times and the James Bond films – Steve McQueen was also a favourite of the de Gaulles.

Charles de Gaulle read a great deal. Although he was sometimes content to skim certain books that had been sent to him, most authors were rewarded by handwritten thanks.

De Gaulle's punctuality derived not only from his military training and concern for efficiency. There was a touch of fanaticism about it. "He was 'trapped' in time like a mammoth in ice," writes Claude Dulong.

But he had moments of idleness that surprised everybody. Sometimes he was seen *doing nothing*. He might be sitting on a chair or standing behind his desk, perfectly erect and motionless, his hands placed in front of him, flat on the wood. A megalith. In those moments, he was reminiscent of a Henry Moore statue, particularly one of them, *The King*. He had to be in the grip of some torment to pace up and down his office with long, stiff, slightly swaying steps, his hands behind his back, pausing in front of one of the windows to turn his eyes on the rather small garden.[5]

The high point of the week, of course, was the Council of Ministers. The General himself chose the venue: Vincent Auriol's former dining-room. The ministers, who arrived at the Elysée at about 9.45 a.m., waited for the opening of the meeting, then sat down – twenty-five on average, tightly packed round the great, green-draped oval table.

At 10 a.m., the President of the Republic made his entrance, followed by the Prime Minister. The General shook hands round the table: "*Cher ami, Cher ami.*" The head of government sat opposite him, the ministers of State – André Malraux on his right – on either side of him. The two secretaries-general, Courcel and Belin, sitting at two small tables, took notes of the discussions, of which they would keep only the decisions taken.

It has been said repeatedly that, under de Gaulle, "nobody said anything" during Council meetings. In his *Mémoires*, the General writes: "Anyone may ask to speak. Permission is always given." Of course, but who dared "speak up" before that monumental personage except on matters specifically concerned with his own ministerial field? Apart from a few youthful dare-devils, like Robert Buron and Pierre Sudreau, and a few intrepid individuals like Jean-Marcel Jeanneney, few dared to do so. Pierre Messmer remembers only three Council meetings (in nine years) that gave rise to genuine discussions, to heated exchanges in which the General's predominance did not put an obstacle in the way of free debate: on Algeria in 1961, after the *putsch* of the generals; on de Gaulle's election victory in September 1962; and, in 1968, on the devaluation of the franc, in which advocates and opponents (led by J.-M. Jeanneney) clashed over a measure that de Gaulle disapproved of, while allowing the arguments to be fought out around him. He liked members of his cabinet "to express an opinion".[6]

In any case, the 1959 government was not lacking in flair. The Prime Minister was Michel Debré. Most of those close to the General testify that nobody in the "household" imagined that the first holder of that hybrid and perilous responsibility could be anybody other than he. Indeed he had been asked by the General to hold himself in readiness for the post as early as November 1958. The founder of the Ecole Nationale d'Administration,* an uncompromising lawyer, an architect of the Constitution, Debré was of all Frenchmen the most passionately devoted to public service and the most capable of extracting from a file the data for a decision.

More will be said about Charles de Gaulle and Michel Debré, harnessed as they were to the Algerian task, but harnessed like the two horses in the torture, pulling one way (*Algérie algérienne!*) and the other (*Algérie française!*) – the General determined to have done with the Prime Minister's determination not to give in. It was a battle almost as fabulous as those earlier ones: Pétain and de Gaulle, de Gaulle and Churchill.

As for his relations with the government, de Gaulle's own words in the *Mémoires d'espoir* say all:

*A new *grand école* or Paris graduate school, devoted to management studies. (trs.)

True, there was a government which "decides the policy of the nation". But everyone knew and expected that it would proceed from my choice and would act only with my blessing. My relationships with my government were thus continuous and extensive. Nevertheless, its role was not usurped by mine. The conduct of the administration was left entirely to the ministers and I never gave orders to officials over their heads... Any member of the government, when he sent me a report, was sure that I would read it, and when he asked for an audience was certain that I would receive him. In short, I kept myself at a distance but by no means in an ivory tower.[7]

It goes without saying, of course, that the Master of the Elysée could not expect of his government the cohesion, discretion and self-abnegation that were the rules of his "household", especially as he did not ignore the need for political balance, the ideological spectrum remaining quite wide, from the moderate left to the militant right, from Boulloche to Soustelle, from Pinay to Buron.

If the Council of Ministers was the big moment of the week, it was the press conference, twice a year, that turned the cameras on to Charles de Gaulle, his "household" and his government. The best description of the General-actor is that of Gilbert Pérol:

Before walking on, there was a long meditation in his office. For days, for weeks almost, working on a text that would then be delivered without hesitation, not so much because it had been learnt by heart but because it had sunk into its author by a long labour with the pen. In fact, the General was more capable than most of playing the game of the entirely improvised dialogue and his art of repartee, his sudden lashings out, his actor's inspirations came over marvellously in such a situation. But, when invested with the supreme responsibility, regarding himself, literally, as "France speaking", he refrained from improvisation.

I waited for the General alone in the gallery that, from behind, led to the still empty platform on which all eyes were turned. That heavy outline seemed to me to be even more than usually impressive at such moments; in a pink file that he held in his hand were the notes that he would not consult and which he would give me afterwards. An officer of the republican guard drew the curtain, revealing on the right the members of the government, the Prime Minister at their head, and, on the left, representatives of the state, civil and military; opposite, the huge crowd of journalists. The General looked round the room, without seeing anything, because of the lights turned on him. The rite was beginning. The long monologue lasted for an hour and a half, sometimes for an hour and three quarters, during which I was haunted by the idea of a possible pause, a "crack-up", since I knew how exhausting the performance was for him. And it ended, as it had begun, in the General's office, alone. He called for me and asked me always the same ritual question: "Well, what did you think of it?" I got out of it as best I could, under the General's amused eye, and, as always, I spoke with the frankness that he expected of me. Indeed at that moment, relieved and at peace like a woman who has just given birth, he tended to be indulgent.

He could show indulgence to his confidant, but to his colleagues, adversaries, fellow-citizens or foreigners, he offered words to men who could not answer back.

Assured as he was of his own legitimacy, he also needed to revive that legitimacy by contact with the people, through provincial tours or visits abroad (which were sometimes the guarantee of his authority for rebels at home). From Epinal to Rouen, from Tananarive to Mexico City, when the ritual gestures had been performed, the speeches made, the masses said, one always came back to the essential thing – what Pierre Viansson-Ponté has called the *bain de foule*, the act of bathing in the crowd,

> the moment when the General found himself in contact with the population. One would see him leave the platoon of officials, push aside the police and detectives and rush into the mass of people like a rugby player in the middle of a loose scrum. To say that he mingled with the crowd would be an understatement: he plunged into it, he wallowed in it, he was literally dissolved in it. He stood out not so much because of his height but because of the movement of which he was the centre. He put on this show for the inhabitants of London, Milan, Algiers and Dakar, as well as Lille or Perpignan. We would stop in the street where he would pass Algerians carrying retractable knives, activists armed with loaded revolvers and even madmen carrying hypodermic needles. None of this mattered to him: he led a charmed life, believed in it and needed contact with the crowd as an ever renewed demonstration of his invulnerability, as proof of his ascendancy, like a bathe in the Fountain of Youth.[7]

On television, de Gaulle had the eyes of an elephant: full of cunning and rancour, enormous wisdom and cold anger; the face, which age had ceased to line, but which it now chiselled in planes, like the summit of some old mountain or Rodin's Balzac, made pink by the weather, twisted by invective, rounded when called upon to be paternal and joking. Then there were the forearms, which he thrust forward, like tanks over the slopes of Abbeville.

Before the cameras, the people that looked at him, dazzled and irritated, this great solitary man gave himself up to his favourite alchemy: he replaced facts by their representation, things by the ideas that he wanted to offer of them, he scratched about in history for raw material for his history; he seized on the real, making it give rise to his dream, with such talent, such determination and such contempt that he turned that dream into a sort of reality.[8] It was not only General de Gaulle's good fortune that the arrival of television coincided exactly in France with his – second – arrival. It was also that his astonishing oratorical talent suited so perfectly – and in so unexpected a way – this incomparable means of communication.

CHAPTER TWENTY

"To Walk or to Die?"

General de Gaulle's views on Algeria have been called ambiguous, complex, devious, contradictory. But though he twisted and turned, there is at least one point on which he always spoke with the utmost clarity: the need for the army to win the war prior to any discussion of the fundamental problem. For de Gaulle, whatever the destiny of Algeria might be, it could not be built on a French defeat. Only when the victory had been won would the victors hold out their hands. He said it all in a conversation with Colonel de Boissieu on 4 June 1958: "Tell your comrades that above all we must win the battle on the ground, then they must leave things to me. I shall try to find the most French solution."[1]

In his *Mémoires d'espoir*, de Gaulle sums up his intentions at the time:

> In appointing General Challe* as Commander-in-Chief and in separating military action and civilian affairs at the top level, I expected operations to take a dynamic turn which would result in our undisputed mastery of the field. I studied with him and approved his plan of action, which consisted in concentrating the requisite forces for an offensive against each of the rebel pockets in turn, reducing them one after another.[2]

The political significance of the revision carried out by de Gaulle with the retirement of Salan and the mission given to Challe is clear. By throwing the army into the offensive, de Gaulle loosened the army's grip on him. It allowed him to breathe. Everyone had his own job: some had to fight battles, others had to take political decisions. After ten months of manoeuvres, de Gaulle recovered a lost political arena. This was made all the easier in that Paul Delouvrier was a Delegate-General infinitely closer to him than his predecessor in terms of outlook, intelligence and culture.

He was offering the formidable army at Challe's disposal – close on half a million men, 50 000 of them professional soldiers, paratroops and legionaries hardened by battle in Indo-China and Algeria – an offensive mission, rather than the job of acting as a combination of policemen and social workers of the kind previously given it by Salan. This was to break with a kind of so-called revolutionary warfare that he despised, to free himself from a yoke that he abhorred and, by successes on the ground, to increase his ability to bargain with the enemy.

Just as Charles de Gaulle and Maurice Challe launched their crack troops into an attack on the djebels, the Army of National Liberation (ALN), formed out of

*General Challe replaced General Salan. (trs.)

commandos lacking modern weapons, seemed to be disintegrating. In early 1959, the best Western military observers were in agreement on this point.

There were many reasons for this decline. The first must be credited to the French military chiefs. Whatever reservations might be made about the conduct of the psychological warfare by such men as Colonels Argoud or Godard, nobody can question the efficiency of their anti-terrorist campaign, especially since the most powerful organizer of the Algerian uprising, Abane Ramdane, had been liquidated in Morocco in December 1957, by a group of his rivals. For a long time concealed, and partly revealed in May 1958 under the guise of a "death on the field of honour", the murder of the Kabyl leader had spread a wave of doubt, rancour and disarray through the FLN, even at the lowest level. Demoralized by the liquidation of Abane, left leaderless in Kabylia by the "purge" instigated by the French secret service, the ALN was suffering even more, at the beginning of the year in which Challe and de Gaulle wanted to have done with it, from a terrible feeling of confinement. Indeed the French General Staff had just carried out the operation that it had been dreaming about for two years: the sealing off of the two frontiers, with Morocco and above all with Tunisia. Without the aid coming from those two countries the FLN felt stifled. Cut off from its two areas of supply, the ALN was unable to sustain itself.

Lastly, the eruption of the de Gaulle phenomenon represented a final trial for the Algerian nationalists. However one sees it, the return of this individual profoundly affected a people particularly susceptible to mythology and to the warm, chivalrous way in which the great visitor addressed them. Did his ambiguous words fulfil the expectations of those Algerians whose sole purpose was the creation of an independent state? Of course not. The pessimists even saw them as the supreme trick of French domination. But, on the whole, the Muslim community listened with emotion to that voice that spoke to them of equality, rights and human dignity, that addressed them in a tone of respect, referring to their courage, their hopes and their future.[3]

In early 1959, the images of Charles de Gaulle and the FLN were seen by the majority of Algerians as two rival possibilities. They represented two separate routes to emancipation: one gradual, the other sudden. That the second should be felt as more natural did not rule the first out of account. So, for a time, the FLN lost its monopoly on hope. It suffered from this all the more in that its weakness was becoming apparent. That is why many of those with whom I have spoken over the past ten years declare that 1959 was the worst year of the war.

On the French side, success followed success. But the army that was winning its war was also a disorientated army. This is what Jacques Soustelle, the leading spokesman of *Algérie française* says:

> In subversive warfare, political positions are as important as military measures and actions. So the army in Algeria, deprived of that essential weapon, represented by a clear political line, found itself rather in the situation of an army in 1940 that had neither tanks nor planes. The rebellion only recovered its strength because of the "cancer of doubt" gnawing away at the Algerian people.[4]

The former Governor-General blames this "cancer of doubt" mainly on the Paris press, which, he writes, "constantly supported the propaganda line of the FLN, which had already been widely taken up by the subversive Soviet and Arab radio stations. At the United Nations, the criticism of our enemies was little more than extracts from those Paris papers, placed end to end."

In that great debate, moreover, General de Gaulle found few followers within the army of which he, constitutionally, was the supreme commander. About this time, an assassination attempt had been made against Colonel de Corta, an old Free French activist, that very nearly cost the lives of himself and his daughter. At the Centre des Hautes Etudes Militaires only a few rare Gaullist officers were willing to be associated with an official demonstration of sympathy, which was traditional in such circumstances. The others refused to make any gesture of solidarity towards that officer: he had a reputation as a faithful follower of the head of State.

One of the arguments most often advanced by those who rejected the arrangements initiated by de Gaulle was that there was no freedom of choice: a chain of public and private commitments bound the French army to Algeria for ever. It was what might be called the "Oath" theory. No one formulated it better than Jacques Soustelle:

> "Are you leaving or staying?" There is no officer who, assuming command of his post in a village, has not been asked this question by the local notables. What it meant was: "If the village raises the French flag, if this or that family head agrees to become mayor, if we send our sons and daughters to school, if we hand out weapons of self-defence, if we refuse to supply the *fellaghas* roaming around the djebel with barley, sheep and money, will you, the army, be here to defend us from reprisals?" If they answered "no", all they could do was go back to the nearest port of embarkation. Anyway, the orders that they received from their superiors, from their Commanders-in-Chief to their area commanders, was always the same: "France remains and will remain." So don't let anyone say that in committing themselves the officers committed only themselves. It was the whole army that made that oath: an oath that no one had the right or power to untie.[5]

There was another factor that helped to turn most of the officer class against General de Gaulle: they felt that the head of State constantly identified them with the defence of the interests of European colonization – when, in their own eyes, they were acting, as much against the old "order" as against the nationalism of the FLN.

On 24 June 1958, André Malraux, the Minister of Information, had declared at a press conference (censored in Algiers) that, although torture had certainly been practised, such excesses would now be forbidden, and that the Commission for the safeguard of individual rights and freedoms had been set up again. On the ground, however, it was difficult to notice any change – the use of "tough questioning" remained at the discretion of the commanding officers: in sectors where the officers had made it quite clear that they were against it, such "interrogation" remained forbidden. In late 1959, recalling Pierre Chatenet to the Ministry of the Interior, de Gaulle gave him strict instructions to ensure that there was to be no resort to this type of "interrogation".[6] But Chatenet did not have the right to look into what was taking place in the villages of the Constantinois.

Was the decision that de Gaulle took, at the beginning of summer 1959, to bring back into question the membership in the Republic of twelve French departments, and thus to allow the dismemberment of the "national territory", as fateful as that of June 1940? In each case he knew that both his honour and his life were at stake.

The decision of 1940 was the outcome of thought over several long days; that of 1959 was arrived at over several months. In August 1958, de Gaulle confided to Edgar Faure in his office in the Hôtel Matignon: "The most common mistake, for all statesmen, is to be absolutely convinced that at any given moment there is a solution to every problem. During certain periods there are problems that have no solution. This is the case at present with Algeria."[7]

We know that de Gaulle the historian, the intellectual, was convinced that Algeria would be independent sooner or later. But there were several levels, several sides to Charles de Gaulle. There was the man of thought, who meditated on the great currents of history and confronted the obsolescence of the colonial system. This de Gaulle knew that Algeria would sooner or later be an independent State. There was also a de Gaulle who as French general was passionately attached to the nation's glory and heritage, as he showed between 1940 and 1946, who found nothing more repugnant than to "abandon" anything.

Then there was yet another de Gaulle: the politician. Called back to power because of a riot by French Algerians, guided and inspired by the army, who had made Jacques Soustelle his right-hand man and who had as a majority in the National Assembly a group of deputies committed to a French Algeria. This third de Gaulle, the man of circumstances, realized that there was scarcely anything in common between what he knew and what he could do. And since he hated nothing more than immobility, inaction, he groped his way from the offer of the "peace of the brave" to elections in which he would like to have seen the expression of an Algerian nationalism in its most benign form. In this way he tried to escape from the state of inertia and, if not to shape a policy, at least to lay down gradually the basis of one and to give himself the means to carry it out.

In 1958, therefore, there were several de Gaulles facing Algeria – an historian, a general defending his territory, a politician considering five or six possible policies and a tactician keen to save his boat from being wrecked on the rocks.

But the person, ideas and temperament of the Prime Minister had an even greater influence on the direction of the General's thinking than those of the army leaders. I have already quoted from documents in which he describes the close relationship that bound him to Michel Debré, whom he called his second-in-command. They were institutional, professional links, but they were also personal, one might almost say emotional ones. It is surprising that so intelligent a man as Michel Debré, and one apparently so well-informed about General de Gaulle's intentions, was able to believe for so long that he was loyally serving his leader by making declarations and gestures that ran quite contrary in spirit to the line followed by the founder of the Fifth Republic.

It has often been alleged that General de Gaulle betrayed the army by his "double-talk", one language for Paris, another for Algiers and the army. What man's words were more publicized, more repeated, whether he himself had delivered them or they had been made public with his authority? On the subject of Algeria, de Gaulle lived with a microphone in front of his mouth and a camera under his nose. This does not, of course, mean that he always said the same thing.

But what has seldom been noted is that this very visible, audible de Gaulle was constantly "interpreted" by a group of men who gave their comrades on the ground and in the military establishment a so-called authorized version of the political line given out by the head of state. De Gaulle allowed this practice to continue for a long time and must, therefore, be held responsible for the deception.

In the government itself, the most diverse tendencies were represented. The most determined integrationist view was expressed by the inventor of that policy, Jacques Soustelle. Maurice Couve de Murville, on the other hand, did not conceal his conviction that there was no solution other than Algerian independence; the Foreign Minister, to whom the General was most attentive, was originally the only member of the government, apart from Jean-Marcel Jeanneney, who dared to reveal such certainties.[8]

Between these two extremes, ministers like Guillaumat, Jacquinot or Triboulet remained attached to the idea of *Algérie française*, while Malraux and Michelet were in favour of radically new formulas, an emancipation that did not exclude very close association with France. Fairly close to these positions were those of Robert Buron, Paul Bacon and Louis Terrenoire. Pierre Sudreau showed his liberal spirit on every occasion, as did André Boulloche, a convinced socialist. As for Antoine Pinay, though favourable to the status quo, he was not as overt and determined a supporter of *Algérie française* as his conservative friends would have liked.

There was another essential factor in de Gaulle's decision: the Delegate-General in Algeria, Paul Delouvrier. Before being France's representative in the European Coal and Steel Community, he had been the financial expert for most of the leaders of the Fourth Republic. Starting work in Algiers on 19 December 1958, he soon realized that he was no more than an executant. At the risk of being reproached by de Gaulle (who had said to him: "Don't look across at Tunis, that's my business"), he established contacts with Ferhât Abbâs and with the Moroccan leader Mehdi Ben Barka, who confided to him: "The man you should talk to is Ben Bella."[9] In short, Delouvrier was not a man to oppose talks, whenever General de Gaulle decided upon them. He was to prove very susceptible to the Algiers atmosphere. But, on the whole, he was to be a very effective representative of Gaullist power on the other side of the Mediterranean. "If only the General had always made such good choices," Alain de Boissieu now says.[10]

From the political point of view, the General's ideas did not allow much room for movement either. What did the FLN want? De Gaulle was still very far from agreeing to deal with this "external organization", but he did want to know what the enemy's aims were. At this time there was almost nobody capable of telling him, and the debate in the press and in political circles was more concerned with the conduct of the war and the moral and legal questions that it raised than with the conditions for a political solution. What is clear is that French public opinion was evolving; until the end of 1958 a majority had been in favour of *Algérie française*, but there was a growing anxiety about the need to fight. One has only to consult the French press, from September 1958 to September 1959, to perceive the growth of a doubt, an impatience, an expectation. General de Gaulle was sensitive to this, if only because those were also his feelings.

Moreover, it so happened that just prior to the UN session, France was preparing to welcome President Eisenhower, certainly the most popular foreign politician with French people. Nothing was more alien to Charles de Gaulle's mind than to take a decision of national interest in order to please the Americans, but it is true that his own inclination to reach a political solution to the Algerian conflict was strengthened by a concern to persuade his allies of the validity of his overall strategy. And how could he better persuade his American guests of this strategy than by speaking of self-determination?

It was in July 1959 that General de Gaulle finally decided to declare the right of the Algerians to self-determination. Among many signs, one is particularly notable: on 22 July on a visit to Algiers, General Petit, one of the architects of 13 May, who became the military *directeur de cabinet* at Matignon, told Colonel Argoud of "the Prime Minister's anxieties about the outcome of the Algerian affair. M. Debré seems to have lost his fine assurance."[11]

Between 17 and 23 July de Gaulle had talks with two African leaders, Modibo Keita (future President of Mali) and Léopold Senghor (future President of Senegal), who were trying to persuade him that there could be no Franco-African association without the recognition of a clear path towards independence. General de Gaulle's decision seems to have crystallized on reading a document written by his adviser, Bernard Tricot. With a view to a political solution of the conflict, this specialist advocated the organization of a referendum allowing a choice between independence and autonomy "within a Franco-African whole".[12] The term "self-determination" was not used.

On 31 July, the General received Dag Hammarskjöld, Secretary-General of the United Nations, at the Elysée. De Gaulle, who did not care for that remarkable man, if only on account of Hammarskjöld's supranationalism, led him to believe that France was preparing a profound revision of her Algerian policy. *L'Express*'s comments on this meeting were: "General de Gaulle has drawn up a programme of action that would place Algeria 'in a state of self-determination'."[13] Perhaps it would have been better if de Gaulle had also informed his own government of what he was thinking. On 12 August, de Gaulle invited his ministers to reflect on the Algerian question and to convey what they had concluded at a meeting on 26 August.

Jacques Soustelle's account of this "memorable Council of Ministers of 26 August 1959" is striking.

> I can still see the long Council table at which I sat to the right of Michel Debré. Opposite, the President of the Republic, flanked by André Malraux and Louis Jacquinot. Beside me was Couve de Murville and further on Sudreau; at the end of the table was Giscard d'Estaing.

The Prime Minister spoke first, declaring that France had strategic, economic, and political interests in Algeria and the Mediterranean which she must maintain if the French Community were not to collapse. How was this to be done? "By guaranteeing democratic expression for Algeria," Debré replied.

Everyone spoke in turn. Some, like Boulloche and Sudreau, believed that an "innovation", an "initiative", before the UN session was necessary. Bernard Cornut-Gentille, on the other hand, considered that France should not go beyond the stage of the "peace of the braves", if "Arab ambitions were not to spread" throughout the Maghreb. And he warned his colleagues against the "cowardly relaxation" that might result in "abandonment".

Michelet suggested relaunching the peace appeal and said that the lawyers should find a formula binding the Algerian State to France. He even declared: "We must never haul down the French flag in Algiers, but I can see nothing wrong with some other flag flying beside it, just as at Lille the Flemish standard flies next to the tricolour." Antoine Pinay said that, in principle, we must keep Algeria. Guillaumat – to my surprise – opposed any change. "The Algerian personality," he said, "does not exist." According to him, any relaxation of French authority in Algeria was out of the question.

All in all, the Council seemed more or less equally divided between advocates and opponents of any "initiative", the advocates indeed often giving rather different interpretations of what that initiative should be. A minority favoured the creation of an autonomous Algerian state, a minority was against it, and another group followed the Prime Minister in the direction that he had indicated at the beginning.

Before bringing the session to an end, the President of the Republic said more or less: "Thank you, gentlemen. In this sort of thing one has to keep walking or die. I have chosen to walk, but that doesn't mean that we may not also die."[14]

Jacques Soustelle says nothing here about the important contribution of Jean-Marcel Jeanneney, who came out unequivocally for the rapid independence of Algeria. He spoke with such clarity that, after the Council meeting, he went over to the Prime Minister to ask him if he had not scandalized the head of State. Without concealing his own disagreement, Debré said: "No. In fact, you are the closest to his own thinking."[15]

The next day, General de Gaulle, accompanied by Pierre Guillaumat and General Ely, set out on that tour of Algeria referred to above. Visiting the soldiers, he was able to assess the military risks that might stem from the decision he was about to take. On 28 August de Gaulle had a discussion with General Massu, who, hearing him speak of the self-determination of the Algerian people, countered with the opinion of the Europeans in Algeria. De Gaulle replied: "Ils m'emmerdent."* Later, a furious Massu declared to his officers: "De Gaulle isn't eternal."[16]

---

*Somewhat stronger than "they're getting on my nerves" or "they make me sick". (trs.)

It was only during the fourth day of his trip that Charles de Gaulle was to expose the broad outlines of his plan to the military leaders. He made it clear that:

The Algerian problem could not be solved until we eventually reached an understanding with the Algerians. That we would never reach an understanding unless they themselves desired it. All the colonized people of the world were throwing off the yoke and that we must act in Algeria only for Algeria and with Algeria and in such a way that the world realized this. I concluded: "As for yourselves, mark my words! You are not an Army for its own sake. You are the Army of France. You exist only through her, for her and in her service. It is I who, in view of my position and my responsibilities, must be obeyed by the Army in order that France should survive."[17]

Maurice Challe took in General de Gaulle's words without blinking an eyelid. He immediately found the answer: the aim expounded by the head of State was to make the Algerians accept French culture. Accompanying the visitor to the helicopter that was to take him to Talergma, where he was to take the plane for Paris, the Commander-in-Chief asked the President of the Republic if he had interpreted his words aright. De Gaulle turned to Delouvrier: "And what do you think?" The Delegate-General replied that if the Algerians were given a free choice they would choose to be themselves. De Gaulle looked at him steadily and said: "Whatever you think, the ballot-boxes will decide."[18]

The visit of Dwight Eisenhower to Paris contributed to the shift de Gaulle was making to his policy on Algeria. To be able to win over such an ally, on the eve of what had become an annual trial of French policy in Algeria at the United Nations, was obviously tempting. As it so happened, the expected shift in policy did coincide with the visitor's expectations. From then on, Eisenhower was to play an encouraging role.

On 2 September the two men talked about Algeria.* Charles de Gaulle outlined the main points of his self-determination plan. The visitor was won over entirely. ("He opened his heart to Eisenhower," Geoffroy de Courcel declares.) That afternoon, during a more official meeting, in which de Gaulle was surrounded by the Prime Minister, the Foreign Minister, his Ambassador to the United States and the Secretary-General at the Elysée, the American delegation let it be known that the United States regarded the French plan sympathetically. But no promise was made concerning the American vote at the United Nations.

The only point of disagreement concerned the public communiqué, which the visitors wanted to be written in such a way as to make it clear that they had been consulted about the General's Algerian plan: neither de Gaulle, nor Debré, nor even the senior civil servants who for years had claimed at the United Nations that Algeria was an internal French affair could agree to this. Eventually, it was decided

*According to Alain de Boissieu, Washington had already been informed of the Elysée's intentions.

that the communiqué was to give no indication that Paris wanted to win Washington's encouragement on Algeria: it stated quite simply that North Africa had been discussed.

So everything was ready. General de Gaulle had consulted his ministers and achieved an at least apparent acquiescence from the first of them and the warm approval of several others; he had got discipline imposed upon the dissidents within the UNR; he was assured of the good intentions of the most powerful of his allies,* had gained support for his ideas from the Secretary-General of the United Nations, thus disarming the opposition of that organization; and he was assured of the prior approval of several of the leaders of the Algerian revolution, whose consent was vital if he was ever to put an end to the war.

On 16 September 1959, at 8 p.m., Charles de Gaulle appeared on French television. There had been warnings that he was to speak of a very important matter. He was wearing civilian clothes and when he began to speak it was in a solemn tone.

He began, as he always did, with homage to his own power. Unity had been recreated, new institutions set up, balance restored, the community given a firm foundation, independence assured. "And yet France is still faced with a difficult, bloody problem: Algeria." It must be solved, de Gaulle went on, not by "sterile simplistic slogans", but "by the free choice of the Algerians themselves". Having recalled the "universal suffrage" and "the economic and social development" agreed to by France, Charles de Gaulle paused and, raising his tone still further, declared:

> I regard it as necessary that a course towards self-determination should be proclaimed as from today. In the name of France and the Republic, by virtue of the powers accorded me by the Constitution to consult the citizens, providing God gives me life and that the people listens to me, I commit myself to asking the Algerians what they wish finally to be, and all the French to accept the choice they decide upon.

The speaker went on to say that this question would be put to "individuals" four years after the end of fighting. But on what themes and what terms would this choice be proposed? The General submitted three possible options:

> Either: secession, an incredible, disastrous end to the question that would bring with it appalling poverty, terrible political chaos, the widespread killing of individuals, and, before long, the bellicose dictatorship of the Communists. That devil must be exorcised by the Algerians themselves.
>
> Or: complete Francocization with equality of rights; the Algerians would be able to accede to all public responsibilities, living, whatever their faith and culture, on the same footing and at the same level as all other citizens, becoming an integral part of the French people from Dunkirk to Tamanrasset.

*This said, the United States was to abstain at the time of the vote.

Or: a government of the Algerians by the Algerians, supported by French help and in a close union with her as far as the economy, education, defence, foreign affairs are concerned, the internal government of Algeria being of a federal type, of such a kind that the various communities, that live together in that country, can enjoy certain guarantees...

Having thus laid down the framework for self-determination, de Gaulle denounced an "insurrection" that no longer had any meaning, except for "a group of ambitious rabble-rousers determined to establish their totalitarian dictatorship by force and terror" and who must not hope that the Republic would deal directly with them, "thus setting them up as the Algerian government. There is no chance of France lending herself to such an arbitrary decision. The fate of the Algerians belongs to the Algerians, through universal suffrage. With them and for them, France will guarantee the freedom of their choice."[18]

It was the most important speech that Charles de Gaulle had devoted to Algeria. It was also the one whose implications were greatest: in twenty minutes, he had said farewell to *Algérie française*.

As for the presentation of the three possible options, it is clear that although he coated the second with the idea of "Francocization", and although he drew a somewhat gloomy picture of independence – by this route which he was granting to African societies that had been no more states in the past than had Algeria, he did so both to "soften up" the army, which could not bear to be treated as a target, as well as to bring out the merits of the "third way".

The broadcast had an enormous effect. In mainland France, there was a clear majority in favour of the de Gaulle initiative – though it was denounced by the extreme right, 20 per cent of the UNR deputies and the PCF (which was to change its mind three months later on the eve of Nikita Khrushchev's visit to France – Moscow now regarding the General's Algerian policy favourably).

Reactions in Algiers were obviously negative. Since the eve of the celebrated Council of Ministers of 26 August, Jacques Soustelle had bombarded Prime Minister Debré with notes warning him against any change to the status of Algeria. Delicately pointing out to his indignant friends that to reject self-determination would be to suggest that one did not trust the wish of the Algerians to choose Francocization, he refused to resign. He was to wait another four months and riots in Algiers in which his supporters were to flout legality and provoke the massacre of French police before withdrawing from a government that, according to him, had delivered a criminal blow to the nation's vital interests.

The response of the GPRA came a week later, on 28 September. It was complicated: reaffirming that it was the exclusive representative of the Algerian people, and that without its agreement there could be no "return to peace", the GPRA congratulated itself that "the Algerian people's right to dispose of its own destiny has at last been recognized" and declared itself ready "to enter into discussions with the French government in order to work out the political and military conditions of the cease-fire and guarantees for the application of self-determination".

So the GPRA had expressed its acquiescence, in principle, to self-determination. It had reservations as to the conditions of application and demanded that the integrity of Algerian territory must be recognized: that meant that the Saharan departments of Oasis and Saoura must be included in the vote, whereas de Gaulle spoke of consulting only the "twelve Algerian departments". But whatever divergences there may have been in the two points of view (for Paris, the cease-fire as the conclusion of pacification opening up the way for consultation; for the GPRA, negotiations with a view to a cease-fire before the vote), self-determination was now recognized as necessary by both parties. For the first time, a common basis had been found and a political solution now seemed possible. On 20 November, to general amazement, the GPRA appointed five leaders who had been held in French prisons since 1956 as representatives in any talks. It was a decision that ran huge risks of damaging the chances of putting an end to the war. The General himself regarded this gesture as "almost crude".[19]

Why this sudden move on the part of the GPRA? According to the excellent Algerian historian, Mohammed Harbi, then a close colleague of Ferhât Abbâs, this decision showed that "in the Algerian camp, as in the French camp, the internal situation was such that it was impossible to give up double-talk".

The United Nations debate was approaching. Would General de Gaulle lose the fruits of his efforts? Letting it be known that France would not take part in the debate, he did not await the conclusion with too much apprehension. A highly subtle African motion, which if it had been approved would have placed Paris in a difficult position (it requested "the two interested parties to engage in talks" with a view to allowing "the Algerian people its right to self-determination", thus placing the French State and the FLN on the same plane), did not receive the two-thirds majority required for its consideration.

De Gaulle had expected more from his bold initiative (we know that he had taken the UN vote as the pretext for moves against certain of his military opponents). But he had opened up the breach. Thus 1959 was to allow him both to affirm the military mastery of his forces on the ground and, at one blow, to restore his moral and political position regarding Algeria on the international plane. But it was at a price: the door opened for the independence of that country failed to arouse the support of those responsible for French rule in Algeria, or the majority of the officer corps in the army.

De Gaulle would now have to snatch the Algerian peace from his own supporters, civil and military.

CHAPTER TWENTY-ONE

The Reaction in Algiers

The proclamation of Algerian self-determination ran counter to the wishes of three-quarters of those who had brought de Gaulle to power eighteen months before. On 1 October, Pierre Lagaillarde roared down the corridors of the Chamber: "You must choose between de Gaulle and *Algérie française*." Léon Delbecque, for his part, declared: "Blood will flow. I shall stop de Gaulle getting out by the side door."[1]

At the Assembly, a plot was being hatched with a view to overthrowing the government on 15 October. But when the Prime Minister defended the policy of self-determination with a conviction unexpected of him, even stressing the effort that the government was making to assist the leaders of the "rebellion" to discuss conditions for a cease-fire, he won an overwhelming success: 441 votes to 23.

Lucien Neuwirth, regarded by most of his "13 May" companions as a traitor since he had come round to the policy of self-determination, announced that "commandos of assassins from Algiers have crossed the Spanish frontier. The list of those to be killed has been drawn up." François Mitterrand was to escape from the threats that faced him night and day by means of a simulated murder in the gardens of the Observatoire. De Gaulle, by opening the way for a political solution, ran the risk of starting the civil war in Paris that he had avoided in Algiers a year earlier.

Within the government, however, de Gaulle saw the rise of an opponent more dangerous than Soustelle: Antoine Pinay, his Finance Minister. The very idea of a confrontation between these two seems unlikely, because they were so obviously unequal, but the withdrawal of this popular individual from the government could only weaken de Gaulle's position with the Conservatives. On 3 November, General de Gaulle announced at the Ecole Militaire that France would shortly leave the "integrated organization" of the Atlantic Alliance. This cannot have made Pinay's place in the government any easier as he had been a fervent advocate of the alliance.

On 8 November, de Gaulle faced his ministers and commented on a speech he had just made, stressing the reserve to be taken with regard to the Americans who, in his view, would sooner or later retreat behind their own frontiers. How could a country base its security on such an alliance? How could they not do everything possible to organize a defence of Europe, the principal element of which would be a specifically French force?

Suddenly the sugary tones of Antoine Pinay were heard: "*Monsieur le Président,**

---

*Antoine Pinay was the only one to use this formula, rather than "mon Général". (trs.)

if I understand you rightly, you have condemned the very principle of NATO."

De Gaulle, surprised, turned his deathly face upon him: "The Finance Minister is interested in problems of foreign policy?"

"Yes," replied Pinay, "I am interested in problems of foreign policy. As far as the economic and financial sector is concerned, we do not have the means to defend ourselves alone. We have no real possibility of creating a strike force and we must prevent the departure of the Americans at all costs."

Charles de Gaulle cut him short: "Thank you, Monsieur Pinay. Gentlemen, the session is over." And to general amazement, he left, without shaking his ministers' hands.[2]

Pinay's resignation did not come until two months later, but the worm was in the fruit. From then on, de Gaulle had to confront the open dissent not only of his second most important minister, Soustelle, but also of Pinay. The anti-Gaullist party in Algiers did its best to exploit the crisis: de Gaulle was frightened, isolated, discredited, and facing ruin. He was endangering the unity of his own country, cutting himself off from the Americans, breaking with the world of money and alienating the army.

So the first days of January were, like those of May 1958, bristling with secret meetings, plans, hasty trips back and forth across the Mediterranean. De Gaulle took no notice: he left Paris to stay for a few days with his wife at the abbey of La Celle in the Var, which had been turned into an hotel, where perhaps he would meditate on this irony of history that would make him, de Gaulle, the liquidator of French power south of the Mediterranean. There is nothing to suggest that this retreat led him in any way to alter his policy. On the contrary. But in so far as de Gaulle had up to this point chosen, decided and acted as if the fate of Algeria depended upon his will alone, now he would have to negotiate each decision, each step, each move – and underneath each stage there might be a mine. It was to be the supreme test of his skill at diplomacy and the art of ruling by words.

In early January 1960, Algiers was practically on fire. A dozen or so individuals (among them Ortiz, Lagaillarde, Sérigny, Argoud, Godard, Delouvrier and Challe) were preparing for a confrontation, some to overthrow the power of the government, others to save it. As for Massu, the man who held the armed forces, he no longer knew which side he was on – loyal to de Gaulle yet abhorring his policy.

The rebels' camp swarmed with colourful characters. At this point, two of them stood out: Joseph Ortiz, known as *Jo les gros bras* (Big Arms Joe) and Massu's Chief of General Staff, Antoine Argoud, who had a long-standing hatred of de Gaulle dating back to Vichy: de Gaulle paid this hostility back in kind, always referring to Argoud as "that little colonel, what's he called? Ragout?" Small Argoud may have been, but like an enraged cheetah, never still, shrill, explosive, his head always buzzing with some idea or another and always ready to condemn something in twenty words.

Jo Ortiz was the owner of the Forum café, the nerve centre of Algiers. He had a face like a Byzantine emperor's, his overweight body forced into a light alpaca suit, sporting a huge signet ring, with the muscles of a nightclub "bouncer". "He was a man of the underworld", it has been said. "Evil tongues said that he had interests in houses of ill repute that prospered on account of the heat of the climate and the presence of half a million soldiers. He was a fascist."[3] The shock troops of his Front National Français (FNF) sported on their many-coloured shirts the insignia of the Celtic cross, with overtly racist references.

Pierre Lagaillarde, who had been one of those responsible for the overthrow of the Fourth Republic on 13 May 1958, had been elected a deputy. In the eyes of the French people of Algiers, one could not sit with the *pourris*.* On 15 October, he used parliamentary indemnity to yell from the tribune in the Assembly that de Gaulle would end up in the high court. That lean wolf had kept acquaintances with the Algiers Bar, in the university and in the army. His electrifying eloquence, his short reddish beard, his piratical appearance, his paratroop uniform always won over opposition. In three weeks, he had gathered round him thirty men he could rely on. He had not had more on 13 May 1958. When Crespin, Arnould and Lefèvre, not to mention Delbecque, were pushed aside or forgotten, he emerged in the front rank of the firing line, his finger on the trigger and always ready to deliver a stirring word. Apart from Argoud, the soldiers tried to be discreet but they were not averse to coming into contact with "M. Jo". So much so that, in the activists' camp, it was often whispered that the owner of the Forum café was a double agent and that Colonel Godard, head of the detective squad, used him both as an informer and as a provocateur.

The main target for the movement fermenting in Algiers was the right to self-determination. The enemy was not only de Gaulle, not only a policy, not only the questioning of *Algérie française*, but democratic principles themselves, parliament, the Republic. The movement of May 1958 had only one aim: to get rid of a government and to appeal to the army to ensure that Algeria remained part of France: the conspirators of 1960 aimed to change the regime. The new power that would be set up – and which had eyes and ears in almost all the Parisian centres of power and influence – would not be deflected by hostile majorities and popular demonstrations: from Dunkirk to Tamanrasset, a hundred French departments would be mobilized to crush the traitors.

In that climate of imminent catastrophe, made worse by the revival of FLN terrorism – scores of Europeans had been murdered, some of them very elderly – all that was needed was a pretext to trigger the event. On both sides, it was known that General Massu was in a sense the keystone on which the two opposing forces braced themselves – containing the anger in Algiers, which he shared, putting a brake on the initiatives of the head of State, to whom he remained loyal. Who had an interest in removing that keystone: the Algiers conspirators, so that they could be free at last to act, or de Gaulle, by removing from his path the symbol of convergence between the Algiers crowds and the army?

On 15 January 1960, General Jacques Massu received the German journalist Hans Kempski, who represented the Munich newspaper *Suddeutsche Zeitung*. Kempski was a former paratrooper and had already published reports on Algeria that were favourable to the points of view of the French General Staff. Massu was a good subject for a sensationalist reporter competent enough to ask the right

*Literally, the "rotten", i.e. "the corrupt". (trs.)

questions. No agreement had been made regarding publication, no veto had been expressed, and Kempski was equipped with a discreet tape-recorder.

In short, Massu went along with it. "We don't understand President de Gaulle's policy any longer. The army could never have foreseen that he would carry out such a policy. Our greatest disappointment has been to see General de Gaulle become a man of the left." More imprudent still, Massu confided to Kempski that the army "was urging the Europeans to form paramilitary organizations and was supplying these groups with weapons". This was no longer a matter of Jacques Massu's personal feelings, but a major departure from the *raison d'être* of the officer corps.

The interview with Massu was published in Munich on Monday evening, 18 January. All the international agencies reproduced large extracts from it next morning: "Massu against de Gaulle". In Algiers and in Paris, things were reaching fever pitch. Challe hastened to deny those "statements devoid of any foundation". Massu made no comment: he might curse Kempski, but he knew very well that his interviewer had done no more than reproduce what he had said.

General de Gaulle's reaction to the statement made by his "companion" was all too predictable. On 19 January he wrote to the Prime Minister: "The interview given by General Massu cannot, of course, be tolerated. At the time at which I am writing to you, this general ought already to have arrived in Paris or, at least to be on his way, on the government's orders, in order to explain himself. It being understood, of course, that, after due punishment, he will not return to Algiers."[4]

Pierre Guillaumat, the Armed Forces Minister, was to try to save Massu by asking the general to come up with a denial or at least a semi-disavowal. De Gaulle, Guillaumat assured him, was not insisting that the criticisms made of him should be denied, but wanted Massu to withdraw what he had said about the army's views of his policy. Massu agreed, but on the key question of morale in the army, he paid homage not to General de Gaulle's authority, but to that of General Challe. It was, it has been said, a suicidal denial.

De Gaulle had not waited to receive Massu's text before delivering these hard words to Guillaumat:

> Nothing is more important than the authority of the State. Now that authority has been publicly challenged by General Massu, challenged in my person, General Massu must not return to Algiers. We shall see whether this decision causes any local disturbances. Such disturbances cannot be anything other than limited and circumstantial. The abasement of the State and the consent of de Gaulle would be irreparable.[5]

A meeting of the Algerian Affairs Committee, arranged for the next day, 22 January 1960, at the Elysée, aroused a great deal of interest. De Gaulle chaired that key meeting in uniform. He summoned twenty-three individuals – ministers, generals, senior civil servants. The reports given by General Challe and Paul Delouvrier had a sense of urgency and anxiety. The Europeans and the army had to be reassured, or they could expect the worst. De Gaulle was unconcerned, laconic. Reassure whom? Only the policy outlined on 16 September would "reassure" Algeria in the long term.

Delouvrier spoke next. He presented a file on the activism of the Algérois, the formidable machinery of the FNF set up by Ortiz – a file that Colonel Godard, informed from day to day of its progress, had handed to him only two days before. The situation was explosive, he said, not only on account of that seditious machinery, but because the European minority felt that they had been abandoned.

The time for conclusions came. The policy of 16 September was sacrosanct, but there would be no "negotiations" with the FLN. The Algerian Affairs Committee would meet regularly. Special courts would be set up to ensure a speedier repression of terrorism. The newspapers waging campaigns against the army would be prosecuted. Furthermore, General de Gaulle announced that he would be going to Algeria on 5 February. Delouvrier and Challe tried to make a final appeal to the General in favour of Massu.

"Massu? No, I'm going to look after him," said de Gaulle.

Challe spoke of resigning: "Without Massu, I no longer have the means of guaranteeing order in Algiers."

"Come now. You have the army, the police, my support. I'll give you Jean Crépin* to replace Massu. For the sake of the authority of the State, Massu cannot go back to Algiers. For the sake of the authority of the State, you must go back there. So I am investing you with full powers. If you have to use force, use it. You are master of your means."

Leaving the Elysée, Paul Delouvrier summed up his thoughts to Michel Debré: "I'm glad to be leaving. You, in your offices, you can't do anything. General Challe and I are going to get ourselves killed!"

That evening, however, General Massu telephoned Algiers to try to calm his supporters. "I've been the victim of a plot," he told Antoine Argoud. "But despite the disagreeable methods used against me, I consider that my transfer was necessary. Preach calm in Algiers. There mustn't be a riot."

Massu managed to see de Gaulle the following day. He has given an account of that in a book in which his very natural concern to play the best part is matched by an evident sincerity. He argued that self-determination was "not appropriate to Algeria". De Gaulle replied, "I don't know what the political solution is yet. But the Algerians don't want us, they want us to leave: who is telling you that I shall not make my choice known when the time comes? No one has done more than I for the Muslims. Only I can save Algeria. France cannot live with half a million of her children in Algeria for fifty years!"[6]

The meeting between the sovereign and the centurion lasted little more than twenty minutes: but it was long enough for the occupants of the offices next door to remember the furious shouting. There is even talk of a watch-strap smashed by a furious punch! François Flohic has said that just as Massu crossed the Aide-de-Camps' room after leaving the President's office, General de Beaufort, head of de Gaulle's private General Staff, went up to him and tried to express his solidarity

*An old Free French combatant, one of Massu's comrades in the 2nd armoured division under Leclerc.

"with a gesture, from which Massu quickly disengaged himself".[7] That says a lot about the state of mind of many of the men around Charles de Gaulle.

Leaving the Elysée, Massu called Argoud on the telephone. According to the authors of *Barricades et Colonels*, it was to take back the call for calm that he had sent the day before. The dismissed general concluded: "It is up to those out there to judge what to do. Yesterday I told you that you mustn't do anything. Today I'm not expressing any opinion!" It was a message sent to prepare a riot.

The general strike was declared by the Algérois conspirators for the following day, 24 January. Pierre Lagaillarde barricaded himself in with a few dozen well-armed men in the university perimeter. From this defensive position they defied army and police to remove them by shooting on men who "wanted to remain French". It was a clever tactical move. The Ortiz plan consisted of seizing public buildings, which the army would not defend. His organization's three thousand thugs would be enough. Thus by holding Algiers they would win over the General Staff. What they would do after that remained to be seen. Susini, Ortiz's young assistant, described their aims thus: "The time has come to bring down the regime. The revolution will start in Algiers and reach Paris."

For the great day of 24 January not to degenerate into another 13 May, Challe and Delouvrier set up the "Balancelle plan", whose benign name made it clear that it was a matter of confronting with flexibility the challenge of the FNF: the 10th Paratroop Division, under the orders of General Gracieux, was recalled to contain the explosion, while backing it. It was a formidable and ambiguous weapon. But there were also the military chiefs responsible for order in Algiers and the surrounding countryside, General Coste and Colonel Fonde: the first was a disciplined officer, the second a highly militant Gaullist, one of Leclerc's old comrades. They had at their disposal four companies of the CRS (riot police) and twenty units of mobile police under the command of Colonel Debrosse, an incorruptible servant of the State.

The tragic day of 24 January 1960 showed General de Gaulle that he had under-estimated the determination of the Algérois, the discipline and fidelity of the centurions and the personal influence he exerted over both.

The worst had already happened, when, about 8 p.m., the General was informed at Colombey of the temporary balance sheet for the day: fourteen dead on the side of the forces of order, eight on the side of the demonstrators, as well as 200 wounded. At 6 p.m., two CRS columns (1000 men) began their march to the University and to the bazaar, around which Ortiz had gathered hundreds of partisans. Beginning from the roofs overhanging Ortiz's headquarters, the machine-gun fire began almost at once. Three riot police were soon on the ground.

Fonde and Debrosse had expected two paratroop regiments to flank the progress of the forces of order: they waited in vain. "We had no orders," Broizat and Dufour, two commanding officers, objected. And the soldiers whose mission it had been to impede the movements of the UTBs and the various columns of rioters, especially on the edge of Bab-el-Oued, let them through, though refusing to support them. At nightfall, the carnage could only be interpreted as a defeat for General Challe and for de Gaulle: blood had been shed, Ortiz and

Lagaillarde were holding firm, and the general strike was paralysing the city.

Around midnight de Gaulle returned from Colombey to the Elysée, where he was joined by the Prime Minister, who had rushed back from Brittany. With them were the Ministers of the Interior, Pierre Chatenet, and of the Armed Forces, Pierre Guillaumat. The latter pleaded for caution. Chatenet and Debré were firmer and persuaded the General to try once again to appeal to the insurgents' reason before giving an order to "clean up Algiers". De Gaulle agreed to write and to record a dramatic appeal, which would be broadcast every hour on the hour from Radio Algiers:

> The riot that has just begun in Algiers is a bad blow for France. A bad blow for France in Algeria. A bad blow to France before the world. A bad blow to France within France. I solemnly call upon those who have risen up in Algiers against the nation, misled as they may have been by lies and calumnies, to return to national order. Nothing is lost for a Frenchman when he rejoins his mother, France. I express my profound confidence in Paul Delouvrier, Delegate-General, in General Challe, Commander-in-Chief, in the forces that are under their orders to serve France and the State, in the Algerian population, which is so dear to us and which has suffered so much. For my part, I shall do my duty.

At the request of Paul Delouvrier, the General had introduced a reference to "a solution that is French", but his appeal remained unanswered. In mainland France, of course, the operations ordered by Ortiz and Lagaillarde had horrified public opinion. The head of State knew that he had the country behind him. But it was not the people's approval that would give him the means of bringing the Algérois insurrection to its knees without causing the deaths of dozens if not hundreds of insurgents and members of the forces of order.

At the Council of Ministers, called for Monday afternoon, de Gaulle was categorical: "The insurrection must be beaten." But how? Several ministers – Michelet, Sudreau, Buron – believed the response needed to be harsh. Malraux advocated dropping a carpet of tear-gas on to the two insurgent bastions. Soustelle cut in: "And why not the atom bomb?"

The Prime Minister was sent on a mission to Algiers. As a former supporter of *Algérie française* he might be listened to by at least a few of the army chiefs. Having in his pocket a letter from the General giving him power to liquidate the insurrection and to punish the ringleaders,[8] he landed with Guillaumat at the Maison-Blanche at 1 a.m. on 26 January. After a glance at Lagaillarde's barricades, he shut himself up at army headquarters with Challe and Delouvrier. The head of State's instructions were unequivocal: put down the sedition, by force if necessary. Was that possible? The generals and colonels were more or less unanimous: neither the officers nor the men would march against those rebels.

Michel Debré saw Colonel Argoud, surrounded by several of his friends:

"What is to be done?"

"Get General de Gaulle to give up the idea of self-determination."

"And what if he refuses?"

"General Challe will have to take charge of the situation."

"And what if he refuses that too?"

"I can see no other solution but a junta of colonels."

Debré emerged from this conversation shaken. "Short of sticking a revolver in his stomach, we couldn't have gone any further" was how one of the colonels summed up that extraordinary nocturnal meeting with the Prime Minister.

On Tuesday 26 January 1960, before listening to Debré's report, Charles de Gaulle was to receive his old Saint-Cyr comrade, Alphonse Juin, the marshal who had been asking for a meeting for some weeks. The discussion was at first as stormy as that of the 23rd with Massu. The visitor hammered out his words: "You have no right to fire on those men. If you do, I shall take up a position against you!" "I don't have the right to allow the authority of the State to be flouted!" the President replied. Then things calmed down. De Gaulle put his head between his hands and, in a broken voice said: "The trouble is, we're too old. I'm an old man, I'll be dead soon." But suddenly, taking a grip on himself, he added: "I shall not give in! I shan't give in to riot!"

Debré then appeared, back from Algiers, still suffering the effects of the night's excitements. What he had come to understand was that the problem was primarily a military one. For Debré, what he had ascertained during that frenetic night was that if self-determination could not be abandoned, then the least that could be done was to announce the government's wishes for the most French solution possible.

"I will not give in, I will not change my policy," the General repeated. He was not averse to pacifying words, to a solemn affirmation that France would not abandon the French of Algeria. But, when Michel Debré offered his resignation, he rejected it out of hand: "You're joking, Debré! There is no question of changing one iota of my policy. And no question of resignation. You will stay beside me, if necessary on the steps of the Elysée, waiting for the paratroops to land."

De Gaulle's feelings of anxiety and abandonment were such that several ministers were considering forming a sort of crisis cabinet, on the basis of a determined support of the President of the Republic and of his Algerian policy. Jean-Marcel Jeanneney suggests that the group was not very large: Malraux, Buron, Sudreau, Joxe, Michelet, Frey and himself. If the worst happened, they arranged to meet in Belgium![9]

During the whole of the "week of the barricades", de Gaulle had felt the State giving way beneath him, threatened by a few extremists in Algiers, encouraged by a few hundred officers and a few thousand shock troops, plotting with them to defend a cause that they placed above service to the national community, preferring territorial realities to the spiritual, historical, abstract legitimacy that he embodied.

On Wednesday 27 January, General de Gaulle received General Crépin, a faithful follower whom he had promoted to replace Massu. Having listened to Crépin very attentively, de Gaulle replied with a series of observations that the visitor noted down: "The European Algerians don't want the Arabs to choose ... The Muslims don't want to be Bretons ... I can't lay down the future form of the status of Algeria. Integration won't work, I don't even know what it is. Is Francocization possible? ... There can be no question of firing... The military headquarters must be put outside Algiers. We must think about it... If the Army collapses, it will be Algeria and France that will collapse."

De Gaulle had launched his *idée-force*: when besieged, power must strike out! In the late afternoon he telephoned Delouvrier at the Palais d'Eté in Algiers. He urged him to leave the city, to take Challe with him and to leave the army to face the mutiny; however complicit the army were in their actions against the State, faced with the absence of any authority they would turn against each other.

The following day, 28 January, Paul Delouvrier and Maurice Challe slipped out of their besieged residences and travelled thirty kilometres to Reghaia, the headquarters of the airforce, where they made their headquarters. De Gaulle had rediscovered the sense of movement, the imagination, the initiative that he had shown throughout his career. But once again it was through words that de Gaulle was to act. He announced that he would be giving a broadcast on 29 January.

A storm had just broken over Algiers when Charles de Gaulle appeared on the television screens. His face was pale and wax-like, his head shaken like a tree in the wind, his voice at first hesitant, but gaining in assurance as he progressed. It was the air and tone of the Grand Inquisitor. Three hours earlier, Argoud, Ortiz and Lagaillarde still believed that they had forced him to bend and to accept *Algérie française*. Now, after five days of uncertainty, anxiety, disappointments, came the language of uncompromising power:

> If I am wearing uniform to speak to you today on the television it is in order to show that I am doing so, not only as head of State but also as General de Gaulle. In the name of France, I have taken the following decision: the Algerians will choose their destiny freely. Self-determination is the only policy worthy of France. It is the only possible outcome. It is the policy decided on by the President of the Republic, decided on by the government, approved by parliament, adopted by the French nation. But there are two categories of people who do not want this free choice.
>
> On the one hand, there is the rebel organization that claims that it will lay down its arms only if, prior to doing so, I give it privileges concerning the political destiny of Algeria. This would amount to erecting it as the sole valid representation and to erecting it, in advance, as the government of the country. That I shall not do.
>
> On the other hand, certain people of French origin are demanding that I abandon self-determination, that I say that everything has already been settled and that the fate of the Algerians is already decided. That I shall not do either.
>
> Self-determination is the only way by which the Muslims will themselves be able to exorcise the demon of secession. As for the shape of this or that French solution, I intend that they be worked out at leisure, once peace has been restored.

Having made the subtle concession of committing himself to some "French solution", he then launched an appeal to the soldiers for discipline:

What would the French army become if certain elements succeeded in placing conditions on their loyalty? It would be an anarchic, pitiful feudal band. Now, as you know, I am the supreme authority. It is I who bear the destiny of the country in my hands. I must, therefore, be obeyed by all French soldiers. I believe that I will be, because I know you, because I have esteem for you, because I love you, and because, for France, I need you. No soldier must be associated at any time, even in a passive way, with the insurrection. If he does so, it will be regarded as a serious offence. In the end, public order will have to be re-established. The means employed to ensure that force remains within the law will have to be of various kinds. But your duty is to attain that aim. I have given, I am giving, the order for this to be done.

He paused, as if made breathless by his efforts. Then, once again, the old tree began to move:

Lastly, I address France. Well, my dear, old country, here we are together once again, facing a grave trial. By virtue of the mandate that the people have given me and of the national legitimacy that I have embodied for twenty years, I ask you all to give me your support.

While the guilty men, who dream of being usurpers, use as a pretext the decision that I have taken with regard to Algeria, let it be known everywhere that I shall not go back on it. To cede on this point and in these circumstances would be to destroy the assets that we still have in Algeria, but it would also be to abase the State before the outrage that is being offered it and the threat facing it. France would be no more than a poor, dislocated toy floating on the oceans of adventures.

How pitiful everyone else seemed that evening! There was the State and there was that feudal band of soldiers who claimed to dictate the policy that France should follow. On the evening of 29 January, the question was settled. Peace had not yet come to Algeria, but de Gaulle was still the master of Paris, and France was once again the capital of France.

On the night of Sunday 31 January, Colonel Dufour, who the week before had failed to give his support for the CRS, persuaded Lagaillarde to bring out his men in order and armed. He, the leader, would have to answer for his actions before the law and he gave himself up with dignity, while Joseph Ortiz slipped away, in disguise, reaching first the Oranie then the Balearic Islands.

At noon, General de Gaulle telephoned Delouvrier: "Well?" "Lagaillarde has just surrendered." "Thank you, Delouvrier." A Council of Ministers met in the afternoon. The head of State, who revealed no sense of triumph, recalled harshly that all the guilty men would be punished, "irrespective of their rank".

The actions taken consisted of the dissolution of extreme right-wing organizations and the arrest of the ringleaders. One might add the removal of Soustelle; the resignations of Cornut-Gentille and Guillaumat, the Armed Forces Minister who had failed to rise to the occasion; the dismissal of Challe, who had also proved unequal to his task, and of Colonel Godard, head of the Sûreté, who, knowing everything about the plot, revealed it only the day before the uprising.

For a year, de Gaulle had refused to contemplate the idea that he might have serious problems with the army. "When I talked to him about it," says Delouvrier, "he shrugged his shoulders." The day after Lagaillarde's surrender the Delegate-General was summoned to the Elysée. He already knew that Challe had been dismissed. He expected the same treatment.

> Usually when one entered the General's office, he got up, walked a few steps towards you and greeted you before sitting down again. That day, even before greeting me, he declared: "I told you they wouldn't obey!" I was exasperated and couldn't stop myself answering: "*Mon Général*, I think it was I who told you!" That calmed him down: "Sit down, monsieur." We talked about things for over an hour. It was the first time that we had ever really discussed the problem. And at the end of it all he asked me to resume my post in Algiers.[10]

On 2 February, the National Assembly voted by 441 to 75 to give full powers to a government that had changed its composition. Louis Terrenoire replaced Soustelle at the Information Ministry. At the Armed Forces Ministry, de Gaulle replaced Guillaumat with Pierre Messmer, an intrepid fighter for the Free French, whom he had esteemed as a High Commissioner in Africa. It turned out that Messmer had just lived through the week of the barricades in Algeria at El-Milia, and noted that, outside Algiers, the army "was holding".

For the first time in the history of relations between Algiers and the mainland, it was Paris that had won. Thanks to the institutions? Thanks to the grip and eloquence of Charles de Gaulle. It was not the State that had won, simply by its authority and the law, but the inventive, unbending genius of an utterly exceptional individual, a soldier for civilians and a civilian for soldiers. De Gaulle now knew that peace in Algeria would come about through peace with the army.

Zigzagging to Peace...

On 3 March 1960, Charles de Gaulle left Paris for what the Press were to call the *tournée des popotes*.* He was not only the man who had defeated Joseph Ortiz: he could claim a much greater success, for on 13 February the first French atom bomb was exploded. The man who in 1945 had made what was almost a forced entry into the camp of the victors – who had got France a seat on the Security Council of the United Nations, who had restored the franc and, in a few summer months, had built up a republican monarchy capable of taking decisions, if less capable of debating them – now had the atom bomb, brandishing France as one might a torch at the opera, or the falconer his falcon.

What was surprising about the announcement of this French success was not so much the success itself as the relatively little effect, given the prospects thus opened up, that it had in French military circles. Just as, twenty-five years before, Major de Gaulle had come up against a General-Staff conservatism that favoured the Maginot line against the use of tanks, the General of 1960 was to find an officer corps more attentive to the words of Antoine Argoud on how to "topple" a Kabyl village by shooting terrorists on the public square than to the world-wide problems of nuclear deterrence.

As he set out to meet the soldiers, de Gaulle had yet another weapon in his hand, another "iron in the fire", as he liked to say: he had established his first contacts with the FLN. While one of his emissaries was talking to Ben Bella and his fellow-prisoners, Georges Pompidou, supposedly on behalf of the Rothschild bank, was taking soundings at Tunis and in Switzerland.

On 3 March, then, the head of state's helicopter landed at Hadjer-Mafrouh, on a rocky peak of the peninsula of Collo, near Constantine, one of the permanent battlefields of the war.

Plans for the General to visit Algeria had been around for two months. Originally it had been planned for 5 February, but his advisors had argued that it would have been suicidal to go then, just as they said it was suicidal now. Nevertheless, de Gaulle insisted on going; the only restriction he allowed himself was to limit his visits to airfields, enabling him to make contact with active units.[1] From post to post he stopped off, surrounded by soldiers, listening to the accounts of the heads of the Troisième Bureau, bombarding them with questions and listening with fascinated interest. And, occasionally, he spoke to the combatants. A despatch sent to Paris on 3 March triggered off a sort of earthquake. According to Geoffroy de Courcel, de Gaulle was talking again of *Algérie française*. René Brouillet wrote:

*"Tour of the messes". The General hated this term, which gave him an opportunity of accusing the press of "always abasing everything".

Our conversation was more relaxed the next evening. In the Sud-Algérois, where the General stopped off, Geoffroy de Courcel saw the Paris and Algiers journalists and he was thus able to assess the response of the Paris press, to realize the extent of the excitement that I had warned him of the day before. But he still had to convince the General of it. Although Geoffroy de Courcel, as a witness, knew what he had heard, the General, with even more certainty, knew what he had said and what he had not said. His reaction was, consequently, to refuse to get excited by something that neither had existed nor did exist.[2]

Louis Terrenoire, the Information Minister, who was then accompanying the head of State, wrote in his book *De Gaulle et l'Algérie* the essence of what the General had said and repeated throughout those three days:

No capitulation. The war may last a long time yet; it must be intensified. Independence? I call that secession, it would mean chaos and misery. Anyway, independence in the strict sense of the word no longer has any meaning in our world. Cut off from France, Algeria would lose its means of existence. You must push pacification to the end, that is to say, to the victory of arms.
  Win the war! Complete your mission! Smash the fellaghal!
  We shall not take Algeria back to the days before insurrection. France must remain in Algeria. In what form? That will depend on the Algerians, when they are able to express themselves freely. Algeria herself will settle her fate. It is in the nature of things that an Algerian Algeria should be linked to France.

Given the circumstances – the military setting, the days immediately after the barricades, disillusionment to be overcome – it was a tougher version of the speech of 16 September.
  Who really knows what the General had said to his soldiers? Perhaps not even those standing closest to him, Geoffroy de Courcel, Louis Terrenoire and Jean Mauriac, a journalist at the Agence France-Presse and son of the writer. De Gaulle was too much a "man of circumstances" not to allow them to colour, even to give direction to his words. Moreover, he himself believed that he had never used the words *Algérie française*.
  The fact remains that in politics the first impression, even if it is rarely correct, is often the most lasting. For a long time public opinion was to associate that tour with the idea of a repudiation, a recovery by the army of its old leader. Robert Buron, one of the General's ministers and most faithful followers, was not alone in wondering anxiously in what direction his leader, a "prince of equivocation", was going.[3]
  In early spring 1960, General de Gaulle's position was far removed from the idea of *Algérie française*, but it was fluid: the Algerians will choose to have their own State and we must be prepared for it and make that State a lasting associate of France. But could he achieve this by talking to the FLN?
  Between Paris and the provisional Algerian government, the steps taken par-

ticularly by Georges Pompidou were making progress. But, as we have seen, the provisional government was not the whole of the FLN. Its parliament, the National Council of the Algerian Revolution (CNRA), was to demonstrate the mistrustful turbulence peculiar to all assemblies that no popular vote has endowed with unquestionable representativeness. Sitting in Tripoli, from 16 December 1959 to 18 January 1960, the members of that body had found General de Gaulle's initiative an opportunity to re-animate legendary conflicts between its various tendencies. What emerged from those tumultuous sittings – and the French secret services gleaned a great deal of what was going on, though, misleadingly, it predicted the break-up of the FLN – was the maintenance of Ferhât Abbâs as president of the GPRA (a post that Belkacem Krim was scheming to obtain); the loss of influence of Krim, who was forced to exchange the prestigious Military Affairs portfolio for the dangerous one of Foreign Affairs; and the appearance at the head of the new, now centralized, General Staff of Houari Boumediene.

On 18 March 1960 Edmond Michelet, the Minister of Justice, who had already given proof of his sympathy for the emancipation of Algeria, received a discreet visit from a *cadi* (justice of the peace) from Médéa, a small prefecture close to Algiers, who had been sent to him by his friend, Procurator-General Schmelk, himself reputed to be a liberal. This Muslim magistrate came with a message from the leaders of Wilaya IV (the fourth province of Algiers in FLN terminology) giving him power to make contact with the French authorities on the mainland. Why? To let it be known that although the GPRA and the politicians of the movement had their reservations, the combatants were favourable to accepting General de Gaulle's offers and wanted to discuss them with his representatives at the earliest possible time.

Michelet persuaded Debré that the approach from Wilaya IV had to be followed up. Once informed, de Gaulle immediately decided not to ignore this overture. After all, he could not be accused of duplicity with respect to the FLN since he had never failed to declare that the FLN was merely one of the elements of fighting Algeria and could not arrogate to itself exclusive representation of the people struggling for its freedom.

Furthermore, the GPRA was not being "duplicated". The head of Wilaya IV, Si Salah, who soon became the central figure in the affair, informed Tunis of his approaches. And on several occasions, Si Salah made it plain that he wanted to win the support of Ben Bella. So de Gaulle appointed two emissaries, Colonel Mathon, a member of the Prime Minister's staff, and Bernard Tricot, his adviser at the Elysée. They set out for Médéa and on 28 March met three of the leaders of Wilaya IV, Lakhdar, Abdelhalim and Abdellatif, who talked of their "animosity towards the people outside" whom they accused of not paying sufficient attention to the problems of the combatants. They gave Bernard Tricot "the impression of men who wanted independence, but who might be satisfied with an autonomy in which their country would enjoy both freedom and the aid of France".

Then began a series of talks at the prefecture in Médéa on 31 March, 31 May, and 2 June 1960. From one meeting to another, the French representatives came to understand the aims of their opposite numbers, who were joined at the third meeting by Si Salah himself. To begin with, they talked about technical problems, such as the fate of the combatants. Then they got on to the political prospects of close cooperation between Algeria and France. Elections? Why? Did not the choice of "solution 3" of 16 September 1959, association, require elections? Lastly, if you insist on a formal consultation... What struck the two French representatives was both the competence and the authority of their opposite numbers. On 9 June, Si Salah, his military assistant Mohammed and his political adviser Lakhdar travelled to Paris in the greatest secrecy. At 10 p.m. they were taken – without being searched* – to see de Gaulle at the Elysée. It must be remembered that they were three leaders of a rebellion against the French State.

Bernard Tricot gives a good account of the meeting. "General de Gaulle was standing behind his desk, the rebel leaders approached and gave a military salute. The General, who had not moved from his place, sat down. The fellagha, Mathon and I, to the right and left of the desk, did likewise. Behind the not quite shut door, which sometimes squeaked weakly, I suspected a vigilant presence."

General de Gaulle opened the discussion with a reminder of his propositions of 16 September: "France no longer has any political manifesto to defend Algeria. It is up to the Algerians to decide on their fate."

Lakhdar: "The Algerian people recognizes the merits of self-determination. Furthermore, our first contacts have made it possible to lay the foundations of a technical agreement between us."

Mohammed: "The central difficulty concerns the laying down of weapons."

De Gaulle: "It is not a matter of surrendering weapons, but of allowing the administration to put them into store."

Lakhdar: "It is our wish that the cease-fire that would come about should extend to other combatants. We need safe-conducts for Kabylia and for Tunis."

De Gaulle: "I agree to contacts within Algeria. Not for Tunis. The important thing is to build up a new Algeria, that calm should be re-established, with the agreement of all, combatants and non-combatants."

De Gaulle then declared that he would address the GPRA in a forthcoming speech, but the present contacts with the visitors should continue in secret. Si Salah then spoke of the trust that this meeting inspired in him.

De Gaulle concluded by saying that he hoped to see the visitors again and, once the fighting had ceased, to shake their hands. "I am not doing that today, but I salute you!"

As they went out to the garden, Tricot asked Si Salah, Mohammed and Lakhdar if they were satisfied with the meeting: "Yes," they said, "it's a great guarantee for us."

The success of the negotiations now depended on the response of the GPRA to the General's speech. The leaders of Wilaya IV, who had been sent a copy of it, found it perfectly acceptable. If Tunis replied in a negative or dilatory way, the talks concerning a cease-fire with Wilaya IV would continue; if the GPRA agreed to negotiate, contacts with the Wilaya would be suspended, to be taken up again later if necessary.

The affair had a sinister conclusion. Si Salah's military assistant, Mohammed,

*De Gaulle was opposed to it.

was to have Lakhdar assassinated at the end of June and Abdellatif a few weeks later. And it is said that he was also responsible for an appalling massacre of women and children on the beach at Chenoua.

Si Salah returned from Kabylia to his Wilaya in September. At first he was kept under armed guard, then freed and given new responsibilities, only to be killed on 21 July 1961 during an encounter with the 22nd Battalion of Alpine Chasseurs near Bouira. Mohammed himself was to be killed by the 11th Semi-Brigade of shock-troops in the suburbs of Blida on 8 August 1961.

The Si Salah affair is one of the favourite themes of Charles de Gaulle's political enemies. It has even been suggested that he himself had Si Salah liquidated. Others criticize de Gaulle for giving priority to the political negotiations with the GPRA as proposed on 14 June 1960 (having excluded the possibility of such negotiations in September 1959 and January 1960) over the military talks, which would have demonstrated the success of the Challe plan and crowned the victory of the French forces. According to these critics – whose arguments are sometimes disturbing – it is because he rejected a solution within a French framework of a type that Si Salah and his friends would have accepted that the founder of the Fifth Republic preferred to talk to the FLN, thus dashing the hopes shared by the leaders of Wilaya IV and the General Staff in Algiers.

General de Gaulle's defenders might reply that, far from undervaluing the attempt made by the men of Wilaya IV, the head of State went out of his way to encourage it by receiving Si Salah and his companions at the Elysée, which he had always previously refused to do for any of the other Algerian nationalist leaders; and that he instructed his trusted assistant Bernard Tricot to pursue the matter with the utmost diligence and that, consequently, Tricot devoted three decisive months, from March to June 1960, to these talks and later wrote up a detailed account of them.

It should be added that the negotiators of Wilaya IV did not claim to be in opposition to the leaders of the FLN. Criticizing their slowness in seeking a cease-fire, Si Salah regarded his approach as a complement, or rather a preparatory phase of one that would be carried out by the leaders in Tunis – and, as Bernard Tricot shows very well, he did not rest until he was in communication with the leader of the prestigious Wilaya III, Mohand Ou el Hadj (a faithful representative of Belkacem Krim) or with Ben Bella or with Tunis.

On 14 June, four days after receiving Si Salah at the Elysée, the General launched his appeal to the GPRA, which seemed to short-circuit the operation that he had begun with Wilaya IV. In his book,* Tricot does not explain as well as one would like how Charles de Gaulle saw the connection between the two approaches. Did he himself distinguish them as clearly as history has done? Did he just give in to his passion for "having two irons in the fire"? Or did he use his meeting with the leaders of Wilaya IV only as a tool, to be used against the leaders in Tunis?

At noon on 14 June 1960, in the Salle des Fêtes of the Elysée, Charles de

*Les Sentiers de la Paix.

Gaulle recorded his most important speech on the Algerian question since that of 31 January, and one of the most brilliant he ever made.

> The genius of the century is also changing the conditions of our action overseas, leading us to bring an end to colonization. It is entirely natural that one should feel nostalgia for what was the Empire, just as one may regret the gentle light of oil lamps, the splendour of the navy under sail. But there is no valid politics outside realities.

So France must put an end to colonization. As for Algeria, the General took up his position on the straight, unambiguous route laid down on 16 September: self-determination, which he continued to link to the cease-fire:

> Once again, I turn, in the name of France, to the leaders of the insurrection. I am saying to them now that we await them here in order to find with them an honourable end to the fighting that is still continuing, to settle the destination of the weapons and so guarantee the fate of the combatants. After that, everything will be done to enable the Algerian people to make its voice heard in a calmer atmosphere. The decision will be its alone. But I am sure that it will take the sensible course: to carry out, in union with France and in cooperation with the various communities, the transformation of Algerian Algeria into a prosperous, fraternal country.

I can still see myself listening to the speech with my colleagues in the offices of *Le Monde*, a newspaper hardly suspected of Gaullist conformism. Leaving the premises, I went to a meeting in favour of peace in Algeria, organized by the left-wing parties. But, that evening, only the words of the man from the Elysée seemed to carry any weight or impress themselves in the memory.

And it seems the GPRA reacted in much the same way. This time, they could no longer fail to respond. De Gaulle had decimated the Wilayas of the ALN; he had smashed the barricades; he had begun talks with an important group of combatants; and today he was talking of an "Algerian" Algeria of tomorrow, not yet as a state, but already as a "country".

On 20 June the answer arrived from Tunis: the GPRA, acknowledging the "progress" in General de Gaulle's position, declared that it wanted "to put an end to the conflict" and had decided to send "a delegation presided over by Ferhât Abbâs to meet General de Gaulle". Meanwhile, an emissary would come to Paris to prepare the meeting. Everybody – both in Paris and in Algiers – knew that there would be difficulties. But was not the end in sight?

This splendid convergence of views was to lead to the most cruel of the many misunderstandings that were to dog the long march towards peace in Algeria. The GPRA had appointed two men of great ability, well aware of the French scene: its spokesman, Ahmed Boumendjel, and Mohammed Ben Yahia, a close colleague of Ferhât Abbâs. On the French side, less political figures had been chosen, Roger Moris, Secretary-General of the Committee of Algerian Affairs, and General de Gastyne. The place chosen for the meeting was the prefecture of Melun.

The failure of the attempt to reach peace in June 1960 arose from a double misinterpretation; on each side, the situation was analysed in a clumsy manner. On the French side, the mistake is to be found in Louis Terrenoire's book: "In Paris, after the speech of 14 June, so prompt and unequivocal a response by the GPRA was not expected. The thinking was that the opposing side was likely to be much more demanding than in fact it was."[4] Placing the affair in the light of the talks with Si Salah, the French leaders saw it as proof, firstly, that the combatants wanted to put an end to the fighting and, secondly, that the GPRA had poor control over its troops and still less over its cadres, and was being "duplicated" by one or other of them. And it was still thought that Tunis was unaware of the meetings with Wilaya IV – this was responsible for the Elysée's underestimation of the GPRA's ability to get their way with de Gaulle.

On the Algerian side, just as many miscalculations were made. The FLN emissaries made demands such as freedom of movement, freedom to speak in public, to hold press conferences even though the fighting was still continuing in Algeria. The two envoys of the GPRA, who had many personal friends in France, especially in the legal fraternity, the press and the universities, believed that these assets would automatically favour them. This was to underestimate the hostility to their cause felt by a large section of public opinion, which would have turned a meeting of the press into a major battle.

None of the four negotiators at Melun has left a precise account of what was said. Their clearest contribution, it seems, was to warn their guests that it was unlikely that French public opinion would change and that this meeting would be kept a secret.

In a letter in which he replied to questions that I had asked him on this matter, Saad Dahlab, who was to become the architect of the negotiations on the Algerian side, wrote: "Melun was one of de Gaulle's tricks! It is quite possible to believe that it was an attempt (the umpteenth) to divide the FLN, the GPRA and the rebels. Melun was what might be called a ruse. There were neither real talks nor real meetings with men truly responsible for French policies. Nothing was ready for a negotiation."

However, in his *Autopsie d'une guerre*, published twenty years after the event, Ferhât Abbâs writes that "the process of negotiation began" at Melun. "Nothing could now stop it. In this respect Melun was a beginning."[5] This could hardly sound more reasonable, but it bears little relation to his reactions at the time: indeed, Abbâs had initially declared on 5 July, in Tunis, that the hour had come for "armed combat", because "independence is not offered, but taken".

It is difficult to appreciate the climate that reigned over the summer and autumn of 1960, when progress towards a political solution turned into panic. Hence the depression that suddenly gripped the advocates of peace and the euphoria that reigned on both sides among those who wanted the war to continue. The conflict resumed with redoubled force. In Algeria, the FLN unleashed a campaign of terrorism that culminated in August with a massacre of Europeans on the beach at Chenoua. And, as in April 1958, the ALN executed prisoners on 12 August 1960. Those two crimes revealed the strength of the enemies of negotiation, who were as active on the FLN side as on the French.

Meanwhile, the GPRA began a major diplomatic offensive: Ferhât Abbâs visited Moscow and Peking in the autumn; and at the United Nations, Belkacem Krim asked for international supervision of the referendum for self-determination. There were also overtures to the Arab world, from which came many urgings not to negotiate. None of this pleased de Gaulle, who reacted by saying that it was impossible to negotiate as long as the fighting went on. On 5 September, during a press conference held at the Elysée, he repeated his views, in his husky voice: "One does not talk if one does not leave one's knives in the cloakroom."

On all sides, then, the signs against a negotiated solution were piling up. Passions were further inflamed by two symbolic trials. One was of the Jeanson organization, which had given help to the FLN and which was run by the philosopher Francis Jeanson, a close friend and colleague of Jean-Paul Sartre. The other was of the leaders of the January barricades, Lagaillarde and Susini, at which Colonel Argoud made a vehement speech against de Gaulle. At the same time, 121 leading figures in literature and the arts (including the daughter of André Malraux,* a member of the government) claimed the right of soldiers to conscientious objection to the war in Algeria. Here and there alliances were being formed between advocates of *Algérie française*, like Jacques Soustelle and Georges Bidault, old left-wing intellectuals like Albert Bayet and Paul Rivet, and extreme-right organizations such as Jeune Nation and more or less marginalized soldiers like Colonel Trinquier.

The return of parliament after the summer recess brought to a head what has been called the degradation of the civic spirit. Shortly after the opening of the Lagaillarde trial, 207 deputies demanded that he be released from detention. He was only eighteen votes short of the majority needed to pass the motion. The next day, the military court gave him his freedom and he took advantage of it to escape, and, with Susini, joined General Salan, who had sought political asylum in Spain. It was a double insult to de Gaulle and to the State. As in early May 1958, an atmosphere of civil war hung over France, at the very moment when the Algerian nationalists, disappointed by Melun, were opening up to pan-Arab and Marxist influences, while the enormous good will that de Gaulle enjoyed from the Algerian people seemed to be declining rapidly.

Nevertheless, it was the moment that de Gaulle chose to counter-attack, and by a series of initiatives he boldly relaunched the movement towards a negotiated peace. In six weeks, there were to be four decisions that shook Franco-Algerian relations out of the indignant stagnation of the autumn of 1960 towards the peace of early 1961 – progress that could only be impeded by the elimination of General de Gaulle in Paris or by some major shift within the Algerian leadership.

On 4 November 1960, Charles de Gaulle gave a press conference to follow up what he had said on 5 September. The General's words opened up a new stage on the long march towards a negotiated peace that would lead, in the longer or shorter term, to the independence of Algeria. The solution of this "affair that has lasted for a hundred and thirty years" could only be, according to de Gaulle, an "Algerian Algeria".

---

*Florence, who became the wife of the film director Alain Resnais.

That means an emancipated Algeria, an Algeria in which the Algerians themselves will decide their own fate, an Algeria in which responsibilities will be in the hands of Algerians, an Algeria that, if the Algerians so wish – and I believe that is what they want – will have its own government, its own institutions and its own laws. The Algeria of tomorrow, as it will be decided on by self-determination, may be built up either with France, or against France. France will not oppose the solution the ballot box produces, whatever it may be. If that turns out to be a hostile break, we will certainly not use force to remain beside people who have rejected us, though of course we shall take the necessary measures to safeguard on the one hand those Algerians who wish to remain French and on the other our own interests.* But if – which I believe with all my heart and all my mind – what we shall have is an Algeria in which the Muslim community and that of French descent cooperate with the guarantees intended, an Algeria that chooses to be united to France, for the economy, technology, education, defence, as is only sensible, then we shall provide for her material and human development the powerful and fraternal aid that we alone can provide.

De Gaulle then reminded the leaders of "the external organization of the rebellion" that he had always invited them to take part in talks concerning the organization of the future consultation, and in the "supervision of the vote" in concert with international observers. But although he put forward in bold detail the outlines of self-determination and the concept of an Algerian Algeria, de Gaulle's tone became harsher when he spoke of his partners at the short-lived Melun talks, who were responsible for "bringing appalling chaos to the region. It would, no doubt, only lead to the benefit of the totalitarian empires that the rebel leaders have chosen as protectors. Do they not see that, under such protection, they would be forceably dragged towards a Soviet Algeria?"

The two words "Algerian Republic", Pierre Viansson-Ponté recounts, did not appear in the version that was recorded in the morning and sent on to the Prime Minister: it was during a second recording that de Gaulle slipped in the fateful words.

A military plane, with a mass of extraordinary precautions, carried the film and sound-tape to Algiers, where it was broadcast at the same time as in mainland France, at 8 p.m. It was only when the plane was flying over the Mediterranean and could no longer be stopped that Michel Debré was warned by Brouillet of the "minor change" that the General had finally made to his speech. The Prime Minister protested, but in vain. "In any case, that's how things will end up," said de Gaulle.[6]

This incident reveals how deep the disagreement between the head of State and his second-in-command had become.

Reactions in Algiers were tumultuous, especially on 11 November, when the head of State's Delegate-General was humiliated by an indignant crowd. From

*Did he include the Europeans of Algeria in the category "our interests"?

Marshal Juin, who despite "the fifty-year friendship that bound him to General de Gaulle", protested against this "abandonment of our Algerian brothers", to Georges Bidault, who denounced as "execrable" and "unacceptable" a project that "would not be accepted" and to General Salan, in exile in Spain, the supporters of *Algérie française* were demonstrating their anger.

As for the GPRA, still ruefully remembering Melun, it chose not to see all that de Gaulle was conceding to the Algerian nation and was content to reply that what he had said merely amounted to an "accorded status", intended only "to prevent the Algerian people from expressing itself". What, then, did the men in Tunis want? Independence or power?

It was clear to de Gaulle that Paul Delouvrier had suffered enough in Algiers, and the General decided to replace him with Jean Morin. Though he had long been regarded as an ally of Georges Bidault, Morin declared his willingness to carry out that impossible mission in Algiers. As well as making this change, de Gaulle set the date of the referendum for 8 January. There was nothing like opposition to drive Charles de Gaulle to irreversible initiatives.

On 22 November, a Ministry of State for Algerian Affairs was created and entrusted to Louis Joxe, a man in whom de Gaulle could have every confidence. Joxe had been Secretary-General of his government in Algiers during the war, then, after the Liberation, in Paris, and was now Education Minister. It was a significant decision. It removed Algerian affairs from the hands of the Prime Minister, and brought in a man whose fidelity to the General matched that of Michel Debré, but who also knew Algeria well, having taught there for many years, and whose ideas on the Algerian question were notably "progressive".

With these decisions and changes made, de Gaulle now had to see if they would have any effect in Algeria itself. There was an unknown element: who would represent the Algerian people? Who could speak in its name, at least to organize the consultation of the people in agreement with the French State? De Gaulle considered that he alone could decide and that this decision could only come from direct experience, from going to Algeria in person. During a Council of Ministers on 8 December, the head of State announced that the trip he would be making the following day would have "the character of an inspection". Of course, the itinerary planned avoided Algiers and the larger cities, where the European crowds flanked by the Front pour l'Algérie française (FAF) would not allow an inspection by the man they cursed – though Lagaillarde's escape from his Paris prison was likely to revive their courage.

For what was to be his last trip to Algeria – the last of a head of State in a still-French Algeria – General de Gaulle flew from Orly on 9 December about 8 a.m., accompanied by Louis Joxe, Pierre Messmer, Louis Terrenoire and Generals Ely and Olié, landing two hours later near Aïn-Temouchent, a large farming community in the Oranie. This is how Louis Terrenoire, who kept a journal of that hazardous trip, describes it:

> All round the town hall of Aïn-Temouchent, a large crowd was massed.
> Dense and vociferous, bearing placards with provocative slogans.* On the

*Such as "No to abandonment!", "De Gaulle = treason!"

town hall steps, the General observed those people yelling abuse at him, blinded by hatred and despair, without saying a word. Nevertheless, the spectacle was not entirely unorganized. Muslims had been placed in large numbers in the front rows. They, too, were carrying placards with slogans. Obviously they were the main elements in a stage setting that the General would bring crumbling down with his usual gesture. As there were outstretched hands rather than hostile fists, he plunged into the crowd. Scarcely had he gone a few steps towards a group of Muslims, than their rhythmic cries of *Algérie française* were followed without transition by repeated cries of *Vive de Gaulle!* The placards disappeared as if absorbed by the commotion that swirled round the General. All round him swarmed a mass of fezes and head-scarves. Temporarily caught off balance, the European ringleaders, who had come from Oran, fell silent for a moment, only to resume even more loudly, as if their shouting could make up for the Muslims' change of side.[7]

On 12 December, after visiting Tizi-Ouzou and Akbou, the presidential cortège reached Bougie, where de Gaulle and his team had to take refuge in a sub-prefecture, besieged as they were by a delirious crowd, and where dramatic news reached them from Algiers: confrontations had led to fifty deaths, forty-five of whom were Muslims. The trip had to be cut short. De Gaulle reached Paris the next day, a day earlier than expected, after passing through Batna and Biskra. The "inspection" was over.

So what had taken place in Algiers, and to a lesser degree at Oran or at Bône? From 9 December, when de Gaulle landed in the Oranie, waves of European demonstrators, most of them younger but better organized than those of May 1958 and January 1960, often wearing helmets and carrying truncheons, marched on the GG then on to the Palais d'Eté. Members of the CRS and mobile police contained them more or less, but at the cost of serious losses. The tide was still rising by 10 December.

On Sunday the eleventh as the head of State was confronting the clamour of the European citizens of Bougie (whose mayor, Jacques Augarde, was a liberal), a wave of Muslims swept in from the outlying districts of Algiers to the centre, brandishing FLN flags (green and white, with a red crescent), chanting the song of the mujahidin, "Biladi Biladi" and waving placards bearing their slogans "Long live Arab Algeria, Long live Ferhât Abbâs, Free Ben Bella!"

Europeans and police were hurt, and one of them was killed. The police opened fire on the columns of Muslims marching towards the residential quarters. Soon there were dozens of dead. The figure of fifty given to the General on the evening of 11 December was to be doubled the following day, while the disturbances spread to Oran and Bône. The ordinary Muslim population was now on the move, after having been merely spectators for so long. The shouts of *Vive de Gaulle!* and *Vive l'Algérie algérienne!* turned to *Vive' Abbâs!* and *Vive l'Algérie arabe!* The Algerian Muslims were no longer quite those of May 1958, firstly because the grip of the army was no longer what it had been (the dispersal of the paratroops through the djebels had been ended),* and secondly because, whatever had happened at Melun, the ideas launched by de Gaulle had had an effect and raised hopes.

In his book *Dernier Quart d'heure*, Albert-Paul Lentin, a witness of those dramatic hours, tells how a French lieutenant said to him: "That 11 December 1960 will have been the Muslims' 13 May." A civil servant at the Délégation Générale told him: "There is no need for a referendum now. Today the Muslims have made up their minds." And he added: "The myth of the isolation of the GPRA is collapsing."[8]

In the plane that took him back to Paris a day earlier than expected, de Gaulle told Louis Terrenoire of his impressions. Although he had long tried to bring about an Algerian third force between the party of integration and the party of independence, he was now very sceptical of any possible success in that direction. "We must find an arrangement with the FLN and, in any case, drive them into a corner. That's what I shall do after the referendum." As for the activists, he added, we shall "smash" them if necessary.[9] Greeting those who welcomed him on his return to Orly airport, he declared: "Well, gentlemen, everything that has taken place has cleared the atmosphere." And he repeated some words that he had just used at Biskra: "This trip has allowed me to get the full measure of the problem." The next day he was to say dryly: "Of course it is Algeria that needs France and not the other way around. But if they want to secede, let the devil take them!"[10]

*Decided on by Pierre Messmer six months earlier.

CHAPTER TWENTY-THREE

The Pronunciamiento of the "Four"

One can endlessly debate the various stages in the development of Charles de Gaulle's thoughts and decisions on Algeria. One always comes back to two key dates: 16 September 1959, when, advocating self-determination, he renounced the idea of a French Algeria; and 9 December 1960, when he realized that the Algerian masses had clearly chosen the FLN as their mouthpiece and independence as their aim. Everything else was really no more than a matter of procedure and methods. Will negotiations take place before a cease-fire? And will they be with the FLN alone? Will the new State include the Sahara? Will it remain structurally bound up with France? Will the European Algerians be given guarantees?

In any case, nothing and nobody was going to reverse his decisions, short of killing him or overthrowing him, especially since the crystallization of his own ideas coincided with those of public opinion. As Antoine Argoud wrote at the time: "The French people are tired of the Algerian war. It wants only one thing: to be rid of that 'problem'."[1] To the electors on both sides of the Mediterranean, to give an answer on 8 January 1961 to the double question, "Do you approve the bill concerning the self-determination of the Algerian populations and the organization of public powers in Algeria before self-determination?" he launched one of those skilfully dramatized appeals that had become such a feature of his life for the last twenty years. On Friday 6 January, only two days before the vote, he gave a personalized, almost intimate appeal: "*Françaises, Français*, as you know, your answer is addressed to me. I need, yes, I need to know what is in your hearts and minds. That is why I turn to you above all intermediaries. The matter really is – who does not know it? – between each of you and me." Never before had he tried to gain entry into the conscience of the French people with such urgency, that "need to know", that reference to "hearts", that "matter between you and me".

The results of the referendum proved favourable: 56 per cent of those on the voting register voted "yes", that is to say, 75 per cent of the votes cast. Two days later he analysed the results with his Minister of Information. It was an honourable result. Louis Terrenoire thought that he had regained his serenity, comparing the figures for the 1958 election, calculating the transferences of vote, studying the significance of the spoilt papers. "The most vital part of France has voted yes, the part that believes in the future, the part with the most children, while the 'no's have come largely from the stagnant departments."

But what of Algeria? 39 per cent, obviously Muslims, had voted "yes"; 18 per cent, obviously the supporters of *Algérie française*, had voted "no"; abstentions amounted to 42 per cent following the order from the FLN. This last figure seemed highly significant to de Gaulle: "We must make no mistake, the Muslims have followed the instructions of the FLN." Terrenoire goes on:

> Suddenly General de Gaulle's expression changed and he addressed me in a quite unusual way as *Monsieur le Ministre de l'Information*: "So far I have made a lot of speeches; we must gradually prepare public opinion for what shall surely happen; now it's getting serious, we must keep quiet, because we shall have meetings with the FLN."
>
> "*Mon Général*, you must be fairly well informed as to what the leaders of the uprising think and want?"
>
> "Absolutely not!" was the response, expressed in unequivocal terms and emphasised by a convincing gesture. The General went on: "That's precisely where we have to begin. We mustn't go back to the misunderstanding of Melun. All we know about them is that they are divided."[2]

At the time when the negotiations were to begin, what did the FLN leadership think of General de Gaulle's intentions and of its chances of getting what it wanted? Abdelhamid Mehri, one of the members of the GPRA at the time and later Minister of Social and Cultural Affairs in the Abbâs cabinet, was to give me his impressions.

> Contrary to what many people said and wrote, we were in no way favourably prejudiced towards de Gaulle. We knew that his coming to power was very important, that the enemy had grown bigger. In what direction could this change affect us? We never presupposed that he was any more favourable to us than others – only that he was more serious.
>
> With General de Gaulle, we had decided on a few guide-lines as to how to treat him. First, not to expect from him anything but the strictest realism. No ideology, no feelings, no external (or internal) pressure could, we knew, deflect the line that he had drawn for himself – and which we knew would be a devious one, with a concern only to preserve French interests. Secondly, knowing his tactical imagination, we should never fail to respond to any of his initiatives. Never allow ourselves to be put on the defensive, always send the ball back. With a strategist, an orator and a tactician like him, always keep the debate moving, after a systematic analysis of his texts. For we knew that any refusal on our part to talk to him would be taken as an excuse to intensify the war.[3]

Through the good offices of the Swiss minister, Olivier Long, and his friend, the journalist Charles-Henri Favrod, also Swiss, who had been in contact with the Algerian leaders for years, this opportunity did not take long to materialize. Favrod left Paris for Tunis, bearing a message proposing an official, but secret, meeting, and a reminder to the FLN leaders that "the fundamental problem is that of the guarantees concerning those of French origin remaining in Algeria".

On 16 January, the GPRA let it be known that it was ready "to engage in negotiations with the French government on condition that it would be allowed to consult the Algerian people". As a result, two days later, Paris published a communiqué (written by the General himself) indicating that the Council of Ministers had noted that "the leaders of the rebellion had expressed an apparently more favourable disposition to the possibility of peaceful meetings".

The diplomat Claude Chayet was sent to Geneva where he was to ask a representative of the GPRA these three questions: "Where? When? Through whom?" Having received the answers to these questions, he was to return to Paris.

Chayet found himself face to face with an Algerian representative whom he may not have expected to be so important. It was Saad Dahlab, who was not yet the GPRA's Foreign Affairs spokesman but had already established himself as the key man in negotiations. Clearly bound to tight rules of engagement, Dahlab did no more than note the questions and indicate that he would pass them on to his superiors. The two men agreed that, in two weeks' time and in Switzerland, an official representative of the GPRA would be ready to meet a personal envoy from General de Gaulle.

On 20 February, then, the General's envoy, Georges Pompidou, met the representative of the GPRA, Ahmed Boumendjel. Meanwhile, Mohammed Masmoudi, a minister and spokesman of the Tunisian leader, Habib Bourguiba, asked for an audience with de Gaulle to urge him to accelerate the process and to receive Bourguiba. According to Masmoudi, the General said to him:

> "I'm not blind. I know that the FLN now represents nine-tenths of the Algerian population, in sentiment at least. I recognize that in Algeria it has forged a moral entity, therefore a political entity, therefore a nation. What I am not sure of, on the other hand, is the willingness of M. Abbâs and his friends to negotiate. I know that it is in the interests of the USSR for the war to go on and it is trying to intervene more and more in Algeria. I wonder if it is not already too late for the FLN. I don't mind telling you that if I were convinced that the FLN were in Khrushchev's clutches I would not talk to M. Abbâs and his friends."
>
> "We don't think so, *mon Général!* President Bourguiba is convinced of it. I hope that he will persuade you to share his view."
>
> "I'm glad M. Bourguiba is convinced of that. I shall have some useful talks with him on the question. I note in any case that he is not frightened by the Bolshevization of the FLN. But I may know what he does not know. The Soviet Ambassador in Paris, Vinogradov, with whom I have talked on the subject, left me with the clear impression that his country intended to intervene more and more in Algeria."[4]

Awaiting the Bourguiba–de Gaulle dialogue, the talks continued between Pompidou and Boumendjel. Three meetings took place, in Lucerne on 20 and 22 February and on 5 March at Neuchâtel. Returning to Paris on 6 March, Georges Pompidou confided to Jean Mauriac:

> We have a 60 per cent chance of succeeding. We are very far from the atmosphere of Melun. It seems quite clear that the two big problems are the

cease-fire and the Sahara. We want a truce, a suspension of military activity during the talks. They don't want that at any cost. But we are going to have to give in to them. On the matter of the Sahara, we agree on a shared exploitation of resources, but not on the nationality of the territory. They have obviously no right over the Sahara. But world opinion, on this matter, will support them. Why do we want to keep that desert? For nuclear experiments. This, of course, does not predispose the majority of foreign states in our favour. On the question of the status of the European minority, our position is better. As for Mers el-Kebir, it will remain French. And the General? He's resigned to it. For him, the worst is over. And he knows he has the support of everybody, even the men laying plastic bombs![5]

Between the first two Swiss talks and the third, General de Gaulle received Habib Bourguiba at Rambouillet, on 27 February 1961. To all appearances, everything went very well between two equally flamboyant characters, virtuosos of the verbal joust. The statement released afterwards spoke of "cordial and satisfactory" exchanges, but, on matters of importance, there were two main disagreements.

The Tunisian leader brought up the question of Bizerte, the second city in Tunisia and a French military base: an independent State could not accept a foreign base on its soil indefinitely. De Gaulle promised that France would withdraw "within something like a year". Habib Bourguiba declared that he was not insisting on "an immediate solution of the problem". But what did "immediate" mean?

On the Algerian question, Bourguiba also indicated that he expected his country to benefit from a revision of the frontiers of the Sahara, giving Tunisia control of areas with oil fields. De Gaulle refused to go along with him on this point. In fact, Bourguiba had got no firm answers on either point.

At the same time, news came from Rabat that the King of Morocco, Mohammed V, had died after an apparently successful operation.* The new king, Hassan II, invited Habib Bourguiba and Ferhât Abbâs to the funeral, which took place at Rabat on 1 March. As the head of the GPRA was accompanied by Belkacem Krim, a conference was hastily improvised, on the basis of the optimistic account given by the Tunisian leader of his talks with General de Gaulle. A statement was issued: "the three delegation leaders consider that no obstacle should be put up to the opening of direct negotiations between the GPRA and the French government in the context of complete decolonization" and "declared their perfect agreement as to the proper means of achieving the independence of Algeria".

On 15 March the French government released its statement: "The Council of Ministers has confirmed its wish to see the beginning of talks concerning the conditions for the self-determination of the Algerian populations and related problems." And the next day, in Tunis, the GPRA confirmed that agreement had been reached on a date, 7 April, and a place, Evian, which the Algerians could easily reach from Geneva.

*De Gaulle immediately telephoned to his Ambassador at Rabat: "What nationality was the surgeon?" "Swiss." "Good."

On 29 March, Charles de Gaulle chaired a Council of Ministers devoted to Algerian affairs, but this time he scarcely asked anyone for his opinion. The ministers were simply given a unilateral account:

> We can be patient in the talks that are soon to start. They will be long and painful. On the fundamental question, our position is self-determination: with France or without her. Algeria is confronting her destiny: neither the grenade nor the bomb, neither the knife nor the machine-gun, neither the susceptibilities nor the bluster of the FLN, neither the blindness nor the threats of the activists, no, none of those things will stop it going through according to the logic of our time. As for France, she must now draw on herself, on her own people, for the elements of her greatness and the permanence of her universal vocation.[6]

Meanwhile, he had to confront a new challenge. In early April, a mysterious organization, which signed its tracts OAS (Organisation Armée Secrète) and was clearly supported by high-ranking officers, launched a campaign of terrorist attacks, the most political and most bloody of which involved the death of the mayor of Evian, Camille Blanc, who was getting ready to receive the French and Algerian negotiators.*

No more was needed for de Gaulle to resume the initiative. At a press conference held at the Elysée on 11 April, he declared that "France has no objection to the fact that the Algerian populations are deciding to build up a State of their own and take charge of their country." When a journalist remarked that a retreat by France would run the risk of handing Algeria over either to the USA or to the USSR, he retorted facetiously, for the benefit of the two superpowers: "A toutes deux je souhaite d'avance bien du plaisir."**[7] And he went on to say: "I have smashed the plots that wanted to force me to support integration."[8] It was an imprudent use of the past tense. Equally imprudent was the statement made a week later by his Minister for the Armed Forces, Pierre Messmer, before the American and British press in Paris: "It is out of the question that the army will lose its discipline."[9]

For a year now, each move towards a political solution had triggered off some counter-attack in military circles. Since September 1960, many high-ranking army officers and some politicians had been convinced that only the assassination of de Gaulle or a *coup d'état* could keep Algeria as part of France. It was at this time that Colonel Argoud, the central figure in these military circles, made up his mind: for moral as well as political reasons, he considered it necessary to sacrifice the Head of State, either physically or politically, so that Algeria would remain French.

*OAS leaders have maintained that they did not want to kill M. Blanc: but two bombs had been planted, one under his car.
**As so often, an apparently simple remark by de Gaulle defies adequate translation of its special combination of old-world formality, bordering on stiffness and heaviness, and idiomatic flair. "I hope they both enjoy it" or "I hope they both enjoy themselves there" are quite inadequate. (trs.)

Shortly after Argoud had made his decision, Edmond Jouhaud, now living in Algiers, having left the army, set about drawing together the civil and military forces against the State. As for Maurice Challe, though still in command of forces in central Europe and based in Fontainebleau, he was preparing to resign (which he did in January 1961).

So Argoud, an energetic leader of men possessed of ready intelligence, was desperately in search of a force and a leader to save French Algeria. Flanked by Colonel Joseph Broizat, he frequented the General Staffs, "an honest agent of the *putsch*", he writes, in search of men ready to risk all – career, life, honour – to smash the "executioner" and keep Algeria.

On 1 November, Broizat and Argoud went to see Massu. Although they had learnt that their former superior was trying to get back into favour with the Elysée, they tried passionately to persuade him to assume the leadership of the uprising in Algeria: he alone had the name, the popularity, and the stature to bring over both a large section of the army officers and the urban masses of Algiers and Oran. But he refused to join in the adventure and told his visitors that they were over-excited.

General Salan, too, was working against de Gaulle. He was coldly received at Madrid, where the authorities were hoping for a *rapprochement* with de Gaulle (though he did make contact with Franco's brother-in-law, Serrano Suñer, former Foreign Minister whom the Caudillo had sacked from his cabinet because he had compromised himself too much with the Nazis). Removed from all responsibilities, Suñer was all the freer to put himself at the disposal of General Salan and his companions, Lagaillarde and Susini. It was thanks to him that they were able to reach Algeria when the time came.

But the operation needed a leader. Salan inspired confidence in nobody and the airman Jouhaud was unknown to the soldiers on the ground. The only possible leaders were Massu and Challe. On 9 March, Argoud and Broizat visited Massu again. It was to be "one of the most frightful scenes I have ever known," Argoud writes. Massu warned his visitors against the "madness" that they had embarked on and the two colonels left pouring insults on his head.

On 30 March, Maurice Challe, who had finally left his command at Fontainebleau, received the two organizers of the *putsch*. He was to allow himself to be convinced that the affair had to aim at a military take-over of Algiers by a few battalions of paratroops, but demanded (a) to be the leader, and (b) to decide on the time of the operation himself. The two colonels were so unconvinced of his determination that they asked him as they left: "You won't throw us over?"[10]

On 12 April, the last meeting of the conspirators took place. The coup was planned for the night of 20 April. They could depend on five generals* – Challe, Jouhaud, Zeller, Gardy and Faure – while Gouraud, the commanding officer at Constantine, had given assurances of support. There was no mention of Salan. The junta was joined at last by a key figure, Godard, who was to be the dynamo of the enterprise of which Argoud had been the inventor. And what forces did they have at their disposal? Two regiments based on Algiers, five on Constantine. But the conspirators had received three warnings from particularly competent officers,

*Retired or without a job.

including Major Robin, who questioned whether the officer corps, still less the troops themselves, would rally to the cause. Challe and his men decided not to take account of this prophetic advice.

The conspirators met in Algiers on 20 April. The colonels, who arrived before the generals – only Jouhaud and Gardy were living locally – learnt on landing that the coup had been postponed for twenty-four hours: it would now take place on the night of 21 April. Challe, Zeller and Jouhaud took up position in the basement of a villa. The spearhead of the operation was the 1st Foreign Paratroop Regiment (REP), whose temporary commander was Major Elie Denoix de Saint-Marc (an officer renowned for his character and integrity), and a paratroop unit, the Groupe de Commandos Parachutistes de Réserves Générales (GCPRG), commanded by Major Georges Robin, also an officer with a fine reputation.

When Antoine Argoud landed in Algiers at 11 a.m. on the 22nd, the first phase of the *putsch* had succeeded. The forces committed to the operation were in control of the city's main nerve centres, the civil and military authorities were under lock and key and the three generals had taken up position at the General Staff. But there was a sense of indecisiveness in the air.

In Paris, on 21 April, General de Gaulle's day had been taken up with African friendship: Léopold Sédar Senghor, President of the very recently independent republic of Senegal, was being given an official reception. At 8 p.m., the two heads of State were welcomed at the Comédie Française, where Racine's *Britannicus* was being performed, each of them knowing whole scenes of the play by heart:* that night, de Gaulle and Senghor went to sleep without any immediate worries.

Yet, very late that evening, the Algiers Sûreté and General Gambiez's General Staff were told of strange activity around Zeralda, a paratroop billet, twenty kilometres out of Algiers. Just after midnight – de Gaulle had already gone to bed – Gambiez in Algiers got into his car and drove straight to the centre of the supposed trouble. On the road going down to the centre of the city, he saw coming towards him a column of trucks loaded with men in camouflage. The little general (he was only five foot, three inches tall) ordered them to stop, tried to block the road with his vehicle and told them they would be punished. Unsuccessful in his attempt to halt this convoy, he drove straight to the Forum, where he was apprehended by the leaders of the uprising, together with General Vézinet, army Commander-in-Chief in Algiers, the Delegate-General Jean Morin and Robert Buron, the Minister of Public Works, who had just arrived in Algeria to open a technical school. Morin and Buron were "locked up" in the Palais d'Eté, but, noting that the paratroops had forgotten to cut off the telephone, they alerted Paris.

It was nearly 2 a.m. on 22 April when the head of the Sûreté, Jean Verdier, woke Roger Frey, the Minister of the Interior. Frey immediately warned Michel Debré, who woke de Gaulle at about 2.30 a.m. "Things are moving in Algiers." But, Debré added, Oran was holding firm, Constantine was more doubtful, and all the security forces in mainland France were already on alert.

De Gaulle and Debré took stock of the situation: one minister and two generals had been taken prisoner by the mutineers; two of the most important members of

---

*M. Senghor had been a teacher of literature.

the government, Messmer and Couve de Murville, had left for Rabat where they were attending the scattering of the ashes of General Lyautey, and the Airforce Chief of General Staff, General Staehlin, was in Madagascar. Until the members of the government could meet formally, the head of State took one important decision: Joxe, the Minister for Algerian Affairs, and General Olié, the Chief of General Staff of the Armed Forces, would leave immediately for Algeria with a view to rallying the loyal forces. It was to be a suicide-mission, and they took off from Villacoublay without knowing if they would be able to land.

At 6.30 a.m. the radio broadcast the proclamation to the troops by General Challe, head of the military uprising:

> Officers, non-commissioned officers, policemen, sailors, soldiers and airmen, I am in Algiers with Generals Zeller and Jouhaud and in touch with General Salan* so as to keep the army's oath to ensure a French Algeria, so that our dead may not have died in vain. A government of abandonment is preparing to hand over the departments of Algeria to the external organization of the rebellion. Do you want Mers el-Kebir and Algiers to become Soviet bases tomorrow? I know your courage, your pride, your discipline. The army shall not fail in its mission.

What strikes one about this speech is not that it is lacking in colour or enthusiasm – Challe was no de Gaulle – but that it was only addressed to the members of the armed forces. Thus, from the outset, the *putsch* did not conceal what in fact it was: a military operation, based on the "oath" of the soldiers.

As Challe was constantly to repeat, it was not a question of seizing power, but merely of cutting short the policy of self-determination, of relaunching operations, crushing the rebels and winning the war in order to make Algeria a "French province", once more part of France. Whether, in the meantime, de Gaulle would have been overthrown or whether he would have resigned was not Challe's business: his job – and this was one of the arguments of his defence – was of a strictly military kind, one might almost say a matter of military honour, even if it had political implications.

Commenting on the absence of the Algiers people from his speech, I wrote in *Le Monde* on 27 April: "A Mediterranean crowd has been offered a German-style *putsch*; it is hardly surprising that it did not succeed." The civilian population was held at a distance by Challe, who, by getting his "professional" point of view to prevail, ruined the whole enterprise. Furthermore, the exclusion of the people of Algiers irritated the second-in-command of the operation, Edmond Jouhaud, who was himself one of them and who had been put in charge of "relations with the population".

While Joxe and Olié were flying low over Algeria to avoid radar detection, the navy, commanded by the Gaullist Querville at Mers el-Kebir, remained loyal to the government, as did General de Pouilly, Army Commander at Oran. At Constantine Airforce Commander Fourquet repeated the government's orders loud

---

*This was not true. Salan learnt of the coup by radio.

and clear. In Paris, the police arrested a few notorious activists – from whom they soon learnt the centre of operation in mainland France: General Faure, Colonel Vaudrey, Major Bléhaut, Captain de Saint-Rémy and a few civilians of some note. OAS pamphlets ("The hunt for the traitors has begun!") were found on the conspirators, together with a plan, drawn up by Colonel Godard, involving the take-over of Paris by three military columns converging from Orleans, Rambouillet and Auxerre – a plan that had begun on the night of 21 April, but only timidly, thus giving the police an opportunity of arresting a few dozen young reserve officers travelling from Orléans to Paris, armed, but in private vehicles.[11]

De Gaulle came onto the scene on Saturday at 9 a.m., receiving Michel Debré at the Elysée. The two men decided to summon an extraordinary Council of Ministers for 5 p.m., which would make it possible to evaluate the first results of the Joxe–Olié mission and to declare a state of emergency. Then the General sent his aide-de-camp to Admiral Cabanier, the navy Chief of General Staff, asking him to order the *Picard*, the ship commanded by Philippe de Gaulle, to leave Mers el-Kebir immediately: the mutineers must not be allowed to take the head of state's son hostage.[12]

At 5 p.m. the Council of Ministers opened. "We found the General wearing his moral 'storm' clothes," Louis Terrenoire recounts. "With incredible calm and implacable determination, he announced his intention of applying article 16 of the Constitution without delay." This determination was shared by the Prime Minister, whom several of the General's colleagues found "much firmer than during the affair of the barricades", and by Malraux, who rediscovered his pugnacity. "We shall face them, if necessary, with tanks."[13]

In such circumstances, de Gaulle could not fail to stress, with some sarcasm, how insignificant he considered these rivals with their star-studded caps: "What is serious in this affair, gentlemen, is that it is not really serious at all."[13] Warned by an officer of his private General Staff that he would not fire on the paratroops if they attacked the Elysée, Flohic and his companions turned their office into a bastion and armed themselves to the teeth. The loyal officers also considered it useful to go and check the defences of the military airfields. At Villacoublay, they discovered that the only airforce officer at his post was a flying officer who knew nothing about what was going on!

On Sunday 23 April, Challe made what amounted to a victory speech. Algiers, it was true, was in the hands of the uprising. But in Constantine the situation was less clear, and Bône, Tizi-Ouzou and Mostaganem were in the hands of declared Gaullists. In Oran, Argoud had been no more successful than General de Pouilly in bringing out the legionaries of Sidi-bel-Abbès. Later he was to reproach himself for not having "executed", with his own hands and on the spot, that officer whose "death would have dramatized the situation" and "shown all those who were hesitating that we would stop at nothing".

Then there was a decisive event that doomed the whole enterprise to failure. De Gaulle spoke. Moreover, he was listened to, not only by the people of mainland France, but also by the army in Algeria. The General's speech, broadcast at 8 p.m. on 23 April was to lead to feverish activity in Paris. The rumour had spread that the paratroops would land from Algiers about 10 p.m. and take cover during the night in the Paris region. There was an appeal from Malraux, but also from the trade unions and the PCF, for the formation of a people's army. People were signing on at the Ministry of the Interior. And a picturesque crowd of Surrealist poets, actresses and philosophy teachers, workers, prostitutes, Moroccan labourers and Communist militants, marched off to the Place Beauvau, then to the cellars of the Grand Palais. They had some helmets and equipment, but no weapons.

No one has forgotten Malraux's speech: "Once again, France is living through a historical moment. In three hours, the paratroops should be here, but since you are here, they shall not pass!" This only led to de Gaulle asking Malraux and Frey the following day: "Would you be so kind as to explain to me the reasons for this grotesque tumult that you have organized under my windows?"[14] Although he had placed a few tanks in front of the Palais Bourbon, he had no desire for a popular mobilization launched by the unions. As we have seen, he never believed in the determination and still less in the imagination of the conspirators. On the Sunday afternoon, he remarked to Chaban-Delmas: "Fidel Castro would already have been here. But that poor Challe isn't Fidel Castro."[15]

Writing years later, Louis Terrenoire has much the same story to tell: "On Sunday evening, we were gathered together in the Hôtel Matignon with the Prime Minister. The fearless behaviour of the head of State was not enough to conceal the threat from us, which we believed to be a real one, of a raid by paratroop commandos on the capital, leading to a *coup d'état*."[16]

At 7 p.m. on the Sunday television technicians were busying themselves at the Elysée. The General then made his entrance: he was wearing his uniform again. When he sat down in front of the cameras, those there knew that it was not to offer a compromise.

At 8 p.m., we saw on our screen the old Jacobin inquisitor who, fifteen months earlier, had crumbled the barricades with a few proud barks. That old head was shaking, under the locks of hair. His eyes flashed with fury, his face twisted in anger and his clenched fists were placed on either side of the microphone, like the Colts of the heroes of Westerns on the card table. This is what he said:

An insurrectional power has been set up in Algeria by a military junta.

This power has an appearance, a quartet of retired generals. It has a reality: a group of partisan, ambitious, fanatical officers. This group and that quartet possess a certain expeditious and limited skill. But they see and understand the nation and the world only through their distorted frenzy. Their enterprise is leading straight to national disaster. The State is flouted, the nation defied, our power shaken, our international prestige abased, our place and our role in Africa compromised. And by whom? Alas! Alas! By men whose duty, honour, *raison d'être* is to serve and to obey.

In the name of France, I order that every means, I say every means, be used to close the road to those men, until they are crushed. I forbid any Frenchman and, above all, any soldier to carry out any of their orders. The only leaders, civil and military, who have the right to assume responsibilities are those who have been properly appointed to do so. The future of the usurpers must only be the one that destines them to the full rigour of the law.

So that the misfortune that hovers over the nation and the threat that weighs over the Republic can be alleviated, I have decided to implement article 16 of our Constitution, having taken official advice from the Constitutional Council, the Prime Minister, the President of the Senate, and the President of the National Assembly. From today, if necessary directly, I shall take whatever steps seem to me to be required by the circumstances. I hereby declare, for today and for tomorrow, that I shall maintain the French and republican legitimacy that the nation has conferred upon me, whatever happens, to the full term of my mandate or until such time as I lack the strength or life to do so, and I shall take every means possible to ensure that it remains after me. French men and women, see the course that France runs the risk of going and compare it with what it was becoming once again.

French men and women, help me! [17]

Was this Charles de Gaulle's finest speech? Energy, emotion, everything was there. Those words were acts. Of all Charles de Gaulle's great speeches, it was perhaps the one in which the effectiveness of speech was most strongly demonstrated. Already undermined by their divisions and their lack of vision, the Algiers rebels were to be swept aside by these words. One has to have heard that summons addressed to a whole people to appreciate its power. But simply re-reading it, from the "a certain expeditious and limited skill" to the two cries of "alas!" and that "help me!", which must have won over millions of hearts, leaves each one confused.

The effect of de Gaulle's summons was to be all the stronger in that it was received on the innumerable transistors that the troops – including the paratroop regiments – had with them in Algeria. Robert Buron writes in his *Carnets politiques de la guerre d'Algérie* that the defeat of the rebels was the "victory of the transistors". In his own way, Antoine Argoud acknowledged this when he complained that the head of state's broadcast appeal incited non-commissioned officers to "desertion".

It was in those four hours, from 8 p.m. to midnight, that matters took a decisive turn. Maurice Challe, realizing that Paris had thus robbed him of most of his troops – less than a tenth of the field forces, less than a hundredth of the total numbers had rallied to his enterprise – acknowledged his defeat and decided to put an end to the operation. It had, in any case, become more problematic for Challe since Salan and Susini had taken over the political direction of the coup at the end of that morning: he hated the first and despised the second.

Challe surrendered to the authorities; he was soon followed by Zeller. But Salan and Jouhaud, who had joined Challe at Zeralda before surrendering, made a different choice: they went underground and became the military leaders of the OAS. In the plane that took him back to Paris, Maurice Challe told one of Messmer's colleagues: "De Gaulle will have me shot." The nominal leader of the coup would in fact be sentenced to fifteen years' imprisonment on 1 June 1961.

Charles de Gaulle had won. And he had won because the French people had largely rejected the adventure from the outset and no longer felt anything but exhaustion and confusion over Algeria. "Let's have done with it!" What de Gaulle actually did was to carry out that rather inglorious exhortation. Of course, his firmness, his talent and the collapse of the coup widened his audience and consolidated his popular ascendancy. An opinion poll carried out in the middle of the crisis showed the greatest support that he had ever achieved. To the question "Do you trust General de Gaulle to solve this crisis?", 84 per cent said yes.[18] Even the left-wing newspapers supported him for four whole days. And it gave him even more self-assurance than before. Shortly after being released from his internment in the Sahara, Robert Buron presented himself at the Elysée. He heard de Gaulle say to him: "What do you expect, Buron? There was one factor that they decided not to take into account, a fact that upset all their calculations; that fact was de Gaulle."[19]

In Tunis, in Cairo, in Rabat and in Switzerland, the leaders of the FLN had followed the affair with anxiety. On 22 April, Ferhât Abbâs had warned his compatriots against any "provocation". M'Hammed Yazid, spokesman of the GPRA, did not hide the fact that the fate of de Gaulle was bound up with that of the negotiations. While Bourguiba expressed his wishes for the General's success over the mutineers, the King of Morocco summoned the French Ambassador, Roger Seydoux, to inform him of his decision to have the French bases occupied by his own troops ("They'll fire at you," the Ambassador replied), then to offer the French head of State, if need be, military aid.[20] The position of the North African leaders is summed up by Bechir Ben Yahmed, the editorial writer of the Tunisian weekly Afrique-Action: "The struggle being waged by de Gaulle against the advocates of Algérie française is, for the moment, our struggle."

Better still, the defeat of Challe was followed by a letter sent to de Gaulle by ex-President Eisenhower on 4 May.

Dear General de Gaulle,

At a time when you have just triumphantly overcome the latest crisis that you have had to face in your long and remarkable career, I would like, both as a friend of liberty and a personal friend, to send you, France and the Western world my congratulations on your success.

I have now retired from all official life and I confine myself, therefore, to expressing the feelings of someone who will always hold you in admiration and affection. I pray that every success will crown the efforts that you have made for so long to assure free self-determination for Algeria and that France may continue to benefit from your courageous leadership.*

They were wishes that Eisenhower's successor at the White House, J. F. Kennedy, would have approved of – his sympathy for the Algerian cause is well known. Indeed, he sent de Gaulle a message of sympathy through his ambassador, General Gavin.

*A letter that the Elysée was quick to publish.

So international conditions were more favourable than ever to opening up negotiations between France and the FLN.

The coup reached its legal epilogue on 1 June 1961. Before the high military tribunal set up under Article Sixteen and chaired by Maurice Patin, an old friend of de Gaulle, the accused present – Challe and Zeller – were sentenced each to fifteen years' imprisonment. Only those officers who had refused to surrender (Salan, Jouhaud, Gardy, Argoud, Broizat, Gardes, Godard, Lacheroy) were condemned to death.*

In his *Mémoires*, de Gaulle says that he was "deeply saddened by the human waste" and convinced that the motives of the ringleaders "were not entirely base".[21] Had he read the statement made by Major Denoix de Saint-Marc before the high military tribunal on 30 May 1961?

I have come before you to answer for my actions and for those of the officers of the 1st REP, for they acted under my orders.

Sir, one may ask a lot of a soldier, in particular to die, it is his job. One cannot ask him to cheat, to go back on a commitment, to contradict himself, to lie, to betray, to perjure himself.

Oh! I know, Sir, there is obedience, discipline. This drama of military discipline has been painfully experienced by the generation of officers that preceded us, by our elders. We were thinking of those slogans that covered the walls of all the villages and mechtas in Algeria: "The army will protect us, the army will remain." We were thinking of lost honour.

It is because I was thinking of my comrades, my non-commissioned officers, my legionaries, who had fallen on the field of honour that, on 21 April, at 1.30 p.m., before General Challe, I made my free choice. That is all I have to say, Sir.

What distance did de Gaulle see between himself in June 1940 and that officer engaged in a defiance that certainly had no outcome, absurd and ruinous, but whose motives were not "entirely base"?

---

*150 officers were given various sentences. Five hundred non-commissioned officers were court-martialled. This gives some idea of the participation of the army in the *putsch*: 650 officers out of about 10 000.

CHAPTER TWENTY-FOUR

From One Evian to Another

There was nothing now holding de Gaulle back from negotiations. When, on 8 May 1961, he addressed the French people on the sixteenth anniversary of the end of the Second World War, it was not so much to ask "Algerians of French origin to give up outworn myths and absurd agitations" and "to turn their courage and abilities to the great work that remains to be done" as to proclaim that "we must, yes, we must settle the Algerian affair" and to announce "new meetings at Evian". Thus he had already made two major concessions to the FLN: he had given up any attempt to try to open discussions with anyone else or to persuade the FLN to stop fighting before negotiating.

These two concessions testify to his impatience. Time was passing, the breaches made in the structure of the State had to be repaired, there was the opening of the peace conference on Laos at Geneva and the forthcoming meeting between Kennedy and Khrushchev in Vienna: everything suggested that de Gaulle should rid himself of the "Arab problem" that was dragging him and France down in Algeria.

Two days after the declaration of 8 May, the French government and the GPRA announced that the forthcoming meeting of their representatives would take place on 20 May at Evian. There was no question of other parties, Algerian or European, or of a prior cease-fire.

In Algeria itself, the Europeans, seeing themselves "betrayed" by the army, had exploded with rage. Convinced that they had been abandoned by everybody, the Europeans could see only one way out: the OAS, and the violence this organization proposed. The OAS had been joined secretly by Salan and Jouhaud, as well as by Gardes, Godard and Sergent. There was also Lieutenant Degueldre, who was liquidating those carrying out Gaullist policy. The wave of terror launched by the OAS was to culminate temporarily on 19 May, the day before the Evian talks opened, when more than a hundred people were killed, almost all Muslims. The fine days of fraternization were far away. This campaign of murder was answered by that of the FLN. As soon as the French head of State agreed to give in to the FLN's own violent means, his partner quite ruthlessly used this terrible means of pressure – so much so that the terror carried out by the militants fighting under the flag of the FLN was the equal on some days to that being perpetrated by the OAS.

De Gaulle rejected the idea that the conference should take place on neutral territory, which, by stressing its international character, would have been tantamount to a diplomatic recognition of the FLN. The GPRA delegates refused, for their part, to be quartered in France. So it was agreed that the French delegation should stay at the Hôtel du Parc in Evian, on the side of the lake where the talks would take place, while the members of the GPRA would fly in each day by helicopter from Swiss territory, where the FLN had been given a house at Bois d'Avault.

The French delegation was led by Louis Joxe, Minister of State for Algerian Affairs, and the FLN delegation by Belkacem Krim, the Kabyl underground leader who, a year before, had become the GPRA's Foreign Minister. Joxe had as assistants Bruno de Leusse, Claude Chayet, Roland Cadet, who was very close to Michel Debré, Philippe Thibaud, in charge of information, General Simon, an old Gaullist who, during the *putsch*, had managed to hold Kabylia, and Lieutenant-Colonel de Séguin-Pazzis, a paratrooper regarded as "liberal".

At Krim's side were Dr Francis, his colleague in charge of finance, Ahmed Boumendjel, a veteran of negotiations and his acolyte from Melun, Mohammed Ben Yahia, Saad Dahlab and Taïeb Boulharouf, other already experienced negotiators, Redha Malck, press attaché, and Colonels Mendjli and Slimane, both of whom were overtly hostile to any compromise.

At 10 a.m. on 20 May, a Swiss army helicopter landed near the Hôtel du Parc at Evian. A few moments later, the sixteen delegates – seven French, nine Algerians – were face to face for the first time (without having shaken hands) in the great salon of the Hôtel du Parc, which had been rented for only one month. It was then that the French head of State, who had given his representatives only one order, "succeed",[1] took a three-fold initiative that was to cause a considerable stir: a unilateral cease-fire, the freeing of six thousand FLN prisoners and the transfer of Ben Bella and his companions to the Château de Turquant, near Saumur.

The FLN delegates could hardly be other than very pleased, especially by the last two decisions. But they immediately denounced the truce put forward by de Gaulle as "blackmail". Obstinately attached to the principle laid down five years before at the Soummam Congress (no cease-fire before recognition of independence by France), the men of the GPRA described the French decision as a "crude propaganda manoeuvre" intended to force them into a truce. "Why? Because a regular army might carry out such a reconversion in its own way, but an insurrectional force could not do so, condemned as it was to maintaining its combatants' morale at a constantly high level."

Mohammed Harbi, one of Ferhât Abbâs's advisers, has written that "by the third day, the gap between the French and Algerian positions proved to be unbridgeable. The French representatives demanded dual nationality for the Europeans, territorial enclaves for military bases and rejected any Algerian sovereignty over the Sahara. It looked as if the talks would break down." Personally, I would not exculpate the Algerian delegation, which was constantly looking out for the slightest sign of moderation on the other side.

On 26 May a critical stage in the talks was to be reached. At the specific request of General de Gaulle, the head of the French delegation appeared before a gathering of two hundred international journalists in Evian to explain the French proposals to them. Louis Joxe did this with such mastery of style and content that he won an important advantage. By throwing the new maps of France on the table, by appealing to public opinion to support the French proposals, by thus trying to drag the FLN along with it, to force its partner to discuss, to orientate it in the direction desired by his own side, Joxe marked up several psychological points, but ran the risk of irritating and humiliating the other side.

But no. On 29 May, the FLN delegation brought the discussion back to the subject most likely to achieve a common accord: the preparation for the vote on self-determination. This was not only because it was the official subject of the negotiations, but because it was the ground on which useful work might be done together. Concerning the problems of self-determination, the Algerians insisted on those that were to be placed "before" and "during" rather than on those that had to be solved "afterwards".

After two weeks of talks – which de Gaulle followed closely, being in contact with Joxe on the telephone at least three times a week – progress had been made. But two disagreements were to lead to a breakdown in the talks: the status of the "non-Muslim" minority and, still more, the Sahara, which General de Gaulle had excluded from the negotiations in his speech of 16 September 1959. His position at the outset had been this: France must "keep the oil fields, which we have put into operation, and the bases for testing our bombs and rockets". With this in view, he went on, "we are in a position, whatever happens, to remain in the Sahara, even if it means establishing the autonomy of that huge void".

The Algerian view was quite the reverse. It might be summed up thus: the Sahara is a part of the national territory. It looked as though the arguments would be tough. "In the tenth century, the Fatimides had gone as far as Tafilafet," Boumendjel maintained. "No, no! The extension of Algeria inland was a consequence of the taking of Algiers in 1830," Joxe retorted.

This type of discussion can lead nowhere. Why not turn the territorial conflict round by treating the affair from the point of view of economic cooperation? the French argued. Ahmed Boumendjel intervened to declare that this was "no basis for discussion". If the sovereignty of the Sahara were transferred to Algeria, Algeria would be ready to cooperate with the foreigners. But Krim then cut short his colleague. What was in question, he said, was self-determination, that is to say, the recognition of the "Algerianness" of the Sahara.

No progress seemed possible as long as de Gaulle insisted that Louis Joxe keep the Sahara out of all discussions.[2] The leader of the French delegation had warned the General that until this condition was lifted, negotiations would get nowhere.[3] For the Algerians, this was a real impasse as they had believed at the beginning of the talks that the French had given up all hope of keeping the Sahara.[4] On 13 June 1961, General de Gaulle lost his patience. Ignoring the pleas of his minister, who felt that progress could only be achieved if the head of State allowed him to unblock the question of the future of the Sahara, de Gaulle ordered Louis Joxe, after long and lively discussions over the telephone between Paris and Evian, to break off negotiations *sine die*.

The Algerians were evidently surprised at having to leave before a new meeting had been arranged: although, the day before, they had helped to raise the temperature by demanding freedom for Ben Bella without delay. Their surprise turned to irritation on 29 June when Michel Debré, during a stormy parliamentary debate in which both the indignation of the conservatives and the disappointment of the advocates of peace were apparent, rejected all responsibility for the collapse of talks with the FLN.

So shocked were they by General de Gaulle's decision, and so irritated by his threat to proceed to a division of Algeria, that it was now the FLN leaders who renewed contacts and insisted that a new conference be organized for July, at the Château de Lugrin. They now presented themselves as the most ardent advocates of a negotiated settlement, coming out with several declarations calling for the resumption of talks. After Abdelhafid Boussouf announced a new meeting with his French counterparts to take place the following week, Belkacim Krim declared, on 10 July, "my government is ready to return to the conference table with France, with no prior conditions. We place great hopes on these negotiations, providing France recognizes the territorial unity of Algeria."

Why such sudden haste on their part? Because of the threat of partition? No. The leaders of the FLN did not really believe that.

But Krim's last words give a key to the change in the atmosphere. If the FLN were pressing their partners so strongly to return to the negotiating table it was because a new dimension had just appeared: the entry on stage of Habib Bourguiba of Tunisia, demanding that France give up the base of Bizerte, but also changes to the frontier between the Sahara and Tunisia, which affected in particular the oil zone known as Landmark 233.

According to the Tunisian head of State, it was the French colonial administration that had altered, to the benefit of "French" Algeria, a boundary that had previously been more favourable to Tunisia. Now that the Franco-Algerian agreements were moving towards a fundamental change in the status of the Sahara, Tunis made its claim all the more assertively.

On 5 July 1961, Bourguiba sent a threatening letter to Paris, ordering France to leave Bizerte. The Tunisian leader made it clear that the oral agreement made at Rambouillet with de Gaulle had been annulled by a decision of the admiral commanding the base to lengthen the air strip and so increase its operational value.

Did the decision taken by Admiral Amman really conform to the spirit of the tacit agreement of 27 February? Perhaps not. But it was no more than a technical measure, to which M. Bourguiba responded by pressing hard on the political accelerator. After the failure of Evian, the Tunisian leader saw an endless continuation of a war that was unbearable to his country and foresaw the gradual takeover of the Algerian movement by the revolutionaries. In the resulting confusion, he found an ideal opportunity of playing his trump card.

On 18 July, Tunisian forces began to move on Bizerte, while military detachments occupied the oil fields claimed by Tunis around Landmark 233. Did Bourguiba believe that he had finally convinced the man with whom he had had such pleasant talks at Rambouillet? On 19 and 20 July, the intervention of the French paratroops – de Gaulle thus giving these soldiers an opportunity to avenge their forced inaction in Algeria – caused seven hundred deaths on the Tunisian side. Relations between Paris and Tunis could only worsen, but for the GPRA it was a reminder that, accommodating as he had been at Evian, de Gaulle could become an implacable adversary once more.

Threatened by both the claims of Tunis and the bloody riposte from Paris, the GPRA wanted to return to the negotiating table without the added burden of having to deal with their Tunisian neighbours over the Sahara. But the talks that were resumed on 20 July at the Château de Lugrin came to an abrupt end. This time, it was the FLN delegation that took the initiative to break off the talks, failing to get an agreement on "territorial unity". But Saad Dahlab wanted to end the abortive conference on an optimistic note: "It is not a collapse, but a suspension of talks; the beginnings of an agreement have been reached; what has been achieved must not be lost; we must keep in contact." Yet the two delegations parted with no date for a resumption having been proposed or any means of continued contact having been decided. On his return to Paris Louis Joxe took part in a meeting of the Defence Committee chaired by General de Gaulle. Was the conflict going to extend to the whole of North Africa? In an article in *Le Monde* of 30 July 1961 I believed that I could ask the following question: "Is this a new stage in the Algerian war?"

In fact, nobody wanted it to be so. The FLN did not want it, because it would finally have had to accept the weapons that Moscow and Peking were offering its men, and thus set out on a path that terrified almost all the members of the GPRA. And above all de Gaulle did not want it. Everything he said at the time suggested that what he wanted was "disengagement", provided it conformed to the terms dictated by him.

It became apparent that de Gaulle's aims and tactics seemed to be becoming blurred. The trials of April, the tension produced by the negotiations, the disappointment brought about by their breakdown, and the pressure exerted by the OAS had put Charles de Gaulle in a state which François Flohic described as "exhausted". De Gaulle himself described this "immense fatigue" that overtook him on his arrival in late June at Colombey and which took the form of ill-temper towards his colleagues during a session of the Algerian Affairs Committee. As he left the meeting, he confided to Joxe: "I don't want my house to witness a physical decline. So there are two solutions: my resignation or my death."[5]

In that period of weakness of summer 1961, which took the form of a physical malaise (he was, after all, over seventy), bitterness towards his ministers, the confusion of his Algerian plans, the unexpected brutality of the military reaction to Bizerte, one has to count the painful tension that continued to increase between his Prime Minister and himself. For three years they had been harnessed to the same task, but not always moving in the same direction or in the same spirit. And for three years the Algerian affair had been in their way.

Charles de Gaulle was now considering, by way of disengaging himself from the Algerian trap, an important shift in policy and a renewal of his government team. The FLN were also drawing the consequences of the double break of Evian and Lugrin by proceeding to a profound overhaul of their organization, if not of their strategy. Not that they regarded the result of the negotiations so far as entirely negative. But they thought that the time had come to resume them. From 9 to 27 August 1961, the session of the Conseil National de la Révolution Algérienne (CNRA) led to the removal of Ferhât Abbâs in favour of Ben Youssef Ben Khedda, but, despite innumerable articles published at the time, the behaviour of the FLN did not alter as a result.

The last phase of the disengagement, on 16 September 1961, did not start without de Gaulle assessing the determination of those who regarded Algeria as indissociable from France and who regarded his Algerian policy as nothing short of treason. Indeed, did he ever doubt that his life was in danger?

On Friday 8 September 1961, three days after a press conference during which he set in train a policy revision on the subject of the Sahara, which was to lead to the final stage of negotiations, General de Gaulle suddenly decided, after talking to Louis Joxe, to set out for Colombey at about 6 p.m. He very seldom took a decision so late and seldom cancelled an appointment to do so: but he had invited Charles Morazé, a historian whose company and ideas he appreciated, to lunch at the Elysée that Saturday. This impromptu decision must in any case have had the advantage of throwing off any possible conspirators,* who, for months, had been studying the routes and timetables of his weekend movements with a view to assassinating him.

Shortly before 8 p.m., General and Mme de Gaulle got into the black Citroën DS 21 driven by Francis Marroux, a policeman who was one of the General's two usual chauffeurs. On the driver's right sat Colonel Teissère, an aide-de-camp. Three escort cars followed, containing, among others, Commissaire Ducret, who was responsible for the security of the head of State, and Dr Delamare, a physician.

An hour and a half later, the convoy was driving at about 70 m.p.h. on the Route Nationale 19, about ninety miles from Paris, on a straight piece of road close to Nogent-sur-Seine, between Crancey and Pont-sur-Seine. Night had fallen. Suddenly there was an enormous flash, an explosion, a huge sheet of fire on the road. The car was blown to the left. The driver accelerated and went through the wall of flames. General and Mme de Gaulle did not flinch. Five hundred yards further on, Marroux stopped his car. As he was getting out, he heard the General shout: "Clumsy idiots!" He then enquired how the other passengers in the convoy were and, reassured, said: "Teissère, *en route*." It was 9.35 p.m.

Charles de Gaulle's own very sober version of the event appears in the *Mémoires d'espoir*:

> Leaving Pont-sur-Seine in the middle of the night on the way from the Elysée to Colombey, the car in which I was travelling with my wife, my aide de camp Colonel Teissère, and my detective Francis Marroux, was suddenly enveloped by a huge flame. It was caused by the explosion of a detonating device intended to set off a charge of ten kilograms of plastic** concealed beneath a pile of sand, much more than enough to destroy its "target". Extraordinarily, this charge failed to explode.[6]

The clumsy pyrotechnist, Martial de Villemandy, was arrested shortly afterwards at Pont-sur-Seine. It did not take him long to come up with a confession, but it didn't provide any clues as to who had planned the assassination attempt. Was the OAS behind it? It very soon emerged that the man in charge of the operation was a

---

*The authors of *Objectif de Gaulle*, P. Demaret and C. Plume (Paris, Laffont, 1973), state (p. 141) that the conspirators were tipped off by a colonel working at the Elysée. They do not name him.
**The investigators say it was 30 kilos.

certain "Germain", to be identified only much later as Colonel Jean-Marie Bastien-Thiry.

The day before the assassination attempt, the arrest of a businessman called Gingembre brought into police custody a briefcase filled with documents of little interest, which he had been told to hand over to Raoul Salan, "supreme head of the OAS". But hidden among them was a parliamentary pass on which was written: "Avec confiance. Le 7 septembre 1961." It was signed Georges Bidault.

Why did an organization, having chosen to assassinate its opponents and claiming to strike "where, when and whom it pleased", allow the one man who was supremely responsible for what it denounced to escape, and to be rigorous only about relatively minor officials?

There were three typical reactions to this attempt to keep Algeria French through assassination. First, there was that of the "OAS people". A comment by Pierre Laffont, who was at some distance from them, but attentive to their aspirations, is instructive in this regard:

> In Algeria, the announcement of the assassination attempt had an enormous effect: the OAS could do everything. It was believed that de Gaulle was dead and that his disappearance was being deliberately concealed. When the truth came out, it did not stem the flow of energy: they failed once, next time they would succeed. They "knew" that OAS men were planted in the Elysée itself. They were close to victory.[7]

Then there was the reaction of de Gaulle himself. To Louis Terrenoire, who congratulated de Gaulle on being safe and sound, the General confided with a shrug of the shoulders:

> Obviously the human animal calculates with relief what it has escaped; but, from the speculative and historical point of view, perhaps it would have been better than dying in one's bed or in an accident. It is also true that the political consequences would have been serious and that, from the point of view of public interest, it was preferable for the attempt to fail.[8]

Then there is the reaction of one of the policemen in charge of the anti-OAS struggle, Jacques Delarue. Describing the individuals who, after Villemandy's confession, gradually fell into the police net – a former itinerant photographer, two car salesmen, an electrician, a minor employee at Orly; in other words, a group of perfectly average Frenchmen – Delarue observed that "the anonymous, interchangeable character of our 'regicides' was the most disturbing aspect of the affair". For "people like that can be recruited by the thousand".[9]

As the Evian negotiators went their separate ways on 13 June one word was on all lips: Sahara. And this was even more the case when the two delegations left the Château de Lugrin, on 28 July, on the initiative of the Algerians.

De Gaulle knew that the intransigence of the FLN was based on very strong considerations. He, too, had learnt history by looking at maps. He, too, felt a sort of repulsion for anything approaching partition. But the Sahara offered space suitable for nuclear experiments. As for the oil fields, there was certainly a way of exploiting them without prolonging the war. He had been reasoning in this way since early 1961, well before the first Evian conference. But there was the psychological, mythical and, one might say, structural aspect of de Gaulle's personality.

To give in, to give in again? How far would it go? From concession to concession, would he have to give up all the assets that he had held since returning to power in June 1958? The great disengagement had its imperious logic. But could not de Gaulle snatch that peace without keeping for himself, for his country, the Sahara? He hesitated for a long time. In late 1961, he realized that his dream, sustained by the passionate will of Michel Debré, was unrealizable.

On 5 September 1961, Charles de Gaulle summoned the press to the Elysée once more. Algerian affairs were not the only concern of the day. He was asked no less than fifteen questions, from the status of Berlin to his government's agricultural policy, from relations between London and the Common Market to the mood of the French army. But it was his answer to a question concerning the future of the Sahara that was to cause a sensation.

The head of State declared that France had only two concerns with regard to the great desert: to safeguard her "interests" and to take account of "realities". And what exactly were her interests? They were "the free exploitation of the oil and gas that we have discovered there and will go on discovering", the use of "airfields" and the safeguarding of "communications with Black Africa". Was that all? Yes, because the "reality" was that

> There is not a single Algerian, I know, who does not believe that the Sahara must be part of Algeria and there would not be a single Algerian government, whatever its orientation with regard to France, that would not have to claim unrelentingly Algerian sovereignty over the Sahara. If an Algerian State is set up and if it is associated with France, the great majority of the Saharan populations will tend to attach themselves to it, even if they have not explicitly claimed to be so in advance.

Hence this conclusion, which astonished his opponents and even some of his colleagues: "That is to say that, in the Franco-Algerian discussions . . . the question of the sovereignty of the Sahara has not been considered, at least not by France."[10]

It was a gesture of crucial importance. By assuming that French interests would be safeguarded, the General seemed to have suddenly removed the major obstacle in the negotiations. Can this decision be attributed solely to impatience to be done with it all? His impatience certainly continued to grow and was evident in a scene described to me by Claude Chayet. During a working meeting at the Elysée with the Algerian Affairs "think-tank", and as one of his experts was presenting Louis Joxe with a perfectly well-founded objection, the General suddenly seemed overcome by irrepressible anger and, bringing his two fists down on his desk roared: "Il faut en finir avec cette boîte à chagrins!"*

*Literally: "We must have done with this box of troubles!"(trs.)

On 15 September, Ben Khedda gave a speech and predicted a socialist future for Algeria. He went on to declare that "frank and loyal negotiations, which will allow our people to exercise its right to self-determination and to accede to independence, will put an end to the war and open up the way for a fruitful cooperation between the Algerian and French peoples".

The General was in no hurry to praise these words. But on 2 October, on the occasion of the return of parliament and the lifting of the conditions of Article 16, he gave a speech in which he referred again to "the search for a negotiated agreement". Taking up various themes of the Evian and Lugrin discussions – the constitution, for example, of "a provisional government" and of a "public force" with a view to preparing self-determination – he was resuming the dialogue. But hadn't there been a surprising shift in FLN policy? Whereas Ferhât Abbâs's GPRA seemed anxious not to exploit General de Gaulle's difficulties, believing in principle that beyond appearances to the contrary he was its ally against colonialism, the GPRA of Ben Khedda used any difficulties facing the French head of State as a weapon: whatever weakened de Gaulle strengthened the Algerian leadership.

By allowing a constant threat to weigh over the life of the head of State, by assassinating the agents of his policy in Algiers and Oran, the OAS helped the new strategy of the FLN. Underground, Salan, Godard and Susini seemed to be the masters of Algeria. What an argument for the FLN spokesmen! What you are claiming to offer us, to barter with us, you don't even have!

The GPRA was no longer content to play the OAS tactically against de Gaulle; it seemed more anxious to pacify the European community in order, at some later date, to detach it from the OAS, to make it a positive factor in the search for peace. M'Hammed Yazid declared on 22 October that "at no time would action be taken by the Algerian people against the Europeans of Algeria". A national day for the realization of independence, organized by the FLN on 1 November, the anniversary of the uprising, had as its theme "the cohabitation of the communities".

More skilful than its predecessor on this point, Ben Khedda's GPRA was nevertheless also forced into radicalism by the harassment inflicted by its military wing. While the ministers still held in France were beginning to criticize negotiations that could not go on indefinitely, and which they were still unable to attend, Colonel Boumediene and his lieutenants constantly warned their former ally Ben Khedda against any mood of concession. So it was in very discreet fashion, as if in a mood of mutual shame, that negotiations were begun again, in October 1961. It was another secret meeting, held in Basle between Dahlab and Ben Yahia, on the one hand, and de Leusse and Chayet, on the other, and again in November, near Vevey, with a meeting between Bruno de Leusse and Redha Malck.

It was at this time that the OAS underwent its most rapid development in Algeria, where it could now claim to be representative of the European community, while in mainland France its allies expressed themselves without the slightest reservation. For instance, Georges Bidault announced the creation, under his responsibility, of a CNR (Conseil National de la Résistance). Under the Nazi occupation he had been chairman* of a body bearing the same name and was

*Thanks to the support of the Communists.

therefore daring to identify the Fifth Republic with the Nazis and de Gaulle with Hitler.

But opposition to General de Gaulle's Algerian policy took less radical forms. On 8 November 1961, a group of deputies – including Jean-Marie Le Pen and former Gaullists – pleaded at the rostrum of the Palais Bourbon for the recognition of the OAS as a legal organization, even though it had just murdered Police Inspector Goldenberg in Algiers.

An imposing parliamentary tendency was thus openly supporting the OAS. Had France been closer to civil war for half a century? Jacques Soustelle, now in exile, gave his considerable intellectual backing in an interview which was released on 3 November by the American news agency United Press:

> The present regime in France is a dictatorship tempered by anarchy. At its summit, a single man exercises an unlimited, unimpeded tyrannical power. Below him, the members of the so-called government do not themselves know what will be decided tomorrow by the absolute master and parliament is reduced to nothing. As if all this incoherence were not enough, a witch-hunt has been unleashed, filling the prisons with our best army officers, former members of the Resistance, academics, writers. Freedom of expression has been abolished. As in 1940, I have had to leave my country in order to remain free to think and to speak as I wish. I am in opposition to the regime because I am and remain a republican, attached to democratic liberties and also to political honesty. The present regime is based on a huge deception. De Gaulle has systematically betrayed those who had trust in him, betrayed the army, betrayed the French people, betrayed the Muslims of Algeria.

"What do you think of General de Gaulle?" a UP reporter asked him. "I think General de Gaulle died, between 1951* and 1958, at Colombey-les-Deux-Eglises. Unfortunately, nobody noticed. The man who now bears that name embodies precisely the opposite of what the head of the French Resistance, to whom we owe the Liberation and return of the Republic, symbolized from 1940 to 1944." Soustelle's words give some idea of the hatred and rejection that was being turned at this time on the man of June 1940. And Jacques Soustelle was certainly the best of those who had turned against him.

As autumn 1961 drew to an end, peace seemed even further away. The OAS had become the FLN of the Europeans, the war thus being fought on two fronts, and within the State itself: the assemblies and the ministerial offices contained men who were linked with the bombers of Pont-sur-Seine.

The officer corps had been split by the April *putsch* and the consequent repression.** The most bitter of the officers were not those who had acted and lost and were now in prison, but those who had refused to follow them, not without understanding their motives, and were now accusing themselves of cowardice and

---

*The date when he broke with Soustelle.
**The officers knew that their minister, Pierre Messmer, had done everything possible for it to be less harsh than de Gaulle wished.

opportunism. The fact that 95 per cent of army officers had remained loyal to the State was now a source of great disgust. As 1961 drew to an end, the mood of the army can be grasped in the words of General de Pouilly, the man of Oran who had done more than anyone to impede the *putsch*. "I chose discipline, but I feel ashamed of abandonment."

De Gaulle, the man almost wholly responsible for this situation, chose to confront over three thousand officers on 23 November, at Strasbourg. Why that date, that city? Because it was the anniversary of the city's liberation by Leclerc's forces, the conclusion to an astonishing feat of arms. To summon the élite of the army here was to demonstrate that Gaullism represented the victory of France.

It was several degrees below zero. De Gaulle spoke first of the manoeuvre that had delivered the city to Leclerc, Rouvillois and Massu. Without a note, as if recounting something that had happened only the day before, Charles de Gaulle gave a masterly lesson in which there was missing not a single figure, not even the name of a village or of an enemy unit; he was obviously happy to plunge back into those noble deeds and to remind that army ("to which I have belonged") that he was first of all a great professional and an incomparable teacher of military history.

But of course Leclerc had not been mentioned solely to glorify the lecturer de Gaulle: he was his witness against Salan. However fine the history lesson may have been and however useful perhaps to remind those thousands of motionless, freezing men what man they were standing in front of, he was there above all to demonstrate that the destiny of the army lay here, in Europe, on the Rhine, at the heart of the modern world, and that to bring ruin to the present State was to destroy national defence.

> Everyone can explain to himself – and myself the first – that, in the minds and hearts of certain soldiers, other hopes once flourished, even the illusion that one can by sheer will-power make things what one wishes and the opposite of what they are. But, once the State and the Nation have chosen their way, military duty is determined once and for all. Outside these rules, there can only be, there are only lost soldiers.[11]

How many of those men standing to attention then thought of killing him? How many Argouds, Broizats, Sergents were there among them? They all knew perfectly well that "the State and the Nation" that had "chosen their way" were that huge old man, standing there, topped by his almost white hair, implacable and fascinating, masterly and a little condescending.

This is the secret of what is called power or rather authority. It is not only control over the means of coercion and not just the possession of the art of persuasion. It is something else and it is what, before that compact, freezing, silent and three-quarters disapproving mass, made Charles de Gaulle reign and govern, impose and dispose. He had imposed his authority upon it.

General de Gaulle carried out that taming operation at the height of a crisis that was capable of reviving the resentment of officers attached to the idea of *Algérie française*: for it had as its centre and symbol the man whose name was, more than any other, anathema to those officers who had devoted themselves to the annihilation of the FLN and Ben Bella, a "rebel" who had not even fought in the djebels.

In early November, the five exiles* of Turquant had suddenly attracted the attention of French public opinion by beginning an unlimited hunger strike, firstly out of solidarity with FLN prisoners demanding political status and secondly with a view to obtaining their liberation, so that they might participate in the negotiations. So the Franco-Algerian meeting was to take place, complicated by a massive hunger strike that was making everything more urgent and more sensitive: it involved the lives of individuals now well known internationally – whose names, in any case, were endlessly repeated by the press of the Third World and even that of the United States.

This new turn of events gave rise to a second intervention in the debate, this time from Morocco. It was while they were guests of the Moroccan king, in a plane placed at their disposal, that Ben Bella, Boudiaf, Khider and Aït Ahmed had been rounded up by the French airforce. Hassan II then declared himself their protector and, in order to prevent a fatal outcome, proposed to receive them in one of his embassies.

General de Gaulle's reaction was very negative, for various reasons. Firstly, because he hated the slightest pressure being exerted on him; secondly, because this was behaviour that was likely to arouse compassion on a political matter; thirdly, because he saw the King of Morocco, whom he regarded as a personal ally, suddenly run to the help of his enemies; fourthly and above all because the Moroccan authorities were to allow an action that had no precedent even in the dramatic history of French diplomatic relations – the invasion and sacking of the French embassy at Rabat, carried out while the ambassador, Roger Seydoux, sent appeal after appeal to the royal palace, which was only a few hundred yards away.

The aggression against this fragment of French territory took place on 11 November. That same evening however, Allal el-Fassi, Minister of State and symbol of Moroccan nationalism, proposed a solution: the Moroccans and the FLN would ask Ben Bella and his companions to break off their hunger strike, in exchange for which the prisoners would be placed under the protection of the Moroccan Embassy in France. The following day, the Moroccan leader and two of his colleagues arrived in Paris, with the intention of making such a deal.

On 13 November, the Council of Ministers heard de Gaulle say: "The day they stop cutting people's throats, I shall send Ben Bella to Morocco. Not before." But de Gaulle did opt for a moderate solution: "Ben Bella and his companions would be taken to a clinic in the Paris region, where they would be attended by Moroccan doctors, under French supervision." That same evening, Ben Bella, Khider, Aït Ahmed and Boudiaf ended their hunger strike and, after four days of treatment, were transferred to the Château d'Aunoy, near Paris. There, on 16 December, they received a discreet visit from three emissaries of the GPRA, Belkacem Krim, Ben Tobbal and Ben Yahia, to whom they gave the "green light" for a resumption of negotiations.

With or without Ben Bella, one always came back to the same debate: an

---

*Who had been taken from prison at an early stage of the Evian talks and kept in that château in central France.

Algerian State which included the Sahara. But with or without the FLN? This is what the General said on 26 October 1961, when haranguing his subjugated ministers:

> Realities and our own interests are forcing us to allow the birth of an Algerian State. This State must emerge from the ballot-box, and therefore from a vote on self-determination. But it would be better that it took place after an agreement has been concluded on all outstanding questions, in particular the guarantees to Europeans. At the vote on self-determination, the two questions asked would be the following: 1. Do you want an independent State? 2. Do you want this State to cooperate with France? Self-determination may now be no more than a formality, but it is essential. To achieve it, a provisional power will be necessary; the FLN is free to take part in it. And if nothing of all this is possible, then we shall leave Algeria to itself and we don't need the FLN for that.

On the subject of the Sahara, he said: "Either we reach a suitable arrangement or, if there is no agreement, we shall stay in the Sahara as long as we choose to do so." And he ended with the words:

"Gentlemen, hold tight to the mast, it's going to be a rough passage!"[12]

On 8 January 1962, the principal leaders of the FLN – with the exception of Ferhât Abbâs and, of course, the residents under surveillance at the Château d'Aunoy – met at Mohammedia, a holiday town near Casablanca, as the guests of King Hassan II. Large numbers of journalists turned up. Would the GPRA put its "cards on the table" and inform public opinion either of the progress or of the failure of the secret negotiations? At the end of the meeting, M. Yazid confided to me: "What is at issue between Paris and us is not 'what' or 'how', but 'when' and 'in what circumstances'." And in the statement that was issued at the end of the Mohammedia meeting, the FLN leaders stressed the guarantees to be given to Europeans and to the French State, and referred to an "evolution towards a peaceful, negotiated solution".

From mid-January 1962, de Gaulle could no longer contain his impatience, because he felt that the OAS was gaining strength with each day of the war and that only an agreement with the GPRA could now deprive the OAS of oxygen. Two meetings between Louis Joxe and Saad Dahlab, in a villa overlooking Lake Maggiore in late December and early January, made it possible to open the way to real negotiations. Twenty-three years later, both men have confirmed this to me. Joxe: "It was then that I began to have confidence." Dahlab: "Our talks with M. Joxe enabled us to get to know one another and to explain our ideas to one another with more frankness and clarity."[13]

But that horrible war was not to come to an end before it took on a new manifestation: after the bloody uprising, the unlimited repression, the terrorism of both Muslims and Europeans, the *ratonnades* (or anti-Arab pogroms) and what de Gaulle called the *entrezigouillement* (cutting of each other's throats) between the OAS and the Gaullists, the killing was to reach Paris.

In early 1962, the OAS murders became more frequent: after General Ginestet,

Colonel Mabille, Police Inspector Goldenberg, William Lévy, a leading Socialist in Algiers, it was the turn of Lieutenant-Colonel Rançon, head of the Deuxième Bureau in Oran, the victim of a bomb placed under his bed. On 22 January 1962 a bomb went off in the Quai d'Orsay, causing one death and injuring twelve. The OAS then turned its attentions to André Malraux: the daughter of his neighbours and friends, the Renards, who was only five, was wounded by the bomb that was aimed at him and was to remain half-blind. The senior Gaullist Yves Le Tac, wounded in Algiers by men of the OAS, was brought back to Paris only for an attempt to be made to kill him in hospital.

Then what is usually called the left decided to react. On 14 January, a manifesto signed by former members of the Resistance called for action to be taken against *les factieux*. On 8 February, around the Bastille, some ten thousand demonstrators, belonging mainly to the CGT, the PCF, the Students' Union and the PSU, a small left-wing party to the left of the Socialist Party, chanted "OAS assassins!", when the forces of "order", which had obviously been infiltrated by members of the organization being denounced, intervened. Some of the police attacked demonstrators who had been stuck in a staircase of the métro-station Charonne, where the gates had been shut, with such savagery that there were nine dead, including three women and a very young child. Some years later, researchers found in the archives of the OAS this document dated February 1962: "Provocation operation at the demonstration of 8 February, carried out by a group of thirty men, divided up into groups of four between Charonne and Bastille. Some of the team were equipped with authentic police truncheons. The rest is well known. Cost of the operation: 90 000 francs."[14]

The funeral of the nine victims of Charonne was to be one of the greatest popular demonstrations of post-war France – the greatest before those of May 1968. The political unity that emerged there between the various "left-wing" elements was to last for a quarter of a century.

The authorities of the Fifth Republic seemed to remain stupefied by this horror. No serious investigation seems to have ever been carried out by the Ministry of the Interior to unmask those responsible for the "operation". Of those nine dead (10 000 francs per head), General de Gaulle said nothing. They had sacrificed themselves neither for him nor against him. *Raison d'état* was not in question. But was his glory?

CHAPTER TWENTY-FIVE

Victory Over Self

On Wednesday 24 January 1962, shortly after 1 p.m., General de Gaulle's dumbfounded aides-de-camp witnessed the ministers leave the Council Room in a manner that could only be described as "explosive".[1] Why were these men who, for the past three years, had seen so much, so agitated? Because they now knew that the decisive debate had begun, that in one or two weeks' time negotiations would begin with the FLN, and at ministerial level – they would soon be held responsible for a policy that would detach Algeria from France for ever: in other words, because of the OAS, they were all under a deferred death sentence.

In Algiers, Oran and Paris, at least thirty-two people had been killed the day before. The OAS now seemed capable of keeping its promise to strike "where, when and whom" it wished. And it was well known, in the circles in which ministers are recruited, that there was not an official body in Paris that did not house a few sympathizers. Each of Michel Debré's ministers could now be a target.

The General cancelled his meetings for Friday 26 January in order to be ready to receive Louis Joxe at any moment. Joxe was delayed, so de Gaulle asked him to join him for the weekend at Colombey where, breaking with his habits, if not with his principles, he would deal with affairs of state.

Joxe did not arrive at La Boisserie until 9 p.m. on the Saturday, when he was received with these words: "Well, Joxe, how are your shepherds getting on?" For the first time at a dinner at that asylum of peace, there was talk of "business", in other words, Algeria. Louis Joxe said that he hoped to reach an agreement that would guarantee that the European population could stay where it was. Until 1 a.m. on Sunday morning, the General and his minister worked in the study in the tower. Next morning, after mass (Joxe had gone back to Paris), the General meditated aloud in front of his aide-de-camp Flohic on French and British colonization, on the work still to be carried out in Algeria and on the future of France.

The meeting that had been announced by the General during the "explosive" Council meeting of 24 January, the principles and broad outlines of which had been laid down during the two Joxe–Dahlab meetings in December and January at Lake Maggiore, presented some tricky problems.

The meeting was to take place in France (General de Gaulle made this a question of principle), near Switzerland, from where, as at Evian, the FLN delegation would come, and at a place that would be kept secret – the OAS, having already assassinated the mayor of Evian, was even keener to liquidate all the protagonists of the operation that would put an end once and for all to *Algérie française*.

A meeting-place was found in the Jura, quite close to the Swiss frontier. It was a mountain chalet called Le Yeti, situated at an altitude of over 1000 metres and normally used as a holiday home for civil servants, in the village of Les Rousses. The Algerian side was represented by four ministers, Krim, Dahlab, Ben Tobbal and Yazid,* and three high-ranking experts, Ben Yahia, who was often in action, Redha Malck, the spokesman of the delegation at Evian, and Dr Mostefaï. On account of his seniority in combat, Belkacem Krim was the official head of the delegation. As for the French side, the General had insisted on flanking his trusted minister, Louis Joxe, with two other members of the government, Robert Buron, Minister of Public Works, and Jean de Broglie, Secretary of State with responsibility for the Sahara.

On Tuesday 6 February, General de Gaulle, flanked by Michel Debré, received the three ministers chosen to take part in the negotiations, in order to give them his instructions. He saw them again on the ninth, in an atmosphere darkened by the frightful episode at the Charonne métro-station. In an apparently calm tone, he gave his final instructions to the three ministers who were about to leave for Les Rousses.

> Succeed or fail, but above all don't let the negotiations go on indefinitely. And don't get too caught up in details. There is the possible and the impossible. On the subject of nationality, don't insist too much that the Europeans should be Algerians *de jure*; your opponents will find it difficult to accept it and our fellow-countrymen will have the impression that we are driving them from France, that we do not regard them as true Frenchmen. Tomorrow the Algerian government will make laws on nationality in a new State. We must make provision that members of the European minority will have three years, say, to exercise their choice. As for the Sahara, don't complicate matters. We can only succeed by letting Algeria decide its own political fate. On the economic plane, try to keep to essentials and on the military plane too. Lastly, do your best.[2]

Robert Buron tells how he spent 9 and 10 February denying press information to the effect that secret negotiations would open in Switzerland, on the 11th, with his participation. On the 10th, he left his ministry by a secret door, more or less concealing his beard under a scarf and, wearing an unfamiliar hat, jumped into his own small Renault 4 and was driven off by his wife. On the motorway, near Orly airport, he was transferred to a larger Peugeot 404, accompanied by two not very talkative police inspectors. The next day, Sunday 11 February, in the late morning, Buron drove eastwards, flanked by his two bodyguards. It was 1 p.m. when they stopped behind a building with its shutters closed, on the road leading to the Swiss frontier, which was quite close. It was Le Yeti. The chalet turned out to be a good shelter for the negotiators, for they were able to work there for over eight days without being discovered and attacked by the OAS.

---

*Who had refused to take part in the Evian talks, believing that they could not be successful and "keeping himself in reserve" for a later, more promising phase.

The Algerians arrived half an hour later on the first day. Dahlab opened the discussions. He assured his French counterparts that, provided the Algerian character of the Sahara was recognized, all questions relating to the exploitation of wealth, transportation and airfields there would be resolved; and as for the participation of the French of Algeria in the constitution of the new state, they would be able to postpone the choice of their definitive nationality and during that period enjoy their Algerian civic rights. On both sides, the Algerian minister concluded, the Algerians wanted an effective and durable cooperation. Agreement "must be easy".

Everything seemed encouraging on the French side. Most of 12 February was devoted to military questions, particularly concerning the French forces that would be maintained during the "transitional" period. Forty thousand men, General de Camas proposed, to which Krim replied that, taking into account the need to maintain order between then and the takeover of the new state, double that would be required. Who would have thought that the most senior of the rebels would end up asking for more French soldiers in Algeria, if even for a brief period?

It was on 13 February 1962 at 8 p.m. that the final phase of the discussions began, the one when, in Buron's words, "each concession will have to be paid for by an equivalent concession". From the outset the French tried to get what was essential to them, guarantees for the Europeans of Algeria. Confrontation was immediate: "You are asking for contradictory things. You cannot play on all the boards at once. You have to choose: either one is Algerian or one is French!"

The French delegation replied that the psychology of the Europeans had to be taken into account. It would be quite impossible to *impose* on French men and women who had suffered so much the status of Algerians as a consequence of the referendum and of the independence that would follow the next day. For a sincere cooperation to be established, these French men and women should not be forced to give up their nationality by an explicit act. The FLN delegation refused this, but it did accept that a compromise formula would have to be found.

On Saturday the seventeenth, an irritated Michel Debré reminded the French negotiators: "The General is getting impatient and doesn't want the discussions to get bogged down. He himself fears the reactions of the army if we make too many concessions in relation to the initial positions. He doesn't want us to break off, but if pushed we must not hesitate to do so."

"Not hesitate" to break off the talks? To resume the war? That was not, of course, exactly what the Prime Minister was thinking, still less the General, who had even agreed to give up the Sahara.

When the Algerians demanded that French numbers be reduced from 550 000 to 80 000 in a year, Buron, a specialist in transportation, replied: "It's physically impossible." "Then there's no solution," Yazid interrupted. Joxe could only ask for an extension of the session to telephone to de Gaulle. This gave him at once a wider margin of manoeuvre on military matters "to counterbalance the discussions on nationality".

It was precisely these discussions that then began, thus giving the French delegation the opportunity of thrashing out, if not an idea, at least a new formula: after three years, those French nationals who remained in Algeria would simply have to "confirm" their names on the electoral list in order to be recognized as Algerians. Dahlab, Yazid and Krim went off for a long private discussion. When they returned, Dahlab declared quite calmly, "we agree" – a very substantial step forward in the negotiations.

On 18 February, at about 11 a.m., Louis Joxe, Robert Buron and Jean de Broglie were sitting round the telephone at the chalet: de Gaulle had called them to give them his last instructions, remarking that Michel Debré was listening in. Joxe summed up the progress that had been made the day before. "Agreement has been reached on the provisional period and on cooperation. I think we shall get guarantees for the minorities. The tough point concerns military questions and the procedure for the cease-fire. They seem to want to go as far as we do, but will they dare to exceed their mandate?" To which de Gaulle replied:

The important thing is to reach an agreement involving the cease-fire, then self-determination, providing that this agreement does not involve sudden upheavals in present conditions relating to the material and political interests of the Europeans, the French military presence in Algeria, the practical conditions in which oil and gas will be exploited on the territory and, lastly, the economic, technological and cultural relations between Algeria and mainland France. That, I repeat, that is what has to be achieved today.

As for the details, the General left his delegates room for manoeuvre. What mattered for him was that cooperation should be tried. The consequences would be judged in due course, but the attempt had to be made at all costs.

It was in a calmer spirit, due both to the progress made the day before and the flexibility of the head of state's instructions, that the negotiators began the day of discussions that they hoped would be decisive.

The military problems still kept them busy for several hours, but this was not time wasted. On the subject of the evacuation of the French forces, which Krim wanted to see reduced to 80 000 in six months and evacuated in two years, Joxe proposed eighteen months for the first operation and three years for the second: an agreement was reached on twelve months and three years respectively. Concerning the Sahara, the French demanded use of the bases for seven years. The FLN only accepted four years: final agreement was reached on five. For Mers el-Kebir, Krim, who had shifted at first from a ten-year lease to one for twelve years, ended, after midnight, by agreeing to fifteen years. On Monday 19 February at 5 a.m., the text of the agreement was re-read. Agreement in principle had been reached. Robert Buron had time to observe: "So there we are! Joxe and Krim have just exchanged two brief statements, grey in tone, but which have given a certain relief to both. For the first time we shook hands."

Before going their separate ways, the partners of both camps agreed to have a final meeting, which would be both official and public and which ought to be no more than a formality. The French proposed 2, 3 and 4 March, somewhere near Paris, with the cease-fire then taking place on the seventh or eighth. The Algerians spoke of the meeting that they had already arranged with their CNRA colleagues in Tripoli. It appeared that this meeting did not seem to them to be merely a formal one and that what had been achieved at Les Rousses would have to go through a more severe examination there than through the official machinery in Paris.

On that same 19 February, at noon, General de Gaulle received the three ministers at the Elysée: "You've done your best. Anyway we won't let ourselves be manoeuvred. If anything goes wrong at Tripoli, well, we shall publish the texts, all the texts. International opinion will be on our side. And we'll carry on the fight. Thank you, gentlemen."

The Council of Ministers chaired by General de Gaulle on Wednesday 21 February was intended to study the results of the secret talks at Les Rousses and the draft agreement that Louis Joxe had brought back to the head of state. Joxe opened the session with a seventy-minute report on the work at Les Rousses and on the texts that had emerged from it. His colleagues were surprised at the fullness and detail of the "provisional" agreements. De Gaulle then invited all the ministers and secretaries of State to express their opinion on these texts. Were there any objections?

Nafissa Sid Cara, Under-Secretary of State for Social Affairs, the only representative in the government of the Muslim community in France, described with poignant emotion the fate that awaited all those Muslims who had not rallied to the FLN cause. To which General de Gaulle was content to reply, with more courteous sympathy than apparent emotion: "Do you really believe, Mademoiselle, that the great majority of Muslims are not favourable to independence, which seems to them to be the inevitable solution?"

Maurice Couve de Murville, probably the only member of the Council who had never considered any outcome other than the independence of Algeria, predicted the development of that country towards a revolutionary, totalitarian regime with which cooperation would prove difficult. André Malraux said: "Texts are of no importance: the problem is to know whether we are changing our style of combat. It might be a tough fight, but in the end it will mark a sort of 'liberation' of France. That's where the real victory is, the victory in depth."

Then Michel Debré, much overcome, intervened. First he reacted to the word "victory" used by Malraux. "The term surprised me, but I understand it this way: it's a victory over ourselves." And that wounded man then recalled that he had wanted to give the Algerian problem other solutions, though, he granted, Algeria had never been "French in the same way as France". De Gaulle concluded the meeting:

> For me, it is a culmination, though a culmination is always a new departure. We must take account of the realities of the world. It is an honourable outcome. It was vital to free France from a situation that had brought her so much misfortune. It goes without saying that the agreements will be haphazard in their application. For our part, we shall be loyal to Algeria, making things easier for her, giving her her chance. Then we shall see... The results we have achieved will be put to a referendum and we shall implement them at a later date. Not everybody will agree with them; but among them, the small number, there will be those whose hurt feelings

blind, in perfectly good faith, their reason. As for those who continue to set themselves up against the State, they will have to be subjected to the full rigour of the law. Indeed I think they will be disarmed.*

According to some versions of that Council Meeting, de Gaulle added: "Now we must turn to Europe. For the era of organized continents is following the colonial era."[3]

How did the FLN "parliament" receive their negotiation at Tripoli? What we do know of that rather stormy session of the CNRA is that the negotiators at Les Rousses succeeded in getting their draft agreement ratified by the majority, which was very soon joined by the five leaders held in France, but that they came up against the veto of the turbulent ALN General Staff led by Houari Boumediene, who preached vehemently leftist ideas.[4]

Of course, the opposition of the Boumediene clan, on the one hand, and the fierce resistance of Salan's OAS, on the other, still constituted considerable threats, especially the second. But taking into account the concessions that had had to be made on both sides, the negotiators at Les Rousses might well have felt encouraged to go further and to bring that seven-year war to a rapid end.

On 21 February, on leaving the Council of Ministers meeting reported above, General de Gaulle had called over Michel Debré, Louis Joxe and Louis Terrenoire under the pretext of putting the final touches to the statement. But in fact it was to say something else. Turning to the Prime Minister, who had just expressed his reservations with dignity, he said: "It is really miraculous that we have reached these agreements, for just think: for one hundred and thirty years, they** have constantly been dominated, robbed, humiliated."[5]

But the results of the draft agreement still had to be confirmed at an official conference. Three weeks after the provisional agreement had been signed, both delegations set out for Lake Geneva, not only to seal the result achieved at the talks and to announce them to the public, but to complete the arrangements for the cease-fire.

The meeting was arranged to take place at Evian on 7 March. With each day that passed, the OAS tried its utmost to push the FLN to the limit, to undermine its confidence in its French partners, to terrify French opinion at home: on 5 March alone, over a hundred murders were committed in Algeria, including setting fire to the prison at Oran. Was that peace really out of reach? Setting out for Evian on 6 March, Robert Buron wrote these significant words: "I am very much afraid that on a number of points discussions will have to begin all over again, with men who are even more anxious than we found them at Les Rousses."[6]

Both teams were more or less unchanged. On the FLN side, behind the leading quartet of Krim–Dahlab–Ben Tobbal–Yazid, were the same men, plus Taïeb Boulharouf, a pioneer of secret contacts and a negotiator at the first Evian meeting,

*This version is based on the accounts of Louis Terrenoire and Robert Buron.
**The Muslims of Algeria. (trs.)

and Colonel Mostefa Ben Aouda, whom the General Staff had allowed them to "borrow": a soldier was obviously needed to sign the cease-fire agreement. On the French side, the "return" was noted of an important recruit, Bernard Tricot, an adviser at the Elysée, who had been following – or perhaps rather preceding – the affair for General de Gaulle. With Joxe, de Leusse and Chayet, it was he, in the French camp, who was most familiar with the files.

From a physical and technological point of view the negotiations would be better than those at Le Yeti. The Algerians would come each day from Geneva by helicopter. The French were housed in the annexe of the Hôtel du Parc, on the lakeside. Each delegation would have at its disposal a huge work room leading off a private restaurant. Communications were well organized and a strong military presence had been set up to ensure security.

It had been mutually decided that the talks would be held in secret – the two spokesmen, Redha Malck for the Algerians and Philippe Thibaud for the French, would issue only statements that had been drawn up together, indicating the subjects that had been dealt with. The crowd of journalists could hardly conceal their disappointment.

What did it all amount to, even after an agreement had been signed? The fundamental problem was not the same for both sides. At Evian, there were two key questions, each of the delegations being ready to do anything to get satisfactory answers on those points. For the French, there was the future of a human community to preserve: for the Algerians, there was the transfer of sovereignty to be ensured – in such conditions that the operation would not run into catastrophe on the way.

Looking back on these discussions twenty years later, Louis Joxe recalled[7] that his efforts tended to ensure the European (or, more broadly, non-Muslim) community the means of survival. Had he had too many illusions on that point? He certainly felt that every step forward made at Evian was paid for by a setback launched by the OAS in Algeria: every assassination undermined what had been achieved. But in an interview given in 1982 he said: "We never thought that the French of Algeria could leave: the idea of a French departure had never been mentioned, on either side, during the conference."[8]

Whatever that lucid diplomat's thoughts may have been after the event, the fact is that the struggle that he put up for the triumph of his cause certainly impressed his opposite numbers. Saad Dahlab, whom Joxe has always praised as the best Algerian negotiator, was later to say that what he most remembered of those long and heated discussions was the effort made by Louis Joxe in favour of the Europeans – for whom he had won much more than the Algerian delegation had been ready to concede.

While the French delegates fought hard for their compatriots on the other side of the Mediterranean, those of the FLN fought to accelerate the transitions and ensure the transference of sovereignty. But the themes crossed and dialogue was achieved. In a letter written to me in August 1984, Saad Dahlab recalled:

On several occasions we ran the risk of a breakdown in the talks at the second Evian. The questions were so delicate and Joxe wanted to win at all costs by constantly coming back to the guarantees for the French minority. We did not refuse to give guarantees to the French minority, but if we had accepted the proposals of the French delegation there would have been in the independent Algeria no more than a change of flags and we would have fought a war for seven years and a half in order to consolidate the privileges of the *colons*.

In any case, the opening salvoes on both sides were so tough that Robert Buron noted in his diary on the first evening: "Certainly the atmosphere is very different from that at Les Rousses. I'm not really sure that it adds up to progress." After five days, the discussions, which were at the outset aimed at finalizing the agreements reached at Les Rousses, had turned into a resumption of negotiations, several key questions being unresolved – the exact form that the cease-fire would take, the organization of the transitional period and how quickly the transfer of sovereignty could take place. This was a crucial problem for the FLN, which, even before taking up its responsibilities, had to be recognized as the only authority representing Algeria before her people and French and international public opinion.

Tuesday 16 March began badly with the announcement of one of the most frightful massacres perpetrated by the OAS – one that killed six European and Muslim leaders at the centre of Ben Aknoun, including the Kabyle writer, Mouloud Feraoun, a man of peace if ever there was one. It was a savage blow to any attempt at reconciliation between Muslims and Europeans, to everything that the negotiators at Evian were working towards.

On the evening of 17 March, Louis Joxe, head of the French delegation, called General de Gaulle on the telephone, his companions beside him. According to Robert Buron's notes,

General de Gaulle seemed less serene, less sovereign, too. He did not conceal his disappointment. He was convinced that if we had pleaded our cause better, we would have been able to frighten them. In fact his skill lay in giving us an alternative: either we succeed at last or we resign ourselves to playing a part that he knows we disapprove of. But for us the room for manoeuvre is small if we try to unfreeze our partners without showing them that we have anything in exchange. As for Michel Debré, he is reconciled to the worst. "Yes, I felt sure we'd never pin them down; there's nothing to be done with those people. If you are driven to breaking off the talks, don't hesitate."

It was plain that the risk of failure was now accepted in Paris. And yet, on 18 March, in the late afternoon, Robert Buron could at last scribble these notes at the end of the session:

Well! We're at the end; we put our three signatures at the bottom of ninety-three pages, the fruit of twelve days' work. Exactly a month ago, at the end of the meeting at Les Rousses, I felt great exaltation and my French friends, like our Algerian opposite numbers, shared, I believe, the feeling that comes after the completion of a painful, difficult but necessary piece of work. Today, things are quite different. Today's agreement is not an end for them. It marks a stage; there are many more to come. We had to bring it to an end! In the climate of horror that is spreading through Algiers and Oran, it is necessary to do everything possible to make the best of the opportunity – it is a poor one, but the only one – represented by the ending of the talks. The days to come will be days of madness and blood.[10]

It was a sombre epitaph for negotiations that had ended with the signing of a treaty. General de Gaulle was informed of the conclusion of the agreements at 1 p.m. At 8 p.m., he appeared on the television screen:*

The conclusion of the cease-fire negotiations in Algeria,** the arrangements adopted for the populations that choose to live out their destiny there, the prospect opened up with the advent of an independent Algeria cooperating closely with us, satisfy the reason of France. The solution of common sense, pursued unremittingly for some four years, has finally won over the frenzy of some, the blindness of others, the agitations of many. This is due to our army, which, by its courageous action and at the price of glorious losses and of many meritorious efforts, has guaranteed the control of the ground and established with the populations human, friendly contacts, unfortunately ignored for so long, and which, despite the attempts at subversion perpetrated by a few misled superiors, and the solicitations of criminal adventurers, has remained firm in its duty. But, above all, what is about to be embarked on to win from a deplorable struggle the opportunities of a fruitful future is due to the French people. For it is they who, thanks to their good sense, their strength, their trust, constantly demonstrated to the man who bears the burden of leading the State and the Nation, has made it possible for the solution to mature and finally come to fruition.[11]

It was a balanced, skilful speech, one that praised the army and flattered public opinion, and it did not exhibit too much self-satisfaction, which would have been very inappropriate: for although the cease-fire was implemented by both sides the next day, the OAS immediately broadcast an appeal from Salan giving an order "to immediately commence operations of harassment in the towns against the enemy forces" – that is to say, against the French forces!

On 18 March, in the late afternoon, Ahmed Ben Bella, Mohammed Boudiaf, Hocine Aït Ahmed, Mohammed Khider and Rabah Bitat flew to Geneva, where they met the negotiators before being received in Morocco.

An extraordinary Council of Ministers was summoned by General de Gaulle on 19 March at 3 p.m., three hours after fighting between the French State and the FLN had officially ceased, to examine the text of the law being submitted to

*At the same time as Ben Khedda was broadcasting his message on Radio Tunis.
**To be declared at noon the next day (19 March) by General Ailleret, French Commander-in-Chief, and by the ALN General Staff.

referendum in mainland France. But an even more serious problem was to crop up: that of the appointment of the man who would be given responsibility for implementing the agreements in Algeria on France's behalf (the man that the OAS were already calling "de Gaulle's *Gauleiter*").

At the end of February, after the negotiations at Les Rousses, when he had just given the General an account of the European negotiations concerning the plan that bore his name, Fouchet, once Mendès France's Minister of Moroccan and Tunisian Affairs, was suddenly summoned by de Gaulle: "Would you like to be High Commissioner in Algeria?" But Fouchet refused. A few days later, he learnt that General Billotte, former head of de Gaulle's General Staff in London, had accepted the job. Summoned once again by de Gaulle he praised the choice, but added: "If Billotte is assassinated, I shall be ready to take his place..."

Three days went by. Billotte "raised his terms too high" by demanding the dismissal of Michel Debré. The head of State, who had decided to dismiss Debré in any case, could not allow his hand to be forced by his former Chief of General Staff, whose appointment was postponed. On the eve of the signing of the Evian agreements, Fouchet was urgently summoned to the Elysée. "Billotte has not been assassinated," said de Gaulle, "but I would prefer not to send a soldier to Algiers. Do you still want to be High Commissioner? I give you twenty-four hours to reflect on it." And so Christian Fouchet, Jacques Soustelle's former assistant at the head of the RPF, found himself with the task of putting an end to French sovereignty in Algeria by implementing the agreements signed on 18 March at Evian.

Those negotiations had been so extensive that it may be as well to outline their salient points.

1. Cease-fire and evacuation

In concluding seven and a half years of war, the military agreement specified that "it will put an end to military operations and to all army activities over the whole of Algerian territory on 19 March 1962 at twelve noon". The French army would remain in Algeria until the referendum on self-determination; the ALN, based outside the territory, would therefore remain there over the same period, each side committing itself to avoiding contacts with the opposed forces. A joint cease-fire commission would be set up.

2. Referendum*

The referendum on self-determination would take place between three and six months after the cease-fire at a date fixed by the French government. The only referendum laid down by the Evian agreements concerned the vote of the Algerians, who would be called upon to choose between three options: main-

*The referendum organized on 8 April 1962, being a French affair, was not mentioned in the agreements.

tenance of the status of Algeria as a French department; independence with the breaking off of all ties; independence with cooperation.

3. The rights of the Europeans

Concerning relations between the two states, it was laid down that every individual of French descent living in Algeria would have dual nationality for three years, during which time he would have to choose between two solutions: becoming an Algerian or adopting the status of a privileged foreign resident. The Europeans would benefit from special representation in the Algerian assemblies, in which a number of seats proportional to their demographic importance would be reserved for them.

In Algiers and Oran, cities in which they were particularly numerous, the presidents and vice-presidents of the municipal councils would be compulsorily chosen from among the Europeans. Those French people who wanted to leave Algeria would be able to take their property or the full value of its sale, and then benefit from aid that would be given to the repatriated. In the event of agrarian reform, proposed by the FLN, France agreed to share the compensation given to the expropriated French people.

4. The Sahara

In the Sahara, the rights of France would be safeguarded. For six years, French companies would have a preferential right in the handing out of permits for research and exploitation. A Franco-Algerian technological organization, giving equal membership to both sides, would be set up. It would develop and maintain the infrastructure necessary to the exploitation of the mines and play the role of technological adviser and executive body.

5. Military bases and means

For a period of fifteen years France would keep the aero-naval base of Mers el-Kebir and for five years maintain its installations in the Sahara. The airfields of Colomb-Béchar, Reggane and Im-Amguel, and stop-over facilities in two airports, would be at France's disposal for five years.

6. Economic assistance

Algeria would remain in the franc currency zone. French enterprises set up in the region would continue to carry out their activities. The realization of the so-called Constantine plan – launched in 1958 with a view to the economic development of Algeria – would be continued and France would commit herself to maintaining financial aid.

7. Cultural cooperation

To this economic, financial and technological cooperation had to be added considerable cultural assistance: French schools and lycées, support for the expansion of teaching, research and professional training, were to be made available to technicians and students.

Some of the comments made by mainland French observers are worth recalling. In *L'Express*, the most constant and lucid observer of the war, Jean Daniel, welcomed this "alliance" made between the Algerian revolution and France, adding: "Instead of a peace based on division, on the acknowledgement of a break, or of an internationalization, what we have ended up with is a pact involving assistance."[12]

The parliamentary right reacted differently. A certain M. Lafay, among others, denounced this "capitulation" that "has stained our history for ever". But the real attack on the agreement was made by Jacques Soustelle in *Vingt-huit ans de Gaullisme*:

> These agreements, presented at the time as a masterpiece of diplomacy and as offering "guarantees" to the Algerian population, were in fact merely a camouflage intended to save face and above all to persuade public opinion in mainland France that the abandonment of Algeria could be approved of with a light heart. That agreement had to be knocked up by abandoning everything, including the Sahara, even including the men and women, who were thus handed over to the cruel vengeance of the conquerors.

The overwhelming majority of French citizens nevertheless welcomed the political settlement that had been made at Evian. But public opinion did not show the same satisfaction that had followed the signing in Geneva, eight years earlier, of the agreements on Indo-China. There were two main feelings: the first was relief at seeing the country unburdened, and the young soldiers freed of a duty in which many had begun to realize that not only their lives but also their moral integrity was at stake; the second was a mixture of remorse and rancour towards the Europeans of Algeria, who were identified with the OAS.

International opinion was unanimously favourable. President Kennedy expressed his "admiration" to General de Gaulle, while also congratulating Ben Khedda. Khrushchev, however, chose to congratulate only the GPRA, which thereby benefited from a *de jure* recognition that led de Gaulle to recall his Ambassador in Moscow: until self-determination had been completed, Algeria remained French.*

*The episode gave place to a curious demonstration of the General's diplomatic views. A few months later, the Secretary-General at the Quai d'Orsay, considering that the "penitence" inflicted on Moscow – and also on Belgrade and Warsaw, which had followed the gesture made by the USSR – had gone on long enough, asked that the diplomats be sent back to their posts. He obtained this answer from de Gaulle: "The Russians are majors, and therefore responsible for their actions. They can wait. Similarly the Serbs, who owe us a lot. As for the Poles, yes, let the French Ambassador go back to Warsaw."

The referendum was fixed for 8 April. Forty-eight hours earlier, de Gaulle made a broadcast in which he said that "we, the French people, are about to implement the clearest, the most frank, the most democratic referendum possible".[13] On the French side, the referendum put the seal on the popular legitimacy of the Evian agreements: of the 65 per cent turn-out, 90.71 per cent replied "yes" to the question asked. The result was even more favourable to the General than the specialists had anticipated. Algeria, a hundred and thirty-two years after the beginning of the conquest, had now ceased to be "French".

The following Wednesday, the head of State opened the session of the Council of Ministers with these words: "I am calling on the Prime Minister to speak. He has something that he wishes to tell us." It was Michel Debré's resignation. As significant as the resignation of the Prime Minister was the General's choice of his successor – the pioneer of the solution that had just prevailed, Georges Pompidou.

Why did General de Gaulle choose that moment to thank Debré, after making him endure the long torture of "disengagement from Algeria", which, for him, was like tearing a limb from the body of the nation? Had not Debré himself offered several times to resign, as we have seen, in August 1961? Had he not inundated the General with messages urging him not to give in on French sovereignty in the Sahara, especially a long, emotional letter in December 1961?[14]

General de Gaulle had needed Michel Debré to "cover" him on his right throughout the Algerian negotiations. Whatever fury the Prime Minister had aroused among his former *Algérie française* friends by lending himself to this game, Debré could nevertheless still rely on a clientèle, both civilian and military, that could be directed at the Elysée from Algeria. Now de Gaulle no longer needed him, regarded him as "worn out". It was time to find a fresher lieutenant, one better adapted, perhaps, to the new political situation. For the excitable parliamentary nationalist Michel Debré, an irritating brake on the Algerian negotiations, he was to substitute a jovial manager of men.

Had Charles de Gaulle turned out to be a good negotiator over Algeria? Could he, by addressing them in a different tone, have won better conditions from the men of the FLN, made the transition from French Algeria to an independent Algeria smoother? Pierre Mendès France told me that de Gaulle knew only how to alternate between pressure and concessions, threats and abandonment, without concerning himself with all that lay between those two extremes and on which diplomatic dealing is based. But this is not the opinion of his three closest colleagues at the time – Louis Joxe, Geoffroy de Courcel and Bernard Tricot. Nor is it the opinion of those who, in the opposite camp, had to deal with him, such men as Saad Dahlab, M'Hammed Yazid or Abdelhamid Mehri. They remember a "devious" and "ingenious" adversary.

In view of his exceptional intellectual talents, his energy and his imagination, it nevertheless does not seem that General de Gaulle was at his best in handling the affair. It had been noted that not one of his major concessions to Algerian nationalism was adequately compensated for by a concession from the other side. It is true that, having all the cards in his hand in early summer 1958, he could scarcely have improved on his position. But from 16 September 1959, once he had launched the great work of "self-determination", certain people were surprised that he did not get more in return, even if the ultimate emergence of an independent Algerian State was not in question.

It has to be said that the chink in the armour of Charles de Gaulle the negotiator of Algeria was his impatience to be rid of it. Most diplomats are handicapped by some military defeat, some territorial demands by their generals, or some directive from their governments. De Gaulle had only one enemy: time. Can one go so far as to say that a bad peace in 1961 would have seemed better to him than a good one in 1965? He was constantly overcome by a sense of urgency, considering that no price was too high that would leave him free once again to confront the world.

But, hasty or imperfect or fragile as those Evian agreements may have been, it was he who, in the name of France, assumed responsibility for them. It was he who took the terrible risks. It was he who dragged France out of an apparently endless war and made 19 March 1962 the first day since 1939 when France was no longer at war with anyone.*

---

*In 1945, the war in Indo-China had begun. In 1954, the conflict in North Africa had begun.

CHAPTER TWENTY-SIX

Confronting the Killers

The removal of Algeria from France could not have proceeded without violence. Such were French law, the Constitution, the teaching of our history, moral values and practices, that it was unimaginable that a million Europeans living in Algeria in 1962 could calmly accept either to withdraw to mainland France or to become part of a State overwhelmingly Muslim – whatever guarantees and forms of participation were laid down by the Evian agreements. As Europeans privately convinced of their intrinsic superiority over the Arabs,* as officers who had made Algeria "their" cause, as a tendency in the French nation that saw Algeria not only as part of that nation, but as the launching pad for rebirth and new greatness, the *pieds-noirs* (as European settlers born in Algeria were called) were less than ready to accept the upheavals de Gaulle was imposing on them.

Of course, it required of Charles de Gaulle a great capacity for intellectual renewal and profound political lucidity, given his military background and the generation to which he belonged, to open up Algeria to the ways of self-determination; it required incomparable courage and tenacity to ensure that this solution prevailed against the storm of opposition. But being aware of the specific character of mid-twentieth-century Algeria, which meant that it could not be regarded simply as France, the founder of the Fifth Republic would have been even more inspired if he had also been able to understand the European community better. One may cite, it is true, texts that reveal his awareness of that reality and of the original virtues of the *pieds-noirs*. During his press conference of 10 November 1959, for example, de Gaulle addressed a warm appeal to the Europeans of Algeria to assume a new future:

> You, the French people of Algeria, who have so much and have done so much there for generations, if a page has been turned by the great wind of history, it is up to you to write another. Have done with vain nostalgias, vain bitternesses, vain anxieties, take the future as it is offered and clasp it to you. More than ever Algeria needs you. More than ever France needs you in Algeria![1]

And, again, on 8 May 1961, just after the *putsch*, he said: "What a fruitful task can now be opened up to the Algerians of French origin! With all my heart I ask them, in the name of France, on the very day when we commemorate a victory** to

---

*Camus' early work – reports for *Alger-républicain à l'Etranger* – is particularly illuminating on this point.
**It was the anniversary of the armistice of 1945.

which they contributed so much, to abandon outworn myths and absurd agitations and to turn their courage and abilities to the great work to be carried out."[2]

But it was too late to try to associate, in an emotional, fraternal way, that emotional and fraternal people with the revolution that was taking place. De Gaulle and his colleagues might point to the efforts made by his delegates at Les Rousses and at Evian, in defending the future of that singular people, with an ardour and patience that won the admiration of their opposite numbers. But it was too late. In 1962, the OAS had acquired a sort of nihilistic legitimacy. The die had long since been cast.

It is also true that two of the General's spokesmen, Paul Delouvrier and Christian Fouchet, were able to appeal to the *pieds-noirs*. In both cases, words spoken in the name of de Gaulle reached their targets, perhaps because they came from men who had a real sympathy for that bewildered people, something that was always lacking in the speeches that Charles de Gaulle had addressed to the Europeans of Algeria between 1958 and 1962. One must seek, in that terrible failure of communication, at least part of the explanation for that collective folly that was the OAS. When Major de Saint-Marc, Captain Sergent, Lieutenant Godot, the baker Bouyer, the mechanic Belvisi or the agronomist Watin said that they were taken in and betrayed by the founder of the Fifth Republic, finding in that betrayal an irrepressible thirst for rebellion, they were sincere enough. But any man working in public life at a high level or a high-ranking officer in the army would have had innumerable opportunities, between 1 June 1958 and the speeches of late 1960, to see what de Gaulle's intentions were. How could a Soustelle, such a close follower of de Gaulle's thinking since summer 1940, a Salan, who had talked each week with de Gaulle since June 1958 and had as a close colleague the General's son-in-law, a Challe, how could they tell themselves that they had been abused by a leader whose writings and statements from 15 May 1958 ran quite counter to integration? There were those who wanted to know and to understand – if only to disapprove – and those who preferred to shut themselves up in "their" truth, or in the truth manipulated, at the Elysée or in Algiers. There was talk of misunderstandings. It was, rather, an inability to listen – or, more simply, pure hypocrisy.

At the centre of the great conflict between de Gaulle and the OAS there were, in any case, three radical incompatibilities: between the very idea of independence and the *pieds-noirs*–army view; between General de Gaulle's treatment of the affair and the temperament of the Europeans of Algeria; between that solitary man, devoted to style, order and classicism, and that Mediterranean people with its irrepressible enthusiasms and sudden, unpredictable behaviour, based above all on emotions.

From late 1958, the irritations between de Gaulle and the army began to turn into tension, pressure and defiance; between de Gaulle and the *pieds-noirs*, the misunderstandings were to turn into conflict, conflict into struggle, struggle into a crusade. From the days after the *putsch*, and even more after the Evian agreements, the OAS, by assuming the cause of the *pieds-noirs*, opened up a struggle to the death, sabotaging the agreements with the FLN, and in mainland France attempting to assassinate de Gaulle.

If one accepts that the violence of the rebellion against de Gaulle was largely a reaction of deluded men, it has to be recognized that those indignant victims of Gaullist policy were not all disappointed careerists or country innocents: for example, the historian Raoul Girardet and Major Robin were remarkable men with no long-standing rancour against the man of London.

Raoul Girardet came from a family of soldiers in eastern France. As a very young man he joined the extreme right-wing, nationalist movement Action française. He became a historian, devoting his doctoral thesis to Déroulède, a rather caricatural advocate of French nationalism. In early 1944, he was deported for work with the Resistance. As a Gaullist, he welcomed 13 May 1958 with ecstatic delight. For him it was the epiphany of *Algérie française* – in which he saw not only the preservation of national territory, but an opportunity for France to regenerate herself through the enormous revolutionary effort that the integration of ten million, then under-developed, Muslims would involve in a modern nation state.

For him, there was no doubt: de Gaulle represented that cause. And it is here that we come to the centre of the debate, that misunderstanding that now strikes me as somewhat mysterious between the General and those of his friends who were devoted to the cause of *Algérie française*: two or three verbal "lapses" apart, was it possible not to read in everything that de Gaulle had written in the years 1958–59 a rejection of integration?

But so intelligent a historian as Raoul Girardet told me twenty-five years later that he did not realize de Gaulle's intentions until the autumn of 1960, when he began to speak of the "Algerian Republic". Ten months later, just after the assassination attempt at Pont-sur-Seine, Girardet was arrested after mention of a Professor "Girardot" in the papers of Maurice Gingembre, a leading member of the OAS. He was kept in prison for two months without being charged, or even officially questioned – though he was able to note that a good many servants of the State dealing with his affair did not miss an opportunity of letting him know that they sympathized with rebels like him.

Major Robin was a *pied-noir*. His family had lived in Algeria for a century. Volunteering for active service in 1939, he fought in the Levant, in the Italian campaign and in France as a paratrooper. Hitherto de Gaulle had posed no problem for him. In Indo-China he was initiated into "revolutionary warfare": he observed there a process of ageing among officers who lived on memories rather than research. The competence of these "obsolete officers" became still more questionable during the Suez expedition, followed by experiences in Algeria. Working with Bigeard, at the Centre Jeanne d'Arc at Philippeville, he trained officers for "revolutionary warfare", soon putting his principles into practice in the Constantinois, where he happened to be on 13 May 1958. For him, "de Gaulle was the man capable of giving the army the stupendous mission of turning Algeria into a modern State bound up with France. This was not de Gaulle's vision of the future. So, having failed in the objective, having deceived himself, he deceived others and, from deception to lies, he led us into an impasse in which conflict was inevitable." So Robin was one of the leaders of the 1961 *putsch*; he was arrested, tried and sentenced to five years in prison. Reflecting on the affair twenty years later, Robin said: "de Gaulle lost a great opportunity for France and above all for youth. That man of imagination, who in every circumstance had defended the cause of our country against foreigners, had been incapable of seeing the future that was there for the taking. He had greatness, but he did not have vision."

This reaction should be added to that of those who suffered the bitterest fruits of the French withdrawal in 1962: the reprisals carried out on the populations who had remained attached to France by the FLN or by those known in Algeria as the *marsiens*, the converts to nationalism according to the Evian agreements of March 1962 – who became the advance-guard of the killers.

The story of the massacre of the European populations in Oranie in early July 1962 is still not fully understood. Between 5000 and 6000 people are said to have "disappeared".* Senior members of the French administration at the time tried to remove a zero from those figures. Nor has everything been said about the dreadful treatment inflicted on those Algerians who had served in the French forces during the conflict. An investigation that I carried out for *Le Monde* in October and November 1962 led me to the conclusion that 10 000 Muslim soldiers had been executed or murdered between 19 March and 1 November 1962.

Much larger figures have been put forward by Jacques Soustelle, among others. A more neutral calculation arrives at 30 000 victims, often in atrocious conditions. In a highly credible article in the review *L'Histoire* (no. 53, February 1983), Guy Perville concludes that this figure was "between 30 000 and 150 000" – the last figure arrived at by taking the total number of Algerians in the French army (210 000) and subtracting the number who took refuge in France. It is a rather simple calculation, but it is one that is worth remembering, as we should remember the horror of the executions and torture inflicted on those poor wretches who stayed behind (plunged into boiling water, castrated) as described by General Challe in *Notre révolte*.

The leaders of the new State argued that these were "blunders" and that such violence was not so different from what had taken place in France during the summer and autumn of 1944. This is to confuse very different historical situations. Given the complexity of the situation in Algeria before 1962, the facts of "collaboration" in Algeria can in no way be compared with the collusion of subjects of a sovereign State with a foreign army of occupation. One had to have had a relatively clear political consciousness to be able to detect at what stage the fact of serving in the French army, as a number of the nationalist leaders (including Ahmed Ben Bella) had done with some distinction, constituted a crime. And if the horrors committed during operations belong normally to a repressive regime, the Muslim soldiers who had been guilty of such things against their future fellow-citizens had, by doing so, been carrying out orders incomparably harder than the Europeans. This was also brought out by the Evian agreements, which stipulated: "No one may be harassed, sought, prosecuted, condemned, or made the object of any penal decision, disciplinary punishment or any discrimination whatsoever for acts committed in relation to political events that took place in Algeria before the declaration of the cease-fire."

*Colonel de Blignères, cited by Gérard Israël in *Le Dernier Jour de l'Algérie française* (Paris, Laffont, 1972, p. 384), gave the figure of 6500.

* * *

From the evening of 18 March, when the Evian agreements were signed, the OAS laid down their challenge in a statement: "M. de Gaulle's cease-fire is not that of the OAS!" Directive number 29-OAS, issued under Salan's signature on 23 February 1962 in anticipation of the "irreparable" (i.e. the ceasefire), was then applied:

> I want to cause a generalized offensive. I consider that the population of the great urban centres has reached a degree of structuring and organization sufficient to regard it as a valuable tool. The rottenness of the enemy must be exploited by the entry of the population at the final phase as a human tide. The crowd will be pushed forward through the streets. The final "rush" must be as disciplined as the rest of the manoeuvre. We must smash the military partitioning of the city by systematically opening fire on units of the riot police.

All the dramatic events of the next few days are implied in this text signed by Salan. Another, issued at the same time, specifies that "leading Muslim intellectuals must be attacked. Whoever is suspected of sympathy for the FLN will have to be eliminated" (a few days later, that man of reconciliation, the Kabyle writer Mouloud Feraoun, was assassinated).

And while orders for a general strike were given to the Europeans, the officers and men of an army that had come from mainland France and had tried for seven years to keep Algeria as part of France were given an ultimatum: either come over to the OAS or be treated as individuals "in the service of a foreign State".

All hell was then let loose: at Oran and at Algiers there were "Arab hunts", massacres of supporters of independence; public buildings, libraries and townhalls were set fire to; and there were shootings. On 23 March the OAS declared Bab-el-Oued, the main district of the poor whites in Algiers, an "insurrectional zone", forbidden to the "forces of occupation". A military patrol crossing the district was encircled and allowed itself to be disarmed. But the second refused. The OAS commando opened fire: six soldiers of the contingent were killed, nineteen wounded. The "battle of Bab-el-Oued" had begun. The army launched a terrible response that was not to end until well into the night, while the OAS commandos withdrew, leaving the inhabitants of the district to face the rigours of repression: twenty dead, eighty wounded ... and another seven killed on the army side.

High Commissioner Christian Fouchet landed the next day, 24 March. As soon as he had arrived at Rocher-Noir,* he urged the *pieds-noirs* to break with the Salan organization: "Those who tell you to fire on French police and soldiers are madmen and criminals." De Gaulle reacted violently: "Our army must not be separated morally from the nation. The nation wants the OAS to be crushed. It must be firm. Algiers is in the grip of subversion? Bab-el-Oued is rebelling? Every means is ready. We must spare nothing. We must impose our will!"

*Given the situation in Algiers, the representatives of the State had to be set up at Rocher-Noir, on the coast, twenty-five miles east of Algiers.

General Ailleret and Christian Fouchet could hardly receive a more imperative, less limiting mandate. But the OAS leaders took no notice. They called on the population to gather at the Algiers war memorial, from which it would then march on encircled Bab-el-Oued and "free our brothers".

The crowd began to gather about 2 p.m. No weapons were visible. An hour later, shooting began in the Rue d'Isly. From the recordings made by several radio reporters of that terrible scene it emerges that at least one officer shouted over and over again: "Stop shooting!" If the firing did not stop it was probably because it was kept up from some other quarter. It is no easy matter to apportion responsibility. What is clear is that the OAS leaders took all the risks of the confrontation by urging the crowd on to the streets in accordance with Salan's directives, breaking down the army's barriers on the road to Bab-el-Oued, knowing that the troops were exasperated by the constant attacks that had been made on them for several days. But it has also been proved that the armed forces put in to impede or channel the demonstration were drawn from an artillery unit largely made up of Muslims: Colonel Goubard, the regiment commander, an officer of unquestionable integrity and competence, had specifically requested that it should not be used to maintain order in Algiers.

Thus the massacre of 26 March in the Rue d'Isly (46 dead and 121 wounded civilians) was the combined result of the suicidal strategy of the OAS treating the crowd as a way to manoeuvre and drive forwards and the inexplicable choice of a largely Muslim military unit to confront a demonstration of *pieds-noirs* outraged by the repression of Bab-el-Oued.

Of course, this massacre dealt a terrible blow to the credibility of the OAS, which, after dooming its supporters to the repression of Bab-el-Oued, then sent them to be butchered in the Rue d'Isly. But it was also a moral defeat for de Gaulle: a week after the signing of the agreements that were supposed to bring the war to an end, nearly fifty French citizens had been killed in the heart of Algiers. What was this "peace" that substituted French victims for Algerian ones?

The question became all the more urgent with the OAS's reprisals: ten Muslims were murdered during the night at Belcourt, twenty-four at random two days later. The "Arab hunt" had begun: nine members of the FLN being treated in the hospital of Beau-Fraisier for wounds were murdered in their beds. Dozens of charwomen on their way to work in the houses of their European employers were murdered. The carnage was such that Muslims no longer dared to venture out into European-dominated districts. On some days, there were close on a hundred murders.

But, from late March to 25 April, the OAS suffered irreparable losses: on 25 March, General Jouhaud, its boss in the west, was arrested at Oran; worse still, on 7 April, the former Foreign Legion Lieutenant Degueldre, commander of the "delta" commandos, the spearhead of subversion, was arrested in Algiers. On 20 April it was Raoul Salan himself, disguised as a company manager, who fell into the hands of the official forces. The OAS had lost control of Algiers. But it could still sow terror, destroy the peace and kill off large numbers of its enemies.

The organization constantly changed strategy. Initially devoted to the defence of *Algérie française*, it then took as its task the destruction of "M. de Gaulle's rotten republic". After the capture of Degueldre and Salan, it planned a partition that would allow it to set up the "republic of Oran", to which the European communities of Algiers and Bône might be transferred. Hence the maintenance of the order issued in March: Europeans are forbidden to leave Algeria.

But three factors were soon to cut short this last project. The first was the disillusionment that overcame the *pied-noir* community. Realizing that the strategy of the OAS was essentially suicidal and having no choice between "the suitcase or the coffin", according to the old saying of some nationalist leaders, they chose the suitcase, invading ports and airports in tragic, moving queues. The second was the reaction of the *barbouzes*, the Gaullist commandos sent by Paris, who challenged the OAS for the monopoly of violence. The third was the return on stage of the FLN, which, under Major Azzedine, head of the autonomous zone of Algiers, counter-attacked.

Furthermore, de Gaulle gave exceptional support to Fouchet, flanking him by two men whom he held in special regard, Bernard Tricot, who was appointed "delegate to the High Commissioner", and Colonel Georges Buis, an old Free French fighter and formerly General Catroux's *chef de cabinet* in the Levant, who had given the most striking proof of his ability as a combatant on the ground and who was a well-known advocate of the liberal solution.

At Rocher-Noir a strange communal life was organized that consisted of three elements: the French High Commission, the headquarters of General Ailleret – soon to be replaced by General Fourquet, of the airforce, who had contributed so much to the failure of the *putsch* a year earlier – and the Algerian provisional executive, chaired by Abderahamane Farès, assisted in particular by Dr Chawki Mostefaï, the FLN Ambassador, whose task it was, as Colonel Buis put it, "to bring the independence of Algeria to the baptismal font". French paratroops and members of the ALN were seen side by side and seemed to get on quite well.

Tragic as things were in Algeria, de Gaulle regarded his essential aims as having been achieved. He had already turned back to setting up the Pompidou cabinet, to questions of Europe and the great international debates. But he could not be finished with Algeria yet: there were the legal epilogues of the OAS rebellion and the assassination attempts on his life by the Organization, whose dismantlement, in Algeria, had brought into prominence its branches in mainland France or abroad.

The legal phase of the affair, in spring 1962, while Generals Challe, Zeller and Gouraud were incarcerated at Tulle, mainly concerned Edmond Jouhaud and Raoul Salan. The first was arrested on 25 March and tried between 11 and 13 April. The second, arrested on 20 April, came before a military high court on 15 May. The facts were fairly simple: these two army generals had turned against the State the weapons entrusted to them by the Republic. And this time they had fired on the forces of order, causing the deaths of many civilians and soldiers.

Nevertheless, the case of Edmond Jouhaud was a very special one. Firstly because, as a native of Algeria, he would benefit from the circumstances. Who could not see, without despairing, one's native land turn into a foreign state? Secondly, because this officer had never shown a great deal of political dexterity. Thirdly, because at the head of the OAS at Oran, he tried on several occasions to

oppose the racist excesses of the terrorist strategy: there were several witnesses to
this effect. In any case his signature appeared on none of the texts condemning
hundreds of innocent people to death – whereas that of Raoul Salan did.

None of these arguments in favour of clemency could really be of much use to
the former commander-in-chief who had become the principal leader of the OAS.
It was clear that he disapproved of such horrors as the mortar bombardment of the
Place du Cheval or the explosion of a booby-trapped car, on 2 May, which
together caused the deaths of 120 Muslims. But he had never expressed public
disapproval of any of these crimes. He took responsibility for them in the face of
the law.

Yet, against all logic, it was Edmond Jouhaud who on 13 April was condemned
to death. Raoul Salan got no more than a term of imprisonment on 23 May. The
withdrawal of one jury, between two trials, was not the only thing to provoke this
extraordinary shift, but also perhaps the feeling that the OAS threat was weakening, the reservations of the public ministry that dared not demand the death
penalty and, above all, the extraordinary performance of Salan's principal defence
counsel, Maître Jean-Louis Tixier-Vignancourt – whose oratorical talent was fired
with a hatred for General de Gaulle dating back to Vichy.

In short, Salan saved his head, to the cheers of a public that had been won over
by the OAS. It was the last victory of *Algérie française*. De Gaulle learnt of the
verdict during a reception given at the Elysée in honour of an African head of
government: according to several witnesses, he went pale. Flohic, his aide-de-
camp, saw him go back to his apartment and followed him at once. He found him
furious at this verdict, which he saw as an "affront" to the head of state. To his
close friends, he roared: "It isn't Salan that this court has been trying, but de
Gaulle!" And although he had been "determined to pardon Jouhaud",[3] he now
thought that he ought to "disavow the high court" and "have Jouhaud executed".
Only the execution of one of the main leaders of the OAS, he argued in the
presence of his Justice Minister, Jean Foyer, would avoid discouraging the forces
of order engaged in the struggle against subversion: how can everyone else be kept
in line if the leaders are spared? To which Foyer could reply that, just because the
leader had saved his head, one could not substitute his second-in-command on the
scaffold. The rejection of pardon would seem like "a reaction of irritation and
spite", which, he hastened to add, "was not in General de Gaulle's character and
would tarnish his glory". Georges Pompidou, Pierre Messmer, Pierre Sudreau,
Edgard Pisani all came up with similar arguments, thus putting their ministerial
portfolios at risk. The head of State confirmed that Edmond Jouhaud would be
shot at dawn on Saturday 28 May. But the execution was not carried out. On 3
June, from his prison cell, Jouhaud launched an appeal to his fellow French
Algerians that the OAS should give up the struggle. Was it a gesture suggested by
his defence to save his head? I would prefer to attribute this initiative to the
disinterested credit of a man who was above fear, and sensitive above all to the
safety of his own people. Thus the affair rebounded politically. Jouhaud, who
could be executed at any moment, had become a factor for peace.

On 5 June, at Rocher-Noir, Christian Fouchet received a call from the Elysée.
It was 4 p.m. General de Gaulle, most unusually, was on the line.

"What has been the effect of Salan's acquittal on the forces of order?"

"It has produced a very bad impression on those whose jobs it is to arrest – at any risk! – the OAS leaders."

"Of course! Is it possible to shoot the little ones if one does not shoot the big ones? And is it possible not to shoot the little ones without seeming to be acquiescing in the weakness of the court, and even in the policy of the OAS? Now that Salan has been acquitted, what do you think of the condemnation of Jouhaud?"

"As I have informed you, *mon Général*, I think it is quite useful to gain time."

"For what reasons? Do you really think the publication of the Jouhaud statement* is important?"

"*Mon Général*, this is what I think: for myself, I am an advocate of rigour. But I'm convinced that the publication of the Jouhaud statement will be positive on European opinion as a whole. It will help them to shift over to those who want to distance themselves from the OAS. And, if it has to be published, it has to be published straight away. But then Jouhaud couldn't be shot. It would be morally inconceivable."

"To what extent do the advantages of publication outweigh the inconveniences of weakness?"

"*Mon Général*, if the publication goes ahead, everything changes. Jouhaud is asking the OAS to stop a struggle that has become desperate. If you pardon him, you do not align yourself with the court that judged Salan; it is simply a recognition of a new fact to Jouhaud's credit and has nothing to do with Salan."

"So be it."[4]

That same evening, Christian Fouchet learned that Edmond Jouhaud would not be executed. But the General was to wait for over five months more before making the pardon official (on 28 November).

It had long been an obsession of the OAS leaders to kill de Gaulle. To punish the traitor? To avenge "our dead"? The failure of Pont-sur-Seine could not in any way have discouraged them. At an executive committee meeting of the CNR in Rome in May, Georges Bidault took over the leadership, Colonel Argoud** was put in charge of operations in mainland France and Jacques Soustelle, who had mainly been living in Italy for the last six months, of the theatre of operations abroad.[5] Their aims included "the punishment of traitors" and "the carrying out of legal decisions taken by the executive committee". But these "legal decisions" were soon to be handed over by the CNR to a "military court" – like the "judgement" of 3 July 1962 condemning General de Gaulle to death for "the crime of

*A call for a cease fire.
**Who had escaped four months earlier from the Canary Isles, where he had been deported by the Spanish government.

high treason". As for the operation aimed at the physical elimination of the head of state, Antoine Argoud was extremely frank:

> Despite what may have been said or written, the physical elimination of the Head of State poses no moral problem for any of us. We are all convinced, Bidault the practising Catholic, Soustelle the liberal, like myself, or the *pieds-noirs* in the group, that de Gaulle has deserved the supreme punishment a hundred times over. The only divergences between us relate to the opportunity. The professor (that is what I call Chairman Bidault) is very aware of the consummate skill with which de Gaulle has used the assassination attempt to consolidate his political position. He believes that another failed operation would give him new advantages. He is the only one to think like this.[6]

After 4 May 1962, the date of the arrest of the last important leader of the OAS – André Canal, known as "the Monocle" – the "de Gaulle operation" slipped into the hands of what were more or less fringe groups, the most important of which was the one that its members called "the old General Staff". The central figure of this group was Jean-Marie Bastien-Thiry, the organizer of the assassination attempt at Pont-sur-Seine.

The last phase of assassination attempts either involved trying to kill de Gaulle on the steps of the Elysée during the visit of some head of state, by a marksman at a window of 86 Rue du Faubourg-Saint-Honoré, or during a visit by the President of the Republic to Vesoul on 14 June, the day before the proclamation of the independence of Algeria (3 July 1962). As long as there was still time to stop, by the death of the man mainly responsible for it, the mechanism of dissociation between France and Algeria, the OAS-CNR, Argoud and Sergent, were still concerned with organizing "the execution". Afterwards, when it was too late, the whole project was passed on to men who behaved like exterminating angels, instruments of a divine justice, like Bastien-Thiry, or as revengers of the *pied-noir* people like Georges Watin. Just as much of the activity of the senior members of the CNR had been impetuous and incoherent, that of "Didier", alias "Germain", that is to say, Jean-Marie Bastien-Thiry, was impressive for its rigour, the meticulousness of its organization, his implacable determination and boundless energy. In Bastien-Thiry and Watin, de Gaulle found enemies capable of carrying out the plan that they had made.

Colonel Bastien-Thiry, a graduate of the Ecole Polytechnique, worked in the research department of the Air Ministry. He was a remarkable engineer. A Catholic, he was the son-in-law of Georges Lamirand, who set up the Vichy Ministry of Youth: but his own family had opted for Free France – beginning with the father, an artillery officer who had known de Gaulle at Metz in 1937 and had been an active member of the RPF. A Gaullist until 1959, Bastien-Thiry then broke with de Gaulle over Algeria. From then on, for him, the man who handed over Algeria to "Arabo-Communism" was the Antichrist.

When, on 22 August 1962, "Didier" was setting up the trap of Petit-Clamart, it was his seventh attempt in a few weeks. In May, in the Avenue du Maine in Paris, in June at the Porte de Châtillon in Paris and then at Meudon, and in July in the Orléans region, where de Gaulle attended the wedding of a great-niece, the arrangements were repeated – thanks to information, one of the conspirators was to say, provided by a "mole" in the Elysée, but the innumerable suppositions made on this subject have led to no definite conclusions.* It seems that Bastien-Thiry in fact based his plans on telephone calls from observers placed around the Elysée – especially a certain "Pierre" – as soon as the head of State was expected to make a move.

De Gaulle's security was carefully organized, as we have seen, from inside the palace. But during most of his outings for private reasons he could only bear an escort of one or two cars and two motorcyclists, being irritated by any more obvious protection, telling the Interior Minister, Roger Frey, who begged him to cooperate with his men, "you do your job, I'll do mine."

Since the attempt at Pont-sur-Seine, de Gaulle's security at Colombey had been impressive. In June 1962, the idea of an assassination attempt "from the air" while the General was there in August had been taken seriously. General Delfino had set up "Operation Turtle-dove", which involved in particular: forbidding all flights at any altitude over Colombey-les-Deux-Eglises, within a twenty-kilometre radius; setting up light anti-aircraft batteries around La Boisserie; keeping a fighter on maximum alert from thirty minutes before dawn to thirty minutes after sunset.

For the week 20–26 August, a Major Douchet was in charge. A few days before, his predecessor had learnt that during the General's daily walk one of his grand-sons told him of a big machine-gun he could see (the General's eyesight was very poor). De Gaulle, finding the proximity of this weapon excessive, but unwilling to alter a plan drawn up by experts, insisted that the battery be hidden from view by a small hayrick.

On 8 August 1962, those responsible for the security of the head of State came very close to disaster. It is through information passed on to the authors of *Objectif de Gaulle* that we know the details of this new phase of "Operation Z". Charles de Gaulle had left Colombey that morning in order to lunch with General Eisenhower at the Elysée. Just as the presidential convoy entered the Avenue de Versailles, the three cars of the Bastien-Thiry commando sped from the Rue de la Convention on to the Pont Mirabeau. The "Didier" plan was to slip into the General's convoy, to overtake the General's Citroën DS21 and then open fire on him. But this manoeuvre was ruined quite by chance, since the General's chauffeur, Paul Fontenil, suddenly decided to go along the other bank of the river.

The commando did not consider itself beaten. Bastien-Thiry's vehicles pressed ahead to overtake the General's car, moving in and out and getting level with him. But just as they were there and Watin, with his window down, was getting ready to shoot the General, who was only a few metres away from him, the driver of a Renault 4, forging ahead like all Parisian drivers, came between them. La Tocnaye, the second-in-command of the operation, yelled: "No! There'll be too

*The most serious being that by Jacques Delarue, *L'OAS contre de Gaulle*; attention may also be drawn to *Comment je n'ai pas tué de Gaulle*, by Alain de La Tocnaye, one of the conspirators (Edmond Nalis, 1969), and *Objectif de Gaulle* by P. Demaret and C. Plume.

much of a mess and we won't get out!" At the Trocadéro tunnel, Bastien-Thiry's men gave up the pursuit, sighing somewhat exasperatedly: "It's only our seventeenth attempt."[7] Neither de Gaulle, nor his wife, nor his son-in-law, nor any member of the protection service noticed anything.[8]

Two weeks later, on 22 August, General de Gaulle, who was staying at Colombey, had to spend the day in Paris to chair a meeting of the Council of Ministers. His wife insisted on going with him. He suggested to his son-in-law, who was also on holiday at La Boisserie, that he act as aide-de-camp. There were so many rumours of an assassination attempt that Colombey was on extra alert. After landing at Villacoublay airport – since the affair of Pont-sur-Seine, the General hardly ever went to Paris other than by air – Boissieu took the shortest route, through Petit-Clamart, the Porte de Chatillon and the Avenue du Maine: he did not know that the conspirators had decided to wait for them around the Place Saint-François-Xavier,* – but, caught up in the traffic jams, they had arrived late. Once again the "operation" had failed.

During the Council of Ministers, Roger Frey reported on information coming from various sources concerning new preparations for an assassination attempt on the General. Just after 7.30 p.m. the General got into his Citroën DS19, registration number 543 HU 75. He sat in the rear left-hand seat, beside his wife, Alain de Boissieu having taken the seat on the right of the chauffeur Francis Marroux.** Bonneval (whose place had been taken by the General's son-in-law) and Boissieu had a quick discussion. What route should they take? Meudon, suggested Boissieu. No, said Bonneval: there would be too much traffic at this time. The two men then decided to take the same route that they had taken that morning, through Clamart. It would seem impossible, therefore, that the commando unit could have been informed of the route by a "mole". Everything seems to suggest that "Pierre", Bastien-Thiry's look-out, was somewhere near the Grand Palais: if the convoy crossed the Seine, it had to go through Clamart; if not, through Meudon. That time, it was to be Clamart. He made a telephone call and twenty minutes later, at 8 p.m., the commando was in position in the Avenue de la Libération at the Petit-Clamart crossroads.

Twelve men, ten of them armed with automatic rifles, dozens of weapons and explosives, and four vehicles were there. In a Simca 1000 parked before the crossroads, Bastien-Thiry lay in wait, holding in his hand a copy of *L'Aurore*, which he would wave when the convoy emerged; parked near a petrol station, a yellow van with five men inside, armed with machine-guns: in a Citroën ID 19 was La Tocnaye, flanked by Watin and Prévost, armed with Sterling automatic pistols; and a Peugeot 403 van was being kept in reserve, containing Condé, Magade and Bertin, also armed with automatic weapons. Taken together it represented an irresistible force. Charles de Gaulle would go up in a cloud of smoke.

At 8.08 p.m., as night was falling, and a light drizzle was reducing visibility,[9] Bastien-Thiry saw the head of State's Citroën and the escort car in which sat Dr Degas and the two inspectors, Puissant and Djouder, followed by two motor-cycle

---

*Where de Gaulle spent his childhood.
**The same man who had driven the General's car at the time of the Pont-sur-Seine assassination attempt.

outriders. The copy of *L'Aurore* was waved. A salvo was fired that ought to have brought an end to the Fifth Republic.

This is how Alain de Boissieu, who had the best overall view, describes the scene:

At that moment I think I saw bullets bouncing on to the road. I could see very clearly the van, whose rear doors were wide open. I understood at once and told Marroux to accelerate. I quickly noticed, at the height of the left wheel before the van, a marksman with an automatic pistol. I looked at the automatic pistol, which was moving as a result of the fire. I turned round to tell my parents-in-law to keep down and to see that they had not been hit by the first shots.

Then I peered into the road ahead to see if there might be a way out on the right or left; Marroux followed my look, questioningly. I repeated to him: "Straight ahead, in the middle. Marroux, straight through." At that moment I saw two things that will be engraved on my memory as long as I live: a Panhard coming towards us* and on the avenue to the left a parked ID** with the two side windows lowered and two marksmen aiming automatic pistols at us.

I realized at once that this was a new group of marksmen, I turned round and yelled at the top of my voice: "Father, keep down!" Just at that moment the rear window on his side shattered. Mme de Gaulle had not moved, either during the first series of shots, or during the second, but she agreed to get down when the General had given her the example to do so. I looked behind and saw the ID follow the escort DS, firing shots; it was in front of the two motor-cyclists, one of whom seemed to have been hit and had his hand to his helmet.

Despite the two burst tyres and the gear-change out of action, our DS reached the Petit-Clamart crossroad; I then saw behind us the killers' ID turn into the little Rue du Café de l'Aviation. The DS smelt of burnt rubber and was swaying dangerously like a motor-boat on the sea. I asked Marroux if he thought he could get as far as Villacoublay airfield and he replied that he would try to.

General and Mme de Gaulle had sat up. I looked at them. They didn't seem to be hurt, but they were covered in broken glass. Brushing it off him, the General slightly cut his fingers and, as he touched his collar, I saw a slight trace of blood. I was anxious to stop and examine these two passengers, who had shown such exemplary cool under fire, but who might be mortally wounded in the back, the kidneys or the legs.

The army guard of honour was at Villacoublay and de Gaulle wanted to inspect it as usual. In this way I would see the General standing and, under the pretext of removing the fragments of glass, I ran my hand over his back, his shoulders and chest. No blood. The General inspected those airmen who had heard the gunfire, seen the DS riddled with bullet holes and its windows

---

*The car containing the Fillon family, innocent travellers.
**'La Tocnaye's car.

smashed and were literally petrified with astonishment. More discreetly, I looked at the back of Mme de Gaulle, that brave woman who had won my admiration by her astonishing calm: she had eyes only for her husband. The army doctor, Degas, also looked at my parents-in-law. Our eyes met and he seemed to say: "Nothing to report." We could hardly believe it!

At that moment a rather comic incident lightened the atmosphere of tension. In the boot of our DS there were some wrapped chickens that my mother-in-law had ordered in Paris for the following day's lunch at Colombey, where M. Pompidou was expected. She said to me: "Don't forget the chickens.* I hope they're all right." All the security men, taking the remark to apply to them, looked at one another and smiled with pleasure.[10]

The General's only comment before getting on the plane was: "It was touch and go, this time!" And a little later, telephoning Georges Pompidou from La Boisserie, he said: "My dear fellow, those men shot like pigs!"

The examination of the car** by the security forces was impressive: it had been hit fourteen times. Several of the shots had gone through the coachwork at the level of the passengers' heads and a few centimetres from them. One had gone through Boissieu's seat, probably while he was bent forwards. One hundred and eighty-seven bullets were found on the pavement of the Avenue de la Libération – which was renamed, almost immediately, Avenue Charles de Gaulle – where several shops had been riddled with bullets and where the Café Trianon, itself hit by some twenty bullets, changed its name to Au Trianon de la fusillade.[11]

The police worked fast. The members of the Petit-Clamart commando unit had been able to scatter at first. An hour later, they met up, determined "to try again". Ten weeks later, six of them were in prison. Twelve days after that, on 17 September, Bastien-Thiry himself was arrested. But three of the clumsy killers, including Watin, were never found.

Shortly after Bastien-Thiry's imprisonment, he received this terrible message from his father: "I disown you. You have dishonoured me." General de Gaulle had let it be known that he was inclined to clemency. "Bastien-Thiry is an idiot! He'll get off with twenty years and in five years I'll free him."[12]

Assisted by four lawyers – Maîtres Dupuy, Le Coroller, Isorni and Tixier-Vignancourt – Wing-Commander Jean-Marie Bastien-Thiry wanted to turn his "defence" into the trial of General de Gaulle, questioning both the bases of the Fifth Republic, the whole of the General's Algerian policy, which was termed "genocide" of the European population, and the "tyrannical" power of the head of State. He even went so far as to compare himself to Colonel von Stauffenberg, who, on 20 July 1944, had tried to kill Hitler.

But this impressive indictment revealed its failings when Bastien-Thiry declared before the court that he had not wanted to kill de Gaulle, but to take him prisoner in order to hand him over to his judges! Whereas all his subordinates

*"*N'oubliez pas les poulets, j'espère qu'ils n'ont rien.*" In *argot*, Parisian slang, *poulet* means policeman. Did Mme de Gaulle even know this? (trs.)
**Now exhibited in the Musée Charles-de-Gaulle, at Lille.

recognized that the purpose of the operation was to murder the head of State,* Bastien-Thiry, while alleging that tyrannicide had been justified by St Thomas Aquinas and that a confessor had absolved him of murder in advance,** maintained that this attack had no other aim than to seize the person of the head of State!

Psychiatrists having declared him to be normal, Jean-Marie Bastien-Thiry was, at the end of this acrimonious trial, condemned to death. This presented General de Gaulle with the problem of a pardon. We shall now turn once again to Alain de Boissieu, who recorded General de Gaulle's confidences on the affair:

> The first reproach was that Bastien-Thiry had fired on a car in which he knew there was a woman, Mme de Gaulle, who had nothing to do with the problems of Algeria, or with politics in general. The second was that he had endangered the lives of innocent people, including the three Fillon children. Thirdly, he had introduced foreigners into the affair, namely, three Hungarians, who had been generously rewarded.
>
> Fourthly – in the General's eyes, the most serious – Bastien-Thiry had himself taken no personal risks in the attempt. He had been content simply to raise his newspaper to trigger off the shooting. "He was not in the centre of the action," the General declared with a certain severity. In any case he was to pardon the other men condemned to death, La Tocnaye and Prevost, who had taken such risks.[13]

Some may prefer the thoughts of de Boissieu himself, who, after listing the "reasons" for Jean-Marie Bastien-Thiry's execution, declares that the assassination attempt was "radio-controlled" by certain "political circles" unconnected with the OAS and CNR. And General de Gaulle's son-in-law declares that this accusation, which he does not expand on, but which seems to be aimed at a small number of very highly placed servants of the State, would emerge at the end of a long investigation, one which he is still pursuing.

A few days after 11 March 1963, when Jean-Marie Bastien-Thiry was shot at Ivry while clutching his rosary (not before his father had gone back on his curse and sent a final appeal for mercy to the Elysée), Charles de Gaulle was talking very gloomily with one of his old Free French companions: "The French need martyrs... They must choose them carefully. I could have given them one of those idiotic generals playing ball in Tulle prison. I gave them Bastien-Thiry. They'll be able to make a martyr of him. He deserves it."[14]

Certainly nobody, not even the General himself, emerged unscathed from the affair.

The man who had returned to power in early June 1958 was confirmed in what he had long since known: the Algerian problem had no military solution and it was

---

*Alain de La Tocnaye writes that, until 1 July, he was in favour of seizing the General, but, after the proclamation of the independence of Algeria, he went over to the idea of assassination.
**A Dominican father. La Tocnaye obtained the approval of two religious.

through the ballot box, the redistribution of land and negotiations that any attempt to resolve the problem would have to be made. For him, when he took the affair in hand, the army was not only ill directed, but the subject of scandal. And by taking on the role of the civil power it was committing suicide.

In this respect, the Algerian affair was at the very heart or nerve centre of de Gaulle's system. The fact that the General could not bear seeing the solution imposed upon him by the FLN, that he loathed this amputation, that it pained him as much as it did many others is beyond doubt – though it is true that this undeniable pain was sometimes mitigated by the pleasure of making his arguments prevail over those of soldiers whom he despised, such as Salan, or intellectuals who exasperated him, such as Soustelle.

But, if the settlement of the Algerian affair demonstrates so strongly the originality of Charles de Gaulle, statesman and strategist, it is because it also expresses these two guiding ideas: everything is in movement and every group is defined initially by membership of a nation. For de Gaulle, movement was the key to everything. He was convinced that life is a river, not a dam, and that the water is endlessly renewed. How could the nineteenth-century structure of Algeria survive the immense movement brought about by the emergence of formerly dominated peoples?

He brought Algerian independence to birth, though the operation hurt a lot of people. But he did it. He freed France of her colonies and even that part of her territory that he had come to consider, with fearless lucidity, irreducible to the national future. He did it and became an object of execration for some, of admiration for others, including, when all is said and done, the author of this book.

V

THE WORLD STAGE

CHAPTER TWENTY-SEVEN

The Shores of Europe

It was partly to bring back the French forces to the Rhine that Charles de Gaulle decided on and carried out the immense Algerian amputation. Was this the vision of an old man obsessed by Richelieu and Bainville? Or the vision of a prophet of a Europe in which rivers would no longer be frontiers, and which, once together, would rediscover its inventive genius of the past thousand years?

In grasping the nature of a national community, Charles de Gaulle was a master. He who *is* France speaks better with nations than with men. Between de Gaulle, France and the French, there is a troublesome ambivalence: he is both principle and projection, speech and spokesman. But between de Gaulle and Germany, de Gaulle and Spain, de Gaulle and Poland, there is a sort of majestic familiarity.

The muse of history inspired in this twentieth-century French army officer such a strong attachment that, when deprived of her lessons, he sometimes seemed to vacillate, to be groping his way. It has been suggested that the strained relations between the head of the Free French and Franklin D. Roosevelt are partly explained, in de Gaulle's case, by the fact that he had no "grid" of historical references to assist him in dealing with the United States. This idea might be complemented by its opposite: that the bitterness that often darkened de Gaulle's relations with the British was the result of excessive attachment to a past in which Hastings, Agincourt, Waterloo and Fashoda loomed large.

This obsessive presence of the history of his country in every step he took finds expression in a sort of naivety in this page of the *Mémoires d'espoir* in which de Gaulle justifies the choice of Rambouillet as a suitable setting to receive foreign heads of state:

> I had developed a liking for the latter as a site for such meetings. Housed in the medieval tower where so many of our kings had stayed, passing through the apartments once occupied by our Valois, our Bourbons, our emperors, our presidents, deliberating in the ancient hall of marble with the French Head of State and his ministers, admiring the grandeur of the ornamental lakes stretched out before their eyes, strolling through the park and the forest in which for ten centuries the rites of official shooting and hunting parties had been performed, our guests were made to feel the nobility behind the geniality, the permanence behind the vicissitudes, of the nation which was their host.[1]

If Germany was in the forefront of Charles de Gaulle's political thinking, it was because the human community living on either side of the Rhine belonged perfectly to the historical setting that inspired the author of *Le Fil de l'épée*. Charles de Gaulle was well aware of what had taken place over three or four centuries between the Loire and the Oder, and beyond both. He had the measure of it – and sensed how much of it went beyond measure. He knew what had tempted the Electors of Brandenburg, what Bismarck – whom he admired from extensive knowledge – wanted, what Wilhelm had dared to do. He had weighed the effects of their actions. He had dreamt those dreams, cursed those triumphs, envied those successes, shared the rancour and hatred of his fellow-citizens. Those centuries of history, consisting for many of wars with France, were his raw material, his daily bread as a teacher at the military academy of Saint-Cyr, as a pupil of the Ecole de Guerre, as a fighting soldier, as a prisoner, as a writer – and, when events came his way, they were the *raison d'être* of the man of 18 June.

By education and by history – and also by that indecipherable and explosive mixture of an intellect grounded in technical precision and a soul possessed of immense, stormy aspirations that is the very essence of the German genius – Charles de Gaulle was better armed than any other Frenchman of his time to open up a creative dialogue with those to whom the destiny of Germany had been entrusted. And who better than he could claim to be freed of the obsessions, complexes and doubts that bedevilled so many French minds on that subject?

General de Gaulle's German project, from the time when, as head of state, he could conceive it, decide it and carry it out, makes the positive prevail over the negative. For the two bases of his revenge strategy of 1944–45, the superpower of a unified Reich and the noxiousness of a totalitarianism of the Nazi type, had passed into history.

Since the early 1950s, the federal structure adopted by West Germany, even more than the division that was for a time imposed upon it, marginalizing in particular "Prussia and Saxony" – as the General said – excluded any possibility of reconstituting a great Reich; and the democratic option clearly adopted by the overwhelming majority of its citizens had been consolidated to all appearances by the economic "miracle". This much Charles de Gaulle had understood. But the founder of the Fifth Republic could not be satisfied with a policy based on this evidence alone. He had at one and the same time to dramatize the great reconciliation, confer on it the style of an historical event, turn it into a sort of ceremonial of French forbearance, of the convergence of the oldest Western cultures, the kernel of an autonomous Europe and a buttress to French independence.

What made the German question so important for de Gaulle was that the answers given to it conditioned the three debates that formed the basis of any French diplomacy worthy of the name: national independence, the construction of Europe, peaceful East–West relations. The whole problem was to act in such a way that these three imperatives converged – that is to say, that Franco-German relations should be organized in such a way that a closer bilateral relationship would be matched by a "greater Europe", that a "greater Europe" would be matched by "greater East–West security" and that "greater East–West security" would culminate in "greater independence from the ideological blocs".

In 1959, circumstances looked exceptionally favourable for the grand design that de Gaulle had formed in relation to Germany. Opposite him, on the other side of the Rhine, stood a man who of all Germans would be most favourable to closer relations between the two countries, but of all Germans he was also the freest to take bold initiatives in this area. There was also this factor that was for de Gaulle of great importance: that the great reconciliation between French and Germans was to take shape at a time and in a context in which one of the two partners was, if one may say so, "more equal than the other". Whereas France, restored by years of economic growth (1952–58), rationalized and corrected by the Rueff Plan, by her new institutions, shortly to be liberated from her empire, appeared at the conference table free of any shackles and endowed with maximum assets, Germany continued to suffer from a double handicap: the occupation of a third of her territory by the Soviet Union and her renunciation of making and deploying nuclear weapons on German soil.

In that great historical dialogue, there was, therefore, one man freed of all shackles and another somewhat hemmed in. Hence the accusation so often made, on the German side, of a Carolingian arrière-pensée on de Gaulle's part: friendship, yes, and reconciliation, and interdependence – but on the basis of an implicit hegemony from Paris.

De Gaulle really only insisted on one condition for this joint venture: that it should be brilliant. When so many other diplomats dramatize crises in order to produce rapid solutions, he, in this instance, was concerned to dramatize peace and give it a romantic, theatrical, sonorous brilliance that belonged usually only to situations of tension. For this aesthete-general, peace had to borrow some of the thunder of war, if not quite the smell of powder.

Of course the Bonn partner was not unaware of the slightly unequal aspect of the contract. But, at the same time, Adenauer believed that the agreement would correct his handicap. In terms both of national unity and defence, the German statesman considered that the contract might well pay off. In a race, to set out from the rear often helps one to beat records. A genius for collective action, an ability to work hard, a sense of organization, American favours – Bonn had a lot going for it.

But what preoccupied Adenauer and those around him was not so much the original handicap as the divergences in aim. That de Gaulle could boast, in order to demonstrate his ascendancy, of France's national unity and a mass of strategic attributes that he did not possess disturbed the Bonn Chancellor less than the General's approach to East–West affairs.

For Adenauer, de Gaulle remained that strange character for whom Moscow communism was not the only enemy, in whose eyes it was not unthinkable to ally himself with the Marxist devil, as he had done once when confronting Berlin and was doing so now in his relations with Washington, if France's interests were thereby defended.

I have described the first de Gaulle–Adenauer meeting at Colombey on 14 September 1958, and their immediate mutual understanding. De Gaulle, of course, had many links with Germany. And there was much that he found attractive about the old Rhineland Catholic, strongly conformist as he was, attached to very similar values to his own and whose great age was so reassuring. If, according to the General, "one does not begin a career as dictator at the age of sixty-seven", he had even less to fear from an octogenarian. In 1960, de Gaulle was seventy,

Adenauer eighty-four. The German Chancellor had been in power since the birth of the Federal State eleven years earlier. In order to keep it, he had refused to be elected head of State the year before. For a long time burgomaster of Cologne, that city where the residents on the left bank, Heinrich Böll once told me, say they are "going into Germany" when they cross the bridge over the Rhine, Adenauer, who had dared to advocate the autonomy of his region in 1923, had acquired by 1933 the reputation of a firm anti-Nazi – which resulted in his being stripped of office by Hitler, but did not spare him being subjected to the same insult, in 1944, from the British military authorities. He had preserved a tenacious rancour against the British that was often to surface.

A conservative and a Catholic, he was driven by a relentless anti-communism, which was fed still further by the occupation of the east of his country and of Europe by the Soviet forces and the gradual building up of the Marxist East German state. For him, nothing was more important than the Atlantic Alliance, its cohesion, its power, the union of America with Europe. His ideal partner was John Foster Dulles, whose resignation in 1960 as a result of illness seemed to him to be a disaster.

The odd, imaginative, unpredictable side of Charles de Gaulle's character must have disturbed that bourgeois of fixed habits and principles. There were, of course, times when Adenauer deplored the General's "extravagances" – above all, the withdrawal from NATO. But the personal pact made at Colombey in September 1958 was to resist all reverses. His long political experience convinced the Chancellor that, in any ally, power and vitality were more important than anything, even if they sometimes took disconcerting forms.

His confidence in de Gaulle was based on three certainties. The first was that the French President was genuine in his aim for reconciliation over the Rhineland, which he saw not only as a necessity for France, but as one of the elements of the statue that posterity would raise to him. The Chancellor had appreciated de Gaulle's conviction during the talks at Colombey. The man who was at the Elysée was now a friend of Germany as well as of his own glory.

The second certainty was that de Gaulle was faithful to the West. Of course, swords had been crossed with Roosevelt. Of course, there had been criticisms of the Atlantic Alliance, misunderstandings with Dulles or Kennedy. Of course, there were his overtures to the East. But Konrad Adenauer had appreciated the firmness displayed by de Gaulle in November 1958 when Khrushchev announced the expulsion of Westerners from Berlin and noted that, of Bonn's three Western allies, it was the French who had shown most firmness.

Lastly, he was convinced that de Gaulle had become a good "European". This did not, of course, take the "integrationist" form given to the enterprise by Robert Schuman, de Gasperi and Adenauer himself in the early 1950s, but from the last days of 1958 and the decisions taken by the de Gaulle cabinet to re-establish the franc outlined in the plans of Jacques Rueff, the General's "Europeanism" had been proved along the way. These were measures that enabled France to apply the Treaty of Rome – which the General had come to realize was an ideal framework for the economic development of his country.

If Adenauer had doubted the intentions of his French partner, he would only have had to listen to his friend Jean Monnet, a "European" if ever there was one and hardly suspected of automatic admiration for de Gaulle. Monnet maintained that the combination of the former burgomaster of Cologne and the man of June 1940 was "one of Europe's great opportunities". Monnet was under no illusions as to the General's agreement with his own supranational theses aimed at a United States of Europe. But he thought that, flanked by Adenauer, de Gaulle would be a good worker in that indispensable phase of European transition represented by the Common Market.* And he had no difficulty in convincing the Chancellor of this.

At the time when the great Paris–Bonn dialogue that was to lead to the treaty of January 1963 began, the President of the Fifth Republic was certainly in the Chancellor's eyes the man that I have just described – Germanophile, Western and "European". But de Gaulle's position did have certain features that were disturbing, and although, on Adenauer's side, one "party" supported this Francophile policy without ceasing to be pro-American, there were also factions in Bonn that were not at all favourable to this strategy: there was the Finance Minister, Erhard, who mistrusted over-protectionist European arrangements on the grounds that they would stifle the commercial expansionism of the German Federal Republic; then there was Gerhard Schröder, who was suspicious of the influence of Paris; then there were men like Wehner, who considered that Europe could not progress without a close association with London.

Adenauer's "Gaullism" had to overcome many doubts and many trials. As we have seen, the General did not hide from him, during the first meeting at La Boisserie, that he intended to demand of him not only a renunciation of any change to the eastern frontier (the Oder–Neisse line) by which large areas of Germany had been ceded to Poland, but also "endless patience" with regard to reunification, goodwill in relations with Moscow and a "complete renunciation" of atomic weapons.

Six months later, on 15 March 1959, the withdrawal of the French from the NATO forces dumbfounded Konrad Adenauer, who in his memoirs described this gesture as "extravagant", seeing it as a sign of "disjunction" within the Western alliance that could not but lead to others. This was very perceptive of him. But he added that his French partner was thus showing that NATO had to be reformed: on this point, he wrote, "I agree entirely with de Gaulle's demands".

If the Chancellor recorded in so phlegmatic a fashion his French partner's initiative, it was because at the same time the General was resisting a manoeuvre that the Chancellor regarded as infinitely more threatening: the Rapacki Plan, named after the Polish minister who promoted it. This plan was aimed at creating a neutral zone in the centre of Europe (West and East Germany, Poland and Czechoslovakia). The Poles, the Czechs, and the East Germans would have gained by getting the Red Army off their territory – a great improvement for them, certainly. But Bonn would have lost its American protection. No one, of course, was more convinced than Konrad Adenauer of that other possibility, namely that to de-Americanize the West was not to de-Sovietize the East, because the

---

*Until, as we shall see, turning against de Gaulle, he drew inspiration from the preamble to the 1963 treaty.

fundamental problem was not the presence of nuclear weapons, but the combination of nuclear weapons and the totalitarian nature of power in Moscow.

Exasperated by the attitude of Prime Minister Macmillan, who at this time was the advocate of what was regarded in Bonn as a dismantling of the "United Front of the West", the old Chancellor was relieved to find a de Gaulle whose thinking was removed from any disguised military withdrawal before the forces of the Warsaw Pact – even if the disengagement were reciprocal.

On 29 July 1960, Konrad Adenauer was received by Charles de Gaulle at Rambouillet. Two months earlier, the Chancellor had been received by de Gaulle with a view to clarifying their points of view prior to the "summit" conference that was to bring together the representatives of the USA, the USSR, Great Britain and France two weeks later. The General intended to represent Germany at this conference – he did not say so, but that was the fact of the matter – just as Churchill had spoken for French interests at Yalta.

During the Big Four conference, the Bonn leaders were deeply grateful for General de Gaulle's behaviour in the face of Nikita Khrushchev's "melodramatic" behaviour,[2] exploiting to the utmost the incursion of an American spy-plane over Soviet territory: although host of the three other great powers and extremely keen to associate his name and Paris with the success of that conference, de Gaulle constantly preached firmness to an Eisenhower tempted by Macmillan to seek a compromise with Moscow.

At Rambouillet, de Gaulle threw his cards on the table on the subject of Europe, whose unification would be a union of states that was immediately called a *Europe des patries*, cooperating with a view to being transformed into a confederation. The existing communities would be subordinate to this new political power. Defence would be one of the major themes of this operation and NATO would be reformed under the initiative of the Europeans.

The problems were confronted with extraordinary frankness. Of course, the intention was to begin with a Franco-German agreement. This would have to be a profound one, not one based on equivocations inherited from the past. But was this not to forget that the Europe of which Adenauer had been one of the fathers was based on the idea of integration? Was this not to challenge the old Chancellor?

In his book, Couve de Murville maintains that on this theme of confederation,

> Adenauer expressed his full agreement and, really, the German leaders have never since considered any others. He therefore gave his agreement, even though he was clearly much more interested in an organized cooperation between France and the Federal Republic than between the Six of the Common Market. Like de Gaulle, the chancellor disapproved moreover of the excessive caprices of the European Commissions, their tendency to try to replace responsible governments, while expressing his discontent, for internal political reasons, only in very moderate terms.[3]

Thus the representatives of France left Rambouillet with the impression that they had obtained the agreement of the German Chancellor on the idea of a *Europe des patries* with a confederal structure, despite all the criticism expressed around them.

Nothing of the kind appears in Konrad Adenauer's memoirs: the old statesman concludes his description of events by referring to "obvious misunderstandings".[4]

The two accounts of the meeting do converge on their disagreements over the need to reform NATO, which the General tried to get the Chancellor to endorse, but he obtained no more than a very qualified approval. This is what Couve de Murville has to say on this point:

> The opposition [on the part of the Chancellor] appeared on the subject of defence. For him, the only problem in matters of security was, integration or not, to keep the United States securely attached to Europe. As for nuclear weapons, he still hoped, against all the evidence, that one day they might be placed by the United States at the disposal of the European armies. In short, he revealed a certain irritation on the subject of the French atomic programme.

Atomic discrimination, *Europe des patries*, de Gaulle's criticisms of the Atlantic Pact: these were the causes of Adenauer's doubts, though he constantly defined them as the cornerstone of his policy. Indeed it was at this time that a truly unprecedented agreement in the history of the two nations was signed (on 25 October 1960): it authorized German military activities – manoeuvres within camps, the keeping of supplies and use of airfields – on French territory.

De Gaulle's success in the referendum on Algeria of 8 January 1961 tended to restore Adenauer's confidence in the French leader. Such confidence was all the more necessary in that it was now subjected to three tests – the arrival, in Washington, of a team, under Kennedy, of which he was deeply suspicious, accusing it of "amateurism" – although their attachment to Europe and their concern to remove the threat of Moscow were greater than those of their predecessors; then, in August 1961, the erection of the Berlin Wall, aggravating the division of Germany; and above all, in September, the severe warning given to the Chancellor by the electors of the Federal Republic – disappointed by the defeat encountered at Berlin, by the West and, more specifically, by him. Thus deprived of an absolute majority, Adenauer was forced into an alliance with the Free Democrats, who demanded that Gerhard Schröder be made Foreign Minister. This had the effect of introducing a permanent element of disturbance in relations between Bonn and Paris, since the new minister could see the special relationship between Adenauer and de Gaulle only as an attack on the domestic alliance.

Nevertheless Adenauer insisted on affirming his own authority by giving his approval to what were called the "Fouchet negotiations": these talks had opened on 31 October 1961, in an attempt to implement the idea of a "Europe of States" launched by the French President. Throughout the long negotiations, Adenauer took great care to support the French point of view. But he had no wish to be seen as a "pushover".

After a visit to Washington, Adenauer insisted on meeting de Gaulle and in early December he informed the General that Kennedy had "spoken of the General and of France with great respect". But this was only a way in which Adenauer could voice his reservations about the events of French diplomacy, its "lack of interest", not to say "passivity", in East–West relations, especially on Berlin.

What! roared the General. If France had not stood up to them, the Americans and British would already be negotiating with Khrushchev! When one negotiates with the Russians, one has already given in. And, if Adenauer is to be believed, his host then declared that if Britain, America and the Federal Republic were ready to hand over Berlin, France could do nothing about it, but she did not want to take any part in it.

Adenauer could not bear what was almost an insult and immediately broke off the talks for the day, "very irritated", he comments. One can almost hear an echo of the de Gaulle–Churchill talks of 1942.

For the rest of the talks there was a prudent calm between the two men: they agreed on the need to keep Kennedy better informed about European affairs in Europe, on the urgent need to relaunch the political unification of the continent and on the opportunity of linking Great Britain, but not the Commonwealth, with the discussions. As a result, the statement published on the evening of 9 December 1961 spoke of "a total agreement".

At a time when the reasonable Europe of the Fouchet plan was beginning to totter, de Gaulle and Adenauer were to invent their common response to that collective wreck: it would be a Franco-German agreement, whose weight alone could almost be that of the Europe of the Six. On 15 May 1962, during a press conference, Charles de Gaulle carried out one of those reconversions of which he alone had the secret: he transformed the European failure into an epiphany of Franco-German understanding. When questioned on the prospects of negotiations on Berlin and Germany he replied:

> There is an interdependence between Germany and France. On that interdependence depends the immediate security of the two peoples. One has only to look at the map to see this. On that interdependence depends any hope of uniting Europe in the political field as also in the defence or economic fields. On that interdependence depends, consequently, the destiny of Europe as a whole.[5]

Hence the exceptional brilliance accorded to Chancellor Adenauer's visit to France. It was the visitor who then proposed the signing of an agreement between France and Germany to have regular consultations. "De Gaulle took up the suggestion," Couve de Murville writes. "If, in fact, they [the other members of the Six] persist in their negative position, would the Federal Republic agree to conclude the political union envisaged with France alone? The Chancellor gave his consent, adding that if the others really did not understand the need for a union, we would have done everything possible to enlighten them."[6]

In the chapter of his memoirs devoted to his visit to France in July 1962, Adenauer writes of the dilatory manoeuvres of the European partners that led Bonn and Paris to their agreement: "It would be better than making Great Britain the arbiter of Europe. In the whole of British policy concerning Europe, there is only one thing: Britain could not bear France to become the dominant power."[7]

The old German statesman's account is imbued with two *idées-forces*: that the Franco-German partnership is the cornerstone of European security, but that any move away from Washington is an advantage given to the Soviet Union. But for the General, the Paris–Bonn axis was seen in an almost opposite way: increased independence for Europe.

The French head of State had wanted to dramatize as much as possible this honeymoon between old enemies. On a field exercise at Mourmelon, he paraded before the German statesmen six hundred tanks from both countries. Never since the Germans had created Germany had the troops of both states ever operated together. It was a solemn tribute to the armed peace. Then, standing side by side, the Chancellor and the General attended a mass in Reims cathedral.

This lyrical celebration had to have its counterpart. Two months later, between 4 and 9 September 1962, Charles de Gaulle was in turn the guest of the Federal Republic. Bad Godesberg, Hamburg and Munich were to match Colombey, Rambouillet and Reims. Things were not entirely the same, however, in that, whereas Adenauer was greatly respected in France for a career devoted to bringing the two peoples on either bank of the Rhine together, Charles de Gaulle was a somewhat controversial figure in Germany. Nevertheless, his trip was a triumph.

The political talks between Adenauer and de Gaulle have received less attention than the General's public appearances. He ended all his speeches by raising his long arms to heaven and declaring: "Es lebe Deutschland! Es lebe Deutsch-französische Freundschaft".

"Sie sind ein grosses Volk (You are a great people)," he shouted at his listeners, observing to those around him: "If they weren't still a great people, they wouldn't be applauding me like that!" And he delighted his listeners by comparing their welcome to "the waves of the Rhine, innumerable and powerful". But the climax of his trip came with his visit to the officers of the Military Academy of Hamburg, where he referred to the "solidarity in arms" of the two peoples, in almost provocative terms.

General de Gaulle's triumph assumed such a noisy, exalted form that it could not fail to arouse negative reactions. In the German press, some commentators spoke sarcastically of the "coronation of an Emperor of Europe". In London and Washington, reactions were even sharper – and, in Moscow, these encouragements to German militarism and nationalism were denounced.

The General's triumph was to go too far. When he had recovered from this intoxication, the Chancellor began to ask himself questions. Where, in fact, was de Gaulle leading him? Away from the Americans? It was all very well fusing Franco-German relations like this, but the reactions of the Americans were becoming too unfavourable not to alert a man like Adenauer.

While the Quai d'Orsay sent Bonn on 17 September 1962 a draft text giving more specific form to the offers of exchanges and coordination made by the Federal German leaders, Adenauer was to give a not unfavourable reception to Washington's advances concerning a European "multilateral force". Referring vaguely to the now defunct European Defence Community, this project was clearly a new American attempt to drown the strictly European initiatives, thereby ensuring that Washington would retain its upper hand: "This was precisely what

General de Gaulle had constantly struggled against and what the Franco-German bilateral treaty was to attempt to counter." This did not stop Adenauer signing, on 10 January 1963, an agreement to belong to the "multilateral force".

Konrad Adenauer was caught up in the perpetual balancing-act that characterizes his policies, between the seductions of the French and the tutelary power of the United States. Without questioning the pre-eminence of the American guarantee, would not a strengthening of the links with France run the risk of making Washington doubtful of its mission in Europe? Events were to settle the matter, at least for a time. The crisis caused by the installation of Soviet missiles in Cuba showed everyone that the American strategists could be taken by surprise by Khrushchev and that, in the face of threats from the East, General de Gaulle showed exemplary firmness. Had he not been the first of all the allies of the United States to declare his unconditional solidarity with John F. Kennedy?

Decidedly, the strong man of Paris had a lot going for him: until such time as more light was thrown on American intentions and on the ulterior motives of Britain, the Franco-German treaty would be the starting-point for a powerful Western political structure. De Gaulle having declared on 17 January 1963 that "the Franco-German entente was the very foundation of the foreign policy of France", the Chancellor took the Paris road with the firm intention of carrying these agreements to their end: that is to say, to the signing of a treaty.

The day before the relations between Adenauer and de Gaulle were solemnized, the two leaders had a conversation that the first recounts in moving detail and in such a way as to reveal the extraordinary ascendancy exerted by the General on the old gentleman from Cologne. As de Gaulle was describing to him once again the reforms of NATO that he hoped to bring about, Adenauer replied:

> I remarked that de Gaulle underestimated France's and his own influence. General de Gaulle was highly considered in the United States, where France was greatly loved and esteemed. Perhaps even more than England. I was of the opinion that the Americans needed Europe. Kennedy wanted its advice. I urgently begged de Gaulle to make use of every opportunity that was offered. Personal influence could not change everything, obviously, but it could act on the direction of affairs.[8]

In short, they were to sign a treaty to which the Chancellor wanted to give the most solemn form.

> He meant by that, of course, to stress its fundamental character. Above all, he wanted to bind his successors by a legal act that would guarantee, whatever happened, the permanence of Franco-German cooperation. It would also be the final important act of his political life and he was determined to mark it in some such way. So it was finally decided to transform the initial memorandum into a proper treaty, which would be submitted to the parliaments of both states.[9]

Adenauer faced domestic resistance from Bonn, but there was also displeasure in London (which had just received from de Gaulle a refusal of its application to join the European Community) and in Washington, which saw the treaty as an operation cooked up by France to prevent any attempt by the Americans to resume their control of the "multilateral force".

The enemies of the agreement were not going to wait until Adenauer's back was turned to deliver the worst possible insult to it. "Since this document," wrote the German journalist August von Kageneck, "had no legal value as a unilateral declaration, it practically strangled at birth any hope that this historical agreement between two peoples who had for so long been separated by hatred had given rise to."[10]

Indeed this article stipulated that neither the association between Europe and the United States, nor the common defence in the framework of the Atlantic Alliance, nor the participation of Great Britain in European unification should be harmed. One could hardly counter more meticulously everything that had been the *raison d'être* of the treaty. "It was the negation of European Europe. De Gaulle could only express his disapproval of such a procedure."[11]

The General had decided to forestall matters. A month earlier, meeting Willy Brandt, then only Mayor of Berlin and his party's Vice-Chairman, he had warned him that if the text of the preamble, which had been communicated to him by his Ambassador in Bonn, were adopted by the Federal Parliament, he would take it as a "personal affront". Brandt did not want to deliver a "personal affront" to de Gaulle. But he did want Adenauer to be defeated. Thus the Bonn "Atlanticists", supported if not inspired by those in Washington, London, Brussels, even Paris – Jean Monnet boasts in his memoirs that he had inspired this text* – had won.

On 2 July, on the eve of going to Bonn to pay what was to be his last visit to Konrad Adenauer as Chancellor, the General declared: "Treaties, you see, are like girls and roses: they don't last long. If the Franco-German treaty were not implemented it wouldn't be the first such time in History." And he quoted Victor Hugo's famous line: "Hélas! Que j'en ai vu mourir de jeunes filles."

Well known to be a lover of roses, the Chancellor could not resist replying in kind. When he received the General a few days later, he declared:

> I have read somewhere that roses and girls soon fade. Girls perhaps. But, you see, I know something about roses and the plants that have the most thorns are the most resistant. The Rhöndorf** roses survived the winter brilliantly. This friendship between France and Germany is like a rose that will always produce buds and flowers.

In those last months of 1963, de Gaulle's foreign policy had received some setbacks. There was not only Konrad Adenauer's retirement. Three other factors also played a role: John F. Kennedy's trip to Germany, the French Atlantic fleet's withdrawal from NATO, and the dreams aroused in the Federal Republic by the

*This is strongly confirmed by Maurice Couve de Murville.
**The Chancellor's property, whose rose garden was celebrated.

"multilateral force" invented by the American strategists. All these actions and manoeuvres weakened the impact of France and strengthened the future bonds of Germany with the Atlantic Alliance.

President Kennedy's visit to the Federal Republic, the enthusiastic reception that he was given in the old capital of the Empire, his "Ich bin ein Berliner" speech, had somewhat tarnished de Gaulle's triumph of September 1962. And the withdrawal of French naval forces from NATO could not fail to turn his German partners to dreams of that "multilateral force" in which, Macmillan suggested, the Federal Republic might have access to nuclear weapons.

The "post-Adenauer" period was not one of decline in Franco-German relations. Maurice Couve de Murville has stressed the attempts made by Adenauer's successor, Chancellor Ludwig Erhard, to re-animate the project of a political Europe by the Franco-German initiative. But Germany was less central. Ludwig Erhard did not conceal the extent to which the French initiatives of 1964–66 (recognition of People's China, the leaving of NATO), left him "aghast and terrified".[12] De Gaulle was to show some sympathy for Erhard's successor, Chancellor Kiesinger, who expressed discreetly pro-French feelings,* and also for Willy Brandt, whom he had apparently forgiven for the "terrible preamble" of May 1963.

The treaty, which had been so roughly challenged by the Bundestag, the German press and Herr Schröder's friends, was implemented with honourable care by both bureaucracies and both political classes. And even when de Gaulle took the major risk of cutting himself off from his allies, first by imposing Community agricultural tariffs, which seemed to Bonn to be acts of economic warfare, then by leaving France's chair empty during the Councils of the Community in 1965 over the question of the simple majority at the heart of that body, and finally by withdrawing from the military structure of NATO in 1966, the framework set up three years before nevertheless stood firm. But a period had come to an end. Charles de Gaulle could still talk to Konrad Adenauer – he died in 1967 at the age of 91 – but the season of roses had given way to that of the gardeners.

That trip to the Rhineland and that time of roses marked, in the life of Charles de Gaulle, a most unusual eruption of emotion into the public domain. Was it, in the end, a failure? What purpose was served in the reconciliation of the two peoples, in European construction, in the cause of peace, by that sentimental exaltation, that could not but offend by-standers, arouse jealousies, revive rivalries and sow mistrust? By reducing the settlement of German, European and Western problems to an epic duo, de Gaulle and Adenauer had taken risks that were aggravated by their age and took too little account of the complex structure of the problems treated, of the political societies of which they were only the delegates, if the leading ones.

Did not so many noble declarations, so many promises and gestures, myths revived and memories transfigured, eventually turn against their inventors? Did a task boldly begun in 1950 by Jean Monnet, Robert Schuman and Adenauer, brought to maturity and almost carried through already under the old Chancellor

---

*All the more meticulously in that he had been a member of the Nazi Party.

and men such as Pleven, Mendès France, Pinay and Mollet, have to be dramatized to this extent?

On 24 April 1969, three days before the referendum that was to bring to an end de Gaulle's political life, the General received Maurice Schumann at the Elysée, alerting him to his forthcoming appointment as head of Foreign Affairs. In a testamentary tone of voice, the old head of State declared to the former spokesman of Free France that there could be no French foreign policy which was not "based on the irreversibility of Franco-German reconciliation". They were perhaps the last words that Charles de Gaulle spoke as head of State on diplomatic matters.

Was de Gaulle an anti-European? He has often been described as such, but he could be better described as an unhappy "European". The man whom fortune had allowed to succeed in apparently more dangerous enterprises was condemned, in this area, to carry off only partial, procedural victories concerned with tariffs, useful and lasting as they may be, and unable to convince his partners of the excellence of his master plan: to build a "European Europe" in which the nation states of the old continent would be confederated round a lodestone situated in Paris and manipulated by him, de Gaulle.

It was a splendid plan, but its major fault was to presuppose that France was the heart, the soul, the kernel of Europe; that the shared hope of Europeans, French and non-French, lay in independence rather than in security; and that the influence of France seemed less of a threat to their liberty than the hegemony of the United States. It would have been to break with the vision of most of the men who had invented Europe, from Jean Monnet to Paul Henri Spaak, who saw it much more as the eastern bank of an Atlantic grouping inspired and armed by the United States. Of course, de Gaulle situated his "independent" Europe "within the world of freedom".* But it is clear that the General intended to give that grouping of free peoples an autonomy between the two blocs, being the friend of one, but tending to be open to the other. In any case, he saw its supreme aim as that of an arbiter on a world scale between the two blocs and, in the long term, the means for their dissolution.

If we open the *Mémoires d'espoir* at the chapter entitled "Europe", there is talk, to begin with, for three pages, of France, her misfortunes and her resurrection.[13] And it is only after these reminders that Europe itself comes on the scene, like an extension of that rebirth. There is nothing aggressive, disdainful, still less "dominating" here. But the approach is irresistibly French: the very substance, the hard kernel, of the continent is situated between the ocean, the Alps and the Rhine, and it is on those places marked by the most intense history, at the heart of that permanent battlefield, that the new Holy Roman Empire must be built. One is reminded of Harold Macmillan's remark after de Gaulle's visit to him in 1961 at Birch Grove: "He talks of Europe, and means France."[14]

And in 1961, when proposing his major plan for Europe, the Fouchet Plan, which bears his mark and so obviously expresses his vision of a "Europe of States", he cannot resist proposing Paris as its capital. His Europe is sincere, open, generous, but irreducibly French.

---

*He took care to say "world of freedom" and not "free world", a typically American term.

De Gaulle may not have been wrong to declare that in the absence of any movement coming from the old continent itself, Europe would only build herself up under the protection and influence of the United States – this had been proved over the ten years since he had returned to power.* It might even be right to maintain that the nation-states were still the only true raw material of the unification to be achieved and that the best way towards Europe for its citizens was the *Europe des patries*.

But it so happens, independently of heavy historical memories and Francophobic reflexes, that people almost always prefer a distant authority to too close a guide and that if it becomes necessary to submit to a protector, they prefer one who can give them an effective protection. Furthermore, the concept of the nation-state is too marked by the French genius and the use that has been made of it not to alert mistrust.

For the de Gaulle of 1958 Europe was not a new idea. In March 1944, at the platform of the Consultative Assembly, he had advocated the formation of a "Western grouping, of which the Channel, the Rhine and the Mediterranean would be the arteries", and, six months later, according to Geoffroy de Courcel,[15] on the occasion of a visit by Winston Churchill and Anthony Eden to Paris, on 11 November 1944, de Gaulle suggested the formation of a "Franco-British-European nucleus".

Winston Churchill was soon to respond to this project in the famous speech that he gave at Zürich in late 1946: "The first step towards the resurrection of the European family must be an association between France and Germany. Only in this way, can France recover the moral direction of Europe." And presenting the formation of a "European union" as an "urgent task", the former Prime Minister urged "France and Germany" to "assume direction of it", in which case Great Britain and the Commonwealth, the United States, "and, I am sure, the Soviet Union", would be "the friends and guarantors of that new Europe". More Gaullist than de Gaulle!

Nationalist that he was, de Gaulle did not forget Europe, once it was no longer depersonalized under the aegis of the United States. On 25 September 1949, at Bordeaux, he was even heard advocating a "confederation of the peoples of Europe, comprising all Europeans free to express themselves on the Seine, the Thames and the Rhine". But, observing that Britain seemed determined to hold herself aloof, he proposed incorporating Germany in the larger whole to be built, this incorporation serving as the basis for the Europe desired.

It was not until February 1961 that de Gaulle and Adenauer decided to think seriously about the creation of a "political Europe", well beyond the mere combination of the existing communities (the coal and steel community, the economic commission and Euratom). The setting up of a study body, the so-called Fouchet commission, made a decisive advance possible.

*This is expressed by Jean-Pierre Chevènement in the very Gaullian formula: "The United States of Europe would be the Europe of the United States."

But then the question of Great Britain was posed in the most poignant way. Both German and French representatives agreed that London had come closer to the EEC, that the hypothesis of a radical revision of its relations with the Continent was becoming serious, since the progress of economic collaboration between the Six had forced London to revise the negative attitude that it had had in the early 1950s.

During that summer of 1961, at a time when East and West, in the persons of Khrushchev and Kennedy, were meeting in Vienna (3 and 4 May), before the Berlin Wall was built (13 August) and before the first Algerian conference at Evian had failed (13 June), the great European debate began. Whereas on 4 August the London government officially asked for Great Britain to be admitted to the Common Market, Paris was completing the Fouchet Plan for a European political union on a confederal basis, which was to be put to France's five partners of the EEC on 31 October 1961. When Harold Macmillan received Charles de Gaulle on 24–25 November at Birch Grove, his country house in Sussex, he told him that Britain now wanted to enter the European Community, not for economic but for political reasons. As long as Europe was moving towards integration, to supranational structures, London could not be incorporated in it. But now that there was talk of confederation (in the Fouchet Plan), the British Prime Minister could see no obstacle to Britain's leaving her "splendid isolation".

Thus, by a strange irony, Charles de Gaulle, as the herald of a confederal Europe, found himself promoted to the role of introducing that island kingdom into the Continent. All he had to do, of course, was to object that the United Kingdom was something more than a few islands on the other side of the Channel and that the incorporation, more or less direct, of the Commonwealth into the European "political community" was a "colossal undertaking", which would lead Europe to being no longer Europe.

The real problem had not been avoided either: that of active participation by Britain in the realization of Charles de Gaulle's grand design, the construction of a Europe of States.

But what exactly was the Fouchet Plan, that expression of de Gaulle's vision of Europe? In February 1961, the heads of State and of government of the Six meeting in Paris had formed a study commission entrusted with the task of laying down the foundations for the political union of Europe. This body had met on 6 March. On 18 July, at Bad Godesberg, after clashes between Chancellor Adenauer and the Dutch minister Luns, who maintained that the plans on which France claimed to be basing the preparatory work were insufficiently supranational to be of interest to the Netherlands, the Commission was given the task of drawing up the statutes for a "Union of Peoples". This body, whose work was to be carried out under the chairmanship of the head of the French delegation, Christian Fouchet, examined the French plan, which had been presented by its chairman and usually supported during the sessions by Jean-Marie Soutou, Director of European Affairs at the Quai d'Orsay and a convinced "European".

The plan, which bore the mark of the General himself, was a draft treaty consisting of eighteen articles. An important preamble laid down that it concerned a "Union of States" (a word that in itself was likely to trigger off polemics*), but that the body that would emerge from it would not claim to replace the integrated European committees (the European Coal and Steel Community, the EEC, the European Confederation of Agriculture) that were already in operation and would remain operational "in their respective domains".

Article 1 specified that this Union would respect the "personality" of the "peoples and member States", and article 2 that their cooperation would concern diplomacy, defence and culture (excluding economics). Articles 5, 6 and 7 described the main institutions of the Union: the Council, the Assembly, the Political Commission. The first, formed either by the heads of State or of government of the Six, or by their foreign ministers, must meet three times a year, extraordinary sessions excepted. Its decisions would have to be unanimous.

The parliamentary Assembly, made up of delegations from the existing parliaments, was an institution anticipated by the Treaty of Rome of 1957 – to which the text specifically referred. It had little more than a consultative mission. The real government of the Union would be the European Political Commission, which would sit in Paris and be made up of senior civil servants from each of the member states.

The Union would have no other revenue than that provided by the member states, but it could transfer or acquire property and go to law. The admission of a new member must be approved unanimously. This State must previously have belonged to the Communities set up by the Paris and Rome treaties and have recognized that it shared the aims of the Union (particularly foreign policy).

The French plan could not fail to arouse the hostility of advocates of European integrationism and those governments that espoused this doctrine, namely, those at Brussels and The Hague. The Fouchet plan was put before the committee responsible on 10 November 1961. The German, French, Italian and Luxembourg delegations expressed their approval, with more or less qualification. The Belgian delegation expressed reservations concerning supranationality. The only opposition came from the Dutch delegation, which, according to Christian Fouchet, declared that it could not be "committed so long as Great Britain did not participate in negotiations".

Throughout December the ebb and flow continued, Brussels suggesting a compromise linking entry of a new State into the new Union to membership of the EEC. Then the Belgian government suddenly condemned the whole of the French plan for a "Europe of States" as "constrictive", for "Europe will be supranational or it will not be". Harold Macmillan, after letting it be known that Great Britain wanted to take part in the discussions, which strengthened Dutch resistance, declared that he did not regard the Fouchet plan unfavourably.

"The year 1962 began badly," Christian Fouchet wrote. "After being so close to success, we now felt that a collapse would follow at the first pretext. This occurred with a few amendments proposed by France..."[16] It was much more than a "pretext" that brought on the crisis. There was no shortage of good Gaullists who regarded the modifications then made to the French plan at the instance of

---

*The Commission had been instructed to prepare a "Union of Peoples", as we have seen.

General de Gaulle to be serious reasons for a break, given the Belgian and Dutch objections and the Italians' mistrust.

In a lecture delivered in 1974, Ambassador François Seydoux declared that "everybody, in the Fouchet plan that was being developed, tried to get a little bit more out of it and the General in particular could not resist the temptation to add two or three little touches that looked like nothing at the time, but which did alter the plan a little from what it had been at the outset. Our partners, some of them at least, not the Germans or perhaps even the Italians, but others... were not very pleased."

What were those "two or three touches" given by de Gaulle that were to upset France's partners? To begin with, the Council's decisions would no longer be binding for the states that had taken part in them; the "Political Commission" lost the adjective "European" and the reference to "trust" that the Six owed one another disappeared. But there was worse. In the text that they had reworded, the senior civil servants who made up the Commission had specified that the common defence of the confederated Europe would have the result of "strengthening the Atlantic Alliance" – a salute to the American ally that was indispensable in the eyes of France's five partners. General de Gaulle, re-reading this draft on 17 January 1962, had quite simply crossed out those four words, adding that the Council set up by the French plan would have economic responsibilities, which amounted to placing the Brussels bodies under the hegemony of a new interstate institution on which each member State would have the right of absolute veto. In a few "touches", the General had ruined the efforts of these negotiators who knew that they could succeed only by satisfying both Washington and the Brussels bodies. The French negotiator, Jean-Marie Soutou, noted sadly in his diary: "That's the end of it all."[17]

An attempt was made to save the plan, however. On 15 February, General de Gaulle set off for Baden-Baden to ask for the help of Konrad Adenauer. He had to make two concessions to his host: the treaty would have to declare that the existing organizations would continue, while declaring that the states were not subordinate to the organizations; and it would pay solemn homage to the Atlantic Alliance.

When the discussions resumed on 20 March, at Luxembourg, it was around a third version of the Fouchet plan. Independently of the question of British participation, arguments raged round the appointment of a Secretary-General, to which Paris was hostile. Whether on the question of supranationality or on the British "front", the positions of Paris were challenged. The supporters of the Fouchet plan, beginning with the General and Couve de Murville, made sarcastic remarks about the inconsequentiality of their Dutch and Belgian opponents, who, in their view, acted as champions both of supranationality and of British membership, which were irreconcilable, London having chosen Europe only to the extent that de Gaulle had challenged supranationality.*

Those days of March 1962 were among the most tense, the most complex, but also the most significant in de Gaulle's career: at Evian Louis Joxe and his

---

*An objection that provoked this response from the Belgian, Josef Luns: "If we are going to make Europe in the English manner, we might as well do it with England..."

companions came back each evening fearing that the talks with the FLN delegation were on the verge of collapse, and Christian Fouchet was desperately trying to
save the French plan in the face of the integrationist "Europeans" in Brussels and
The Hague.

Should we see another link between the two discussions? Yes. It is clear that in
the minds of the anti-Gaullists in The Hague and Brussels (or in Bonn) the end of
the Algerian war would increase France's potential on the Continent and that
there was a risk that the already imperious de Gaulle of 1961–62 might be
replaced by an ever-increasingly "dominating and self-confident" General. Hence
the revival of mistrust.

In early April 1962, the Fouchet plan without Fouchet* certainly seemed
doomed. De Gaulle was again to try the impossible: when he met Amintore
Fanfani in Turin and Konrad Adenauer at Cadenabbia, on 4 and 7 April, he
stressed the consequences of failure. He was listened to, not only by the German,
but also by the Italian. "The Italian statesman had sufficient interest for great
issues and sense of the higher necessities of our day to want his country to be a
pillar of European unity together with France and Germany."[18] Furthermore, the
brilliant Italian diplomat, Attilio Cattani, representing his country during the talks,
had just succeeded Christian Fouchet in the chair of the Commission, where his
influence was if anything to favour the French plans.

On 17 April, the six Foreign Ministers met in Paris to discuss compromises on
the reference to NATO and to the organizations in operation: these vague hopes
were swept away by P. H. Spaak, who declared that, without the presence of
Britain, the discussions had no future and that Belgium would not sign the draft
treaty "even if she approved of it as such".

Thus de Gaulle's plan for a European confederation, which demonstrated his
coming round to a certain idea of Europe, was "smashed" on 17 April 1962.
"What a success for Britain!" observed one of the negotiators.

The General's reaction to this failure was certainly not a desperate one. "He
isn't in mourning for the Fouchet plan," one of his closest colleagues confided
to me. This was because he had assessed the extent to which the confederation
would become something of a yoke. He would have to consult Bonn and Rome
whenever he wanted to deliver a snub to Washington! However, it would not be
fair to infer from this that his "modifications" of January 1962 were intended
expressly to demolish his own construction before he had become a prisoner
of it.

The dispute over Great Britain's membership, in the early 1960s, was of a quite
different nature. While everyone had adapted perfectly well to London's decision
to exclude itself from Europe, the question of Britain's ties with the Continent
could not but be asked.

Was Charles de Gaulle right to believe that the history of Europe was a matter
of British manoeuvres to divide the Continent and that its future could there-

---

*Fouchet had been appointed by de Gaulle to Algiers, as we have seen. (trs.)

fore only reproduce this schema, aggravated by London's collusion with the "hegemonic" United States? Was the judgement of Luns and Spaak – like that of Pierre Mendès France and many French "Europeans" – more soundly based? They considered, given Great Britain's role in the history of Western democracy, its defence of liberties on the Continent, and its position to act as a counter-weight to the pre-eminence of the Franco-German axis, that the participation of London was, from the outset, indispensable.

Geoffroy de Courcel, who represented France in London from 1962, reported that whenever he was summoned to the Elysée – about once a month – he always asked the General the same question: "Are you against Britain's entry into the EEC?", to which the General replied that he "hoped" that Britain might "one day" join the Six, provided she "carried out certain transformations".[19] These "transformations" were nothing less than a preference to be given to Europe rather than to the Commonwealth and the assumption of a certain distance in relation to Washington.

Charles de Gaulle did not like England. He admired her. A few pages of his *Mémoires de guerre* have been quoted in which the tribute paid to the British people in wartime is one of the finest that they have ever received. And what more enthusiastic salute was ever given to British democracy than that heard on 7 April 1960 by the members of the Westminster Parliament assembled to listen to the French general, who twenty years before had been the "shipwrecked man of desolation" received in brotherly fashion by Winston Churchill and His Majesty's subjects?

He chose London for his first State visit as President of the Fifth Republic and, on 5 April 1960, was received as a brother-in-arms. It was clear to all those who were with the General on that occasion that this was a "meeting of souls" between the man of 18 June and the British nation. It was a visit that the Crown, the authorities and the people of London had wanted to turn into a festival, a resurrection of the entente cordiale. One has to read the pages that this man devoted to the welcome given him by the capital of the British Empire:

Queen Elizabeth set the tone. On our arrival, she came to Victoria Station with Prince Philip to welcome me and my wife and those who accompanied us, and as we drove through London side by side in her open carriage, the Sovereign went out of her way to encourage with gestures and smiles the enthusiasm of the crowd massed along the route. To give an exceptional cachet to the dinner and reception at Buckingham Palace, she arranged for the first time a glittering firework display around the Palace, and in the midst of the illuminations stood for a long time on the balcony by my side acknowledging the cheers of the vast crowd below. For the gala performance at Covent Garden, the Opera House was garlanded from top to bottom with carnations. At the dinner which I gave at the French Embassy, the entire royal family was present with the Queen. At her invitation, I had the unusual honour of reviewing the Household troops, with the Duke of Edinburgh at my side.

And the visitor even goes on to recall the advice he gave the Sovereign when she asked him what he thought of *her* role in the midst of such uncertainties: "In that station to which God has called you, be who you are, Madam!"[20]

The whole of this description, written years later, is imbued with that irrepressible reverence that French visitors, however republican and chauvinistic they may be, have for British institutions, decorum, great deeds and heroes. It has to be said that sometimes, for all his style, culture and self-confidence, Charles de Gaulle behaved like an average Frenchman abroad, that is to say, like a country-cousin dazzled by all the heraldry, wigs and coaches.

However, what an average Frenchman could not have brought to London was the text of the speech that de Gaulle gave on 7 April 1960 in the Great Hall of Westminster, before the assembled House of Lords, House of Commons, members of the government and trade union leaders. Of course, homage to the nation that had been the first to break the wave of the Nazi assault and to Winston Churchill was only to be expected. What was less expected was the praise given to the British political system:

> This outstanding role in the midst of the storm is owed not only to your profound national qualities but also to the value of your institutions. At the worst of moments, who among you challenged the legitimacy and authority of the State? Today, at Westminster, let me pay to England the homage that is her due, in this respect as in others.
>
> With self-assurance, almost without being aware of it, you operate in freedom a secure, stable political system. So strong are your traditions and loyalties in the political field that your government is quite naturally endowed with cohesion and permanence; that your parliament has, throughout each term of office, an assured majority; that this government and this majority are permanently in harmony; in short, that your executive and legislative powers are balanced and work together by definition as it were. Although, since 1940, you have undergone the harshest vicissitudes in your history, only four statesmen, my friends Sir Winston Churchill, Lord Attlee, Sir Anthony Eden and Mr Harold Macmillan, have guided your affairs over these extraordinary twenty years. Thus, lacking meticulously worked out constitutional texts, but by virtue of an unchallengeable general consent, you find the means, on each occasion, to ensure the efficient functioning of democracy without incurring the excessive criticism of the ambitious, or the punctilious blame of purists.
>
> Well! I can tell you that this England, which keeps itself in order while practising respect for the liberties of all, inspires trust in France.[21]

One may admire and yet wish to keep one's distance from the object of one's admiration. Of course, the extraordinary experience of the war had made de Gaulle question the vague Anglophobia instilled in him by the ideologists of Action française, which he was on his guard against in this area less than in many others. But the stoicism of the British people and his own epic companionship with

Churchill were not enough to sweep away a background of mistrust fed by the policy of the Foreign Office in the Levant and above all by the observation that he made between 1940 and 1944 that, despite her glory, Churchillian Britain was forced to give in to orders from Washington. When he considered the United Kingdom in terms of its policies, intentions and manoeuvres, General de Gaulle always saw the ghost of Roosevelt, the Roosevelt who, in 1943, told his British "friend" that if he did not break with Free France he could see an end to American aid to Britain.

But in that stormy dialogue, the reservations were not entirely on the French side. For the British, mistrust was still strong and more diversified. Above all, it concerned the General's personality and the nature of Gaullist power.

What de Gaulle was now doing was launching into the very undertaking that was most anathematical to the diplomatic traditions of the United Kingdom: the bringing together of Europe under the aegis of a national power, uniting the misdeeds of the Common Market (that "continental blocus", according to Macmillan) with a more or less hegemonic strategy that would give the Continent a political cohesion that was unacceptable to the heirs of Pitt and Lloyd George.

In one of their impassioned meetings, between 1958 and 1963, Harold Macmillan declared to de Gaulle: "You want to rebuild the Holy Roman Empire. We, the Roman Empire!" The difference between the two projects was that the first was continental, whereas the second extended from Carthage to Alexandria, from Thrace to Caledonia.

In 1961, the combination of the Franco-German *rapprochement*, the launching of the Common Agricultural Policy, the first French plans for a political union, and President Kennedy's "Euro-American grand design" forced Harold Macmillan and his colleagues to a major revision of policy: there was now no other path than to join it. To blow it up from within? The accusation was often made in political circles, especially in France and Germany.

No one more than General de Gaulle seemed convinced of the truth of this pessimistic hypothesis. Almost everything he did and said on this question seemed to be inspired by the image of the Trojan horse. The British government was to make more and more moves in their direction, but de Gaulle was constantly to face them alert to any attempt by a Britain ultimately serving the interests of the United States to take over Europe, then sabotage it. He sums up this idea in his *Mémoires d'espoir*: "Having failed from without to prevent the birth of the Community, they [the British] now planned to paralyse it from within."[22]

For Macmillan and his government, de Gaulle sinned by his excessive scepticism. When the British Prime Minister told him that the three greatest nations in Europe would never be led by men so well disposed to cooperating in its organization as the Chancellor, the General and himself, he was obviously not lying.

"Let us bring Europe together, my dear friend! There are three men who could do it: you, Adenauer and I. If we let this historic opportunity pass us by, God knows when and to whom it will ever present itself again!"[23] "These words struck a sympathetic chord in me," de Gaulle adds. But he goes on to point out that he did not believe that Great Britain was in a position to reconcile a membership of Europe with the demands of the Commonwealth and the Americans.*

On 2 June 1962, when received by General de Gaulle at the Château de Champs, Macmillan carried his declaration of European faith further than he had done before. If there was an opportunity for synthesis between the British and French points of view on Europe during General de Gaulle's time, it was certainly then, a few weeks after the strangling of the Fouchet plan and before the American campaign for the MLF (Multilateral Force) radically changed the situation. This is how Geoffroy de Courcel remembers those moments of Anglo-French harmony:

> I remember that when they came out of their private meeting, de Gaulle said to Macmillan: "Tell us what we have agreed on." And Mr Macmillan, full of euphoria and optimism, said: "Well, there are three points on which we agree today and which seem to me to be fundamental: the first, and it is the hardest for a man of my generation to say it, is that we British consider that the Commonwealth no longer has the importance that it once had and that consequently the preferential rights that we have at present with the Commonwealth must gradually disappear. Secondly, we regard French agriculture as a crucial element in these negotiations. We must find an agreement on the common agricultural policy. There is a third aspect: that is that we are the only two European powers that have nuclear weapons. It is normal that we should cooperate in this area to form the backbone of European defence."

"I remember," M. de Courcel goes on, "how, on our way back to Paris, I was in the same car as the British Ambassador, Sir Pierson Dickson, and how we congratulated one another, saying: 'We've made great progress at last. France and Britain must be able to understand one another.'"[24]

That Charles de Gaulle was not entirely fair on the subject is shown by the fact that he removes from his memoirs (except for a very brief allusion) the optimistic dialogue at the Château de Champs, but keeps the very negative one – through his own doing – that took place at Rambouillet, six months later, when he put an end to the British Prime Minister's European hopes.

Before the next meeting between the French and British at Rambouillet five important events were to occur: the proclamation of President Kennedy's "grand design"; the rejection by the Six, at Brussels, of the British offers concerning imports of Commonwealth produce, followed by the postponement of negotiations concerning Great Britain's entry into the EEC; a Commonwealth Conference, in London, at which the Dominions had refused the concessions that London hoped to make to the EEC on the subject of their exports; General de Gaulle's triumphant tour of West Germany, which had brought the French head of state's superiority complex to its height; and, finally, the refusal by Washington to make Skybolt rockets for British use, thereby putting London at the mercy of American pressure against any coordinated independence with France.

*On this subject see the General's confidences to Adenauer, as recorded in the Chancellor's *Memoirs* (III, pp. 308–9).

The British delegation had come to Rambouillet feeling confident. Of course, Kennedy's "grand design", a significant challenge to de Gaulle's "European Europe" (since it amounted to closely binding together both sides of the Atlantic within an egalitarian partnership) could not fail to harden the General's attitude and make his British visitors seem like courtiers of the American President; the United Kingdom's claim, on entering the European club, to obtain a delay of between twelve and fifteen years for the agricultural rules to be applied, was certainly an open challenge to French plans and interests. But, by signing in November an agreement with France to go ahead with the plans to build Concorde, the British leaders, rightly regarding their aeronautical industry as more advanced than that of the French, thought that they had made a gesture that would assist the realization of French ambitions to construct a potent strike force – a *force de frappe* – and hoped that they would be grateful.

At Rambouillet, then, Macmillan and his party had come in principle to talk about Europe. De Gaulle clearly regarded them as solicitants: did he reply, as any negotiator following the classic rules would have done, by a "tit for tat" offer, steering the talks immediately onto nuclear matters, making his agreement to London's entry into the EEC dependent in a sense on British association with French atomic plans? For de Gaulle that was the test: if on this matter London refused to follow him, and to fall back on its American partner, it would prove that this country was not ready, mentally, to be associated with "European Europe", that it was applying to the Community only as a protégé of Washington.

De Gaulle was quick to grasp the significance of the American decision not to supply the British with the Skybolt rockets they needed for their atomic weapons: it had the effect of suddenly weakening London's nuclear potential and putting it at the mercy of White House decisions, unless there was nuclear cooperation with Paris. This is what de Gaulle hoped would happen. But in so far as he was, in this area, the weaker, he would not present himself as a solicitant, except to invite his visitor to take it or leave it: nuclear association involving dominant British participation against Great Britain's entry into the Common Market. Was this exchange offered at Rambouillet?

In his very fair biography of General de Gaulle, Bernard Ledwidge declares that when the British and French diplomats compared their accounts of the Rambouillet meetings they noticed divergences. On the French side, it is maintained that the offer of cooperation was at least suggested by the visitors. On the British side, there is mention only of the charge made by the General on the theme of the incompatibility between Britain and the idea of a "European Europe".

The Macmillan–de Gaulle dialogue at Rambouillet had two witnesses: Philip de Zulueta on the British side and Burin des Roziers on the French. The second categorically denies that British entry into the Market against atomic cooperation was suggested by either side. Above all he remembers both sides mentioning the difficulties of recent months in Brussels, the threats that the Soviet Union had just made to the West (the Cuban missile crisis was only a month old), and the idea of necessary cooperation between London and Paris in various areas, technological, aeronautical and nuclear.

What is clear is that if at this time the General wanted to link his British ally to his plans for developing a European nuclear force independent of the United States, he was wrong not to mention it to his visitor – who he knew was about to be given American offers that were quite incompatible with his own plans. If he had really wanted to bring about this "European atom bomb", why did he not say so clearly to Macmillan at Rambouillet?

The British position was presented in its most anti-Gaullist form by Nora Beloff in *The General says No.** Declaring that the Rambouillet meeting amounted to a "long monologue" from the General listing the reasons why Great Britain was not ready to enter the Common Market, the author describes a Macmillan in the grip of "growing anxiety", seeing his European hopes swept away and asking de Gaulle why he had not expressed his reservations earlier. The General, it seems, gave no answer.

"It would be wrong to say that the Common Market negotiations were broken off at Rambouillet, for the nub of the problem was not confronted," Nora Beloff writes. None of the points in dispute in Brussels was seriously examined. And the General made no reference to a request for aid concerning nuclear weapons. After Macmillan's departure, the General stayed on at Rambouillet and invited some of his ministers to dinner. When one of them asked him if the question of nuclear collaboration had been raised, the General replied: "We scarcely mentioned nuclear weapons."[25]

Ambassador Ledwidge was much less categorical. He recalls honestly that General de Gaulle's argument could be imputed to many other reasons than anti-British feeling. For it cannot be forgotten that when Macmillan arrived at Rambouillet, the Brussels negotiations were at an impasse; the Six considered that Britain did not fulfil the requirements for membership, if only because she was asking for a delay of between twelve and fifteen years to apply the agricultural rules; that the Commonwealth had taken a contrary view, condemning the concessions already made by London to the Six on agricultural policy as excessive; and that the repeated successes of the Labour Party, which was resolutely hostile to the Common Market, showed that the majority of British public opinion was against membership.

Macmillan was certainly sincere in his approaches. But the only opportunity he had of carrying them further would have been to put the deal clearly to his host at Rambouillet: an Anglo-French nuclear association independent of Washington against France's support for London's application for membership of the Common Market. He did not do this, any more than his host had done, except by vague allusions. The important thing about Rambouillet was not that what was said was misunderstood, as that very little was said at all.

In fact, Macmillan and his colleagues had only committed themselves to the great community adventure in so far as they knew that their approaches were supported by Washington. They were not ready to go with de Gaulle as far as a "European Europe" – no more on the nuclear plane than on any other. They wanted to move towards Europe, not move away from the United States. Since his

*Which carried malevolence towards de Gaulle so far as to compare the "enthusiasm" aroused by the General in Germany to that aroused by Hitler.

British visitors did not agree to exchange "more Europe" for "less America", since they wanted both the protection of Kennedy and the keys to Europe held by de Gaulle, since they were clearly hoping to win on both tables, the General would be pitiless. When he left Rambouillet for the Bahamas, Harold Macmillan knew that his European future was blocked, his entry into the club of the Six postponed indefinitely. So it is unfair to blame the collapse of talks on what he was going to agree to sign on the other side of the Atlantic.

It was before knowing the results of the Bahamas talks that de Gaulle gave, before the Council of Ministers on 19 December, the funeral oration for Mr Macmillan's European hopes: "I couldn't give the poor man anything and he looked so sad, so downcast, that I wanted to put my hand on his shoulder and say, as Edith Piaf does in her song: 'Ne pleurez pas, milord!'"

The Anglo-French association, creating a hinge between the United States and that continent, had failed. Could not Macmillan have tried to resist Kennedy's offers in order not entirely to alienate the French President? That is, in a sense, what he bravely tried to do in the Bahamas. Whereas everybody – above all de Gaulle – thought that he had gone to the Bahamas, saddened by the snub at Rambouillet, to bow before the conditions laid down by Kennedy, the British visitor negotiated with his all-powerful hosts not only the direct delivery (without going through NATO) of the Polaris rockets, which were far superior to the abandoned Skybolt, but also the right to use them independently, from Britain's own submarines if "the country's supreme national interests were at stake". Better still, Harold Macmillan had persuaded John Kennedy that France should benefit from the advantages that he had just won for his own country. Indeed, all in all, Macmillan had just imitated his master Churchill, who at Yalta had obtained for France an occupation zone in Germany. But if, in 1945, de Gaulle had reluctantly agreed to pocket the present, he was no longer, in 1962, a man to accept such presents. For him, it was nothing more than a Trojan horse.

De Gaulle's attitude should not be reduced to mere pride. If he rejected the apparently unhoped-for offer from the Bahamas, it was for a number of other reasons. First, he could not bear an agreement that he had not negotiated himself; secondly, the same advantages should be offered to West Germany, a non-nuclear power; thirdly, Polaris was not being given to Paris and London on the same terms – the British would have it directly, the French under American command; fourthly, as France had no nuclear submarines at this time, Polaris was of no use to her; fifthly, the weapons being offered were within the framework of the strange Multilateral Force. Thus what was being offered de Gaulle was a renunciation: a defence that was not "French" or of national inspiration.

All the same, other statesmen would have seen that what the "Anglo-Saxons" were offering was positive (weapons that could be used independently in cases when "the supreme national interests were at stake") even if it meant making the terms of their use more flexible and altering the original framework in which they could be used. But de Gaulle was in no mood to recognize any victories other than those that he himself had won. And, although he gave instructions to his ambassadors in Washington and London to study the offers that came from the Bahamas with care, he was already planning his rejection.

It was on 14 January 1963* that he intended making his position clear. That day, at the Elysée, the international press had been waiting expectantly for the first of his weekly press conferences. Over five hundred journalists and close on three hundred guests crowded into the Salle des Fêtes at the Elysée. The curtain moved and there he was. The ministers on one side, the "entourage" on the other. We held our breath, knowing that in London and Washington Macmillan and Kennedy had asked to be kept informed of the General's words as they came out, knowing that they, too, would probably be targets. We had to wait for a quarter of an hour before the expected question on Great Britain and Europe cropped up. In a serious, courteous tone of voice, speaking rather more slowly than usual, de Gaulle spoke.

Britain is insular, maritime, bound up by its trade, its markets, its food supplies, with the most varied and often the most distant countries. Her activity is essentially industrial and commercial, not agricultural. She has, in all her work, very special, very original habits and traditions.

In short, the nature, structure, circumstances, peculiar to England are different from those of the other continentals.

How can Britain, in the way that she lives, produces, trades, be incorporated in the Common Market as it has been conceived and as it functions?

It has to be admitted that the entry of Britain will completely alter the whole set of arrangements, understandings, compensations, rules that have already been drawn up between the Six, because all those states, like England, have very important peculiarities. So it is another Common Market that we would have to consider building and one that would be presented with all the problems of its economic relations, together with a host of other states, above all with the United States.

It is predictable that the cohesion of all its members, which would soon be very large, very diverse, would not last for very long and that, in fact, it would seem like a colossal Atlantic community under American dependence and direction, and that is not at all what France wanted to do and is doing, which is a strictly European construction.

So, it is possible that one day Britain may sufficiently transform herself to become part of the European Community, without restriction and without reservation, and in that case the Six would open the door, and France would present no obstacle. If the Brussels negotiations do not succeed this time, there would be nothing to stop an agreement of association to be drawn up between the Common Market and Great Britain.

Finally, it is very likely that the evolution peculiar to Britain and the evolution of the world are bringing the English towards the Continent, however long it may take. For my part, I readily believe it, and that is why, in my opinion, in any case, it will be a great honour for the British Prime

*The first anniversary of the main victory of Gaullian Europe, the signing of the agreements for the Common Agricultural Policy.

Minister, my friend Harold Macmillan, and for his government, to have discerned so early, to have had the political courage to declare it and to have made the first steps in putting their country in the way that, one day perhaps, will lead it to anchor itself to the continent.

The superb praise of Great Britain in war with which General de Gaulle accompanied his veto did little to attenuate its harshness, especially as it was followed by a disdainful rejection of the offer made to France by Washington and London to join the Nassau accords:

> To pour one's resources into a multilateral force, under foreign command, would be to contravene that principle of our defence and our policies. It is true that we, too, will be able to take back, in some general plan, those of our elements that have been incorporated in the multilateral force. But how would we do this, in practical terms, in the unthinkable moments of the atomic apocalypse? And then, that multilateral force necessarily involves a complicated network of links, transmissions of interferences within itself, an envelopment of external subjections such that if one were suddenly to remove one integral part of it one would very likely paralyse it, perhaps at precisely the moment when it ought to act.
>
> To sum up, then, we are keeping to the decision that we have made: to construct and, if necessary, to use our own atomic force. That, of course, does not exclude cooperation, whether technological or strategic, with our allies if they so wish it.

"De Gaulle is right!": the only approval that he won abroad came from the *Daily Express*, the organ of the most traditional kind of British imperialism and indeed the most Gallophobic. Most other commentators, in France and especially abroad, supported the sad comments of the *Le Monde* editorial: "General de Gaulle takes delight in those games that frighten or irritate his partners and may give great comfort to the enemy."

That elder statesman, Paul Reynaud, wrote: "France isolated, the Entente cordiale ridiculed, disorder in the Atlantic Alliance, the irritation, if not the enmity of the United States towards us, when it is their presence in Europe that guarantees our liberty, the Common Market, the motive-force of our expansion, threatened with splits. And why?"[26]

Those comments by Reynaud brought a response from the General. Two weeks later, Reynaud received a letter, of which the address, on the envelope, was written by a hand he knew well. He opened it. There was nothing inside. But, on the back, were these few words: "If absent, forward to Agincourt or Waterloo."[27]

The General had good reasons to reject the cosmopolitan Multilateral Force, the two-horned and apparently powerless body thought up by John Kennedy's planners. But however much we may have approved of the tribute paid to the British, many of us, listeners and citizens, would have preferred that praise to have seemed like something other than a consolation prize and to have been more fully incorporated into the decisions of the President of the Fifth Republic.

Charles de Gaulle had chosen to make his hosts of 1940 wait. All that remained was for him to turn the screw a little more, when, a week later, he signed his treaty of alliance with Federal Germany. Harold Macmillan, a good "European" but above all a good Englishman, noted in his diary, on 28 January 1963: "Our whole policy, external and internal, is destroyed. French domination in Europe is now a new, alarming fact."[28]

Seven years before, Gamal Abdel Nasser had brought the career of Anthony Eden to a premature end. In 1963 it was largely the failure of his European policy, brought on by the intransigence of de Gaulle, that brought Harold Macmillan, Eden's friend and successor, to defeat the following year at the hands of the Labour Party.

The General was credited with many comments about Britain's entry into the European Community, notably the celebrated "I want her naked!" – without her American guardians and her Commonwealth cousins. What is certain is that he preferred to humiliate and exile from power a man whom he regarded as highly as Macmillan rather than open the gates to a member who might bring in the American fox. All in all, he preferred to see in Downing Street a man who at first felt quite undrawn to Europe: Harold Wilson. During his visit to Paris in 1965, the new Prime Minister did not even try to pick up the European dialogue. Appearing to anticipate the wishes of the Elysée, he declared: "Personally, the Common Market is of no interest to me. What we must do is set up Anglo-French co-operation."[29] It was then that the manufacture of Concorde was pushed ahead, the initiative to build the Jaguar fighter was launched and there was talk again of a Channel tunnel.*

After the 1966 general election, however, when the Labour Party had discovered Europe and reshuffled its government, George Brown (the new Foreign Secretary) took up negotiations with Europe. He took Harold Wilson on a tour of the six capitals of the EEC to convince them of the sincerity of a new British request for membership. But de Gaulle treated them no better than their Conservative predecessors: for him Great Britain was still not "mature" enough to live in common with the Continent. In 1967 came de Gaulle's second veto.

I would not like to end this account of the relations between Charles de Gaulle and Britain without mentioning the funeral of Winston Churchill, in January 1965 – de Gaulle had wanted to pay homage to his companion-in-arms. Returning to Paris by plane and surrounded by several of his close colleagues, he never stopped talking about the dead man and the people whom he had guided in their severe trials, with unreserved enthusiasm: "What joy it is to see that great nation on its feet again. What other country would be capable of organizing ceremonies of that grandeur? Long live England, gentlemen! She has lessons to teach us."[30]

The Anglo-European party embodied by the Dutchman Luns were to get satisfaction less than two years after the General's retirement in 1969, as a result of

---

*An undertaking to which, in the end, Harold Wilson brought a very Gaullian veto. A great British cartoonist was to depict him, disguised as a general, barring entry to the tunnel with outstretched arms.

Georges Pompidou's presence in power and of a very real conversion in British public opinion. The "integrationists", however, were never to recover from de Gaulle's veto of 14 January 1963. This is what P. H. Spaak has to say:

> The press conference of 14 January 1963 marked a turning-point in the life of the European community. After that, the trust, the spirit of cooperation that had prevailed during the first few years were not to exist in the same way. The unjustified humiliation that General de Gaulle had inflicted on his partners was never to be forgotten. A certain wish for revenge was born. It rose to the surface in 1965.[31]

Was the crisis of 1965 a sequella of that of 1963? Did those who had lost the "battle of Britain" want to make the General pay for his victory by humiliating him in turn on the essential question of supranationality? In trying to force progress towards a "United States of Europe", the "humiliated" party of 1963 was perfectly well aware that it was defying the French head of state.

Professor Hallstein, President of the European Commission (the Community's "government"), advised by a few disciples of Jean Monnet, considered in early 1965 that the situation in France lent itself to an operation that would confer an extra layer of supranationality on the European structures: it was a matter of making the financing of the Common Agricultural Policy (which was very profitable for French farmers) dependent on an increase in the powers of the Commission, thus twisting the rule of unanimity for decisions of the members of the Council of the Ministers of the Six. The calculation of the inventors of the operation – which was opposed by Walter Hallstein's closest collaborator, Robert Marjolin, though he was a very good "European" and not particularly Gaullist – was bound up with the political situation in France. There were to be presidential elections at the end of the year: either de Gaulle would not stand and his successor would weigh less heavily on Europe than he had done, or he would stay and need the votes of the farmers, who were favourable to the Hallstein proposition, because the favourable development of the Common Agricultural Policy depended on it.

The General did not give in, of course. If the farmers' votes went to Jean Lecanuet, a European "integrationist", would de Gaulle have to face a second round? Anyone who believed that he would accept a little supranationality in exchange for the votes of the French farmers failed to understand him. Rather than bow before votes cast at the European Council of Ministers, he decreed that France would no longer participate in the deliberations: this is what was called at the time the "empty chair".*

But, as Jean-François Deniau** observes, "the Treaty of Rome has at least one virtue and that is, if it is difficult to get into it, it is even more difficult to get out of it". Indeed, the General had no wish to detach France from the EEC: he simply wanted to win the argument over the financing of agricultural produce and against the supranationality dreamt up by Walter Hallstein. His re-election in December 1965 would, he believed, allow him to defeat his opponents.

*From June 1965 to January 1966.
**For a long time a European Commissioner.

But what was called the "Luxembourg compromise" in January 1966 suggested that the game had at most only been drawn: a French declaration, condemning the institutional innovation introduced by the Hallstein operation, was "accepted" by the majority, though not adopted on the legal level. As a result the French chair ceased to be left empty.

Meditating on General de Gaulle's European strategy, Alfred Grosser, a fervent but non-sectarian "European", suggests that, given his hostility to integration and his mistrust of American hegemony, the President of the Fifth Republic made a mistake in choosing his preferred ally: it should have been not Bonn, enfeoffed in innumerable ways to the United States, but London, which was capable of a greater freedom of manoeuvre.[32]

This notion has been aired every now and again. But is not this to put tactics before strategy? What the alliance with Germany involved was not, for the General, an *ostpolitik* of which we shall say more later when describing de Gaulle's vision of Europe "from the Atlantic to the Urals". We shall have to return to the Bonn or London dilemma. It will crop up again on the subject of inter-Atlantic relations. Meanwhile the following incident is worth mentioning. Alexandre Marc,* a pioneer of European unification if ever there was one, received, after General de Gaulle's triumphal tour of Germany, an (anonymous) appeal from the Elysée asking him if, in the event of an election for a President of the United States of Europe by universal suffrage, Charles de Gaulle would be elected. His answer was positive, accompanied by a meticulous analysis of positions, country by country.[33]

But that was in 1962, before the great crises of 1963 and 1965.

---

*Who founded and ran for many years the Centre International de Formation Européenne.

CHAPTER TWENTY-EIGHT

Our American Cousins

To appreciate what relations were between General de Gaulle and the Americans one must first take account of what has been said or written by the men who were constantly at the meeting point between the two States, the respective ambassadors in Paris and Washington.

Hervé Alphand, who was profoundly attached to American society and civilization, and had spent a large part of his career in the United States, was the Fifth Republic's representative in Washington for seven years, from 1958 to 1965. Since 1941 he had known how to decipher Gaullist language and reacted strongly against any suggestion that de Gaulle was anti-American: "I have observed nothing of the kind. Rejection of any kind of subjection, demand for equality, irritation sometimes, but nothing that could be defined as systematic hostility. On the contrary, it is situations and circumstances that create agreements, not feelings or wishes."[1]

Do his American counterparts say anything very different? One might reject the opinion of Douglas Dillon, a Francophile, or that of James Gavin, a general appointed to Paris by Kennedy to please de Gaulle and who did indeed please him; but not that of his successor, Charles ("Chip") Bohlen, a survivor of the Roosevelt period,[*] who disapproved of almost all of de Gaulle's initiatives. This great traditional diplomat, with his aristocratic manners ("He's our Lord Louis Mountbatten," Joseph Kraft once told me, with a smile), when questioned by an American correspondent in late 1967 as to whether the sole aim of the General's diplomacy was not "to offend the Americans", replied: "In five years, I have spoken some forty times with the General and I can tell you: I don't at all see that he is anti-American. He likes to speak of relations between the powers as a solar system. He thinks that a small or medium-sized country must not stand too close to a very great power, without risk of being drawn into its orbit."[2]

It is true that this reply does not sum up Chip Bohlen's position or the action that he carried out in Paris between 1963 and 1968. He certainly had more severe things to say about de Gaulle. In his *Witness to History* he repeats a judgement on de Gaulle that he made to President Kennedy's principal adviser, MacGeorge Bundy, on 2 March 1963 (a few weeks after the rejection of the Nassau agreement and the Franco-German treaty):

In the first place it is important to remember that de Gaulle is distinctly a product of that half of France which has been, since 1789, and still is,

*He was in the American delegation at Yalta.

conservative, hierarchical, religious and military. That was one of the reasons for his bitterness against Pétain. He is also the product of French military training pre-World War I in that he tends to approach any given problem from a highly analytical and rather simple point of view. His ignorance of the operation of other countries is, I would say, very great, and this is particularly true of the United States.[3]

Anyone who knew Charles E. Bohlen (as I did) has every reason to be surprised that a man of his quality could have proposed to his government so flat a picture of the man who often received him at the Elysée. The description reads like the despatches written at Vichy by Admiral Leahy.* From this pitiful portrait, the United States Ambassador drew the conclusion that there was nothing to be done to improve relations between Washington and Paris. When he attempts in his book to analyse the reasons for the General's obvious incomprehension of his country, Bohlen suggests first that, for Charles de Gaulle, the United States lacks what it takes to be a stable nation: a military tradition, a religious heritage capable of unifying those groups of immigrants that had come from a dozen countries, civilized values able to correct the prevailing materialism. He adds that what the General deplored above all in Americans was their excessive power, what Senator Fulbright, nevertheless a very good American, was to call the "arrogance of power".

If de Gaulle had wanted to conduct an anti-American diplomacy, it is clear that he would have chosen other men to carry out his foreign policy: from Couve de Murville to Alphand, from Lucet to Roger Seydoux, France was never represented, in his time, either in Washington or New York, except by men who had the keenest concern to harmonize relations between the two States.[4]

It should be observed indeed that, on the American side, Charles de Gaulle's initiatives were welcomed at the White House, even when they were credited with an anti-American significance: thus the "veto" on British membership of the Common Market, the rejection of the Multilateral Force, the denunciation of the Six Day War in 1967, the salute to "Québec libre!", which stemmed in no way from such a state of mind, but from decisions taken, rightly or wrongly, in relation to specific circumstances and strictly French interests.

Furthermore, if the American popular press was prepared to throw fire and brimstone at the "ungrateful", "arrogant", "paranoid" de Gaulle, great leaders of public opinion like Walter Lippmann, Cyrus Sulzberger, Arthur Krock and James Reston, or eminent specialists in foreign affairs or European politics, like Stanley Hoffmann, Nicholas Wahl and Henry Kissinger, have produced many attempts at explanation.

John L. Hess, who as Paris correspondent of the *New York Times* was able to examine the ups and downs of Gaullo-American relations for some time, writes that in all the disputes between de Gaulle and the United States "one can always find at least one argument that proves that he was morally right to act in that way. On all these points, one can show that the positions taken up by de Gaulle were in

**See *De Gaulle: The Rebel 1890–1944*, pp. 343–4. (trs.)

France's greatest interest." But Hess adds more boldly: "What is even more shocking for us Americans is that a detailed examination of each of our controversies shows that the positions taken up by him certainly served the best interests of the United States."[5]

From another, perhaps deeper, point of view, one might quote this fable that I once heard Henry Kissinger invent, one evening, in Washington:

> I have dreamt of a discussion between the two greatest Frenchmen of the period, Jean Monnet and General de Gaulle. The first said to the other: "*Mon Général*, you aren't treating the Americans properly. You raise your voice, you give orders. I treat them gently and get more out of them as a result." To which de Gaulle replied: "Don't be taken in, Monnet! What I *grab* is of much greater value than what you get *granted*!"
>
> For a long time I held Monnet's point of view. Now* I'm not sure that it was not the de Gaulle of my dreams that was right.

The same Kissinger has very pertinently summed up in *The Troubled Partnership* why, on the theme of polycentrism, the allies' right to initiative, the General and the American leaders so often came into conflict:

> Polycentrism does not reflect so much the emergence of new centres of physical power as the attempt by allies to establish new centres of decision. Polycentrism is on the rise not because the world has ceased to be bipolar, but because with respect to nuclear weapons it essentially remains so. President de Gaulle is convinced that those circumstances in which the United States might be prepared to resort to its nuclear weapons cannot be fundamentally affected by his actions. The United States commitment need not be purchased by being conciliatory. President de Gaulle sees little risk and considerable potential gain in political independence. Influence can now be achieved by using another country's protection even for policies not in accord with the ally's preferences. Neutrals enjoy most of the protection of allies and allies aspire to have the same freedom of action as do neutrals.

Examining the General's motives, Kissinger adds:

> Far from being based on an excessive estimate of France's strength, de Gaulle's policy reflects, above all, a deep awareness of the suffering of his people over the span of more than a generation. He judges the merit of a policy not only by technical criteria but also by its contribution to France's sense of identity. His deeper objective is pedagogical: to teach his people and perhaps his continent attitudes of independence and self-reliance. Consequently the dispute between France and the United States centres, in part, around the philosophical issue of how nations cooperate. Washington urges a structure which makes separate action physically impossible by assigning

*This was in 1980.

each partner a portion of the overall task. Paris insists that a consensus is meaningful only if the partner has a real choice.[6]

This luminous book was published in 1965, a year before the General removed France from NATO. But Kissinger's argument might serve as a preface to, if not a justification of, that most important of crises.

It was an alliance, therefore, between independent states, obviously unequal in power, but essentially equal in rights. It was an alliance that would affirm its strength all the more when danger was greatest and the balance most threatened. It was an alliance with a constricting structure, but a contract implemented and constantly revived by free choice.

The relations between de Gaulle and the United States knew three clearly differentiated periods, each linked to the highly contrasted American heads of state, to the reorientations of American strategy, but also to subtle changes in de Gaulle's personality and to shifts in France's military and economic power.

The first period, under Eisenhower, was that of a warm relationship, despite certain divergences. Washington was aware of the nature of the new ally and of the development of his demands, which grew as France recovered.

The second phase (1960–63) coincides with the Kennedy years. It was a period of conflict and argument. Whereas de Gaulle, possessing the atom bomb, triumphant after the 1961 *putsch*, freed of the Algerian burden in 1962, signatory of the Franco-German treaty and declared opponent of the Multilateral Force in 1963, was growing in influence, the young American President was giving dynamism and brilliance, if not always successfully, to American power.

It was only during the third period (1964–68), with the Johnson presidency, that one can speak of crisis. De Gaulle had always been at ease with Eisenhower and Kennedy, but he could make nothing at all of the southern politician for whom France was little more than a sort of senescent kingdom, something of interest to Harvard professors and journalists who specialized in civil wars, but to nobody else. It was not until the entry of Richard Nixon into the White House, with Henry Kissinger in the shadows behind him, that the debate assumed a serene conclusion.

When he became President in 1958, at the age of sixty-seven, Charles de Gaulle was no longer thinking of his conflicts with Roosevelt. His attitude to the United States was not based on experiences at Anfa, Algiers or Yalta, but in the state of subjection into which, in his view, the Fourth Republic had allowed the French nation to fall in relation to her greatest allies. For de Gaulle, it was an intolerable situation, although he regarded the Americans as allies and friends, and freely praised their role as liberators. When President Eisenhower landed in Paris, on 1 September 1959, for a State visit, de Gaulle welcomed him with the words: "Ah! How welcome you are! Whatever happens in the years to come, you will always be for us the Supreme Commander of the Armies of Liberty!"[7]

If one turns to the *Mémoires d'espoir*, one notes that de Gaulle saw the relations between East and West as very different from those existing in 1949, at a time when, having himself called for it, he applauded the signing of the Atlantic Pact. The difference stemmed not only from the fact that the USSR had become aware of the absurdity of an enterprise of conquest, but from the fact that Moscow now had at its disposal "the wherewithal to exterminate America". The two rivals could no longer, therefore, "drop their bombs" except outside their respective territories – in Western Europe, in particular. Thus, for the Western Europeans, NATO had "ceased to guarantee their survival". Hence this conclusion:

> My aim, then, was to disengage France, not from the Atlantic Alliance, which I intended to maintain by way of ultimate precaution, but from the integration realized by NATO under American command; to establish relations with each of the States of the Eastern bloc, first and foremost Russia, with the object of bringing about a *détente* followed by understanding and cooperation; to do likewise, when the time was right, with China; and finally, to provide France with a nuclear capability such that no one could attack us without running the risk of frightful injury. But I was anxious to proceed gradually, linking each stage with overall developments and continuing to cultivate France's traditional friendships.[8]

De Gaulle had not been in the Elysée for three months when he made his first gesture distancing himself from the United States: the French fleet withdrew from NATO. Washington and her European allies reacted as did General Norstadt, the coalition's Commander-in-Chief: the withdrawal of twelve or thirteen warships would not make much difference, but "it is the very principle of the withdrawal that is important".[9]

This was precisely how de Gaulle himself understood it. From now on people must regard France's decision as "important", whether she resumed control of her ships, encouraged Adenauer to cede nothing to the Russians over Berlin, or refused to allow the installation of American bases on her territory or, as in June 1959, the introduction of atom bombs, and lastly whether she was at the centre of the great preparatory negotiations for an East–West summit conference.

For if there was one thing that de Gaulle hated at least as much as the subjection of France to another power, it was the direct, exclusive dialogue between superpowers, avoiding the smaller states. Now that he had real power, soon the bomb and sooner or later an army freed from the African morass, he would do everything possible to prevent France and Europe being reduced to mere pawns in the great dealings by which Moscow and Washington were already thinking of putting an end to the Cold War. He wanted détente, of course, aware that all tension helps to simplify, to bipolarize, to concentrate decision-making in the hands of the superpowers.

On 2 September 1959, Dwight D. Eisenhower landed in Paris. No one who witnessed the talks at the Elysée and at Rambouillet, on 2 and 3 September, does not stress the intimacy and simplicity of the talks, and the warmth of the welcome given the visitor by the people. In his *Mémoires d'espoir*, de Gaulle notes that "large and enthusiastic crowds were there to greet him", adding that Eisenhower was "visibly impressed" and asked how many people had been on the route from Orly to the Hôtel de Ville that morning. "A million at least," said de Gaulle. And the guest, deeply moved, said: "I did not expect half as many."[10]

The best description of the long talk that took place between Eisenhower and de Gaulle on the evening of 3 September at Rambouillet is the one we owe to General (then Colonel) Vernon Walters, the American President's interpreter before becoming military attaché in Paris, then the second in command of the CIA and, in 1985, head of the American delegation at the United Nations. In *Services discrets*,[11] this remarkable expert on French affairs* describes with precision, verve and emotion the dialogue between the two old generals. In it de Gaulle is revealed far more than in his own memoirs.

When the official programme had come to an end, Walters relates, the two generals sat in front of the fireplace in dressing-gowns, and began to reminisce about the war. "Roosevelt thought that I thought I was Joan of Arc," said de Gaulle. "He was wrong. I simply thought I was General de Gaulle."

The French President then came to the subject of French nuclear policy. When his guest raised the objection of the dangers of proliferation and the conditions of the MacMahon Law** de Gaulle replied: "The MacMahon Law! I changed the Constitution of France when I found that it was no longer valid." He then came to the question of French nuclear weapons: "You say that it is dangerous for me to know what a thousand corporals already know. I can't accept that. France intends to remain great. A nuclear weapons programme provides technological knowledge that makes one competitive in innumerable ways on the world market."

And de Gaulle, who had already made an extraordinary gesture to his guest by informing him before anybody else of his decision to grant self-determination to Algeria, demonstrated the trust that he had in him by revealing to him the date (13 February 1960) and the power (sixty kilotonnes) of the French bomb that would be exploded at Reggane. It was then that de Gaulle suddenly came to the nub of the matter:

> You, Eisenhower, would wage nuclear war for Europe, because you know the interests that are at stake. But as the Soviet Union develops its capacity to strike the cities of North America, one of your successors will agree to wage nuclear war only to confront and attack at the same time against this continent. When that time comes, I or my successor will have to possess the necessary means to change into nuclear war what the Soviets would have liked to have remained a classic war.

Adding that he was trying in no way to rival the Strategic Air Command or its Soviet counterpart, but only to complicate, by the existence of another centre of decision, the problems of the Russian strategists if they considered attacking Western Europe, de Gaulle concluded: "The Soviets know me. They know that if I possess the strike force, in order to respond to an invasion of Western Europe, I

---

*He had received his secondary education in Paris.
**Forbidding the communication of nuclear secrets to foreign powers – given the special relations with London.

shall use it, and that will be an extra dissuasion for them. To do that, I have to be unbearable on my own."

Those words sum up the essence of his strategic doctrine: to be "unbearable on my own". The final words affected the American President so strongly that he later confided to Vernon Walters: "De Gaulle isn't entirely in the wrong with his nuclear programme. I'd like to help him in some way or other, but I can't. Anyway, he'll go on with his programme."[12]

And he did. Two months later, the General was to redefine French military doctrine based on national independence, the rejection of Atlantic integration, freedom of initiative and nuclear dissuasion. He had discussed all these things previously with President Eisenhower.

These declarations were received fairly calmly by Washington in order not to put an obstacle to the Western summit meeting in Paris, on 19, 20, and 21 December, that brought together for the first time President Eisenhower, Prime Minister Macmillan, Chancellor Adenauer and General de Gaulle. On 10 November, the French President let it be known that since "indications of détente" had appeared in the East, France had invited Nikita Khrushchev to France in March 1960, and was now favourable to a conference of heads of State.

The conference of the four leading Western powers was dominated by the question of Berlin, since Moscow had demanded the eviction of Western powers from the German city. Like Macmillan, Eisenhower was in favour of reaching an agreement – which was opposed by de Gaulle: "You don't want to die for Berlin, but you can be sure the Russians don't want to either. If they see us determined to maintain the status quo, why would they take the initiative of shock and chaos?" A retreat by the West on Berlin, he argued, would provoke the defection of the Federal Republic, which would then seek its security in the East. Although Adenauer passionately supported him, the General did not succeed in quite convincing Eisenhower.

But on one point at least the gentleman from the Elysée won his case: the Eisenhower–Khrushchev–Macmillan–de Gaulle summit conference would take place in Paris, in May. Better still, Khrushchev's visit to France in March would take place before the General was himself received in the United States in April. Thus the French President would be not only the host and chairman of the conference, but also the man then best informed as to the intentions both of the Soviets and of the Americans.

After a quiet, four-day visit to Canada, de Gaulle was welcomed to the United States on 22 April 1960. He stayed there for eight days, travelling from Washington to San Francisco and New Orleans. It was his third visit to America, the first since 1945.

> In Washington on 22 April we were plunged into the maelstrom of American enthusiasm. I drove beside President Eisenhower to a deafening accompaniment of cheers, sirens and brass bands. A similar welcome, expressing the extraordinary strength of popular feeling, was to greet the French guests from one end of their journey to the other.[13]

The Charles de Gaulle of spring 1960 was received as a brotherly hero by the American people, as a friend of the President, who invited him to his farm at Gettysburg, near the battlefield where, just under a century before, the North had crushed the Confederates from the South. Eisenhower took him over the sites of the great massacre, the visitor showing that he had a detailed knowledge of the events.

The American President spoke only of the forthcoming Paris "summit": "What a splendid exit it would be for me to end up, without any sacrifice of principle, with an agreement between East and West!"[14] De Gaulle did not conceal from him his scepticism, though he did add that he would do everything possible to work for bilateral détente.[15]

The high point of that American journey took place the following day, 25 April: General de Gaulle was solemnly received at the Capitol by both houses of Congress and spoke the few words that, according to Alfred Grosser, "ought to have dissipated crowds of later misunderstandings". Congress gave him a long ovation.

Three months later the two presidents found themselves together again in Paris for the great East–West meeting. But, de Gaulle writes, "the very day on which my letter was on its way towards Moscow, the curtain went up on the bad comedy which was to make the whole meeting abortive".[16] That "bad comedy" was the exploitation by Khrushchev of the American U2 spy-plane affair, the plane having been shot down over the polygon of Russian atomic bomb silos in the Aral Sea.

When, on 15 May, in his office at the Elysée, General de Gaulle learnt from Khrushchev that the Soviet delegation would demand, at the opening of the conference, public apologies from Washington, a promise that such things would not occur again and punishment of the guilty, he realized that the East–West meeting was doomed and told his American and British colleagues so at once. Eisenhower and Macmillan believed that an arrangement might still be found to save the conference, and next day the American President showed him the text of a "soothing" declaration in which he announced that the United States, without going so far as offering excuses, would give up U2 flights.

De Gaulle did not care very much for this attitude. He believed that his firmness was justified when Khrushchev publicly reiterated his remarks, adding what were almost insulting comments on the American President, whose invitation to Moscow the following June was now, he said, cancelled. Would Eisenhower, urged on by Macmillan, go so far as to seek a compromise? However impatient he may have been to move towards détente, Eisenhower was on de Gaulle's side: a conference that opened with a capitulation could only lead to a series of retreats. Leaving Paris two days later after Khrushchev had come out with more insults and provocations, President Eisenhower sent his French host a letter in which he wrote: "I carry away with me from Paris the warmth and strength of our friendship, which I appreciate more than ever, and I cherish for you personally a respect and admiration which I have felt for very few men."[17]

Six months later, the American electors were to make the Democrat J. F. Kennedy their President, not Eisenhower's Vice-President, Richard Nixon. During his visit to the United States, the General had acquired a high opinion of Vice-President Nixon, who struck him as "one of those frank and steady personalities on whom one feels one could rely in the great affairs of State", and in all likelihood he had hoped that Eisenhower's presumed dauphin would be elected. Nevertheless, de Gaulle could not help feeling some fellow-feeling for the newly elected President.

> Chosen to get things done, but elected only by the skin of his teeth; placed at the head of a vast and wealthy country, but one with grave internal problems; by nature inclined to act swiftly and boldly, but hampered by the cumbersome machinery of Federal administration. Entering upon the scene in a world in which American power and glory had spread far and wide, but whose every wound was suppurating and in which a hostile monolithic bloc stood opposed to America; enjoying the advantages of youth, but suffering the drawbacks of a novice – in spite of so many obstacles, the new President was determined to devote himself to the cause of freedom, justice and progress.

Although, in passing, he notes that Kennedy had been "drawn into ill-advised interventions", the author of the *Mémoires d'espoir* concludes: "The experience of the statesman would no doubt have gradually restrained the impulsiveness of the idealist. John Kennedy had the ability, and had it not been for the crime which killed him, might have had the time to leave his mark on our age."[18]

Kennedy had not been in the White House for a month, "still somewhat fumbling and over-eager", when he began a correspondence with the Elysée in which he certainly expected to receive advice, particularly about Africa and Asia. He said as much quite freely to those who worked with him. But the General wanted to establish with the new President a more direct relationship than that possible through messages and ambassadorial despatches. Jacques Chaban-Delmas, President of the National Assembly, who was about to leave for Washington as the guest of the American Congress, was suddenly summoned by the head of state: "Chaban, you will tell me what that young man is like. See him and tell him not to get caught up in the Vietnam affair. The United States could lose not only its forces, but also its soul."

On arrival in Washington, Chaban-Delmas was received by Kennedy. On the subject of Indo-China, he observed an ironic half-smile in the young President's eye. But Kennedy agreed that the question of Laos could be separated from that of Vietnam, and authorized de Gaulle's emissary to present the French arguments in favour of a neutralist solution to those responsible for the area in the Pentagon and State departments.[19]

Combined with the encouraging reports from Ambassador Hervé Alphand, the image of John Kennedy that Chaban brought back to Paris could not but prejudice the General in favour of the new President. And it was in a benevolent mood that, two months later, the old gentleman of the Elysée was to welcome the youngest President in the history of the United States, just after his own victory over the rebels in Algiers – and of Washington's defeat over the Bay of Pigs. All these events tended somewhat to restore the balance between the visitor and his host.

Few of General de Gaulle's writings are more revealing about the relations that he had decided to have with the United States in general and with Kennedy in particular than the instructions he gave Hervé Alphand before the young President's visit.

> The first thing to be said is obviously that France and the United States are in the same camp and will remain so. There can be no question of looking for some other alliance. Then you must find what France can contribute to that alliance. To begin with, an organization of Europe, which without her would be impossible in the economic sphere (that has already been done), the political sphere – we are working on it – and of course defence. But this Europe will not be the Europe that was conceived ten years ago. Europe must have its own defence, based on the defence of the nations that compose it, and allied to America. For that, the Americans must not come and prevent us, with an organization like NATO, from making Europe. Thus each one will have a sense of contributing to the common defence and not of having entrusted that task to America.[20]

On 31 May 1961, John F. Kennedy, his wife Jacqueline and Secretary of State Dean Rusk were welcomed to France. Was it merely a stop-off on a journey that was to take the American President to Vienna, where he had arranged to meet Nikita Khrushchev? No. Although the son of a friend of Roosevelt, the young President was an admirer of the man of June 1940. He was impatient to have his views on Berlin, Africa and Asia.

John Kennedy spared nothing to win over both his host and French public opinion – he was to find that there was no difficulty in doing so. At the press lunch he introduced himself as "the guy who accompanies Jacqueline Kennedy" – who, née Bouvier, took care to speak French, delighting the General. "She has impressed him," an Elysée official confided at the time. He used everything to please them, particularly being funny. When Jacqueline Kennedy asked him which of the famous men he had dealt with seemed to him to have the greatest sense of humour, he replied pleasantly: "Stalin, Madame."

Indeed, one has to read the lines that Charles de Gaulle devoted to that visit. Something like a warm connivance took place: Kennedy "arrived in Paris brimming with dynamism, he and his dazzling and cultivated wife forming a remarkably attractive couple. They were surrounded by an atmosphere of lively curiosity and the welcome they were given by the public was enthusiastic in the extreme".[21]

The talks could not have been more cordial, but were they fruitful? From accounts made public by Bernard Ledwidge[22] and notes taken at the time by André Fontaine, who had good sources, it emerges that the efforts used by both presidents were not enough to bring together views that were very different and sometimes opposed. Almost everything that the visitor said was contradicted by de Gaulle. When he suggested that he did not in any way preclude negotiations with Khrushchev over Berlin, the General pointed out to his guest that any negotiation affecting the present balance of forces, at a time when the Soviet leaders were issuing threats and increasing pressure, could not but increase their appetite. Furthermore, the General went on, if Washington and London thought fit to talk to Moscow, which was their right, France would refrain from doing so until the Russians had demonstrated their concern for peace. "When Khrushchev urges you to change the status of Berlin tomorrow," he concluded, "that is to say hand over the city to him, then hold firm! That is the best service that you can give the entire world, Russia included."

On the subject of the Atlantic alliance, Kennedy could not fail to urge his host in favour of increased cohesion between allies; it provoked what has often been regarded as the first direct warning given to Washington on the subject: the General warned him that although France would remain within NATO as long as the Berlin crisis lasted, she had decided to leave the integrated military organization, while remaining within the Alliance, as soon as the situation had become more normal again.

As for Indo-China, it cannot really be said that the points of view were much closer, except on the subject of Laos, since Kennedy was not against a neutralist solution similar to General de Gaulle's views. But even when they converged on fundamentals, Kennedy and de Gaulle disagreed on the means to be used, means that sometimes conditioned the end.

For the General, the golden rule in Indo-China was the rejection of any military intervention, from any source. The French President had some difficulty communicating to his host the complexity of the problems, the contradictions between the various Indo-Chinese nationalists, the role of China, which was already disturbing all her neighbours and scarcely concealed her disagreements with the USSR. Kennedy remained imbued with the manichean idea (a Communist bloc confronting the free world), which had hitherto had the force of law in Washington.

As the visitor was taking his farewell, de Gaulle gave him this piece of advice, as from a very old, dying sovereign to his son the dauphin:

At the end of the interview, the General said to the President that everybody realized that he had taken over in extremely difficult circumstances. Availing himself of the privilege of age, he allowed himself to suggest that the President ought not to attach too much importance to the advice of others or to "established positions". In the final analysis, what mattered for each man was himself and his own opinion.[23]

The French Ambassador, Hervé Alphand, writes in his notebook that things went "as well as could be expected", that de Gaulle seemed to Kennedy to be equal to his legend, "friendly without being condescending. For the first time, de Gaulle found an American he could talk to."[24] In the *Mémoires d'espoir*, de Gaulle draws a very optimistic lesson from that brilliant, but ambiguous visit:

It emerged that the attitude of the United States towards France had undergone a very decided change. The day was long passed when Washington insisted on regarding Paris as just another of its protégés. Now the Americans acknowledged our independence and dealt with us directly and specially. But for all that, they could not conceive of their policy ceasing to be predominant or of ours diverging from it.[25]

How could American policy cease to be "predominant", given that the powers were so unequal? Moreover, the General's aim was not to weigh as heavily as his monumental partner, but to place the lever of French effectiveness at a point where he could on occasion "diverge" from the mass of troops guided by the American leader.

De Gaulle might believe that he had persuaded Kennedy, when on 12 December 1961 he received a telephone call from him which seemed like a request for approval for a new contact with Nikita Khrushchev, after that earlier, stormy one in Vienna. Far from being won over by this display of good manners, the General replied somewhat curtly (he had been disconcerted by being approached on the telephone, he was to tell his Ambassador Alphand – it was not the way he worked, a dialogue between heads of State has to be prepared, next time he would demand an hour's warning beforehand) that he was opposed to it, and that in any case France would not take part in any talks with Moscow in the atmosphere created by the erection of the Berlin Wall on 13 August.

What in fact is "the heart of the problem", the General asked Kennedy across the Atlantic and he himself answered, without waiting for the President's opinion: "The neutralization of Germany, which would be followed by the neutralization of Europe."[26] This amounted to replacing advice with orders, suddenly reversing the relations and claiming to replace the American protectorate over France with a French right of veto on the Alliance. Kennedy could not but react adversely. The end of the state of grace between them probably dates from that telephone conversation.

In January 1962, John Kennedy received from Charles de Gaulle a supposedly secret letter in which, resuming the themes of the notes sent unsuccessfully to Eisenhower in September 1958, March 1959 and July 1960, then to JFK himself in August 1961, the French head of State proposed a reorganization of NATO. This communication had no more success than the earlier ones.

The arguments between Kennedy and de Gaulle were to continue for eighteen months, in an atmosphere of irritated and combative esteem, on two, often connected, but sometimes separate themes. The first was that of the American nuclear monopoly; the second the independence of Europe.

Even more than Eisenhower, Kennedy was hostile to nuclear forces independent of those of the United States. Many of his actions in 1962 and 1963, especially the plan for a Multilateral Force equipped with nuclear weapons under American command, are explained by an insistence on monopoly that was expressed, in June 1962, by a denunciation of France's "unfriendly" attitude.

As for the nature of the relations between Europe and the United States, Maurice Couve de Murville sums up the disagreements very well: "from the time when a man of Kennedy's class was at the head of the United States and de Gaulle was leading France, these problems appeared at last in simple, clear terms, freed of the uncertainties, ambiguities and contradictions with which others had surrounded them. It was the elementary, fundamental question of whether the Europe that we wanted to build up would be European or Atlantic."[27]

I shall not go into the details of these two confrontations here. But one cannot fail to note the character of the meeting, at once tragic and exalted, for on both sides it was a high idea of their missions that drove de Gaulle to oppose Kennedy's "grand design" and the President to want to "take over" the undocile General.

The following coincidence that marked the opening of the great debate also had a theatrical air: on 4 July, while the first government of independent Algeria was taking power, the President of the United States delivered a famous speech at Philadelphia, offering Europe a partnership, a supposedly equal association: "The United States is ready to sign a declaration of interdependence and to discuss with a united Europe ways and means of forming a concrete Atlantic association."

It was an attractive and generous idea, Couve de Murville admitted. But he went on at once to express the objections felt by the Elysée. Three months before, a political Europe worthy of the name had been stifled at birth. They were now presented with an entity in which the partners would come together "on an equal footing" with America, which alone possessed the power to decide to use nuclear weapons. What distinguished this partnership from the alliance created twelve years earlier, if not the fine style of the new American leader?

Thus that 4 July was the first act of a drama in which the young, powerful god who could lay down the law and a septuagenarian mortal whose pride was as great as his weakness confronted one another. According to an apparently endless contradiction the four acts of the tragedy were: the Nassau accords, France's refusal to be associated with them, the veto on Great Britain's membership of the Common Market, and the signature of the bilateral Franco-German pact.

Meanwhile, a crucial episode was to show that at the moment of greatest danger Charles de Gaulle reacted as a fundamental ally of the United States: when, after its U2 planes had observed the presence in Cuba of Soviet nuclear missiles directly threatening the security of America, John Kennedy had decided, after a week of consultations from 16 to 21 October 1962, to blockade the island, and was anxious to warn his main allies before announcing the dangerous measures taken to the world.

On 22 October 1962, Dean Acheson entered the presidential office at the Elysée, followed by a colleague carrying several rolled-up maps and photographic documents, and embarked at once on the question of Cuba. "I understand that you have not come to consult me," said de Gaulle, "but to inform me." "That is correct," the visitor replied, and went on to inform him that irrevocable decisions had already been taken, while being anxious to show de Gaulle maps and photographs proving that the United States was in the right. "Put your documents away: I've enough to deal with as it is. The word of the President of the United States is good enough for me." And the General agreed that, in order to defend the security of the American continent, the President was perfectly within his rights to decide and to act as he had done. If Kennedy had taken such measures, it must be because it was a matter of vital urgency. And he concluded: "Tell your President that France supports him unreservedly. By acting in this way, the President is simply exercising the right that any nation has to defend itself. We are beside you."[28] The President of the Fifth Republic did not leave matters there. He took the initiative in approaching the European Six with a view to supporting the Americans.

The fact is that General de Gaulle's reaction, which was immediately communicated by the American mass media, restored for a time his image as the faithful ally of the United States. But a few weeks later, not far from Cuba, the Franco-American quarrel was to break out again: in the Bahamas, John Kennedy received a Harold Macmillan still recovering from the rough treatment that he had been given by de Gaulle at Rambouillet. He persuaded the British Prime Minister to join his project for a Multilateral Force integrated into the Washington system, in exchange for delivery of the Polaris rockets under American control. Thus the American President brought Britain back under his own aegis, not without giving himself the luxury of a little humiliation of his French partner by offering him Polaris rockets that the French strike force could not use, and suggesting that France join the MLF system, which the most exuberant of the Gaullist experts, General Gallois, called the "multilateral farce". From now on, there was to be no more than an exchange of blows, culminating on 22 January 1963 with the signing of the Franco-German treaty, which appeared from the outset as an attempt by Paris to snatch Germany from American influence, just as the Nassau accords had turned Great Britain away from the offers of association with France.

It has been said that if the agreement on the MLF made in the Bahamas was improvised in haste, the de Gaulle–Adenauer pact was not a gesture of circumstance, a mere riposte to that made by Kennedy and Macmillan. It was, of course, an operation that had been carefully planned, ever since the Colombey meeting of September 1958, and reshaped as the crises and tensions over Berlin made de Gaulle Adenauer's privileged ally. The 1963 treaty was not an anti-American operation. It was a strictly European operation: but that was precisely why it bothered, even challenged, Washington and the pro-American party in Europe.

The reactions of the American press – and of the press in Europe that echoed it – were so lively, so scathing, that in a press conference on 29 July 1963 the General, who usually took little notice of "hacks", raised his voice: "I admit that for some time the song and dance as far as France is concerned has seemed to me to be somewhat excessive, but these new agitations cannot alter in France what is fundamental in relation to America: friendship and the alliance."

Washington's recriminations found expression not only in the newspapers. Maurice Couve de Murville noted this reaction by John Kennedy to the General's attempt to construct a Europe on Franco-German foundations:

In October 1963 Kennedy told me of his feelings on the matter, criticizing the exclusive character of the Franco-German treaty. "We, too," he said, "are trying to attach Germany to the West. That is why we deplored the fact that your treaty has been made outside NATO and without taking the opinions of others into account." This was to present in an elliptical, but clear way, the whole problem not only of Franco-German relations, but of European construction. Could both be anything other than an appendix of NATO? I replied that it went without saying that the treaty had been signed outside NATO. Although the link of the Atlantic Alliance certainly existed between the European states, it did not take the place of everything for ever."[29]

One of John Kennedy's biographers, Theodore Sorenson, presents the American President's trip to Germany in June 1963 as "Kennedy's most striking and successful response to de Gaulle". The American leader's visit to Germany, and especially to Berlin (where de Gaulle had not gone), was indeed an enormous popular success. Kennedy, dynamic and attractive, reaffirming American commitment to the old continent and the interdependence of Europe and America, succeeded in showing that de Gaulle was not the most popular and influential foreign statesman in Germany.

Commenting on the state of relations then prevailing between Washington and Paris, Couve de Murville writes:

> One cannot underestimate the nature and depth of the crisis that thus marked Franco-American relations during the first half of 1963. It was, in my opinion, by far the most serious of all the crises that occurred during the years 1961–67, although others were just as spectacular or even more so. It was the most serious, because it really went to the heart of things, I mean because it concerned the very nature of relations between America and Europe, including above all, of course, France.[30]

The former French Foreign Minister throws light on the heart of the de Gaulle–Kennedy debate, which was all the more lively and dramatic in that both leaders spoke the same clear, fine language: the nuclear monopoly claimed by the American, the European independence demanded by the Frenchman. Less clear was the third theme of disagreement, which did not always merge with the other two: de Gaulle's wish to avoid a Russo-American summit, which could only lead to a deal in which Europe – in any case, Berlin – would be used as a bargaining counter.

But General de Gaulle had a thought at the back of his mind other than the one of avoiding a new Munich. He wanted to prevent the dialogue of the two superpowers from leading either towards the "neutralization" of Germany, which had its defenders in London but not in Washington, or towards a German status other than the one he had in mind. The General's project may be summed up thus: reunification being postponed indefinitely, the Federal Republic would be linked first to the West through the French umbilical cord, Paris ensuring the nuclear cover of her special ally. In this way the General acted as a kind of hinge between Germany and the West, which gave him an eminent position on the Rhine, a central role in Europe and a vital function in relations between that Franco-German Europe and the United States.

The summer and autumn of 1963 saw incidents that dug the ditch deeper between the two Allies: de Gaulle withdrew his Mediterranean fleet from NATO (a gesture justifiable at the time by the requirements of communications between France and Algeria); and the other three nuclear powers (USA, USSR, Great Britain) signed in Moscow the treaty forbidding nuclear tests, to which France refused to adhere.

When questioned twenty-three years later on the mood of the Kennedy team towards General de Gaulle after rejection of the MLF and the "grand design", MacGeorge Bundy told me:

The President profoundly regretted those disagreements. He continued to admire the General and often wanted to consult him. We all had great regard for his lucidity, his vision, his experience. We wanted to have a dialogue with de Gaulle – though we deplored his determination to challenge the American nuclear monopoly, to which Robert McNamara above all was firmly attached. We didn't regard him as anti-American: we simply realized that his opposition to the United States was of use to him and we regarded that attitude as a tactic, which we didn't hold against him.[31]

Just before his assassination, however, Kennedy was thinking of meeting the General again. On 23 October 1963 he invited Hervé Alphand to dinner to learn from him the reasons for French "acrimony" and to tell him of his wish to receive de Gaulle in 1964. It could only be a working·visit, Alphand observed, for the General did not want to be received in Washington. Jacqueline Kennedy suggested Hyannisport,* adding: "It's our Colombey." But the President added that it would all end with a "military parade in Washington, whether the General wanted it or not". For, he added, "the two most popular men in the United States are Churchill and de Gaulle". From this, the Ambassador concluded that the General's visit would serve the President's electoral aims.[32]

On 22 November 1963, Charles de Gaulle learnt of the assassination of John Kennedy at Dallas. He was to be the first to announce his intention of attending the young President's funeral. The next day, de Gaulle chaired a meeting of the Council of Ministers. When he came into the room, he refrained for once from shaking the hands of the members of the government. He sat down, looking very serious, and without moving his chair towards the table, as he usually did, he stood behind it and said slowly: "John Fitzgerald Kennedy has been assassinated. He was one of the very few leaders of whom it may be said that they are statesmen. He had courage and he loved his country."[33] It was a tribute without precedent and one that was never repeated.

Ten hours later, he was standing in uniform, granite-like, beside the grave in Arlington Cemetery.** All eyes were on him. When colleagues of the assassinated President thanked him for coming, he replied: "It's a tragedy. I'm merely carrying out the wishes of all the French people. There is intense emotion everywhere in France."[34]

He was the first statesman to be received by the President's widow who, wondering what she might give the visitor as an expression of the dead man's esteem, suddenly snatched from the nearest bouquet a flower, a white marguerite, and held it out to the General. De Gaulle only took it out of his jacket pocket when he got back to the Elysée.

These words and these gestures were to have no significant political repercussions. Like the other heads of State present in Washington, the General had the

*The family home of the Kennedys near Boston.
**His hosts tried to persuade him to travel in an armoured vehicle. But they came up against a categorical refusal. "It was one of the most pointless negotiations that I have ever had to carry out," MacGeorge Bundy said.

right to a few moments' conversation with the new President, Lyndon B. Johnson. Nothing of note was said, as we shall see. The visitor had no need of this hasty conversation to realize that the spell that had at first worked between JFK and himself – however little it had actually produced – was now broken.

This was not to stop Maurice Couve de Murville from concluding the chapter that he devotes to relations between Kennedy and de Gaulle with these words: "When all is said and done and in spite of everything, the presidency of John Kennedy will remain, in the minds of French people, associated with the idea that they have always had of their relations with America."[35]

It would be absurd to say that the increase in disagreements between France and the United States from the end of 1963 can be put down to a failure in communication between the French General and the former Texas senator. Far more serious factors played their part. But just as the replacement of Adenauer by Erhard as Chancellor affected, but did not profoundly alter, Franco-German relations, just as when Harold Wilson entered Downing Street relations between London and Paris became even worse, the installation of Lyndon Johnson in the White House erected an additional screen between American power and its French partner.

Indeed their relations got off on the wrong foot. It began on the very evening of the Kennedy funeral. Johnson received de Gaulle in a small office in the State Department and said to him: "It's agreed, then, that you'll come and see me?" The General considered that as he was visiting Washington the American President should come and visit him in Paris. In order not to say no, he replied simply: "I take note and we'll see." The new President took this as an acceptance and summoned the journalists to tell them that de Gaulle would be the guest of Washington in February. De Gaulle thought fit to deny it.[36]

The failure of communication between the two leaders is to be placed well above such matters of temperament, background and language: there was a total divergence in their interests, which is well summed up by Maurice Couve de Murville: "It was during Johnson's presidency that the United States began gradually, but overtly, to show less direct interest in European affairs. Vietnam became Johnson's almost exclusive preoccupation. What he wanted from Europe was not to have to think about it, so that he could concentrate on what was becoming more and more the most important thing."[37]

On Vietnam, China, Latin America, in all these areas, from the first months of the Lyndon Johnson presidency, General de Gaulle came up against the feelings, if not the views, of his Washington partner. In February, it was the recognition by France of the People's Republic of China, which was seen as a betrayal of Western solidarity to the Eastern "bloc" – whereas it was now obvious that such a gesture would not be at all to Moscow's taste.

On 29 August 1963, de Gaulle declared that the solution to Indo-Chinese affairs would not come about by military intervention, but by a political settlement based on the utilization of the states of the peninsula. This was condemned in Washington as a stab in the back. Worse: in March 1964, an exchange of fire between a few North Vietnamese ships and two American destroyers in the Gulf of Tonkin enabled President Johnson to get from Congress a declaration on which he was to base his massive intervention in Vietnam in 1964: the interpretation in Paris of the affair was so sceptical that Johnson and his colleagues felt very bitter about it. From now on, the word Vietnam stood between the White House and the Elysée like a screen and a challenge.

But dialogue was still possible. On 16 December 1964, Dean Rusk, on a visit to the Elysée, was advised once again by General de Gaulle not to commit American forces on Asian territory and to seek peace through an international conference. There was nothing very new about that, no worsening of relations. But later in the conversation, the General came out with a formula that opened up new prospects for widening disagreements. When, in 1968 or 1969, France would have a genuine deterrent force, he said, we will have to consider coordinating our nuclear forces, "if we are still allies, as I hope we shall be".[38]

In each of these affairs, one can find reasons to justify de Gaulle's behaviour and to see it much more as a concern to defend the interests of France, or the independence of Europe, than to challenge the American giant in order to look more important himself. Furthermore, in several areas, such as China and Vietnam, what he proposed was as much in the long-term interests of the United States as in those of France.

The only case, it seems to me, in which de Gaulle displayed purely negative anti-Americanism, and which amounted to an unfortunate use of past disappointments, concerned the celebration of the twentieth anniversary of the Allied landing in Normandy on 5 June 1964. By refusing to take part in it himself, and, what is more, excluding France from the celebrations on the pretext that he had not been at the centre of Operation "Overlord",* the former leader of Free France puzzled, even infuriated, those who saw him as more than the President of the Fifth Republic, more even than the leader of a heroic movement that was often ill-treated by its allies, but above all as the symbol of a France that had continued to live in struggle and in hope.

Finally, two crises brought the leaders' anger to boiling point, but still more that of the American mass media and public opinion: there was the crisis that triggered off the French campaign against the privileges of the dollar and the crisis brought about by France's leaving NATO. Hervé Alphand once told me:

> Really, in all these "crises" between de Gaulle and the Americans, there was only one that made it difficult for me to play my role as a link between France and the United States – and that was the dollar crisis. There I felt that the Americans had been given a terrible blow. That ungrateful de Gaulle was not content to detach himself from them, to talk pleasantries with the Communists, to give them lessons on morality and political wisdom: he was even going to try and undermine American prosperity, to affect the wallet of every citizen of that free society!

*He relented in 1967 for the celebrations of the fiftieth anniversary of the Battle of Vimy, at which thousands of Canadians fell.

The affair went back two years, to John Kennedy's time. During a conversation in June 1976 Hervé Alphand has recounted how, although he had been given no instructions to do so, he tried to explain to Kennedy the drawbacks of an unlimited issuing of dollars and an artificial maintenance of the price of gold. He came up against blank incomprehension on the part of the President: "I've made a commitment to maintain the price of gold at 35 dollars an ounce and no President of the United States will be able to change that," Kennedy objected. He added that the revaluation of gold would suit two states: the Soviet Union and South Africa.* Why favour two countries so unworthy of consideration? To which Etienne Burin des Roziers added:

> Even before the press conference of 1965, the problem had cropped up as a result of our conversions from dollars into gold. The General wanted gold to represent 80 per cent of our reserves. He also wanted gold to be in the cellars of the Bank of France rather than in the Bank of England or Fort Knox. So we repatriated gold, which was a very complicated and costly operation, especially in terms of insurance. In the General's mind there was probably a memory here of the war when the problem of the gold of the Bank of France had played an important role.

It was during his press conference of 4 February 1965 that General de Gaulle launched his SOS about the system set up in 1922 at the Genoa Conference, when the dollar and pound sterling were given the privilege of being regarded as equivalents of gold in all international payments. But, de Gaulle went on, things have changed since 1922. And even since 1945. And the General deduced from these premises the following argument, which unleashed a veritable storm:

> The convention whereby the dollar is given a transcendent value as international currency no longer rests on its initial base, namely, the possession by America of most of the gold in the world. The fact that many States accept dollars as equivalent to gold, in order to make up for the deficits of any American balance of payments, has enabled the United States to be indebted to foreign countries free of charge. Indeed, what they owe those countries, they pay, at least in part, in dollars that they themselves can issue as they wish, instead of paying them totally in gold, which has a real value, and which one possesses only if one has earned it. This unilateral facility attributed to America has helped to spread the idea that the dollar is an impartial, international sign of exchange, whereas it is a means of credit appropriated to one state.[39]

Against the privileges that the Gold Exchange Standard gave Washington and which furthermore was creating inflation in the United States and internationally, what measures could be taken? But, of course, a return to the gold standard. And the calling, by the International Monetary Fund, of a conference of the ten most powerful Western holders of credit would make it possible, said the General, to

*Both great producers of gold.

manage to substitute a new international monetary order for the dangerous, out-moded one based on the Gold Exchange Standard.

After that press conference, there was an almighty rush to get to every available telephone. Meanwhile, behind his curtain, surrounded by a few colleagues, the old gentleman asked Gilbert Pérol jokingly: "Do you think it went all right?"

Three months later, Hervé Alphand entered the General's office at the Elysée and found him "happy in the middle of the catastrophes that he foresaw".

De Gaulle: Well! It can't be very pleasant, given the weather, to be French ambassador in Washington!

Alphand: I'd rather say that, thanks to you, it's interesting.

[The diplomat, who had to stress the deterioration in Franco-American relations, brought up the question of the future of NATO.]

De Gaulle: NATO will disappear as far as we're concerned in 1969. We shall announce this at the beginning of next year in order to give the time necessary for the indispensable arrangements to be taken, for, after that date, there will be no more foreign forces on French territory, apart from those that we want to have and they must be under our supervision.

Alphand: But aren't you striking at the Alliance itself, at the Atlantic Treaty?

De Gaulle: Yes, the Atlantic Treaty will disappear too. It will be replaced, if our partners so wish, with bilateral agreements; thus we shall also be able to conclude one with the United States, one with Britain, one with Germany. They will contain a clause according to which, if one of the countries is attacked, the other will come to its help with all its forces.

Alphand received that revelation like a punch in the stomach. It questioned the very structure within which he had been practising his profession for the past seventeen years. "I found myself, humbly, in an opaque fog," he notes.

A renunciation of the Alliance, in order to replace it with highly improbable bilateral pacts, would lead to the disintegration of the Europe of the Six, an end of American friendship. Perhaps the genius was concealing the light that only he could perceive? Was I in the presence of a star that was falling, despite the strength of his personality and character?[40]

Hervé Alphand himself told me that he had tried to argue against what the General had just said: "The United States will refuse to sign a bilateral pact." To which de Gaulle had simply replied: "Oh! It really doesn't matter. If things get bad – which I don't think they will – we'll find ourselves together all the same."[41]

Charles de Gaulle had not kept his Ambassador in Washington informed of the decision that he had been planning for so long. George Ball, Under-Secretary of State – and regarded as being one of the most anti-Gaullist in the American government, because he was very attached to Jean Monnet's idea of Europe – had heard him say, during a visit to the Elysée in May 1966, that France was going to leave NATO, adding, "There would still be a *de facto* understanding for common defence, even if no signed treaty existed."[42]

Meanwhile, de Gaulle constantly gave arguments to those who denounced his "anti-Americanism" that was shocking for public opinion. Thus, speaking on television on 14 December 1965, he certainly faced up to the subject:

I am called anti-American. In fact, who has been the ally of the Americans through and through if not the France of de Gaulle? There has been no other, and if necessary, if misfortune were to occur and if the freedom of the world were in doubt, who would automatically be the best allies if not France and the United States, as they have often been in such cases?... I am not saying that the Americans are anti-French, because they have not always gone along with us. I don't always go along with the Americans, for example, in the policy that they are carrying out in Asia.

Whether it had really been worked out, or whether he was simply testing the ground, his project of an Atlantic *tabula rasa*, which was obviously challenged by Couve de Murville and the Quai d'Orsay, and by Prime Minister Pompidou, was not even touched on during his decisive press conference in February 1966. Did he really believe that he would quite simply abandon the Alliance?

Maurice Couve de Murville himself, who was not given to laughing out loud, either by temperament or upbringing, very nearly did so when asked about the question: "This affair of leaving the Alliance and having bilateral pacts is just fiction, pure fiction! The General was not above deliberate provocation, even with colleagues. But he never seriously considered* leaving the Alliance!"[43]

It was the time, let us not forget, when General de Gaulle, who had finally decided during the summer of 1965 to stand for re-election as President, was highly irritated when an American (spy?) plane flew over French nuclear installations at Pierrelatte on 16 July 1965. That was why he came back on several occasions to the subject of national sovereignty in a country's "sky".

At a deeper level, de Gaulle was also struck by the fact that the complete revision of American strategy, away from the doctrine of massive reprisals defended by Dulles to that of flexible response (invented by Robert McNamara), had been gradually put into operation from late 1961 (under Kennedy) to early 1966 without the Europeans being consulted. In short, on 21 February 1966, in the Salle des Fêtes at the Elysée, Charles de Gaulle, who had been re-elected two months earlier as President of the Republic, declared to the international press:

Without going back on her membership of the Atlantic Alliance France will, from now to the final expected fulfilment of her obligations,** continue to modify in turn the present arrangements in practice, in so far as they concern her. What was done yesterday in this respect in several areas will be done tomorrow in others, while implementing, of course, the desired arrangements in such a way that the changes are carried out gradually and so that her allies are not suddenly inconvenienced as a result. Furthermore, she will

*Nevertheless, in spring 1966, the Foreign Minister confided to one of his close colleagues: "The General has become very impulsive!"
**On 4 April 1969, the twentieth anniversary of the signing of the Pact in Washington.

be willing to work out with certain of them, as she has already done on certain points,* the practical relations of cooperation, either now or in the eventuality of a conflict. This naturally goes for allied cooperation in Germany. All in all it is a matter of re-establishing a normal situation of sovereignty in which what is French, in terms of land, sea and air forces, and any foreign element that happens to be in France, will from now on be solely under French authority. This does not represent any kind of break, but a necessary re-adaptation.[44]

The reaction of the American press was vehement. There was talk of French "ingratitude", though Mike Mansfield, leader of the Democrat majority in the Senate, pointed out that de Gaulle's gesture served the purposes of the United States by forcing NATO to reform itself.

Two weeks later, Ambassador Charles Bohlen was called to the Quai d'Orsay to pass on a message from General de Gaulle to President Johnson in which it was stated, in sharper terms than at the Elysée press conference, that France "proposes to recover entire exercise of her sovereignty over her territory, which is at present infringed by the permanent presence of allied military elements and no longer to place forces at the disposal of the Atlantic Organization". To which the American President was content to express his concern, assuring the French President that such action would "seriously affect the security and well being of the citizens of all the allied countries".

On 1 July 1966, the representatives of France left the military bodies of NATO, which withdrew from Paris to Brussels, while continuing to take part in the work of the Alliance Council. On 1 April 1967, all the American and Canadian bases were evacuated from French territory. A serious problem remained: if foreign planes were forbidden to fly over France, NATO would be cut into two sections, one in the north and one in the south, by a zone formed by France, Switzerland and Austria (the last two being neutral). In order to benefit from the long-distance radar location systems, France agreed to allow flights over her territory.

But the atmosphere continued to grow heavier between Washington and Paris, being constantly poisoned by comments made on Vietnam by those who, to a greater or lesser degree, were associated with the General. Indo-China had become the very centre of Lyndon Johnson's strategy and it was the favourite target of the General and his associates. It was in this climate that General de Gaulle's trip to the Soviet Union took place between 20 and 30 June 1966. The cordiality of what he said from Moscow to Novosibirsk and Volgograd aroused cries in the United States of a "reversal of alliances" – which was to take moods for realities.

Thus things went from bad to worse, until, in March 1968, Lyndon Johnson's speech, in which he announced both a partial cessation of bombing of North Vietnam and his decision not to present himself at the elections at the end of the year. Although Hanoi's response did not exclude contact with Washington with a view to putting an end to hostilities, de Gaulle greeted Johnson's statement as

*Notably on the matter of the withdrawal of the French fleets from the Mediterranean, then from the Atlantic.

"courageous" and declared that it was moving "in a positive direction".

"These words were enough to trigger off a wave of gratitude in the United States," Hervé Alphand commented. "Once again I have to admire de Gaulle's vision, that combination of instinct and reasoning." Indeed, there were more and more indications of a thaw between the United States and France. A change of men was to contribute decisively to this. Who could have said that the divergences on fundamentals, which had poisoned relations between Lyndon Johnson and de Gaulle far more than incompatibilities of temperament, would not produce the same effect between Nixon and the General? And yet the change was a radical one.

The new President had been Eisenhower's Vice-President and as such had taken part in the very warm welcome given by the United States to the General in 1960. Furthermore, de Gaulle, as a result of that foresight that sometimes guided him, had insisted on inviting him during two of his private visits to Paris, remarking to his close colleagues that Nixon had "a future", whereas, between 1962 and 1967, he was regarded by all as "finished". Lastly, the new President had as his defence adviser the most notorious of the "American Gaullists", Henry Kissinger.

In the book that he called *Leaders*, Richard Nixon draws an extraordinarily favourable portrait of General de Gaulle. Whether Charles de Gaulle's advice helped to make him realize that recognition of China was a necessity, that the war in Vietnam was more harmful to American interests than any political settlement could be and that, since he could not wage war on the USSR, he had to build up a sort of peace with her, or whether this new direction came quite simply from Henry Kissinger, the fact is that Nixon constantly tended to attribute his successes to the beneficent influences of the General. "When I became President, de Gaulle and I closed the breach that had developed between France and the United States. Unlike some of my predecessors, I did not scorn de Gaulle's advice and counsel but welcomed it, for I knew I could profit greatly from his experience and wisdom in world affairs."[45]

In February 1969, Richard Nixon was received in Paris on an official visit. He admits to having been dazzled by the splendour displayed around him by the old gentleman of the Elysée, the "magnificent dinners" at Versailles or the Elysée. But above all he stresses the ten hours of private talks that he had with the General.

After so many storms and conflicts, after so many disagreements and silences, after so many challenges and anathemas, things certainly seemed to be going well. Here is Nixon's description: "An aura of majesty seemed to envelop him. During our meetings, his performance was breathtaking. No leader I met could surpass his remarkable ability to discuss any subject or any part of the world with such competence, intelligence, and at times profound insight."[46] Some weeks later, the great reconciliation was to take an emotional form when the General attended the funeral of Dwight Eisenhower. He left with an invitation to make a State visit to the United States "as soon as possible". But we have already reached March 1969. And a month later, the old leader was to find himself with minority support during the referendum of 27 April – and he left for Colombey.

Richard Nixon repeated his invitation, in terms that were indeed very elevated: "In this age of mediocre leaders in most of the world, America's spirit needs your presence." The retired French President replied:

Your gracious official message and your very warm personal letter touched me deeply. Not only because you occupy the office of President of the United States, but also because they are from you, Richard Nixon, and to me and because I have for you esteem, confidence, and friendship as great and as sincere as it is possible to have.

Perhaps, one day I will have the occasion and the honour to see you again; in the meantime I send you from the bottom of my heart all my best wishes in the successful accomplishment of your immense national and international task.[47]

Two weeks later, General de Gaulle's last diplomatic decision consisted, on 4 April 1969, of renewing, by tacit agreement, the Atlantic Pact, which had just expired.

Was this the gesture of an enemy of the United States?

CHAPTER TWENTY-NINE

To the Urals

Was de Gaulle an anti-Communist? Of course. And not at all. Of course, in that all his background and education were directed against Marxism. Not at all, in so far as ideologies counted for little in his view of the world.

In early summer 1941, as soon as he heard of the opening of hostilities between the Reich and the USSR, he sent a telegram to London in order to place Free France at the side of Russia, urging his colleagues to demonstrate to the Soviet Ambassador, Mayski, the active support of the French Committee of National Liberation – while recalling "the abuses and even crimes of the Soviet regime". This calm distinction between alliances and ideological and moral rejection was to be the constant basis of Gaullist diplomacy towards the East.

Throughout the war, relations were to remain good between Moscow and Free France. We have already seen how rough the confrontation of December 1944 between Charles de Gaulle and Joseph Stalin on the subject of Poland was. De Gaulle returned to Paris irritated at Stalin's rejection of his views on the dismemberment of the German Reich, an irritation that could only revive the role played by the Soviet dictator in the preparation and progress of the Yalta Conference.

By January 1946, de Gaulle could no longer conceive of the Soviet Union as anything other than a regime of oppression with a lust for power. With the creation of the RPF in April 1947, he took as his permanent target "that colossal instrument of domination": thus in the Rennes speech he prophesied that the West would be overrun by "cossacks", which were separated from Paris by only "two stages of the Tour de France bicycle race".

From 1953, de Gaulle made his attacks more subtle. The end of the Korean war had shown that Moscow knew how to control its enthusiasms, while the project of the European Defence Community, which was as much anathema to de Gaulle as to Moscow, brought their concerns, and sometimes their words, together. From month to month, especially after the end of the fighting in Indo-China (July 1954), the General ceased to be the Grand Inquisitor of the socialist camp.

Soon an unexpected individual, Sergei Vinogradov, Soviet Ambassador in France, turned up at Colombey, readily declaring that he was a Gaullist and muttering strange things here and there: for example, that General de Gaulle might, one day, return to power. Then came May 1958. The new leadership showed unexpected respect for a man who had been so perspicacious, who told everyone to call him "Vino" and went around Paris looking, with his rather fleshy face, like a hedonist recovering from some excess.

Throughout the Fourth Republic, relations between Paris and Moscow had been bitter, intermittent and awkward. To the rifts due to the Cold War – punctuated by Big Four conferences in which Mr Dulles's sermons echoed Mr Molotov's propagandist thunderings – had been added the war in Indo-China, while the activism of the French Communist Party stirred up the already painful frictions between the various states. The USSR was nothing more than the potential enemy of the Western states, which had the United States as their leader.

At the beginning of his reign, Charles de Gaulle embarked on no radical revision of French diplomacy, and although he had certainly decided that when he wanted to speak to Moscow he did not have to go through Washington and that he would challenge the system of blocs, thereby ensuring the independence of France, he still considered Russia as the only potential enemy. She was an enemy that skilful diplomacy must try, in the medium term, to turn into a peaceful partner. But we cannot examine the various stages of the relations between the General and the Soviet Union without stating two essential facts: the founder of the Fifth Republic had underestimated ideological factors in the policies of Moscow and her satellites and underestimated the risks of world conflict.

When de Gaulle spoke to Khrushchev or Brezhnev, he spoke to "Russians" (who happened, in fact to be Ukrainians) and also to "Europeans" and to "Whites". The ideological dimension of the debate eluded him completely, but he had made a point of ignoring it. This underestimation of ideological factors led the General to make certain miscalculations about Vietnam or the outcome in Poland or Czechoslovakia, for example. But it found partial justification in the great Sino-Russian quarrel.

Another permanent element in the General's diplomatic thinking was the refusal to take seriously the threats against world peace. A man who had been so pessimistic at the time of the Berlin blockade, then during the Korean war, the man who had then confided to Claude Mauriac that only the American nuclear shield had saved Europe from invasion, was now, from 1958 onwards, convinced of the irreducibly peaceful character of the balance of terror.

It is as much in this underestimation of Communist dynamism and of Russian imperialism, as in a feeling of humiliated irritation caused by the heaviness of the system of Atlantic protection, that we must seek the motive for General de Gaulle's diplomatic reorientation. If the threat was merely illusory, if since the disappearance of Stalin the big bad wolf was no longer quite so bad or really a wolf, and if, moreover, one believed that one had the capacity to make him think, why accept the heavy restrictions of a foreign-led coalition in peacetime? Why remain locked up in the heavy armour that one had put on at a time of great fear when things had become much calmer? Finally, since war had proved to be impossible, did there not remain only one course of action: to turn the armed truce into the peace in which the world had lived since 1945?

And who would be better equipped to make peace than an old strategist at the head of an old nation bringing new vigour to an old, exhausted continent? Russians, Poles, Hungarians, Prussians, Saxons would take more notice of an old reader of Voltaire and Michelet, a man who had fought at Verdun and on the Vistula, a man who had talked to Stalin and Sikorski, than of Professor Rusk.

Would the Russians not dare to? First it had to be proved. I have already referred to the crisis triggered off, on 27 November 1958, when the Western powers received a Soviet note suggesting that they should leave West Berlin, where their occupation was based on Inter-Allied agreements defining the system of occupation in Germany until such time as a peace treaty had been drawn up. De Gaulle immediately became the advocate of uncompromising resistance. When Ambassador Vinogradov dropped his paternal tone and began to offer threats, de Gaulle cut him short: "Well, *Monsieur l'Ambassadeur*, we shall all die, but so will you."

The socialist camp still seemed to him to be the place where plots were hatched against France. Of course, by inflicting two terrible electoral defeats on the French Communists, in September and November 1958 (when they were reduced from 20 per cent to 10 per cent of the electorate), he loosened the grip that the PCF had had over his predecessors.

Although he was aware of the benefits to be obtained from the summit conference then being proposed by Moscow – represented by him, France could plausibly occupy a seat in the first rank – he cunningly delayed giving his approval, while declaring, to applause from the socialist camp in France, that the Oder–Neisse line now marked off Poland from the West.

It was only on 10 November 1959, at a time when his offer of self-determination for Algeria had improved his image throughout the world, that he declared that he could see "some indications of relaxation" now that "Russia admitted that a conflict, from whatever side it came, would lead to general annihilation".[1]

Having spoken on the theme of the harmlessness of a Russia based on the development of a purely geopolitical conflict, the General announced that Nikita Khrushchev had accepted his invitation to come to France in March 1960. Meanwhile, a conference held in Paris in December between Eisenhower, Macmillan, Adenauer and de Gaulle had laid down the broad outlines of what might be the East–West summit proposed by Moscow.

In his *Mémoires*, de Gaulle took almost as much trouble in the account of that visit to Paris of Khrushchev as he had done over his own visit to Russia in December 1944. De Gaulle was there to meet him at Orly, of course. In the *Mémoires*, he comments:

> Adopting the air of a good-natured family man, he had arrived with his wife, their son, their two daughters, and their son-in-law. Wherever he went, he appeared friendly, alert and nimble in spite of his rotundity, full of laughter and friendly gestures. Bordeaux, Lacq, Arles, Nîmes, Marseille, Dijon, Verdun, Rheims and Rouen. I was anxious that he should go to the provinces and meet the French people. There, as in Paris, he showed himself cheerful and homely, mainly interested in technology and industrial output.[2]

They talked a great deal, the visitor and he, "and not by way of idle chatter". De Gaulle made it plain from the outset that he wanted to discuss only "the national interests of our two countries and the ways in which we can reconcile them": "many divergences of view" emerged, but "they did not provoke any serious clashes". The General found his guest "relaxed and easy-going", especially when they were alone. "However great the differences between us in origin, training and conviction, we established a genuine man-to-man rapport."

The visitor tried to intimidate his host by asserting that the East German Republic would continue to exist and would never be absorbed by West Germany. "You are certainly not in any hurry to see Germany re-united," Khrushchev slipped in. Then why should not France recognize Pankow,* which could, once a peace treaty had been signed with Moscow, make it impossible for the West to remain in Berlin, unless they turned the Western sectors into a "free city"? Rid of its occupiers, this would settle its affairs with the German Democratic Republic.

"Icily," de Gaulle recounts, "I gave Khrushchev to understand that the threat he was brandishing did not impress me very much. If you do not want war, do not take the road that leads to war." Against such a threatening approach he offered détente "among Europeans, from the Atlantic to the Urals", with a view to taking "the sting out of the German problems".

To bring the dramatization to a proper conclusion, the General so arranged matters that the announcement of the explosion of the second French atom bomb was made during a private meeting with Khrushchev at Rambouillet. He gave the news to his visitor, adding that he was "anxious for him not to learn of it from the news agencies". The visitor, de Gaulle wrote, "replied to me affably and with a characteristic human touch: 'Thank you for your consideration. I understand your joy. We felt it, too, not so long ago.' Then, after a moment: 'But you know, it's very expensive!'"[3]

There follows the odd account of boating on a lake at Rambouillet, on to which de Gaulle took Khrushchev, Kosygin and an interpreter.

> Khrushchev shouted: "Kosygin, you can do the rowing, as usual." Kosygin seized the oars. Jokingly, I asked the Soviet Prime Minister: "By the way, when do you work yourself?" To which he replied: "But I don't work! A decree of our Central Committee has ordained that after sixty-five – and I'm sixty-six – one should only work six hours a day and four days a week. That's just enough for my journeys and my audiences." Then, pointing to Kosygin, who was rowing the boat, he added: "He's the Plan!"[4]

What de Gaulle does not relate in his *Mémoires*, but which his son-in-law Alain de Boissieu has told me, is that in the middle of the lake, as if he had wanted to be heard only by the General, the oarsman, the nymphs and the water sprites, the fat little man from Moscow seized the hands of the Gallic giant and said, in a rather worried way: "We're both Whites, you and me."[5]

The visitor had already admitted that he was trying to grapple with the Asian multitudes. He left for the Kremlin, "friendly and cheerful once more, leaving me, I must confess, impressed by the strength and resilience of his personality, disposed to believe that, after all, there was a chance of peace in the world and a future for Europe, and reflecting that something of profound importance had occurred in the time-honoured relationship between Russia and France".[6]

In less than two months, things were to be different. The President of the Fifth

*A district in Berlin which served as the capital of the GDR.

Republic had so arranged matters that the summit conference would take place in Paris, under his chairmanship. A date had been fixed for it: 16 May. But two weeks earlier an American spy-plane had been brought down while photographing Soviet launching pads over the Aral Sea. On 15 May, he was at the Elysée, flanked, for this peace conference, by the formidable Malinovski, the "rockets marshal": and the text that he handed at the beginning to his host, demanding apologies, punishment of those guilty and a commitment that such a thing would not happen again, already sounded like the death-knell of the summit.

"It was clear," writes de Gaulle, "that the Soviets wanted either to inflict a spectacular humiliation on the United States or to extricate themselves from a conference which they now no longer desired after having clamoured so loudly for it."[7] And as the visitor went on to describe the misfortunes that might strike the allies of the United States, the General "retorted sharply", daring to make a comparison that must have put the Soviet leader beside himself with rage, if he was not already so. Twice already in his life he had seen "the defeat of a country that had taken the risk of going to war in the certainty of winning it". Khrushchev went on, denouncing the "provocation" of the American spy-plane. De Gaulle cut him short: "Espionage is undoubtedly a deplorable practice. But how can it be avoided when two rival powers, heavily over-armed, give each other the impression that they may reach for their guns at any moment? At this very moment a Soviet satellite is passing over France eighteen times in every twenty-four hours."

When Khrushchev realized that Eisenhower would refuse to be humiliated, he summoned a "press conference" that was so quickly infiltrated by Communist militants that one suddenly found oneself plunged into a provincial election meeting, full of sound and fury: a meeting in which the head of the second most powerful nation in the world, crimson with fury, thundered aggressively, yelling at those who contradicted him: "To those who are barracking me, let me say this: if they come up against the Soviet Union, we shall barrack them so loudly that they'll no longer recognize their bones!"[8]

In any case, the Soviet leader's petulance had the effect of ruining a conference to which de Gaulle had attached great importance, if not hopes: a conference at which he was host and chairman. It would have been a sort of revenge for Yalta. How could he not resent Khrushchev's sabotaging his diplomatic mission and, what was worse, doing so at the apparent orders of Marshal Malinovski and the military plan?

However little importance he attributed to Khrushchev's outbursts, de Gaulle could not fail to find in it support for the rigid opposition with which, for months, he approached any projects for world-wide negotiation. What was the point of talking before the Eastern bloc showed a new, more conciliatory attitude and did something to help create a climate of détente before the dialogue could take place? Then suddenly, on 13 August 1961, the Wall went up, ending any communication between the two Berlins, east and west. But with the last breach in the iron curtain now filled, Moscow had ceased to dream of invading the West and was turning the key in order to avoid the worst. It was recognition of defeat, firstly psychological, secondly strategic, in so far as the East, which had once claimed to be chasing the West from Berlin, was now resigned to defending only its own slice of the cake.

At the Elysée, the building of the Berlin Wall was seen as a renunciation by Moscow of its most ambitious aims, as an end to the crisis opened up in November 1958 by Khrushchev, as a withdrawal in fact. It was a victory for the status quo that had been tenaciously defended by the General. However cruel it might be to German hearts – Adenauer took it as an irreparable defeat – the crisis was also a bitter one for the stormy strategist in the Kremlin.

After the sabotage of "his" Paris summit of May 1960 and the final shattering of his old friend in Bonn, de Gaulle could hold a great many things against the Soviet leader in the early 1960s. Not least was that provoked by the Algerian affair. Although with some caution, the Moscow leaders constantly encouraged the representatives of the Algerian independence movement. Ferhât Abbâs and Belkacem Krim were received with official honours in Moscow. And, curiously enough, the very settlement of the affair, which should normally have improved relations between Paris and Moscow, actually caused renewed friction. When Khrushchev thought fit to congratulate the GPRA for concluding the Evian agreements, as if it were a treaty between states, even if Algeria still remained French territory, de Gaulle recalled his Ambassador in Moscow.

So we are very far from that "reversal of alliances" that de Gaulle's most vigilant detractors were beginning to detect. For de Gaulle, "Russia" was no longer anything more than an aggressive power stupidly engaged on the geopolitical terrain of its enemy and Khrushchev a clumsy adventurer who thoroughly deserved the lesson that Kennedy was planning to give him in the Caribbean.

De Gaulle was to show no more willingness to accommodate the Soviets on European territory over the next few months: the treaty signed with the German Federal Republic, on 2 January 1963, was very badly received in Moscow. On 5 February, the Soviet government published an official protest against the agreement for cooperation between Paris and Bonn. The refusal of France to join the American-Soviet treaty, signed on 27 July 1963 in Moscow with a view to forbidding nuclear tests in the atmosphere, did nothing to improve what were already bad relations between Paris and Moscow.

The General's interest in the Eastern world was increased when the cracks between the two branches of the Communist world began to appear. This breach first appeared in the summer of 1960, between Russian and Chinese delegates at the Congress of the Rumanian Communist Party. The difference appeared first on the theoretical plane, around the interpretation of Lenin's view of imperialism: Moscow regarded it as capable of development, while Peking saw it as intrinsically perverse and bellicose. But, to the profound satisfaction of de Gaulle the historian and strategist, this debate between sociologists and ideologists was soon to turn into a more classic conflict between appetites for power and national ambitions.

From the comments of August 1960 on the nature of capitalism, they had moved to deliveries of tractors interrupted, atomic secrets forbidden, conditions for settling the Cuban Missile Crisis criticized, prospects for disarmament denounced, then to skirmishes over the possession of the banks of the Amur river. What an excellent illustration of de Gaulle's theses! As soon as they could be "treated" nation by nation, interest by interest, ambition by ambition, those Communists became interesting partners for the General. So the Elysée, on 27 January

1964, suddenly recognized the People's Republic of China, the first Ambassador of the Fifth Republic, Lucien Paye, arriving in April. It is extremely doubtful whether Moscow was pleased by this. But Khrushchev had expended too much energy advocating such decisions – had he not given emphasis to his arguments by banging his shoe on the desk at the United Nations? – to be able to allow himself any signs of irritation. Furthermore, although the General's gesture served the interests of the Chinese heretics against Moscow, it also revealed a freedom with regard to Washington that Soviet diplomacy would be able to exploit.

This new course coincided oddly with the withdrawal of Khrushchev, which, to say the least, had been hastened by his colleagues. Oddly? Yes. For no one seemed better qualified, in the East, to implement the détente that had been in the air for months than the excitable little Ukrainian. This, at least, was how de Gaulle saw him.* When he learnt the news, he was in Rio de Janeiro, talking to the local archbishop. "Sic transit gloria mundi, Monseigneur," he sighed and he began to dream, perhaps, of the long reigns of Peter and Catherine.

The year 1963 was certainly the great diplomatic turning-point. In any case, it was the year in which Jean Monnet saw the General turn away from Europe, when Maurice Couve de Murville situates the origins of the thaw in the East, when John Kennedy was succeeded by Lyndon Johnson, Konrad Adenauer by Ludwig Erhard, when Washington, London and Bonn tried to breathe life, against de Gaulle, into the shapeless, unviable, absurd Multilateral Force.

Let us try to imagine the de Gaulle of that period. He sees himself isolated, countered by his most recent allies, who were indeed surprised by the withdrawal of the French Atlantic fleet from NATO, which the General had decided on without even consulting Bonn, as he was duty-bound to do by the treaty signed on 22 January. But he was also unable to join the Moscow treaty on the supervision of nuclear tests, not only because his application would strangle the French strike forces at birth, but because he saw in those Soviet-American talks a return to the system of double hegemony that would throw France and Europe back into the vague herd of nations under the influence of one or the other.

In almost total contradiction with his allies and neighbours on the future and structures of Europe, de Gaulle declared on 31 December 1963 that France, "because she can, because everything invites her to do so, because she is France, must carry out in the world policies that are on a world scale". And what could his country do "in the world", if not make her "contribution to the maintenance of peace"?[9]

> Without ceding to the illusions in which the weak indulge, but without losing the hope that men's freedom and dignity will everywhere win the day, we must envisage a time when, perhaps, in Warsaw, Prague, Budapest, Bucharest, Sofia, Belgrade, Tirana and Moscow, the communist totalitarian regime, which still manages to imprison peoples, might gradually come to a development reconcilable with our own transformation. Then, prospects

*According to the sagacious Couve de Murville, who showed some relief at Khrushchev's departure.

matching her resources and capacities would be open to the whole of Europe.

So the long march towards the harmonization of relations with the East was undertaken in 1964. At first it seemed to take the form of constant visits to France by the heads of government of the Warsaw Pact countries: but, of course, this was only after Moscow had opened up the way, with a visit to Paris, in February 1964, by Nikolai Podgorny, President of the Supreme Soviet of the USSR. For, in this domain, it was French doctrine that nothing would be done that seemed to challenge the Soviet Union. For nothing was more contradictory to de Gaulle's religion of independence than the idea that he required some kind of Soviet visa to talk to Warsaw. The thinking in Paris at this time is well described by Maurice Couve de Murville:

> We were well aware of the limitations of such an opening, laid down in advance by the possibilities of development of the regime to which those countries were subjected. One could hope for a liberalization to take place gradually, and traditions for such still existed, at least in some of the countries, in Poland and Czechoslovakia, for example. But nothing would be conceivable without Soviet agreement.

Thus, Couve goes on, there was no question "of trying to detach them from Russia. This enterprise would not only have been unrealistic because it would be doomed to failure, but contrary to the very interests of those states, to which it would have brought nothing but trouble and misfortune." What was thought possible in Paris was "to reawaken old friendships that would be directed against nobody, to offer those nations locked up in their world, in some sense segregated for the past twenty years, the possibility of opening to the outside, of establishing new relations with it, in short to find new conditions for their life and development".[10]

As we shall see, in certain instances the ambition of de Gaulle seemed to go beyond these modest intentions. Where Poland, probably, and Romania, certainly, were concerned, he seemed to suggest to his guests that they should seek inspiration in their relations with Moscow in his own behaviour with Washington. Not that he identified Russian oppression with American protection: but independence is a state of mind (sometimes based on an illusion), rather than a range of defined powers.

With Moscow, a commercial agreement was signed (October 1964), accompanied by an interesting exchange of messages between de Gaulle and Mikoyan, then nominal head of the Soviet state. The General's is significant: "We have been able to note that, despite accidents of history, our two nations are profoundly bound together in a lasting friendship, by the conviction of possessing a common heritage and by mutual cordial interests."

What is surprising in these years 1964 and 1965, is not so much the reorientation of Gaullist diplomacy, but the essentially favourable view the Kremlin had of the French President. Had the Kremlin come to believe, through the researches of its Ambassador Vinogradov, that the General was willing to move much further towards the East?

It so happened that in March 1965 the man who had been called the most "Gaullist" of the Soviet ambassadors in Paris was recalled to Moscow and replaced by Valerian Zorin. Was this a way of putting a stop to the whole business, the end of a sort of "honeymoon"? Not at all. By replacing "Vino", that subtle specialist in French affairs, with Zorin, Moscow had not decided to cut short its special relations, but rather to give them a less verbal, more political dimension. Zorin was one of the two or three great figures in Russian diplomacy. With him, good attitudes had to be turned into tangible benefits.

De Gaulle did not let his old visitor to Colombey leave, however, without addressing to him a farewell toast of a kind that few diplomats from the East have received from the lips of Western leaders. Stressing the personal role played by Vinogradov in the development "of the widening zone of understanding and cooperation" between "Russia and France", the head of State praised "the centuries-long sympathy and natural affinity" between "the French and Russian peoples" and "the need for coexistence and peace between our two peoples". It was much more than the diplomat himself had expected, he confided, delightedly, as he left his colleagues.[11]

But when, on 27 April 1965, the General assembled the French people before their television sets in order to outline before them the relations between France and the world, he remained extremely discreet on the matter of openings to the East. Reminding his audience that there could be no question of "repudiating our friendship for the American people" and welcoming the close ties between the Six of Western Europe, de Gaulle proposed to resume "with the countries of the East, as they emerge from their crushing constraints, the relations of active understanding that bound us to them in the past".[12]

How much of this was dream and how much reality? At a press conference held at the Elysée on 9 September 1965, he remained very laconic on the subject, saying no more than: "We attach great importance to the new course that our relations with Russia are taking." And, having finally decided to seek re-election as head of State in December 1965, he was content to recall, during his last appeal to the electorate, that "we wish to pursue, with understanding and cooperation in every field, the vast undertaking of *rapprochement* with the East, that has so happily been begun".[13] To Hervé Alphand, who asked him what he expected to do about the Soviet "advances", he replied:

We are not supplicants. They will have to say precisely what they are thinking. I still don't know how much to place on it. It is true that Russia's satellites are gradually freeing themselves from her grip and turning towards us. In Russia itself, the revolutionary thrust has been stopped. So it is not inconceivable that one day we might have certain agreements. But the Russians must give new, clear proof of their wish for *détente* and understanding.[14]

Any Western leader with any breadth of vision could have subscribed to that in early 1965. A year later, the same diplomat, having meanwhile become Secretary-

General at the Quai d'Orsay and preparing to visit Moscow, notes that de Gaulle "has not changed". When Alphand asked him to assess the implications of "the USSR's smiles, its offers in the scientific and economic fields", the General replied that the aim was still "to create European solidarity from the Atlantic to the Urals", provided "we see Moscow extend her smiles to Bonn" and "to try to remain on good terms with the United States", adding that he saw nothing wrong with that. So there would not be between Paris and Moscow any "treaty of alliance or non-aggression", but only "a new improvement in the climate of our relations" – and agreements on technical cooperation.[15]

Was this the great operation described as a reversal of alliances? It is true that, some days earlier, on 7 March 1966, the General announced to Lyndon Johnson that he was withdrawing French forces from NATO. So there was no need for anything as formal as a treaty for Moscow to feel closer to Paris. But French troops remained in Berlin; the development of the French *force de frappe* was speeded up; more joint projects with Peking were planned.

The big event, of course, was to be General de Gaulle's visit to the Soviet Union between 20 and 30 June 1966. Planned the previous year, the trip had to be postponed on account of the presidential elections in France. So it was a Charles de Gaulle endowed with a seven-year mandate at the age of seventy-six who landed in Moscow.

In his speech on arrival, he greeted the "yearning for peace" of "that great Russia, which I saw during earlier, troubled times, in the grip of a war effort that was to ensure her victory and, for a large part, that of France and our allies". He announced that his visit would be "an opportunity for the two countries, to bring their relations closer in the economic, cultural and scientific domains", but also, "I hope, to concert their action with a view to assisting the union and security of the continent, as well as balance, progress and peace throughout the world".[16]

The welcome given by the Russian people to the French leader was on the whole much warmer than the one he had received twenty years earlier, though the *Figaro* correspondent in Moscow, Nicolas Chatelain, who was of Russian origin and familiar with local atmosphere, denied that "the crowds swarmed towards him".

The programme that had been laid on for him suggested that the greatest care had been taken to interest and to honour him. Leningrad, the beauty that came from the West; Kiev, the cradle of national power; Volgograd, once Stalingrad, a reminder of the common struggle against Nazism; Novosibirsk, the symbol of the great march to the virgin lands of Siberia; Akademgorod, a city of scholars, a tribute to universal culture; lastly, as a special favour, the space centre at Baikonur, where he was the first foreign head of State to be received. He was given exceptional "treatment" and he received it as such, pouring forth pleasantries and praise.

It would soon emerge that, apart from Vietnam and opposition to German nuclear weapons, the respective positions of the two governments were peacefully, but totally, opposed. Everything that de Gaulle said was imbued with a sense of movement, revision, rejection of the status quo. Everything that came out of the Kremlin was static, conservative, opposed to revision, a defence of established positions. In the days of Khrushchev, de Gaulle was able to parry with another imaginative individual, sometimes finding himself in the situation of having to defend established structures; with the new leadership, he came up against a wall of unyielding courtesy.

The visit ended with a rather dull joint declaration, the setting up of a Franco-Soviet "grand commission", which would meet at regular intervals to give new impetus to the exchanges, the installation of a "red telephone" (in fact a tele-printer) between the Kremlin and the Elysée, an invitation to the Prime Minister, Kosygin, to visit France: there was nothing very new in all that. Détente was going well enough, understanding was possible on a few points, cooperation was spread-ing into the technological domain. But what had these pleasantries in common with the great dialogues with Eisenhower, Kennedy or Adenauer?

Politeness? Even here, things are only relative. A few weeks earlier, in Berlin, commenting on the General's decision to withdraw France from the integrated organizations of NATO, Leonid Brezhnev said to his colleagues Gomulka and Ulbricht: "De Gaulle is our enemy. He is very cunning, but his policies are causing a weakening of American positions in Europe."[17]

The General has been criticized for his "naivety" with regard to the USSR. Who could believe that ideology would gradually give ground to the traditional motives of the Russian state? This criticism was put notably by the great expert in East–West relations, Charles Bohlen, but, in the last words of his book, the American diplomat nevertheless pays involuntary homage to the General: "The only hope, and this is a fairly thin one, is that at some point the Soviet Union will begin to act like a country instead of a cause."[18]

We can hardly conclude this account of General de Gaulle's policy to the East without making some attempt to elucidate that strange slogan – "Europe from the Atlantic to the Urals" – which has caused so much irritation to commentators.

One day, when asked by his Ambassador in Washington to explain it to him (poor Alphand was so often urged to do so there), General de Gaulle refrained, for once, from enclosing himself in some Jovian cloud and actually tried to throw some light on the phrase:

> For such a Europe to be possible, great changes will have to take place. To begin with, the Soviet Union must no longer be what it is, but Russia. Secondly, China is threatening her eastern frontiers, in Siberia. And what could happen in a certain number of years? The phrase is intended to show to the Russians that the creation of a Western European Union is not directed against them, is not part of the Cold War; it sustains a certain hope among East Germans, Czechs, Poles, Hungarians. It represents, however, only a historical anticipation.[19]

Those words were spoken in September 1962, and what lies behind them is at one and the same time a geographical approach to the problem, a historical judgement on the Soviet Union, that colonial empire built up over five centuries by the tsars of

Muscovy (thus he compared the Siberia of the Russians to the Sahara that he had himself given back to its African mother), and lastly, a certain view of Europe.

It was a Europe that could not be bound within the frontiers of the Common Market. He might denounce "British insularity", but it was not because Britain was an island that it had to be kept waiting at the doors of the EEC; it was because she was still too tied up, in his view, with Washington: but he also knew that, if detached from that allegiance, she had her place beside Italians, Germans and French just as, if freed of their ideological and imperial chains, the peoples of Eastern Europe would be members of that vast community of which he certainly hoped, by being its prophet, to become the inspirer and arbiter.

In short, what de Gaulle meant was that ideologies are merely traps to catch nations and that these nations, when revealed to themselves, would find that there was much more in common between the readers of Tolstoy and those of Balzac, those who went to see Shakespeare and those who listened to Smetana, the disciples of Kant and followers of Copernicus, between the companions-in-arms on the Somme and at Monte Cassino,* than between political commissars from Minsk and Shanghai, and perhaps between football players in Turin and baseball champions from Los Angeles.

In short, General de Gaulle was a "European" much more by school, book and museum, than by systems and treaties. He believed that poets were greater unifiers than ideologues, artists and soldiers more creative of convergences than technocrats. He believed Chekhov and Bartók to be greater than Jean Monnet – and perhaps even than Karl Marx.

Where he was wrong, perhaps, was in believing that he knew God's purposes, by decree of Providence, and that these were carried out by Frenchmen – by one Frenchman above all.

---

*Where the Poles were in the majority (of those killed, at least 49).

CHAPTER THIRTY

With Two-Thirds of the World

In the great redeployment of French diplomacy carried out by General de Gaulle, circumstances, of course, played an essential role. One positive one was the peace signed with the Algerian rebels: the other, more negative ones were the failure of the Fouchet plan, the crisis with London, the tension with Washington. The West did not want de Gaulle's Europe. The General did not want an American Europe. Not given to immobility and little inclined to play the role of a wasp against the window pane, he sought a field of action elsewhere. But the way was shut towards the East: there was little chance of a diplomacy of détente that would allow France to play the role of pioneer in the great encounter with Moscow and her satellites. Not content with throwing the Big Four Paris conference of May 1960 into confusion, shamelessly intervening in the Algerian affair, then terrorizing the world in Cuba, Khrushchev pretended to see the Franco-German treaty of January 1963 as a threat to peace.

Caught between a cantankerous West and a bad-tempered East, what could the protagonist of a diplomacy of movement do if not seek allies and partners through the other "two-thirds of the world"? Until 19 March 1962, such a project was out of the question. Of course, his return to affairs had aroused some hopes in the Third World. Of course, the proclamation on Algeria's right to self-determination of September 1959 had placed de Gaulle on the side of emancipation, and the various stages of decolonization brought an end to the war and to France's imperial vocation within view. But it was the signing of the Evian agreements that brought down the walls between France and the "proletarian" nations: from that point on, everything was possible, with Algeria soon turning from being an obstacle into being a link.

So in spring 1962, freed of the Algerian burden, Charles de Gaulle stepped up his long march towards the southern hemisphere. Although France's map of Africa was now more or less settled, Asia was to give an enthusiastic welcome to the General's two major initiatives (his appeal of 29 July 1963 in favour of a political settlement in Vietnam and recognition of China) and Latin America gave a warm welcome to the visitor who, twice in 1964, crossed the Atlantic to walk in the steps of Simón Bolívar.

Then there was the United Nations. In the sixties, the Third World used the New York organization for political manipulation on a world scale. Outclassed in bilateral relations, exploited, manipulated and divided, the Afro-Asian and Latin American states found in Manhattan a sort of soundbox or rather a permanent court of appeal. There their powerlessness created numbers, their very poverty carried weight. Refracted by that rostrum, that press, those procedures, weaknesses became virtues: however small they might be at home, there they were in the majority.

Whoever ignored the UN robbed himself of access to the Third World. We know that de Gaulle had done nothing, for years, for that forum to grant him any kind of credit and that in 1960 he even went so far as to speak, contemptuously, of that *machin*, that "thing". But the decolonization of French-speaking Black Africa removing any source of major conflict, the entry into the UN of ten former French colonies in October 1960, and above all the emancipation of Algeria transformed relations between France and the UN in two years. From 1962 the President of the Fifth Republic enjoyed increasingly relaxed relations with the United Nations, overcoming many of his doubts and not disdaining to take an active part in Security Council debates, for which France's representatives, Armand Bérard or Roger Seydoux, were surprised to receive his personal directives.

And what of Asia? De Gaulle could not fail to regard it with respect. Two thousand million people with five thousand years of history, infinite spaces from Sinai to Kamchatka. It was a Gaullian horizon.

When Charles de Gaulle returned to power in June 1958 Indo-China was still on the eve of her great upheavals. In Vietnam, Ngo Dinh Diem felt the first effects of the disturbances caused by his authoritarianism, on the one hand, and the intrigues and infiltration from Hanoi, on the other; in Cambodia Norodom Sihanouk gave new dynamism to his neutralism by recognizing the People's Republic of China; as for Laos, the very precarious balance in which it had lived since the Geneva Conference of 1954 was broken by a *coup d'état* led by the pro-American Marshal Phumi Nosovan.

From 1958 to 1962, the situation in Vietnam continued to worsen after the setting up (December 1960) of the National Liberation Front, the Vietcong, and by the escalation begun by the Americans.

The feelings aroused in the General by the gradual engagement of the United States in Indo-China were not only inspired by respect for the right of peoples to dispose of their own fate, or even by his quasi-prophetic vision of the consequences of such an operation. All this was certainly there, but it was combined with an old bitterness. Haunted twenty years earlier by the prospect of France's being a victim, he could not but be disgusted by Kennedy's America taking in hand the very Indo-China so pitilessly lost by the Fourth Republic. A real Americanophobe would probably have been delighted to see the United States sink into such a morass, the various stages of which de Gaulle had predicted with such implacable lucidity – seeing it as an opportunity for greater freedom of action in relation to the trapped giant. But however much he wanted to free himself from the grip of the Western superpower he was even more attached to the idea of détente as he saw the American commitment in Indo-China, on the frontiers of a China in turmoil, as a threat to world peace.

The policy applied by the General in Indo-China between 1962 and 1969 certainly might have seemed less coherent if it had not been applied by such experienced diplomats, especially Etienne Manac'h, who, before becoming Ambassador to Peking, was for ten years director of Asian affairs at the Quai d'Orsay. Competence, energy, clarity of mind, and the temperament of an educator were the characteristics of a man who had played a determining role in the background, informing, urging, criticizing, gaining the respect of the American specialists whom he often consulted.

This Indo-Chinese strategy, begun in relation to Laos in 1962, emerging fully in relation to Vietnam in 1963 and reaching its culmination in Cambodia on 1 September 1966, was based on three ideas: that no military intervention in Asia could serve the cause of the West; that neutrality, extended at least to the whole of Indo-China and better still to the whole of South-East Asia, would be the best expression of a balance threatened by the regional preponderance of China, the greed of Hanoi and Russian penetration in Vietnam; and that France, given her local experience and the personality of her President, was best placed to get these views applied.

Whatever one thinks of this last idea, the first two articles of this "doctrine" have since been recognized as judicious. Their first point of application was Laos. After the "pro-American" coup of Marshal Phumi and the "neutralist" coup of Captain Kong-Le, an international conference that met during the summer of 1962 in Geneva set up a formula for government resembling the "three princes" (the communist Suphannuvong, the conservative Bum Um and the "neutralist" Suvanna Phuma), with a view to establishing a regime "independent of the two blocs".

Throughout this affair, French diplomacy played an encouraging role. The solution, of which Couve de Murville was one of the inspirers at Geneva, was regarded as one of General de Gaulle's diplomatic successes. Had he not pleaded for an outcome of this type during John Kennedy's visit to Paris in April 1961? And did he not constantly praise Prince Sihanouk's Cambodia for choosing the doctrine of the "golden mean", rejecting domination by either Americans or Communists?

The General did not throw himself into this crusade at once. For three or four years, given the limited nature of the American commitment, he gave the benefit of the doubt to the South Vietnamese government of Ngo Dinh Diem. He sent his Finance Minister, Antoine Pinay, to visit Saigon in the summer of 1959. The visitor came back even more "Diemist"* than he had set out: they had to support that little nation "faced with communist aggression". De Gaulle believed that he could hear in this echoes of American propaganda and thought that Antoine Pinay was trying to give a new direction to his diplomacy. Relations between Paris and Saigon turned sour soon after.

On 29 August 1963, two months before Ngo Dinh Diem and his brother fell under the blows of a junta of very different officers, de Gaulle suddenly announced his feelings about Vietnam to the world. He said that France was well aware of "the value of that people". Addressing "the whole of Vietnam", he recalled that she had "chosen the means" of attaining her unity and that France was ready to help her. Without making explicit reference to neutrality, the General thus advocated a reunification without victor or vanquished and proclaimed the

---

*I accompanied the minister on that trip and can testify to the euphoria in which the excellent M. Pinay bathed.

right to "self-determination". Having established diplomatic relations with People's China and declaring, on 31 January 1964, that the fate of Indo-China had played a great part in the decision that he had taken, he said:

> There can be neither war nor peace in Asia without China being involved in it. Thus it would be absolutely inconceivable without her to have any agreement on neutrality relating to the states of South-East Asia, a neutrality that, by definition, ought to be accepted by all of them, guaranteed on the international plane, and which would exclude both armed agitation, supported by any of those states or any other, and multiform information from outside, a neutrality that certainly seems, in the period in which we live, to be the only solution compatible with the peace and progress of populations.

By establishing relations and opening up a dialogue with Peking, de Gaulle had reanimated a situation previously blocked by Sino-American intransigence.[1] This was the view expressed by the London *Observer*: "De Gaulle has just entered the scene in the affairs of Asia like a diplomatic ice-breaker."[2]

Not wanting to see in this any more than a "challenge" from France, the Americans and their Indo-Chinese allies reacted in a very negative way. While President Johnson declared that the neutralization of the two Vietnams could not be a solution and that there was nothing else to be done other than "to intensify operations", at Saigon the hesitant junta that had seized power on 1 November was overthrown by new generals who declared themselves to be determined to bet everything on the war effort, denouncing "neutralism" as the invention of a France accused of "fishing in troubled waters". In April 1964, a pro-American *coup d'état* in Laos destroyed the experiment of the "third way" that had emerged from the Geneva Conference, two years earlier. Thus, having been removed from the scene by Washington and her allies, de Gaulle was to be picked up by their enemies.

On 24 January 1966, Ho Chi Minh, the North Vietnamese head of State, sent an extremely urgent letter to the General. Recalling that France had been a signatory of the Geneva accords, the old Hanoi leader wrote: "Faced with the extremely serious situation created in Vietnam by the United States, I hope that the government of your country will fully assume its obligations with regard to these accords and that Your Excellency will use his prestige to help stop in time any new American interventions in Vietnam and in Indo-China."

The American bombing of North Vietnam, having been broken off for a time, was resumed with increased intensity. In February 1966 de Gaulle replied to Ho Chi Minh, stressing the national and international dimension of the conflict. On the first point, the French President referred to "eventual reunification", and hoped that South Vietnam would elect at last a "representative government, which will not be possible as long as the war continues". On the second point, he advocated a return to the 1954 agreements, in favour of "the independence and neutrality of Vietnam and a non-interference in its internal affairs, which is contradictory to the present situation".[3] And, lest there be any doubt about it, Charles de Gaulle took up the same theme again in the press conference that he held at the Elysée on 21 February 1966:

The conditions of peace are well known [the Geneva agreement of 1954]. Fundamentally, it is an understanding and, to begin with, a meeting between the five world powers, France, for her part, having already organized her external relations in this direction – you understand what I mean.* Locally, it is the end of all foreign intervention in Vietnam and, as a result, the neutrality of the country, France, after some experience, having once agreed to withdraw her troops and being all the better today for having done so.[4]

There was no response from Washington. The General then, in his own way, dotted the "i"s and crossed the "t"s. One can hardly claim that his decision to leave NATO was dictated above all by a concern to give Washington a "lesson"or even by fear of being dragged by her great allies into the Far East conflict. But, as one of his advisers in Asian affairs, Jean Sainteny, a former representative of France in Hanoi,** remarked some weeks later, it was only a few days after a new intensification of the American bombing of North Vietnam that the General announced his decision concerning the Atlantic Organization. He had declared at a meeting of the Council of Ministers: "We are not disposed to accompany the Americans into every adventure that they think fit to throw themselves into."[5]

Prince Norodom Sihanouk, the Cambodian head of state, was in June 1964 the guest of de Gaulle, who seemed, by showering him with honours and respect, to want to sacralize him as the pioneer of Indo-Chinese independence. He certainly knew how to return the compliment: when Charles de Gaulle made his first appearance in the Far East, the visit was turned into a sort of fireworks display of militant neutrality. They were astonishing hours for all those who witnessed them.*** We saw a de Gaulle who was constantly surprised, which was rare, or moved, which he seldom showed. Entering the stadium of Phnom Penh where, on the steps, a set of panels manipulated by the spectators suddenly turned into a giant effigy of him, he murmured: "It's incredible, incredible." And, the same evening, during the concert, for which Prince Sihanouk composed the opening piece, he listened delightedly to the waltz from *Faust*, confiding to his neighbour, Princess Monique: "It was to such tunes that I danced with young ladies when I was at Saint-Cyr."[6]

"A State worthy of the name has no friend," de Gaulle was fond of saying. General de Gaulle did, however, find a friend in Prince Sihanouk, the man who, in order to govern his country better, gave up his throne. In the least sentimental career of any statesman, sentiment was to play a surprising role. How had this old man been able to absorb his hosts' political and psychological outlook to hit the bull's-eye every time he opened his mouth?

Prince Sihanouk and Cambodia were, it will be said, consenting prey. The surprising thing is that de Gaulle should have taken such meticulous care to create an almost musical harmony. And why did he take so much trouble? Here he was France, in search of a new destiny: Sihanouk was offering him the opportunity, the

*A reference to the recognition of Peking.
**Under de Gaulle, then under Mendès France.
***Including the author. I have based the following pages on articles written for *Le Monde* and *Le Nouvel Observateur*.

site, the echo of his voice. So he could interpret, in an Asiatic mode, his passion for independence and challenge, the love, too, of a certain France, which was rather refreshing at a time when most of the allies of the United States had become docile.

What was he looking for here and what was he offering? He was throwing a bright light on Cambodia that would make it less vulnerable to attack. He was offering recognition of its neutrality and of its threatened frontiers, which was vital to Prince Sihanouk. What struck him, at Angkor, was not the proliferating, twilight charm of that forest of faces, it was the political power that was expressed by the canals and dams, the temples and pools: a royal art that derived both from Thebes and from Versailles. In short, the General had the impression that Sihanouk's architects no longer considered themselves capable of erecting such proud monuments. But they had built a stadium, vast enough to hold the 200 000 people who had come to see and to hear Charles de Gaulle.

Sihanouk spoke first, pointing to de Gaulle: "Our world today, in which so many peoples are victims of injustice or are subjected to acts of warfare, has the greatest need of modern 'St Georges', who don't employ the spear or sword, of course, but take up courageous positions on the political and diplomatic plane, 'St Georges' who dare to defend, even against their allies' wishes, justice, law and peace."

Facing his giant portrait, facing the people, the gymnasts, the choristers and uniformed youth, General de Gaulle, who had donned his uniform to speak of peace, then stood and spoke in a style that astonished many of those who heard him by its haughtiness, crudity and frankness. De Gaulle was not a man to be frightened. But had he ever addressed a belligerent country in such a fashion? Suggesting once again negotiations on the basis of the Geneva Conference of 1954 with a view to re-establishing peace in Indo-China and establishing neutrality there, the General said:

The opening of such far-reaching and difficult negotiations would depend, of course, on America first taking the decision and undertaking to repatriate her forces by a reasonably fixed date. France is saying this in the name of her experience and her disinterest. She is saying it by reason of what she once did in this region of Asia. She is saying it on account of the exceptional, two centuries-long friendship that she has borne America, of the idea, which so far she had always made hers. That she was the champion of an idea that other countries were to pursue as national destinies. She is saying it, taking into account the warnings that Paris has been giving Washington for so long.

Lastly, she is saying it with the conviction that, given the power, wealth, influence to which the United States has now attained, the fact of renouncing a distant expedition in a distant land, once it appears to be without either benefit or justification, and to prefer to it an international arrangement organizing the peace and development of an important region in the world, would not in any way wound their pride, contradict their ideals or harm their interests. On the contrary, by pursuing a way that accords so well with the genius of the West, what an audience the United States would rediscover from one end of the world to the other and what an opportunity peace would find everywhere else! In any case, if we do not reach that point, no mediation will have any prospect of success and that is why France, for her part, has never thought and does not think now to propose anything.

Let us leave to one side the challenge to the Americans and the ease with which such essential elements in the affair as the responsibilities of both France and Hanoi in the Vietnamese chaos were passed over in silence. There remained a grandiose exhortation to Washington, based upon a parallel that presupposed that Lyndon Johnson was willing to see the world as Charles de Gaulle did and that a nation whose military budget was practically unlimited could act as France had done in 1954 or 1962. There remained, too, an idea: that of a date to be fixed for the disengagement, given which the advocates of peace, in the Communist camp, guaranteed that they could then begin negotiations.*

Sihanouk was jubilant: "This time the General has burnt his boats, has committed himself completely to our side, has ceased to be a spectator sickened by war; he has become a combatant for peace."[7] His American listeners, on the other hand, did not conceal their irritation: "What has the General got to say about the responsibilities of Hanoi and the Vietcong, of Peking and Moscow? And does he really think that we are waging a colonial war here, as France had done before 1954?"

What was more telling than the imperious tone in which his speech had been delivered was the confidences that the General made that evening to his colleagues. It was clear enough that he was under no illusions as to the effectiveness of his intervention. If he had believed that he had succeeded, it is clear that he would have committed both France and himself completely to mediation. There remained the bitter beauty of the words and the historical wisdom that they expressed, the shock to the imagination, the support thus given to a vast sector of American opinion that, from Walter Lippmann to Eugene McCarthy, had been saying nothing else and the support given in dozens of Third World capitals.

Would he have been given such a welcome if he had not, thirteen months before, already made himself a spokesman for the Asian masses? By announcing the establishment of diplomatic relations between France and the People's Republic of China (to the detriment of Taiwan) on 27 January 1964, de Gaulle had acquired in the Far East – including India and Japan – unrivalled credit.

He had reflected on and prepared the move at great length and he had carried it out alone. It was, as Edmond Jouve shows, one of those affairs in which the General's skill appears most constantly, where his "hand" is most visible – a taste for secrecy, a sense for the moment, a concern for consultation, suddenness in decision, the art of dramatization.[8]

The terrain had been prepared by Charles de Gaulle's predecessors in the 1950s: at the Geneva Conference of 1954, Pierre Mendès France had met the Chinese Prime Minister Chou En-lai, whose efforts to reach a peace settlement had seemed extremely promising. But the support then brought by Peking to the

---

*A spokesman of the Vietcong, whom I met that same evening at Phnom-Penh, assured me of this.

Algerian rebels had blocked the process – not to mention the threats of repercussions from Washington should any rapprochement between its allies and the Chinese revolution occur. But there was, of course, the obstacle of Chiang Kaishek. General de Gaulle, so attached to the memory of the common struggle against the dictatorships of the 1940s, was the last person to ignore the rights of the head of the Chungking government that had resisted the Japanese invader.

In short, de Gaulle had made the recognition of Peking a long-term project, which the settling of the Algerian conflict might make possible sooner or later. In 1957, the General had read a book written, on his return from a stay in China, by the former head of government, Edgar Faure. Its title, *Le Serpent et la Tortue* (The Snake and the Tortoise),[9] was inspired by one of Mao's poems. In his book Faure advocated the establishment of a diplomatic link between France and People's China. The author had sent a copy to the General and had received a response "entirely favourable to your point of view", though accompanied by the usual reservation, "If France had a State!"[10] In 1960, she had one. It was then that the General invited Faure to "come and talk to him about the Chinese problem". Should "something" be done in the direction of Peking? Edgar Faure advised prudence, as long as the Algerian conflict, which divided the two capitals, had not found a solution.[11]

Three years later, Faure was summoned once again to the Elysée: "Are you still in favour of waiting?" Faure said that he was not: not only had the Algerian conflict ceased to be a screen between the two countries, but the Chinese were in difficulties "on account of their friction with the Soviets". What better time to hold out a hand? And as the author of *The Snake and the Tortoise* told his host that, as it happened, he had just been invited to China, the General declared: 'Yes, you will go to China. But you will go as my representative."

The two men immediately drew up a meticulous plan involving two visits – one, on the way out, to Prince Sihanuk, and the other, on the way back, to Mr Nehru – which would cover the traces of the real purpose of these journeys. And the General gave Edgar Faure a personal letter accrediting him to the Chinese authorities.

Landing in Peking in late October 1963, accompanied by his wife Lucie, the General's emissary noted that the Chinese leaders treated him as a negotiator. It was Chou En-lai who took the affair in hand and, with Faure, drew up a protocol agreement that the French envoy took it upon himself to sign *ad referendum.**

A visit to Mao Tse-tung having put the most solemn seal on his mission, Faure left for Europe, stopping off at Delhi, from where he sent the Elysée the text of the draft agreement. The General received his envoy on 22 November 1963, the same day as the assassination of President Kennedy – which they both deplored, for, writes Edgar Faure, "it had vaguely occurred to us that the Americans might try to take advantage of our initiative, especially as far as Vietnam was concerned. I think that could have been the case with the Kennedy administration."[12]

Given the death of the young President, the two men agreed that the conclusion of the affair would have to be in January 1964. But they did not ignore the obstacle

---

*That is to say, so long as the approval of the authorities was given.

that always lay between the resumption of normal diplomatic relations between Paris and Peking: the official relations between France and the government of Taipei, headed by Chiang Kai-shek.

De Gaulle found it distasteful to have to humiliate his wartime ally, and the operation proved to be all the more delicate in that, in order to put de Gaulle into an embarrassing position, Washington urged Chiang not to break with France.[13] On 24 December, the President of the "Republic of China" (Taiwan) wrote to his French counterpart warning him against the initiative that, he had learnt, was being planned in Paris. On 14 January 1964, de Gaulle replied: "It is indeed true that in the fairly near future my government will enter into diplomatic relations with the government established in Peking. I am quite aware that the announcement that I am making to you will no doubt not fail to disappoint your expectations. But France cannot ignore any longer a fact that has been established."

Not only to mitigate the harshness of the blow, but also to ensure that his wartime ally would not put him in an embarrassing situation by refusing to break off diplomatic relations first, de Gaulle sent two emissaries to Taipei on 28 January: General Peshkov,* who had represented him to the Chungking government during the war, and Colonel Guillermaz, a well-known Sinologist. Chiang asked the French envoys to persuade de Gaulle to postpone his decision: was it so urgent to give the Communists such a present?

It was no use. On 24 January, Peshkov and Guillermaz reported to de Gaulle on their mission, from which it emerged that Chiang Kai-shek was more pained by his decision than determined to stand in its way. A discreet mission by Jacques de Beaumarchais** to the Chinese Ambassador at Berne made it possible to complete the text begun in November by Edgar Faure, and a joint statement was simultaneously published on 27 January in Peking and Paris, specifying that the two governments had "decided to establish diplomatic relations" and, therefore, to exchange ambassadors "within three months". The Peking government thought it useful to add that France's gesture implied a rejection of the theory of the "two Chinas" and a recognition of Taiwan as "an integral part of China".

However frequent and insistent were the rumours aroused by the comings and goings between Paris and Peking and the allusions made by the General or by M. Couve de Murville to a renewal of Franco-Chinese relations, this statement caused a sensation.

On 31 January 1964, a year and a few days after saying "no" to Kennedy and Macmillan, the founder of the Fifth Republic was to say a solemn "yes" to the heroes of the Long March.

China, a great people, the most numerous people on the face of the earth, and a vast country; a State older than history, constantly determined to be independent, striving unceasingly to centralization, instinctively turned in on itself and contemptuous of foreigners, but aware and proud of a perennial immutability, such is the eternal China.[14]

*Son of Maxim Gorky.
**Director of European affairs at the Quai d'Orsay, very close to M. Couve de Murville.

A lesson in geopolitics in the old style. After paying tribute to the historical role of Chiang Kai-shek, who had "tried to channel the flood" of revolution, recalling that the progress since carried out thanks to "enormous efforts" by China was not accomplished without "terrible sufferings by the people as is always the case with a communist system", the General presented the diplomatic act that had just been carried out as quite "normal" and "necessary", "self-evident" and "reasonable".

The consequences were less marked to begin with, more bitter later: when the embassy led by Lucien Paye,* a former education minister, was at last bearing its first fruit two years later, the cultural revolution turned China into a witches' cauldron – which was not at all in tune with the peaceful, rational aims of the French head of State. And it was Henry Kissinger and Richard Nixon, disciples in their own way of the General, who in 1972 were to collect the fruit of the operation begun eight years before in Paris.

Charles de Gaulle was not to see this culmination. Neither Nixon nor Kissinger failed to acknowledge him as the pioneer. The first saw this as one of the elements of the General's portrait that he painted in his *Leaders*. The second confided to several French listeners (of whom I was one), one October evening in 1980, that the establishment of Franco-Chinese relations in 1964 had opened up the way for his own initative, that trip to China in summer 1971 that suddenly transformed diplomatic prospects in Asia.

Charles de Gaulle's approach to Latin America followed very closely the opening up of his relations with Peking. It was during the "Chinese" press conference of 31 January 1964 that he announced his forthcoming visit to Mexico City.

> France may turn to other countries, which, in other continents, are develop-
> ing, and which attract us instinctively and naturally, and which, wishing to
> give an appropriate support to their evolution in accordance with our spirit
> and way, may wish to associate ourselves directly in their progress and,
> reciprocally, take part in all that France represents.

He concluded: "That is what we hope to discuss shortly with M. Lopez Mateos, the President of Mexico." The same President was received on an official visit to Paris in March 1963.

Why this reorientation of Gaullian diplomacy towards a whole horizon that had hitherto been unfamiliar to him and in which France's interests and involvement were much less obvious than in Africa or Asia? It must not be forgotten that, under the crucial impulse of Jacques Soustelle, in 1940, Latin America had played a positive role in the history of Free France (which Uruguay and Peru were the first states to recognize); and that some of the greatest Latin American writers, such as Miguel Angel Asturias, had become passionate advocates of the Gaullist cause.

De Gaulle was not a man to be unaware of the extent to which French culture

---

*Who was preceded, as chargé d'affaires, by Claude Chayet, a former negotiator with the Algerian FLN.

had impregnated the Brazilian, Peruvian or Chilean intelligentsia, nor that the sombre memories of the intervention in Mexico of the French Second Empire had been counterbalanced, in that country, by attachment to the France of which de Gaulle had given proof. And in so far as all the steps then taken by the General, freed by the peace in Algeria but impeded by his European neighbours, aimed at challenging the American hegemony, what better fulcrum could be found for that diplomatic lever than Latin America? By going to Latin America de Gaulle was demonstrating the multipolarity of the world and the pluralism of his own diplomacy.

President Lopez Mateos was the first Mexican head of State to be officially received in Paris. There were positive and negative aspects to such a trip. On the positive side there was the fact that in the eyes of the Latin American crowds, de Gaulle seemed like a *caudillo* in love with independence, a fearless "horseman" – even as another Bolívar (who had nourished his plans for Latin American liberation in Paris). It was not yet the period when harsh dictatorships were to spill their blood in Argentina, Uruguay and Chile; soldiers were still associated with the century of Enlightenment. A general's uniform was not, therefore, a negative factor.

As for the support that de Gaulle claimed to be offering to the Mexicans in their desire to free themselves from Washington, there were plenty of Mexicans who regarded it as untimely: did they not owe their prosperity to their great neighbours? It was one thing to denounce their encroachments, to call them *gringos*. But was it not better to live under their protection than be exposed to some revolution?

No sooner had de Gaulle landed in Mexico City than, on the central square of the capital, the Zocalo, into which 300 000 excited people had crowded, he roared out some fifteen sentences in Spanish, concluding with a "Marchamos la mano en la mano", which amounted pretty much to the "Je vous ai compris" speech of Algiers and triggered off a similar response. This reached new heights of delirium, leading to demonstrations that terrified those responsible for security the following day, during the French President's visit to the University of Mexico City. Before the General's car reached the gates, where the Minister and Rector were waiting for him, students blocked the vehicle, hoisted the General out of his car and bore him in triumph to the amphitheatre. "We were all shoved about, grabbed, knocked over," Ambassador Offroy recounts. "I found myself next to a reporter who was yelling: 'This is Europe No. 1. I am standing on the belly of a Mexican general.'"[15] Jean Mauriac, who followed all Charles de Gaulle's trips, had to admit that he had never been so afraid for the General's safety.[16]

The General himself was delighted. This was not bathing in the crowd, it was diving into the sea. And, certain now that he had won his bet, he said to Raymond Offroy, as he got into the plane bound for Guadeloupe: "Put up a French flag for me here, at the gates of the United States!"

The General's second Latin American visit was six months later, between 20 September and 16 October. In a little more than three weeks, travelling by plane or on the cruiser *Colbert*, de Gaulle was to be the guest of ten South American states – Venezuela, Colombia, Ecuador, Peru, Bolivia, Chile, Argentina, Paraguay, Uruguay and Brazil.

It was a moving trip, not only because it brought dream and reality together, but also because we were later to learn that this man of seventy-four had carried out that exhausting programme with a probe fixed in his bladder – five months after being operated on, delivering two or three speeches a day, part of them in Spanish.

He marked his arrival at Caracas on 21 September, with a denunciation of "hegemonies", praise for national independence and a tribute to the attitude adopted by Venezuela to Free France. The following day he was at Bogotà, where he visited Bolívar's house and recalled, before the country's parliament, the role that the ideas of the French Revolution had played in the emancipation of Colombia. And at Quito, dominated by a junta of four generals, he vaunted the "decisive strengthening of our Latinity": he had come out with the word that was to ruffle a few feathers in largely Indian countries like Bolivia and Peru, where he was to call next.

Here and there he was reminded that independence did not necessarily involve the renunciation of the United States. At Lima and at Cochabamba in Bolivia, he pleaded for stabilization in the prices of tropical agricultural produce. At Lima he referred to "those most disinterested of men, the soldiers", who were to hold on to power there for nearly twenty years, and he advised the Chileans to adopt the procedure of referendum. They did so six months later – without, in any case, there being any apparent link between this constitutional innovation and the leadership that they were to endure thereafter.

Passing through the Magellan Straits on board the *Colbert*, de Gaulle landed at Buenos Aires on 3 October. Warned that several of his hosts, from Lima to Santiago, had regretted that he spoke not so much of cooperation with Europe as with France, he referred to "the old world that, recovering from its divisions, will show itself once again to be the great source of human reason". But, the visitor added, "we are in the century in which Latin America, marching towards prosperity, power and influence, would see its day arrive, as Bolívar predicted". He could not go to Paraguay without appearing at the side of the sinister dictator Stroessner and, in Uruguay, he received an even more friendly welcome than elsewhere. He ended his dazzling tour in Brazil, at Brasilia where, taking account of the close links between the regime of General Castelo Branco and the United States, he modified his calls for independence with a few reminders of the realities represented by American organizations and the proximity of the United States. The General was content to say in his end of year speech on 31 December 1964 in Paris: "We have made ever closer contacts with Latin America, a continent with a very vast future and one particularly close to us in mind and heart."

The general impression left by this visit is that of a challenge thrown at the United States, but anyone who re-reads or reflects upon the texts and accounts of witnesses will rectify this: what was striking, especially after his visit to Bolivia, was the visitor's prudence, his concern not to offend his allies in Washington – whether this reserve was or was not dictated by what his hosts had not failed to tell him of the firmness of the links that bound them to Washington.

Keen to be reconciled with the Latin American masses, did de Gaulle think of embracing Cuba after the revolution? The Algerian war had long kept Castro and his supporters at a distance from Paris. Once the Evian accords had been signed

and the political support given by de Gaulle to Kennedy during the Missile Crisis
had been forgotten, there was talk of contacts, of visits to Paris by Che Guevara.
There was even talk, after these contacts, of deliveries of French arms to Cuba.
But seven years earlier a curious diplomatic episode had taken place that says a
great deal about Franco-Cuban relations, and also about Franco-American relations during the Eisenhower period. This is what an informed French diplomat
has to say on the matter:

> In 1959, I received a visit from a Cuban emissary who came and explained to
> me that the United States had cut off all supplies to his country. Since so
> much of the fabric of the Cuban economy was of North American origin,
> nothing worked in his country any more and the crisis was assuming
> catastrophic proportions. So Castro's government was asking France to take
> the situation in hand by helping Cuba to get her economy working again.
> Cuba, moreover, was able to pay for any such aid with her exports of sugar
> and was not therefore asking for financial help. I summarized this meeting in
> a note that was to reach the Elysée, where General de Gaulle jotted down his
> comments on it: he agreed in principle, but added that we would have to get
> the green light from Washington, since Cuba was "in the strategic zone of
> interest of the United States". This note came back to me and my depart-
> ment made approaches to the American Embassy in Paris. Some weeks later,
> I received a visit from an American diplomat who told me: "Thumbs down.
> In Washington we don't think the Cuban regime will last more than six
> months."[17]

The fact that Paris was to comply with the American diagnosis of the Cuban
situation shows just how limited Gaullian neutralism was, and the nature of de
Gaulle's "anti-Americanism".

To the credit of de Gaulle's Latin American policy, one must put the operation
to save Régis Debray, who had been captured along with some Bolivian rebels by a
crack squad of soldiers who rarely showed any mercy and who had just killed Che
Guevara. Handed over to General Barrientos, whose reputation made people
tremble, Debray was saved by the personal intervention of General de Gaulle to
the Bolivian authorities. The President of the Republic put his reputation at risk in
order to save one of the heralds of the Latin American revolution.

Was de Gaulle really the promoter of a world-wide "third force", of what was
already called the Non-Aligned Movement – a diplomatic expression of the realities that cover the Third World? Was de Gaulle a neutralist, in search of a middle
position in the name of which he might have stood between the hegemonic
superpowers?

I would be tempted to refute this interpretation by quoting this or that statement
– or this or that act – of the General, if I had not discovered, during a visit to
Yugoslavia, a curious document: the message addressed to General de Gaulle on 7
March 1968 by Marshal Tito. The father of the Non-Aligned Movement was
inviting the French head of State to a conference on this theme to take place at
Belgrade the following summer – a project that was to be ruined when the Soviet

Union invaded Czechoslovakia. Tito's letter to de Gaulle was not a formal invitation. Nevertheless, it was a discreet invitation and was expressed in a tone that implied that for the Yugoslav marshal, de Gaulle was now sympathetic to this "constructive programme of independence and economic progress".

By not responding to this appeal, was de Gaulle showing that non-alignment did not concern him? Or that, in order to achieve it, he could not align himself with a Communist? It should be noted that a few weeks later, in May 1968, his attention was occupied with other subjects. Not, it should be said, that the tumult in Paris made him postpone his last trip abroad as head of State to Romania, which was also concerned with non-alignment and was sometimes called the France of the Eastern bloc. The words exchanged with Ceauşescu at this time would not have come as a disappointment to Marshal Tito.

But what is this? De Gaulle a neutralist, de Gaulle breaking with the United States, de Gaulle transformed into a European Nehru? No. Whatever his long-term views were, circumstances diverted the General from such an adventurous choice. Just before leaving office, the founder of the Fifth Republic was going to try to get closer to London and to renew France's adhesion to the Atlantic Treaty. However difficult he may have been, de Gaulle was to remain to the end – despite what might be called the nuclear vertigo – an ally of the West.

CHAPTER THIRTY-ONE

The Nuclear "I"

For de Gaulle, the possession of nuclear weapons was always more than a symbolic gesture: it was the essential attribute of national independence. No State could decide its fate without possessing the ultimate weapon. There was no sovereignty without the terror inspired by the memory of Hiroshima. Everything that he had wanted to be, everything that he had been – and everything that he suffered from for not having been – required that he endow himself with this irreplaceable asset. Nuclear power was, therefore, entirely commensurate with Gaullism.

Nobody had understood better or more quickly than he the equalizing or levelling power of the nuclear bomb. Furthermore, the person who was invested with the power to use it became a unique being, a solitary individual as the true leader ought to be, endowed with a power that could not be shared. In an inviolable France, de Gaulle was without equal. The absolute dream was realized. There was no Jupiter without lightning. Without Jupiter, what would the lightning amount to?

The possession of a nuclear capability fulfilled the Gaullian project. But it did not proceed from his system. Some time before de Gaulle became President, the French atom bomb was in gestation. So necessary had it seemed that the Fourth Republic had launched France into that adventure. Thus, just prior to the presidential elections of 1965, a pamphlet published by the Gaullist party, the UNR, could remind the electors that "de Gaulle has invented nothing, he has merely accelerated an evolution that had become irreversible".

From Charles de Gaulle's point of view, everything went back to the conversation he had, on 11 June 1944 in Ottawa, with two French scientists, Bertrand Goldschmidt and Jules Guéron, who had been working for many months in Montreal with an Anglo-Canadian team extracting plutonium from the supply of "heavy water" transferred in 1940 from Norway to France, then to Britain* and, finally, to Canada. Goldschmidt and Guéron, although not working directly on the weapon itself, had taken the initiative of warning de Gaulle (who, of course, was kept in the dark by Washington and London) of what had to be called "apocalyptic work". The two French scientists believed that they had a right to inform de Gaulle not only because Free France represented an important element in the shared resources, but because the research partly originated in France: it was in Paris that artificial radioactivity had been discovered by Frédéric and Irène Joliot-Curie, in 1934;** and it was in Paris, too, that the principles of the nuclear reactor

*On board the *Milan*, 16 June 1940, on which Charles de Gaulle had also embarked for his second trip to London.
**A discovery that won them the Nobel Prize for Chemistry in 1935.

had been discovered in May 1939, by the team of physicists at the Collège de France: Joliot, Francis Perrin, Hans Halban and Lev Kowarski. The explosions of August 1945 obviously seemed to de Gaulle as foreshadowing a new world. Without concealing either the terror he felt or the admiration he had for the way in which the United States had used its monopoly, he decided very quickly not to allow France to be outside that research. On 18 October 1945, a few days after the publication of an article by a strategist whom he respected above all others on the nuclear revolution, General de Gaulle set up the Commissariat à l'Energie Atomique (CEA), entrusting its direction to Frédéric Joliot.

The CEA seemed, at this time, to be working solely in the direction of civil energy. The General had just declared: "as for the bomb, we have time". Frédéric Joliot, who had just joined the Communist Party, did not conceal his hostility to the military use of the atom. Whatever thoughts General de Gaulle may have had, he never doubted the loyalty of the man whom he had put at the head of the CEA and said as much to Joliot's assistant, Francis Perrin, himself a militant socialist and opposed to the militarization of nuclear energy.[1]

The structure and functioning of the CEA reflected the extraordinary importance that General de Gaulle attached to it from the outset: it was practically exempt from that fundamental rule of public administration represented by the supervision of expenditure by the Finance Ministry. It was an extraordinary privilege and one that meant that it continued to enjoy generous funding. Sensing that the Commission was gradually moving towards military research, Joliot denounced these aims as early as 1948, with such insistence and so publicly that, in 1949, he was removed from his post and replaced by his friend Francis Perrin. But his wife, Irène Curie-Joliot, continued her work for the CEA.

It was Félix Gaillard who gave the organization its decisive thrust. First, in 1952, while Secretary of State in the Pinay government, he got a five-year plan of nuclear research adopted; then, on 11 April 1958, just before the collapse of Pinay's government, he took the decision for the first French atom bomb to be exploded in early 1960. Pierre Mendès France also played an important role in this, first by setting up on 4 November 1954 a preparatory commission concerned with the nuclear explosion (whose scientific adviser was Yves Rocard, father of the future Prime Minister, Michel Rocard), then by defining at an inter-ministerial committee meeting, on 26 December of the same year, the arrangements for the manufacture of the bomb.

No one was better informed than the General of the progress of research. The director of the CEA was now Pierre Guillaumat, a Gaullist sympathizer, and the head of the information service was Olivier Guichard, a trusted colleague of the General's. So he was able, at his press conference of 7 April 1954, to come out very firmly in favour of the manufacture of atomic weapons by France.

Another source of information and inspiration appeared very soon, and in the oddest way. General Pierre Gallois, a former Free French veteran, an airman with a fertile mind and fearless imagination, was then one of the assistants of General Lauris Norstadt, Commander of NATO's airforces and a man well informed in atomic matters. This American officer encouraged his French colleague to relate to de Gaulle the development of the nuclear debate, regarding it as absurd to keep so experienced a strategist outside such considerations. This suggests that not all those responsible on the American side insisted on excluding France.

In the evening of 2 April 1956, Pierre Gallois turned up at the Hôtel La Pérouse bringing documents, maps and tables built up over the past three years to illustrate NATO's research. At the end of a two-hour exposition, he was surprised to hear de Gaulle respond with the tone and vocabulary of an old hand. Quite clearly, the General had kept scrupulously up to date with current research.

How can anyone who has read *Le Fil de l'epée* and *Vers l'armée de métier* be in any doubt that Charles de Gaulle was attentive and open to this kind of research or thinking? And at a time when the means at France's disposal were no longer what they were, who could be more pleased than he at the idea of possessing the equalizing power of the nuclear bomb? Possessed by a firm hand and a strong will, the shortest but sharpest sword could represent a powerful dissuasion equal to that of Wotan's spear. Moreover, Gallois pointed out, the very smallness of the power involved would be a safeguard. In the past, the great size of a territory and population gave a country an advantage in recruitment and capacity for manoeuvre; now, by virtue of proportional deterrence, to be a small target gave a country an advantage over a huge aggressor.

It should come as no surprise, therefore, that the General's return to power was followed by a flood of decisions concerning the acceleration or promotion of the nuclear effort. On 2 June 1958, a man was appointed to head the Armed Forces Ministry whose name – as we have seen – later became identified with the CEA, Pierre Guillaumat. On 10 June, the Commission for Special Weapons was set up under an officer who, with Generals Crépin and Buchalet, had been associated for five years with every development of French nuclear weapons, General Ailleret. In April 1958, the military specialists had been ordered to plan an explosion to take place in early 1960. On 12 July, de Gaulle summoned General Buchalet and ordered him to begin work, assuring him that absolute priority would be given to the undertaking. De Gaulle emerged from their talk convinced that things were well on their way and that they would soon have to go over into thermonuclear research. For in so far as the weapon that France would have at her disposal was "a political means to sit at the table of the Great Powers",[2] he considered that he would be able to derive full advantage from that conquest only if the asset that he brandished was not undermined by those possessed by his potential partners: the United States for the past six years, the Soviet Union for the past three years, and soon Great Britain.

The decision to go over from nuclear to thermonuclear research was not adopted without debate. The resistance to the project put up by Pierre Guillaumat was significant. The Armed Forces Minister maintained that it went well beyond the financial resources at his disposal – unless the nation put an end to all military activities in Algeria which he, Guillaumat, did not favour at all.

Passing over opposition, General de Gaulle decided "to initiate the carrying out of a programme that would lead to thermonuclear weapons, in particular by the construction of a factory for enriching uranium into isotope 235 by gaseous diffusion", at an inter-ministerial committee held on 16 July 1959.[3]

It was also a time that saw the publication, in the form of a vigorously argued doctrine, of the project of one of its inspirers, General Pierre Gallois, *Stratégie à l'âge nucléaire*.[4] This book was often regarded as a reflection of de Gaulle's own thinking, whereas in fact it was rather one of its sources and perhaps the most stimulating.

De Gaulle himself had chosen to publicize his decisions and the strategy that he had adopted in two forms; that of a lecture at the Ecole Militaire, to officers of the various institutes of advanced studies on 3 November 1959; and that of a press conference, held at the Elysée a week later. He told the officers at the Ecole Militaire:

> The view of a war and even of a battle in which France would no longer act on her own behalf, and in accordance with her own wishes, such a view is unacceptable. The system that has been called "integration" has had its day. The consequence is that we must quite obviously be able to provide ourselves, over the coming years, with a force capable of acting on our behalf, what is commonly called a "strike force" capable of being deployed at any time and in any place. It goes without saying that the basis for such a force would be atomic weapons – whether we made them ourselves or bought them – but, in either case, they must belong to us. And since it is possible to destroy France from any point in the world, our force must be so made that it can act anywhere in the world. In the domain of defence, this will be our great work over the years ahead. The possible use of such a force must be an essential object of your studies and work.[5]

On 10 November, the General summoned the press to the Elysée. His exposition was devoted to détente, of which, it seemed to him, there were "a few signs" in the East. But someone questioned him about the French nuclear tests in the Sahara that had been the object of strong criticism in the United Nations. It was an opportunity to make an uncompromising confession of faith: "If anyone asked France to give up her atomic weapons, while others possessed such weapons and were developing enormous quantities of them, there would be no question of her taking up the invitation." Without recognizing that "the sort of balance that has been established between the atomic power of the two camps is for the moment a factor in peace," de Gaulle wondered about "what will happen tomorrow", raising several hypotheses from the most predictable to the most appalling, "some sudden advance in the development of space rockets" that would challenge "the peaceful intentions" of one of the two camps, or a situation in which, "the political *données* having completely changed, those powers possessing the nuclear monopoly come to an agreement to carve up the world" or, again, a situation in which, agreeing to spare each other, they agree "to crush the others".

Having given free vent to his fears – collusion between the superpowers over the head of and at the expense of Europe, or transformation of the old continent into a battlefield by the two monsters – General de Gaulle ended by saying that France, "by giving herself nuclear weapons, is rendering a service to the balance of the world".[6]

The statements made by Charles de Gaulle could not fail to bring out into the open a question that always invited sharply divided answers. We shall see that the reactions of the United States, then of France's other allies, and finally of international opinion would vary according to the personalities of the leaders involved, the relation of international forces and circumstances – the Third World, at first very hostile, eventually saw the French bomb, before the Chinese bomb, as a sort of symbol of non-alignment.

It was quite normal that Washington should have the greatest reservations about France's entry into the nuclear club. The *ultima ratio* of modern strategy, the nuclear decision, was the exclusive attribute of the head of State and, moreover, of the leader of the Atlantic Alliance. When Paris reserved the right to use this or that part of her forces, Washington might feel irritation, seeing it as a sign of the dispersal of allied forces. But the arrival of a new centre of atomic decision, especially in the hands of an individual like de Gaulle, posed the American leadership a problem in the starkest way. Nuclear strategy required centralization, if not a monopoly of decision-making. By challenging – if only with a still weak and outdated weapon – Washington's ultimate power of decision-making, de Gaulle was upsetting everybody's presuppositions and plans.

Of course, the British had already had atomic weapons for seven years, but although the British had not resigned themselves to it, by the end of the 1950s London had accepted the integration of its atomic forces and their handing over to the strategic needs of NATO. Often at the forefront of discoveries in weapon technology, the British felt increasingly dependent on the Americans for warheads.

Is it certain that the French acquired a nuclear capability against the wishes of her allies? Although it is undeniable that the French bomb was regarded, under Eisenhower, with a mixture of incredulity and, once testing had begun, of irritation, then under Kennedy and Johnson of increasing irritation, not all the signs coming from the other side of the Atlantic confirmed this.

It is true that the MacMahon Law, passed in 1946, forbade the communication of any information on nuclear matters to anyone, allies or not. Seven years later this text was amended to benefit the British, when Washington, disconcerted by the explosion of the Soviet thermonuclear bomb of 1953, chose to appeal to all. Only London benefited regularly from this flexibility, but exceptions were made. Francis Perrin recounts how, in the early 1950s, Robert Oppenheimer, one of the three or four "fathers" of the new weapon, told him: "You ought to make an 'A' bomb. It would be good for France. And it isn't very difficult. All you'd need is a metallurgist endowed with a little imagination."[7]

Jean Renou, for a long time director of public relations at the CEA, tells how Admiral Strauss, the "big boss" of the Atomic Energy Commission, had tried in late 1957, during talks with Pierre Guillaumat, to dissuade his French colleague from continuing with the construction of the bomb. Then, seeing that his arguments were not getting very far, he concluded: "Anyway, I can see you'll build that isotopic separation factory at Pierrelatte, and I shall shout all the same 'Vive la France!'"[8]

At the same period, a French delegation, led by Admiral Barthélemy and General Buchalet, set out for the United States with a view to negotiating the buying of an atomic submarine, obtaining a delivery of enriched uranium and visiting the test sites in Nevada. Washington refused to hand over a submarine, but agreed to the visit to Nevada and the delivery of uranium 235 with a view to feeding the engine of an experimental submarine on land.

In fact, there were groups in the United States that thought very differently on the matter. The one led by Admiral Strauss had become convinced that some of the French arguments were well founded. On the other hand, the group led by Admiral Rickover opposed any transfer of technology, raw material and information to France. Learning of the explosion of the French bomb, Admiral Rickover growled: "There's been a leak."[9]

When de Gaulle decided to make the Mirage IV, the first French jet capable of carrying a nuclear payload, it was noted that if it were to have optimal range, this machine would need supply planes, the best being the American C135s. Washington did not object to a deal being made between Boeing, the manufacturers of the plane, and France. This shows that the Rickover type of opposition had been modified. General Curtis Le May, Chief of General Staff of the US Airforce, said: "Since they've got the Mirage IV, they might as well have the best possible equipment!"

Lastly, on the subject of raw materials, it was noted that whenever French officials tried (at least until 1960) to obtain uranium in countries over which the United States had a greater or lesser influence, the price suddenly rose as if by magic. But if the Americans had really wanted to put significant obstacles in the way of the manufacture of the French bomb, they could clearly have done more.

The crucial decision was taken by the Debré government on 17 March 1959: "Absolute priority will be given to the realization of the strike force and to the manufacture of the atom bomb." All those who were associated with it – Pierre Guillaumat, Pierre Messmer, Francis Perrin, Generals Buchalet, Maurin and Ailleret – have testified to the privileges, psychological as well as financial, that the General made available to the scientists and technicians associated with the nuclear programme. This is what Guillaumat has to say: "I was often struck, and even troubled, by General de Gaulle's indulgence towards the engineers. Some took advantage to write veritable 'letters to Father Christmas', knowing that, whatever resistance ministers might put up, they could count on the agreement of the General." And Pierre Messmer, his successor, says: "General de Gaulle was excessively indulgent towards the engineers. As the Armed Forces Minister at the time, I sometimes found the CEA extravagant, but was practically always forced to sign blank cheques. The General invariably said: 'When you want something, you have to be prepared to pay for it.'"[10]

Several witnesses have described him, during the trip that he made in September 1966 to Muroroa to attend "Operation Betelgeuse", the explosion of the last French "A" bomb before the thermonuclear ones. For reasons both technical and meteorological, the explosion had to be delayed. He was in a terrible mood. "When the first glow appeared," Francis Perrin recounts, "it was red, which seemed to mean to us that it was a failure. There were two seconds of despair: then we heard over the radio of a British patrol plane: 'The French have done a damned rough explosion!' That's how we learnt that the operation had succeeded."[11]

When the mushroom unfolded, Pierre Messmer goes on, General de Gaulle roared out, "C'est magnifique!", which expressed "the admiration he felt for the work of the engineers, their success justifying the indulgence he had shown them".[12]

Research in this area had long been marking time. How were they to pass from the nuclear to the thermonuclear, from fission to fusion? In *Le Mal français*, Alain Peyrefitte, who was Minister of Research and Atomic and Space Affairs from January 1966 to April 1967, reports a conversation that he had with General de Gaulle in January 1966, which shows that his "indulgence" had found limits:

> "Find out why the CEA has not yet managed to make the 'H' bomb. It's going on for ever! It has just been explained to me that it will take several years more. I can't wait more than two or three years! I won't see out this seven-year term. I had to present myself, to make sure we won. But I shan't go on to the end. But before leaving I want the first test to have taken place. Are we to be the only one of the five nuclear powers that hasn't reached the thermonuclear stage? Are we going to let the Chinese outstrip us? If we don't get there while I'm here, we never will."
>
> "How long are you giving me?"
>
> "Until 1968 at the latest."
>
> Those responsible at the CEA cried: "Mission impossible!"[13]

At this time, they were not considering the manufacture of the "H" bomb for a very long time – and that on condition that the principle of "fusion" was discovered in 1968. If the General managed to overcome the resistance of those who wanted to keep to the nuclear method, if the political or politico-military problem was resolved, those in charge of the military applications of the CEA could not solve the technical problem without, they said, uranium 235, or the giant computers that the United States kept for themselves.

"Every now and then, after a meeting of the Council of Ministers," Alain Peyrefitte recounts, the General would say: "Well? What about your H bomb?" An "H Committee" brought together each month, around the Minister, the leading lights of the CEA: Francis Perrin, Robert Hirsch (Pierre Guillaumat's successor) and Jacques Robert, director of DAM (Direction des Applications Militaires). It was no use. Shortly afterwards there took place what Peyrefitte calls: "The vicious circle of renunciation" and it took place at Matignon and at the Armed Forces Ministry. Why couldn't they be content with an "A" bomb made bigger or more efficient? Wouldn't the deterrent effect be the same? This type of argument soon proved to be absurd, taking into account the methods of investigation at the disposal of France's rivals, partners and enemies, and taking into account the fact that deterrence is based only on credibility. Urged by de Gaulle to get out of this vicious circle, the Minister for Research asked his scientific advisers, Jean-Luc Bruneau and Edmond Parker, to find the specialist in scientific synthesis who, according to him, would alone be able to bring together the multi-disciplinary data of the affair. They drew his attention to a young physicist named Roger Dautray, who had been winning a reputation for himself in a laboratory of the CEA at Saclay. "He was," Peyrefitte recounts, "exactly the type of man we needed:"

[He had] an exceptionally gifted brain, capable of assimilating rapidly all the disciplines necessary to the synthesis and mastering them, of understanding the language of the various kinds of analysis involved and bringing them together. I advised Robert Hirsch to entrust him with the scientific direction of the affair: around him, we would form a new team. Robert Hirsch did his skilful best to solve the delicate human problems involved in such a reorganization.*[14]

Things went well. Dautray was able to take in hand the results obtained by researchers at the Direction des Applications Militaires, such as Billaud, Carayol and Dagens. In a very short time the pace of work increased rapidly and a complete synthetic and systematic view of the weapon emerged. Soon everything converged on very clearly defined objectives, culminating in the formula of the thermonuclear weapon. So well had things gone that a year later de Gaulle saw the fulfilment of the wish that he had so passionately held and peremptorily expressed: the first two French thermonuclear bombs were exploded in August 1968.

What role had de Gaulle played in this process? The pressure exerted on his colleagues – beginning with his Prime Minister, Armed Forces Minister and Minister for Research – had been decisive in three domains: that of place (his insistence made it possible for France to use at Mururoa a test centre that would be usable for several decades), that of time (his demands succeeded in wearing down resistance in his own lifetime and succeeded before the arrival of less determined individuals), and that of the nature of the weapon. At the time when the decision was taken to pass over to the thermonuclear weapon, the objective seemed to be the search for higher energies for the French nuclear weapons (to pass from kilotonnes to megatonnes). In fact, looking back, we now see that what made the thermonuclear formula possible allowed France to make her weapons smaller, to hold several thermonuclear weapons in the head of a single rocket, each having its own aim, what is called the MIRV, or multiple independent re-entry vehicle.

Charles de Gaulle rarely felt the need to justify the "absolute priority" that he gave to nuclear weapons either to French public opinion or to his allies. On 10 November 1959, stress had been laid once and for all on equality of rights. France could not be excluded from the atomic club. It therefore seemed to him to be quite useless to make any plea for nuclear weapons.

General de Gaulle's first argument** – no national independence without the supreme weapon – might be regarded as the only one. If it is true that the fate of the world, that is to say the future of the nations – or groups of nations – depends on this type of weapon and if it is proved that France can produce it, then it is not

*A solution that Peyrefitte's successor at the Ministry, Maurice Schumann, had the merit to keep and complete.
**I have tried to summarize here the arguments collected from some of the General's close colleagues and advisers. This does not mean that I share them. I shall omit here the debate on the fundamental questions, which in no way influenced Charles de Gaulle's decisions.

conceivable that our country could renounce it. What destiny has a people whose salvation depends on the good will of another – even if there is not the shadow of a doubt that this other people would come to its aid?

From 1940 to 1945, Charles de Gaulle had had to beg his allies for the means to fight. When one examines de Gaulle's motives for establishing an independent French nuclear capability, one may forget those years too easily. Anything was better than having to beg Roosevelt's successors to be so kind as to give him the means of taking Paris, of saving Strasbourg or liberating Royan. For him, anyone who depends on the decision of a foreign power or of a body like NATO, which is totally manipulated by a foreign power, cannot be free. In time of war, of course, powers of coordination have to be conceded to some new Eisenhower, but, in the meantime, he could not bear that the decision to make peace or war, or to live freely, should depend on another power.

Mention should be made here of an episode that helped to anchor de Gaulle in his determination. In September 1958 he decided to find out what the disposition of NATO troops was in France. He invited General Norstadt to come and expound for him the broad outlines. Norstadt agreed and, in the presence of his Allied General Staff, he made an extremely brilliant exposition of it. De Gaulle congratulated him and asked the American general to tell him the locations of nuclear weapons in France and secondly, what the targets for those weapons were. "I'm afraid I cannot answer those questions unless we are alone," said Norstadt. "Very well," said de Gaulle. The entourages of the two generals left. "Well?" "Well, General, I'm afraid I can't answer your questions." "General," de Gaulle concluded, "this is the last time, I am telling you, that a French leader will hear such an answer!"[15]

What is one to think of a country that, in order to *survive*, hands itself over to another? What is the point of protecting oneself against invasion, enslavement, annihilation, if, when all is said and done, our life, our freedom, our fate depend on a Senate majority in Washington, on elections in Iowa or North Dakota?

De Gaulle's argument very soon became more serious as a result of what might be called a climate of suspicion, which arose in September 1959 during the Eisenhower–de Gaulle talks. The General's suspicion might be summed up thus: I, de Gaulle, know that you, Eisenhower, would dare to risk the survival of your country in order to safeguard Europe: you have already proved your devotion. But what of your successors? Will they take the risk of devastating American cities so that Berlin, Brussels and Paris might remain free?

From then on, General de Gaulle was convinced that recourse to nuclear weapons was conceivable, on the part of the power making the decision, only if the national "sanctuary" was in danger. Hence the terrible hypothesis of a common decision by the two superpowers not to attack one another directly, and to confine their quarrel to the area between the Elbe and the Atlantic.

Would this notion be too offensive for the leaders of the Atlantic Alliance? It usually took a different form in the General's statements: that of an arrangement between the new superpowers to settle in terms of bombs not exploded, but counted, non-battles calculated in terms of respective potentialities, as in negotiations between Chinese generals in the time of Sun-Tse, or the fate of Europe in a chess game – Russian knights and American rooks arbitrating, in the heavy silence of absolute co-deterrence, the destiny of the old disarmed continent.

This suspicion, which led him not only to refuse to turn France into an American protectorate, but even to doubt Washington's will to guarantee that protection automatically, was enriched by de Gaulle with arguments ranging from the indecision of his Western allies when faced with Khrushchev's threats over Berlin to Washington's hesitation in resorting to the atomic ultimatum during the Cuban Missile Crisis, via the revision of American strategy, abandoning in 1962 Dulles's theory of "massive retaliation" for Robert McNamara's "flexible response".

It was at this time that General de Gaulle's "suspicion" deepened. Directly threatened by Khrushchev's audacity in installing missiles under his nose in Cuba, John Kennedy did not dare to brandish the supreme threat, ensuring that discussions only involved conventional weapons, as McNamara proudly makes clear. Exactly how "flexible" would the response be if it were not Miami and Washington that were under threat, but only Rotterdam, Milan or Strasbourg? And on that occasion the United States had been represented by a team of bold, ambitious young men, impatient to restore American greatness, to stand up to Soviet power.

Others preferred to see in this affair a demonstration of Kennedy's authority as possessor of nuclear power, of his ability to keep his major assets in reserve, of his virtuosity in playing at a kind of restrained, postponed deterrence. De Gaulle was not unaware of this aspect of things. What he remembered of the crisis above all was that the White House team suffered from what might be called a strong nuclear retention and that if one's fate were in their hands...

De Gaulle's argument took on new force when he noted that the American administration had radically altered the strategic principles of the "Alliance" without the slightest consultation with its allies. To shift from "massive reprisals" – which automatically justified an atomic response to an attack from Europe by the Soviets – to this "flexible response", which presupposed a study case by case and blow by blow, according to scenarios worked out by the brilliant Washington team of MacGeorge Bundy, Walt Rostow, Alan Enthoven, Henry Kissinger, Tom Schelling and Hermann Kahn, involved a radically new set of perspectives for Washington's European allies.

Without consulting or even warning them, Defense Secretary Robert McNamara, in an address to the Atlantic Council in The Hague in May 1962, then in a speech to the University of Michigan on 16 June, made official the strategic transformation decided on by the Pentagon from massive reprisals to flexible response – while condemning in passing, and without the least accommodation, the nuclear forces of the British and French allies, which, the Americans feared, might be guilty of an "unflexible response". So the European allies were deprived of the automatic threat of a nuclear response to Soviet attack and urged to show their willingness to make their own response flexible. It did not need any more to confirm de Gaulle in his mistrust.

It was a mistrust that was to become deeper as the Americans increased their presence in Vietnam, gave their unconditional support to the most risky initiatives of Israel, or involved themselves in Latin America. By committing themselves to so

many peripheral undertakings, were the American leaders still the credible sen-
tinels of Fortress Europe? Should not the old continent, beginning with France,
now look after its own safety?

So de Gaulle had a great many arguments to justify the decision that he had
taken. But since those arguments had not proved wholly adequate, he was to
introduce the domestic interests that would favour the possession of nuclear
weapons. The first concerns the French army, both its moral health and its level of
technological development. In most of his addresses to the army, from 1959
onwards, de Gaulle stressed this great mission. Deprived of Algeria, the army was
being offered the world of scientific discovery, high technology, strategy on a world
level. The army was not entirely convinced by this swap of Mururoa for Algiers,
but the airforce and above all the navy were quick to see the justification.

Charles de Gaulle took little notice of all the debates, indictments, denunci-
ations and warnings that the creation of the French nuclear capability gave rise to.
For him, the important thing was to obtain it and to be able to brandish the tool of
national independence. Since early 1959, he had been informed by his experts at
the CEA that the explosion could take place, in early February 1960, on a site to
the south-west of Reggane, in the Tanezrouft desert in the middle of the Sahara.
And the General was sufficiently confident of his right and of the technical
preparation of the affair to inform President Eisenhower, on 2 September 1959,
five months ahead, of the date, place, nature and power of the explosion.

This is how General Buchalet, who for ten years was associated with the
development of the operation, describes it: "On 13 February 1960, dawn was
breaking at the far end of the Reggane firing range. We were all sitting, wearing
dark glasses, with our backs to the tower on which the experimental mechanism
was supposed to explode. We heard the countdown. At that point, an important
figure sitting next to me leaned over to me and said: 'Are you sure you're really
going to have a nuclear explosion?' A good question!"[16]

That morning, de Gaulle – who had scarcely emerged from the tragic week of
the barricades in Algiers – would be receiving Bruno Kreisky, then Austrian
Foreign Minister. He was woken half an hour earlier than usual by his aide-de-
camp: the explosion had succeeded. On 13 February 1960, at 6.30 a.m., France
joined the atomic club – even though, in the opinion of such experts as General
Crépin, this had been no more than an "experimental" test.[17]

Less than an hour after the Reggane explosion, de Gaulle's joy exploded in the
form of a fourteen-word statement that, for once, because it was an event without
precedent in national history, borrowed at least one of his few words of foreign
extraction: "Hurrah for France! From this morning, she is stronger and prouder."
On 25 February, he declared to the crowds in Languedoc: "If France must have
allies, she has no need of a protector!"

By rejecting the Americans, de Gaulle assumed a role comparable to that of a
detonator. France, now the owner of an independent nuclear deterrent, might
force her greatest ally to employ its own nuclear weapons, even if she didn't wish
to, should France herself encounter a threat from the Soviet Union.

Some of the best French specialists believed that France should play this ingenious role, notably General Beaufre[18] and Raymond Aron, who once wrote that the threat "to use French force as a detonator is the only deterrent function it can fulfil in the present situation".[19]

A determined adversary of this view was Pierre Gallois, who quoted a remark made to him by Harlan Cleveland, former United States Ambassador to NATO. When a French officer confided to Dean Rusk, John Kennedy's Secretary of State, that French nuclear weapons had no other objective than to force the Americans to "go to extremes" if they hesitated to respond in this way to a Soviet attack against any part of Europe, Rusk replied quite simply that, in such circumstances, Washington's reaction would be quite simply to warn the Soviet leaders of the origin of the missiles that had been directed at them and to assure them that the Americans would not have resorted to them.[20]

Although such an account over-simplifies the exchanges on which the essentially psychological game of deterrence rests, it certainly draws attention to the limits of the "detonator" tactic. De Gaulle had no need of this role: his vision was higher and on a broader front. He was not content with the function of a provocateur, any more than that of a protégé.

De Gaulle was not claiming to be giving France, or himself, a nuclear "doctrine". But the military corps, which he had launched into this venture – and which had gone into it with some reluctance, just as twenty-five years earlier over the introduction of tank divisions – demanded at least an overall scheme and directives. It was with this in view that Pierre Messmer, the Armed Forces Minister, formed the Centre de prospective et d'évaluation (CPE) in 1962.

Forty months later, this group produced a thick document which Messmer thought so interesting that he passed it on to General de Gaulle. The General let it be known, through the head of his military office, Admiral Philippon, that he approved of its conclusions, though he observed that by over-stressing the "potential" aspect of the conflict one ran the risk of demobilizing the military corps. It stressed above all the autonomy of French decision-making.

It was from this global panoply that de Gaulle built up his thinking on the subject. In his eyes, the independent nuclear capability that France had acquired aimed to establish her autonomy in decision-making in the event of a threat of conflict. Of course, those who conceived the French nuclear strategy certainly did not claim that it would always work on its own. In their view, it could be included in a much wider system, either with a view to massive reprisals, or to one of the stages of the "flexible response". But then that flexibility would not be decided unilaterally by the USA, but in Paris. The multipolarity of action, therefore, brought out national sovereignty in a collective context. If it was a question of risking the survival of the national community, no one should take the place of the man whom the French had elected to do so.

Although it was necessary to design a nuclear doctrine that expressed Charles de Gaulle's thoughts on the matter, there would be talk of "deterrence by the weak on the strong", such as had been described by General Gallois in *Stratégie de l'âge nucléaire*, and which consisted of laying down the ratio between the stake represented by a given country and the capacity for destruction at its disposal. Provided it permanently protected its instrument of deterrence from enemy attack, the State in question could create a situation in which its ability to take reprisals was equal to or exceeded the value of the objective that it represented.

De Gaulle, who, if Pierre Guillaumat is to be believed, was in the grip of "apparent hesitations" and, at one time, was thinking of "what he called the drop-by-drop" method (if you destroy Metz, I shall raze Kiev), seems to have rejected it in the mid-1960s at the time of the CPE report.

France had the means of practising "minimal deterrence" as soon as she had at her disposal the elements of "nuclear coercion", which would have the potential to destroy the enemy's means of retaliation – an aim that had been abandoned by both superpowers, contenting themselves with the notion of Mutual Assured Destruction (MAD).

A medium-sized nuclear power like France – or Britain, or China – did not have sufficient means to practise flexible response. It could exert pressure only by displaying an extreme and immediate threat. It was a strategy that was simple, inflexible and short, unless it were inserted into a larger whole. But it was at this point that one came up against the fundamental principle of independent decision-making. Moreover, that inflexibility and shortness could not operate without a good supply of psychological energy.

If it is admitted that deterrence is the product of two factors, a weapon and an aptitude to decide, the (relative) weakness of the weapon must be partially compensated for by the personal credibility of the decider. De Gaulle was not weak. But the adaptation of the weapon of deterrence must be constant, both to the means of the potential adversary and – de Gaulle could not have failed to think of this – to the personal credibility of the deciders to come.

So we are far from the oblique strategy of the "detonator", further still from a distribution of the tasks that would consist in reserving to France, or to any other power allied to the United States, the use of the tactical nuclear weapon. This idea alone could not fail to be anathema to de Gaulle, whose thought was essentially strategic.

Hence the differences that arose between de Gaulle and his American allies, first from 1962, when Robert McNamara condemned the possession of non-American nuclear weapons, especially those of France, which he could not integrate into his strategy of controlled response, then, after 3 August 1963, when Paris refused to join the nuclear non-proliferation treaty signed in Moscow between the two superpowers and Great Britain.

If, in other areas, General de Gaulle's policy towards the United States, which might be defined as harassment without break, assumed a rather artificial tone that fits MacGeorge Bundy's description of it ("We realized that this attitude suited him"[21]), the nuclear debate was of fundamental importance. John Kennedy realized as much, and that was why he spoke of an "unfriendly attitude" towards the United States.

That Washington should have insisted on minimizing the affair did not mean they were uneager to solve it. This is confirmed by a small book published in 1962 by Walter Lippmann,[22] in which the most "Gaullist" of the great American commentators differs from the General, whom he accuses of having made his nuclear capability "a stratagem that would commit the United States, while leaving the nuclear initiative to Western Europe". This amounted to turning de Gaulle's denunciation of the American nuclear monopoly back on the General himself.

The most judicious appreciation of the Gaullian question was offered by Mac-George Bundy in a letter of 16 May 1962 to Raymond Aron, who published it in his *Mémoires*:[23] "We believe that centralized control and indivisible response are by far the least dangerous means of building up the West's nuclear defense and that we could alter our present policy only for reasons of exceptional seriousness. We do not perceive the same sort of constraining requirement in the case of the French independent nuclear effort." But he added: "France has the right to undertake that effort. We may regret it, but it is not up to us to oppose it."

Firmer still, but less courteous, is the overall criticism made of this French strategy by the German politician Lothar Ruehl:

> In France, the armed forces, nuclear or non-nuclear, cannot thus be conceived in terms of independence since those terms are imagined and not real. The French armed forces can only be conceived, armed, organized, deployed and led in terms of the probabilities of a conflict in Europe from which France could not subtract herself. In reality, it is not a question of "deciding" sovereignly on the conditions in which France would or would not participate in the defence of Western Europe. For France, national security is not a function of independence, but, on the contrary, of dependence on the European system that is the very basis of her existence.[24]

In the eyes of that perspicacious German, de Gaulle and the French strategists who shared his ideas were either innocents or fools.

The American strategists continued to claim, as an absolute right, what they called the "three Cs": command, control, communication. All three were anathema to General de Gaulle's thinking: although he may have been able to accommodate himself to "command" in time of war or extreme crisis, he was not prepared to accommodate himself to "control", even that of the American nuclear stockpile placed under the rule of the "double key" (American and native), which was removed from France, at his request, in the early 1960s, and still less to the monopoly of "communication" enjoyed by Washington, that is to say, to the exclusive responsibility of exchanging with Moscow "signals" likely to deter, and of negotiating peace and the future of mankind. Let us quote here these lines by Maurice Couve de Murville:

> The peculiarity of atomic weapons is that they can only be national. The responsibilities implied in their possession are indeed those that cannot be divided, even if one wanted to, and that has never been the case. What State would consider being one day dragged into nuclear war, that is to say, risking its own destruction, by the use, outside its own decision, of weapons that it had handed over to a friendly power?[25]

On all these points disagreement was fundamental. For, as Alfred Grosser has observed, it is an "insoluble" problem:[26] the atomic poker game, with its inextricable scaffolding of "signals" and "gestures", is so played out in men's brains, and probably in so short a time, that it must, it seems, be concentrated in the hands of a single power – a power that, in the case of the West, the President of the United States cannot but claim.

But, Grosser adds, this situation is, for every lucid statesman thus excluded from the decision-making, "unbearable"[27] – especially if he happens to be a war leader who, from 1940 to 1945, witnessed the hasty retreat of France's allies at Dunkirk; the refusal of the United States to join the battle until it was forced to do so; and the fact that he had been excluded from all the strategic decisions concerning his country until the autumn of 1944. How, with such a cruel experience of "flexibility" and of the limits of coalition, could de Gaulle not have tried to arrange matters in such a way that in future France could work out her destiny other than in collective terms?

Nevertheless one is right to deplore that by thus assisting nuclear proliferation, France helped to turn the world into a jungle, haunted by suicide and annihilation. In an essay published at the time of the first French thermonuclear explosion, Léo Hamon* drew a sketch of "an atomic democracy" based both on "the end of the nuclear duopoly" and on the plurality of atomic powers. Within that five-member directory, the British, French and Chinese would obviously not be the equals of the two superpowers, since the equalizing power of the atom operated only in a period of deterrence not in its use; but they would help to found a "democracy in the ancient style", a "divided and open oligarchy"; citizens, moved by "prudence" rather than by "virtue", would act "under the supervision of the greatest number with real, but limited initiative and latitude of action". To conclude, this experienced lawyer asks, "Is democracy really anything else?"[28]

Already serious up until 1966, then envenomed by the withdrawal of France from NATO, the nuclear debate between the Western powers was brought to its climax with a definition, provided by the highest French military authorities, of the so-called "all-round" strategy, by which France seemed to slip from being an awkward but circumspect ally to being a neutral, supporting some sort of diplomatic and strategic "third way" – the "great leap forward" of the Gaullist strategy of deterrence.

We are in the early months of 1967. The United States is getting bogged down in the Vietnamese adventure. In Britain a white paper has just been published showing a renewal of the British will to power, especially on the Rhine. In France, for three years, a draft law sketches out a nuclear weapons programme that, according to de Gaulle and his experts, has culminated in the development of an SNF (Strategic Nuclear Force) whose credibility has been recognized for a year.

De Gaulle had placed General Charles Ailleret at the head of the French forces not only because he was in the forefront of those developing the bomb, but also because this great technologist possessed such intellectual brutality that the head of State used him as a sort of bulldozer. There was one man who would not flinch and who would break down any resistance in the army.**

*Professor of Law at Dijon University, former Information Minister. (trs.)
**As he had already done, ruthlessly, as Commander-in-Chief in Algeria (1961–2).

On 20 January General de Gaulle visited, as he did every year, the Institut des Hautes Etudes de Défense Nationale. What he heard there convinced him that most of the future heads of the French forces had understood nothing of the revolution in the concepts of national defence that the nuclear bomb had ushered in. Many spoke of nuclear weapons as a more sophisticated form of artillery! This attitude so disappointed and irritated him that he decided to draw up a directive summarizing the new principles of French strategy. This document, written in de Gaulle's own hand, remained confidential. It is of exceptional interest. It is one of the texts in which the General's profound views are best expressed. Unfortunately, it cannot yet be quoted word for word, but what follows may be taken as a faithful paraphrase of the original.

According to de Gaulle, the mission of the French Armed Forces would be "to be able to intervene at any point in the world, carry out an action at sea or around our own territory, and put up resistance on the national territory". In order to carry out that mission, the General added, "four* large groups of forces were to be formed, during the period 1970–80", whose essential element was "a long-range thermonuclear force capable of striking wherever necessary on the surface of the earth in order to obtain irreparable destruction in any of the great states".

According to Charles de Gaulle, this amounted to a complete system: thermonuclear bombs, intercontinental ballistic missiles, seven or eight rocket-launching submarines, "circumterrestrial" bombers, communications satellites. It was, he stressed by way of conclusion, "a planetary system".

This "planetary" directive disconcerted a good number of de Gaulle's colleagues, military and civilian. At least three of them have told me that the word "excessive" was repeated in a number of offices at the time and that the more daring of them referred to the directive's author as "unbalanced", "ageing", even "deranged".

At least one of them remained undismayed: General Ailleret, who considered the unimaginable mission entrusted to him without flinching.

The Chief of General Staff set to work. While doing his utmost to drive on the technical realization of the project, he wrote at de Gaulle's request an article intended to circulate the ideas of the presidential directive of February. This was to be the article which achieved some celebrity when published on 1 December 1967 in the unofficial *Revue de Défense Nationale* under the title "'Directed' defence or *tous azimuts* ('all-round' defence)". It made all the greater stir in that it was preceded by a drawing showing the national hexagon exploding into a hundred flashes of lightning moving in all directions: one could hardly depict better a France left alone, cut off from the rest of the world and, like Cyrano de Bergerac waving his sword at the wind, delivering blows on universal enemies.

Indeed the article did not need this provocative image to astonish its readers, who as it turned out were more numerous than the regular subscribers to that serious publication:

If France wants to be able to avoid the risks that might threaten her, she

*The other three being an intervention force (which was to become the FAR), an Air-to-earth Battle Corps and an Operational Defence of the Territory (DOT).

must have at her disposal significant quantities of megatonne, long-range ballistic missiles capable of deterring those who might wish, from whatever part of the world, to use us or destroy us in order to assist in the achievement of their war aims. To be the strongest possible in an autonomous and individual way and to possess one's own high-capacity, long-range weapons capable of deterring any aggressor from wherever he may come is clearly an entirely different formula from one in which one is constituted, for the same financial effort, as a complementary force of that of the leading member of an a priori alliance.*

General Ailleret observed that this formula would not prevent France, in a situation in which deterrence would not be enough to prevent war, from "incorporating herself as best she can" in an alliance, while remaining "free to conduct her actions". He went on to point out that it was not possible to know from which direction might come the "danger that will threaten the generations that will follow ours". "Our autonomous force" ought not, therefore, to be "pointed in a single direction, that of some a priori enemy, but be capable of intervening everywhere, be therefore what we call, in our military jargon, 'all round'." So France's objective must be to form "an all-round, world-wide thermonuclear force".[29] The reactions were stormy, right up to the head of state's close colleagues. To dare to suppose that the American ally might one day become a justifiable object of French thermonuclear weapons! Such an outrageous, absurd supposition could only come from a soldier keen to show that he was more Gaullist than de Gaulle.

But it soon became quite clear that the Chief of General Staff's article was merely the reflection of talks that he had had at the Elysée. Several witnesses, such as Admiral Sabbagh, of de Gaulle's private General Staff, and General Bourgue, Ailleret's closest colleague, have confirmed** that the article had been closely read and re-read by the head of state.

Furthermore, at least three texts by de Gaulle are enough to remove any lingering doubts about General Ailleret's fidelity to the Gaullian "doctrine". The first is the speech given to officers of the military schools on 3 November 1959: "Since it is possible that France may be destroyed, from any part of the world, our forces must be so constructed that they can act on any part of the earth..." The second of these texts is the directive for the long-term plan for 1970–80 quoted above, in which General de Gaulle spoke of "a long-range thermonuclear force capable of striking everywhere".

For greater clarity, General de Gaulle was determined to deliver the fateful words himself, on 27 January 1968, before members of the Institut des Hautes Etudes Militaires. The text that follows*** is based on notes taken by several members of the audience. It was given to me by General Bourgue, who was then in charge of studies at the Ecole Militaire.

*Which is what Great Britain does.
**Particularly at the conference at Arc-et-Senans, September 1984, and then later in conversation with the author.
***Le Monde gave a somewhat abbreviated version of this speech, but one that was "authorized" by the General's General Staff.

I should like to take advantage of my visit here to deal with what has been called the all-round strategy, about which a great deal has been said recently. Yes, we are making atomic weapons. These weapons will form a completely new defence system, involving a military reshaping and a reshaping of power, which cannot be compared with anything we have so far known.

It is a long-term affair. We are doing it not for tomorrow, but for generations to come, within a completely new system of deterrence and defence. And in that long space of time, who can say what the evolution of the world will be? In twenty years, who will govern the United States and with what system? Who will govern the USSR? And Germany? And Japan? And China? Who can say what will be happening in South America and in Africa? Surely no one.

Given all these uncertainties, we are manufacturing our own nuclear weapons system. And it is not the first time in our history that it has been done in this way! In his day, Vauban fortified all the frontiers of France, the Pyrenees, the Alps, our ports and even Belgium. We went everywhere, we waged war everywhere, we entered Madrid, Berlin, Moscow. We waged war in Europe, in the East, in America, in Asia. There is no reason why this strategy, which has always protected us against everything, should not go on.

By definition, our atomic weapons system must be all-round. You must know this, you must see this and your studies and your outlook must adapt to it.

The "all-round" nuclear strategy was certainly the one that de Gaulle wanted to give France in 1967. Must it be seen as the expression of a policy of "armed neutrality"? The question was asked at the time by a listener of General Ailleret's at the Institut des Hautes Etudes de Défense Nationale. The Chief of General Staff replied more or less as follows:

We are not Switzerland, which, if Norway was attacked by the Russians, would declare that it was nothing to do with her. France is not saying that. If certain values, our independence, our survival were in question, if Soviet aggression were unleashed againt Europe, France would be instantly at war. But we want to intervene only at the decision of the French government, of the French people. We do not want to intervene because we belong to an alliance.

A month later, on his return from a visit to Madagascar, General Charles Ailleret was killed in his plane as it was taking off from the airport of Réunion. However little credence one may give to the idea* of those who saw it as the result of an assassination attempt perpetrated by secret services (French, or others hostile to the direction that French strategy was taking), one was to observe a slight shift on the part of the French army chiefs.

*Collected in a book entitled *Mort d'un général*. General Bourgue, Ailleret's closest colleague, who followed the investigation very closely, categorically excludes any hypothesis involving murder.

So the new Chief of General Staff, General Michel Fourquet, took up position in turn, on 3 March 1969, before a gathering at the Institut des Hautes Etudes de Défense Nationale. This lecture was not published by the *Revue de Défense Nationale* until May 1969, just after Charles de Gaulle's departure for Colombey: but it had been written in symbiosis with the head of State at a time when his retirement had not begun. Entitled "The Use of Different Systems of Forces in the Context of Deterrence Strategy", this study places the stress firmly on France's commitment "against an enemy coming from the East". It defines the mission of the operational forces as a "test" of the adversary's intentions before resistance takes the form of nuclear "escalation", and distinguishes between various forms of battle capable of triggering off the French deterrence, not excluding that it might one day operate in other cases than that of a violation of national territory.

Is this, therefore, if not a revision in depth, at least a modification of the idea of the "all-round strategy"? General Poirier, the leading French theoretician of deterrence, denies this. He maintains that General Fourquet's article tends to insert Ailleret's somewhat rigid and technocratic expression into a wider, more flexible system, and above all to articulate the nuclear strategy in an overall prediction that is also based on other weapons (classic and tactical nuclear) and on a more complex play of forces. "It does not represent," General Poirier concludes, "a slipping away, still less a revision, but rather a widening and an elucidation."[30]

General Fourquet says very much the same. In a letter that he wrote to me in January 1986, the former Chief of General Staff maintained that there was no difference or shift of view in the two texts, but only a difference of "circumstances".

It should be pointed out that his predecessor's article was published with the intention of wrenching the French officer corps from their spirit of "dependence" on the Atlantic General Staffs, which "profoundly irritated de Gaulle". "In 1969," General Fourquet goes on, "the army was beginning to accept the new state of things, the setting up of our nuclear forces was advancing apace, and it seemed necessary to me to orientate minds in the right direction and to say clearly that the danger of war lay in the East."

All the same, we cannot exclude the possibility that between the time at which Ailleret was writing (1967) and the time when General Fourquet delivered his lecture (3 March 1969), an inflection had occurred in Charles de Gaulle's strategic thinking. Did he take into account the reappearance of a preferential enemy, after the invasion of Czechoslovakia by the USSR, at the same time as Washington was looking for peace in Vietnam?

Whatever were the "Atlantic" modifications made by General de Gaulle to his nuclear strategy, the *idée-force* remains, at the time of his retirement, that of a deterrence "by the weak of the strong", proportional to the scope of the modest means at the country's disposal and of the more limited objective that it represented, aiming to "sanctuarize" national territory and only incidentally to contribute to the overall defence of the West – autonomy of decision excluding neither solidarity nor allied cooperation.

An adaptation of the "all-round" strategy? We know that Charles de Gaulle was not a man to resist change. There is abundant proof of the renewal of the Franco-

American alliance between 1967 and 1969. Even before the talks between Richard Nixon and Charles de Gaulle, the extreme cordiality of which has already been described, before the revision of the Atlantic Pact in March 1969, the agreements between Ailleret and Lemnitzer (the American Supreme Allied Commander in Europe), defining the forms of cooperation between the two commands, had been signed in February 1967 – less than a year after France left NATO.

Admiral Sabbagh, who stressed the "gestural" aspect of de Gaulle's supposed neutralism and the trust that the American military leaders had always had in de Gaulle, described to me with great vividness the final ups and downs of those tough Franco-American negotiations. It was at Rambouillet, during a hunt to which he had invited General Lemnitzer, that de Gaulle won from the American army chief recognition of the usefulness of the French nuclear force for European security, at the same time as he was renovating or rather readjusting his views on the Alliance.

Suddenly de Gaulle, who as always, was unarmed, pointed out to the visitor a pheasant in full flight. The American put his gun to his shoulder and, swinging round to keep the bird in his sights, found himself almost face to face with de Gaulle who, pushing the barrel of the gun aside said: "You'd have been in a mess if you'd shot me." Back at the château, the two men defined the reciprocal views of the Alliance and the use of nuclear weapons. Then, taking Lemnitzer to see the great room of the château, de Gaulle stopped in front of a tapestry illustrating the fable of the wolf and the lamb. "France," he said, "will never be the lamb again!" Lemnitzer burst out laughing. "If he is laughing," said de Gaulle, "it's because he has understood..."[31] The Ailleret–Lemnitzer agreements remained secret. Those who have been able to learn their contents have declared that the tests placed France very far from the "neutrality", the "non-engagement" that have so often been discussed.

Was it a schizophrenic strategy, then? At the same time as France was leaving the military structures of NATO and there was talk of the "all-round" strategy, was not bilateral cooperation being set up once more with the leader of the coalition? In fact, one of the General's military advisers told me, one should speak of *non-encagement* ("uncaging"). What de Gaulle rejected was a structure, a "cage", automatically involving France in a conflict decided on by others. "At all times," says Pierre Messmer, who for nine years was de Gaulle's Armed Forces Minister, "he wanted to retain freedom of decision. What he rejected was not the alliance, but automatic commitment in any conflict."[32]

The decision to use nuclear weapons amounts, as it has been written a hundred times, to the apocalypse. Charles de Gaulle, a Christian armed with the most intrepid political cynicism, did not regard himself as unfitted to be the man handling the lightning, living by that very fact, he confided to friends, in "a terrible and perpetual perplexity".[33] If any man in France, over the past few centuries, was capable of regarding this quasi-supernatural mission without paralysing fear, it could only be the author of *Le Fil de l'épée*.

It was a decree of 14 January 1964 that made the head of State the chief in nuclear matters, specifying that the strategic nuclear force should intervene "on orders from the President of the Republic, the President of the Defence Council and Supreme Commander of the Armed Forces". This text was the object of virulent criticisms from the opposition, on 24 April, during a debate in the National Assembly, notably from François Mitterrand, who demanded that this power of decision should be in the person of the Prime Minister.*

The bomb is not an abstraction in the life of a man who has been invested with that terrible responsibility. It inhabits him, haunts him and follows him like a shadow – a very physical shadow, that of the ordnance officer who accompanied de Gaulle, following him wherever he went, carrying a cassette that would put him into immediate contact at any moment with the nuclear headquarters at Taverny, forty kilometres from Paris.

How is the political authority** that is alone authorized to trigger off the nuclear attack recognized? The problem is solved, according to General Maurin, former Chief of General Staff, by the implementation of modern means of transmitting images between the President of the Republic and the centres of operations – means that are protected against any intrusion.[34] The coded figure that enables the President of the Republic to trigger off the nuclear firepower changes at regular intervals. Under de Gaulle, says Alain Larcan (a close colleague of Pierre Messmer), it was written by General de Gaulle on a small piece of white card carried inside a medal that he wore in his waistcoat pocket linked by a chain to his buttonhole and which he kept by him during the night.

If he had decided to live in the Elysée, which he did not care for, it was largely because all the warning systems – and systems for checking errors, based on three computers in the Armed Forces Ministry in the rue Saint-Dominique – were linked to it, and could not be guaranteed in the same way elsewhere.

The image of the decider not being sufficient to authenticate the faithful directive, the voice of the Head of State was required to complete reception of the order given. The officer responsible for the strategic nuclear force, General Madon, then General Mitterrand,*** knew Charles de Gaulle's voice well enough for no mistake to be possible. Nevertheless, Admiral Sabbagh goes on, when the Mirage IVs were put into service, General Madon asked how the "decider" would be identified during an operational flight. "Come now, Madon," said de Gaulle, "you know my voice, don't you?"[35]

For nuclear firepower was also a nuclear "I".

---

*Twenty years later, François Mitterrand, when confronted by Jacques Chirac as his Prime Minister, was to maintain precisely the opposite view.
**A power that, unlike the case of the United States, may be delegated, in France, to the Prime Minister or to his colleague in charge of the armed forces.
***François Mitterrand's older brother.

CHAPTER THIRTY-TWO

The Prophet Challenged

By virtue of its absolute nature, nuclear fire power carries within it and in those who hold it, its own threat. Because it involves the most audacious intellectual speculations, exalts imagination, destroys distances and gives the weak a supposed ascendancy over the strong, it incites in its holder a sort of *hubris*, a sort of excess.

So grandiose was de Gaulle's project for Europe that he had neglected local contingencies, the immediate reality of power ratios. The man whose fundamental strategic rule had always been to take account of circumstances rather than of a priori plans was now being less attentive to facts. Thus we see him, during that year of 1967, entering a sort of planetary drift, in strategic matters, the Near East or his relations with his Western allies. The vision was still dazzling. But a new intemperance and sometimes a disconcerting distance from reality were perceptible.

Nineteen-sixty-seven was the year when the General, who a few months before had removed France from NATO, now considered that she had at her disposal a deterrent force credible in all places and noted that the aggravation of the American involvement in Vietnam ran the risk of spreading to Cambodia despite his solemn warning at Phnom Penh. De Gaulle acted during those months as if France had no other rules and obeyed no other laws than those of her isolated salvation and that he himself was invested with a universal mission.

From the Near East to the American continent, this high-voltage de Gaulle disturbed, annoyed, inspired and exposed himself to all manner of condemnations, seeming to find in them material for new challenges. What he was to lose in support, he regained of course in new loyalties, broadening the diplomatic space opened up by the settlement of the Algerian affair and the challenge to the American adventure in Vietnam.

But the splits that then appeared between the head of State and French public opinion were of a breadth that went well beyond the simple gap between a superior mind and the timid reactions of public opinion. Great diplomacy cannot be the reflection of a majority, the fruit of public opinion polls: it is in its nature to be in the advance guard. But it cannot run against the current.

Relations between General de Gaulle and the State of Israel were perhaps, until mid-May 1967, the best that the founder of the Fifth Republic had ever had with any national community.

Before the proclamation of the Jewish state, Free France had established very friendly relations with the Zionist organizations. In London, de Gaulle had received their most authoritative spokesmen. In Palestine, François Coulet, then the General's trusted adviser in Algiers, had set up a radio station, "Levant-Free-France", together with combatants from the Jewish legion; it was in Jerusalem that those who fled the Vichyite Levant to join de Gaulle came together and it was in the struggle against Dentz's troops at the side of the Free French that Moshe Dayan lost an eye in 1941.

Of course, considering at this time the likely effect of the division of Palestine on future relations between Jews and Arabs, de Gaulle had shown some anxiety about Israel. The politician in him had doubts about the long-term prospects of the Zionist enterprise. But its intrepid, visionary, but also real nature could not fail to make him favour the founders of the state. That epic challenge, that hope in action was essentially similar to his own enterprise.

During the crossing of the desert, and until his return to power, he was well disposed to Tel Aviv. He applauded the Suez expedition of autumn 1956, criticizing only the inadequacy of the forces used, the unpreparedness of the British; and several of his best-known colleagues, Soustelle, Palewski, Chaban, Debré, had very friendly relations with the Israeli leaders.

His return to power was accompanied by various "slow-downs" in Franco-Israeli cooperation: he conveyed his doubts to Maurice Couve de Murville about the closeness of the relations that had been established by the general staffs of the two countries during the Suez expedition and the Algerian war. The high-ranking Israeli officers had entry into all the departments in which French defence plans were drawn up, particularly in the areas of information and nuclear research: the atomic station at Dimona, in the Negev, where uranium was turned into plutonium, was a sort of annexe of Marcoule or Pierrelatte. Military supplies to Israel remained as abundant as ever and at a very high technical level. Seventy-two Mirage IIIs were delivered in 1961. A contract for a further fifty was granted in 1966. Tanks, helicopters and patrol boats were then delivered or sold by France to Israel, whose leaders, throughout those years, maintained friendly and trusting relations with the Fifth Republic. In fact, writes the Israeli historian Samy Cohen, France "was much more pro-Israeli than she had been before 1954".[2]

The resumption of friendly relations with the Arab world after the Algerian war focused above all on Egypt. The crisis opened up over Suez, revived in 1961 by the incarceration in Cairo of several French diplomats and teachers accused of espionage, was receding: in 1965, Marshal Abdel-Hakim Amer, Egyptian Defence Minister and a close colleague of Nasser's, was received at the Elysée. The Arab world had applauded Charles de Gaulle's many demonstrations of independence from Washington. But could this *rapprochement* with the Arab world – which did not at this time have important implications regarding oil – be carried out without a radical revision of France's privileged relations with the Jewish state? There is nothing to suggest that before 1967 General de Gaulle thought so. He claimed to be forging links with the Arab world without denying Israel. We should quote here the eloquent lines from the *Mémoires d'espoir* in which Charles de Gaulle expresses the mixture of admiration and anxiety that Israel inspired in him at this time.

David Ben Gurion came to see me more than once. I had developed an immediate liking and respect for this doughty warrior and champion. He was the personification of Israel, which he now ruled, having presided over her foundation and her war of independence. I could not fail to be attracted by the grandeur of an enterprise which consisted in re-establishing an autonomous Jewish nation in a land which bore the traces of its fabulous history, and which it had owned nineteen centuries earlier. Humanly, I was gratified that the Jewish people had found a national home, and I saw it as some compensation for all the sufferings that they had endured during the ages, and which had reached a hideous climax in the massacres perpetrated by Hitler's Germany.

Speaking clearly of the "Jewish people", recalling that it had been "re-established" on land that it had "owned nineteen centuries earlier", de Gaulle was giving approval to the theses of Zionism and expressing the reasons why the great majority of the people in the West approved of the creation of the State of Israel. But what the General goes on to say – and it was written, we must remember, after his retirement – could not fail to be contentious:

But while the existence of Israel seemed to me to be more than justified, I considered that a great deal of caution was called for in her handling of the Arabs. The latter were her neighbours, and would always remain so. It was at their expense and on their lands that Israel had set herself up as a sovereign state. In doing so, she had wounded them in their religion and their pride. For this reason, when Ben Gurion spoke to me of his plan to settle four or five million Jews in Israel, which could not contain them in her present frontiers, and revealed to me his intention of extending these frontiers at the earliest opportunity, I urged him not to do so. "France," I said, "will help you to survive in the future as she has helped you in the past, whatever happens. But she is not prepared to provide you with the means of conquering new territory. You have brought off a remarkable achievement. Do not overdo it now. Rather than pursue ambitions which would plunge the East into terrible upheavals and would gradually lose you international sympathy, devote yourselves to pursuing the astonishing exploitation of a country that was until recently a desert, and to establishing harmonious relations with your neighbours.[3]

David Ben Gurion did challenge certain elements in this passage, notably Charles de Gaulle's warning against a massive immigration into Israel. We should quote here the excellent description of Franco-Israeli relations in the years 1963–67 by Abba Eban, then Israeli Foreign Minister, in his *Autobiography*:

The adherence of this strong figure to Israel's cause had given us great pride during the nine years of his regime. I had recently become uneasy about some gaps in the structure of French-Israeli relations. Our Embassy had advised me not to worry. To question the assurances given by de Gaulle

31. The "King's House".

32. Inspection of Algeria (August 1959). Colonel Buis, one of the first Free French soldiers, later a four-star general, presently in command of the "Lesser Kabylia" area, explains the situation to de Gaulle. On de Gaulle's left, General Jean Olié, head of military cabinet; Pierre Guillaumat, Armed Forces Minister; Jean Mauriac, son of the famous writer François Mauriac, represents the Agence France-Presse; Paul Delouvrier, High Commissioner in Algeria.

33. The Algerian barricades of January 1960.

34. The pronunciamiento of the "Four". From left to right: André Zeller, Edmond Jouhaud, Raoul Salan, Maurice Challe.

35. Evian, 1961: the French negotiators around Louis Joxe. From left to right: Claude Chayet (Quai d'Orsay); Bernard Tricot, de Gaulle's special advisor for Algerian affairs; Roland Cadet (Conseil d'Etat); Louis Joxe, Minister for Algerian Affairs; General Jean Simon, commander of the "Greater Kabylia" area; Paul Thibaud, spokesman.

36. Evian, 1961: the Algerian negotiators around Belkacem Krim. From left to right: Major Slimane (wearing sunglasses), Ahmed Boulharouf, Major Mendjli, Ahmed Francis, Belkacem Krim, Saad Dahlab, Ahmed Boumendjel (hidden) and Mohammed Ben Yayia (far right).

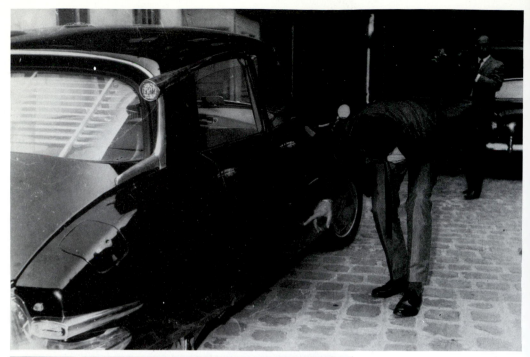

37. After the Petit-Clamart assassination attempt (22 August 1962): one of the fourteen bullet holes in the General's Citröen DS.

38. Michel Debré and Georges Pompidou: one leaving, the other arriving. Behind Debré, Christian Fouchet, later Education Minister and Interior Minister.

Two sketches, the first [FACING PAGE] from *Le Canard Enchaîné*, depicting de Gaulle as the Sun King, being greeted by courtiers at Versailles; the second [LEFT], by the famous cartoonist Tim, depicting de Gaulle as Don Quixote.

39. *"Charlot, des sous!"* was the slogan of the great strikes of 1963.

40. Khrushchev at Rambouillet (1960), before the May Storms. On de Gaulle's right, Michel Debré, then Prime Minister.

41. The General at Westminster: the eulogy for British institutions.

42. The Kennedys at the Elysée, a Franco-American honeymoon. With the Kennedys and Charles de Gaulle, Yvonne de Gaulle and Michel Debré.

43. Adenauer and de Gaulle in front of Reims cathedral: reconciliation.

44. In Mexico City, "*la mano en la mano!*". In the car, President Lopez Mateos. "*La mano en la mano*" (hand in hand) was a phrase used by de Gaulle in his speech to the Mexican people.

45. Dakar, buoyed up by the warm African welcome.

46. A few minutes before
speaking the celebrated words
"*Vive le Québec libre!*", standing
beside Daniel Johnson, the Prime
Minister of Quebec.

47. In Warsaw, between Gomulka
and President Ochab: too soon?

48. Under Prince Sihanouk's
parasol, in Phnom Penh.

49. The press conference, the ultimate ritual. Present are André Malraux, Minister of State and of Culture; Georges Pompidou, Prime Minister; Maurice Couve de Murville, Foreign Minister; Roger Frey, Interior Minister; Edgard Pisani, Agriculture Minister.

Jean Effel's sketch: "*Moâ!*" is a phonetic attempt to convey an exaggerated, self-important "*Moi!*"

— MAO...   — MOÂ!

50. Being interviewed by Michel Droit, editor of *Le Figaro Littéraire*.

51. The dauphins on the starting-line: left, Valéry Giscard d'Estaing, Finance Minister; right, Georges Pompidou, then Prime Minister.

52. May '68. Cohn Bendit: "*Dix ans, c'est assez!*" ("Ten years are enough!") Daniel Cohn Bendit was the student leader during the "events" of May 1968.

53. "*Mais non!*" Left to right: Michel Debré, Robert Poujade, former Environment Minister, André Malraux.

54. Return from Baden-Baden: his mind was made up.
Landing at Chaumont airport, 6 p.m., 29 May 1968.

55. With Maurice Couve de Murville who epitomized France's "rank".

56. With André Malraux who epitomized France's message.

57. Opposite Quimper cathedral:
irremediable words. De Gaulle announces
that the referendum will take place
during the following spring.

58. In front of Anne de Gaulle's grave,
with his wife, Elisabeth and Alain de
Boissieu. Anne de Gaulle, the third child,
had been seriously handicapped.
Elisabeth, the elder daughter, married
Captain (later General) Alain de Boissieu.

59. The memorial service at Notre-
Dame: seventy heads of State and heads
of government. From left: President
Podgorny of the USSR, Archbishop
Makarios of Cyprus, King Baudoin of
the Belgians, Grand Duke Charles of
Luxembourg, Charles, Prince of Wales,
President Tsiranana of Madagascar,
Houphouet-Boigny of the Ivory Coast,
Léopold Senghor of Senegal, Diori
Hamani of Niger, unknown, Richard
Nixon, out of the picture, was the next
on the right.

60. The funeral at Colombey. Behind
the celebrants, Mme de Gaulle and her
daughter, Admiral Philip de Gaulle (de
Gaulle's son), General de Boissieu.

would arouse his irritation – and not only his. The trade in aircraft and other equipment was flowing. A new agreement for fifty Mirage V aircraft had been signed in the summer of 1966.[4]

Thus, in the months preceding the crisis of 1967, Gaullist diplomacy was defined, on the one hand, by a controlled cordiality towards Israel, which was advised to act with prudence, but was constantly resupplied with weapons, and on the other by a gradual, but definite, *rapprochement* with the Arab world. This rebalance was in accordance with the nature of things and the Israeli government and public opinion in that country seemed to accept it. How could de Gaulle not be satisfied by that skilful navigation, in accordance with the traditional policy of his country, with its interests and perhaps with future moves towards peace? Hence a quasi-dogmatic position in favour of peace that alone would preserve the skilful balance to which de Gaulle had contributed. But, for once, this prudence took insufficient account of circumstances.

On the one hand, there was the strategic impatience of an Israel secretly harbouring the aspirations expressed by David Ben Gurion, who was preoccupied with the deliveries of Soviet arms to Damascus and Cairo, and disturbed by the growing unity of the surrounding Arab world which might, one day, turn on the Jewish state. The diversion of the waters of the Jordan, a gesture that many Arabs regarded as a *casus belli*, only helped to make the future seem more unsettled.

Did the governments of Ben Gurion and his successors really comprehend the character of the Palestinian claims that were then beginning to rise to the surface? It would not seem so. In leading Israeli political circles, people at this time claimed to see in this Fatah, which was finding an organizational shape in the Palestine Liberation Organization, only mercenaries or the *harkis* of Arab heads of state. Meanwhile, in London and Paris, voices could already be heard warning that this was an expression of Palestinian aspirations.

So it was de Gaulle who urged the Israelis to maintain a politico-military status quo, which he regarded as favourable to their cause – but at the same time he could perceive the gravity of the threat that lay behind the rhetoric employed by the various Arab groups, namely, the return of the Palestinian repressed. And perhaps it was because he was so aware of this that he stressed that Israel should be careful not to give the seething discontent of the Palestinians and the Arab world an excuse to boil over.

How did the Israeli strategists see things at the beginning of that year? If President Nasser was constantly manoeuvring to prevent his colleagues in Damascus, Amman, Baghdad or Algiers forcing him into a war, he could avoid neither joining the Syrian-Iraqi-Egyptian federation nor signing with Damascus, on 4 November 1966, a defence agreement that bound him more closely than ever to the turbulent leaders of Syria – where, nine months earlier, the "revolutionary" general, Salah Jedid, had seized power by brandishing the aim of liquidating Israel.

At the same time, Soviet military supplies were flooding into Syria, where growing numbers of Palestinian commandos of Al-Assifa (the military branch of the Fatah), expelled by Nasser because their anti-Israeli activism had exasperated him, were setting up their headquarters. These commandos were infiltrating

Israeli territory. Thus Jerusalem's anxieties were soon to be focused on Damascus.[5]

I shall not go over in detail the history of the Six Day War. I shall simply recall the sequence of actions and reactions, which go back to the pre-war operation of the Israeli airforce; on 7 April, they brought down some twenty Syrian planes; on 9 May, the Israeli Prime Minister, Levi Eshkol, announced that the "Syrian aggression" would be thrown back; on 13 May, Nasser was warned by the Soviets that Israel was massing troops* with a view to an imminent attack on Syria. Nasser then suddenly found himself called upon by his allies to come to their help; and on 15 May an important Egyptian contingent was sent into Sinai.

From mid-May until 5 June, it was the Arab party that was to take the most obvious initiatives and the ones most susceptible to driving its adversary into action: on 16 May, the Egyptian Commander-in-Chief asked the United Nations contingents, which had been installed at strategic points in Sinai since 1957, to withdraw in order to allow Egypt's own troops to go into operation in the event of a conflict. (These UN forces were stationed along the frontier between Israel and Egypt only on the territory of the latter country, as a result of an exchange of letters between Secretary-General Dag Hammarskjöld and President Nasser, it being understood that the latter could at any time ask for the withdrawal of those troops – Israel having refused to receive them on her soil.)

U Thant, the new Secretary-General of the United Nations, agreed at once, without even trying to gain time. Nasser, who seemed anxious above all to make a gesture to save face before his Syrian allies and the Arab world, had been sucked into the conflict. On 20 May, the Egyptian forces took up position at Sharm el-Sheikh (a locality commanding the Straits of Tiran, gateway to the Gulf of Aqaba, of which Egypt controlled one bank and in which Israel had built the port of Eilat) while the War Minister obtained (or thought that he had obtained) assurances of unconditional support from Moscow. And on 22 May, called upon to do so by propaganda coming from other Arab countries, the Egyptian Raï announced the blockade of the gulf, a gesture that Golda Meir, Israel's Foreign Minister, defined as a warlike gesture.**[6]

On that 22 May then, war or peace would be decided by President Nasser. He knew that he had taken a major risk. And what he said over the next few days seemed calculated to remove the last doubts of the Israeli strategists: the blockade of the Straits of Tiran provided an opportunity for acting. But when the Council of Ministers met in Jerusalem on 23 May, the advocates of negotiation won a delay: the best known of them, Abba Eban, the Foreign Minister, set off that very evening for Washington in order to obtain the support of the United States in raising the blockade of the strait, the only non-military outcome that would allow Israel to emerge decently from the crisis. Abba Eban was also given the mission, before

*Information that rested, it has since been discovered, on estimates exaggerated – consciously or not – by the Soviet Union.
**The three Western powers (including France) had let their support for this position be known. But Moscow had denounced it, as also had Cairo, which had refused to recognize the gulf as "an international waterway".

meeting President Johnson, of having talks in Paris with de Gaulle, who was regarded as a special friend by the Israeli leaders.*

De Gaulle, considering the consequences of a conflict with Maurice Schumann, chairman of the Foreign Affairs Commission in the National Assembly, listed three: an aggravation of international tension that would allow the Soviets to get a foothold in a region from which they had hitherto been excluded; a resurgence of the Palestinian problem, which would now assume dimensions that would change its very nature; the awareness, by the Arabs, of the power of a weapon that they held, but which they had not yet used: oil.

What makes a policy great is not only that it is based on long-term views. It is also that it takes account of the immediate or medium-term realities of a situation, the human, psychological elements that go to make up the background. In this instance, de Gaulle "the long-term seer" was admirable. But he might be criticized much more for his sense of immediate realities. It is one thing to detect the syndromes of an illness, quite another to treat it in such a way that the organism rejects it. And in late May 1967, the diagnosis was impeccable, the prognosis, as we shall see, more questionable.

As he was landing in Paris, on the morning of 24 May, Abba Eban was anxious: he had noted that the French spokesman had hardly reacted to the blockade of the Gulf of Aqaba. Whereas Washington and London had assured Jerusalem of their determination to oppose Nasser's gesture, no such declaration had emerged from Paris.[7]

Before quoting from Abba Eban's very convincing account of his talks with de Gaulle from his *Autobiography* I shall give the General's own version of what was said, which he made public six months later during a press conference:

> "If Israel is attacked," I then told him in substance, "we shall not let her be destroyed, but if you attack, we shall condemn your initiative. Of course, I have no doubt that you will have military successes in the event of war, but, afterwards, you would find yourself committed on the terrain, and from the international point of view, in increasing difficulties, especially as war in the East cannot fail to increase a deplorable tension in the world, so that it will be you, having become the conquerors, who will gradually be blamed for the inconveniences."[8]

Here is Abba Eban's account:

> General de Gaulle received me with grave courtesy. Authority flowed from him like a steady tide. Even before I was seated near his desk – uncluttered by papers or telephones – he said loudly, "Ne faites pas la guerre." At that moment we had not even been introduced. We then exchanged greetings and the General went on as if completing his previous sentence, "at any rate, don't shoot first. It would be catastrophic if Israel were to attack. The Four

---

*It was only in Paris that Mr Eban was to receive the invitation to go to London, where, contrary to his expectations, he was to be given a warmer welcome.

Powers must be left to resolve the dispute. France will influence the Soviet Union toward an attitude favourable to peace."

The case that Abba Eban made to the General was very clear: it was because Israel had arrived at a turning-point in her history that her government had wanted to consult her "great friend" France. The tension was composed of three factors: Syrian-based terrorism, Egyptian troop concentrations in Sinai after the departure of the United Nations forces and the blockade of the Straits of Tiran, an aggressive act that must be rescinded. In 1957, France had given the most energetic definition of Israeli rights in the Gulf of Aqaba. The French declaration had even included recognition of Israel's right to defend herself physically against the blockade. Without Eilat Israel would be stunted and humiliated. And Eban concluded: "Israel without honour is not Israel."

These last words seemed to shake the General, the Israeli minister goes on. De Gaulle then asked him an anxious question: "What are you going to do?" "If the choice lies between surrender and resistance," Eban replied, "Israel will resist. Our decision has been made. We shall not act today or tomorrow, because we are still exploring the attitude of those who have resumed commitments. If Israel fights alone, she will be victorious, although the price in blood may be heavy."

The General's answer was short. On no account must Israel be the first to attack. "I replied that we could not be the first to 'open hostilities' since these had already been opened: Nasser's blockade and declaration were acts of war. Whatever Israel did would be a reaction, not an initiative." Reaffirming that he upheld the freedom of the seas and that an international agreement on the straits should be sought "as in the Dardanelles", de Gaulle observed that since 1957 there had been several incidents of which the blockade was only the latest. Since Israel had not always "accommodated" the Arabs, tension had increased. Apparently sceptical as to the potential of a demonstration of strength by the Western powers, the General added that Israel's adversaries were hoping that Israel would open hostilities. "Israel should not satisfy these expectations."

Abba Eban reminded the General that French help and friendship had done much to reinforce Israel's strength and spirit. De Gaulle replied that it was this friendship that now moved him to give the advice that he had formulated. Israel, not being "sufficiently established to solve all her problems herself", should await the results of international consultation before undertaking anything. France would continue to work for a strong Israel. Eban pointed out that sometimes inaction is more dangerous than action, which drew the solemn reply: "De Gaulle understands the dangers which arise from inaction, but I advise you not to be precipitate. Do not make war." And the two men took their leave.

The bitterness then felt by the Israeli diplomat found discreet expression in the statement that he made on leaving the Elysée ("The blockade is a pirate's act. A world which resigned itself to such acts would be a jungle") and more clearly in the telegram that he sent to Jerusalem, which he sums up thus: "France was disengaging herself from any responsibility for helping us if we chose early resistance."[9]

Couve de Murville, who was a witness to this meeting, writes: "After that meeting, it was obvious that nothing would stop the process that had been put in train.""¹⁰ At about the same time, however, after a meeting of the Council of Ministers, the French government conveyed to the other three great powers the offer of a "diplomatic consultation" or a "conference" on the means of re-establishing free circulation in the Gulf of Aqaba and restoring calm to the region. Washington accepted; Moscow, after two days of reflection, refused, alleging that there was no crisis!

But the crisis worsened on 29 and 30 May; first following an incendiary speech by President Nasser (in which he asserted that it was no longer a matter of this or that strait, but of "the rights of the Palestinian people", and that consequently "the aggression suffered by Palestine in 1948" had to be wiped out); then from the signing of a mutual assistance pact between the Egyptian leader and his old adversary, King Hussein, who suddenly placed his army under Egyptian command. Thus that encirclement of Israel that had haunted Israeli leaders from the outset had been carried out. It wasn't surprising, therefore, to see a Cabinet of National Union formed in Jerusalem in which not only was Moshe Dayan given the defence portfolio, but even Menachem Begin became a member. After a meeting of the Council of Ministers on 2 June, de Gaulle released the following statement.

> France has committed herself in no way to any of the states in question. She considers that each of those states has a right to live. But she considers that the worst eventuality would be the opening of hostilities. Consequently, the state that is the first to resort to arms would not have her approval, still less her support.

Whereupon it was decided that France would place an embargo, dating from 5 June, on deliveries of weapons to the states of the region – Israel and seven Arab countries.

The reaction of most of the French press was of surprise. Public opinion, which was manipulated only slightly by the very diligent Israeli propaganda and which was all the more effective in that the behaviour of the Arab leaders was more provocative, reacted by showing its sympathy for Israel. Far from encouraging Charles de Gaulle to revise his position by taking into account what amounted to a sort of spontaneous referendum in favour of Israel taking place in full view, this pressure from the media had the effect merely of stiffening his resolve, of poisoning him with the venom of suspicion: was not the reason why the French press was showing such excited sympathy for Israel the result of the influence of so many eminent Jewish commentators? We shall have to return to this point only too often.

The Israeli government decided to act. On 5 June at 8.30 a.m. – in order to deceive the expectations of the Egyptians, who had been expecting an attack at dawn for three days and had raised the alert only a few minutes before – the Israeli airforce launched an all-out attack on Egypt's airfields: in one hour, Nasser's airforce was annihilated and the main Arab country earth-bound before battle had even begun. The fate of the war was already decided when, at 10 a.m., the Ambassador, Walter Eytan, came to inform de Gaulle of the outbreak of hostilities. Jacques Foccart, who had also come to inform the General, was surprised to hear raised voices as he waited in an antechamber. Then, following the diplomat into the General's office, he heard de Gaulle sigh: "They've just launched a colonial war. They'll win it very quickly. But they won't settle anything that way."[11] The provisional verdict of history was not to shake the Great Judge: after inspiring the statement from the Council of Ministers on 15 June, which condemned the "aggressor" – Israel – and refused to accept any *fait accompli*, he instructed his Foreign Minister to denounce Israel's attitude before the National Assembly, then before the assembly of the United Nations.

A few days later, General de Gaulle commented on the episode in the presence of a number of parliamentarians on the occasion of a reception at the Elysée, on 22 June. "Of course, the Israelis are admirable people. But I told them: 'Don't attack!' They have done so. And I'm annoyed with them for that."[12] He was to repeat the same observations several times in the course of the summer, notably on 13 July: "We told the Israelis not to start a conflict. Now, France does not recognize her conquests. We have been pushed into a position similar to that of the Soviets, but for different reasons. Our policy is to maintain good relations with the Arab countries, so that they will not have them only with the Soviets."[13]

None of the General's arguments is unimportant. None, however, was strong enough to win support. Firstly, because he seems to have taken no account in this case of the unbearable stress under which the Israeli people had to live after the blockade of the Gulf of Aqaba, on 22 May, when Nasser increased his threats and such individuals as Shukeiry and Ahmed Said were yelling for the death of Jews. Secondly, because all the measures taken by Egypt and the other Arab States against Israel had shifted relations between Jerusalem and her neighbours from a state of peace to imminent war.

To call "aggressor" a party that could not bear such pressure and, harassed with provocations and half-strangled, accepted an escalation of the situation and shed the first blood, is not entirely fair. But one has to take into account this judgement of an American diplomat, Charles Yost, to whom President Johnson had given a final peace mission in late May. Drawing on the lessons of his unsuccessful approaches, that competent observer writes that "no government had any intention of starting a war in spring 1967, [but] the reactions of all the States concerned [Syria, Egypt, Israel] were excessive".[14] If the Israeli leaders proved unable to control their superiority, it was largely because they felt "deserted" in the affair of the blockade, where they had right on their side, by their Western allies and above all by France.

But qualifications are to be made and we must try to find the reality behind the accusing words. Was the embargo on weapons for Israel as strongly laid down as General de Gaulle seemed to suggest? Jean-Claude Servan-Schreiber,* a fervent Gaullist and ardent supporter of Israel, feeling unable to resign himself to seeing his Israeli friends deserted by France, decided to be at their side, as a voluntary worker, while the young men of Tsahal were fighting. He arranged with Admiral Limon, who was in charge of buying weapons in France, for a seat to be reserved for him in a plane bound for Tel Aviv that would land in Paris on the night of the

*Cousin of Jean-Jacques Servan-Schreiber and brother-in-law of Pierre Mendès France.

5th. But, the traveller observes, that El-Al Boeing, whose seats had been removed, was filled with "munition rockets and spare parts for the Israeli airforce's Mirages".[15] Was this flexibility or non-execution of orders? The same Jean-Claude Servan-Schreiber was to be given an interesting explanation from the head of state. Why had he left for Israel in the middle of a war and attended a military march past in Jerusalem on 2 May?

"I'm a friend of Israel."

"And I suppose I am not a friend of Israel! But I wasn't there. I told them not to attack. They always go too far!"[16]

The quarrel between the founder of the Fifth Republic and Israel was resumed at a press conference held five months later at the Elysée, during which de Gaulle addressed a few sentences to Israel that, without questioning the historical and moral legitimacy of the State founded in 1948, placed it in the dock.

On 27 November 1967, de Gaulle once more summoned the international press to the Elysée. Since the stormy meeting of 14 January 1963, which had given him an opportunity to place Britain outside Europe and to reject the American Multilateral Force, he had lost a large number of sympathizers. But however restive it may be, the international conclave is always impatient to see a great virtuoso in operation. No feeling seemed more propitious for the demonstration of his talents than the Middle East conflict.

> Many people wondered, even many Jews wondered whether the establishment of that community on lands that had been acquired in more or less justifiable conditions and in the midst of Arab peoples who were profoundly hostile to it would not lead to incessant, interminable friction and conflict. Some people even feared that the Jews, hitherto dispersed, but who had remained what they had been for all time, that is to say an élite people, self-confident and dominating, might not, once it was gathered together on the site of its ancient grandeur, change into ardent, conquering ambition the very moving desire that they have felt for nineteen centuries.

One could feel a shudder go through the room. The words "élite people, self-confident and dominating" had gone through the audience like an electric shock. What he went on to say hardly lowered the tension:

> We saw appear a State of Israel that was warlike and determined to expand. On 22 May, the Aqaba affair, unfortunately created by Egypt, was to offer a pretext to those who were dreaming of breaking loose. Israel, having attacked, seized, in six days of combat, objectives that she wanted to attain. Now she is organizing, on the territories that she has taken, an occupation that cannot but involve oppression, repression, expropriation, and there has appeared against her a resistance that she, in turn, describes as terrorism.[17]

Everything that he had said was calculated to infuriate the Israelis. A harsher criticism could hardly be made against them. This interpretation of the facts was perfectly defensible, but de Gaulle, involved in the search for peace, weakened his diplomatic position by giving so unilateral a version of the affair.

"An élite people, sure of itself and dominating." Apologists for the head of State remarked at once that this formula could only have, de Gaulle being what he was, a positive significance. Of course, as a historian, de Gaulle might see these words as a tribute; but as French head of state, he must have known that many would see them as venomous. Three days later in *Le Monde,** there appeared a cartoon by Tim showing an Auschwitz deportee crucified on the barbed wire, the caption being those words of Charles de Gaulle's. And a month later, Raymond Aron published a small pamphlet, *De Gaulle, Israël et les Juifs,*[18] which constituted a noble and vibrant answer to the General's words. Posing the question of whether, by using words so laden with antisemitic connotations, de Gaulle was not attacking the behaviour of very many French Jews who, in June, had chosen to demonstrate their solidarity with Israel rather than imitate the critical reservations of their head of state, Aron wrote:

> I agree: I didn't care for the gangs of young men going up the Champs-Elysées shouting "Israel will conquer", nor for the Jews before the Israeli Embassy. I didn't care for the ex-advocates of French Algeria or those who felt nostalgia for the Suez expedition who pursued their war against the Arabs through Israel. What has happened made the reverse, of which General de Gaulle has been not so much the initiator as the interpreter, inevitable. But as a French citizen, I claim the right, accorded to all citizens, to combine allegiance to the national State with liberty of beliefs and sympathies. For believing Jews, Israel has a quite different significance than it has for me; but I would despise myself if I allowed them to be alone in defending a freedom that would mean less to me than to them.

By using such words about the Jewish people, was not de Gaulle reopening those wounds and reviving quarrels that were all the more intense because less than five years had elapsed since the Algerian war? He knew very well that the exodus of Europeans had brought together in France itself tens of thousands of North African Jews, who were less assimilated to French culture and to the national State than the contemporaries of Raymond Aron or Claude Lévi-Strauss and all the more attentive to the fate of Israel.

Indeed General de Gaulle tried on a number of occasions to remove the negative implications of his words of November 1967 that simple souls as well as commentators from the opposition had detected in them.

On 1 January 1968, after a reception given in the Elysée, the General asked Rabbi Kaplan to stay after his other guests had left, and in a small drawing-room of the palace he began a conversation with Kaplan that included these two significant remarks:

> *Charles de Gaulle*: It was justified praise of the Jewish people. I, an anti-semite! You know what my relations are with Jews!
> *Jacob Kaplan*: Nevertheless, what you said gave arguments to the anti-

---

**L'Express* considered it too controversial.

semites. Is there, in your view, an incompatibility between the duties of Jews, as French citizens, and their declared sympathy for Israel?

Charles de Gaulle: No. The sympathy of French Jews for the people and land of Israel* is quite natural.[19]

The day after this conversation, the Rabbi published the following statement:

The President of the Republic expressed surprise at the emotions aroused by his declaration about the Jewish people. In his view, it has been wrongly interpreted. For him, it was a justified praise of the value of the Jews. For my part, I was anxious to make it clear that our position in favour of Israel was not to be interpreted as an act of dual allegiance. By showing concern for Israel, French Jews are no less absolutely French. I am happy to say that the President of the Republic agrees with this, and that, for him, there is no problem on the matter.

Charles de Gaulle's opinions about Israel during those years may be summed up by his words, "They go too far." They were the words that Malraux heard whenever he took it upon himself to plead Israel's cause to the General.

The correspondence of late 1967 between David Ben Gurion and General de Gaulle showed that, beyond the bitterest exchange of condemnations, there was a profound convergence. To a letter from the Israeli leader, protesting against the reference to a "self-confident and dominating" people, de Gaulle replied that Israel had certainly gone beyond "the limits of necessary moderation", but that he continued to regard her as "a friendly and allied state".

However little understanding it showed for Israel and however shocking it may have been for large sections of French Judaism (and for many non-Jewish French citizens), did not the policy defined and implemented by General de Gaulle lend itself to a more favourable judgement, from the point of view of national interest and from that of international peace?

Six years after the event, the great Harvard political scientist, Stanley Hoffmann, when he was asked about this after a lecture given at the French Institute for International Affairs, in Paris, on 18 September 1973, replied as follows:

In the Arab-Israeli conflict, it seems to me that the position adopted by the General was perfectly justified, sensible and defensible in all kinds of ways. As to the importance that there was, that there is, in carrying out an Arab policy, in being the political power that can speak to the Arab countries in a way that the United States and Great Britain cannot, I have no reservations: that policy seems to me to be entirely sensible, though it has been very misunderstood in the United States.

One may have more reservations than Stanley Hoffmann about the affair and yet, like him, acknowledge the profoundly judicious aspect of this strategy, which went

---

*He said "land" here, not "State".

much further than a concern to protect oil supplies and to open up markets: by striving to maintain links between the Arab world and the West, de Gaulle was quite obviously working for world peace and against the takeover of the Arab world by the Soviet Union.

It was to win the votes of Arabs that Charles de Gaulle, in June 1967, challenged, from top to bottom, the privileged relations existing between France and Israel. But he did win those votes. A whole school of Egyptian* or North African commentators tried of course to point out that the General had been moved only out of concern for French interests – political and material interests. But such judgements, in a society in which realism, less vulgarized than in the West, still has the virtue of novelty and appears like the ultimate wisdom, have nothing pejorative about them and are intended to point out that there are lessons to be drawn from such behaviour. In a thesis devoted to the image of General de Gaulle in the Arab countries in 1967, Armand Pignol points out that the character presented by the press in Cairo or Beirut is always great and strong, called noble (*nabil*), and victorious (*nasir*), compared to the eagle or the lion and automatically placed among their friends, as opposed to Israel and the USA.[20]

The day after the press conference of 27 November 1967, the dithyramb was still in full spate: in the Lebanon there was talk of the "Napoleon of the century"; in Cairo, they praised the *caid-al-azim*, the "great chief". And Nasser declared that "de Gaulle is the only Western Head of State on whose friendship the Arabs can depend". He went even further, on 15 February 1968, when he declared that "under the leadership of that great patriot, regarded as one of the major figures of this century, France has adopted the position that accords with justice and peace". In the Cairo newspaper *Al-Maussawar*, Alya-el-Solh (daughter of a Lebanese Prime Minister assassinated twenty years earlier, after one of General de Gaulle's representatives had had him imprisoned in 1943), wrote that "de Gaulle belongs to that class of history builders who have accurate intuitions, express well based prophecies and see the future from afar off".

And, to conclude, there is the funeral oration published on 14 November 1970 after the death of Charles de Gaulle by the celebrated Ihsan Abdel Koddons in the most popular weekly in the Arab world, *Akhbar-el-Yom*: "He was the man who, against the slogans, opted for realism. A friend neither of the Arabs, nor of Israel, but only of France. And because he despised pressure, the Zionists brought him down from within."

If de Gaulle had wanted to barter the affection of the Arabs against the admiration of the Israelis, he certainly succeeded. But we know that that was not – and never was – his purpose. A friend neither of the Arabs, nor of Israel, but only of France. But did he keep intact, in all its elements, the friendship of France?

---

*In particular Mohammed Hassanein Heykal, the famous editorial-writer of *Al Ahram* and a confidant of Nasser.

CHAPTER THIRTY-THREE

The Legacy of Louis XV

When in 1940, in London, de Gaulle appealed to the solidarity of the "French Canadians", he suddenly knew much more about America than did most of his compatriots. In particular, one may suppose that he was better informed about the indifference with which the July monarchy allowed the British government to crush the rebellions of 1837, that he attached particular importance to the thousands of Canadian soldiers killed on French soil at Dupuy in 1917 – and that the fate of the French colonists abandoned in 1763 did not square with the idea that he had of France.

If we must pause for a moment at his appeal to the "French Canadians" on 1 August 1940, it is not because it was derived from particular familiarity with the problems of Quebec: it is because de Gaulle, so alone and resourceless, resigned himself here to a veritable appeal for help. But he was soon to learn that although "French Canada" was quite capable of forgiving the "betrayers" of 1763 – those *maudits français* (or *mozzi frança* as they called them) who had abandoned them, it was not the handful of republicans, many of them freemasons, who were continuing the fight under the symbol of the Cross of Lorraine that they would forgive, but rather the pious State of Vichy, which was represented by Pierre Dupuy.

Quebec, then, wanted to acknowledge only that France that was attached to her kings and priests and, consulted by referendum, refused by a majority of 71 per cent to accept conscription to go and fight in Europe. By sending Father d'Argenlieu on a mission to Quebec, de Gaulle was certainly trying to give Free France an image more in accordance with the wishes of the Quebec people. But in 1945, the condemnation of Pétain looked to the Québécois like a repeat of "the assassination of Louis XVI", a new crime committed by that same atheistic France that guillotined her kings and wallowed in the sins of the flesh.

The first contact that the head of Free France had with Quebec (between 11 and 13 July 1944), just after his visit to Franklin Roosevelt in Washington, was nevertheless a warm one. Impressive crowds greeted him at Quebec and Montreal. He was to speak, in his *Mémoires de guerre*, of a "wave of French pride" and "unconsoled pain". But it was not a welcome to lead him, the following year, to include a further visit to Quebec in his second visit to Canada: in August 1945, he went no farther than Ottawa.

And it was only during an official visit to the United States, in April 1960, that Charles de Gaulle became, after Vincent Auriol, the second French head of State to visit Canada. He was welcomed by the Conservative Prime Minister, John Diefenbaker, who had been his guest in Paris sixteen months before, and General

Vanier, one of Charles de Gaulle's old wartime companions, representing the British crown as Governor-General.

At the time when de Gaulle was thus renewing contact with Canada, his ideas on that country were still vague. In fact, what did that "duality between the two peoples cohabiting without merging", to quote one of his speeches of the time, mean? In the *Mémoires d'espoir*[1] he tells us that he told Mr Diefenbaker that since one of those "two peoples" was French, it had "the right to self-determination". He could not have gone much further, in this domain, without seeing that his friend Governor-General Vanier, "French Canadian" as he may have been, had declared himself to be more faithful than anyone to the British crown.

In fact, that third visit to Canada (and second to Quebec) seemed rather disappointing to his companions. In *Une politique étrangère*, Couve de Murville describes the Quebec of 1960, still under the thumb of Maurice Duplessis, an uncompromising conserver of the language, the family, ethnic separatism and the Catholic religion.[2] François Flohic, de Gaulle's ADC, noted the "lack of interest of the population in the General and in France". Indeed, as the national anthems came to an end before the monument that had been raised on the battlefield where General Wolfe defeated Montcalm, Colonel Martin, Governor Gagnon's ADC, said to him: "So it was you, you accursed French, who abandoned us."[3]

Yet, around 1963, a certain mutual interest between Paris and Quebec was perceptible. One after another came a French exhibition in Montreal, a visit from André Malraux, and the setting up of a section of the French radio and television service in Quebec. For two years, at the head of the Liberal government, Jean Lesage had begun his "quiet revolution", which tended to drag the country out of its clerical, backward-looking mummification by re-establishing contacts and friendships. The new slogan, "Masters in our own house!", meant that the Quebec people were now determined, without questioning federalism, to affirm their internal autonomy with relation to Ottawa.

How much did de Gaulle's awareness of the aspirations of the Quebec people owe to a letter addressed to him, on 10 July 1963, by the writer Gérald Robitaille?

Have we forgotten *what losing one's soul* means? I am not using those last words in a religious sense. I am inviting the whole world to come and observe it. What could be more moving than the spectacle of a people that condemns and curses itself, that abases itself and says thank you whenever, after a bitter struggle, it is given back what was stolen from it and belonged to it by right. As soon as one sets foot in that poor colonized country, one feels caught up by that horrible system that can really only be compared to shifting sands. Camus said that it was by accepting to live as a slave that one betrays one's brothers. Here, for the moment, and let us not prejudice the future that may still hold surprises in store for us, one can only live as a slave. So I hope that despite your heavy tasks, you will deign to give your attention to this humble request.

In January 1964, the Canadian Prime Minister Lester Pearson, who had won for himself a prestigious position on the international diplomatic stage, was warmly received by General de Gaulle. De Gaulle was to refer to the fate of "our people established in Canada", who "never fail to interest and move us very deeply". Five months later, on 1 June 1960, after the presentation of the credentials of the new Canadian Ambassador, Jules Léger, a note written by the General himself was distributed by the Agence France-Presse, indicating that "France is present in Canada not only by her representatives, but also because many Canadians are of French blood, French language, French culture, French spirit. In short, they are French in everything except sovereignty."[4]

On 10 October 1964, Queen Elizabeth visited Quebec in a deathly silence, broken by a few demonstrators who were dealt with by the police in such a way that the local press had to call that day the "Saturday of the truncheon". A few weeks later, on 22 February 1965, a Royal Commission on bilingualism and biculturalism (known as the "BB Commission"), which the federal government had had to set up under pressure of events, divulged the first results of an eighteen-month investigation, from which it emerged that the claims of French Canadians to equality were justified and that Canada was going through, as a result, "the gravest crisis in her history".[5] A month later appeared the book that Daniel Johnson called *Equality or Independence*. Mr Johnson was not a member of some small, extreme political movement: he was the successor of the venerable Maurice Duplessis as head of the very conservative National Union. But there were also excited, eloquent, fearless militants of the overtly separatist movement, the Rassemblement pour l'Indépendance Nationale (RIN), which acted as a sort of ice-breaker, though such autonomists as the barrister François Aquin, the journalist René Levesque, and the senior civil servant Claude Morin let their impatience be known.

At the same time a sort of Quebec lobby was formed in Paris bringing together such Frenchmen as Philippe Rossillon, former director of the Gaullist movement Patrie et Progrès, the diplomat Bernard Doran, Xavier Deniau, who was in charge of the expansion of French-speaking, the former colonial administrator Martial de la Fournière, and such Québecois as André Patry and Jean Loiselle, who kept communications open between Montreal and France. It was a veritable network. When, in April 1966, Daniel Johnson, the man who had introduced the term "independence" into the political life of Quebec, succeeded Jean Lesage as head of the government, the ground was already well prepared. And it was then that the problem of Charles de Gaulle's visit to Quebec arose.

The opening of the International Exhibition at Montreal was fixed for the end of July 1967. About mid-1956, the new Quebec government was working out with the federal authorities the programme for receiving heads of State and of government. Although all the invitations were sent out from Ottawa, Quebec reserved the right to invite the French head of State. At first, de Gaulle expressed strong reservations. What would he be doing at a "fair"?

In April 1967, the fiftieth anniversary of the battle of Vimy, at which ten thousand Canadians died, there was an unfortunate incident: de Gaulle, invited after the Duke of Edinburgh, responded to this lack of correct procedure, by "snubbing" the ceremony. The General was on the point of abandoning the trip – especially as his colleague, Gilbert Pérol, who had been sent to Ottawa to study precisely what the visit would consist of, had been given "the most unfriendly, the least cooperative" welcome that he had ever been given in seven years of similar experience.[6] Then a suggestion was made that delighted him: he should go to Montreal by sea.

On 17 May 1967, the head of the Quebec government, Daniel Johnson, landed in Paris. Charles de Gaulle received him twice at the Elysée, on the 18th and the 20th; though to the European French he may have seemed, with his rural manner and outlandish accent, somewhat exotic, he had, in his own way, a subtle mind, and turned out to be a man of firmly held convictions. The General liked him at once, convinced that he could hardly be dealing with a more authentic representative of a long-lost past. Johnson was perfectly well aware of how to persuade the General to come and lend a strong hand to his enterprise of freeing the Quebec people. Three sentences were enough to convince him: "*Mon Général*, Quebec needs you. It is now or never.[7] Our people will receive you with all the honours and affection due to your rank and person."

Charles de Gaulle believed in a slow process, from Duplessis to Lesage, from Lesage to Johnson. And now, suddenly, he was being urged to realize that 1967 was the decisive year, that Quebec had given herself six months to persuade Ottawa to agree finally to a constitutional reform recognizing that equality of French-speakers that had been recommended by the (largely English-speaking) "BB commission", but which, given the ratio of forces between English and French Canada, only reinforcement from outside could enable Johnson to achieve.

Excited as he always was by this cause, de Gaulle was well aware that federalism, however inequitable it may be, is not colonization. It is a way of keeping under control somewhat backward children, "natives" who could do better if they learnt English and respected the queen; it was not an oppression, it was a sort of vassaldom, corrected by the liberalism of the gentlemen from Westmount and their tolerance for the self-government of others. Why shouldn't they be free to speak the patois of Molière in their farmyards? Provided the Montreal banks were branches of the Toronto ones.

De Gaulle was too much of a nationalist, too much of a centralizer, too much of a Catholic and too imbued with the "civilizing mission of France" not to see this as a mixture of cunning and humiliating condescension. He had been too involved with colonial affairs not to improvise a semi-colonial interpretation of the Canadian situation. For him, that preponderance of the Anglo-Saxon world over a fragment of the French people, that fossil that had survived in a pure state from the centuries of the Valois and the Bourbons, who spoke the language of Molière's peasants, was unbearable.

That was it. He would go, and all the more willingly when he learnt that the federal authorities in Ottawa did not at all care for the fact that de Gaulle had been invited by the Quebec government,* when the federal constitution laid it down that this type of relation belonged to Ottawa, nor that the General would be arriving by sea and would enter Canadian territory on board a cruiser, repeating the royal progress by which Jacques Cartier had opened up to Europe the immense spaces

---

*Which six months earlier had set up a ministry "of Inter-governmental Relations" (thus avoiding the phrase "Foreign Affairs").

of North America. So many symbols, so many reminders, so many challenges!

As he set out from Brest on 15 July 1967, had Charles de Gaulle read the book that had just been published by Gérard Bergeron, Professor of Political Science at Laval University, Quebec, *Le Canada français après deux siècles de patience*?[8] It was a summons, expressed in the most friendly way. According to that Quebec professor, the people who had been abandoned in 1763 had waited long enough: it had the right to demand that France come and lend it a hand, not to be separated from Canada as a whole – that was a matter to be discussed among the Quebec people themselves, then between them, Ottawa, and the other "provinces" – but in order to be able to choose freely.

In short, de Gaulle was ready to set sail from Brest. To Xavier Deniau, a French politician with an interest in the affairs of Quebec who had come to greet him on the quayside, where the motor-boat that was to take him out to the *Colbert* was waiting, he declared: "I'm going to be listened to over there." Three days before, he had confided to General de Boissieu: "It's the opportunity to make up for France's cowardliness." Five days later, landing on the south bank of the St Lawrence, he was to complete those words. Receiving Jean Mauriac in his cabin in the *Colbert*, he declared: "I've decided to go quite a long way!"

The visit began with a problem, which it is difficult to believe was entirely innocent: the officer sent by the federal government* to receive de Gaulle, Commander Plant, did not speak a word of French. It was a way, perhaps, of reminding the visitor that it was not Montcalm, but Wolfe, who had won the battle of Abraham Plains in 1759.

On the morning of 23 July, the *Colbert* was moored at Anse-au-Foulon, the quay situated at the foot of the Quebec citadel from which, in 1759, French Canada had come to an end. At 9 a.m. – it was Sunday – de Gaulle, in military uniform, set foot on the quay where he was received by the Governor-General of Canada, Roland Michener, and the Prime Minister of Quebec, Daniel Johnson.**

Over a small platform, crowded with important figures, floated three flags, the French, the Canadian (with the red maple leaf) and the Quebec (with the blue fleur-de-lys). The military band, wearing red jackets and bearskins, played *God Save the Queen*, interrupted by boos, then the *Marseillaise*, which was taken up in chorus by a large section of the nevertheless carefully chosen public. From the very outset, those who were there were amazed: a referendum was beginning that would continue for three days and swell into a plebiscite.[9]

The visitor delivered a few words, expressing his "esteem" for the Governor and his "friendship" for "Canada as a whole" and to the Prime Minister "the immense joy" that he felt in being "chez vous au Québec". Then he got into the Governor-General's car, in which he drove to the citadel. There he changed to the car of the head of the Quebec government: from then on, he made his way through a human tide, before taking, in front of the City Hall, the *bain de foule*, as he had done from Pont-à-Mousson to Brazzaville and from Marmande to Phnom Penh,

---

*The federal government had authority over the rivers and their banks.
**The whole of the account that follows owes much to two films made during those three days by Quebec television.

with such evident delight. It was from a mass of heads, arms and shouts that he emerged to deliver, first in the City Hall, then in the square, two short, but highly significant speeches.

In the first, he praised Quebec as "the capital of French Canada" and declared, with more boldness, that here "a French Canadian élite is emerging ever more active, more efficacious, better known". Then, on the square before the municipal building, in the midst of the crowd, he was heard in turn to shout out, in an enthusiastic uproar, that "we are at home here, after all!" and that "at this moment, the whole of France sees you, hears you and loves you!" Lunch was taken in the garden of the Quebec seminary attached to Laval University, near the church of Sainte-Anne-de-Beaupré, where he attended mass. After a reception on the rear deck of the *Colbert*, there was the official dinner at the Château Frontenac, during which the expectations of the Quebec people and the contribution of the visitor were defined.

Daniel Johnson's speech might be summed up in two words: help us! De Gaulle's must be quoted at greater length, because it is in a sense an exposition of the motives for a highly premeditated act, of which the "Vive le Québec libre" was only one, if the most strident, form it would take. There were "three essential facts" that defined French policy.

> The first is that a portion of our people after, two hundred and four years ago, the inconsolable sovereignty of France had been snatched from this soil, maintained itself where it was and where it is still. The second fact is that your determination to survive after taking on the character of passive resistance, has now assumed active vigour by becoming the ambition to seize every means of emancipation. The third dominant fact is that as Quebec reveals herself and grows, relations will revive and multiply between the French living on the banks of the St Lawrence and the French living in the basins of the Seine, the Loire, the Garonne, the Rhône and the Rhine. What was kept alive here by sixty thousand French people, who have now become six million, gives exemplary proof to all French people of what our powerful vitality can be.
>
> We are assisting here, as in many regions of the world, at the advent of a people who want, in every domain, to make up their own mind and to take its fate in its own hands. The French part of Canada now intends to organize, in conjunction with other Canadians, means of safeguarding their substance and independence in contact with a colossal State that is their neighbour.

It was a key speech and one that – written in Paris, re-read by Pompidou and Couve – went further in a sense than a mere "Québec libre". For what de Gaulle was advocating, on that Sunday evening, was not only the freeing of Quebec from the rules of an over-protective federalism, but an incitement to the whole of Canada to free herself from the tutelage of a colossal neighbour.

The strange thing is not that Anglo-Saxon opinion should be indignant at a few words spoken on the balcony of Montreal, it was that it did not react more to those sentences delivered the day before, which went further and questioned, not only the weight of Ottawa's protectorate over Quebec, but the docility of federal Canada to the pressure or mere influence of her great southern neighbour. What de Gaulle was describing that evening in the Château Frontenac was not only "Québec libre", but an active, liberating Quebec.

Perhaps the boldness of 24 July found its source in the quiet reception of the 23rd. If they took it so calmly, perhaps it was because they hadn't understood? If he were to shake them out of their lethargy, perhaps he would have to hit them harder, or in a different way? In the tone not of a sacred orator, but of a popular tribune. "Certainly, that Sunday evening," Pierre-Louis Mallen writes, "everything was explained. And yet nothing was. If the deaf were to hear, he would have to shout."[10]

Opened in August in 1734 by the Grand Voyer (Inspector-General of Roads) of New France, the Chemin du Roy linked Quebec to Montreal by following the left bank of the St Lawrence: over 270 kilometres it crossed the old colonized lands, the villages and towns on which the rural genius of Champlain's heirs had been lavished.

De Gaulle, who had slept on board the *Colbert*, got into Daniel Johnson's open car before nine o'clock, Captain Flohic sitting next to the driver. On the edge of the city a triumphal arch had been set up. Twenty more were to follow, as they entered each township. And on the roadway itself were fleurs-de-lys. Everywhere, the crowds were enormous.

Six stop-offs were planned along the way, at Donnaconna,* Sainte-Anne-de-la-Pérade, Trois-Rivières, Louiseville, Berthierville and Repentigny, where, each time, in response to the mayor's speech, the General had to address the crowd. There were many additional stops, caused by the congestion in the villages. In each of the localities where a reception had been organized, de Gaulle was surrounded and lifted out of his car. And, each time, after the mayor's speech and some singing from the local schoolchildren, he embroidered on the theme of Quebec "at last master of its own fate".

After Trois-Rivières, the world capital of paper manufacturing for newspapers, where the party had lunch, the enthusiasm grew wilder. "During the afternoon," François Flohic recounts, "things took a quite different turn; was it a result of the bison steak served at Trois-Rivières? One felt that the morning's formal welcomes were over: contact was now without intermediaries."[11] Everywhere the crowd burst spontaneously into singing the *Marseillaise*, bringing visitors and visited together. The closer they got to Montreal, the denser and more enthusiastic the crowd became. Many tried to stop the General's car by placing themselves in front of it. They were already an hour late.

At Louiseville, the mayor could no longer control himself: "*Mon Général*, for us you are not only a great man, but an old friend!" And at Berthierville (or was it Repentigny?) the school choir, consisting largely of girls, declaimed: "That general, that general, is made of gold, is made of gold!"

And from village to township and from town to town de Gaulle repeated the same message:

*The name of the Huron chief brought back to France by Jacques Cartier.

It is France's duty to help you. She has owed you something for a long time. Well, France wants to pay you back what she owes you, by the assistance that she will give your development. That is why my friend M. Johnson and I have concluded agreements of cooperation. Thus your élites, your scientists, your engineers, your managers, your technicians will contribute to the progress of the old country, to the progress of France.

He was applauded everywhere. De Gaulle travelled the last fifty kilometres before arriving in Montreal standing in the car, forced to do so by the enthusiasm of the crowd.

In the city, from the Rue Sherbrooke (twenty kilometres through the city) to the Rue Saint-Denis and the Hôtel de Ville, where the visitor was expected, the crowd amounted, according to the estimates of the press, to half a million people. In the photographs of the General's arrival in the square in front of the Montreal Hôtel de Ville, one can see, surrounding the car as it cuts through the crowd, the placards of the Rassemblement pour l'Indépendance Nationale, one of whose slogans is: "Vive le Québec libre".

"The cheering drowned the fanfare," Pierre-Louis Mallen recounts. "I saw him, two steps away from me, without being able to hear him, as in a silent film. We were bathed in a huge continuous clamour, consisting of thousands of shouts of 'Vive de Gaulle', 'Vive la France!', 'Le Québec aux Québecois!', 'We shall have our French state', 'France libre!', 'Québec libre!'"[12]

On the steps of the Hôtel de Ville, the mayor, Jean Drapeau, who, as inventor of the exhibition, was the man responsible for those crazy days, received the visitors. To the General, who, very moved, thanked him for the "indescribable" welcome that had just been given him, the mayor, well known as a federalist, replied calmly: "It is the welcome that a great cosmopolitan city gives a great man."[13]

Charles de Gaulle was not a man to allow himself to be reduced in this way to the rank of a touring Caruso. Outside, the crowd roared its greeting, chanting rhythmically the two syllables of his name, alternating them with the three of "Québec libre!" De Gaulle then said to Drapeau: "I must answer them. I must talk to them from the balcony." "But, *mon Général*, the guests await you on the terrace and they want to hear you." "No. It is to them, the people cheering me, that I want to speak." "But there is no microphone on the balcony..." "No microphone?" Then, as if by chance, Paul Comiti, his bodyguard, took the General's arm and led him to a microphone that (unknown to the mayor, who had been determined to avoid that contact – two hours before, he had cut off the sound) had been hastily put back by technicians, who may have belonged either to Radio Québec or to the French Radio team organized by P.-L. Mallen.*

And so Charles de Gaulle stood, between the tall grey Corinthian columns, facing a sort of barracks called Fort-Ramsay and a column on which was placed a rather poor statue of Nelson. Below, twenty yards away, the crowd had tried to force its way into the relatively small square known as the Champs-de-Mars. The

---

*Fifteen years later (April 1982), Jean Drapeau told me, in his office, how staggered he had been to see that accursed microphone emerge on the balcony of his town hall.

shouts from the crowd became deafening. "Vive de Gaulle! Le Québec aux Québecois!" It was 9.30 p.m., on 24 July 1967.

There is a recording of that speech of twenty sentences that was to go round the world, spreading the name of Quebec. It is worth attending to. What is striking about it is its tone, which is not at all exalted, but rather friendly, familiar, almost bantering. There were the two statements that caused a scandal. "I'll let you into a secret, but don't repeat it. This evening here, and all along my route, I found myself in an atmosphere exactly like that of the Liberation." The comparison aroused indignation in the English-speaking world, and shocked many of those who knew what the last word meant to de Gaulle. What? The Quebec people compared with the French under the occupation? We know that the General was not really making such a parallel. He was not comparing historical situations, but moments of rejoicing.

But the form chosen by Charles de Gaulle, that "secret" whispered into the ears of the world, could not fail to offend his federal hosts. Whatever one thinks of the "Québec libre" that was to follow, those words about "liberation" seemed indefensible.

Then came the conclusion of "the call from Montreal", that "Vive le Québec libre" which was to cause so much fuss. That peroration was made up of five exclamations: "Vive Montréal! Vive le Québec! Vive le Québec libre! Vive le Canada français et vive la France!"

The next day, an English newspaper in western Canada wrote that de Gaulle had addressed the Quebec people "as Hitler had addressed the Sudetens* in 1938". That comparison does not hold either. The visitor's tone, as is proved by the recording and the photographs, had nothing exultant about it.

Before going back to the content of the affair, before describing the first reactions that it provoked, we should analyse what drove General de Gaulle, a responsible statesman, to launch those four words that, as he could not fail to realize, would arose keen emotion because they had become one of the slogans of the pro-independence groups, especially the RIN. None of the officials of that party that I have spoken to, beginning with Pierre Bourgault, its principal organizer, or Louise Beaudouin,** conceal the fact that one of their aims was to condition the General, throughout the day, by repeating those words over and over again, from Trois-Rivières to the Rue Sherbrooke, and in the Champs-de-Mars.

"We had not hoped for so much from de Gaulle," Pierre Bourgault admits. "When we heard our cry from his lips, we were drunk with joy and absolutely amazed: so it isn't Johnson that he is supporting, we told ourselves, it's the RIN, us!"[14]

Does that mean that General de Gaulle had been subjugated, intoxicated, conditioned by a group of politicians and that it was under a sort of spell that he had given voice to the famous slogan? Attempts have been made to compare it with his "Vive l'Algérie française!" of 6 June 1958 at Mostaganem. In both cases, after

*The minority of German origin in Czechoslovakia, which Hitler demanded be re-attached to the Reich – a concession that he won at Munich.
**Minister of External Relations of Pierre-Marc Johnson's government in 1985.

a series of carefully prepared speeches, he had come out with the phrase that had been rhythmically repeated to him and which he had so far refrained from saying. One may prefer to place the answer at a higher level and relate it to another slogan that the General had used two days before that of Mostaganem, nine years before that of Montreal, the celebrated "Je vous ai compris!" In both cases, the visitor, bombarded by a slogan expressing the profoundest feelings of the crowd, which had come not to praise him, but to identify with him, to identify him with it, to commune with him, had become so imbued with the spirit surrounding him that he "understood", reflected and echoed the cry repeated a thousand times.

The four words spoken on the balcony at Montreal set concentric waves in motion. Yet general euphoria did not reign in the French delegation. François Flohic notes that around him people looked contrite and that, when he asked Maurice Couve de Murville if he had heard the General's speech, he got this answer: "Yes, he was wrong to speak."

Among the Quebec political class, the independentists were triumphant and, though Mr Johnson and his friends in the government, rather scared, soon decided to take advantage of the visitor's "breakthrough", the liberal opposition, as a whole, faithful to federalism, looked glum. Its leader, the former Prime Minister, Lesage, was to make so strong an attack on Daniel Johnson, who, in his view, had imprudently provoked the storm, that a few leading individuals immediately left his party and joined the independentists: one such was François Aquin, a well-known lawyer and member of parliament.

René Levesque was to follow this example later before founding the Quebec Party. When I asked him, sixteen years later, about Charles de Gaulle's effect on the life of his country, M. Levesque, then Prime Minister, replied: "It did not orientate my decision to join the struggle for sovereignty – on the contrary, it wasted us three months. But he gave incredible publicity to our cause. The whole world was suddenly interested in us. One of our young friends from Quebec, a social worker in Lima, suddenly saw Indians gathering round him: "You're from Quebec, aren't you? The country General de Gaulle talked about.'"[15]

The historian Michel Brunet, who teaches at the University of Montreal, made this comment on the "crazy day", 24 July 1967: "I watched the event on television. When de Gaulle came out with those words, I told myself at first, 'He's joking, the Old Man.' Next day, when urged by my students, three-quarters of whom were independentists, to take up position, I criticized the excessiveness of the General's words – but even more the hateful, racist reaction of the English-speakers, as we saw their mask drop, to reveal their naked superiority complex!"

Some of the Canadian English-speaking press were content to denounce de Gaulle as a "quarrelsome old man", a "reactionary", a "mean-spirited, chauvinistic" politician, a "dictator", an "ageing, self-satisfied statesman", or simply as "senile". But there was also mention, in the *Montreal Star*, of a "furious elephant".

What, then, was to be the reaction of the Ottawa government? Maurice Sauvé, who was then a member of Lester Pearson's federal government, described those tumultuous hours to me:

I listened to the Montreal speech with some irritation, thinking that the "old man" was wandering and would trigger off a huge crisis. So much so that when invited the following day, the 25th, to Vancouver, I telephoned on the evening of the 24th to the Prime Minister to tell him that I was cancelling my trip in order to be present at the extraordinary cabinet meeting that would surely be called for that morning. To my great surprise, the very phlegmatic Pearson advised me not to change my plans: he anticipated no exceptional cabinet meeting. It was my French-speaking colleagues in the cabinet, Marchand and Trudeau* in particular, who mobilized Pearson against General de Gaulle's intervention. In such instances, French-speaking Canadians can be more federalist than the English-speakers. And it was by giving in to their pressure that Pearson hardened his tone and took responsibility for a statement, the terms of which we had discussed for three hours. One of the unfortunate aspects of that crisis was that it set Pearson against France, which he was ready to approach in fact as a counter-weight to Washington and London.

Note that our government had some responsibility for the antipathy that de Gaulle felt for it: Ottawa refused to deliver uranium to France (whereas we sold it to the British and Americans) on the grounds that we had excluded Tokyo from those markets. Why treat Paris like a former enemy, rather than as an ally? On that point, de Gaulle was right.[16]

The statement issued by the Ottawa cabinet, after the angry deliberations described by Maurice Sauvé, could not but reflect a compromise between the Prime Minister's concern not to exaggerate the incident and the determination of the "hard-liners" (Marchand and Trudeau above all) to be firm. Lester Pearson, speaking in French before the television cameras, declared that

some of the President's declarations tended to encourage the small minority of our population whose aim is to destroy Canada and, as such, they are unacceptable to the Canadian people and her government. The Canadian people is free, each Province in Canada is free, the Canadians do not need to be liberated. We attach the greatest importance to friendship with the French people. I hope that the discussions that I shall have later in the week with General de Gaulle will show that this is a wish that he shares.

As the Canadians were listening to their Prime Minister's statement, Charles de Gaulle was preparing to give a banquet in the French pavilion of the International Fair, which he had visited that morning. Just before sitting down to eat, he learnt blow by blow of the Ottawa statement and of the defection of the federal Minister for External Affairs, Paul Martin, who was boycotting his invitation. He hardly showed any trace of emotion.

Meanwhile, Daniel Johnson had been able to get soundings as to Quebec's response to the speech from the balcony at Montreal: after recovering from the initial shock, the reaction of public opinion was expressed by the editorial-writer of

*The future Prime Minister.

La Presse, a large-circulation daily, regarded as moderate: "The welcome given to General de Gaulle by a usually undemonstrative population," wrote Guy Cormier, "is equivalent to a plebiscite. Life and liberty being the two greatest goods in this world, one might wonder what was so scandalous about that 'Vive le Québec libre!' When de Gaulle celebrates free Quebec he is expressing one of the strongest aspirations of our time."

De Gaulle whispered to Johnson, in the tone of a kindly visiting uncle, "I don't think either of us has wasted his time. Perhaps something has happened. If, on this occasion, the President of the French Republic has been able, who knows, to be useful to the French people of Quebec, he will be deeply pleased and France with him, believe me."

The Quebec Prime Minister then said boldly: "Language and culture are not the only gifts that France has bequeathed us. There is another that we value even more: that is the cult of liberty. We would no longer be French if we were not in love with liberty. Large or small, all nations have a right to life and control over their own destinies."

Mr Johnson could hardly have taken up the "Vive le Québec libre!" with greater swagger, or authenticated it more clearly. Hitherto the slogan had been that of the young members of the RIN; the man with the moustache and manners of a backwards farmer now made it the slogan of the Quebec majority that had recently elected him.

So Quebec "followed". Armed with that essential consent, General de Gaulle turned back to Ottawa. Was he to take notice, in the response of the federal authorities, of the "unacceptable" or the "let's talk all the same"?

It was clear that Mr Pearson was right in a formal sense – de Gaulle had, in the strict sense, interfered in the internal relations of a foreign state. It was no less clear that the visitor had good arguments as to substance at his disposal: the majority of the Quebec people aspired to a status that reinforced their personality as a profoundly original "people", whose relations with Ottawa could not be quite the same as those enjoyed by Alberta or Manitoba, and whose relations with France could not remain those that one would have with any purely foreign state.

That substance should come before form, de Gaulle was so certain that he did not wish to see, in the text issued by Lester Pearson, anything more than a hypocritical rebuff to the man who was simply telling the naked truth. But he could not draw the consequences of the negative elements of the Ottawa text without alerting his Prime Minister to them. Woken at five in the morning (it was midnight in Montreal), Georges Pompidou learnt that the General would not be going to Ottawa, where, he considered, he had just been declared *persona non grata* and that, when he had completed his Quebec programme, during the following afternoon, he would return straight to Paris. His later statements were to confirm this: de Gaulle had no wish to go to Ottawa. So, about 9 a.m. on the following day, 25 July, while an article appeared in *The Times* of London, which the normally placid Couve de Murville described as "outrageous" (it referred to "the slow, sad process of decline of a Head of State adrift") and while the Paris press expressed not so much enthusiasm as a sort of reverential terror, General de Gaulle visited the Montreal métro, which had just been built by a French firm. He was besieged by journalists: would he be received in the federal capital? "It's the first time since 1936 I've been in the métro," he replied.[17] But he pursued his programme like a diligent visitor: at the University, where, before the staff flanked by Cardinal Léger, Archbishop of Montreal, he entered the great amphitheatre, filled by students who had broken off their vacation to hear him, and delivered a speech to which he had attached great importance and which he had written in Paris.

Extolling "that great totality that I call French, that great totality of intelligence, feeling and reason" indispensable to the balance and "progress of the world", de Gaulle stressed the training of the élites needed by the "Canadian fraction of the French people in that vast, new country, the neighbour of a colossal State that, by sheer size, can put your own entity in question". That phrase "colossal State" again! What the Americans had forgiven him for in March 1964, in Mexico City, before the great tensions caused by the challenge to the hegemony of the dollar, France's withdrawal from the military structures of NATO and the dropping of Israel, was now regarded as a crime. The American press took up the arguments of *The Times*: How could they put an end to the excesses of that senile agitator?

There was one last confrontation, at the Hôtel de Ville of Montreal, between Charles de Gaulle and Jean Drapeau. How was Drapeau to come out of it, caught as he was between the good-naturedness that was his trademark and his federalist convictions, which had been so insulted by the "Québec libre"? Sixteen years later, M. Drapeau defended himself to me for having "wanted to give a lesson to so great a man", who had since shown him "innumerable instances of friendship".[18]

The fact is that Jean Drapeau's speech was a fairly clever mixture of good-humoured civilities and pained remonstrances. He had done his duty. When he sat down, his face red with his efforts, observed with amusement by those who knew him well, the cumbersome visitor rose slowly to his feet.

First he amused himself with a history lesson: they were all there, Cartier and Champlain, Maisonneuve* and Jeanne Manse,** Montcalm and Levis, and, of course, "the conquering English". And then he reached the present day: "During my trip – as a result of a sort of shock, about which neither you nor I could do anything, it was elementary – and we were all seized by it, I think I was able to reach what concerns you at bottom. In particular the destiny of the Canadian-French or French-Canadian people, as you will." And Jean Drapeau had not recovered from his emotion when he heard: "And as for the rest, all that swarming, wrangling, scribbling mass has no historical consequence in great circumstances."

After that contemptuous attack, he was to find a conclusion of a more elevated, nobler tone in the testamentary style: "When I have left you, I would like you to have kept the idea that the presence for a few days of General de Gaulle in this rapidly evolving Quebec, this Quebec that is taking hold of itself, this Quebec that is making up its own mind, this Quebec that is becoming master of itself – that my trip, I say, has been able to contribute to your enthusiasm."[19]

At Dorval airport, though no announcement was made, several hundred people

*Founder of Montreal.
**A nun and nurse to whom there are many statues in Quebec.

were waiting for him, including, at the foot of the steps leading up to the plane, Daniel Johnson and Jean Drapeau. They could not stop the crowd approaching and cheering him. There were a lot of journalists there, too. One of them took a photograph that was published next day in one of the most important English-speaking dailies, *The Gazette*. But those responsible for that honest publication had cut off the bottom of the picture, thus removing anyone else but de Gaulle himself; de Gaulle appeared alone, on the last step, about to enter the plane. The caption of that ingenious picture read: "Nobody waved goodbye".

The head of state's plane took off shortly before 4.30 p.m., the arrival being expected in Paris the following day at 4 a.m. While Madame de Gaulle was plunged in a book, the General summoned in turn in the sort of small private sitting-room that had been set up for him colleagues and travelling companions, including a few journalists. Jean-Daniel Jurgenson, director of American affairs at the Quai d'Orsay, found words calculated to move the traveller. "*Mon Général*, you have paid the debt of Louis XV!"

"I'm going to be dragged through the mire," de Gaulle confided to his travelling companion. "You've seen the foreign press. Wait till you see the French press. Mind you, what I did, I had to do."[20]

Several articles in the Quebec press and several comments made, years later, by the leaders at the time have already been quoted: from this it emerges that there was certainly an "appeal" from a pro-independence minority (about 8 to 10 per cent of the potential voters) and understanding or support from a majority of "French Canadians" wanting greater liberty or equality. These are some of the implications of an opinion poll carried out shortly after the General's trip by CROP (Centre de Recherches sur l'Opinion Publique) of Montreal.

It emerged from that poll that almost 70 per cent of French Canadians thought the visit had been a success, that a little under 60 per cent considered that de Gaulle had not interfered in the internal affairs of Canada, and 65 per cent that by advocating the liberty of Quebec he had not incited the province to secede from Canada as a whole.[21]

In Paris, the two main leaders of opinion, *Le Monde* and *Le Figaro*, had taken up or were taking up a position against the head of state's initiatives over Quebec. The first (26 July 1967) questioned above all the procedure of de Gaulle's intervention and the form taken by the appeal delivered from Montreal's Hôtel de Ville. In *Le Figaro*, André François-Poncet, former French Ambassador to the Third Reich, then to Fascist Italy, a member of the Académie Française, thundered in indignation, denouncing the visit as "humiliating", a "misadventure incurred by the French Head of State", and even more the "revolutionary character" of his action.

Ever since there was such a thing as French diplomacy, the Head of State, before setting out on an official visit abroad, submitted the text of his speeches to the Head of Government and to his Foreign Minister. The personal regime has overthrown these customs. The General had certainly not prepared his oratorical interventions.* He abandoned himself to his

---

*We know that this criticism is not well founded, except in relation to the speech from the balcony of the Hôtel de Ville in Montreal.

inspiration. He let himself be carried away by his enthusiasm. He was led astray. Unfortunately, he is not modest enough to admit his error. He will persist in it.[22]

The atmosphere that met the General on his return is well described by Alphand:

At four o'clock in the morning, at Orly, we awaited the General's return from Quebec. All the ministers were there. Some did not conceal their irritation. "He's crazy," said one. "This time he's gone too far," said another. Then the great man appeared, tired, but smiling, raising his arms to heaven at the sight of all those people assembled at that ungodly hour, and they all forgot their reservations, hence that photograph in which everybody is laughing, as if we were all congratulating ourselves on a good trick played on a pal.[23]

The photograph published in *France-Soir* that day shows a bantering, almost hilarious de Gaulle and twenty astonished men, in the grip of an attack of the giggles. Even the most reserved of the travellers, Maurice Couve de Murville, who had been forced to acknowledge that in three days his country had altered three important alliances, infused a little Québecois enthusiasm into his colleagues' hearts. To the closest and most faithful of them, who was no less a Gaullist than he and who remarked a few hours later, "This time, the General went too far!", he replied, his eyes on some distant horizon, "If you had been swept up as I was in that wave of enthusiasm, you would understand better. It was unimaginable, that Chemin du Roy, unimaginable."

Two days after his return to Paris, de Gaulle was to receive great comfort from Montreal – in the form of a government statement from Daniel Johnson, who dismissed once and for all the allegations of newspapers accusing the visitor of reviving an almost extinguished fire:

General de Gaulle received a triumphal welcome from our population. The Quebec government is delighted that we invited him. Taking up ideas that had been expressed many times by recent Quebec governments. He greeted the conviction that is more and more that of the Quebec people, that it is free to choose its own destiny, like every people in the world.

So it was as a man who knew that he was approved by those whose part he had taken that General de Gaulle chaired the meeting, on Monday 31 July, of the Council of Ministers, where around the green table, a leaden, vaguely disapproving silence reigned. The General spoke:

I had already been to Canada on three other occasions. But the fact of French Canada had not yet crystallized. This time I was seized by the French upsurge, so widespread, so impressive, even more than I had imagined it to be. For two hundred years, the French Canadians have lived closed up upon themselves, without contact with us. They no longer wanted that domination, but they had not become aware. I took cognizance in the name of France of that evident pressure of the French Canadians. I did not tell them to rebel! In fact, they must conclude arrangements with their neighbours: the Americans and the English. Those arrangements can only be made on the basis of freedom and independence. To begin with, there must be a State. And Ottawa? I couldn't go there and anyway I was not very keen to do so. Of course, the Anglo-Saxons are furious. That's understandable. That the Anglo-Saxon press is furious at the revelation of the French fact is obvious, too. But that the French press should join in is incredible. *Le Monde* is a scandal. Anyway, our press is in the final stage of degradation. Especially as I said nothing to offend anybody. After all, it was France that populated Canada and forged its soul and spirit. Things aren't settled yet. They're only just beginning. It's a great matter, it's a matter of culture, the universities, a generation determined to become its own boss in its own country.[24]

Better perhaps than all those public texts are the few sentences spoken to his aide-de-camp Jean d'Escrienne about his Quebec adventure.

If you had seen those French people, who had been waiting for so long for a gesture, a word, some support from France to help them get out of their unacceptable condition. No, I could not disappoint them! So I turned on the switch and things will now pursue their course, I think! In fact, it may have been a little premature: but, I'm old, it was then or never, and I grabbed the opportunity. Who, after me, could have said that, if I had not? And it had to be said![25]

The conclusion of the affair was to be drawn by de Gaulle on the occasion of a press conference held on 27 November 1967, which saw the now celebrated description of the Jewish people as "self-confident and dominating", which, for the first time for five months, put the Quebec affair somewhat in the shade.

It is obvious that the national movement of the Canadian French and also the balance and peace of Canada as a whole, and even the future of relations between our country and the other communities of that vast territory, and even the conscience of the world, which has now been aroused – all that demands that the question be resolved. Two conditions are required. The first involves a complete change of the present Canadian political structure, as it resulted from the Act granted a hundred years ago by the Queen of England, by which the "federation" was created. In my opinion, that will lead inevitably to the advent of Quebec as a sovereign State, master of her own national existence, as of so many peoples, so many other States in the world that are not as viable or even as populated as that one would be. Of course, that State of Quebec would have to regulate freely and on an equal footing with the rest of Canada in order to master and exploit a nature that is very difficult over such vast expanses and to confront the strength of the United States. The second condition on which the solution of this great problem depends is that the solidarity of the French community on both sides of the Atlantic should be organized. In this respect, things have already begun. The next meeting, in Paris, between the Quebec government and the government of the Republic must, we hope, give even greater momentum to that great French work that is essential in our century. Indeed in that work all the French people of Canada who are not resident in Quebec and who number a million and a half will have to take part in conditions that will have to be worked out.[26]

It is easy, eighteen years later, and almost ten years after the referendum of 1980 that expressed the refusal of the majority of the Quebec people to set out towards independence, to reject the prophet's grand vision. Perhaps because he had ignored or underestimated three important factors in the situation: the progress that had been made since 1960 by the French Canadians, under Jean Lesage, then Daniel Johnson, slow progress, but progress that led many of its beneficiaries to consider the radical strategy of the French President as over-adventurous; the American nature of that people, French in origin and language but profoundly Americanized in its way of life and proud to take part in the epic of the New World; lastly, the federalist impregnation of the society that, unlike the old country in Europe, with its tireless Cartesian outlook, could accommodate itself quite happily to a mixed sovereignty, or various national personalities coexisting under the same crown, where a door may be both open and shut.

One thing is worth mentioning here on the matter of de Gaulle's underestimate of the "Americanness" of the people of Quebec. In the answers to the August questionnaire published among other papers by *Le Soleil*, one notes that the French Canadians did not care very much to be called "Canadian French", by the visitor. Québecois? Certainly. French Canadians? Probably. But French, no. By what right did the old country, which had dropped us so long ago, now claim to be our nation?

A few days before his death, de Gaulle remembered, the Mediterranean Paul Valéry wrote these words about French Canada capable of inspiring a bold initiative:

> What has been done in so many centuries of searching, misfortunes and greatness must not perish. The fact that there exists a French Canada is a comfort to us, an incalculable element for hope. French Canada affirms our presence on the American continent. It shows what our vitality, our endurance, our capacity for work can be. It is to French Canada that we should convey the most precious thing we have, our spiritual riches.

How could such a text not induce active enthusiasm in de Gaulle? And what would have been his reaction if he had read these sentences written by Arnold Toynbee in *Civilization on Trial*: "If mankind as a whole awaits a happy future, then I would willingly predict that there is a future in the old world for the Chinese, and in North America for the *Canadiens*.* Whatever mankind's future in North America may be, I am sure that those French-speaking Canadians will in any case be present at the conclusion of the adventure."

The adventure: it was a British writer who whispered the last word to us.

*In French in the original.

VI

THE STATE GENERAL

CHAPTER THIRTY-FOUR

Limitations of a Grand Design

One day in late summer 1967, Hervé Alphand, Secretary-General at the Quai d'Orsay, noted in his diary:

> The General's popularity seems to have been affected by events. His enemies reproach him for his lonely pride, his *rapprochement* with the Russians and Arabs, his mistrust of the Anglo-Saxons; he is good with the poor and quarrels with the rich; he abandons his old friends for new ones of dubious reputation; he offends received ideas and conventions. His opponents consider him to be made of rock and ice. He must live long enough for circumstances to prove that, alone in the midst of this ocean of protests and rancour, he saw things aright.[1]

It was the period when Valéry Giscard d'Estaing, an important figure of the regime, denounced that "solitary exercise of power". It was the time when, according to the British press, the General was suffering from a sclerosis that would not spare the old gentleman long enough to demonstrate the accuracy of his prophecies. It was the time when American journalists were denouncing the "homicidal madness" of that "ungrateful old man".

But the old storm-maker had not yet blown his last. On 6 September 1967, he set out for Poland. If there was one journey that he had to undertake it was that one. Not so much on account of the memories that he allowed himself to evoke, those associated with his stay there from 1919 to 1921, as of the history and strategic situation of that frontier country. Was it not the fate of Poland that, on 8 and 9 December 1944, well before Yalta, had been the subject of the altercations between Stalin and him that carried within them the inevitable splitting of Europe that he now hoped to repair? Could his "Europe from the Atlantic to the Urals" find a better and deeper response than on those lands where a Slav people, thoroughly imbued with the West, had not ceased for a century to shake off the alternate yokes of her neighbours? It was there that he had to go and declare that only détente would allow the independence of medium-sized nations and that once the terror had been removed, they would be able to recover their autonomy.

The climate was established from the outset.* At Okacie airport, he greeted, in Polish, the detachment presenting arms with, "Greetings, soldiers". The reaction was enthusiastic. The enthusiasm grew as the days went by, when it became clearer that the man of "Free Quebec" had not come to those lands implacably

---

*I make use here of a few memories of that trip that I wrote up for *Le Nouvel Observateur*.

hammered by colonizers to advocate resignation to the order set up at Yalta. On the second day, for example, the visitor let fly a well-directed arrow at the politics of the power blocs. At the Belvedere Palace, before the three principal officers of state,* he declared as if it were self-evident: "France always wanted an independent Polish state, while others have not always wanted it. For us, you are a popular, secure, respectable and powerful reality, in a world that must be one of balance and independence; you are a people that must be in the first rank."

Of course, none of us who were there at his visit to the camp at Auschwitz could forget it. We had seen de Gaulle elsewhere, fearless or sovereign, exalted or playful, merry or episcopal. But there he was simply the distressed survivor of a drama so immense, so utterly excessive that one could not but be overcome with emotion. Birkenau 1, Birkenau 2, those two camps that were the capitals of death. Rather than our own memories, let us quote those of an observer who was much closer to the General, his aide-de-camp, Jean d'Escrienne:

> I don't remember ever seeing the General so "caught off balance", so incapable of expressing what he felt, as he was at the end of that visit, when asked to sign the Golden Book. He was sitting there, outside, at a small table on which the book had been opened on a blank page. He put on his spectacles, picked up his pen and remained for several seconds uncertain and silent before writing. I was standing, to his right, quite close to him and saw him write at last, a third of the way down the page, in two lines, "Quelle tristesse! Quelle pitié." Then he paused, once again unable to find his words for quite a long time. Finally, before the words "Quelle tristesse", he wrote two more words, "Quel dégoût", added an exclamation mark, then sank once again, for several moments, into his thoughts. At last, as if he really did not know how to end it, after "Quel dégoût, Quelle tristesse, Quelle pitié", he wrote again, "Quel espérance humaine!", signed it and dated it.[2]

On Sunday 10 September, the local leaders at Gdansk gave a luncheon in his honour at Sopot, a nearby seaside resort. At the end of the meal, the General rose to his feet. Three years before the strikes and demonstrations that were to open up a new chapter in the history of the Polish people, the General declared before the local officials:

> You have it in you to be a great country. Now that your misfortunes and difficulties regarding frontiers have been overcome by your victory, which is also ours, you must look ahead. France has no advice to give Poland, but it has enough friendship and respect for her to be glad of the new vocation that is yours. She hopes that you will see a little further, a little bigger perhaps than you have been allowed to so far. Without any doubt you will overcome the obstacles that now seem to you to be insurmountable. You all understand what I mean.[3]

The reaction came the following day, in Warsaw. This time, it was Gomulka himself, who, before the Polish Diet, delivered to the stormy tempter the sternest

---

*Ochab, Cyrankiewicz and Rapacki. The Party leader, Gomulka, had not yet turned up.

niet that a visitor to Poland had ever heard. The door was being slammed shut: "Renascent Poland has drawn all the conclusions stemming from her historical experiences. The Alliance with the Soviet Union, combined with the treaties concluded with the Socialist States of Eastern Europe, is the cornerstone of the policy of the People's Republic of Poland."

The "historical experiences" of his country had led Gomulka to prefer the Russian protectorate, strengthened to the west by East Germany, to any innovation. General de Gaulle regarded that strange Poland with some surprise. Had that historian of European tensions misjudged the power of the Communist ideology?

Thus de Gaulle learnt that between the Atlantic and the Urals there had passed and would pass, for a long time to come, only those currents that the masters in the Kremlin controlled. He now knew that Moscow's grip would not be loosened and that, although one may keep one's distance from Washington, the only "distances" known to Moscow were those that her tanks had to cover in twenty-four hours.

Was it there, at this time, that the General's "grand design" collapsed? The speech he gave a few hours later on Polish television seemed flat and dry. What he talked of now was "peace" and "cooperation". Any appeal to another destiny had been excluded. And even the very words that he spoke in Polish, at the end, sounded more nostalgic than exalting.

Next day, Maurice Couve de Murville, calm and collected, received at the French Embassy the twenty or so French journalists who had followed the trip. And when asked whether the General was not too disappointed by the rejection that the head of the Polish Party had just given him, the minister put on an air of great astonishment and replied that since nothing had been suggested to Mr Gomulka that in any way resembled a distancing from Moscow, the General could not have felt any disappointment in what he had said. To believe that would hardly have been flattering to Charles de Gaulle.

Had communications between de Gaulle and Gomulka broken down when the General left? Not if we are to believe Jean d'Escrienne, who was close enough to the General and his host to have heard the Polish leader whisper a few words to the visitor as he left. After "thanking him for what he had said during the visit", he added: "I hope it will be possible one day." One day?

Not all the international efforts of the President of the Fifth Republic at this time can be summed up as so many brakes on those who wanted to act and acceleration given to those who did not. It was not because Paris had been chosen as the site of the conference between Washington and Hanoi to put an end to the Vietnam war that de Gaulle should be presented as a peacemaker. His Phnom Penh speech, because it denounced only American responsibility, was not of a kind to bring him a role as mediator or arbiter. But de Gaulle had done enough to open up the dialogue, during the months leading up to the conference, for Washington to agree to its being held in Paris.

Raymond Aubrac, a former companion of Jean Moulin, Commissioner of the Republic at Marseille, had become friendly with Ho Chi Minh during the Vietnam conference at Fontainebleau in 1946. Twenty years later, Henry Kissinger, meeting him at a conference, told him that Washington was beginning to wonder about the possibility of a negotiated solution. Could he sound out Hanoi? De Gaulle encouraged Raymond Aubrac to go to Vietnam with his friend Hubert Marcovitch. At Hanoi, the two French visitors were given only a confirmation: an end to the bombing of the North was the prior condition to any dialogue. When, sixteen months later, Henry Kissinger was in the White House, at the side of Richard Nixon, he knew that he had at his disposal a Paris link in case a political solution to Vietnam came into view. The idea was accepted by the new President. During his talks in 1967 with General de Gaulle in Paris where, he indicated, "we shall devote a lot of time to Vietnam", the man who was not yet the principal Republican candidate for the White House heard de Gaulle express the wish to see the United States withdraw from Vietnam, but not precipitously – not "in a catastrophe".

Before the man in whom he had placed his trust took his responsibilities in Washington, de Gaulle was to intervene once again in the Vietnam debate. On 31 March 1968, Lyndon Johnson, giving in at last to the urgings of Clark Clifford, announced both the cessation of American bombing over most of North Vietnam and his decision not to seek a second term as President. De Gaulle reacted at once. Realizing that these gestures might do something to reverse the situation, he took the initiative of a statement greeting the "courageous" position of the American President.

We do not know how much General de Gaulle was responsible for the decisions taken towards peace in Vietnam by those two men who admired him so much, Nixon and Kissinger. Marginal though it may have been, the influence exerted by the French President on his American counterpart cannot be dismissed.

13 May 1968 might have been regarded as a glorious day in the implementation of Gaullian strategy: at the very moment when in Paris, near the Etoile, the heads of the American and Vietnamese delegations, Averell Harriman and Xuan Thuy, the poet-civil servant from Hanoi, faced each other for the first time, the General himself had gone off to Bucharest, where Nicolai Ceauşescu, the only head of government in Eastern Europe who had dared to put the interests of his own country before Moscow's directives, awaited him.

On the one side, peace; on the other, independence. But, on that same day, the demonstrating students occupied the Sorbonne and 300 000 of them chanting "Dix ans c'est assez"* launched the most wounding challenge to the Elysée by making that 13 May 1968 not the climax of Gaullian diplomacy, but the beginning of the decline of the Gaullian Republic.

As a result, that visit to Romania very nearly did not take place. Throughout the morning and afternoon of the 13th the Romanian chargé d'affaires in Paris had awaited from the Elysée news of a postponement of the trip. Yet, that night, Maurice Couve de Murville had achieved, against the opinion of the Interior Minister, Christian Fouchet, the decision to maintain the visit to Bucharest exactly as planned. The General, so attentive to the signs of greatness, so anxious to make France appear at the four corners of the earth, hesitated right up to the last

*"Ten years are enough", a reference to 13 May 1958.

minute. He chose, as always, the bigger risk and, on the morning of 14 May, flew to Bucharest.

Of the General's reception there, François Flohic remembers above all the precautions taken by that highly policed regime to conceal not only its guests, but also its leaders from popular curiosity. De Gaulle and his party were lodged outside the city, "in total isolation".4 It was only at the end of the trip, on the road back between Craiova and Bucharest, that a huge, vibrant crowd was able to hear him speak.

From the moment that he set foot at Banéàsà, he had fixed his aim: "Let our Europe begin to re-establish herself in independence." And, that evening, confronting all the representatives of the East European states, he elaborated: "How is one to admit that, for countries as burdened with reason and experience as those of our Europe, a situation can endure in which many of them find themselves caught between two opposed blocs, bend under one external political, economic and military direction and endure the permanent presence of foreign forces on their territory?"5 Here, "as in France", the permanent presence of foreign forces had come to an end, and de Gaulle was purely and simply challenging the Soviet Empire. Russian, East German and Bulgarian diplomats applauded him: but they had less reason to do so than the Queen's representatives had had, ten months earlier, in Ottawa.

Was that encounter between rebels the culminating point of Gaullian diplomacy? One may take it as such, especially if one does not forget that decline follows the high point. A great foreign policy can only rest on a solidly based nation. From May 1968, despite the electoral triumph of June, the Fifth Republic was too beset by unknown quantities for the General's liberating message not to be greeted with growing scepticism.

Paris had greeted the Prague Spring with great sympathy, qualified by the prudence that comes with the realization of a long-cherished dream. That President Novotny, a docile Stalinist, a symbol of the Europe of hermetically sealed blocs, should give up his post to old General Svoboda (whose name means freedom), was regarded as the beginning of a scenario that might have been written at the Elysée, especially as the initiatives then taken by the new Party Secretary, Alexander Dubček, certainly confirmed what de Gaulle had said in Poland ten months earlier. And if Czechoslovakia became free, was not the great dream of a Europe from the Atlantic to the Urals beginning to take shape?

De Gaulle, a man who had never recovered from the hideous humiliation of Munich and the Nazi occupation of Czechoslovakia, had pleasant memories of his talks with Eduard Beneš, the chief architect of Czechoslovakia, in London, during the war: and Prague had been the first liberated capital where he had wanted to be represented, sending Leclerc, the liberator of Paris, there. If only that high place of liberties and European civilization, that first victim of Hitler, could regain her freedom of decision, the fate of Europe might be transformed.

On 1 May, a festive Prague gave its support to Alexander Dubček and his liberal friends, Smirkovsky, Cisar, Cernik, Kriegel; but, a few days later, Dubček was summoned to Moscow by Leonid Brezhnev. He could not refuse the Soviet leader permission for the great Warsaw Pact manoeuvres to take place at the end of June in Czechoslovakia – nor, once the exercises were over, could he stop the Red Army staying. Among the satellites, he found two at least willing to urge Moscow to be understanding, the Romanian Ceauşescu and the Hungarian Kádar. But the Pole Gomulka very soon joined the "repressive" side.

Furthermore, there were rumours that there was something far more likely to upset those old Bolsheviks than the measures of liberalization adopted in Prague: there was talk of contacts between Prague and the Federal German Republic. There was talk of a neutralist hypothesis, a "Romanian way" for Czechoslovakia, of a revision of the Warsaw Pact. *Pravda* even referred to caches of American weapons. These rumours continued to make Dubček more and more out of favour in the Kremlin and to weaken the position of his friends in the socialist camp.

Two meetings between leaders of the Soviet bloc, at Cierna Nad Tisou and Bratislava in late July and early August, gave hope that a compromise would be reached, on the basis of the internal gains of the movement, that would open up a "Hungarian Way" rather than a "Romanian" one in Prague. But, while Dubček constantly warned his colleagues against "provocation", the welcome given to Tito and Ceauşescu by the Prague population was an affront to Moscow.

De Gaulle observed this process with a vigilance combined at first with hope, but very soon with anxiety. When, in early July, Jean-Marie Domenach, a writer whom he respected, asked to see him after returning from Prague, he told him that all his sympathy was with Dubček and his supporters. But he added; "It's all very fine, but they're going too quickly, and too far. The Russians will intervene, then, as always, the Czechs will give up fighting and night will fall once again over Prague."[6]

On 20 August, just before midnight, troops flown in by air and Soviet tanks occupied Prague and the provinces without encountering any opposition. The Kremlin propaganda machine considered that it would be better to declare that the operation had been carried out "at the request" of leading figures in the Czech state: but the accomplices of the operation, Bilak and Indra, did not dare to show themselves until much later. Although vehement protests were made against the invasion, the reformist leaders, led by Dubček, asked their people not to resist the aggressors. Five months later, the student Jan Palach set fire to himself on a square in central Prague.

The statement published after a meeting of the Council of Ministers in Paris was expressed in the strongest terms:

> The armed intervention of the Soviet Union in Czechoslovakia shows that the Moscow government has not abandoned the politics of blocs that has been imposed in Europe as a result of the Yalta agreements and which is incompatible with the right of peoples to dispose of themselves as they wish. France, which did not take part in those agreements and which is not adopting that policy, takes note of and deplores the fact that the events in Prague not only constitute an infringement of the rights and destiny of a friendly nation, but are of a nature to undermine détente in Europe, which she herself practises and urges others to do so, and which alone can ensure peace.

Alain de Boissieu, who was then spending a holiday at La Boisserie, has some interesting comments on his father-in-law's reaction to the Prague events:

> Before reacting, General de Gaulle waited to find out whether the Czechs had defended themselves militarily. Hours passed and we learnt at Colombey that no unit of the Czech army, either on land or in the air, had fired a single shot at the invaders. Of course, there had been hostile and courageous demonstrations by the populations of the cities, but nothing from the armed forces. That scandalized de Gaulle, who observed to me that East German police had fought in Berlin against the Soviet tanks, that the Hungarian army had done as much, that if such an invasion had taken place in Yugoslavia or Poland, the army would probably have opened fire. "What can you do for a nation that does not want to defend itself?"[7]

Moreover, General de Boissieu relates how his father-in-law, when put in possession of very precise information about the threat of a Soviet invasion on the occasion of the "great manoeuvres" of early July, had immediately warned General Svoboda, whom he had known personally since 1941. Svoboda had replied that he thanked him for the information, but that, when alerted, Mr Dubček had replied that General de Gaulle, "being a capitalist officer is utterly ignorant of the Marxist mentality and that the Soviet Communists would not dare to invade Czechoslovakia".[8]

Seventeen years later, Etienne Burin des Roziers who for a long time had been his closest colleague at the Elysée, drew this conclusion from the Prague affair, from Charles de Gaulle's point of view: "It was a very hard blow for him. His view of the future of Europe involved the re-establishment of our traditional relations with our friends in the East. He considered that détente provided the best hope of emancipation on offer. Obviously, the Prague affair smashed that hope."[9]

The old gentleman faced that terrible catastrophe calmly and no one was less inclined than he to reveal the signs of any discouragement. But something was shattered in his great hope. Something was corrupted in the prospects that he held out so nobly to the East. Five years of effort to file down the Iron Curtain and so restore to the states of central Europe their role as link between East and West, their cultural duality, their political ambiguity, had come to nothing.

Did this amount to a return or reconversion to the West? If the socialist camp was so firmly established that a mediator burnt his fingers when he tried to extend a hand, and if the Third World was typified by the ill-temper of the Chinese press (which now called the French state, four years after the effusions of 1964, an "imperialist clique"), by the Arab rejection (which his defeat in June had plunged into greater despair than ever) and by the statements of African and Madagascan "clients", there was little alternative but to draw into that reorganization of the Atlantic Alliance and of Western Europe that were the immediate zones of action of French diplomacy. De Gaulle was going round in circles.

But although de Gaulle wanted to turn once again to his allies and neighbours, his efforts were not particularly well received for all that. In his memoirs, Etienne Manac'h expresses the view that the General was not to recover from the great shocks of the previous summer. "Everyone had got bolder and attacked him. He no longer carried weight. Events killed off his policy."[10]

Nevertheless, in that autumn of 1968, there were a few signs of a possible improvement in relations between Paris and Washington, on the one hand, and between France and Britain, on the other. The two English-speaking capitals had sent new ambassadors to Paris, whose dynastic character were likely to seduce General de Gaulle: from Washington arrived Sargent Shriver, J. F. Kennedy's brother-in-law,* and from London, Sir Christopher Soames, Winston Churchill's son-in-law.**

On the American side, there was, with each day that passed, greater appreciation of the almost day-to-day cooperation with French experts in the preliminary phase of the negotiations with Hanoi. A reading of the diary of Etienne Manac'h, director of Asian affairs at the Quai d'Orsay, is illuminating from this point of view: not a day passed but this inspirer of Gaullist policy in Indo-China also inspired American diplomacy.[11]

Relations between the Americans and de Gaulle might be analysed as a series of crises and disagreements against a background of traditional sympathy; relations between the British and de Gaulle were, since the advent of the Labour Party, more like an underhand guerrilla war of unappeased jealousies and cleverly cooked up plots.

On the French side, several factors – one personal, another tactical, a third fundamental – were to urge a revision of this *mésentente cordiale*. Firstly, there was the arrival at the Quai d'Orsay of Michel Debré, a thoroughgoing anglophile. Secondly, there was the prospect of a re-negotiation of the British application to join the Common Market: at the pace at which things were going, marked by the decline of General de Gaulle's personal authority, there was a strong risk that the "smaller" European members would manoeuvre things in such a way against him that he would have no alternative but to give in to British membership or leave the Community.

The third reason for this *rapprochement* was the deepest: the rise in power, and self-confidence, of West Germany. London and Paris had never had such friendly relations than when confronted by the expansion of German power. On the other hand, the de Gaulle–Adenauer axis, from 1958, had alarmed British diplomacy. From 1966, the tone adopted by some of the Bonn leaders, such as Franz Josef Strauss, or by such great European bureaucrats as Walter Hallstein, led people to think in London that the risk of disequilibrium no longer lay in Paris, and that the axis symbolized by the de Gaulle–Adenauer treaty of 1963 had been broken. So, in November 1968, at a time when France was shaken by a monetary crisis which demonstrated the supremacy of the German economy, London gave a favourable reception to the idea thrown out by Michel Debré of a Franco-British dialogue on European affairs.

*He married Kennedy's sister, Eunice.
**He was Mary Churchill's husband.

Charles de Gaulle took things in hand and invited the British Ambassador to lunch on 10 January: it would be surprising indeed if he could not recreate a favourable climate with Churchill's son-in-law. For a number of reasons, the meeting was postponed until 4 February, the eve of a trip by the British Prime Minister, Harold Wilson, to Bonn – a circumstance that was to play an important role. Anyway, the luncheon at the Elysée, which was attended only by General and Mme de Gaulle, the Ambassador and Lady Soames, and which was preceded and followed by two long private discussions, made it possible to start a dialogue that had become rare between representatives of Britain and France.

Speaking in the most friendly terms, the General described to his guest the "European" Europe that he would like to see arise. Recalling that he was still fairly sceptical about Britain's membership of such a whole, he agreed that more thoroughgoing bilateral negotiations than those that had hitherto taken place ought to be opened up with London, with a view to seeing whether, on economic and monetary problems in particular, "the two governments might solve their differences of views". And he said that, if everybody was in agreement, he would agree to study a profound transformation of the Common Market with a view to making room for Britain.

Concerning political and military affairs, which did not directly concern the EEC, de Gaulle went on, a reorganization of the Alliance might be worked out, one that would give a privileged position to the four European powers that possessed proper armies: France, Great Britain, West Germany and Italy. When Ambassador Soames* objected that such a project took little account of the existence of NATO, the General replied that that body would not last for ever, that the Americans – while remaining allies of Europe – would one day remove their military presence from the Continent and that consequently the Europeans would have to organize their own cooperation.

According to de Gaulle, discussions on these different points had to involve all the interested parties. But they might begin with bilateral and secret negotiations between Paris and London. If progress were made, others could be brought in. Although there was nothing really new in what de Gaulle had said, Christopher Soames could not fail to be struck by the sudden pre-eminence given to relations with Britain by the man who had been responsible for the vetoes of 1963 and 1967. Did this amount to a revision, a reconversion, a rebirth of the *entente cordiale*, or just a relaunching of it?

According to Bernard Ledwidge, then minister at the British Embassy, who was very closely involved in these discussions, Soames immediately telegraphed a detailed account of the meeting, recommending that a favourable response be given to his host's idea. Although the General had spoken to him "off the record", Soames considered that "the potential importance" of what he had said was obvious – that this initiative was a "consequence of the events of May '68" or that it was the occupation of Czechoslovakia by the Russians that had "inclined him to open the doors of Europe to Britain".[12]

---

*Since the late Lord Soames refused to cooperate with me, this account owes much to those of André Fontaine (*Le Monde*, 11 March 1969) and Sir Bernard Ledwidge (*De Gaulle*, pp. 392–7).

Although the General had spoken to him in private, Soames thought fit to check his account with the General's colleagues. First Bernard Tricot, then Michel Debré, having learnt the contents of his text, considered that it concurred, with the exception of a few phrases, with the account given by the General himself. To begin with, the partners were in agreement as to the broad lines of that report, the use of which was to become the object of what was to be called "the Soames affair" – though unjustly, since the Ambassador was the victim, not the author, of the machinations that were to ruin the resumption of the Franco-British dialogue.

Soames's communication had interested the Prime Minister. But the Foreign Secretary, Michael Stewart, who did not even try to conceal his Francophobia, spoke at once of a "trap". This is how Bernard Ledwidge describes the situation: "Michael Stewart and his officials were eager to tell all to the Five and to the Americans. Their attitude was a striking proof of the 'depth of distrust' that then existed at the Foreign Office towards de Gaulle."[13]

"Distrust" is an understatement. One should speak rather of animosity, since the diplomats in question, serious and informed men as they were, credited de Gaulle with the only fault that they could not, so far, tax him with: hypocrisy. That those responsible for British diplomacy had found in de Gaulle so much to complain about, the brutality of his methods, the boastfulness of his speeches, even his sudden fits of anglophobia, is understandable enough. But who had ever acted with more abrupt rudeness? The *combinazione* that Mr Stewart and his team claimed to discover here was, initially, the result of their antipathy. Indeed Bernard Ledwidge relates how, as soon as he was informed by the General of the talks with Ambassador Soames, Couve de Murville (then Prime Minister) told him that London had not failed to inform Bonn immediately. "It was untrue at the time," the British diplomat comments, "but prophetic!"

Perhaps the advocates of trust might have won over those advocating sabotage if Harold Wilson had not, on 11 February, been the guest of Chancellor Kiesinger in Bonn. Could he keep the Elysée's secret? Michael Stewart persuaded him to spill the beans. He did it, according to Ledwidge, "briefly", on the 11th. It is understandable that Wilson did not think it loyal to keep silent before Kiesinger. But the facts are even stranger. The following day the Foreign Office ordered its Ambassador in Paris to warn the Quai d'Orsay that Harold Wilson had taken the initiative to reveal to his German colleague the tenor of a confidential meeting that Mr Soames had had with de Gaulle. According to André Fontaine, Soames had asked the President of the French Republic on 4 February if the proposition was to remain confidential and had agreed that it could "be made public once the conversations had begun": there was no question "of informing anybody in the meantime".[14]

On 12 February, receiving from Mr Soames the warning of the communication made to Kiesinger, Hervé Alphand was forced to sum up the British action thus: "In fact, the answer that France expected had first been given to the German chancellor."[15]

Even stranger still is the fact that Bonn's "leak to the summit" was to be the one organized by the British Foreign Office over the next few days. The British ambassadors to the other five countries of the Common Market were ordered to convey to the governments to which they were accredited a summary of the report drawn up by Christopher Soames after his conversation with the General. Worse still, Michael Stewart's colleagues and some of Christopher Soames's even went so far as to systematically distort the Ambassador's report, giving it a more anti-American and anti-European character. No less than three "reports", "doctored" by Michael Butler,* were sent off from Paris.

According to André Fontaine, those who had "touched up" the report had taken out of the original text the negative answer given by de Gaulle to Soames when asked if London would have to leave NATO in order to be as "European" as he wished. Thus amended, de Gaulle's proposal became a plan to destroy both NATO and the EEC.

But the Foreign Office was to go further still. When a fairly vague mention of a difference of opinion had been made in *Le Figaro* of 21 February 1969, London was worried that Paris might "bring out" her version of the affair. Bernard Ledwidge recounts:

> The British reply was extraordinary. The Foreign Office was not content with giving its version of the proposals, or refusing to comment at all on the grounds that the talks were confidential. Instead, it took the unprecedented step of issuing the full text of Soames's account of his discussions with the General, and describing it as an agreed record. Such treatment of the text of a confidential diplomatic exchange with a foreign head of State is perhaps without precedent in British history. It was accompanied by guidance to the press to the effect that de Gaulle seemed to be contemplating the break-up of both the EEC and NATO, whereas it was British policy to strengthen both organizations.[16]

It would be quite impossible to attempt to describe the General's furious reaction. It will be no less vain to suppose that he did not acknowledge some responsibility in that unfortunate exchange. Could he expect that the country of Pitt and Churchill could overlook the snubs of 1963 and 1967 and not resort to one of those acts of revenge that only very old families and very old diplomatic services are capable of exacting?

Sir Christopher Soames, turned in spite of himself into a tool of revenge, and who could quite rightly consider that he had been manipulated by his minister, considered resigning.[17] He did not do so and was surprised to see that the ostracism that fell upon him from the Elysée was lifted before the General's retirement.

During a confidential talk that he had at that time with Jean Mauriac, the British Ambassador expressed his confidence in a resumption of dialogue. "I still expect a sign of hope. I've fallen off the horse, but I shall get back into the saddle."[18]

* * *

*Who, in the offices of the Quai d'Orsay, spoke so insultingly of General de Gaulle that Paris had to ask London to recall him.

Failure to the East, failure to the West. In those first weeks of 1969, which were to see him bring an end to his extraordinary career, did Charles de Gaulle see his "grand design" in tatters? To answer that question, we would have to define, in a less approximate way, what the Gaullian project was outside France itself, which, as an absolute prerequisite, he had built up into a state whose monarchical style impeded neither its productive vigour in many areas, nor its capacity for renewal, nor, in the final analysis, its democratic vitality.

In thirty-three impassioned, illuminating and contradictory pages,* Raymond Aron tried to grasp what he, too, calls the General's "secret". Disagreeing with André Siegried, who, according to him, made "the end of the Atlantic Alliance" the General's major aim, Raymond Aron asks more questions about the General than he gives answers. The only things that he regards as certain on this subject are that de Gaulle underestimated the ideological character, profoundly Communist as well as Russian, of the actions of the East European leaders and that he overestimated the hegemonic character of American power.

It is certainly true that what one might call the "identification of the giants" is, in de Gaulle's intellectual mechanism, what most justifies the accusation of artificiality. It is true that there is a link between the size of a power and its "arrogance". Since 1941, the United States has given some evidence of this, which Raymond Aron tends to minimize. But even if he often declares that France must beware of equating American democracy with Soviet totalitarianism, the General could not resist basing his system on a false symmetry.

It is not only on account of a certain view of history that things have to be said again about the General's behaviour in this field. It is also because he distanced himself too much from public feeling and from the opinion of most of his fellow-citizens. Unlike Alfred Grosser, I can see no "Americanophobia"[19] except as a result of propaganda of the kind produced by the PCF. So the "disAmericanization" of French diplomacy by the General was supported by wide sections of the population only when it did not assume a polemical form.

Trying in turn to define Charles de Gaulle's "grand design", the American political scientist Philip Cerny writes in an excellent book:** "The General was the first great Frenchman to try seriously to break the vicious circle of the politics of the cold war and to show clearly that in a world characterized by thaw and détente, the role of the nation-states and the concept of national interest would become crucial and that the hegemony of the superpowers based on universal hegemonies would decline."

Most attempts to describe Charles de Gaulle's "grand design" – even that of Raymond Aron – fail on one point: they exist only in space. East–West, North–South, oceans and mountain ranges . . . This is to ignore far too much what was an essential element in it: time. The Gaullian project was also a race against the clock, a struggle with the hours, the days and the years. The General was no sooner installed in the Elysée than he confided to his colleagues: "I arrived ten years too

*Of his *Mémoires* (pp. 418–50).
***The Politics of Grandeur*, Cambridge University Press, 1980.

late" or "I'm ten years too old". He was constantly obsessed by how little time he had to carry out his fundamental aims.

So he ran post-haste from the "peace of the braves" to Evian and from Bonn to Quebec, haunted by the fear that he had not got France out of the Algerian trap fast enough, that he had not been able to construct in time the European confederation of which Paris would be the epicentre, of not having transformed the Atlantic Pact into an egalitarian system of transatlantic military cooperation, in which France, present on both sides of the ocean as a result of its cultural roots in Quebec, would play the roles both of Mercury and of Minerva. So, in order to pile up so many projects, so many ambitions on top of one another, or rather inside one another, he had constantly to move faster, constantly double his bets, shout a little loudly here, give too harsh a lesson there, and there venture into the unknown or contradiction.

When considering the "grand design", we must always refer to the time factor, think in terms of accelerations, delays, one thing leading to another. And it is this that is not entirely accounted for in the inevitable thematic presentation that one has had to adopt in the interests of clarity of exposition, for the policy on the Rhine, the re-deployment of the Atlantic Alliance or the search for détente in the East were conceived and can only fully be explained in terms of interaction, succession and connection, as operations growing and developing out of one another.

Shaped by the French authors of the classical age, Charles de Gaulle, a man of letters as well as a man of action, took as his models the masters of tragedy, whose rules of unity concerned time as well as place. A single action: the re-establishment of France as a subject and protagonist of History. A single place: the world. A concentrated period of time: the decade that opened at the point at which he had gathered into his hands the builder's tools, the decade whose end coincided more or less with his eightieth birthday – chosen, according to his son, as the time when he would retire. And just as Pierre Corneille rushed around, shouting at the top of his voice and losing his breath, to contain within the temporal unity of a single day Roman wars and the falls of empires, Charles de Gaulle tried to confine within a few feverish years enough action to furnish the chronicles of a few generations of scholarly Benedictines.

If the Gaullian project was profoundly marked by time, it was modified according to "circumstances". So we must distinguish here between those elements of the "grand design" that were constant, irreducible, the hard kernel, and what was, willy-nilly, capable of modification, reorientation and even abandonment. The following five propositions belong to the hard kernel.

France will no longer depend on anybody, recovering her full sovereignty and disposing of her autonomy of decision in every domain, above all in the strategic. Any system of supranationality – military within NATO, economic, monetary and a fortiori political through the various Brussels bodies – must, as far as France is concerned, be abolished.

The freezing and organization of the world into two blocs corresponds neither to the nature of things nor to the interests of the various peoples, in the first instance, the French people.

At the centre of those constellations and configurations, Europe has a mediating vocation, as a result of her incomparable experience and her role as the motive-force of modern civilization, a role that she will exercise better if the nations have kept, within the community, their creative originality.

But, even if united and reconstructed, Europe must not assume the role of a self-satisfied arbiter. To the two-thirds of the world still in the grip of poverty and conflict, she must bring active, massive cooperation, for reasons based as much on a strategy for peace as on human understanding.

For peace was now the aim, even the constant imperative of all politics. Now dominated by the nuclear age, war is the evil hypothesis that must be warded off at all costs. Admitting its possibility, as General de Gaulle did, can only help one to comprehend its full horror.

The strategists of the Elysée added to those golden rules a panoply of variable geometry, more or less accommodated to internal and external circumstances – the appearance and disappearance of individuals or majorities ruling in Washington, Moscow, London or Bonn, conflicts that blew up here or there, economic, monetary or political crises, scientific or technological innovations.

In three areas at least, the "grand design" had, so to speak, shifted or hesitated: firstly, the balance in Europe, secondly, in relation to the two superpowers, and thirdly, in relation to the all-round strategy.

The Gaullian Europe, the so-called Europe of "nations" or of "states", was a classic project for confederation expressed by the Fouchet plan, which came to birth in Paris in 1961 and was strangled in Brussels in 1962. It was based on a Paris–Bonn, or rather de Gaulle–Adenauer axis.* Did Charles de Gaulle believe, then, that he was building on rock? He was the last man to ignore the fact that Konrad Adenauer's career was coming to an end. He saw, around the old Chancellor, another generation moving and asserting itself, another type of man, one that knew that "the German economic miracle" was not only that of a determined and inventive people, but that of a capitalism geared to American power.

Nonetheless, he chose not to give precedence to the human relationship over sociological facts, and, beginning with his understanding with the old gentleman from Rhondorf, to make the Franco-German alliance the cornerstone both of the future of France and of the revival of Europe. And not content to bet everything on what was truly a dazzling alliance, he claimed to detach his ally gradually away from the "other alliance", that on which West Germany had based her security: with the United States.

Here the whole Gaullian view was based on erroneous premises. When everybody, outside his circle of intimates, told him that, however strong and deep the Franco-German reconciliation was, one thing could not be asked of the Federal Republic: to choose between Washington and Paris – de Gaulle persisted. As a result, four months later, a "preamble" to the treaty was signed that made the German preference for Washington absolutely clear. When the French (Gaullian?)

---

*I use this word, which happens to be useful, in the knowledge that, for many readers, it may be historically painful.

project was to get Bonn to adopt its own distance from Washington, the West German project began to use France as an additional bargaining-counter with the United States. That a man as perspicacious as Charles de Gaulle did not sense that, will remain one of the mysteries of that mysterious career.

We have already analysed the choice made, in the late 1950s, for the German alliance against the *entente cordiale* with London. Why, in order to reject British advances, did de Gaulle speak on several occasions of an "American Trojan Horse"? Referring to that debate, MacGeorge Bundy, the inspirer first of J. F. Kennedy's, then of L. B. Johnson's diplomacy, told me: "A Trojan Horse? But it was in Bonn, not in London. The links of the Germans with us were much deeper and more indissoluble than those with the British. De Gaulle may have succeeded in distancing Macmillan or even Wilson from us. But not Erhard or Kiesinger, who constantly reminded us that, for them, the Atlantic Alliance had primacy over any other consideration."[20] So it was only in the last months of his reign that the old sovereign considered readjusting his aim and holding out a hand to London, even if it was cruelly refused.

That revision of the "grand design" was not the only one. What he had seen during his various trips in the East (in 1966, 1967, and 1968) led de Gaulle to carry out some revisions that, especially after 1967, were to darken the relative optimism that had made him hope for a relaxation of the totalitarianisms and prepared him for a renewal of the Western Alliance, of which Nixon and Kiesinger were to be the artisans and beneficiaries.

There was, of course, a lot of gesturing and pretence about the setting up of the French strategy of dissuasion in the 1960s. "We found it very hard to believe in some sort of armed neutrality," one of General de Gaulle's closest colleagues once confided to me. It took less effort for such men to remember, with the signing of the Ailleret–Lemnitzer agreements, Richard Nixon's visit to Paris and the renewal of the Atlantic Pact, in April 1969, that France remained, for all her moods of quarrelsome nostalgia and dreams of grandeur, a cornerstone of Western defence.

Charles de Gaulle had realized that the demolition material of one policy would help him to build an alternative diplomacy. The rubble resulting from his undermining of a certain form of American alliance would be used to try to build his policy of détente with the East and cooperation with the Third World.

Thus a new configuration that must be called the General's "grand design" emerged. Certain that whatever happened the American nuclear umbrella would remain over Western Europe and that France's strategic and economic position gave her an importance such that, whatever happened, she would be protected, he set about building, around France, a Europe, a bundle of nations and crossroads of continents capable both of offering peace to the East and of cooperating with the South.

If one accepts that General de Gaulle's "grand design" was, for ten years or so, the building up of such a France, the ally but not the protégé of the United States, the inspiration of European confederation whose member states would choose Paris as its dynamo, and the instigator of an opening to the East that would have involved the erosion of the two great blocs and the return of a multi-polar system in which the old nations saw the opening up of endless prospects for mediation, arbitration and conciliation – one is led to rather disappointing results. The East, at the time of his death, was still sealed. The West still clung to America.

But if one prefers to see the General's "grand design" above all as a pedagogical purpose, a wish to teach the French to walk with heads held high once more, then a much more positive judgement may be passed on the enterprise. As Emmanuel Berl put it, "He de-ridiculized France." Expressed in more solemn tones, this is also the opinion of one of the foreign diplomats who was to have a most stormy relationship with Charles de Gaulle from 1940 to 1965, Lord Gladwyn, United Kingdom Ambassador in France from 1954 to 1960:

A sort of Nietzschean superman beyond good and evil, he was to have more influence on his contemporaries than any man since Cromwell. Even Churchill was a less extraordinary man. But however remarkable they may be, statesmen are fallible. De Gaulle seems to have overestimated the means at France's disposal to a catastrophic degree. But after the heroic period there came for France a more normal role within Western society. In this sense, de Gaulle's great contribution was to free his compatriots from an inferiority complex based on defeat and occupation.[21]

CHAPTER THIRTY-FIVE

Belote and Poker

The man whom de Gaulle appointed to succeed Michel Debré is to play a major role in the rest of the story. One eye more open than the other, which was often half-closed under the effect of humour, attention or smoke; one tended to blue, the other to grey; under his thick black eyebrows, they seemed to be lying in wait. They might express ironic humour or gaiety. But they remind me of a Persian proverb: "Beware of the man whose face is not lit up in a smile." They were the eyes of a guard or an examiner. The bottom of the face was quite different: it expressed an easygoing love of life, a certain epicurean hedonism. It has often been said that General de Gaulle, by virtue of the strangeness of his genius, which seemed at once medieval and far reaching, was untypical of the French people: the most illustrious of Frenchmen was also the most untypical. The same could hardly be said of Georges Pompidou. His physical appearance, his speech and his behaviour expressed so many traditions and customs that it was almost as if he had been drawn by the illustrator of some French encyclopaedia. Less fertile material than his predecessor, Michel Debré, for the historian of ideas, he was certainly richer for the sociologist and observer of human behaviour. In all that, of course, it was the Midi that predominated. Since the end of the Third Republic, few southerners had reached high office: Pétain and de Gaulle, Pleven and Schumann, Mollet and Pflimlin, Laniel, Coty and Debré were almost all from the northern half of the country.

But a man is not only what his face reveals of him, nor what is suggested by his background, his accent or tone of voice. He is what he does, and it is this that was interesting about the new Prime Minister. How does a man, without being elected, become Prime Minister? The example of Georges Pompidou was not a typical one. For although the first half of his career was exemplary, following closely on the traditions of republican morality, the second seems to belong to the literature of the improbable, to chance meetings and the favour of a great man. His family were peasants from the Auvergne; his father, who had been seriously wounded in the First World War, and his mother were both schoolteachers. His education took him to the Ecole Normale Supérieure,* as a result of a first prize in the competitive entrance examination. He taught first at the Lycée Saint-Charles, in Marseille, then in the great Latin Quarter Lycée Louis-le-Grand. That was certainly how, under the Third Republic, a minister, or even a President, made his way.

A year in the private office of the head of government at the Liberation, even

---

*One of the *grandes écoles*, or élite bodies of the University of Paris. The ENS specializes in the training of teachers in the humanities. (trs.)

though he had held no rank in the Resistance, a job as "Director of Research" at the RPF headquarters, in which he distinguished himself by his efficiency, seven brilliant months as head of General de Gaulle's private office while President of the Council (in 1958), two missions to the Algerian FLN in Switzerland, a refusal to serve as Finance Minister, preferring instead to continue at the Rothschild Bank – and there he was, Prime Minister.

Napoleon once declared that he wanted only happy men as marshals. Was it this that drew Charles de Gaulle's attention to Georges Pompidou, rather than to anyone else? Perhaps we should see the new head of government in April 1962 as a symbol, or rather as an emblem, of the art of succeeding. Just by looking at him, millions of French people could already see themselves as ministers. One can see easily enough why the ordinary French people liked him. What did the General think?

> Georges Pompidou seemed to me capable and worthy of conducting affairs at my side. While his intelligence and wide culture kept him abreast of ideas of every kind, he was by nature inclined to concentrate on the practical side of things. Though he admired brilliance in action, risk in a venture and boldness in the exercise of authority, he himself tended towards cautious attitudes and a circumspect approach, while at the same time he excelled in grasping the basic issues in every problem and finding a solution. Thus protected from above and supported from below, but moreover self-confident beneath his circumspection, he grappled with the problems of the day, exercising, as occasion demanded, the powers of comprehension and the tendency to scepticism, the talent for exposition and the inclination to hold his tongue. In the light of my position and my knowledge of the man, I placed Pompidou in office.[1]

It is an excellent thing that a head of State is able to define his relationship and his differences with his closest colleague with such sagacity. But why did de Gaulle appoint a man to head his government who had never subjected himself to any election, not even a local election, thus making him the first unelected head of government in the history of the French republics? To understand that choice, we must consider the Charles de Gaulle of spring 1962, still recovering from battles that had been waged with only mixed success, but stirred by the battles to come.

A few weeks earlier, the Evian agreements had put an end to the Algerian war. Would he now take a rest? Of course not. As he said to a close colleague in June 1961, "As soon as peace is concluded, they'll try to get my skin. Then I'll attack."[2]

The Algerian tragedy had given the General a consular mandate that those who had given it to him obviously expected to last as long as the mission. With the task carried out, the General suddenly cast a shadow over the proceedings. In that spring of 1962, he had not forgotten autumn 1945, when a resuscitated parliament tried to put the handcuffs of an "imperative mandate" on him.

There were at least two aspects to the choice of Pompidou. One, purely negative, was the setting aside of a Prime Minister who, for over three years, had served him with diligence, efficiency and unlimited self-abnegation, and whom, as de

Gaulle himself testifies, he fully appreciated. But Pompidou said publicly that he was "worn out". Freed of the Algerian problem, that eminent man, whose ascendancy over the political class had continued, under trial, to increase, ran the risk of assuming at his side such importance as to form, at the summit of the State, a sort of two-headed monster.

For a long time a senator, a fervent admirer of the British system, Michel Debré had done everything possible in 1958 to construct a "rationalized parliamentarianism" – which the General was wise enough to accommodate himself to, though he often considered that the second word in the term assumed too much importance and the first not enough: he would have preferred a "rationed" parliamentarianism.

The choice of Georges Pompidou meant above all that the General was declaring quite unambiguously that he, and only he, was master. To promote a trusted subordinate in this way who was unknown to the public and above all to the electors was to demonstrate in the crudest possible way that from now on parliament was no longer the source of power. And so, on 13 April 1962, Georges Pompidou's employers at the Rothschild Bank freed him for the service of the state: he was asked to form a government. The principal innovation in relation to the Debré cabinet was the appointment of five MRP ministers, including the chairman of the movement, Pierre Pflimlin, and Maurice Schumann. But Guy Mollet had conveyed his refusal, and a few eminent individualists, such as Edgar Faure, still had reservations.

Though a skilful negotiator, Georges Pompidou did not at first reveal the gifts of a great parliamentarian. His first appearance, before that unindulgent audience, was not remarkable. Did he put too much stress on the supremacy of the head of state? He might maintain that his aim as Prime Minister was to establish "trusting relations" with the parliament, but it looked as if it would be difficult. Only 259 deputies, as against 247, gave him their confidence. It was a close thing, but the General may not have been so displeased. By letting the newcomer into their club with such ill grace, the nation's elected representatives helped to justify the presidential choice. A Pompidou winning the enthusiasm of parliament might have acted as a brake on the great operation that was beginning.

No sooner had a month passed than he had to face his first disappointment: at his press conference on 15 May, de Gaulle had made fun of the advocates of European integration. M. Pflimlin, Mayor of Strasbourg, the European capital, resigned, together with his four MRP colleagues.* Georges Pompidou's "parliamentary opening" had misfired. The General commented that those party men "go off like ants in a procession".

Gaston Monnerville, the President of the Senate, warned that his counterpart in the Palais Bourbon, Jacques Chaban-Delmas, had been consulted by the head of state on a possible revision of the constitution, addressed a warning to the Elysée against any attempt to infringe the rights and powers of the assemblies. From then on the Senate was in a state of alert. M. Dumas, minister concerned with relations

---

*On 13 June, in the Assembly, would be read a *European Manifesto* signed by 293 deputies, which was a veritable declaration of war on de Gaulle. But the "European" plotters would not dare to act on their words.

with the parliament, declared on behalf of the government that "neither the Prime Minister nor the government are at present considering proposing any institutional reform to the President of the Republic".[3] This did not stop the rumours from multiplying.

The General summoned to the Elysée Professor Vedel, Dean of the Faculty of Law, in Paris, a celebrated constitutionalist, and for long an advocate of the election of the President of the Republic by universal suffrage. De Gaulle approached the subject as if out of politeness. Vedel launched into it with obvious pleasure, though he added: "If the head of State were chosen in this way, his powers would be such that he would have to give up the right of dissolving parliament." To which the General replied: "Give up the right of dissolution! Do you think the Executive can make itself heard by the Assembly if it doesn't have dissolution at its disposal?"[4]

From the corridors of the assemblies to the offices of newspaper editors and to the Elysée itself, rumours, suppositions, denials, warnings, confabulations and soundings followed one another throughout that summer until late in the day of 22 August 1962, when, in the rainy half-light of a crossroads in the outer suburbs, fourteen high-calibre bullets went through the car driven by Francis Marroux carrying Yvonne and Charles de Gaulle and Alain de Boissieu from Paris to Villacoublay.

When did Charles de Gaulle become an advocate of the election of the head of State by universal suffrage? It is a subject of inexhaustible debate. The theory that he had long held this idea was not demonstrated on past form: he had twice rejected the idea, when he called on people to vote "no" in June and October 1945, and twice in a positive way in the texts written or supervised by him, the Bayeux programme and the Constitution of 1958. It has been asserted, first by Léon Blum in an article published on 21 June 1946 in response to the Bayeux speech, that "for the head of the Executive thus conceived, the extension of the electoral system would not suffice. Since all sovereignty necessarily comes from the people, one would have to go down to the *source* of sovereignty, that is to say, put the election of the head of the Executive to universal suffrage. That is the logical conclusion of the system."[5] So, since 1946, de Gaulle seems to have been an advocate of this form of election, if his comments on the question in the *Mémoires d'espoir* are to be believed.

> For a long time I had felt that the only way was the election of the President of the Republic by the people. It is true that, speaking at Bayeux in 1946 about the regime which France needed, and then directing the proceedings and debates in which the Constitution was elaborated in 1958, I had not yet specified that the head of State should be elected by universal suffrage. However, for the sake of the future, I was determined to finish off the edifice in this respect before the end of my second-year term.[6]

There are many people (including the chairman of the RPF or the head of government in 1958) who maintained that at least until the early 1960s the idea of electing the head of State by universal suffrage aroused de Gaulle's mistrust. Thus the American political scientist, Nicholas Wahl, who had several opportunities to discuss this subject with him, came to the conclusion that "de Gaulle was opposed to that system; first, because it went against the grain to copy American political practices; secondly, because he thought that this system would strengthen still further the grip of the parties on political life; and lastly, because he did not believe electors capable of carrying out so important a choice directly."[7]

That this type of presidential election was not envisaged in 1958 cannot be attributed solely to the General's distrust of it. Firstly, because the prime architect of the constitution, Michel Debré, had the same doubts. What if a Communist candidate were to win the election? But the main reason for rejecting that solution was above all because, the French Community being what it was and Algeria still part of the Republic, the election of the head of State would have depended in an exaggerated way on the overseas vote.

Hence that rather heteroclite electoral college, bringing together several types of electors, those celebrated "intermediaries", those "notables" for whom the General cared little, preferring "the people" to them, but who nevertheless, in December 1958, confirmed his legitimacy. But it so happened that the very composition of that college of 80 000 grand electors was to play a role in the upheaval of 1962.

"Among the reasons that led the General to wage that battle," one man who was at the centre of the debate, Pierre Sudreau, told me, "don't ignore this one: from soundings that he had had carried out, it emerged that the college that had elected him in 1958 was planning to make Antoine Pinay his successor."

The plan for electing the President by universal suffrage had formed or matured in the General's mind as the Algerian war was coming to an end. Although the idea of a *modus vivendi* with the political class had crossed the General's mind, the assassination attempt in August showed him the way: he was being forced into a fight. One reads in Alain de Boissieu's memoirs[8] that "certain politicians knew that General de Gaulle was on the point of announcing his project for electing the President of the Republic by universal suffrage. If that reform were carried out, it would mean an end of rule by parties. The assassination attempt at Petit-Clamart was organized in my opinion to prevent the General from carrying out his plan. It was from much more important individuals than the leaders of the OAS that Bastien-Thiry received his orders." If, writing so coolly some years later, a man who was so intimate with the General could write those accusing words,* it must be because the Elysée did not reject the possibility of a "political" plot.

Throughout this affair, we must remember that although de Gaulle embarked upon an operation of "constitutional revision, whose purpose is obscure, whose advisability is dubious and whose procedure is openly contrary to the texts",[9] it was because he considered that he was in a state of war with the political class – and, more specifically, with that most symbolic of all political figures, the President of the Senate. According to some of the General's colleagues, he suspected the holder of that office, Gaston Monnerville, all the more because the sudden death

---

*For which no proof has emerged since.

of the head of State would make him, for a time at least, the first citizen of the Republic.

That barrister from Guiana, a compatriot of Félix Eboué and, like him, a former member of the Resistance, had had, in various spheres, an exemplary career. A friend of Pierre Mendès France, a left-wing Radical, a good public speaker, a distinguished lawyer, he had been elected seven years earlier as President of the Senate, which made him the second citizen in the State. In late May 1958, he had been a key figure in the implementation of the peaceful procedure that, two days later, brought de Gaulle to the Elysée. Thus he regarded himself as one of the godfathers of the regime, and therefore of the General – with whom, for four years, relations had been friendly. But, since the project for constitutional reform seemed to infringe the powers of the Senate and of its President, Gaston Monnerville appeared, in that summer of 1962, to be at the heart of parliamentary society, its best-informed and most vigilant guardian.

So nobody was more alarmed than he when, on 29 August, after a meeting of the Council of Ministers, the Minister of Information, Alain Peyrefitte, read a statement that had clearly been written by de Gaulle: "General de Gaulle stressed the need for the Republic to ensure, in whatever circumstances, the continuity of the State and the maintenance of republican institutions. He confirmed before the Council of Ministers his intention of taking the necessary steps in that domain and to that end."

This time, the decision would not be long in coming, especially as, from 4 to 9 September, Charles de Gaulle would be making a tour through Germany. Three days after his return, de Gaulle chaired a meeting of the Council of Ministers that speeded up the process and gave it a decisive orientation: the statement conveyed his intention of "proposing to the country to decide by means of referendum that the President of the Republic would henceforth be elected by universal suffrage". So it was to be a referendum! Legal objections were piled upon the political ones: "He has no right to do that! Constitutional revision is incompatible with the referendum procedure!" We shall come back to this debate, but suffice it to say for the moment that it was on 12 September that the great battle began from which that Fifth Republic was to emerge transformed into a presidential monarchy.

The ministers were summoned on 19 September: but not simply to sit there or to accept the technical decisions of the various men responsible and the political decision of the only Politician, as usual, but this time to express their opinions: as on 22 August 1959, as on the eve of his announcement to the world that the right of Algerians to self-determination would be recognized, Charles de Gaulle wanted to know the feelings of his ministers. This time, they were not in fact being asked to express an opinion, but to give their agreement or their resignation. The day before a battle, the General did not consult; he checked that his General Staff agreed with him. One important defection was announced even before the meeting: Pierre Sudreau, the Education Minister, let it be known that he disagreed not so much with the question of election by universal suffrage, as on the procedure chosen, the referendum. This was all the sadder for de Gaulle in that Pierre Sudreau was one of the few men with whom he had rather more than professional links. The General had even said to him, before he took his leave: "Why are you leaving me, Sudreau? You would be Prime Minister."[10] Sudreau gave in on only one point: he would not announce his resignation before the Council of Ministers.

Asked for once to express their opinions, the members of Georges Pompidou's cabinet showed that the ministers of the Fifth Republic could behave as true citizens. Although most of the members of the UNR and the "General's men" (Malraux, Palewski, Fouchet, Couve de Murville) almost all demonstrated their spirit of discipline, there were some – Frey, Peyrefitte and Foyer – who made suggestions and delivered judicious warnings. And there were also ministers – those regarded as being "on the left", by reason of their political background and certain of their actions (Gorse, Pisani) – who expressed divergent views, not to mention Pierre Sudreau, who did not mince his words, and gave that meeting of the Council a dramatic tone.* Louis Joxe made some wise suggestions in passing:

> In due course the constitution will have to be altered to take into account the imbalance introduced by the election of the President of the Republic by universal suffrage. Seven years is too long. It should be reduced to five, perhaps to coincide the legislature with the Presidency of the Republic. Thus we would be assured of a sort of agreement between the President and the Assembly. In any case, the President of the Republic's power of dissolution should be abolished.

Roger Frey presented more direct criticisms. In his view, "the reform should have gone through the Assembly". If that resulted in failure, then the Assembly should be dissolved before proceeding to the referendum. Edgard Pisani caused something of a shock by asking whether or not there was any need for a Prime Minister: "Is such a thing justified? I very much doubt it." (One can imagine what kind of look, from under his bushy eyebrows, Georges Pompidou gave him: relations between the two men were not improved.)

So the only categorical opposition to the project came from Pierre Sudreau. The Education Minister attacked not only the procedure, but the very idea itself. "This reform," he pleaded, "makes the imbalance of powers worse, it is inopportune and even dangerous. This project will revive opposition, at a time when the Algerian war might have allowed it to die down. General de Gaulle, who has a vocation as a unifier, will appear as a divider. Furthermore, it will open the door to adventure after his disappearance."

It was no use. Georges Pompidou flew to the help of the project by maintaining that, if one did not resort to a referendum in such a matter, "one may well wonder why it was created". The General then brought the discussion to an end on a pleasant note, making a few formal concessions: he would not resign before his mandate came to an end only to get himself elected by universal suffrage, and the President of the Senate would still take over presidential duties on a temporary basis in the event of a vacancy in the office.

Of all the discussions that he chaired the General had remembered above all the

---

*This account of the Council of 19 September 1962 owes a great deal to that of André Passeron, but also to the memories of Georges Gorse, Pierre Sudreau and Edgar Pisani.

words of Pierre Sudreau, "It's almost a challenge!" The following day Charles de Gaulle appeared on television. It was his most revealing statement yet on the subject of institutions.

> The keystone of our regime is the new institution of a President of the Republic appointed by the reason and feeling of the French people to be the head of State and the guide of the State and the guide of France. Far from the President's having, as in the past, to be confined to an advisory and representative role, the Constitution now confers on him the illustrious burden of the destiny of France and of the Republic. Without altering in any way the respective rights, or the reciprocal relations between the executive, legislative and judiciary powers, as they are laid down by the Constitution, but with a view to maintaining and strengthening our institutions in the face of factious enterprises, from whichever side they come, or the manoeuvres of those who, in good faith or bad faith, would seek to bring us back to the disastrous system of former days, I believe therefore that it is my duty to make the following proposal to the country: when my seven-year term comes to an end, or death or illness interrupts it before that end, the President of the Republic will henceforth be elected by universal suffrage. By what method should the country express its decision? I reply: by the most democratic way, the referendum. It is also the most justified way, for national sovereignty belongs to the people and it belongs to it obviously, in the first instance, in the constitutional domain. Our present Constitution specifies that the people exercises its sovereignty either through representatives or through a referendum. Although the text makes provision for a particular procedure in cases where revision would take place in a parliamentary context, it also makes provision, in a very simple, very clear way, for the President of the Republic to be able to propose to the country, by means of a referendum, "any draft law" – I stress, "any draft law" – "bearing upon the organization of the public powers", which, obviously, embraces the election of the President. The draft law that I propose will be submitted to the French people, therefore, in accordance with the Constitution that, at my suggestion, it has given itself.

So, having posed the problem in his own way, de Gaulle was given wide approval by public opinion, pleased at being now called upon to choose the man to hold the highest office of State. Apart from the UNR and the Comte de Paris, all the organizations, parties and movements, all the most celebrated politicians, active or retired, immediately denounced the illegality of the procedure envisaged by the government draft law and the inevitable consequence that it would lead to personal power.

The most vigorous protester was Gaston Monnerville. On 30 September, at Vichy, the President of the Senate declared that he would vote "no" to "a deliberate, intended, premeditated and outrageous violation of the Constitution, which I call a breach of the Constitution".

A breach, really? The word was to set the tone for the whole "no" campaign, whose stridency was to equal that caused by the Algerian war. So much so that, on 1 October, the Council of State laid it down, by an almost unanimous vote, that the procedure chosen by the government did not conform to the Constitution.

The reform announced by General de Gaulle aroused two kinds of rejection, one on the content, the other on the procedure. And the first type of opponents were themselves divided into two groups: those who condemned the principle of the election of the President by universal suffrage, which might be thought to lead to the establishment of a presidential regime (without the guarantees, of a parliamentary or federal type, with which the American system counterbalanced the development of personal power) or, according to the more vehement, to dictatorship; and those who accepted the principle, but only if there was a revision in the balance between the different powers of the State. To this group belong the two most famous French constitutionalists, Georges Vedel and Maurice Duverger. To the first belonged almost all the members of the political class that did not have a declared allegiance to de Gaulle.

The reform of 1962 was not a *coup d'état*; it was not to install the dictatorship of the General or his successors, and its most ardent opponents came round to it in the end. But although those opposing the proposal on grounds of "content" were not proved right by history, the criticisms of the procedure adopted to get the reform demanded by General de Gaulle implemented have never entirely disappeared. One might cite the fundamental arguments of a specialist whose criticisms, on this matter, have all the greater strength in that he was for years the most celebrated advocate of the election of the head of State by universal suffrage, namely, Georges Vedel. For the former Dean of the Paris Faculty of Law,* it was not possible to proceed to a revision of the Constitution of 1958 while ignoring its article 89, which was wholly devoted to this subject. This article laid it down that any measure of this kind must be passed by both chambers, before being subjected, either by referendum, or by the approval of both assemblies meeting together. Thus, Georges Vedel goes on, the Constitution of 1958 "unequivocally excludes, with a view to altering the Constitution, any direct recourse to a referendum that has not previously received parliamentary approval".[11] Admitting that General de Gaulle and his advisers believed in good faith that the referendum procedure could be based on article 11 of the Constitution, which allowed the head of State to subject to referendum "any draft law bearing on the organization of the public powers", Georges Vedel rejects this argument. A "draft law", he reminds us, has nothing to do with a "constitutional revision", and article 11 "may be used in relation to legislative matters, but not constitutional ones". And he concludes: "There can be no question but that the procedure chosen was unconstitutional."[12]

Some lawyers, however, have come to regard this as a secondary fault, in view of the positive aspects of the reform. Thus, commenting twenty-three years later on the Homeric battle of 1962 and the arguments then being exchanged, Maurice Duverger confided to me, in December 1985: "We were right to denounce the procedure imposed in 1962 by the General: it was unfaithful to his own constitution. But it was in order to get a reform adopted that, in fact, some of us regarded

*Since 1973 a member of the Constitutional Council.

as positive. On reflection, and if I am to be quite honest, I believe that in the situation in which General de Gaulle then found himself, I might have acted as he did."[13]

The confrontation between the government and the political class reached a climax when the National Assembly, after having heard a message from de Gaulle asking for its "confidence", then after a motion of censure declaring that "the President of the Republic is violating the Constitution, of which he is the guardian" and "is thus opening up a breach through which some adventurer might one day pass in order to overthrow the Republic" was called upon to decide on the fate of the government. It put Pompidou in a minority of 280 votes against 480 on 5 October. For the first time in the history of the Fifth Republic, the National Assembly inflicted the most dramatic rejection on the head of State.

De Gaulle had done everything possible to save the Pompidou cabinet: his televised speech brought to bear on the elected representatives the pressure of a public opinion that he knew was sensitive to the appeals of an eloquence dramatized by every possible means:

> The attempts perpetrated or planned against my life have forced me to make sure that after me, as far as I am able, there will be a sound Republic, which implies that it is sound at its summit. French men and women, the draft law that I am subjecting to you proposes that the President of the Republic, your President, should be elected by you. Nothing is more republican. Nothing is more democratic. For my part, each "yes" from each and every one of you will give me direct proof of your trust and encouragement. For, believe me! I need it for what I can still do, as, yesterday, I needed it for what I have already done. It is your answers that on 28 October will tell me whether I can and whether I must continue with my task in the service of France.

The General seemed indifferent to the defeat of his Prime Minister. He received Pompidou, accepted his resignation, told him to remain in his job and told him that he had decided to dissolve the Assembly. But the decree of dissolution could not be published until he had consulted the presidents of both assemblies. So, before seeing Jacques Chaban-Delmas, he had to face Gaston Monnerville.

According to the usher at the Elysée, there had never been a shorter meeting. De Gaulle was standing behind his desk. "*Monsieur le Président du Sénat,*" he began, "the Constitution places me under a duty to consult you. I am now doing so." "*Monsieur le Président,* I believe the dissolution to be necessary, but a new Prime Minister must be designated." "*Monsieur le Président du Sénat,* thank you."

Most of the press followed the politicians in their criticisms. Some great editorial-writers, such as Hubert Beuve-Méry and Raymond Aron, preferred to stress the "uselessness" of the crisis, its artificial character. Why had de Gaulle, having scarcely recovered from the Algerian troubles and the assassin's bullets, chosen to open up this institutional crisis? In fact, whatever one thinks of the General's theses and of his methods, nothing could have been less "useless" than this debate on essentials.

"It was for this reason that I committed myself to the uttermost," de Gaulle writes in his *Mémoires d'espoir*. Without risk? No. The prospects for the referendum were not, at first, so favourable to the General.

At the height of the campaign, when the opposition was constantly brandishing the threats of dictatorship and totalitarianism, a new blow struck the General. On 19 October, the Council of State, which had already condemned his project for constitutional revision, annulled the contents of the decree of 1 June 1962 setting up the military court of justice – which, having already condemned to death several assassins of officials, was preparing to judge one of the leaders of the OAS on the mainland, André Canal, who had been mixed up in most of the assassination attempts on de Gaulle. It did not help his morale.

A week before the vote, he was talking to Roger Frey, Minister of the Interior: "Everyone is against my draft law. The officials, but also the notables and all the parliamentarians. In short, the political class in its entirety. So, for all that, if I get 65 per cent of the votes cast it would be a triumph." "And what if you get only 60 per cent?" "Then... that will be a success."[14]

Circumstances, once again, were to come to the General's assistance. On 22 October, six days before the vote, the Cuban Missile Crisis broke out. If it did not lead to war, it was a crisis involving the greatest possible degree of international tension. In such events, everyone knew that de Gaulle was irreplaceable. The few gestures that he made, the way in which he behaved, with calculated brilliance, at Kennedy's side, everything tended to raise his prestige. And he did not hesitate to take advantage of it when, on 26 October, he launched a final appeal to the citizens:

> All the parties of the past, whose blindness has been cured by nothing that has happened, are asking you to answer "no"! At the same time all the factions, employing every means so that my death or my defeat may bring back a state of great confusion, which would be their ignoble opportunity, also want you to vote "no"! French men and women, I feel sure that you will say "yes"! I am sure because you know that in our world, which is such a dangerous one, France could not survive if she were to fall back into the impotence of yesterday.

Throughout the night of 29 October, the results did not look too good. Would de Gaulle get a clear enough mandate to continue with his task? About 2 a.m., Roger Frey declared that with 62 per cent of the votes cast and 47 per cent of registered voters, the "yes" vote had won the battle. But the following morning the General let it be known that he preferred to stay at Colombey "to reflect". Pompidou and Joxe telephoned La Boisserie. De Gaulle was still evasive. Yet on the Tuesday he was at the Elysée, drawing an initial conclusion from that ambiguous verdict: "When I was dreaming, I thought '70 per cent'. When I was reasonable, I said '65 per cent'. I am disappointed to learn that it was 62 per cent." But the following day, the statement that he issued was more enthusiastic in tone: it noted that "the main aim of the referendum has been achieved by the fact that the head of State must now be elected by universal suffrage". The Assembly having been dissolved, everything now depended on the electoral battle, set for 18 November. Roger Frey declared that the government could consolidate its majority, provided de Gaulle himself joined in the battle.

General de Gaulle in an election campaign? Four years earlier, he had rejected the very idea with sovereign haughtiness: "I don't have anything to do with electoral matters!"[15] But then the referendum had given him (on 28 September 1958) 80 per cent of the votes cast. He had to go down into the arena.

On 7 November he lashed into the enemy, those parties "that no longer represent the nation" and committed himself to the side of the "Gaullist" candidates who, suddenly, united for battle: André Malraux founded and publicized with his jerky eloquence an "Association for the Fifth Republic", which brought together the two branches of official Gaullism, the one on the right, the UNR (Union pour la nouvelle République) and that on the left, the UDT (Union Démocratique du Travail).

Their opponents tried to organize a similar operation. On 9 November, Guy Mollet, whose anti-communism had seemed, for five years, to be his *raison d'être*, suddenly declared at the second round of the elections that he would vote for a PCF candidate against a Gaullist. This move towards the resurrection of the Popular Front would certainly bring seats to both parties of the left. But it also helped to swing the uncommitted to the conservative side.

18 November 1962 was the date of one of the greatest political victories that the General ever won. Not only because those who supported him obtained outright nearly 32 per cent of the votes cast – which no party had been able to claim since the war – but because his most important opponents were personally eliminated: whether they were the men who had attacked the constitutional revision,* or the last upholders of *Algérie française*, whom he might well suspect of having been mixed up to some degree or other in the plots against his rule. On 21 November, at a meeting of the Council of Ministers, de Gaulle gave full vent to his pleasure: "We'll now have a bit of peace for several years. I wanted to smash the parties. I was the only one who could do it and the only one to believe that it was possible at the time I chose. I've been proved right against everybody. I declared war on the parties. I shall refrain from declaring war on the party leaders." There was a brief silence, then he went on: "All they want is to regain a ministerial appointment."[16]

The second round, as the majority system was designed to do, further accentuated the tendencies found in the first. *Le Monde* summed up the situation thus: "The General-President has just won the war that, taking every risk, he himself imposed."[17] Under his name, 229 candidates of the UNR-UDT,** most of whom were unknown, were about to enter parliament, where they would form the largest group that had ever been seen in a normally elected French assembly and possess an absolute majority, with the support of Valéry Giscard d'Estaing's thirty-five "independent republicans". Taken as a whole, the candidates sporting the "Fifth Republic" label won 42 per cent of the votes cast – enough to give the impression of a landslide.

After the meeting of the Council of Ministers of 28 November, de Gaulle

*Except Guy Mollet, who was saved at the second round by the support of the Communists.
**They were to be joined by four deputies from overseas.

expressed "his satisfaction that the French people had, to a very large degree and in solemn circumstances, given its approval to the policies that the President of the Republic has pursued, through the government, for several years". The night before, he had insisted on speaking on the occasion of the funeral of René Coty, the man who had opened the legal gates of power to him and whose final political gesture had been to oppose his constitutional proposals. The General preferred to stress the first episode and recalled how, refusing to cling to "a system adrift", René Coty had acted in such a way that "the rupture in the State" and the "split within the nation" were avoided. So, de Gaulle concluded, "the respect of the nation surrounds his memory".[18]

The victor exploited his victory by reforming the Pompidou cabinet that, defeated on 5 October, won on 30 December 268 votes against 116 in the Assembly. His New Year greeting was, therefore, quietly victorious.

The best conclusion of the great debate that turned the monarchical republic into a republican monarchy was drawn by de Gaulle himself, when, commenting on the results of the November elections to a visitor, he said: "You see, the so-called heads of the so-called parties would, of course, have preferred to go on playing *belote*. But I forced them to play poker. And nobody is better at it than me."[19]

In March 1963 France was at peace, not having fired a shot in a year for the first time since the beginning of the century. Their faces blackened with coal-dust and wearing their miners' helmets and blue overalls, thousands of men had come from Charles de Gaulle's native province, marching between two rows of warm sympathizers, surging from the bank of the Seine between Concorde and the Pont Alexandre III: for a time, the General caught sight of them from his window in the Elysée. They were miners from Les Houillères du Nord and they were demonstrating their anger.

For two weeks, a requisition decree signed by the General at Colombey was directed at the strikers who, on 1 March, had decided to stop work for an unlimited period. But it had not been successful: the strike continued and was now turning into a demonstration. In a sense, it was the most serious failure that he had had for five years. What is more, it was a failure that he took as a personal affront: had he not nationalized the Les Houillères mines in 1945? Had he not brought them back to life?

What was in question was the society and economy of "his" State. For some, Gaullism was simply a new version of the monarchy of the *Grand Siècle*, for others a resurgence of Bonapartism. But there were also those who saw Gaullism as the form of transition adopted in France by an industrializing society. Thanks to the catastrophic circumstances of 1940, then of the dramatic ones of 1958, and thanks to the appearance of an exceptional individual, that ambiguous system would allow the old political structures of the State to adapt to the economic transformation begun in the mid-1950s.

The sociologist Serge Mallet wrote in 1963 that Gaullism appeared as "the agent both of a revolution of structures and a channelling of that revolution, as the apparatus of a circumstantial break, but also of a continuity of the State ensuring without major disorders the enormous transformation in progress and making it possible to coordinate its various phases and tendencies". Thus the General and his supporters could be seen as responding to a profound need in French society, felt, according to our sociologist, "not only by the leading groups, but also by particular social groups, which, while in a subordinate position, had an interest in permanent economic expansion, that is to say, the workers and technicians in sectors of modern industry". Hence the strictly tragic character of the social confrontation of March 1963. By allowing itself to get involved in an emotional face-to-face confrontation with the miners of the Nord, symbolically representing the working class, the triumphant regime of late 1962 had suddenly found itself shifted to the anti-social, repressive right.

Curiously enough, Charles de Gaulle, not usually in the habit of mixing feelings with political decisions, especially where particular social groups were concerned, and still less inclined to self-criticism, evokes that "sad episode" in a tone of nostalgic confession. He was not "in the least happy" to see

> the diminution of the role that had been imposed on our collieries. I was well aware of the stupendous toil that generations of miners had expended in order to develop the patrimony which I myself had decided to nationalize after the Liberation. As a man of the north myself, I had a particularly high regard for these workers. Besides, my brothers Xavier and Jacques and my brother-in-law Alfred Cailliau had been mining engineers. But here, too, I must consider only the general good of the country. And then I must admit that I had the illusion that in the last resort the miners would not wish to take the responsibility of inflicting great damage on the French community. Alas, it was not to be.[20]

Whoever tries to describe the economic strategy of de Gaulle must never lose sight of the melancholy of the sons of factory-owners in the Nord, bathed in a paternalism which, in this area, placed its hope in the Christian democracy of the 1930s – and which saw in every worker one of those soldiers abandoned by their leaders in 1940. He was a man who did not care for those who owned wealth; he despised the bourgeois and hated capitalism. But he was also a leader who upset working-class political movements, rejected the concept of the working class and saw the economy as a weapon for the powerful. Hence his nostalgia for a "third way" between Marxism and capitalism, which continued to haunt him until 1969, the dream of a "participation" begun in the days of the RPF, when it was known as "association".

In this area, three principles dominated General de Gaulle's thinking: the preponderance of the role of the State, the priority given to defending the franc, and budgetary rigour. By 1965, the General could take advantage of a strictly balanced budget. As for the franc, given new parities in 1958, the General could declare enthusiastically that "The strength of a country's currency is an index to the world of the true effectiveness of its economy, on which its policy depends. At home it is the essential condition of honesty in relationships, moderation in desires, serene acceptance of one's lot, and the whole social and moral order."

The replacement of Debré by Pompidou was not, in this respect, a simple matter of one man taking over from another. To begin with, relations between the General and Pompidou were not the same as those that had existed with Michel Debré. From 1959 to 1962, the Prime Minister had had the upper hand in such matters. Absorbed by the Algerian war and diplomatic questions, the General interfered very little. From April 1962, de Gaulle – flanked by a Secretary-General who was highly knowledgeable about economic and social affairs, Etienne Burin des Roziers – was at the centre of all such decisions. It was the end of the Matignon's reserved area.

From 1963 onwards, hardly a month passed without Charles de Gaulle letting it be known that he regarded the government's reaction to the economic troubles as inadequate. It was the head of State himself who took the initiative in summoning to the Elysée several cabinet committees concerned with steps that might be taken to improve the economy. Seven meetings of this type were to take place before the end of the year. When he threw himself into the struggle for stabilization, during the summer of 1963, General de Gaulle was waging a very personal battle, one for which he assumed responsibility in an even more original, more direct way than in 1958.

In late July 1963, when all the economic indicators drew attention to accelerating inflation, while the deficit in external trade was increasing and the rise in prices was exceeding the rate, then regarded as disturbing, of 0.5 per cent per month, the General, who had spent time at Colombey examining figures, noted that "the good resolutions seemed to be losing their edge".[21] He would take sterner measures. In the *Mémoires d'espoir*, written when he had retired from office, he indicates that "Georges Pompidou seemed less convinced than I was of the prime importance of the stability of the franc" and that Valéry Giscard d'Estaing was "somewhat shaken by the realization that his task of promoting the general interest would entail firmness and severity towards each particular interest".[22]

The General then wrote an urgent letter to the Prime Minister, demanding the summoning of two meetings of cabinet ministers, on 30 August and 7 September. Pompidou and Giscard "immediately set to work with their colleagues, hastily summoned from their holidays, in some instances resorting to the police to discover where they were".[23] And the first measures of what was to be known as the second "stabilization plan" were announced, on 12 September 1963.

Comparing "his" 1963 plan with that of 1958, Giscard d'Estaing was to declare at the Palais Bourbon: "In 1958, we had to find a level for the currency; today we have to maintain the existing parity; in 1958 the State proposed a rise in public fares; today it is taking measures to halt rises; in 1958 the plan proposed to take back some of the things acquired by the citizens; today it is only moderating the developments to come." The 1963 plan could not be as drastic on the social plane as that of 1958. France had emerged from the atmosphere of tragedy prevailing in 1958. The electors – who had been promised by the Gaullist candidates that 1962 would be a "social year" – would not have put up with such reductions at the expense of their standard of living. Hence the hybrid nature of the 1963 plan.

The stabilizing effects of the plan of September–November 1963 are generally acknowledged (the 6 per cent rise in prices fell to 3.6 per cent in six months) and a balanced budget could be presented in 1965. Many of those who recognize its merits in the short to medium term think that Giscard d'Estaing's error (encouraged in this by the General) was to maintain the cure for too long and not to have prepared the way for an emergence from it in good time.

Declaring himself to be an unreserved advocate of that policy of rigour, the author of the *Mémoires d'espoir* states his constant aim to be "to maintain the franc at the rate I had fixed, when I took it upon myself to set France on the road to recovery".[24]

It was not until 1966 that France emerged from the phase of stagnation brought on by the 1963 plan: it was, said the opposition, a policy of "unemployment on a pile of gold". The day after the grudging re-election of de Gaulle in December 1965, the formation of the third Pompidou government was to bring about the removal of Giscard d'Estaing and his replacement at the Rue de Rivoli by Michel Debré, an advocate of economic stimulus and movement. Pompidou had urged the General to make that choice.

Curiously enough, in the debate between the two men who were General de Gaulle's two principal colleagues at the time, it was the one who had so far seemed most attached to the plan and its rigours who had been eliminated and the one who seemed least bound to that policy who remained in office. Can this paradox be explained by recalling the choice made by de Gaulle in 1945 in favour of the economic liberal Pleven against the planner Mendès France? No: the circumstances were very different. By opting once again in 1966 for the man who seemed, by taste, temperament and training, the least attached to constraints, de Gaulle realized that he was giving preference to a man, not to a policy as he had done in 1945. This time he himself would be in charge of the overall economic direction. And the "line" that he had drawn was the one symbolized by the Fifth Plan.

The years between the legislative elections of 1962 and the troubles of 1968 have left many, such as François Bloch-Lainé, with "the memory of a great opportunity lost",[25] that of a bold redistribution of the fruits of expansion. The composition of the Fifth Plan team – Massé, Ripert, Delors – aroused hopes of a movement in that direction. The Fifth Plan was to be both the major ambition and the driving force of Charles de Gaulle's second seven-year term: it was to sink in the storms of 1968. But his two main ambitions, to reinvigorate French industry, a process which had begun, and the incomes policy, which he had only outlined, were to be the main aims of the next seven-year term. The first had been achieved; the second hardly begun.

It was one of the most typical expressions of his genius that de Gaulle had ever embarked on. Always tending to pose problems in voluntarist terms, and obsessed by the short time he had left to complete his work, he gave impetus to a policy that has been labelled "too tough" rather than yield an inch on inflation or accept the slightest delay in the industrialization of the country.

Until then, the "economist" in de Gaulle was scarcely coherent with the rest of his character. Of course, there, too, he was fearless in adversity, quick to come to a decision, ready to embark on a new course, hostile to private interests, intransigent on the matter of independence. But it all added up to a rather defensive policy and one that could be carried out by conservatives.

And what of the Plan? Of course, he had seized it from the hands of its creator, the flexible Jean Monnet, and became its unyielding champion. In a letter written to the Prime Minister on 24 July 1965, he came down in favour of an overtly interventionist approach: "It goes without saying that the Plan will be of value only to the extent to which it is actually carried out and that our economic policy must be *directed* year after year with a view to attaining the aims laid down. Planning, indeed, can only have effect if it is *directed*. This observation should make persistent doctrinal discussions on this subject pointless." And he favoured this interventionism in every area: "Where private enterprises are concerned, it is true that we must urge them strongly to modernize their capital equipment and move towards whatever regroupings are necessary."[26]

Hence the setting up of the Committee for Industrial Development, whose chairman was the senior civil servant in charge of the Plan. It was to be one of the motors of the vast movement of concentration introduced to speed up modernization and capital investment, but also to face up to international competition and to check the over-rapid expansion of American investments, attracted by the French economic "boom" indicated by all the experts from 1960 onwards.

At first these concentrations concerned the public enterprises: the banking sector (the setting up of the BNP), then insurance, the oil companies (ERAP) and the aircraft construction enterprises (SNIAS). In the sector that did not depend on the state, similar tendencies were appearing, but more cautiously.

General de Gaulle, recounts Alain Prate, was not automatically against any foreign participation in French enterprises, but he was against the transfer outside France of the decision-making of important enterprises. Hence the struggle that he put up to prevent the takeover of Jeumont-Schneider by Westinghouse and the Fiat-Citroën merger (which failed). What his financial adviser calls "the General's fits of anger", caused by operations of the kind involved in, for example, the takeover of Simca by Chrysler, helped in the formation of a number of large, wholly French industrial groups.

In other fields, General de Gaulle's authority was to be exercised more unambiguously. Here, in his directives and reactions, one detects an explosive mixture of irritated nationalism and modernist intuitions that do not amount to a real policy, but were the beginning of an industrial strategy that was to be carried out by Georges Pompidou. That is why the Fifth Plan will be remembered not so much as the framework for a bold decade of modernization (1965–75), but rather as the expression of an honourable awareness of the need to redistribute the surplus value of economic growth. This is how de Gaulle described that ambition in his press conference of 4 February 1965: "If we are to avoid imbalance, all social categories must advance at the same pace as the whole, so that each has its own share. This elementary harmony, which must be envisaged by the Plan, is all the more necessary in that the French economy is now developing on the basis of stability." Although the General did give some impetus and erected a few barriers in the domestic domain, his fine feelings, on social matters, rarely went beyond a declaration of intent.

How can one not be struck by this contradiction? Whereas the text of the Fifth Plan presents as its aim a policy "that expresses the will to contribute to a more equitable distribution of income", at the same time, in the absence of the necessary social consensus, the government let it be known that it was not possible "to consider for the time being the application of a contractual incomes policy".[27]

Although it is true that an enterprise must be judged by its results, any attempt to assess those stemming from the totality of measures taken at the General's direct initiative between 1963 and 1968 comes up with ambiguous conclusions.

A rate of growth oscillating around 5 per cent (slightly behind the one anticipated by the Fifth Plan), industrial development of the order of 7 per cent (higher than that envisaged by the Plan), progress in investment estimated at 8.7 per cent, price increases held under 3 per cent until 1968: the insistence on balance coming from central government did not affect economic dynamism adversely.

But there were areas in which these principles were not respected. In agriculture, the almost revolutionary spirit of enterprise shown by Edgard Pisani opened the way to the necessary adaptations and new directions, while the French negotiators in Brussels were preparing the structure of a common agricultural policy, the arrangements of which were to prove highly profitable to the producers: but French rural society, shaken to its foundations, subjected to sudden initiatives and unexpected appeals, above all ill-prepared for change, reacted with wild-cat strikes and semi-insurrectional actions such as the seizure of a police station at Morlaix in June 1961. No systematic policy of industrialization could fail to cause terrible upheavals in the peasant world.

And what of the failures? Firstly, the building industry was woefully behind, especially in the area of housing. In 1968, the regime was in ill-repute on this point. For fifteen million poorly housed people, 370 000 homes were built a year: for the Paris region, 70 000 a year, whereas the Fourth Plan had provided for 100,000. But above all there was the increasing disparities in the incomes between wage-earners and the better off: 4 per cent growth for the first, 13 per cent for the second in 1968.

Charles de Gaulle did suffer from his relative powerlessness in economic and social affairs. To his old London companion, Léo Teyssot, who would come to see him at the Elysée, he remembered: "You know what they're like, so tell me why what I do, in this area, doesn't percolate down to the masses."

CHAPTER THIRTY-SIX

A Dictator in the Second Round

At the Elysée, the press conference was coming to an end.

"How is your health, *mon Général?*"

"Quite good. But, don't worry, one day, I shan't fail to die."

On 4 February 1965, ten months after a surgical operation which had provoked a wave of anxiety throughout the country, just as the assassination attempt of 1962 had done, Charles de Gaulle wanted to remind people that the hero could make light even of death. Why should he not amuse himself imagining how the little men would cope when suddenly confronted by the problem of so monumental a succession? All those who attended the press conference held by Charles de Gaulle on 31 January 1964 had sensed that he was deploying, expressing, representing that concept of immortality before their eyes. Once again, the General was before us.

De Gaulle could create an event by concealing his plans for his own future: were France and the world already asking themselves about his intentions? Would not the "successor", to whom the referendum of 1962 had promised overwhelming legitimacy, not be himself? But, on 31 January 1964, he preferred to create the event, by redefining the nature of the powers of the head of State. That dazzling exposition has been called a "veritable unwritten Constitution, so much does it differ from the text of 1958".[1] When one journalist asked him for his opinion on the functioning of the Constitution, he was given this dazzling "answer", which certainly amounted to a constitutional revision:

> A Constitution is a spirit, institutions, a practice. The spirit of the new Constitution so arranges matters that, while keeping a legislative parliament, power is no longer in the hands of party supporters, but proceeds directly from the people, which means that the head of State, elected by the Nation, is its source and its holder. That is what was achieved, as everybody knows, when I resumed direction of affairs, and when I assumed the functions of President. It is what has been simply confirmed by the latest referendum. It is true that, concurrently with the spirit and with the text, there is also the practice. This, of course, has fallen mainly to men. As far as the head of State is concerned, it is obvious that his personal equation has had its effect and I doubt if, at the outset, this was not expected.

Having, in passing, rejected any recourse to the presidential system that has "up to the present, operated, as best it could, in the United States", then confirming that the President of the Republic could not be elected at the same time and above all for the same period as the deputies in order not to be mixed up with the struggle of the parties, and finally removing any notion of a "diarchy" at the summit of the state, he recalled solemnly that "the President is obviously the only one to hold and delegate the authority of the State", and then added the following sentences, which have been the object of interminable and impassioned commentaries:

> Though it must be clearly understood that the indivisible authority of the State is entrusted entirely to the President by the people that has elected him, that there is no other authority, ministerial, civil, military, or judicial that is not conferred and maintained by him, and finally that it belongs to him to adjust the supreme domain that is his with those that he attributes to others to manage, everything contrives, in normal times, to maintain the distinction between the function and the field of action of the head of State and those of the Prime Minister.

He then concluded: "Our Constitution is a good one. It has proved itself for over five years. Let us keep it as it is."

One has to have heard that epic statement of personal sovereignty to have any notion of what certainty armed with a conception of history can be. One cannot have heard those incandescent words without feeling them to be an immense restoration of the centuries of monarchical power. Good lawyers such as André Hauriou saw it as a quite different Constitution,[2] while Hubert Beuve-Méry wrote, the next day, that "rarely has the theory of absolute power been expounded with such indulgence".[3]

Charles de Gaulle did not re-establish the monarchy, or found the Third Empire, or establish a dictatorship, or abolish parliament, or even reduce the Prime Minister to the role of a head of cabinet, and, as soon as he was put into a minority by the people, he withdrew. A republican by history and a democrat for want of anything better, he did not act in the manner in which he had defined his role as the "sole source" of the "indivisible authority of the State". But those phosphorescent words exposed his flank to polemics, which raged all the more freely in that circumstances were to come to their aid.

For some weeks de Gaulle had known that he could not put off indefinitely an indispensable operation: he was suffering from an adenoma of the prostate. At his age, his surgeon and friend, Professor Aboulker, reminded him, the operation incurred no risk. But there was the immobilization, the time lost, the gossip. They had managed to keep the secret of a probe in the bladder, even during the tour of Mexico in March. Only members of his family, the Prime Minister, the Secretary-General at the Elysée and his private secretary were informed. On 16 April, the head of State went into the Hôpital Cochin, where he was operated on by Professor Aboulker the following day at 8 a.m. The rumour of the hospitalization began to spread in the early afternoon. It was not until the evening that a statement written (the day before) by the General's own hand was to reveal that an operation had taken place and that it had been successful. Together with this text, Etienne Burin des Roziers, Secretary-General at the Elysée, had been sent a sealed envelope bearing the words: "Not to be opened until after my death. But you will give me back this note the day after tomorrow, if, as I expect, everything goes well."[4]

Article 21 of the Constitution lays it down "by virtue of a specific delegation of authority and for a specific agenda, the Prime Minister may chair the Council of Ministers in the place of the President of the Republic". The event forced de Gaulle to implement it. As if doped by the showering of such responsibilities on his head, Georges Pompidou had no sooner chaired a meeting of the Council of Ministers than the parliamentary arena suddenly opened up before him to prove that he was a first-class debater. On 24 April, seven days after the operation at the Hôpital Cochin, the Prime Minister had to face a considerable challenge: François Mitterrand, who was already the most pugnacious of the opposition leaders, launched into an accusation:

I can see that one may prefer this or that form of representative regime, a parliamentary regime or a no less democratic one of a presidential type, but it seems to me difficult to accept that the parliamentary regime established in 1958 has not undergone since that time a decisive mutation. The articles of the Constitution according to which "the government determines and conducts the policy of the Nation" and "is responsible before Parliament" are now void of meaning. The present regime, in which you appear sometimes as a discreet head of government, sometimes as a Prime Minister, reminds one more of the relations between a master of absolute power and his favourite than of a Constitution valid for all citizens.

But the sensation of the debate was not the vigour or brilliance of the accusation, which were expected by everybody, but Georges Pompidou's reply:

Is the Prime Minister reduced to the role of a non-entity? Forgive me, but I don't think so. In any case, I regard the role of head of State as fundamental, but I would not continue to carry responsibilities if I were not fully in agreement with him on all aspects of policy, which it is my task to carry out, with the government, whose action I approve.

The speaker then had his audience on the edge of their seats when he delivered a semi-confidence: "I regard it as an elementary duty for a Prime Minister never to reveal publicly the divergences that, in this or that circumstance, might arise between the head of State and him." That was something new. There were frowns on the Gaullist benches; wonder on the others. Then Pompidou moved on to the counter-attack:

The truth, Monsieur Mitterrand, is that you remain faithful to the Fourth Republic. You remain faithful to a way that was nevertheless marked by disasters and dishonour. On the peaceful benches of the opposition, like the émigrés of the Ancien Régime on the shores of England, you await impatiently the time to return to the State, without having learnt anything, or forgotten anything. But the future is not yours. It does not belong to ghosts.

Whatever the conditions of the political struggle may be tomorrow, the country will give its confidence only to those who unreservedly are committed not to allow the condition of its stability to disappear: a head of State who really is one. As M. François Mauriac wrote recently,* the French people does not know what it wants, but it knows what it does not want. And what it does not want is to fall back into your redoubtable hands. If it were ever tempted to forget that, you would always be there, thank God, as a reminder.

From that day, 24 April 1964, the Prime Minister began to be seen as a possible dauphin. "You must get yourself known, Pompidou. Travel, speak to the French people, show yourself to foreigners." However naïve the former employee of the Rothschild Bank may have been, how could he see himself otherwise than as the heir presumptive when, at the General's urgings, he visited Sweden, India or Japan? No one can confirm that de Gaulle welcomed with unequivocal satisfaction the demonstration of non-vassaldom given by Georges Pompidou during the brief withdrawal of the "sole source of power", and that he cared at all for the reference by his Prime Minister to possible "divergences" between the Elysée and Matignon. De Gaulle always liked to have several irons in the fire. In any case, he now had one plausible heir. This did not impose or exclude anything or anybody. Pompidou would be kept in reserve. No more, no less.**

As the electoral year of 1965 came into view, Charles de Gaulle does not seem to have posed the problem to himself in other than personal terms. To accept a second mandate or to get elected a reflection of himself: that, for him, was the only dilemma. The man who regarded as quite inadequate the 62 per cent of "yes" votes at the referendum of October 1962 did not for a moment envisage that the opposition could intervene in "his" problems. The rather poor results of the municipal elections of March 1965 do not even seem to have disturbed him. The UNR had not succeeded in making the expected "breakthrough", as the RPF had done in 1947. This, declared the General at a meeting of the Council of Ministers, was because the French had not felt that issues of great national interest were at stake.[5]

But the head of State's phlegm came close here to a lack of vigilance. However, the signs were multiplied that, though crushed in November 1962, the opposition parties had, since late 1963, shown a certain vague aspiration to existence and, more important, an attempt to find unity or convergence. Realizing that such formulas as the "*cartel des non*" of 1958, which had been revived in 1962, led only to failure, parties, movements and political clubs tried to set up against the Great Sorcerer a character that was less phosphorescent, of course, but more modern in style and more European in inspiration: hence the creation of "Monsieur X". The mask of anonymity was soon to be snatched away: it was Gaston Defferre, former Socialist minister, now mayor of Marseille. He was the man who might bring

*In *Le Figaro littéraire*.
**But it should be noted that when Pompidou became President in 1962, he declared to Maurice Schumann: "I never imagined, for a moment, that the General's successor could be anyone other than I" (interview with the author, April 1986).

together all the forces that occupied the political landscape between Mount de
Gaulle and the Communist peak. A poor speaker, but a good administrator, this
sporty, open, forthright *bon vivant* aroused little enthusiasm, but less rancour.

In the eyes of General de Gaulle, Gaston Defferre was probably the least
dislikable of politicians. He had been a brave member of the Resistance, a declared
supporter of the General's Algerian policy, a sworn enemy of the OAS, and had
played little part in the struggles against the constitutional revision of 1962;
Defferre was certainly one of the leaders of the left that the Elysée would like to
have associated in some "social opening" on the theme of participation.

In spring 1965, after the municipal elections, Gaston Defferre became the
official candidate of the Socialist Party for the presidential elections. But everyone
knew that that was not his major aim. Any reflection on the removal of General de
Gaulle had to set out with the idea that the left was not in a majority in France and
that the key to victory was to be found in the centre: from the MRP to the Radical
Party and to the less conservative (and non-Gaullist) fringe of the Independents.
Hence the idea of federating those forces. Plans for such a "great federation",
which were to be loyally supported by most of Gaston Defferre's possible rivals –
Pierre Mendès France, François Mitterrand, Maurice Faure, if not, in the final
hours, Jean Lecanuet – were not to be a success.

However much the candidate demonstrated his moderation, his flexibility, his
anti-communism, he remained nevertheless a Socialist. Neither on political
institutions, nor on Europe, nor on the social programme did the allies have any
difficulty in reaching an understanding. But the SFIO had certain great principles,
one of which was secularization, which the Secretary-General of the SFIO always
managed to bring up when agreement was in sight. So he turned once again to the
hypothesis of an appeal to Antoine Pinay, who scared all those who did not want to
break definitively with the Communists and secularized education.

By the middle of June everything seemed once again possible. Of course, on 15
June, at the home of Jacques Duhamel, a rising star of the Radicals, a very heavy
cloud blew up when Jean Lecanuet said that "the MRP electorate is tempted by de
Gaulle". Meanwhile, Guy Mollet made constant references to the contacts that
Jean Lecanuet was having with the Communists, whose votes were indispensable
to him if he were to be elected. Lecanuet then denounced the collusion between
Mollet and the Gaullists. It seemed that the "Great Federation" was so great that
it would have to expel its two extremities on the grounds of treason.

Nevertheless, a meeting was arranged for the evening of 17 June, at the home of
Pierre Abelin, a leading member of the MRP. There then arose a problem that
had not cropped up so far, that of nationalization. Albert Gazier, the spokesman of
the SFIO, supported by Defferre, suddenly turned it into a major theme. Lecanuet
was opposed to it. Mollet called on the great ancestors to bear witness. Lecanuet
then said: "If the Federation is formed, it can only function after the presidential
elections." (In other words, it could not be used as an electoral mechanism in
support of a Defferre candidature.) There were angry reactions, accusations that
Lecanuet was planning his own candidature.

Abelin tried hard to get the discussion moving again, but to little effect. Mitterrand then intervened: it would be a mistake, he argued, to include an explicit

rejection of Communist votes in the Federation's programme. There was an explosion. Guy Mollet asked round the table: "If you have the choice, will you prefer to elect a UNR candidate rather than a Communist?" Maurice Faure, approved by the MRP members, gave a clear "Yes". "Then," the Secretary-General of the SFIO cut in, looking very pleased with himself, "No federation is possible."[6]

On 18 June, at dawn, the "great federation" was buried. Meanwhile, Charles de Gaulle had his own reflections. He had successfully come through the operation in April, but his eyes were troubling him. And his age, of course. A few months before, Maurice Schumann had confided to Jean-Raymond Tournoux: "I've just seen de Gaulle. I doubt the General will ask for a second seven-year term in 1965. He still seems to be haunted by one thing. I wouldn't use a comparison that he did not make in my presence, but I'm sure he's thinking of the ageing Pétain."[7]

Mme de Gaulle did her utmost to persuade her husband not to ask for a second term. Several close colleagues heard her say that "the General's true friends must urge him not to stay at the Elysée". Thus, what did he mean when, on 31 December 1964, he confided to journalists that in 1965 "people won't be bored"? Then there was this: "The election will take place in December, as laid down in the Constitution, unless I disappear before that." And at Melun, on 17 June, vaunting the successes of his seven-year term, he declared: "One must be blind or in bad faith not to recognize it. But the world is in no doubt. Then one must go on. That is what the country wants as it wanted it yesterday. We shall draw all the consequences from that and so will I."

On 28 June, he invited to the Elysée the four men whose opinions he most valued (apart from Etienne Burin des Roziers, his Secretary-General, whom he saw every day): André Malraux, Gaston Palewski, Michel Debré and Georges Pompidou.* Each of them knew that he was there to express his opinion on the fundamental matter of the General's decision. It was a sounding of the miniaturized Gaullist planet to which the sovereign had summoned his chief advisers, taking care to balance the mystics (Malraux and Debré) by the politicians (Palewski and Pompidou), the ardent by the prudent, the eloquent by the cunning, the "interested" (Debré and Pompidou) by the disinterested (Malraux and Palewski).

The most ardent advocate of the candidature was Michel Debré. De Gaulle could not withdraw at the normal end of his mandate, like just any president. It was up to him, and to him alone, to decide when he would go, in terms not of a calendar, but of his historic mission, taking account of the situation of France at home and abroad.

Almost as persuasive was Gaston Palewski. Stressing the head of State's health, which, for a man of seventy-five who had been operated on in the spring of 1964, was excellent, the General's former *directeur de cabinet* concluded: "Too many things remain to be done for Charles de Gaulle to give up now." The head of State cut him short: "There are always things to be done."

---

*Couve de Murville was in Brussels, where he represented France.

The two most subtle contributions were those of Georges Pompidou and André Malraux. Pompidou did not try to silence suspicions by too enthusiastic a speech and weighed up the arguments on both sides – which the General took, it seems, as an invitation to go. (Four years later, he was to confide to François Flohic, in Ireland, that Pompidou had tried to dissuade him from putting himself forward.[8]) André Malraux's contribution was that of a sage – in tone fairly close to that of Pompidou. He, too, tried to bring out the risks that a second mandate might bring to the historical image of Charles de Gaulle and the advantages of a withdrawal, leaving the General as the nation's ultimate recourse, the politician being in the Elysée and the mystic at Colombey. But this was, he said, to conclude in favour of a renewing of the head of state's mandate, taking account of forthcoming events in the diplomatic and military fields.[9]

The Knights of the Round Table had spoken. The General was content to conclude: "I'll think about it."

The following day, 1 July, one minister saw a "haggard-looking" Couve de Murville leave Brussels: the evening before, he had had to break off negotiations on the financial settlement of the Common Agricultural Policy. The decision, advocated by Couve,[10] was immediately adopted by the head of State even before the Prime Minister had been informed of it: France's chair would remain empty. It was a serious crisis. It amounted to cutting France off from all her neighbours. Furthermore, the repercussions, in the country, would be harmful: the rural world, having done well out of the Common Market, realized that it had become an essential element in its expansion.

That year, 1965, was certainly turning out to be an eventful one. Here was a situation worthy of him. Confronting the Brussels Five, who, weary of France's pretensions to rule Europe, were now forming a coalition against her, was not the time to retire. Would a Pompidou be capable of facing up to such schemings against France? Would not Charles de Gaulle's enemies, the Spaaks, the Lunses and the Schroeders, get it into their heads that they had finally "got him"?

Throughout August, the General gave no inkling of his intentions. De Gaulle had resumed his long walks in the forest of Les Dhuits and on the Malochère road. He was getting ready. He had not yet said anything to Georges Pompidou. Since 29 June or 1 July, the Prime Minister had suspected something; but nevertheless he had chosen, that summer, to give himself an image closer to that of the average Frenchman, to spend his holidays not at Saint-Tropez, but at Fouesnant, in Brittany, among people with small savings, shrimp fishermen and large families. In other words, electors.

It was on 4 September, according to his *directeur de cabinet* that the Prime Minister was informed by General de Gaulle of his decision to ask for a new mandate. What is more, Michel Jobert goes on, "he was asked to keep the matter private".[11] For the head of State, who always believed in the tactical virtues of secrecy, silence and surprise, kept his world (except Pompidou, Peyrefitte and Burin des Roziers) in suspense.

On 9 September, he held his weekly press conference, the first since 4 February – the one when he had remarked that "I shan't fail to die". He was no sooner sitting in front of the green-covered table than he was asked: "*Monsieur le*

Président, can you tell us if you expect to present yourself at the elections on 5 December?"

"I shall tell you at once that you will know, I promise you, before two months are up."*

This was to be as provocative as one could be towards the press, public opinion and politicians. To say the least, the laughter with which that joke was received was tinged with irritation. In the end, that strategy of feint did not go down well. François Mitterrand realized this and decided to get things moving. He had made up his mind three days before, he writes in *Ma part de vérité*.[12] After sounding out the intentions of the Communists once more, he in fact took his decision on 25 August, with three certainties, three conditions in his pocket: that the SFIO would support him; that the PCF would not put up a candidate against him; that he would have the support of Pierre Mendès France. From 25 August to 6 September he patiently obtained all these "necessary visas".[13] He then decided to surprise everybody. On 9 September, just as de Gaulle was playing fast and loose with his listeners at the Elysée, a statement was issued from the "candidate of the left" announcing his candidature. The day after that the setting up of a Federation of the Democratic and Socialist Left, in which the various currents of the left, non-Communist opposition had come together, was announced. The Mitterrand candidature was orientated firmly on the left, thus raising the ghost of the Popular Front. A candidate from the centre has to find his place. Europe having become, after the break with Brussels, an essential issue in the campaign, the name of Jean Lecanuet, chairman of the MRP, was an obvious choice.

Opinion polls in September gave Mitterrand 11 per cent of voting intentions and, in October, 2 per cent to Lecanuet, who, in seven weeks, would multiply that figure by 8. Television had a lot to do with this, as did the talent of those two competitors, who at that time were the only ones capable of offering any challenge to the President on that ground.

The significance of Mitterrand's candidature was not lost on de Gaulle. Not that he thought that he had the slightest chance of winning, with or without the support of the PCF. Since he had made up his mind, the General thought that he would not have to fight much of a battle. He considered that he had broken the electoral power of the PCF in 1958 and felt sure that he would get 70 per cent of the votes (in the first round).[14]

But Mitterrand's candidature gave him the impression that a personal challenge had been laid down. Since 1962, the deputy for Nièvre had become the most militant enemy of his regime – with the possible exception of Gaston Monnerville. He was, in any case, the most constant and most brilliant of them. He was the author of *Le Coup d'état permanent*, published the previous year. He was the man who, on 24 April of the previous year, on the rostrum of the Assembly, had drawn up a major case against the type of power defined on 31 January 1964.

On 26 October, at a meeting of the Council of Ministers, de Gaulle announced with some solemnity: "I shall address the country on 4 November, at 8 p.m. Please forgive me if I say no more. For me, it is a question of conscience." And so, on 4

*The election was to take place in two months and twenty-six days.

November, the feast of St Charles, in the late morning, the blue vans of French Television were parked in the courtyard of the Elysée. Alone in his office, the General re-read a text that he had written some ten days earlier at Colombey. At 6 p.m. precisely, the General delivered the first words, his head moving up and down and from right to left, like a war horse about to charge:

> Twenty-five years ago, when France was rolling into the abyss, I felt it my duty to assume responsibility for leading her until she was freed, victorious and mistress of herself. Seven years ago, I thought it my duty to return to its head in order to preserve it from a civil war, to avoid a monetary and financial crash and to build up with her institutions corresponding to the needs of the time and of the modern world. Since then I have considered it my duty to exercise the powers of head of State in order that an unprecedented stage in her internal development, to the advantage of all her children, may be completed, to recover complete peace and to acquire in the world a political and moral position worthy of her. . . . Today, I believe it my duty to be ready to continue my task, fully aware of the effort that this involves, but convinced that at present it is the best way of serving France.

The head of State's statement was the first item, of course, in the broadcast of the evening news. By 8.04 p.m., the French people knew at last. The last sentence alone immediately became the focus of comment, private and public, overshadowing at first the one that was later to be the most criticized: "If the frank, massive support of the citizens commits me to remain in my office, the future of the new Republic will certainly be assured. Otherwise no one can be in any doubt that it will crumble at once and France will have to undergo – but this time without any possible recourse – a confusion of the State more disastrous still than the one it once knew."[15]

Mitterrand, who held a public meeting at Lyon, got up to speak only after having heard the General's address. He seemed very cheered by it: "Since I am fighting personal power, I shall also fight the man who embodies it. The pawns are on the chessboard. De Gaulle offers himself. Then so do I!" Meanwhile, Jean Lecanuet published this brief comment: "A President of the Republic has no right to say that without him the regime comes to a stop and France gives up."[16]

At the Elysée, they were not entirely happy about that entrance. This included the General himself: "It was too long, too much like a lawyer's plea," de Gaulle sighed. But, as far as he was concerned, it had all been said, or very nearly. He could not campaign: on 3 December, two days before the vote, at the very time when the debate was closing, he would have the last, brief word. The electoral regulations gave him, and his opponents, the right to two hours of screen time: he did not use it. The Minister of Information, supported by pleas from Georges Pompidou, Jacques Chaban-Delmas and Roger Frey, urged him to speak – but to no avail. The General was sure of what he was doing.

On the morning of 30 October, Mohammed Tahri, a politician of the Moroccan left, telephoned *Le Monde** to warn that his friend Mehdi Ben Barka, the

*To the author of this book, to be precise.

organizer of the most militant opposition to King Hassan II and Secretary-General of the so-called "Tricontinental" conference, which was to meet in Cuba a few weeks later, had disappeared the day before. Colleagues on *Le Monde* alerted the Quai d'Orsay and the Ministry of the Interior. The Ben Barka affair had begun.

On 2 November, the brother of the man who had disappeared, Abdelkader Ben Barka, laid a charge of kidnapping and sequestration. A can of worms had been opened: gangsters, double agents, informers, hired killers, spies in the royal palace at Rabat, police manipulated by extorting gangsters – it was the dark side, the obscene side of two states, two societies, Moroccan and French, involved in a common crime – at the top of which was the formidable personality of General Mohammed Oufkir, a former creature of the French protectorate who had become King Hassan II's Minister of the Interior and adviser.

On 3 November (the day before General de Gaulle's declaration of his candidature), it was learnt that Mehdi Ben Barka had been seized on 29 October about noon in front of the drugstore at Saint-Germain-des-Prés and taken to Fontenay-le-Vicomte, to the house of a gangster called Boucheseiche, after which all trace of him had been lost. It then transpired that Mohammed Oufkir happened to have been passing through Paris on 30 October: and there was the same minister appearing on 3 November, first at a cocktail party given by the Minister of the Interior, Roger Frey, on the occasion of a training course in France for Moroccan civil servants, then at a dinner given for the same occasion at the Villa Saïd, before returning to Morocco the following day.

On that 4 November, certain investigators made a series of discoveries that seemed nothing short of incredible: still alive or already dead after torture, Mehdi Ben Barka had been transferred by plane to Morocco on the night of 30 October. General Oufkir had quite obviously organized the kidnap and supervised the "interrogation" at Fontenay-le-Vicomte. The plane carrying Ben Barka or his corpse to Casablanca overnight was allowed to leave Orly without any checks. Two policemen, Souchon and Voitot,* had themselves, together with criminals, taken part in the kidnapping disguised as an arrest.

It is hardly surprising if, on that 4 November, a member of the *cabinet* of the Minister of Foreign Affairs, Philippe Malaud** was sent to Morocco where, accompanied by the French Ambassador, Robert Gillet, he presented to the King the information that had been gathered in Paris about the affair and conveyed France's regrets. The Moroccan Interior Minister was directly involved, in France, in a criminal affair: in his country's name, General de Gaulle demanded extradition. The two diplomats came up against a brick wall. Hassan II had heard of nothing. His minister had merely stopped off in Paris for twenty-four hours, between 3 and 4 November, at the invitation of the French authorities. The report sent to General de Gaulle put him in a fury. Not only had that "little king", who owed everything to France, beginning with his father's throne, which he had

---

*Who were to be able to prove that their good faith had been surprised, though nevertheless they remained involved in a criminal operation.
**Malaud was to become leader of an extreme right-wing political organization.

assumed four years before in rather dubious circumstances, settled his accounts with his enemies on French soil, but he was making a mockery of him, de Gaulle! And on the very day when he had just announced to the world that he was going to continue with his task.

Two days later, de Gaulle wrote and immediately published a letter addressed to Mehdi Ben Barka's mother. It was a very fine letter, and a very explicit one, which concluded: "I can assure you that justice will be carried out with the greatest rigour and the greatest speed."

The letter, and the revelations in the international press that Mohammed Oufkir had been directly involved, showed that de Gaulle regarded himself as directly involved in that incredible scandal: a foreign minister, of a supposedly friendly country, coming to Paris to kidnap, torture and perhaps murder the leader of the opposition, who was about to return to his country and had gone to the meeting at Fontenay-le-Vicomte convinced that he would be meeting there the King's most respected adviser, Ahmed Belafredj. Furthermore, Mehdi Ben Barka was not only the leader of the Moroccan left, but also one of the most influential figures in the Third World, with which the Elysée had friendly relations that it was trying to strengthen. Three days after the publication of the head of State's letter, the *Gazette de Lausanne* described the kidnapping of Ben Barka as "a personal affront to General de Gaulle" by Morocco.

It is very difficult today to get any idea of the nature of the relations between Ben Barka and the General's colleagues. De Gaulle himself, having received the Moroccan leader shortly before the declaration of the right of Algerians to self-determination, in 1959, had not taken kindly to the interpretation later given of his words by the visitor. But in the development of the Elysée's Third World policy, just prior to the Conference of the Three Continents in Havana, de Gaulle could not fail to see Ben Barka as an asset in his game.

On 11 November, after the meeting of the Council of Ministers, Alain Peyrefitte, when asked if the General had spoken on the matter, told journalists: "Yes. He did speak, as he does on all important problems." Important because certain of his colleagues ran the risk of being seen as implicated in the affair? No. For the General, responsibility lay at two levels: on the higher, the Moroccan side, and on the lower, the French side, involving criminals, killers, police informers and stupid or ill-informed civil servants.

A few weeks later it emerged in the press that in one meeting of the Council of Ministers (probably on 11 November) Roger Frey had revealed that Ben Barka had telephoned him, on 28 October, on the eve of his departure from Geneva for Paris, asking him if Oufkir was in Paris: to which the minister appears to have answered no, which at the time was correct. During the parliamentary session of 8 May 1966, which gave him an opportunity of presenting a detailed account of the official thesis on the affair, Roger Frey made an indignant repudiation of that "lie": "I never said anything of the kind at the Council of Ministers, for the very good reason that I did not know M. Ben Barka and have never heard the sound of his voice." During the same meeting in May 1966, Roger Frey made another statement, which seems relevant:

There is another particularly odious accusation: it has been said and repeated that the government had wanted to stifle the affair on account of the presidential election. One has only to bring the dates together. The kidnapping took place on 29 October. Lopez* was arrested on 4 November, El Mahi** on the fifth. Souchon and Voitot on the eleventh. Bernier*** on 26 November. Everything was known during the presidential campaign and the election took place on 5 December. So what is all this?

It is a fact that there was no shortage of revelations from the press and official circles throughout the campaign. What is surprising is not the holding back of information, but that the candidates should have made so little of a scandal that could not fail to rebound on the reputation of the Gaullist State. It is easy enough to believe that Lecanuet and Pierre Marcilhacy, an old-style liberal, were overcome by embarrassment. But what is astonishing is that Tixier-Vignancourt, a specialist in muck-raking around those in power, should have kept silent. Did he think that if he lifted the veil he might lose a client? Only François Mitterrand decided to refer to the episode by allusion to the one in which Dreyfus had been the unhappy protagonist. And he did so in a very discreet way. On 17 November, during a press conference in Paris, he declared that the Ben Barka affair had exposed "the unhealthy activity of certain members of the political police who carry out the government's dirty work, if not on their own account".

Then on 16 December (between the two rounds of the election), before the television screens, he returned to the matter of the "complicities" that had emerged in the Ben Barka affair, in which, he believed, people "around the Minister of the Interior" were implicated. The candidate of the United Left concluded: "I think General de Gaulle cannot know everything, cannot say everything, cannot supervise everything."

That is as far as things went during the presidential campaign. Not that the "affair" was over: it was to re-emerge again in January 1966 (with the attempt to arrest Georges Figon, the inventor of the trap into which Ben Barka had fallen on 29 October, which ended with his "suicide"; the arrest of the secret agent Le Roy, known as "Finville"; the retirement of the boss of the SDECE, the secret service, General Jacquier; the orders issued for Oufkir, his assistant Dlimi and his agent Chtouki to report to the police). Never had the honour of de Gaulle's republic been so much in question.

De Gaulle's anger derived not so much from the involvement of two or three secondary figures in the affair as from the penetration of the system by bodies hostile to his policies or keen to get a footing in France. What the investigation revealed was that the "Fortress Fifth Republic" had been infiltrated on all sides and that French territory was being used as a field of manoeuvre for ill-intentioned powers. As one of his closest military colleagues told me twenty years later, "The

*Who worked for Air France: linked to the secret service, he acted as a go-between and assisted the departure of the plane from Paris to Casablanca.
**A Moroccan spy.
***A journalist who was involved in planning Ben Barka's trip to Paris, and in the film that was then being planned.

Ben Barka affair was for him as terrible a spotlight on the vulnerability of the system as the *putsch* of April 1961."

The General said nothing. Mitterrand did his best, mastering television technique with some difficulty; Lecanuet tried "to oppose the image of the conquering son to that of the father", keen to reassure people; Tixier-Vignancourt, the candidate of the extreme right, shook the screen with his Gascon peasant's laugh; Marcilhacy spoke like a liberal lawyer; de Gaulle kept silent.

A large, pale-blue poster presented de Gaulle's image on walls throughout France: he looked old, a figure from the past. "You must speak, *mon Général*," Peyrefitte insisted. "You still have nearly two hours' broadcasting time. Personalize your appeal. You saw Lecanuet: he burst through the screen presenting himself to the viewers: background, age, profession, family. It had an effect." "Well, Peyrefitte, you really want me to stick myself in front of the screen and say: my name is Charles de Gaulle and I am seventy-five years old! I'd be a laughing stock!"[17]

All his colleagues urged him to speak. Then there were the opinion polls: on 25 November, ten days before the vote, the IFOP gave de Gaulle only 51 per cent of intended votes. This was 20 per cent less than three months before! If it went on like that, there would be a second round, rumour had it – even in leading Gaullist circles. On the morning of 3 December, when Charles de Gaulle was getting ready to deliver his final appeal to the country, the polls cast an even darker shadow over the analysts at the Elysée. They gave 44 per cent to the General, 25 per cent to Mitterrand and 15 per cent to Lecanuet. A second round now seemed inevitable.

On Friday 3 December, de Gaulle still had eight minutes' television time to turn the situation round, as had all the other candidates. Was it the compulsory brevity, the challenge that was thrown out to him, the sort of impasse in which, suddenly, he found himself? It was not the first time that we have seen him rise to the occasion under trial. This time Charles de Gaulle spoke. He spoke not of his opponents, but of the affairs of France:

> Where are we going? Five essential problems, which used to be concealed beneath pretence and equivocation, since nobody was capable of solving them, have now been solved. The institutions, once designed to make government powerless, have now given us a head of State and a government that lasts and governs, and a parliament that effectively and worthily exercises its legislative power. Decolonization, which divided the French people, alienated us from the rest of the world and undermined our army, has now been carried out. Peace, which we had, in fact, not known for at least half a century, has now returned. Inflation, which undermined our economy, our finances, our currency, and, from the social point of view, maintained constant insecurity and perpetual injustices, has now been overcome. Lastly, independence, which was being stifled under a mass of lying myths, has been restored.

De Gaulle had rediscovered the tone of the statesman. That evening, comparing him with the other five candidates, he seemed to us to be the best. But it was too late. When he set out for Colombey, on Saturday 4 December 1965, General de Gaulle was no longer under any illusions. The latest opinion polls – those of the IFOP of 30 November – gave him 43 per cent of the votes, as against 27 per cent to Mitterrand, 20 per cent to Lecanuet and 7.5 per cent to Tixier. He now knew that he had been wrong to confuse an election with a referendum, and that in getting 70 per cent of the votes, three months earlier, he had confused factors that were brought together under his name only in exceptional circumstances and heavily underestimated the terrible rancour that had grown up against him during his fabulous career.

On that Sunday, 5 December, Colombey was buffeted by the storms that the General was so fond of. So he gave up the walk that had been planned and shut himself up in his tower until 5 o'clock, when he had tea with Mme de Gaulle. At 8 o'clock they turned on the television set. It became clear almost at once that the head of State would have to face a second round: 44 per cent... 43.9... 43.7... 43.8, with Mitterrand given over 32 per cent and Lecanuet just under 16 per cent.

They were about to go in to dinner, around half-past eight, when the telephone rang. It was Etienne Burin des Roziers: "Yes, *mon Général*, it will mean a second round." De Gaulle grumbled and said that he would be staying at La Boisserie the next day to "reflect", and hung up. Two hours later, there was another call. This time, the advice did not come from an old, faithful friend, but from the professionals – it was from the Hôtel Matignon. Supposing the General "cracked". Supposing, in his anger, he repeated what he had done on 20 January 1946. They knew that Charles de Gaulle was capable of suddenly abandoning everything.

There were three men who spoke to him from the Hôtel Matignon: Georges Pompidou, Louis Joxe and Alain Peyrefitte. Pompidou pleaded with him to continue the fight. He sensed, at the other end of the line, a grief-stricken man and heard nothing but recriminations, a mixture of self-criticism and rancour.

Louis Joxe, too, had to listen to the old man's indignant outpourings: "I shall retire. They don't want me any more." "*Mon Général*, it was only to be expected. The way the campaign was run. A number of candidates. You can't give up the struggle."

Peyrefitte thought he was listening to "a youth who had been punished, knocked about and was dying to inflict further punishment on himself". He piled up the arguments. For the first round, 44 per cent was enormous, looked at coldly, it was a good result, considerable room for manoeuvre, certain victory.

De Gaulle grumbled and hung up. But, quite obviously, Peyrefitte's arguments had had an effect.[18] And when, an hour later, Pompidou rang back to Colombey to read to the General the official comment that he wanted to issue, de Gaulle cut him short. He would go on grumbling, sulking, but he would also go on fighting.

On the Tuesday morning, it was a man who had already made up his mind who went back to Paris by helicopter: he was in a hurry now. He had read the newspapers, the evening before, especially Jacques Fauvet's article in Le Monde – which he hated, while recognizing the correctness of his analysis. "An election, even a presidential one, is not a referendum. The General tried to ignore it. Today he has paid for doing so."[19]

That evening, he worked with Georges Pompidou, who suggested a denunciation of the "divider" Lecanuet and an attack on the "Popular Front" aspect of the candidacy of Mitterrand, "a prisoner of the Communists". "Out of the question," de Gaulle interrupted.

> Lecanuet is out of the game. Quite pointless to mention his name. As for the charge against the Popular Front, it would be absurd. The analyses show that I have got 10 per cent of the workers' votes. If we stress the Mitterrand–PCF collusion, we shall lose that electorate to our opponents. There must be no question of a right-wing campaign against a left-wing one. That's just what Mitterrand wants. We shan't make him a present of it.[20]

And it was a de Gaulle "who looked ten years younger", according to some ministers, who, on 8 December, chaired a surprising meeting of the Council of Ministers, which he opened with words that seldom fell from his lips: "I was wrong!" He even went further: "It was I, and I alone, who confused an election with a referendum. I would be lying if I said that I had not been hurt." But he added, in the most natural way in the world: "Of course, I'm holding on!" He then repeated what he had said to Pompidou: it would be a debate in which he would do everything possible to avoid losing the working-class votes that he had obtained in the first round. "Mitterrand says that he is on the left, but when it's a question of San Domingo* or the Plan, I am the left!" And he concluded: "In the first round, the French let themselves go. In the second, they're serious."[21]

From then on, the campaign for the vote of 19 December was carried out at full stretch, but under the sign of Gaullism rather than that of the UNR, of André Malraux and François Mauriac rather than Georges Pompidou. A public meeting was organized for 14 December at the Palais des Sports, from which the political leaders of Gaullism, beginning with the Prime Minister, were kept to one side. It was Malraux who harangued the masses in the style of the populist meetings of 1948; then Maurice Schumann rediscovered the throbbing voice that he had used in broadcasts from London during the war to denounce the "dagger-bearing plotters", of whom Mitterrand was the leader. The great sociologist Germaine Tillion and François Mauriac spoke in favour of "candidate de Gaulle" – whose words to a visitor were repeated: "They call me a dictator: has there ever been a dictator presenting himself at the second round of an election?"

Meanwhile, François Mitterrand began the complicated negotiations to persuade the other candidates to withdraw in his favour. Jean Lecanuet agreed, after much persuasion; Tixier and his supporters in the OAS and the more-or-less fascist extreme right offered their support without conditions. By accepting these votes, was not the chairman of the Federation of the Left driving into abstention more democratic electors than he was gaining votes from the extremists? He did get the support of Vincent Auriol, Jean Monnet, Daniel Mayer and even Jean-Paul Sartre.

But it was on the television screens that the fate of the campaign was decided.

---

*Where the United States intervened against a "left-wing" power and were criticized by the General for doing so.

There was no question, for de Gaulle, of accepting a face-to-face challenge – as Valery Giscard d'Estaing was bravely to do in 1981. On Saturday 11 December, de Gaulle appeared, delivering, in a quiet tone and in a simplified setting, a carefully studied, carefully written speech in which he denounced "all the pretences, all the tricks of a former time", a time when "a system was so paralysed by its scandalous games" that "our country was called the sick man of the world". "No," he concluded, "the future is not there! The future is with the new Republic whose very purpose is not to split, to divide the French people, but on the contrary to bring them together."

Seeing himself on the screen, on Saturday at 8 p.m., de Gaulle found himself too abstract, too intellectual, confronting a pugnacious, incisive Mitterrand. What could be done to liven up his speeches, to make them more human? Maurice Schumann, Gilbert Pérol, head of the press department at the Elysée, and Alain Peyrefitte, the Minister of Information, all suggested that he should "personalize" his speeches. "What? You want me to appear in front of the French people in pyjamas?" No. But why not choose the form of a dialogue? "Have yourself interviewed, *mon Général*," Schumann suggested. By whom? De Gaulle already had visions of having to face one of those rebellious journalists. A name came to Peyrefitte's lips: "Michel Droit". The General breathed a sigh of relief. There was a man who would at least be respectful.

The dialogue was a lively one. Michel Droit, though a devoted supporter, knew his job: the "tougher" he was, the better de Gaulle would be. His questions were very astute. The first drew attention to a contrast between the "idea of France" held by the author of the *Mémoires de guerre* and the idea that he had of the French people. And the answers came thick and fast, more and more lively. The General became involved in the game, came to life, raised his voice, relaxed, smiled, waved his long arms about, slapped his thighs, produced vocal effects that overflowed with vitality, sparkled with sarcasm.

Turning to everyday life, he referred to homes where "the husband goes out on the spree, the boys put their feet on the table and the girls don't come home at night", to the detriment of the "housewife". When, as the twenty-eighth minute passed, Michel Droit indicated to him that he only had two minutes left, he played by the rules like a professional. When he had finished, he gave a cunning wink to his interviewer and remarked: "I think I took three minutes, didn't I?" It was he who "wanted more".

They then embarked immediately on the second part, in which they would deal with foreign policy. He launched into the subject of Europe. "Of course, one can jump onto one's chair and caper about shouting 'Europe! Europe!'" – and he himself started capering about like a performing elephant. It was all quite astonishing. He then added, quite carried away: "There are those, the choirboys who have drunk some of the altar wine, who yell in favour of a supranational Europe." His advisers began to look gloomy.

They broke off again, for lunch. In the afternoon, he was even livelier than in the morning, clearly having a better time than he had ever done during his seven years of life at the Elysée. This time, he referred to his opponent, whom he called *ce personnage* and, taking the viewers into his confidence, declared: "If I am elected on Sunday, I shall not stay for very long, but, whatever happens, I will have fulfilled my destiny."

It was all over. It was a superb performance and those who witnessed it agreed that, with ammunition like that, he could not fail to win. But there were two objections. The first came from Alain Peyrefitte: that arrow launched at the MRP ("choirboys who have drunk some of the altar wine") was really a present to Mitterrand. All right, said the General. Cut it out. Then someone queried the phrase "I shall not stay for very long", if elected. Was it useful to tell the electors that their vote would bring to office only a temporary president? There, too, de Gaulle agreed: the words were cut.

The final comment of that monumental candidate, before going up to his private apartment, was: "You see, once I get started, I could chatter on like that for several hours."[22] On Friday, 17 December, between 8 and 9 p.m., de Gaulle was getting more and more benevolent: "I'm not saying I'm perfect or hiding my age." And Mitterrand, the "challenger", became more and more incisive: "The fundamental choice is between personal power and the republic of citizens." The die was cast: all the opinion polls were more or less 55–45 in favour of de Gaulle.

On 19 December, the rain did not keep the electors at home – there was an almost 85 per cent turnout. The forecasts were confirmed to a few decimal points: 54.6 per cent to 45.4 per cent. Everything could now go back to normal. The General-President was back in office. According to the psephologists, he owed his victory to women and those over forty. He still "held" the East, the West and the North, but Mitterrand won more votes south of the Loire.

The effect produced on the head of State by this considerable turn-around was surprising, given that he was such an old hand. "De Gaulle will never be the same again," Viansson-Ponté observed. "He had to behave as a candidate, rejoin a world of parties. He has desacralized himself, brought himself back from the mystical plane to the political plane. He had wanted a plebiscite. At first he played the game as if it were a referendum. The second round was a blasphemy, a mere postponement."[23]

At a meeting of the Council of Ministers on 22 December 1966, the General, who seemed rested, calm and relaxed, declared: "The regime had to go through the trial by fire. It has emerged well tempered." But Georges Pompidou knew very well that, throughout those feverish days, the General had examined whether it would be opportune to replace a Prime Minister who had not been able to spare him the affront of 5 December, comparing the virtues and talents of possible successors, Maurice Couve de Murville,[24] Michel Debré, Jean-Marcel Jeanneney and Edgar Faure.[25]

And the threatened Prime Minister demanded, for his part, the head of Valéry Giscard d'Estaing. Pompidou could no longer bear[26] his Finance Minister dealing directly with the Elysée and systematically ignoring decisions coming from Matignon, thinking that by doing so he was pleasing the General – who, in fact, defended him and accepted the sacking (on 8 January 1966) of that young man, whose relaxed competence dazzled him, only with ill grace.

In his end-of-year speech de Gaulle claimed that "we have put an end to doubts, gropings, abandonments".[27] How he needed to believe that, as, at the age of seventy-five, he was approaching the last stage.

Was it to be another de Gaulle, for another seven-year term? Of course not. On that face of fissured granite, the wrinkles were certainly deeper; under the eyes, the bags were heavier, the lenses in his spectacles had been made even thicker and, during the interview of 13 December, he had had to "retake" part of it, because, as he was confronting the French people, his eyes in theirs, he had failed to see which was the right camera. His walk, too, was more hesitant and the effort required to get out of the DS 21 that brought him back from Colombey, on Mondays, cost him more with each month that passed. With each month that passed, there was a slight diminishing in his capacity for work. His working days no longer exceeded six hours, often less. He knew how "to save himself". He spent more and more time with his family, or in front of the television.

In any case, he tended to allow the Prime Minister's field of action to grow wider – in other words, he went back to how things were at the time of Michel Debré. From 1959 to 1962, as we have seen, apart from the three great affairs of Algeria, foreign policy and strategic redeployment, the head of State had left his Prime Minister's hands free: he was the master of the parliamentary game, the head of the administration, the man in control of the economy.

With Michel Debré's successor, the General had worked differently at first. Georges Pompidou had been his *directeur de cabinet* from June 1958 to January 1959. From April 1962, for three years, he had become so again – though he had risen in esteem, from April 1964, on account of the General's absence and his brilliant parliamentary performances, which were almost on a par with those of his predecessor.

In January 1966, although he had suffered from the electoral setbacks of December and felt that the risks of a disgrace comparable with that inflicted upon Michel Debré in 1962 were increasing, Georges Pompidou came back to the Hôtel Matignon stronger and bolder than ever. He knew that plans for changing the Prime Minister were still under consideration at the Elysée, where the Secretary-General, Etienne Burin de Roziers, was no friend of his. "It's bad enough that he regards me as too conservative, but he also regards me as the second figure in the State," Pompidou grumbled to his close colleagues. Never mind, he had rightly sensed that the General wanted to extricate himself from affairs a little more. And the space abandoned by the Elysée would now be occupied, since he had got rid of Valéry Giscard d'Estaing, by Pompidou.

Was this not to inflict a yet heavier cross on himself? It was he who had suggested to General de Gaulle that Giscard should be replaced by Debré. Did Pompidou want to put his predecessor in charge of Finance lest he take over the Hôtel Matignon? The fact is that, at his suggestion, because a job had to be found for him and the Quai d'Orsay could not be taken away from Couve, Michel Debré was given an enlarged Ministry of Finance and Economic Affairs, where his influence increased by virtue of the fact that de Gaulle had appointed, to Social Affairs, a man well-known to be his friend, Jean-Marcel Jeanneney.

Subtle psychologist though he was, and possessing no illusions about men, Pompidou had not gained from the exchange. And it is not out of the question that the General watched his embarrassment with some secret pleasure. In Giscard, the Prime Minister had got rid of an ambitious politician of a classical type. How, on the other hand, could one control that solid block of concentrated ardour, fierce determination, vehement conviction that was Michel Debré?

Contrary to appearances, the affair was not primarily about economics. Of course, it was not insignificant that Debré, like Colbert, believed that the State is "the best economist of France", whereas, for Pompidou, the virtues of the market and *laissez-faire* required only minor corrections. If de Gaulle had decided to risk his glory in the adventure of a second seven-year term, it was obviously not in order to act as referee at some Pompidou–Debré duel. Other issues required his attention, all of which tended to enhance France's influence in the world. And six weeks later, on 7 March, the President of the French Republic sent President Lyndon Johnson a message informing him that since France no longer belonged to the integrated structures of the Alliance, the presence of American troops and organizations in France was no longer required.

Had Charles de Gaulle got himself re-elected for any other purpose? Was not that a premeditated gesture? Indeed, everything seems to suggest that when Gaston Palewski had reminded him that he "still had things to do", both adviser and advised were thinking of the same thing. But the nuclear affair required no less attention. In 1960, the possession of nuclear weapons, which had been planned under the Fourth Republic, became a fact. De Gaulle did not want France to remain on the threshold of the atomic club. If the great powers possessed thermonuclear weaponry, then France could not be without it. From now on, then, did only the great affairs of State hold his attention? And future visits to the USSR, Vietnam, Israel, Quebec? Alas, no. The political landscape was too encumbered with lesser matters requiring his attention.

Three months after his kidnapping, Mehdi Ben Barka had still not been found. Nobody was now in any doubt that after being tortured* at Fontenay-le-Vicomte, he had been killed, either in the Paris region or in Morocco. The investigation, which the imperious terms of de Gaulle's letter to the mother of the disappeared man could not fail to have activated, led the police to the refuge of Georges Figon, regarded as the inventor of the trap into which the Moroccan leader had fallen. But just as they were about to seize him, the men of the Sûreté found only a corpse. Was it suicide? The investigation was to reveal that the bullet that had killed him had not been fired at point-blank range. How could the press not refer to the Stavisky affair,** in which the protagonist had ended in the same way?

The scandal returned with even greater violence three days later when a member of the police, Souchon, the tool of the kidnapping of Ben Barka, revealed that he had informed his superiors of his involuntary participation in the crime as early as 3 November. "Sanitary" measures were quickly implemented: the suspension of Marcel Le Roy, the departmental head at the SDECE, the secret service,

---

*General Oufkir was trying to find the number of a safe that Ben Barka had had in Switzerland, where, among other things, he kept important documents concerning revolutionary movements in the Third World.

**A crook whose activities, in early 1934, had compromised a number of politicians of the Third Republic.

followed by his arrest; replacement of General Jacquier, his superior, by General Guibaud; an international warrant for the arrest of General Oufkir and his assistant Colonel Dlimi;* and recall of the French Ambassador in Morocco, which led to a symmetrical gesture from Rabat.

The affair was a direct blow to the Gaullists. One day, it was Maurice Clavel, who, in a defence of Georges Figon, published an indignant article in *Combat*. The following day, several well-known Gaullist signatures were to be found at the bottom of an "appeal for the truth about the Ben Barka affair". François Mauriac wrote in his column in the *Figaro-littéraire*:

> I don't want anyone to have reason to believe that I agree with those Gaullists who, in order to fire on de Gaulle's ministers, waited for the ambush to take place. Yes, an ambush. Who can doubt it? Just before, or just after the murder of Ben Barka (I can't find the date of the visit), a Moroccan friend, who knows what is going on, told me about close links between General Oufkir and the American secret service. I have no idea whether this is true or not. The fact remains that for once those services carried off a magnificent double coup, against the "Third World", by getting rid of Ben Barka, and against de Gaulle. If the American secret service is innocent in this affair, then the devil must have been acting for them.[28]

This idea – which Washington immediately denied – was to crop up again and again. Indeed, it could hardly have reassured General de Gaulle, since it suggested that the French secret services had been infiltrated by those of the United States, with or without Moroccan intermediaries. In the gesture of withdrawing from NATO, which the French head of State was to carry out a few weeks later, there was also an element of the exasperation that he felt when discovering – or believing that he was discovering – this abusive form of the American "presence" in France.

Not all the Gaullists believed that those mainly responsible for the scandal were from the United States or Morocco. And the opposition was even less disposed to do so. Gaston Defferre published in *Le Provençal* the following attack:

> It is from the President of the Republic that all powers emanate. [...] The electoral campaign and the elections were an excellent opportunity to seize the sovereign judge. [...] That is what he would no doubt have done, if he had had nothing to fear, if he had had a clear conscience. [...] This in itself proves how much General de Gaulle feared that this file would be opened to the light of day. By acting in this way, he has accused himself.[29]

De Gaulle was less affected by these attacks from his opponents than by the criticisms from a friend such as Emmanuel d'Astier de la Vigerie, who commented thus on the affair: "For my part, I believe that if de Gaulle was taken in, if he made a mistake, he wants to, and he can, rectify it. De Gaulle is not a totalitarian leader who does not acknowledge his errors until he is overthrown".[30]

*Both of whom died tragically, the first killed after a failed *coup d'état* against the king, in 1972, the second in a mysterious road accident.

Whether or not he regarded this as an appeal, the General could not keep silent for much longer. Between 15 January and 15 February, revelation followed revelation. A long-anticipated press conference, on 21 February, gave him an opportunity at last to throw light on the affair. From the outset, he announced that he would speak about the Ben Barka affair. Very quickly he was asked a question, but in a polemical tone that he had not expected: "Why did you not think it right, when seeking people's votes, to inform the country?"

"It was the result of my inexperience!" The exposition that followed clearly defined the affair as Moroccan, as a result of the implication of Hassan II's Interior Minister, and Franco-Moroccan, since the kidnapping of Mehdi Ben Barka "took place on our territory" and was "perpetrated with the complicity of agents or members of the French secret service and the participation of criminals recruited here".

"On the French side"? According to the General, "what took place was a vulgar affair involving subordinates". Vulgar it may have been, but "subordinates"? Is that an accurate description of Le Roy-Finville, the SDECE's "Head of Research"? The General maintained that the only thing that he could be criticized for was "silence" concerning the activities of the informers that he employed.

In short, Charles de Gaulle recognized the "serious" deterioration in relations between France and Morocco, but not actions that were pretexts for "frenetic attacks on the public powers" organized particularly by those who had suffered from Gaullist networks "at the time of Vichy, then, again, at the time of the OAS".[31]

Of course, the affair had a most serious effect on relations between France and Morocco, as well as on those with America. Moreover, it added a touch of bitterness to the relations between de Gaulle and his Prime Minister. Addressed during a meeting of the Council of Ministers with a somewhat intemperate "You aren't keeping your services under control!",[32] Georges Pompidou was deprived of responsibility for the SDECE, which passed to the Ministry of the Armed Forces – a decision that could only appear as a punishment. Finally, it gave further material to an opposition that was to attempt to exploit those sorry "blunders" against the majority, during the electoral campaign of 1967.

Everything seems to suggest that the main purpose of the plot was, for General Oufkir, to prevent the return to Morocco of Mehdi Ben Barka (his worst enemy), whose entry into the government was being considered by certain royal advisers – though Ben Barka himself had thought fit to deny such suppositions. The second purpose of the plot was probably to deliver to the Americans information concerning the pro-Third World strategy inspired by the Moroccan leader, which was to be developed further a few weeks later in Cuba. By thus killing two birds with one stone, Oufkir thought that the support that he enjoyed in many French organizations (former residents in Morocco, services infiltrated by the Americans, the survivors of the OAS anxious to hit the Gaullist regime below the belt) would give him impunity and freedom of manoeuvre.

Whether the King in Rabat authorized the operation, having sent out signals to Ben Barka only to catch him, or whether – caring little if he came into conflict with France – he had been double-crossed by his Interior Minister, the fact is that the manoeuvre as a whole could only damage de Gaulle. At the time when he was carrying out an overall revision of his relations with Washington (France left NATO in March), de Gaulle could only wish for a parallel "correction" to be made in Morocco – where collusion between Oufkir and the CIA was an embarrassment to the development of his policy towards the Third World. Did Hassan II's minister want, by getting rid of a personal rival, to sabotage at the same time an inconvenient Gaullist diplomatic operation?

Did the "affair", which did not reach a judicial conclusion until June 1967, in the meantime so poison French public life as to allow the opposition to deliver decisive blows at the regime? I do not think so. From autumn 1966, the left had ceased to treat it as a warhorse. The extreme right, which loved this kind of situation, could not derive any benefit from it; the big loser of the presidential election of 1965 (with 4.5 per cent of the votes cast), Jean-Louis Tixier-Vignancourt, was also in court: his client, Antoine Lopez, got the maximum penalty, eight years. All in all, it would be tempting to draw from that sinister episode the same lessons as François Caviglioli in the conclusion to his brilliant reportage *Ben Barka chez les juges*:

> The State did not stifle the Ben Barka affair. On the contrary, it brought it before the public, animated, amplified by a clever play of mirrors. It turned it into an endless riddle. It involved the whole of French society in it. It added absurd, unreal elements to it. The public had got "wise" to it. The State had had the skill to flatter it, to give it the wink: you see, I'm not hiding anything from you. But what do you expect me to do? That's life. The State is a clever teacher.[33]

The General's second seven-year term was to be marked by more significant actions than this underworld festival. Take this diagnosis by one of the new organizers of what Giles Martinet has called *le Système Pompidou*:[34] "The economic and social policy of the regime had not ceased, since 1962, to be the soft underbelly of the Fifth Republic. But it was above all following the presidential campaign of 1965 that criticisms began to accumulate on every side." It appeared in effect that, whether as a result of the Prime Minister's attachment to the principles of *laissez-faire*, or as a result of conflicts between senior officials in the Finance Ministry and those responsible for the Plan, or tensions between Valéry Giscard d'Estaing and Georges Pompidou, "the best years of the Fifth Republic had been wasted".[35]

Taking in hand the French economy, would Michel Debré infuse it with the expected vigour and reanimate the sense of social justice that Charles de Gaulle regarded as one of the major themes of his historic message? One cannot reply in the negative without first trying to understand why a "party", that of the Gaullist left, which could claim the patronage of the head of State, the sympathy of the Secretary-General at the Elysée, an alliance with the Finance Minister, supported by his colleague at Social Affairs, was in under two years reduced to intentions possessing no future.

It would be too easy to incriminate the Prime Minister, as does Louis Vallon, who made this denunciation the theme of a pamphlet, *L'Anti de Gaulle*.[36] The Paris deputy wrote in the heat of action, defying an all-powerful man, powerful enough in any case to have him expelled from the UNR.

A more distanced analysis of the conflicts of that time confirms that although the Hôtel Matignon opposed several social reforms then being proposed, the reformists lost the battle because they did not operate on a united front. If, to cite one of Jean-Marcel Jeanneney's striking phrases, "de Gaulle could not do to Pompidou, in the social field, what he had done to Debré over Algeria", was it because he did not find, in this area, men like Joxe, Delouvrier, Crépin and Tricot?

However different or divergent they may have been by temperament and history, "Debréists" and "Left Gaullists" shared a common objective here that could hardly have failed to bring them together and then to get them to seek an alliance with such progressive technocrats as Edgard Pisani. But nothing of the kind occurred. Michel Debré seemed more concerned not to allow himself to be overwhelmed by his Minister of Social Affairs in the field of family legislation and to confine him to administration alone, than to wage this particular battle side by side with him. As for Jeanneney himself, who, as we have seen, was anxious not to "betray Pompidou", he expressed to de Gaulle reservations so serious about the projects of Louis Vallon and René Capitant that they were interpreted by the General as expressions of pusillanimity. When de Gaulle praised to him the plans for worker participation in the running of enterprises, Jeanneney merely raised objections dictated by prudence and reason.[37]

Everything suggests that General de Gaulle, who had long been searching for a solution, had studied Marcel Loichot's suggestions ("pancapitalism") and conceived of "participation" as a system challenging the power of the employers. What he had in mind, says M. Jeanneney, was the sort of spontaneous democracy in the enterprise that would have involved the workers not only in profits, but also in some decision-making.

The General's plans went further than most of those of his supposedly "leftish" advisers. But what was it that meant he could not bring himself to wage against Pompidou the kind of battle waged against Debré seven years before? He allowed the champions of social reform to use up their energies against the very reasonable politician operating at the Hôtel Matignon, considering that it was a crack-brained notion to challenge the power of the employers. "About ten times a year," Michel Jobert recounts, "the Prime Minister summed up, for the benefit of General de Gaulle, his attack on the projects that were being circulated by the 'Left Gaullists'. Each time it only took ten minutes to convince him of the stupidity of those ideas. But, each time, he had to begin all over again."[38]

However, on 12 July 1965, a law had been passed "defining the modalities by which the rights of wage-earners to a share in increases in the assets of enterprises as a result of self-financing" would be recognized. A few weeks later Marcel Loichot's *La Réforme de l'entreprise* appeared.[39] Louis Vallon summed it up to me by this quotation from Chesterton: "What I reproach capitalism for is not that there are capitalists, but that there are not enough of them."[40]

The Gaullists with a bias towards the left had launched their offensive. It was to end, on 17 August 1967, with no more than a modest "ordinance" concerning the interests of wage-earners written at the Hôtel Matignon by Edouard Balladur, of all Georges Pompidou's advisers the least favourable to this type of project. The Elysée had hardly lifted a finger to support the "left Gaullists". Was this because of the departure of Etienne Burin des Roziers for the French Embassy in Rome? The new Secretary-General, Bernard Tricot, considered quite simply that the State was very badly placed to intervene in the working of enterprises. So the great reform ended up as a discreet ordinance. And the General was content with this conclusion: "All those lawyers know is how to drown themselves in their own spit."[41]

Charles de Gaulle never accepted that his great social projects would forever be drowned in lawyers' "spit". He was to relaunch the battle in 1968, then again in 1969, on a different plane – and once again lose it before a single engagement. For it is the case that, in politics, actions are not to be measured by the intentions behind them, or by the powers at one's disposal, but by one's determination to carry them out. What career best demonstrates that than Charles de Gaulle's?

In fact, the real question is this: did the General really have, in the strict sense of the term, a "social policy"? Bernard Ducamin, who was at the Elysée from 1964 to 1969 as one of his advisers in this area, says that he did, declaring that he "placed social problems at the centre of his concerns".[42] Should one not speak rather of noble wishes, at least of "social intentions"? In order to explain the poor results, M. Ducamin blames the inadequacy of those in charge, though he does recognize the "worth" of Capitant, Vallon and Le Brun.* "Really," he adds, "what was lacking was a Malraux of enterprise reform."[43]

Gaullism had no sooner won the elections of 19 December 1965 than it was seized by a fear of what Jacques Fauvet called the "third round", that is to say, the legislative elections expected for March 1967. It was clear from the beginning that the General had delegated all responsibilities for the operation to his Prime Minister, firstly because it was a principle with him not to "get mixed up with electoral matters", and secondly, because Pompidou had shown, between the two rounds of the presidential elections, exceptional qualities as a political manager.

Before the party machinery could be put in place for the confrontation of March 1967, debate was concentrated on the question of relations between the executive and legislative powers, in the event of a reversal of the majority in the National Assembly. Hitherto the system, whether parliamentary in spirit as from 1959 to 1962 or presidentialist in tendency as from 1962 to 1966, had been marked by the fact of the majority: holding powers that he had defined as even more hegemonic on 31 January 1964, General de Gaulle had majorities in the Palais-Bourbon that he would have regarded as automatic if Debré's cabinet had not been burdened with acute crises and if Pompidou's first government had not been overthrown in 1962. But would the opposition become a majority in the Assembly? If François

*Pierre Le Brun, leader of the CGT, who supported, in this and a number of other areas, the General's "social ideas".

Mitterrand, a bigger figure since his campaign of August 1965, won a dominant position in the Assembly, he would, as everyone knew, make life extremely difficult for the General and his government.

One speech opened the debate. It was delivered by Alain Peyrefitte (who, having moved from the Information Ministry to that of Research, had the General's ear as much as ever). It suggested that in the event of a conflict between the President and a freshly elected Assembly, the fundamental legitimacy would remain, in de Gaulle's view, on his side.

A few months later, Peyrefitte, accompanying de Gaulle on the tour of the Pacific that was to enable him to view the French nuclear explosion, wanted to be quite clear on the matter, and, taking advantage of the long hours spent on board, questioned the President of the Republic on what he expected to do in 1967. "Why not dissolve the present Assembly? You would catch everybody on the wrong foot."

"I shan't do that. The present majority has allowed me to govern. I have no reason to penalize it by dissolving it. And, anyway, suppose these elections are not favourable to us. I couldn't dissolve it again within a year.* On the contrary, if this legislature serves out its term, I shall be able to dissolve the new Assembly when I like."

For Charles de Gaulle, there were two kinds of legislative elections. There were those that followed the normal constitutional timetable, in which he did not consider that he had any part to play. The separation of powers had erected a sort of screen between the hegemonic executive and the legislative, referred to as "487 local elections". He did not go so far as to claim that this type of election did not concern him, as we have seen, but it was a parallel procedure, which he simply hoped would give him a secure tactical flank. It was not "his" game. It was Pompidou's business. Elections called by him, as in 1962, after the referendum and dissolution, were a quite different matter. Then he was himself involved. It was his decision that the French were called upon to approve. Here, there was no longer a separation of responsibilities. Legislative elections of this type became a "super-referendum", a mode of appeal or confirmation of his legitimacy.

On the basis of the ten million electors who supported his name on 19 December 1965, and of the impetus thus given to his "federation", François Mitterrand had built up an electoral coalition that everyone regarded as capable of endangering the parliamentary majority. The aim of Pierre Mendès France's former Interior Minister was to make his Federation of the Democratic and Socialist Left (the FGDS) the necessary meeting-point of all the forces of the non-Communist Left, then the axis of an alliance that would bring in on its left the PCF and on its right those so-called "progressive" republicans, with a view to forming an "alternative majority".

On 21 December 1966, François Mitterrand, on behalf of the FGDS, and Waldeck Rochet,** on behalf of the PCF, signed an agreement that put an apparent end to the twenty-year divorce between the two great families of the

*Article 12, paragraph 4, of the Constitution.
**Who then tried to de-Stalinize his party on the lines of the Italian model, and to loosen the Soviet grip on it. His ensuing illness put an end to that attempt.

French left. They were joined by the small left-wing socialist party, the PSU (Parti socialiste unifié), formed by a merger of a few left-wing groups. This alliance, however loose or ephemeral, obviously changed the election prospects.

The election campaign opened on 13 February. It was only on the day before the campaign opened and again after it had closed, on 4 March, that de Gaulle deigned to speak to the electorate. The government's election campaign was run by an "Action Committee for the Fifth Republic", including Roger Frey, Olivier Guichard, Pierre Juillet, Jacques Foccart and Jacques Baumel. Pompidou worked hard, taking up challenges launched in his direction by François Mitterrand at Nevers and Pierre Mendès France at Grenoble, after opening the campaign with an impressive meeting on 31 January, in the Palais de Sports, where he was flanked, on the platform, by André Malraux and Jacques Chaban-Delmas.

On the eve of the vote, opinion polls gave 35 per cent to "Fifth Republic" candidates, 25 per cent to the FGDS and 15 per cent each to the centrists and the Communists. On the evening of 5 March, the government was in a position to claim victory: the Gaullist candidates had won 37.7 per cent of the votes (close on 8.5 million votes, 20 per cent more than in 1962). Clearly the UNR and its satellites were appearing more and more as the dominant force in French political life. This progress was won at the expense of Lecanuet's democratic centre – which the General savoured as a delicious revenge.

But the optimism of Matignon was tempered by the revival of the Communist Party, which, with over five million votes and 22.5 per cent of the electorate, was almost back at the level it had enjoyed before the Fifth Republic, while the FGDS, with 18.7 per cent, showed that the alliance with the Communists – the fruit of which could only be collected at the second round – had not made moderate voters desert it.

But with the second round Georges Pompidou could not conceal his disappointment: the defenders of the Fifth Republic certainly won 42.6 per cent of the votes cast, but the "Popular Front"-type coalition had proved so effective that it was claiming 46.4 per cent. And when the new Assembly met, it had to be admitted that, since the PCF had risen from 41 to 72 seats, and the Mitterrandist federation from 89 to 120, while the "Fifth Republic" had dropped from 276 to 232, the government had retained only a very slender majority: 245 seats (including 43 ambiguous Giscardians) against 242.

Alain Peyrefitte gives a good description of de Gaulle's reaction:

After the elections, when we had to wait until the early hours of the morning for the results from the Wallis and Futuna [Pacific] islands to know whether we had a majority of even *one* seat, the General said to me banteringly: "So *you* have won *your* elections! It's a pity! We would have seen how one can govern with the Constitution!" For the General, the presidential mandate conferred sufficient legitimacy to get through a bad patch, providing one avoided the reefs by resorting to the people's arbitration – by dissolution, referendum, or even resignation followed by his own candidature, that is to say, by having his legitimacy confirmed by the people.[44]

CHAPTER THIRTY-SEVEN

Under the Paving-Stones, the Abyss

During the storms that swept the history of France during the last quarter of a century, de Gaulle often seemed to be the man who brought, if not ordinary wisdom, at least lucidity of vision and firmness of purpose. But in the tempest that swept over France in May 1968, de Gaulle succeeded rather in adding to the confusion, increasing the illusions of some and the disarray of others. He was not the conqueror of the tempest, but was rather borne aloft by the storm, the weakness of his opponents, the general fear – and, in the end, his genius. A man usually so firm in extraordinary circumstances, so much at ease in danger, was seen to be confused, hesitant, passing from brutality to disarray, from the temptation to resign to a determination to stamp out chaos, risking too much, then dreaming of abandoning everything, evasive, constantly moving about rather than remaining in one place.

After ten years of exercising more or less undivided power which he had used with an inimitable mixture of sovereign haughtiness, *bonhomie*, crudity, boldness and skill, Charles de Gaulle had triumphed over all his opponents – politicians, colonels, terrorists and Eurocrats. The Gaullist success, in the legislative elections of March 1967, had been poor, but the General kept his majority. He was about to enter a grandiose twilight, to become the first French sovereign since Louis XVIII to complete his reign to the last breath. Then came May 1968.

On 28 April de Gaulle sighed to Captain Flohic: "It doesn't amuse me much any more; there's nothing left to do that is difficult or heroic."[1] In a similar spirit the editorial writer of *Le Monde*, Pierre Viansson-Ponté, wrote a still-famous article entitled, "France is bored".[2] The first crisis involved the State. It was the time when the sociologist Michel Crozier developed his theses on France as a "land of command" and a "blocked society". Hierarchies, bureaucracies, conformisms: the regime was ossifying into a huge, prosperous enterprise, in which the bosses by divine right assumed the double face of an old soldier of genius and an intelligent managing director more skilled in management than keen to renovate.

During the first meeting of the Council of Ministers that year, on 11 January 1968, Jean-Marcel Jeanneney crudely put his finger on the wound: the "tentacular bureaucracy" and its most fearsome agent, the Finance Ministry, "omnipresent, omnipotent". The accusation was so strong that it aroused, in that very conformist circle, profound embarrassment and an irritated reaction from the minister most directly in view, Michel Debré – a personal friend of Jeanneney. When received a few days later at the Elysée, Jeanneney asked General de Gaulle to forgive his "outburst". "Not at all," said de Gaulle. "You're perfectly right. That's where the evil lies. It had to be said." And when Jeanneney remarked that compared with the feverish situation in the United States, France was calm, the General cut him short: "It won't last!"[3]

The second crisis was economic and social. Not that French production had suddenly lost its efficiency. Growth, which had been held back by the stabilization plan between 1963 and 1965, had resumed and was close on 5 per cent (as was inflation), the standard of living was rising overall, the franc was recognized as a stable currency. But in 1967 France suffered the effects of the German crisis, which itself owed a great deal to the French plan of 1963. In January 1968, growth was beginning to fall off. Unemployment had risen to 226 000, which seemed considerable at the time. Brittany had been shaken by violent peasant demonstrations. And, as Michel Jobert reminds us, there were in 1967 "four million working days lost as a result of strikes, an absolute record".

But the measures to stimulate the economy then taken by Michel Debré proved to be effective. In April, the indices were again favourable: but the muted crisis of 1967 had affected confidence and exposed the fragile condition of the economy. That fragility had an effect on an industrial workforce that was in the midst of transformation and which, given the requirements of growth, had swept up *en masse* young people, farm workers and immigrants. Indeed the demographic data were an essential element in the situation. In *La France déchirée*, Jacques Fauvet notes that from 1965 the post-war generations were beginning to exert strong demographic pressure capable of upsetting the present balance. Combined with serious international crises such as the Vietnam war and with a vast world-wide youth movement deeply shocked in April 1968 by the attempted murder of the young German revolutionary, Rudi Dutschke, and various other factors, the feverish state of the student world had first appeared, in 1965, in the Paris suburbs at Antony, where young people had resorted to violence when the free movement between male and female accommodation that they demanded had been denied.

The following year, at Strasbourg, the "Situationist" group took over the student organization and published a pamphlet denouncing "poverty in the student world", demanding "revolution in everyday life". In 1967, the epicentre of the earthquake returned to the Paris suburbs, this time at Nanterre, where a new arts faculty had been built, the embryo of a "model university" that had sprung up in what looked like a vast building site.

In the constant disputes, reported by the university authorities to the Education Minister, Christian Fouchet, then, from April 1967, Alain Peyrefitte, there soon intervened another member of the government, François Missoffe, Minister of Youth and Sport, who, a few months earlier, had published a report on "youth today" revealing a naivety bordering on caricature: the report presents young French people between fifteen and twenty-five as dreaming only of economic promotion, social integration and bourgeois virtues. Hence the astonishment of the minister when questioned by a red-headed student – it was understandable that he should not yet know his name, Daniel Cohn-Bendit – who criticized him for ignoring students' sexual problems. Missoffe thought that he had made a clever move when he invited his interrupter to cool off by plunging into the swimming pool.

A month later, a "sexual riot" broke out when a crowd of male Nanterre students marched to the girls' halls of residence. In late March, after anti-American demonstrations during which the American flag was burnt, several students were arrested: Daniel Cohn-Bendit and several dozen of his comrades then seized lecture halls and declared the birth of a new movement, to be known as the "movement of 22 March", which was to be the kernel of the great upheaval of May.

The crisis deepened on 3 April, after a meeting of the Council of Ministers at which university reform involving entry by selection was decided on: the word "selection" held threats of exclusion, which was taken by the student movement as a kind of challenge.

The temperature continued to rise at Nanterre, where the crisis found both its pretext, selection, and its framework, the "movement of 22 March". On 2 May, finding that he could not control the situation, Dean Grappin decided to close the university. He was encouraged to do so by Christian Fouchet, who, the day before, at the Elysée, had heard General de Gaulle say: "Fouchet, we must put an end to those incidents at Nanterre!"

But the closing of the campus had the result of immediately transferring the "angry young men" from Nanterre to the Sorbonne, where they set up on the morning of 3 May. Taking as a pretext threats from those they call *fafs* or *fachos* (i.e. fascists) of the extreme right-wing group "Occident", they tore up the paving stones of the university courtyard in order to erect barricades. The student revolt had entered Paris.

In the afternoon, Alain Peyrefitte summoned Christian Fouchet: "The university rector Roche has asked me to use police to evacuate the Sorbonne." Both ministers, and the prefect of police, Maurice Tricot, with whom they were conferring, were aware of the gravity of such a step. But Peyrefitte pointed out that "the rector had already signed a written requisition order". Furthermore, both men were aware that they would be acting in accordance with the views of de Gaulle. As for Pompidou, he had just left, on 2 April, for Iran, despite several warnings sent to him by Fouchet.

The evacuation of the Sorbonne by the police transformed student unrest into a popular uprising. What had been started by the "22 March" Nanterre students was to explode in the government's face. May 1968 had begun. And it began badly for the Fifth Republic: the Sorbonne was occupied, hundreds of students had been stopped and questioned by police, thirty were being held in custody, ten had been given suspended sentences, twenty had been wounded, four imprisoned.

De Gaulle was not entirely taken by surprise by the "student revolt" of May 1968. Alerted by his adviser for educational affairs, Jacques Narbonne, he was anxious about the over-population of the universities and believed selective admissions to be necessary. But Pompidou, a former teacher, shrugged his shoulders, saying, in late 1967, that "the greatest success of the five years of the regime has been education". The General, who had been entirely won over by the ideas of his adviser, had respect for ministerial functions and responsibilities: furthermore, it was Fouchet, an old companion from London days, who was in charge.

Narbonne, who had discovered that most of the resistance to his suggestions was to be found in Matignon, tried to influence Pompidou: without more strict control, there would be a catastrophe. The Prime Minister listened to him politely, but replied: "I'm not the man to put French youth into barracks."[4] As a consequence, during innumerable inter-ministerial meetings, de Gaulle and Pompidou were to witness, in silence, several exchanges between their respective champions: on the one side, Narbonne and on the other, a minister manipulated by the teachers' organizations and anxious above all not to attract the students' condemnation.

In April 1967, de Gaulle said to Peyrefitte: "You'll be there for five years. Or at least work as if that were the case." Later, he added: "Specialization and selection must be pushed through." The more Peyrefitte studied the files, the more convinced he became of this. In November 1967, at Besançon, he declared: "It is as if the University were organizing a shipwreck, to pick up the swimmers who have escaped drowning."[5] But what direction should he take himself, between the reformers of the Elysée and the laissez-faire attitude at Matignon?

Charles de Gaulle did have a university policy. But he had no sense of the complexity of the student affair, seeing it, at first, as no more than unruly behaviour by anxious young men on the eve of their examinations. "Childishness" was the word he used. The problem was in the hands of three men: the acting Prime Minister, Louis Joxe, the Garde des Sceaux, Christian Fouchet, and Alain Peyrefitte. To this trio, haunted by the fear that the regime might be stained with blood, was added a prefect of police, Maurice Grimaud, a lover of literature and modern painting, who was all smiles and good will. If the "angry young men" had chosen provocation in order to arouse repression, they would have been hard put to it to gain their ends with those men.

But the evacuation of the Sorbonne, on 3 May, was carried out with a heavy hand. The memory of the brutal acts committed on that occasion was to be a permanent source of anger as was the imprisonment of four students, arrested and tried the following Sunday. No theme is better suited to a demonstration than "Free our comrades!" So on 6 May, the slogan rose up, spread and filled the Latin Quarter. The "comrades" were not liberated, but sentenced to two months in prison: a few barricades were erected, a mere hint of what was to come; teargas transformed the Boulevard Saint-Germain into a vale of tears. By the middle of the night, four hundred wounded had been counted among the demonstrators, two hundred among the police.

"No May Day was to be as brutal," Christian Fouchet wrote.[6] But "there is no question of giving in," the General had said to his Interior Minister the evening before. On the Thursday, the General put an end to his Education Minister's wish to negotiate by placing a personal, explicit veto on it, even going so far as to telephone Fouchet directly, forbidding any such action. His orders were the same as those at the time of the Algiers barricades: "Power does not retreat!" But the two affairs were not of the same kind. By rising to his full height, de Gaulle did not help to stop the revolutionary riot.

On 9 May, UNEF* called not only on the students, but also on workers to attend a great demonstration on the Place Denfert-Rochereau, against the imprisonment of the three students. And what about the workers? The PCF and the CGT, the Communist-dominated union confederation, forbade their members to respond to this invitation: after all, had not Georges Marchais denounced "the German anarchist Cohn-Bendit" in the columns of *L'Humanité*? He did not actually write "German Jew", but that is what the readers read between the lines. It led to what was to become one of the most popular slogans in May: "We're all German Jews!" And on 13 May, during a public meeting, Cohn-Bendit was to denounce "the Stalinist scum". From the earliest stages of the movement, then, Communists and *gauchistes* (Leftists) confronted one another without mercy.

The night of 10 May 1968 will remain, for history, the night of the barricades. Fouchet, convinced that he was acting in accordance with de Gaulle's wishes, had first thought of forbidding the UNEF demonstration. Grimaud persuaded him to allow it to take place, while opening up negotiations. The government might consider freeing the condemned students, amnesty them and reopen the Sorbonne if all demonstrations ceased.

An incident that was very typical of those times was to put an end to the talks. About 11 p.m., a radio station announced that the rector, Roche, was negotiating with Cohn-Bendit in his office at the Sorbonne, which students had been prevented from entering. An astonished Peyrefitte and Fouchet telephoned Roche. "Why are you talking to Cohn-Bendit?" "What?" "Have you got a fat little redhead with blue eyes with you?" "Yes." "Well, that's him! Throw him out!" The time for accommodation was passed.

Between midnight and 5 a.m., barricades were put up from the Place Edmond-Rostand to the Val-de-Grâce, from the Place Monge to the Boulevard Saint-Michel and from the Place Maubert to the Rue Mouffetard. Confrontations soon took on the appearance of a veritable street battle. Between the Luxembourg and the Sorbonne there was a constant drama of Molotov cocktails, teargas, marches and counter-marches of men in blue helmets and shouting youths, their faces covered with scarves, their hands loaded with missiles. Cars were on fire, girls were singing, the wounded were leaning against the barricades.

De Gaulle, whose reactions on hearing the reports can be imagined, nevertheless went to bed before 11 p.m., informed that negotiations, which he did not really approve of, were under way with the "troublemakers". It was thought that he approved of them in principle, provided they brought a return to calm. Throughout that terrible night, nobody dared to wake him up – not before 5.30 a.m. in any case and the seizure of the last barricades.

The fact is that at 2 a.m., while two *arrondissements*, the 5th and the 6th, had been turned into a battlefield, when anguished appeals were sent to the government by leading university teachers – François Jacob, Jacques Monod, Alain Touraine – appalled at the carnage that they saw, when the Prime Minister was in Afghanistan and the General asleep, Louis Joxe, the man of peace in Algeria, the

---

*The Union Nationale des Etudiants de France, inspired by the PSU, and infiltrated by Trotskyites and a few anarchist groups.

man of peace everywhere, was faced by a terrible decision: to order five hundred riot police to charge through streets that were remembered only for books and laughter – to march on youths, political rebels perhaps, but so young in their angry night.

At 2.10 a.m., on 11 May, he gave the order: the charge began and the barricades fell, one by one, to accompanying shouts of "CRS – SS", with little regard for history. But, on that night, who showed regard for anything? Certainly not the "forces of order": exasperated, they struck out in all directions, sometimes savagely, especially towards the end of the night. At 5.30 a.m., when the last barricade fell, Cohn-Bendit gave the order, by radio, to disperse.

At last Joxe dared to wake de Gaulle. When, flanked by Fouchet and Messmer, he entered the General's office, in the Elysée, around 6 a.m., he was able to announce that order had been restored in Paris. The story of the night made gloomy reading: 376 wounded, a third of whom were members of the "forces of order", close on 500 individuals arrested, more than a hundred cars burnt out. And furious excesses on the part of the police that, blown up by the press, could not but reflect badly on the regime. Nevertheless, the fact that, throughout May, there was not a single life lost must clearly be credited to those same "forces of order".

The General "made no comment on the way things had turned out", writes Fouchet. However, his whole attitude during the following day suggests that he acknowledged that Joxe, Fouchet and Messmer deserved credit for the restoration of order – by whatever means. He does not even seem to have held it against them that they did not dare to confront the head of State with his supreme responsibilities at a time when the regime itself was in question. But it was a close thing: one has only to imagine what the reaction throughout the country would have been if there had been a single young death that night!

In the stunned Paris of the day after the riots, the atmosphere was almost everywhere more relaxed. Had we gone completely mad? Here and there talks were begun. Louis Joxe, still in a state of shock, went to see the General and tried to urge a more gentle approach. That day, he had four talks with him: one on the telephone, three at the Elysée. The minister had a peace plan. He proposed reopening, from the following Monday, the faculty at Nanterre and suggested that, in accordance with legal rules, the gaoled students should be released. "We cannot treat those youths as rebels," he said.[7]

As the hours passed, the General reflected on these arguments. When Alain Peyrefitte in turn came to plead for a compromise at about 6 p.m., he got a better reception. During that afternoon of Saturday 11 May, as Pompidou's return to Paris was expected hourly, de Gaulle was working out a policy consisting of tactical withdrawal and strategic threats.

Pompidou landed at Orly at 7 p.m. The ministers who had gone to meet him, he was later to observe, looked "pale and scared", with "catastrophe written all over their faces".[8] He hinted that he had "his own ideas", but refused to confide them to journalists before he had seen de Gaulle. Anxious to show that power had returned with him, he did so fully and with impressive promptness. The speech that he had written in the plane and delivered that very evening on television was a stinging rejection of what had been done over the past week. The Pompidou plan was a joyful capitulation. When he informed three of his ministers – Joxe, Fouchet and Peyrefitte – of what he intended to say, he was told, especially by the first, that de Gaulle would disapprove of his plan. Nevertheless, he did win the old gentleman round. "Our conversation was short. I immediately obtained the agreement of the President of the Republic to my proposals."[9] One would like to know what magic words he used. Later, de Gaulle was often to criticize his acceptance of that "capitulation". Fouchet comments that it was on 11 May that the regime committed suicide.[10] In fact, de Gaulle seems to have been less convinced by arguments than carried away by the dynamism, the decisiveness, the vigour of a man whose freshness contrasted with the exhaustion and gloom of the men whom he had been seeing all day.

Pompidou went on television and delivered the speech that he had written – apart from a few changes – between Kabul and Paris: "I have decided that the Sorbonne should be freely reopened as from Monday, lectures resuming at the request of the rector and deans. Also from Monday the court of appeal will, in accordance with the law, consider requests for the freeing of the imprisoned students. Those decisions are inspired by profound sympathy for the students."[11] Pompidou expressed no "sympathy" for the State employees and police who, during the night of 10 May, had done the "dirty work", and whose actions the head of State had approved. The speech and the decisions that it announced were to be greeted ten years later by Jacques Chirac* as those "of a statesman who dared to expose himself" and who "faced up to everything".[12]

From that evening of 11 May, Pompidou was no longer the Prime Minister: he was now the only minister. All the others were to fall into the trap as a result both of their exhaustion and of the Prime Minister's compulsive need to devour potential rivals. Suddenly, from being practically deserted between 2 and 11 May, Matignon absorbed the entire State. So much so that Fouchet could write of Pompidou's return: "This brings to an end, as far as I am concerned, the story of May 1968."[13]

The only men who drew the correct conclusion from the situation were first Peyrefitte, who, on 13 May, brought a resignation letter to Matignon (which Pompidou handed back to him, saying, "Stay in *my* team!", with the result that this resignation was not made known until 28 May) and Michel Debré, who did likewise on 25 May: but things had come to such a pass that the resignation of the Finance Minister was hardly noticed!

Meanwhile, the man of Matignon took a grip on everything. He was the real Interior Minister – and even the prefect of police lost many of his powers of decision to Pierre Somveille, a very capable policeman and a trusted colleague of Pompidou's, who directed operations from a radio-van installed in the Matignon courtyard.

At once Justice, Finance, Information and Education Minister, Pompidou did not govern, he did not reign, he monopolized power as nobody had done since the Napoleon of the Hundred Days – tirelessly, joyfully, taking responsibilities, decisions and risks in every field, surrounded by an iron guard, consisting of Jobert,

*Then Under-Secretary of State assigned to the Prime Minister, and a close colleague.

Balladur, Chirac and Juillet, around whom what was left of the State apparatus gathered and returned to life. It was a total recovery, an unlimited acceptance of responsibility: it is to that team, and to no other, that the credit or blame for what happened from 11 to 29 May must be attributed.

The Pompidou peace, declared at 11 p.m. on Saturday 11 May, lasted only for another day. On 13 May, as the students were flooding into the Sorbonne, the twenty-four-hour strike called by the CGT, the Confédération française démocratique du travail and the teachers' unions paralysed public services – the private sector to a lesser degree. At about 1 p.m., around the Gare de l'Est, there gathered the first elements of an enormous cortège that, from 3 to 6 p.m., was to reach Denfert-Rochereau, from the north to the south of Paris, a flood of 300 000 demonstrators, in which the rebel student leaders – Cohn-Bendit, Sauvageot, Geismer – eclipsed the union leaders Descamp and Séguy, who themselves were more prominent than the political leaders, Mendès France, Mitterrand, Daniel Mayer and Waldeck Rochet.

It was a relatively calm demonstration, rather more amused than indignant, punctuated by shouts of "58–68, ten years, it's enough!", "Au revoir mon Général!", "Charlot, des sous!" – hardly the cries of an insurrection. Though still stars of the street, would the erecters of barricades now be organized, hemmed in, before being eliminated? This is what Pompidou thought; one of his justifications after the event for the decision to reopen the Sorbonne was the behaviour of that crowd. If the university had remained closed, it was obvious, in his view, that that enormous mass would have launched an attack. "I preferred," he wrote, "to give the Sorbonne to the students than to see them conquer it by noble struggle."[14]

A few thousand students, refusing to disperse at the Place Denfert-Rochereau, turned off towards the Champ-de-Mars and seemed to have made up their minds to cross the Seine (towards the Elysée?), over the Pont Alexandre III, which was guarded by only a few dozen police. At that point, writes Michel Jobert, "I thought anything could happen. If the crowd had pushed on that pitiful barrier, no one, at that time, would have given the order to fire. It could have got through and in its wake history would suddenly have speeded up."[15] Informed of this crowd movement by an anxious colleague, de Gaulle muttered: "Don't worry, Flohic, the Communists will keep them in order."[16]

Well, the worst was avoided. But, all the same, 300 000 people in the street might be enough to put off the five-day trip to Romania, where the General was expected next day. Should he leave? Pompidou's escapade in the East had had nothing but beneficent effects. De Gaulle summoned Fouchet in the early evening of 13 May. "Stay, mon Général," begged the Minister of the Interior. "The affair is still too hot." The General was shaken. How could he inflict such a disappointment on the Romanians, who, beyond the Iron Curtain, confronting Moscow, had done so much to echo his challenge to hegemonies and "blocs"?

Around midnight, Pompidou and Couve de Murville arrived. They agreed with each other: there was no question of cancelling, or even of postponing so important a diplomatic visit. De Gaulle's mind was made up: the trip and the timetable would stay as they were. Bucharest was less than four hours away from Paris by plane. Bernard Tricot would keep him informed of the situation in France, hour by hour. And the Prime Minister would be given a delegation of powers that would strengthen his authority still more.

On Tuesday 14 May, at 7.35 a.m., the General left for Bucharest, announcing through the Minister of Information, Georges Gorse, that he would address the country on 24 May. Two hours later, the workers at the nationalized Sud-Aviation factory at Nantes seized their boss and began a wild-cat strike that was to serve as a model for many others. The student rising suddenly took on a social dimension.

From Romania, where, four times a day, he received calls from Jacques Foccart, Bernard Tricot or Xavier de La Chevalerie, his *directeur de cabinet*, de Gaulle anxiously followed developments. When, on the morning of 17 May, he learnt that the Odéon had been occupied, the General lost patience. What were "they" doing in Paris? He would have to cut short his visit. When consulted, Pompidou tried to dissuade him: the situation was a very shifting one, the strikes movement was not "mature". So he should continue with his programme.

On the morning of 18 May, General de Gaulle could no longer contain himself: he decided to leave that very day, in the afternoon. His Bucharest hosts made it clear that they understood his reasons perfectly well. Those ministers who were there to receive him could hardly forget the General's reappearance in the Orly night. He was furious and let everyone know it. "De Gaulle has only to turn his back," he roared, "and everything collapses!" Each of them, according to rank, was on the receiving end: Peyrefitte with that "student bedwetting", Fouchet with "mess everywhere!",[17] Gorse with his information that "falls apart the moment you touch it". It was, in Philippe Alexandre's words, "a long hour of anger, in military language". The General concluded with this more civilian declaration: "Play time is over!"

He took Pompidou to the Elysée and with him launched into a rough explanation that was to continue until midnight. Because the General blamed him for letting things become so bad, the Prime Minister offered his resignation, this time in unambiguous terms. The General rejected it out of hand: "One does not abandon one's post in the middle of a battle. First the war has to be won. Then we'll see."[18]

Next day, the General summoned to the Elysée those ministers "responsible for order": Pompidou, Fouchet, Messmer, Gorse and Grimaud. Previously warned by Pompidou, the other four visitors expected a rough session. They had to endure all the anger of the previous night, but expressed more coldly, more fiercely, in more reasoned fashion. With implacable bad faith, isolating those five days of absence as if they had not been preceded by a week in which he himself had let things slide, he roared: "In five days, ten years of struggle against rottenness in the State have been lost. In five days, we have come back to the worst days of political manoeuvring! It is true that for the past six years* we have done nothing, foreseen nothing, been content to live from week to week. Ah! What a fine state you'll all be in when I'm no longer here!"[19]

Pompidou took the storm of abuse without flinching. The others' turn would come. They were informed – in the terms of a note dated 19 May at 1 p.m., of

*That is to say, since Pompidou had been Prime Minister.

which Georges Pompidou was to publish a facsimile[20] – that "the Odéon must be evacuated within twenty hours", that henceforth the ORTF (French Radio and Television) must "use as news only information that has been properly confirmed" and that if the police force is "traumatized", as Fouchet assured him it was, "then the only thing to do was to give it a shot of brandy!"

The Minister of the Interior had the genuine courage and sense to object that the enforced evacuation of the Odéon would not take place, in so short a time, without casualties, that the police would have to consider shooting, that if any of the students were killed the situation would surely get worse and that it would therefore be better to temporize. To which the head of State replied sharply that a minister of the interior cannot do his job properly if he excludes the idea of shooting at people. However, having had his say, the General agreed to postpone the operation for a few days.

Having thundered at his subordinates, de Gaulle now shut himself up in the Elysée to write the speech of 24 May, on which he now placed all his hopes.

Like everyone else, but with more concern and more anger than anyone else, de Gaulle confronted two major phenomena: the authority of the State that seemed to be on the point of collapse and the national economy that had entered a coma. It was a great body that had lost its nervous system and whose circulation had seized up. The France that he had picked up, ten years before, lying by the wayside, half-dead, was now falling to pieces in his hands. A third phenomenon was emerging that de Gaulle, protected as he was by his colleagues, could hardly perceive, but which his supporters could not fail to acknowledge: there was disaffection, detachment on the part of a growing number of "Gaullists". Jacques Vendroux, the General's brother-in-law, noted on 21 May that during a meeting of the parliamentary "Gaullist" group he had heard "odious remarks". Vendroux's depression deepened when Waldeck Rochet, the Secretary-General of the PCF, informed him, loudly enough for everyone to hear: "Above all, insist that he doesn't give in. He mustn't go!" To be rejected by UDR deputies and supported by those of the PCF!

One body that was still functioning, in spite of everything, was the Council of Ministers. It met again, under the General's eyes, at 10 a.m. on 23 May. With serious, depressed or worried faces, they examined the old face of their leader, looking for signs of the great internal collapse. That Thursday, they did not find any. Not at all.

De Gaulle spoke: it was a vigorous, straightforward statement that concealed nothing.*

> I am going to tell you what I think of the situation. The country is in the midst of a transformation. There is fear neither of war nor of misery. When the French are no longer afraid, they challenge the authority of the State. The country is caught up in a movement that it cannot understand, that of mechanical, technological civilization. If it is young people who are express-

*I have used here – together with interviews with Georges Gorse and Olivier Guichard – several passages from the account of that meeting published in *Le Mois de mai du général*, pp. 118–37.

ing their disturbed reactions first, it is because the University is no longer adapted to its purpose. But, as always, we shall show the way. As always, France is exemplary. We could have done a lot of things in the educational field and in that of public order. There is no point in going over that again. In any case, this situation cannot go on any longer, unless we allow the State to be swept away. We must both re-establish public order and negotiate without compromising the most important thing, the security of the nation.

De Gaulle then presented his plan for a referendum: "The country must tell us: we trust you to reform the University and to amend the economy in favour of the less fortunate – by ensuring the participation of employees in the running of enterprises. If the answer is in the negative, the President of the Republic would consider that his task was over."

There were a few last-minute crossings out and a final reading over, then, on 24 May, at noon, the television crew arrived at the Elysée. He read his address: seven minutes. The tone of his voice seemed calm. But, when the film was played back on the monitor, everyone looked disappointed. Everyone turned to him: he seemed to have understood. But he didn't ask to record it again. No one dared to suggest that he should. He shook hands with them all, thanked them briefly and left. Did he already know that it was a "flop"? Yet the text is not unworthy of him – it is simple, lucid, forward-looking.

Everyone understands, of course, what the implications of the present events, in the educational and social fields, amount to. They are so many indications of the need for a transformation in our society and it seems clear that such a transformation must involve a more extensive participation by everybody in the running and the results of whatever activity directly concerns him.

Of course, in the upheaval that we have today, the first duty of the State is to ensure, in spite of everything, the elementary existence of the country and of public order. It has done so. It is to assist in the resumption of activity, especially by making whatever contacts might facilitate it, and it is ready to do so. But, without any doubt, there is also a need to alter structures. Many obstacles, at home and abroad, have already been overcome, others are still blocking the way of progress. Hence the profound disturbances, especially among the young. A tide of disorder or abandonment. Our country is on the verge of paralysis. In view of the quite exceptional situation in which we find ourselves, I have decided to submit for the approval of the Nation a plan giving the State and, in the first instance, its head, a mandate for renewal.

The University must be reconstructed in terms of the real needs of the country's development and of the actual working possibilities of young people. Our economy must be adapted, by improving the living and working conditions of employees, by organizing their participation in the running of affairs. This is the aim that the Nation as a whole must lay down for itself.[21]

And the head of State concluded by reminding the nation that if he was not given a majority in the consultation organized on this theme for June, he would resign.

One has to have heard those wise words, standing in the middle of the militant, sarcastic, long-haired crowd, assembling near the Gare de Lyon, to appreciate the extent of the Great Wizard's failure that evening. His words fell flat. To an audience that for three weeks had lived in a whirlwind of lyrical, sexual, ideological challenges, in which Bakunin, Che Guevara and the Red Guards of Peking mingled with Rimbaud, Antonin Artaud and Jean Genet, to that militant crowd that had become enraged once more, de Gaulle's speech sounded like a piece of eighteenth-century prose in a surrealist meeting.

The failure was all the more serious in that the address, specifically intended to turn the nascent revolution into reform, triggered off a further spate of violence. That night of 24 May was to be the most terrible in the month because it marked the outbreak of the new Commune: until then confined to the Left Bank, it now swelled, crossed the Seine, reached the *beaux quartiers* and the Bourse. That night was not only to make the General doubt his own ability to control any situation, it also convinced large sections of the bourgeoisie that "the old man" was no longer a safe bastion.

The next four days, from 25 to 28 May, were to be for the General a sort of descent into the underworld. The night of 24 May had already been a night of agony. "I'm the problem now. What they want is my departure." For the first time, de Gaulle refused to go to bed and chose to stay up until dawn. The radio crackled with worrying news: the Bourse was on fire, paving stones were being removed from the streets again, Paris was terrified – so much so that the General's advisers came to an agreement, by telephone, to advise the General to send in the troops. But de Gaulle rejected these suggestions.

On 25 May, at 11 a.m., de Gaulle received the credentials of the new United States Ambassador, Sargent Shriver, the husband of Eunice Kennedy, one of the assassinated President's sisters. The situation must have seemed gloomy indeed for the General, when confronted by that splendid American, to come out with little more than a few doom-laden words: "The future, *Monsieur l'ambassadeur*, does not depend upon us. It depends on God, on God alone. Everything seems to suggest that it will be troubled. Perhaps dramatic."

Immediately after the United States Ambassador, the Minister for Youth and Sports, François Missoffe, arrived. He found the General unrecognizable, declaring that "It's all over." The stunned visitor tried to plead for firmness. But de Gaulle interrupted him, referring to "threats of totalitarian communism", of the failure of the French people to react. The Minister for Youth left the Elysée deeply shocked and immediately rang Pierre Messmer: "I've just left the Elysée. It's catastrophic. You must see the General." Messmer went to the Elysée in the early afternoon: "I found myself," he says, "in front of a man with no 'sense' of the future. But he was less depressed than he had been that morning, with Missoffe."[22]

On the evening of Sunday 26 May, the General had a talk with his son, Philippe, who had recently been transferred from Brest to Paris, to study at the Institut des Hautes Etudes Militaires. As a fellow sailor, Captain Flohic asked his old friend how he had found his father. "Obviously, my father is tired," Philippe de Gaulle replied. "He's old and he isn't sleeping, or very little. But he assured me that he would not give up."[23] But he must have felt confused, to say the least, to allow Pompidou to take charge, as he did, of the negotiations that were about to open and which "serious people" expected would bring the crisis back at once into an area of reasonable debate. In his speech that Friday evening, de Gaulle announced that "contacts" with a view to a resumption of economic activity had been made. The contacts that had been made for several days with the CGT by the Secretary of State, Jacques Chirac, were thought to be promising.

What is surprising here and reveals the extent to which the balance of forces had shifted between the Elysée and Matignon was that Pompidou had declared to the General: "I'll take over all responsibility for the affair, on condition that I'm spared Debré." It was not only the Finance Minister who was thus being removed from negotiations on which the balance of French production and currency depended, but the most faithful of all the General's colleagues. Michel Debré stormed, resigned, warned the General that ten years of Gaullist financial policy was about to go up in smoke, but to no avail: de Gaulle submitted to the *diktat* of his Prime Minister.

In two days of almost incessant negotiations, Pompidou, who had announced, from the outset, that the aim was to "get France back to work", showed, together with his talents as a negotiator, "incredible endurance and competence".[24] The General had given him *carte blanche*: he made full use of it, accepting from the outset a 35 per cent increase in the guaranteed minimum wage, which the employers' representatives seemed to accept without flinching, together with an immediate wage rise of 7 per cent (plus 3 per cent in October), a reduction in working hours (to be negotiated), and the "revolution" that would come about by a revision in the relations between employers and employees. In 1936, the Popular Front government did not implement many more reforms in so short a time.

After this, Pompidou went off, on the morning of Monday 27 May, about 7 a.m., to get a bit of rest. Before he left, the union leader Georges Séguy remarked: "It's a fruitful agreement." In two days, they both thought, the country would be back at work.[25]

What must de Gaulle have thought of those negotiations? What few clues there are seem to suggest that he regarded the talks as inevitable, and that if one had to soil one's hands with such matters, it would be better to leave the job to Pompidou: the General clearly believed that it would be one of the last jobs done by that particular Prime Minister. In any case, he had told him: "Settle at whatever price."[26]

Having signed the draft agreement, Georges Séguy and Benoît Frachon, the two CGT representatives, headed for Billancourt, where over 12 000 workers were gathered in the central yard of the Renault factory. They knew that they would have a tough job to persuade their listeners that these agreements fulfilled the aspirations of a proletariat which had seen, like everybody else, that over the last ten days a shift had occurred in the balance of forces. Were the agreements "fruitful"? Yes, in normal times, Georges Séguy's listeners thought. But in a situation in which the authority of the State and employers had collapsed, why be content with so reasonable a booty? Séguy and Frachon, the old revolutionary, were certainly given a hard time by the militants. There would be no return to work at that price.

A few months later, Georges Pompidou was to comment severely, during an evening at Claude Mauriac's, on the behaviour of his partners: "Once again, those Communist idiots let themselves be had."

Pompidou was warned, at 11 a.m. on 27 May, that work would not resume in the Renault factories. Once again the Prime Minister saw that his strategy of compromise had failed. That afternoon, at 3 p.m., the Council of Ministers met at the Elysée. "It was the saddest meeting for ten years," Tournoux writes.[27] Nevertheless, Pompidou did not accept defeat. He suggested that the reaction in the Renault factory might be untypical. Work could resume. Perhaps.

That afternoon, it was the General who looked like the man who had been defeated at Grenelle. Several ministers remember a head of State completely "at sea", in a state that Philippe Alexandre describes thus: "De Gaulle's mind is elsewhere. His shoulders are hunched, his forearm stretched out over the Council table. He stares at the ministers gathered around him without seeing them. Of the discussion, concerning the referendum, he only takes in a few phrases here and there... The referendum will not take place. De Gaulle is already in mourning for it."[28]

The following day, 28 May, at noon, François Mitterrand announced his candidature for the presidency of the Republic in the event of the post falling vacant. General de Gaulle's principal opponent at the elections of 1965 added that he had already chosen his Prime Minister, Pierre Mendès France. Thus, in those few hours during which de Gaulle had maintained an atmosphere of unrelieved gloom, politics had undergone a resurrection. It was a triple resurrection. To begin with, there was the resurrection of the Communists, who, as guarantors of order in agreement with the representatives from Matignon, had lost the battle on the union level and had suffered two rejections, at Billancourt and Charléty. They called for a demonstration to take place on 29 May intended to measure up to these challenges: it would be the opportunity, if not to seize power,* at least to affirm their ascendancy. It was a resurrection for the parliamentary leaders, Mitterrand and Mendès France. And, above all, it was the resurrection of Georges Pompidou.

The fiasco at Grenelle had not weakened his authority. So strong, so active, so self-confident did he seem at that time that the failure was imputed to a lack of realism on the part of the proletarians who had broken with the union organizations, rather than to him. On that evening of 27 May, when, at the meeting of the Council of Ministers, de Gaulle had "covered" him, he returned to an Hôtel Matignon besieged by visitors who might, tomorrow, be courtiers. "Monday 27 May," Anne and Pierre Rouanet write, "was the birthday of a Pompidouism that was now distinct from Gaullism. And was now irreconcilable with it."[29]

That evening, Pompidou consolidated still further his own power, if not that of

---

*It would be easy enough to take power, its spokesmen remarked at the time, but how would they keep it?

the state. Indeed it was then that he arranged, in view of the great Communist demonstration to take place on 29 May, the presence of considerable numbers of troops, which, like the General, he had so far refrained from deploying.

The hypothesis of a recourse to armed force had been studied. On 16 May, Pompidou had taken steps to implement a possible call-up of reservists. On 19 May, shortly after his return from Romania, de Gaulle had summoned Pierre Messmer to enquire into the mood of the soldiers. The minister had assured him: the Algerian wounds were healing, the army was loyal.

In fact, the civil power had available at Satory, on the edge of Versailles, a very strong unit, known as the "armoured gendarmerie", one thousand highly trained troops endowed with easily manoeuvrable and effective AMX 13 tanks. That force was still in reserve, to be used only in the event of a real "armed uprising of an insurrectional character".

Another unit that was often talked about during those days was the 2nd Brigade at Rambouillet, which was on manoeuvres on 10 and 20 May in Champagne, at Mailly camp. Once the exercise was over, the tanks at Rambouillet returned to barracks, near Paris, not by railway – as usual – but, because of the strike, by road. On its way, it made a detour, which was entirely planned, via Fresnes and Petit-Clamart! The sound of those "caterpillars" created a sensation that may have had an effect on ensuing events. Concerning the feelings, the morale and the possible role of the army of May 1968, one could not do better than quote the following description given to me by General Fourquet, then Chief of Staff:

> At first the army regarded all that disturbance with astonishment, then with anxiety mingled with a touch of disgust. But it was haunted by the obsessive fear that it would be asked to intervene. Because it had no wish to be mixed up with so political an affair, one bordering on civil war, and because it was perfectly aware of the risk that one could take by confronting demonstrators with twenty-year-old youths whose nerve might break and cause a catastrophic situation. Facing up to demonstrators was tough, very tough. This being the case, it was my duty to expect the worst and I had brought to the camp at Frileuse units composed solely of active troops (including naval commandos), who would have been able, if need be, to relieve the riot police in their exhausting task. But I was never asked to bring the army in, as such, though a few panicky individuals in ministerial offices might have leapt at the idea.[30]

The fact remains that those around the Prime Minister were dealing with this *Kriegspiel*. During the account of those days that he made to François Mauriac, six months later, Pompidou remembers his feelings and thoughts at that time: "I had reached the stage when I might have to be forced to shoot. It was terrible..." But he also says: "I found it fascinating to take personal charge of those measures."[31] Fascinating? There's nothing like an intellectual to be attracted by the use of force, in all its forms. And if there is any doubt as to the Prime Minister's determination on the eve of the great Communist demonstration of 29 May ("Communism was the enemy. I was at war," he told Mauriac[32]), one need only quote from Jacques

Chirac writing of his former leader in *Le Monde* on 30 May 1978: "He took it upon himself, and himself alone, to organize the tank units at the gates of Paris."

On 28 May, Charles de Gaulle saw six more people: Michel Debatisse (the leader of the farmers' union*), General Fourquet, the journalist Michel Droit, the Prime Minister, the Minister of the Interior and, lastly, his son, Captain Philippe de Gaulle.

Michel Debatisse arrived at 4 p.m. He was not at all known to the General, nor was he even a supporter. His impressions are all the more significant, therefore. According to the accounts that he published of the meeting, de Gaulle, for over an hour,

> showed me how everything was lost, that France's enemies, at home and abroad, were in league, that the game was up. I tried to reply, to tell him once again that many French people were depending on him, on him alone, to get them out of such a mess, that he must speak. He replied that he had already done so and that it had done nothing. Anyway, nothing could be done. That was the end of our meeting. I was dumbfounded, anxious and no doubt showed it. At the door, I spoke to the General again, repeating that, in my opinion, he ought to speak again. It was at that moment that a strange event occurred that contradicted everything that I had just heard. The General shook me by the hand, put his left hand on my shoulder and said, adding nothing more: "Well! Debatisse, I'll speak."[33]

Georges Pompidou left a lively and to all appearances authentic account of his meeting with the head of State in his *Pour rétablir une vérité*:

> In the evening, after dinner, I had a meeting with the General. I found him tired. "Are you sleeping?" he asked. "Yes, when I've time." "You're lucky." He asked me what I thought would happen. What I said was more or less this:
>
> "The Communist Party demonstration is going to be an important demonstration. The problem concerns its intentions. Is it going to try to organize a really revolutionary action? It's possible. The fact that the march starts from behind the Hôtel de Ville may suggest that it is thinking of seizing it and doing a re-run of the Paris Commune. In that case, if you agree, I shall bring in the tanks, which are ready. But, all in all, I don't think so. In my opinion, the PCF analysis is that the situation is not a revolutionary one. So I think it will stick to a show of force to remind everyone that it alone has the big battalions and, consequently, is alone capable of taking power if the State collapses. In that case, I think the crisis is over and we've won, public opinion having had enough."
>
> "You're an optimist," he replied. "Anyway, from the outset, you were too optimistic."
>
> "In what way was I wrong?"

*The FNSEA (Fédération nationale des syndicats d'exploitants agricoles).

"You told me you'd get an agreement with the CGT."

"I got that agreement. It was the CGT that couldn't get it approved and that's why the PCF is now trying to regain control. It will cost a little more, but we'll get there."

I left without realizing how exhausted, and even discouraged the General was.[34]

Christian Fouchet's turn came at about 9.30 p.m. The General confided to his faithful colleague: "Sometimes I think I'm going to fall to pieces!" When the head of State admitted to him that he was unable to sleep "with all those grenades going off around him", Fouchet said: "Then go and sleep at Versailles! Like Thiers advised Louis-Philippe in 1848." "I'm not Louis-Philippe!" de Gaulle muttered. But he looked his visitor straight in the eyes and said: "It may well be that among all those crazy kids at the Sorbonne and Odéon, some of them are right."[35]

An hour later, Fouchet called Pompidou to ask him if he did not think that there was "something odd" about the General, who seemed to have "something up his sleeve".[36] The Prime Minister had not noticed anything. Reputations can be curious. Fouchet was noted for his "heaviness", Pompidou for his finesse.

Meanwhile, it is true, a scene had taken place that seemed to have made up the General's mind. During the afternoon, Mme de Gaulle, while shopping near the Madeleine, had been recognized and roughly insulted by a man. According to General de Boissieu,[37] his mother-in-law had been insulted in a large store by a group of unionized assistants. In any case, the General's wife had been deeply shocked. This is François Flohic's account: "Mme de Gaulle really can't take any more. At dinner on Tuesday evening, the 28th, she literally cracked up so much that the General, leaving the dining-room, had dinner served in the sitting-room next to his bedroom."[38] De Gaulle, of course, had known every kind of tribulation and insult in his time. But he found it quite intolerable that anyone should insult his wife. He had not allowed the presence of Yvonne de Gaulle in the car attacked at Petit-Clamart six years before to influence his decision regarding Bastien-Thiry. However, the incident of the afternoon of 28 May did influence the decision that he was making.

On the evening of 29 May, de Gaulle summoned his son, Captain Philippe de Gaulle. He handed him two letters, one of which contained, it seems, what might be called "his last wishes". Then he warned him that the head of his military office, General Lalande, had been ordered to take them – the General's son, his wife Henriette and their three children – the following day, by plane, to the headquarters of the French forces at Baden-Baden.

Did the General reveal his own plans to that very privileged confidant on that evening of 28 May?* It seems likely that, even with those closest to him, he had left room for manoeuvre. Earlier, the General had telephoned to his son-in-law, Alain de Boissieu, who was then commanding the 7th Division at Mulhouse, asking him to come urgently to see him in Paris. Since the journey by road would be too long,

*This was obviously one of the questions that I would have asked Admiral de Gaulle had he given me the honour of seeing him.

Boissieu took a helicopter in the early hours of the morning on 29 May. He would be at the Elysée in the morning. Meanwhile, he telephoned his direct superior, General Hublot, commander of the 1st Army Corps at Nancy, to warn him of this mysterious mission. That evening, he would receive from that officer and from General Beauvallet, Military Governor of Metz, messages for General de Gaulle that were to play a part in the rest of the story.

De Gaulle went back to his bedroom. He had made up his mind – at least to take everyone by surprise – a surprise intended to create anxiety, to focus on him the general anxiety in which the whole country lived, by means of the most meticulous dissimulation, aimed at everyone, friend or enemy, even those closest to him.

Before embarking on an account of that prodigious day – especially as it was to last from 7 a.m. on 29 May to 4.30 p.m. on 30 May – let me simply quote from these few precepts that the author of *Vers l'armée de métier* formulated in 1934: the real leader must know "how to put his own camp on the wrong scent, to mislead purposely those very people whom he is thinking of using", "to make people believe that he is where he is not", in other words to surround himself "with a thick veil of deceit".

That extravagant day of thirty-three hours, ending with the eighty-nine minutes spent at General Massu's residence in Baden, almost seems to have been constructed like a classical drama, complete with unity of time. The construction, however, was only apparent. The author of *Le Fil de l'épée* certainly had a plan, even several alternative ones. But he was not always in control of the action. At certain times, he himself was led, swept up by the wave, submerged by exhaustion and doubt, ready to give up.

The facts that marked that day of 29 May 1968 have long been known, even if the exact timetable and even some of the stages have sometimes been questioned. But the interpretations of de Gaulle's behaviour, on 29 May 1968, are of two opposing types: there is that of disarray and that of tactics. To take only those who were directly involved and who have taken the trouble to express their views on the matter, the first includes General Massu and above all Georges Pompidou. The second comprises General de Boissieu and Captain Flohic. According to the first, de Gaulle literally sought refuge at Baden-Baden and was brought back into action only by the exhortations of General Massu. According to the others, the head of State, throughout the entire day, was carrying out a lucidly worked-out plan, of which the stay in Baden was merely one episode, if not a detour, the meeting with Massu, planned in France, having a clearly determined strategic aim.

At 7 a.m. on 29 May, Xavier de La Chevalerie, the head of State's *directeur de cabinet*, was urgently summoned to the Elysée. He arrived at 7.30. The General received him standing in the small sitting-room. La Chevalerie, who saw the President of the Republic every day, was nevertheless struck that morning by his paleness and by the exhaustion that had clearly left its mark on his face. "I'm done in, dead-beat," the General told him. "I'm going off to rest and sleep a bit at Colombey. Present my apologies to M. de Courcel: I won't be able to see him today for lunch as arranged."[39] Half an hour later, in his office, Charles de Gaulle received General Lalande, head of his military office, to give him a strange mission: Lalande would leave at once to learn of the intentions of the three great military leaders in the East commanding between them the "battle corps": General Beauvallet at Metz, General Hublot at Nancy and General Massu at Baden-Baden. He would go first to Baden-Baden, putting into Massu's care his son, daughter-in-law and three grandsons, whom he would take with him.

At 9.15 a.m. it was the turn of Bernard Tricot, Secretary-General of the Elysée, to receive the head of State's instructions: the next meeting of the Council of Ministers was postponed to the following day, Thursday at 3 p.m., after the brief stay at Colombey that the General had decided to spend with Mme de Gaulle.

Georges Pompidou, who, before leaving for the Elysée, chaired a meeting at which were decided the civil and military measures required to maintain order before the CGT demonstration, planned for the afternoon, was given the General's message passed by Tricot. Suddenly seized by "extreme anxiety", he leapt to his telephone, called the Elysée and asked Tricot to arrange a meeting with the General immediately. The Secretary-General was evasive. About 11 a.m., Pompidou rang Tricot back: "I must see him before he leaves!" Ten minutes later, the Prime Minister was surprised to hear a voice at the Elysée declare: "General de Gaulle speaking. Listen, my dear fellow, I feel tired. I must be alone and rest. To step back a bit to see things more clearly. So I am going to Colombey, but I shall be back tomorrow."

"It's serious, *mon Général*, because I'm not sure that you will come back."

"Of course I will. I shall be there tomorrow in the early afternoon for the Council of Ministers. (A pause.) And even if I don't come back ... I'm old. You're young. You're the future. People would look to you. But I'm telling you: I'll be back. *Je vous embrasse*." De Gaulle hung up, leaving Pompidou dumbfounded.

Matignon may have been plunged into anxious confusion, but the Elysée had become once more an engine room: indeed a meeting had just taken place between de Gaulle and de Boissieu, to which we shall return, and which forms the first turning-point of that zig-zagging day. Up till then, from the missions given to La Chevalerie, Tricot and Lalande and up to the *au revoir* to Pompidou, everything or almost everything seemed to suggest a withdrawal on de Gaulle's part. Almost everything: for Lalande had not only to take Philippe de Gaulle and his family to shelter in Germany, he had also to contact the three men in command of French forces in the east – Massu, Hublot, and Beauvallet. That must mean that de Gaulle was up to something.

Concerning the meeting between de Gaulle and de Boissieu, de Boissieu recounts, in a book published fourteen years later,[40] how, after de Gaulle had said that "I'd better go home to write my memoirs," he got up and declared to the General: "*Mon Général*, it is not your son-in-law who is standing in front of you, but the commander of the 7th Division who has a message to convey to you on the part of the general commanding his army corps and the general commanding his military region." Rather surprised, the visitor continues, de Gaulle in turn rose to his feet: their talk continued with both men on their feet.

The mood of the military chiefs then described by General de Boissieu was that of excited expectation: each of them was determined "to defend the country against anyone, whether the attack came from without or from within".

"Good," said de Gaulle. "But most of your troops are young national servicemen."

"I shall do everything I can to gather together a regiment of regular-army volunteers in my division if you have any particular action to undertake. If, for example, you gave me orders to seize the Odéon. The army would not understand why the State should allow itself to be kicked around any longer."

"What would the attitude of the army be if we had to go as far as a trial of strength?"

"The army has never been so disciplined. It awaits its orders."

"Good, I shall see whether Massu thinks the same,* then I shall speak from Colombey, Strasbourg, or somewhere else. The State will be where I am. In fact I'm leaving Paris; if the Communist demonstration diverges and moves towards the Elysée, there won't be anything here any more; they'll be attacking an empty palace." Then the head of State handed his son-in-law the two letters: one similar to the one that he had already given him before his trips abroad, the other containing instructions for Georges Pompidou, "In case something serious happens to me that prevents me from carrying out my responsibilities. Or death."

"Should I warn General Massu of your intention of meeting him?"

"Yes, but not from Paris, you will do it from Colombey. Here you must say nothing to anybody. I want to plunge the French people, including the government, into doubt and anxiety in order to regain control of the situation."

"Where shall I tell General Massu to go to meet you?"

"Oh yes, to Le Dabo** or to Sainte-Odile*** – that high point will impress people's minds and its choice will please the Alsatians."

"But I'm afraid it won't be possible to land your helicopter at Le Dabo or Sainte-Odile. The weather's bad in the Vosges."

"Well, in that case, tell Massu to meet me at Strasbourg-Entzheim airfield."

"And if I can't reach General Massu? Or if atmospheric conditions are bad over Alsace?"

"Well, in that case, I shall go all the way to Baden, then I shall spend tonight in your home at Mulhouse, unless I can't get back by road to Colombey, in the late afternoon."

"Jacques Foccart is waiting for me outside your office. What shall I tell him?"

"Nothing, you mustn't say anything to anybody, nor make any telephone calls before arriving at Colombey. I shall be far away at that point, on my way

---

*General Massu was the only one of his peers, entrusted with large-scale "operational" commands, who showed no intention of supporting the head of State over the previous few hours, as, for example, other Free French generals, such as Vaginet at Lyon and Simon at Marseille, had done.

**A pass through the Vosges, taken by the Leclerc division to capture Strasbourg.

***A convent dedicated to the patron saint of Alsace.

to Alsace. If there is a leak, it doesn't really matter, but since one of the alternatives might take me to Baden, I don't want the German press to be alerted to the fact."[41]

What we have here, then, is de Gaulle emerging from his melancholy as the sovereign strategist, the version propagated by a certain school of thought. Taken literally, what could be more Gaullian than this manoeuvre? The General had overcome his early-morning fatigue and the news of the army given him by Boissieu had stimulated him to new activity. Before seeing Boissieu, de Gaulle had summoned Captain Flohic, in uniform. The ADC on duty that morning was Colonel d'Escrienne. But, says Flohic, he wanted to take a naval officer, who, he thought, would feel freer in relation to the military chiefs – all army men – whom they would meet that day. In any case, the officer was surprised at being asked to wear uniform: never had he, as an ADC, left for Colombey other than in "civvies". Arriving at the Elysée, about 10.40 a.m., Flohic met Boissieu, who remarked cryptically: "If you need petrol, there's a good man at Orge, between Chaumont and Châteauvillain..." What did that mean? Flohic's surprise increased when the head of State said to him: "Without letting anyone see, take maps covering the area east of Colombey." "Has provision been made for funds?" Flohic asked. "Everything has been arranged."

Another precaution was taken, this time by Mme de Gaulle: the day before, she rang her brother, Jacques Vendroux, asking him to come and collect, on the morning of 29 May, petite Jeanne (the housemaid at the Elysée) and take her to her home, in the Nord, "for a few days". During the journey to Calais, the girl was to tell the Vendrouxs that the de Gaulles' departure for Colombey, that day, was "quite different" from usual, that "a lot more things were packed than usual" and that she was afraid that "it meant that they would be going away permanently".[42]

After signing and handing to Bernard Tricot a document delegating the chairmanship of the Council of Ministers to the Prime Minister if such a meeting were required before the following day,[43] the General, followed by Mme de Gaulle and Flohic, left the Elysée at 11.30 a.m. A quarter of an hour later – there were no cars in the streets of Paris, supplies of petrol having dried up – they were at Issy-les-Moulineaux, where two helicopters were awaiting them. The General, his wife and Flohic got into the first. In the second were Inspector Puissant, the bodyguard Paul Teissier and Dr Menès (the physician who accompanied the head of State on all his trips, taking with him impressive blood transfusion equipment). As he left, the General was nervous, complaining that there was too much luggage, that it was too long, that "we've been seen".[44]

They set out for Saint-Dizier, fifty kilometres north of Colombey, half-way to the eastern garrisons. It was there that the final itinerary would be decided according to information conveyed by Boissieu from Colombey. But when they landed, they found that there was no news waiting for them: General de Gaulle's son-in-law had been delayed by a breakdown and, because of the post office strike, had been unable to contact Baden-Baden by the international line.

After refuelling, the two helicopters took off for the east. Having no news from Boissieu, and therefore from Massu, the General asked Pouliquen to radio Baden-

Baden. But the pilot only had at his disposal frequencies that had been prear-ranged on his equipment, those that were indispensable for the Paris–Colombey journey.

This moment of uncertainty is worth looking at more closely. The General's plan, already so heavy with uncertainties, had just suffered a hitch. The silence of his son-in-law disconcerted him. That crucial phase of the process was one of the simplest and now it could not be carried out. So he hesitated for a moment.

Sitting at the front, beside the co-pilot, de Gaulle being behind with his wife, Flohic could communicate with the General, in the surrounding din, only by scribbling on the back of an envelope. Suddenly, in the General's hand, he read: "Residence of the Commander-in-Chief of the FFA".* So Baden-Baden was the objective, though they had been unable to warn Massu. It was 1.15 p.m. The Michelin maps were not very precise, Flohic notes, but they were flying low to avoid radar: they could see where they were going. At 2.20, they crossed the Rhine to the north of Strasbourg: and soon, there before them, was Baden-Oos. They landed at 2.40.

The ADC immediately telephoned the Commander-in-Chief's residence, which was quite near. Mme Massu answered the telephone and got her husband:

"This is Flohic, *mon Général*, we're here."

"Who's we?"

"General and Mme de Gaulle. I would ask you to mark out your lawn with beacons..."

"Look, I'm naked in bed and I am having my siesta. Give me five minutes to get ready."**

Just as they were taking off for the residence, Flohic was surprised to see two light planes land, out of which emerged General Lalande, Philippe de Gaulle and his family. There was no time to waste. Two minutes later, the two helicopters landed at the residence. General Massu was standing to attention on the lawn. It was 3.01 p.m.

De Gaulle emerged wearing a dark grey suit, and launched into the attack at once: "It's all up, Massu..."

What he said, which is quoted by the author of *Baden 68*, is confirmed by Flohic, who was standing two steps away and, before moving away, heard Massu's first reply: "You can't be serious, *mon Général*! A man with your prestige still has means at his disposal."[45]

The two generals talked for a while on the lawn. For between ten and fifteen minutes, Flohic thinks. Then they went into Massu's office, where their talk continued for another twenty minutes, interrupted at about 3.30, when the visitor was brought some food. In thirty-five minutes, in such circumstances, a great deal can be said. What General de Gaulle said is summed up thus by Massu in his book: "It's all over, the Communists have provoked a total paralysis of the country.

*Forces Françaises en Allemagne – French forces in Germany.

**General Massu denies saying any such thing. In his book, he describes himself as lying on a sofa wearing a pullover, with the *Figaro littéraire* over his face. As an old colonial, Massu was much given to the siesta. What is more, the evening before, he had magnificently entertained, with vodka, Marshal Koshevoy, the Soviet Commander-in-Chief in Germany, well into the night.

I'm not in charge of anything any more. So I'm withdrawing and since I feel that I and my family are threatened in France, I've come to seek refuge with you, in order to decide what to do. I told my son to join me here with his family. Pompidou may have been wrong, at the beginning, to settle with the students, but he's been very good since. People don't want me any more." De Gaulle then inquired as to how to reach Strasbourg and went on: "We only have to warn the German authorities of my request for hospitality." And he suggested that the French Ambassador at Bonn, François Seydoux, should be warned of his presence.

While de Gaulle replenished his resources (an omelette, a glass of water, two cups of coffee) his host, who thought that he looked "a little less tense than when he arrived", continued the plea that he had begun beside the helicopter:

> For the country's sake, for your own sake, you cannot give up like this. You will be criticized for this departure and your image will be tarnished. Everything that has been done over the past ten years cannot disappear in ten days. You will open the floodgates and accelerate the chaos that it is your duty to control. You are dealing with fifteen thousand individuals determined to wage in our country a struggle that is taking place throughout the world. You have been sickened by it, but you have seen other such times, since 1940. You must fight till the end, on the terrain that you have chosen. If you leave power, it must only be after consulting the people.
>
> There will always be time to resign. But without running away beforehand, because the front is in France and, for you, in Paris. General de Gaulle is an old fighter and must fight to the end. I don't believe for a moment there is any physical threat to you. Anyway, it would be better to be a victim of such an eventuality than run away from a risk of that kind.

Massu also reports saying to de Gaulle something that does not appear in his book: "*Mon Général*, it's too bad, what can you do, you're in the shit and you must stay there. Go back to it. You can't do anything else. You're still in it and have got to stay there."[46]

"My efforts lasted over an hour," Massu goes on, adding that during his plea he found time to inform his two aides-de-camp, who were waiting in the neighbouring sitting-room, of the difficulties of his task. In an interview given fifteen years later, one of those two officers, who was then Captain Richard, relates what Massu had said to them: "We aren't out of the wood yet. He's as stubborn as a mule and determined to drop everything. He has described the Apocalypse to me."[47]

Suddenly, Massu goes on, "He got up. He came over to me and embraced me: 'I'm going! Call my wife! As for my son, he can decide for himself what he must do.'"[48]

One of de Gaulle's closest, most faithful and most constant colleagues described him to me as "cyclothymic". Simulated or not, depression and exaltation took extreme forms with him. In his depressive statements there was, of course, genuine worry – which its very expression helped perhaps to banish, to purge. But there was also the wish to test the person he was speaking to. Taking account of what had been said that morning between the head of State and his son-in-law, one would be tempted to minimize the role played by that conversation at Baden-Baden – if other factors did not support the "pessimistic" thesis of the advocates of Gaullian disarray.

The General's account of Baden does not refer to a conversation that took place about 3.30 p.m., probably after the first phase of the Massu–de Gaulle dialogue, between the head of State and François Flohic. No sooner had the ADC entered the drawing-room than he made this comment, which says a great deal about the lamentations directed to Massu: "Now that I am no longer present on French territory, the Constitutional Council will announce my fall." This does not seem to suggest that the stay at Baden was regarded at the time as a mere stop-over. Flohic judiciously notes that the body referred to was chaired by the General's faithful friend Gaston Palewski,* who would not have been excessively impatient to take such steps. But, all the same, that comment did not come from a tactician who had crossed the Rhine only to sweep back to Paris.

In the dining-room next door, Mme de Gaulle was lunching with Suzanne Massu. Quite obviously, a certain understanding had grown up between the two ladies: as we know, Mme de Gaulle was very much in favour of her husband's retirement. That connivance was rather crudely expressed in a remark made by Mme Massu: "One does not repeat 18 June at seventy-eight!"** This certainly shows that, among those around Massu, not everybody was so keen to see Charles de Gaulle's career continue much longer.

That theme of the prolonged retirement, of a lasting withdrawal, cropped up several times during those eighty-nine German minutes. During his brief talk with Flohic, de Gaulle asked him to contact the French Embassy at Bonn to warn it of his presence in the Federal Republic. But there was the more serious problem of how to approach the German authorities. On that point, this is how General Edouard Mathon, Massu's Chief of Staff, puts it:

> At 4 p.m., I was called into the office, where the head of State was with General Massu, who ordered me to summon General Karpinski, who represented the Federal government to the French General Staff in Germany, to warn him of General de Gaulle's presence. After five or six minutes, I had to report back that I had failed to contact him. "So we must summon our Ambassador at Bonn," de Gaulle said to Massu. This mission was given to Captain Richard.[49]

There are other arguments in favour of the "disarray" thesis: the amount of luggage and the fact that Mme de Gaulle set herself up in one of the bedrooms. This is what Georges Pompidou has called "the arrangements made for an extended stay" at Baden.[50] Moreover, quoted on several occasions by her husband

---

*Fifteen years later, Gaston Palewski described to me, ecstatically, that "flight of the General, who was absent but all the more present, the only person you missed and without whom everything seemed depopulated".

**Quoting these words to me in January 1986, François Flohic added that Mme Massu had said the same thing to Philippe de Gaulle.

in *Baden 68*, Mme Massu commented that the luggage was so heavy that "the boys had to make several journeys to bring it into the house".[51]

That luggage amounted to what could be carried by two helicopters, each of whose "boots" was comparable to that of a normal car. Furthermore, the medical equipment brought by Dr Menès occupied almost all the useful space of one of the machines. In fact, Flohic remarks, there must have been one large suitcase and two smaller ones.[52] This was much more than the de Gaulles took for their weekends at Colombey, but less than Suzanne Massu suggests.

It should be added that Mme de Gaulle brought with her a small case containing family jewels. Knowing what the standard of living of the de Gaulles was, one may assume that it did not amount to a great deal: but one may see this as an indication, if not proof, of a decision on the General's part to take a long retirement. As for the installation of Yvonne de Gaulle in one of the bedrooms of the house, there can be no question but that Mme de Gaulle, after the exhausting trip in the helicopter, appreciated this opportunity to take a rest.

This leaves the setting-up of Philippe de Gaulle and his family at Baden-Baden – where, having arrived by plane at the same time as the helicopters, they were to stay close on two weeks. It is here that we have the strongest arguments of those who believe that by setting foot in Baden-Baden, de Gaulle was seeking refuge rather than planning some manoeuvre. This is how François Flohic puts it:

> Philippe de Gaulle went to Baden on the orders of his father, who was not only President of the Republic, but Supreme Commander of the Armed Forces. It could only be a precaution taken by the General, who did not want to leave his son as a hostage in Paris, in case he wanted to plan some action from Strasbourg or Metz. Previously, during the Generals' *putsch* in Algiers, he had sent me to the Naval Chief of General Staff instructing him to arrange for *Le Picard*, of which his son was captain, to leave Oran. If the General had chosen retirement, he would not have mortgaged his son's career without his consent. And, if that had been the case, Philippe de Gaulle would not have agreed to follow his father into exile. At the time of the departure from Baden for Colombey, Philippe asked his father to take him back with him to La Boisserie. The General replied: "There's no room for you. I shall call you if I need you."[53]

As we have seen, it was shortly after 4 p.m. that Charles de Gaulle suddenly stood up in front of Massu and declared: "I'm leaving..." It took another half-hour to organize everybody and to refuel the helicopters. De Gaulle spent the time trying to make sure that he had made the correct decision. Leaving the drawing-room, he took General Mathon to one side:

> "What do you think of the situation? Do you think I'm right to go back?"
> "*Mon Général*, I think the situation is difficult, tense, but not desperate. I think General de Gaulle has overcome worse situations!"
> "You're talking like Massu, who has just persuaded me to go back to Paris..."

"Whatever your future is, *mon Général*, I do not think your place is in Germany."[54]

De Gaulle then turned to Colonel Moniez, Massu's *chef de cabinet*, and asked him the same questions. He got more or less the same answers. It is curious, all the same, to think that de Gaulle had such a need to be reassured, encouraged, urged on. At 4.25, they walked towards the helicopters, which were ready to take off from the lawn. Massu comments:

> I reflected on that extraordinary visit. I noticed that it had taken place in such a way as to prove that the General, having lost his patience with events in Paris, wanted to get away from the capital, but certainly not to plan some kind of military intervention with the Commander-in-Chief of French forces in Germany. The subject never cropped up. I can only conclude, in all modesty, that, knowing that my wife and I were faithful and devoted to his person, and having at my disposal the geographical situation in which he had placed me two years before, the General had been driven by the "Paris mess" to take a break at Baden.

Before getting into their helicopter, General and Mme de Gaulle took an emotional farewell of their children and grandchildren. Suzanne Massu walked back to the house with Philippe de Gaulle, who "repeated over and over again that he could not make sense of the manoeuvre. His father, he said, had not explained anything clearly to him. 'It's either my father or anarchy,' he muttered several times."[55]

Was it a "depression", a "stop-over" at Baden? Who, whether witness, chronicler, analyst, supporter or adversary, can say the last word about that strange escapade in the Black Forest? We can, in any case, cite two crucial remarks made by Charles de Gaulle himself. On 1 June, he confided to Georges Pompidou: "For the first time in my life, my nerve failed me. I am not very proud of myself."[56]

What precise importance should be attached to what he said on the evening of 29 May, at La Boisserie, to Flohic, who asked him what would have happened if he had not decided, that afternoon, to return to Colombey, and then to Paris? "I would have informed Kiesinger* of my presence in Germany. I would have stayed there for a time and then I would have gone to Ireland, the country of my maternal ancestors, the MacCartans, then much further. In any case, I would not have come back to France."[57]

On the specific role of Massu, one cannot ignore what General de Gaulle said to Mme Massu during a luncheon at the Elysée on 8 November 1968, before several dumbfounded witnesses: "It was Providence who put your husband on my way on 29 May. It had considerable consequences at the time and perhaps incalculable ones for the future."

Massu the saviour of Charles de Gaulle? General Buis, who commanded the

---

*The Federal Chancellor. As we have seen, this "information" did not go beyond the project stage.

Trier Division not far from Baden and who was informed confidentially of the event the following day, considers that the Commander-in-Chief of French forces in Germany rendered, on that day, "a considerable service to France". However, he goes on, advice is only one element in a choice of action. "The decision is all important. That old man of seventy-eight, near his end, worn out with struggles on a world scale, was able, wounded as he was even more in his heart than in his spirit, to pull himself together in less than an hour and to take on his shoulders once more the very heavy burden, which suddenly seemed light, that he had for a moment put down on the roadside."[58]

Was Baden merely a detour, "to see Massu", given the impossibility of the planned meeting in Alsace, during a vast manoeuvre to regroup both the civil and military authorities, centred on Strasbourg or Metz? Some days later, speaking to Jacques Chaban-Delmas, Charles de Gaulle confirmed that he had planned a reconquest from Strasbourg. "A single cannon shot would have been enough – in the air, of course!"[59] Here, too, the description seems too simple. One cannot deny, in view of what certain witnesses have said and given General Massu's concern to aggrandize and ennoble his own role, that Charles de Gaulle, on arriving at Baden-Baden, for a period of forty or fifty minutes, as on a number of occasions in previous days, underwent a failure of nerve. Nevertheless, he made several attempts to get out of it: twice, in the course of the darkest hour, he asked Massu, and then Flohic, if it was possible to reach Strasbourg – that is to say, to act, to raise a standard.

One incident is worth mentioning here. Three days after his return to Paris, de Gaulle received M. Jeanneney, his Minister for Social Affairs. His only comment on the episode was this: "As I flew over Lorraine, I felt that I could not abandon 'them'."[60] Anyway, what is the point of going over and over the various possibilities when everything is said in a sentence spoken the following day by a completely restored de Gaulle when addressing the French people whom he claimed once again to be bringing together: "For the past twenty-four hours, I have considered every eventuality."

We left a highly anxious Georges Pompidou being "embraced" by a de Gaulle who had just told him that he was leaving for Colombey. For twenty-four hours. What did that mean? Michel Jobert, who was present at the time, speaks of Pompidou's "almost clinical interrogation as to his leader's intentions". Around the Prime Minister there was a great deal of coming and going. Gaullist "barons", big and small, wondered, opined, confabulated, prophesied. But that was only the beginning.

At 2 p.m., Bernard Tricot was announced. This is how Pompidou described the meeting to the Mauriacs: "Tricot, livid, came into my office saying; 'The General has disappeared.' 'What do you mean, disappeared?' 'Well! Yes. He was supposed to arrive at Colombey at half-past twelve. And at half-past one his helicopter was still not there. No one knows where he is.'" In his book, Pompidou writes: "I let out a cry: 'He's gone abroad!'" But, to return to Mauriac's version: "He said nothing to me about it! He said nothing to the Prime Minister. I spent some frightful hours there." Were those hours so frightful? Certainly. The Prime Minister remained in ignorance for a little under two hours. As soon as he heard the news, he alerted Messmer, of course – hinting that the General might have been kidnapped by a military movement – and pointing out, rather harshly, that he was "responsible" for the head of State, the Supreme Commander-in-Chief.

When did the army learn of the route taken by the two helicopters? General Fourquet, then Chief of General Staff, recounts: "I immediately telephoned to the Commander of Air Defence to know if there was any trace of the General's Alouette helicopter. The answer came back very quickly: Baden. I immediately warned my minister, Pierre Messmer. And I rang Massu."*

The Prime Minister, too, it seems, had considered "every eventuality". From the formation around himself of a "government of French unity" to an appeal to the people. Since the General had abandoned him, why should he take on the burden? But we should cite here the evidence of Olivier Guichard, a witness of those feverish hours and a good Gaullist: "Georges Pompidou never demonstrated so much loyalty and sense of responsibility as on that day."[61] In any case, the Prime Minister cannot be held responsible for the comments of this or that colleague – for example, Jean-Luc Javal, who said, in the presence of a senior television official: "It's time we got rid of the old fool."[62] Six months later, talking of the General's disappearance to François, Jeanne, Claude and Marie-Claude Mauriac, Pompidou could not contain his rancour: "It was unthinkable." To which his wife added: "I shall never forgive him for it."

The two helicopters that had taken off from Baden at 4.30 p.m. landed at Chaumont – twenty kilometres from Colombey – at 6 p.m. Twenty minutes later, the gates of La Boisserie opened to let in two police cars – which shows that the de Gaulles' return was not expected so early.

The General immediately telephoned Bernard Tricot who heard the celebrated: "Je me suis mis d'accord avec mes arrières-pensées,"** a superb summing up of that day of offensive retreat. De Gaulle added, in the most natural tone in the world, that he would be returning to Paris the following morning and that the meeting of the Council of Ministers would take place at 3 p.m. as scheduled. Pompidou in turn was telephoned at about 6.30 p.m.: "The voice was firm. He confirmed that he was back and that the Council of Ministers' meeting would go ahead. He seemed to be saying: You see, you were wrong to worry."[63]

Having thus closed the Baden episode and indicated that his programme (apart from one detour) was still what it had been on the morning of 29 May, de Gaulle regained his serenity. With his wife and Flohic he went for a long walk in the park, where they talked "of nothing but flowers, trees and poetry".

He returned to the drawing-room. Unusually, the General did not shut himself away to work in his tower. Apparently, only one thing mattered to him: the television news, which he awaited with growing impatience. Like all French people that evening, he noted that the information services were still on strike. But, at 8

---

*Who, two days later, sent his adjutant, General de Rougemont, to present an account of the episode of 29 May to the Minister of Defence and to General Deguil, head of the military office at Matignon.

**Meaning, roughly, "I have reached agreement with my reservations". (trs.)

p.m., a news reader announced simply that General de Gaulle was at his home, in Colombey. The remarkable thing is that he seemed reassured to hear it – especially as he had just learnt from the radio that the great Communist demonstration was quietly dispersing around Saint-Lazare. There would not, after all, be a march on the Elysée.

Flohic noted that, next morning, as soon as he was up, the General went to his study, where he prepared the statement that he would issue that afternoon. "He seems very determined. Once again, the air of his Boisserie seems to have been beneficial."[64]

The helicopter took off at 11 a.m. They reached the Elysée at 12.30. To Bernard Tricot, who found him rejuvenated and told him so, de Gaulle confided: "I needed to breathe in some good air. I slept well. I'm in good fettle." One witness remarked: "He has put on his 1940 boots." Pompidou rang, asking to see him. The General put him off until 2.30. First he had to "tune the strings" with his own staff. Foccart, who was one of its inventors, came to tell him about the demonstration planned for the Champs-Elysées in the afternoon. The General would receive the Prime Minister before the Council of Ministers meeting, arranged for 3 p.m. After the meeting, at 4.30, he would address the nation, on radio only. And the march would begin before 6 p.m.

Charles de Gaulle was himself once more. But the situation had not suddenly been turned round. The Gaullist party as a whole had not suddenly regained its confidence with the return of the General. The miraculously restored leader was yet to work a miracle. On the morning of 30 May, Jacques Vendroux noted: "Most of our friends in the Assembly are in a pitiful state of depression. The wind of defeatism blows stronger and stronger."[65] The press for that day may be summed up in two headlines: "The General is alone" in *France Soir* and "Tomorrow's Tandem" (Mitterrand and Mendès) in *Le Monde*.

At 2.30, Georges Pompidou was at last face to face with the head of State. He had a letter of resignation* in his pocket and had already talked about it to Bernard Tricot, who had warned the General about it. "Out of the question!" de Gaulle insisted. "If you go, I'm going too."[66] Pompidou, who felt that he "did not have the strength to insist on his resignation",[67] then listened to the General as he read the speech that he had written that morning at La Boisserie. It was de Gaulle at his best: a reminder of his legitimacy, a tribute to his Prime Minister, a denunciation of the "totalitarians", a threat to resort to article 16, a call for "civic action"...

Excellent, thought the Prime Minister. But despite his repeated urgings, de Gaulle was still not announcing the dissolution of the Chamber, which, in Pompidou's view, was now an absolute prerequisite. The Prime Minister then pleaded with consummate talent and impressive conviction.

> The General insisted on repeating: "We cannot have elections. The proof is that I couldn't have the referendum." I replied that the two things were very different, that a referendum on some such vague subject as regionalization hardly aroused interest and in no way corresponded to the country's anx-

---

*Published in facsimile in his book, p. 198. In it he makes no reference to his bitterness.

ieties, that to make it practically impossible by strikes would not antagonize public opinion, whereas the people would never agree to having elections, an ancient form of popular consultation, deeply rooted in people's minds, prevented in this way. In the end, seeing that I was not convincing him, I declared: *"Mon Général,* you are asking me to stay. I am asking you for a dissolution." The General looked at me, then picked up a sheet of paper and wrote a letter to Monnerville, the President of the Senate. He was thus conforming to the Constitution, which laid it down that the presidents of both assemblies had to be "consulted". I added that it was pointless to consult M. Chaban-Delmas,* since he shared my opinion entirely and had authorized me to say so. We went into the Council meeting.[68]

It was a short meeting. The General swept into the room like a gust of wind. Hardly had he sat down than he began to read the text that he had amended during his conversation with Pompidou. The ministers looked at one another, dumbfounded. Gorse, who was still Minister of Information, had laid on a tele-vision van. But the General had chosen the radio. A reference to 18 June 1940? Because the technical imperatives of television would mean wasting too much time? These reasons have been raised: but the best reason, which we did not understand at first, was that nobody or almost nobody watched television in the middle of the afternoon, whereas everybody – in office, workshop or car – could turn on the radio at that time.

It was 4.30. The weather was fine. From every open window, from every car radio, in every street, at every crossroads, the old voice resounded, as if it came from far off. "It's Zeus!" Maurice Grimaud murmured.[69]

Françaises, Français, as the possessor of national and republican legitimacy, I have considered over the past twenty-four hours all the eventualities, without exception, that would allow me to keep it. I have made up my mind.

Given present circumstances, I shall not withdraw. I have a mandate from the people and I shall fulfil it.

I shall not change the Prime Minister, whose value, solidity and ability merit the homage of all. I shall propose whatever changes seem to me to be useful in the composition of the government.

Today I am dissolving the National Assembly. I have proposed to the country a referendum that will give citizens an opportunity of authorizing a profound reform of our economy and universities, and, at the same time, to say whether or not they still have confidence in me, by the only acceptable way, that of democracy. I acknowledge that the present situation makes such a procedure materially impossible. That is why I have postponed the date. The legislative elections will take place as laid down by the Constitution, unless certain men intend to gag the entire French people, by preventing it from expressing itself as they are preventing it from living, by the same means that they are preventing the students from studying, the teachers from

*President of the National Assembly.

teaching and the workers from working. Those means are intimidation, intoxication and the tyranny exerted by a party that is a totalitarian enterprise.

So if this situation of coercion continues I shall have to seek other ways than the ballot box to maintain the Republic, in accordance with the Constitution. In any case, civic action must be organized everywhere and immediately to assist first of all the government, but, at a local level, those prefects who have become Commissioners of the Republic. Indeed France is threatened with dictatorship, that of totalitarian communism exploiting the ambition and hatred of rejected politicians.

Well! No! The Republic shall not abdicate. The people will recover its balance. Progress, independence and peace will prevail, together with liberty.[70]

They were fighting words. Were they an incitement to civil war? The strategist knew that there was no risk of triggering one off, that those martial preparations and those threats were even less seasonable than his project of 24 May. He also knew that there was no better target than the Communists when he wanted to gather the crowds behind his name: in 1947, he used the same theme to raise the strength of the RPF. And it was a new RPF that was to rise up from the paving stones.

The idea of responding to the endless marches of students and workers with a great Gaullist demonstration had been proposed for several days by various kinds of Gaullists. Jacques Foccart and Roger Frey, chief "mechanics" of the Fifth Republic; ex-servicemen's organizations; Paris parliamentarians, Pierre Krieg, Michel Habib-Deloncle, Louis Terrenoire and Jean de Préaumont; lastly, the Association for the Support of the Action of General de Gaulle and its organizers, Pierre Lefranc and Yves Lancien.

That Thursday, an hour after General de Gaulle's speech, the Place de la Concorde began to fill up. Around 6 p.m., from the windows of a building in the Rue Royale* we could see the crowd, getting thicker, move towards the Etoile. The demonstrators arrived from everywhere, dressed very differently from those who, for a month, had swamped Paris. Were they more exasperated by the disorder than faithful to de Gaulle? Who could say? In any case, six days later, Raymond Aron wrote in *Le Figaro* that it was a "victory of the party of order, which is broader than the Gaullist party".

The slogans were very political, from "De Gaulle is not alone!"** to "Down with the Communists!", from "Mitterrand, charlatan!" to "Clean out the Sorbonne!" (I did not hear the frightful "Cohn-Bendit to Dachau!", which some witnesses heard and which, in any case, did not reflect the spirit of that march.) At its head was Malraux, a sort of icon with rebellious forelock, arm in arm with Michel Debré, an ecstatic Michelet, a Maurice Schumann walking on air, Joxe rather surprised by the surrounding atmosphere, Missoffe, Poujade, Sanguinetti,

---

*Where, greatly surprised, I happened to be standing.
**A reference to the headline in *France-Soir* referred to above.

Messmer, a jovial Vallon, a Chaban livelier than ever at the head of his light cavalry from the Palais-Bourbon. Not far from him, François Mauriac on the arm of his son Jean, saying how he was living through one of the great moments of his life. It was a triumph. How many were there? 500 000? 700 000? Certainly more than there were Leftists on 13 May between the Gare de l'Est and Denfert, or Communists between the Bastille and Saint-Lazare.

Was that regime, which had been dislocated by a student demonstration, to be saved by a march of its supporters? No. It was already saved by the unexpected combination of the strange tactical genius of an old man and the exhaustion of an exasperated people.

In the end, the victory went to de Gaulle.

What better deceiver is there than the sincere deceiver, the man who hesitates between two forms of deception – deception of himself and deception of others? How could that storm-tossed de Gaulle, who, from his helicopter, hesitated between offensive and abandonment, history and his home, action and inaction, not surprise Pompidou and his own son, the French people and the world, the historian and even himself?

A victory? Yes. But it was a disturbed, bitter and shared victory. This is what the judicious Guichard has to say: "It was certainly the General who had been at the heart of those chain reactions. But, by abandoning the direction of operations on 11 May to Georges Pompidou, by choosing the wrong subject and language on 24 May in his address on the referendum, by accepting the elections of 30 May, he was preparing the secret files of a trial to which he would constantly subject himself."[71] De Gaulle was no longer quite himself. From now on, there were intercessors, advisers between his dream and himself.

CHAPTER THIRTY-EIGHT

The Three Hundred Days

On 7 June 1968, General Massu was received by Georges Pompidou at the Hôtel Matignon: "You and I have saved the Republic," the Prime Minister said. "I could have held out, but I needed a president. You sent him back to me."[1]

Did the remark ever come to de Gaulle's attention? In any case, he could hardly have been unaware of the new climate around him. For many, the Elysée was no longer anything more than a temporary mausoleum. In one month, the engine-room had crossed the Seine: it was now with Pompidou at Matignon.

The overriding aim of those three hundred days, from Georges Pompidou's electoral triumph to the April referendum, was a return to normal life. How was this done? Through television. On 7 June, de Gaulle reappeared on the screen, looking a little thinner, but lively and determined, less brilliant, less forthright, but, on the whole, himself. That, at least, was the opinion of the general public. He could not avoid explaining the strange episode of Baden-Baden: "Yes, on 29 May I was tempted to resign. And then, at the same time, I thought that if I left, the threat of subversion would spread and destroy the Republic. Then, once more, I made up my mind. On 30 May, having told the country what I had to say, I realized that my appeal had given the signal for salvation."

Let there be no mistake: de Gaulle did not come back to be the symbolic object "sent back" by Massu to Pompidou. He had his own ideas, his own plans, which, once again, he outlined. With great vigour, he advocated participation: "We must walk resolutely in that direction; we must. For my part, I am determined that we shall."[2] He knew that his Prime Minister was opposed to it. And the first gesture that he made, to mark his "restoration", was, in this sense, a snub to Pompidou. Circumstances required a cabinet reshuffle: those who had suffered most from the May events, and they were in the first rank – Fouchet, Joxe, Peyrefitte, Gorse, Missoffe – had to be removed. The General then took advantage of the situation not only to give the Finance Ministry to Maurice Couve de Murville, who switched jobs with Debré, but above all to impose on his Prime Minister, as Garde des Sceaux, the minister who sat on his right, the man whose presence might be most disagreeable to him, and who was the most noted champion of social participation, René Capitant.

The last outbursts of the student revolt, which had spread to certain groups of workers, caused four deaths, on 10 and 11 June: two workers at Sochaux, a *lycéen* at Flins and a policeman at Lyon, which, after the event, proved that Christian Fouchet,* the Interior Minister in May, had been right to be prudent. They gave

---

*Replaced on 31 May by Raymond Marcellin.

the government the opportunity of reacting harshly to a new "night of the barricades", on 12 June, which was to be followed by the evacuation of the Sorbonne and Odéon so urgently demanded by de Gaulle on 19 May. Those operations coincided with the freeing of the OAS leaders, Raoul Salan, Antoine Argoud, among others, and the return to France of Georges Bidault.

The main aim of Pompidou's government was to make sure that the elections, planned for 23 and 30 June, would give them a good majority. Before the first round, General de Gaulle – who, as we know, prided himself on "having nothing to do with anything electoral" – confined himself to a sentence calling on "the French people to unite in their vote around the Republic's President". But, on the day before the second round, he committed himself more fully: on 29 June, he made a television broadcast, asking electors to demonstrate their "massive determination" by giving parliament "a strong, constant and coherent majority" in order to implement "the necessary policies. That is the way that we must follow and that my vocation and mandate command me to show you." On the following day, the "strong, constant and coherent majority" that he had asked the French to give him did in fact emerge: 360 seats out of 485. (The *Fédération de la gauche*, the centre-left alliance, lost half its seats, as did the Communist Party and Jean Lecanuet's centre group. Pierre Mendès France very nearly lost his seat at Grenoble.)

Did this amount to a plebiscite for the founder of the Fifth Republic? That was precisely how de Gaulle saw things himself. During his decisive meeting with Georges Pompidou, who, between 2.30 and 3 p.m. on 30 May, had persuaded him to abandon a referendum in favour of elections, the Prime Minister had used this argument: "If the referendum is lost, then you are the victim. In the case of elections, I am." "And what if we win the elections?" de Gaulle replied.

The General gave an ambiguous welcome to the electoral fireworks of June. "They were the elections of frightened men!" he is supposed to have remarked. One good, long-standing Gaullist remarked: "There was one happy man: Georges Pompidou. And there was one unhappy man: Charles de Gaulle." In any case, the Prime Minister informed the head of State of his desire to resign. The General's response was an invitation to dinner. It is said that, during the meal, de Gaulle turned to Mme Pompidou and remarked: "It appears that your husband and I won the elections." In his *Pour rétablir une vérité* Pompidou rejects the remark as mere "gossip" and adds that their host remarked to his wife, in a quite different tone: "Madame, I can tell you that your husband held firm."

The problem concerns both the content of the debate and the individuals involved. It concerns the personal relations between President and Prime Minister, the hierarchy set up between them by the Constitution and by practice, by history, too, and by what might be called the historical mystique of Gaullism. De Gaulle hated mixtures of this kind. He himself possessed legitimacy. So when, in the case of Pompidou, he began to see not only a wish to carry out the power entrusted to him by another, but the birth of an "authority", he began to reflect. The nature of the relationship was changing.

Furthermore, the stature of the Prime Minister was beginning to obscure that of the head of State. That was bad enough in itself. But was the increased value accorded to Pompidou well founded? De Gaulle weighed things up. The Prime Minister who took control of the situation on 12 May did, of course, demonstrate courage, imagination, skill and coolness of nerve that all those who worked with him at the time have acknowledged. De Gaulle himself was the first to do so.

But was not a man to whom he had delegated full powers for six years not responsible when catastrophe occurred? Did not the man of order that he had chosen prove to be above all a man of concessions? On several occasions, during this period, the General was heard to remark severely, and with an air of surprise, that *it was thought that they had to reopen* the Sorbonne on 11 May and that it was thought that they had to accept the unions' demands on 26 May. Unfair? Ungrateful? Sovereigns tend to be both.

So much for the past. Now there was the future. There was a divergence, which some believed to be fundamental, on the question of participation. The head of State put the question to the Prime Minister, who recounts the conversation thus:

"Pompidou, are you determined to introduce, with me, participation?"

"*Mon Général*, I could only answer you if I knew what participation was. If Capitant is to be believed, it amounts to Sovietization, the setting up of rule by assembly in every enterprise. If that is what it is, then I am not for it."

"But that's not it at all. Capitant is mad. It involves associating the workers in the activity of the enterprises, giving them information about that activity. We'll talk about it again."

We went into the Council meeting and were never to speak about it again.[3]

On 1 July, Pompidou went to the Elysée to report on the election results. He made no attempt to conceal his pleasure. But when the General asked him: "Have you come to any conclusion about your intentions?", he confirmed that he did, indeed, intend to step down. The General seemed annoyed, but did not make any attempt to dissuade him: it was not his style. However, de Gaulle did give the impression to various colleagues that he wanted to keep the Prime Minister in his job. "Several times he returned to the attack to keep him," says Xavier de la Chevalerie, his *directeur de cabinet*, adding, "We told him: '*Mon Général*, he is tired.' 'Tired? Then let him take a weekend off!'"[4]

That afternoon, Pompidou assembled the victorious army of three hundred UDR deputies at the Hôtel du Palais d'Orsay. What he said there seemed, to some, to express reservations. He urged them "to organize the majority in such a way as to make it the government's valid interlocutor". What did that mean? Why was the head of the executive trying to promote the interests of the legislature? Was he presenting himself as the leader of the parliamentary majority? Did he envisage a transfer of responsibilities?

It would not seem that the General welcomed this initiative. So, two days later, at a meeting of the Council of Ministers, he counter-attacked, not on the form, but on the content. After praising the French people for the trust that they had placed in the regime and in its institutions, de Gaulle greeted "the great movement that is carrying the country towards participation". This was to give the elections that had been forced upon him by Pompidou the significance of the referendum that he had himself planned.

Whereupon Pompidou tried once again to convince Bernard Tricot of the sincerity of his offers of resignation. The Secretary-General at the Elysée has not forgotten either the attitude or the words of the Prime Minister: "I've had enough! The very idea of reforming a government, consulting, asking this man, dropping that one. I can't face all that again! The General must realize that I'm tired." Georges Pompidou added: "One day I shall be called upon to succeed the General. There must be a break between the two. I must remove myself, so that people will want me all the more when the time comes."[5]

"Friday 5 July was for me a very trying day," Georges Pompidou recounts. "Various people came, one after the other, begging me to stay on... My departure was 'unthinkable'. It was a betrayal. Nevertheless, I held firm."[6]

That evening, Pompidou received a visit from Couve de Murville, who, having just left the General, told him that his resignation had been accepted, but that his successor had not yet been chosen.

When he got back to his home, on the Quai de Béthune, Pompidou had to face the pressure of his family, which had hitherto kept out of his political life, but which had suddenly come together to beg him to alter his decision. He seemed to be hearing the same thing on all sides and many of those who were involved have reported that his departure was seen as "an act of cowardice" and a gesture "against the country's interests".

Georges Pompidou had a sleepness night. On Saturday morning, 6 July, he decided to ring Tricot to inform him that, all things considered, he was "resigned to going on". He sensed that Tricot was "embarrassed". They would ring him back.

He invited Pierre Lazareff, editor of *France-Soir* and a friend of everybody, to lunch. His guest arrived at Matignon very early. His eyes twinkling behind his thick spectacles, Lazareff had the look of the pressman who is making history before telling it: "Well, what are you going to do when you are no longer here?" Pompidou went pale: "What? What have they told you?" The journalist did not have time to explain. Tricot was on the telephone: "When I told the General about your call, he cried out: 'That's really too stupid. He's too late: I've just offered the post to M. Couve de Murville.'"

Georges Pompidou said that he felt "wounded" by the fact that the General had not been as "frank" with him as he had been with the General. He blamed his own "extreme naïvety" for not perceiving "Couve's profound ambition".[7] Yet, three times in a week he had begged the General to let him go. If de Gaulle had made up his mind beforehand, then he and Pompidou were in agreement. Had Couve also known for long that he was likely to be the next Prime Minister? Maurice Couve de Murville denies this firmly. "Never, before Friday 6 July at 10 p.m., had the General offered me Matignon. Neither in 1965, nor in 1967, nor during the trip to Romania in 1968. I heard rumours, suppositions. But I was never made a precise offer."[8]

De Gaulle was too much of a French writer not to have a taste for antithesis. Six years before he had replaced the nervous Michel Debré with Georges Pompidou. And now he was replacing that peasant from the Auvergne, who, in Paris, had consorted with the artistic avant-garde – abstract in painting, concrete in music –

and whom the demands of power were gradually leading back to the Catholic Church, with a tall, thin Protestant who seemed to have come straight out of a story by the young, puritanical Gide. The deep, earthy tones of the deputy for the Cantal would give way to the ethereal, smooth, impalpable voice of a reader of Victorian novels.

The new Prime Minister had been able, during his five weeks at the Finance Ministry, to realize that the damage done by the events of May was not merely superficial. In 1985 he told me:

> One can have no idea today of the demoralized state into which the May events had thrown business circles, now terrified by the wage increases. Neither the resurgence of 30 May nor even the elections had brought a decisive recovery. There were still strikes. Confidence remained very muted, the wounds deep. We were dealing with an economy in a state of shock. Only a policy of very liberal credit could bring it back to life. Fortunately, the abolition of the last of the European customs barriers, which came in according to the rules of the Common Market, on 1 July, did not have any serious effect. Up to the last moment, we did wonder. Given the crisis from which we had emerged, would it not be better to ask our partners for a postponement? The General decided the matter: "Let's get on with it!" It all passed off very well.[9]

In the search for new resources, Couve and his Finance Minister, Ortoli, who had been very close to Pompidou, were not content to raise the income taxes of two million citizens: they decided to adopt a measure that had long been considered and always rejected, given its unpopularity: a huge increase in inheritance tax, which, when proposed on 2 October, came up against strong resistance from the Assembly three weeks later.

In that summer of 1968 the major issue, however, was university reform. It had been the students who had put the match to the explosive that had very nearly toppled the regime. The regime would ensure its survival, or at least its rebirth, only by giving a bold, overall solution to the problems of education.

To set this counter-fire going, de Gaulle chose an ingenious pyrotechnician: Edgar Faure. A former President of the Council, the excellent negotiator of recognition of People's China, and Agriculture Minister, he had become one of the sages of the regime when the General called him to square the university circle. With François Furet as one of his principal advisers, the new minister based his reforms on three themes that were nothing short of revolutionary in the France of that time: autonomy, interdisciplinarity and participation. Faure had to face shouts of "Anarchy!" and "Soviets!" when, from 3 to 10 October, before the National Assembly, he defended his *loi d'orientation*, which was passed (by 441 votes for and 39 abstentions, including Christian Fouchet, who had been minister from 1963 to 1967).

The most curious thing about this whole affair was the attitude of de Gaulle himself. During a press conference held at the Elysée on 9 September, the head of State, who had for so long been a conservative in this area, became the advocate of

Edgar Faure's reforms, which, he said, ought to be "deep" and "involve and grant many things at once".[10] Why? Because Faure's law was the first application of the principle of participation. The reshaping of the universities could not be carried out, he now said, unless "masters and students are both directly concerned" and their representatives are "appointed by all".

The attempt at economic revival initiated by Maurice Couve de Murville was based on the idea of an "accompaniment of expansion", which was expressed in a bold credit policy. Although, on 29 June, de Gaulle had clearly demonstrated his usual inclination to rigour, in order "to prevent price rises, inflation, the fall of the value of the franc", it was a strategy of forward flight that was adopted under pressure from the business and professional organizations, in order to keep, they said, the promises made at Grenelle and to prevent a situation in which there would be "one million unemployed in October". Hence a policy of intensive expansion, which led to a dangerous monetary expansion. To the set of measures that the Prime Minister had undertaken, "creating both a threat and the means of escaping it",[11] was suddenly added the rumour of an imminent revaluation of the mark, clearly a danger to the value of the franc. Capital poured out of the country in ever greater quantity. So November 1968, which put the French exchange rate on the rack, turned out to be the monetary equivalent of May.

On 13 November, General de Gaulle declared that "the devaluation of the franc would be the worst absurdity". This remark, which was not made to be reported, provoked, in isolation, further fears and therefore speculation on the currency market: it was enough to say that a devaluation would not take place for speculators to imagine at once that it was imminent.

General de Gaulle was not, in principle, hostile to any devaluation. The recovery plan of 1958 involved a very bold one. In early June 1968 he had brought up the idea with his financial adviser, Alain Prate, regarding it as possible on condition that it was linked with an overall revision of monetary parities. But, in late November, the operation looked so much like the death-throes of the franc – and therefore, for him, of France – that he thought it useful to have a final consultation on the matter. "Everyone is playing with inflation," he remarked to his colleagues.[12] Yet five men were to support him in his determination to oppose devaluation: two ministers, Jeanneney and Faure; two senior civil servants, Goetze and Barre; and Alain Prate.

So when the General entered the meeting, at 3 p.m. on 23 November, he was well armed. But which of the ministers believed that the operation was unavoidable? For the past two or three days, the Prime Minister and Ortoli had made it quite clear that pressure from abroad was too strong, that there was no way out.

The time came for each of the ministers to express his opinion. Jeanneney opened with a strong attack on devaluation. Ministers looked at one another. Malraux, of course, was for resistance. Edgar Faure added further arguments. Then Michel Debré spoke, followed by Maurice Schumann, and Michelet. Couve, after seeing the General, had encouraged Jeanneney to be firm: there was nothing more to be done than to draw the conclusions from what had turned into a mass uprising.

General de Gaulle also took the precaution of consulting Raymond Barre, then a member of the European Commission in Brussels, before issuing at 7.45 p.m. a statement that was to amaze public opinion, speculators and the world: "The President of the Republic announces that, following a meeting of the Council of Ministers on 23 November, the following decision was arrived at: the parity of the franc will be maintained."

Next day, at the Elysée, de Gaulle recorded a broadcast. Declaring that the monetary crisis that France was going through was a consequence of the "upheavals" of May and of "people who try to put their own interests before the public interest... There is a price to be paid for odious speculation on the national currency", he said that until the world established "an impartial and reasonable monetary system", he and the government had decided that "we must complete our recovery without recourse to devaluation". As a result, from 26 November, draconian measures were taken at such a pace that they looked like a genuine plan for recovery. Cut after cut was made in public spending. The most symbolic concerned the French nuclear tests in the Pacific.

It was then noted that, in the revised budget, military expenditure had been exceeded for the first time by that for education, the first having declined over ten years from 28 to 17 per cent,* the second rising from 12.5 to 19.9 per cent. A few years before, de Gaulle had remarked to his Armed Forces and Education Ministers that he would consider that they were on the right path when the budget for the second exceeded that for the first. That was now the case.

And what of "participation"? De Gaulle defined it in a press conference on 9 September thus: "In an enterprise, participation must take three distinct forms. For those who work in it, it must first involve direct material advantages in the results obtained, secondly it must mean that they are kept informed of developments in the enterprise on which their fate depends and, lastly, it means their ability to have their practical proposals taken into account."[13]

De Gaulle went on to state that a sketch for what he had in mind already existed: the "enterprise committees" set up under his government in 1945. "Contacts are already being made," de Gaulle added. But, "they don't affect most workers a great deal and yet it is in this area that we must make progress today". Then came the verdict that terrified the employers:

> We must do something like what is done for shareholders who commit their money to an enterprise. The management should receive and welcome periodically proposals from those who contribute their labour. Representatives of each category of the workforce should be elected by its members by secret ballot from freely proposed candidates. The implementation of the laws covering these measures will be supervised by legal procedure, in which, of course, the Factory Inspectorate will have a role to play.[14]

Opposition to such plans began to be organized. Did it take the form of a massive flight of capital? We must refrain from blaming the monetary collapse of November on an organized response from the employers to the "revolutionary" plans of the old gentleman in the Elysée.

---

*Enormous as it is, the cost of nuclear weapons is less than that of conventional ones.

In November, in the midst of the *grande peur du franc*, *Le Monde* published a letter from Paul Huvelin, President of the CNPF, the French employers' confederation, who had negotiated the Grenelle agreements: it referred to "the serious concerns that the plans for participation have given rise to. They look like a threat to the life and development of enterprise. It is perfectly understandable that such a threat should have a direct effect on savers."[15] Was Louis Vallon wrong to see this as "a declaration of war by the CNPF on de Gaulle"?[16]

We are now faced with one of the mysteries of Charles de Gaulle's career. Three months after the press conference, during which he had at last given a clear definition of the participation on which the French people were to be consulted by referendum, it was suddenly no longer a question of the reshaping of relations between capital and labour, but of a transformation of the Senate and of regional development.

On 9 September, de Gaulle presented to France a project aimed at attenuating, if not abolishing, the class struggle by involving workers in the management of enterprises. On 10 December, his minister Jean-Marcel Jeanneney, the last man capable of betraying his projects, spoke only of institutional revisions,* important revisions, of course, but very far from the kind of social revolution that participation seemed to represent for de Gaulle.

The best explanation of why the marginal regions-Senate theme was substituted in the referendum for the fundamental one of social participation is provided by Jeanneney himself. On so serious a subject, affecting the nature and structure of the French economy, the government would only be in a position to propose a sufficiently detailed text to the citizens after several months, at a date in any case when the General wanted to clarify his relations with the French people.[17]

This explanation is probably the right one. It is not convincing for all that. In the cases of the Constitution in 1958 or Algeria in 1962, de Gaulle had ordered his colleagues to work and, in a few weeks, texts appeared that any reasonable person would have expected after several months. Then, to the "Jeanneney argument", we must add this one, suggested by Bernard Tricot: in the end, the General had come round to the view that the enterprise was not an area in which the State would effectively intervene.[18]

He had had to abandon any idea of holding the referendum between 24 and 30 May, but it was still at the forefront of his mind. "In July I had tried to put him off the idea," Maurice Couve de Murville recounts. "I pointed out to him that it would be quite useless and risky. Had he not won a triumphant victory at the elections? Was not our majority of unprecedented solidity? Why throw himself into that adventure? It was no use."[19] A de Gaulle who had acted in a masterly fashion in the affair of non-devaluation was to risk his prestige in a marginal affair in which, for no apparent purpose, he would antagonize an important sector of national opinion.

On 25 December 1968, at Beirut airport, an Israeli commando unit destroyed, without casualties, Lebanon's commercial air fleet. It was, according to Jerusalem, an act of reprisal: an attack had been perpetrated in Athens on an El-Al plane by

---

*Which were also announced at the press conference of 9 September.

Palestinians based in Lebanon. Without consulting any of his ministers, de Gaulle decreed an embargo on all weapons destined for Israel. In this way he demonstrated France's solidarity with the country of which she had always striven to be the protector. What interests us here is the embargo's impact on relations between the head of State and the nation. Few of General de Gaulle's gestures were ever so unpopular. Few of them, in any case, had so seriously shaken the confidence that the French people had placed in him to represent the country in a worthy manner in international society.

Why punish the Beirut intervention when one does no more than regret the infinitely more scandalous one in Prague? Of course, France had less capacity to respond to the USSR than it had to respond to Israel, but gestures do have an effect. Furthermore, de Gaulle's gesture was accompanied by an unpleasant commentary: he denounced Israeli influences in "the information media".

In this affair and the semi-silence over Prague one finds the vices of a system based on the over-concentration of power and the over-exclusive domination of certain areas of decision-making in the hands of one man. Because he was committing France as a whole on a terrain and by means that he alone chose, the Sovereign was putting into question both his own country and what it stood for. He was embarking on dangerous ground, not only as a diplomat, but as the embodiment of a country. In this matter, one finds in de Gaulle something like a lack of a sense of proportion. Just as in the issue of participation, he seemed to confuse end and means, project and procedure.

In early October, on a public rubbish dump at Elancourt, in the Yvelines, was found the corpse of Stefan Markovitch, a former friend and bodyguard of Alain Delon. A few days later, at a cocktail party, Michel Jobert recounts, "two newsmen were whispering: 'It's the Pompidous who're going to cop it!'"[20] The rumour went the rounds. A prisoner in Fresnes gaol called Akow told the examining magistrate that he had taken part a few years before in evenings in which "the wife of the Prime Minister" had mingled with Delon's entourage.

One evening when, as usual, he was chatting with his colleagues, Georges Pompidou called one of them over: "Tell me, Javel, you who know everything that's going on, who is that important politician who, according to the press, is mixed up with the Markovitch affair?" Thus began, in stupefaction, Michel Jobert goes on, "the cruel trial of a man and a family".[21]

Georges Pompidou has himself recounted, with concentrated fury, how the Elysée, Matignon, and the Justice and Interior Ministries had left him in ignorance of the information that was at the government's disposal. Apparently, René Capitant had alerted Raymond Marcellin, the Interior Minister, who had himself warned Couve and Tricot. With a file under his arm, the Secretary-General at the Elysée rushed off, on 1 November, to Colombey, where the General was spending the All Saints' holiday.

On Monday 4 November, at the Elysée, de Gaulle called in as a matter of urgency Couve, Capitant and Marcellin: they decided to do nothing to obstruct the course of the police investigation, a step that would have harmed M. Pompidou as well as the proper running of the State. But did he really declare, at the end of that meeting, "We must wait"? Michel Jobert assures us that he did.[22]

Nevertheless, General de Gaulle did instruct the Prime Minister to warn his predecessor. But, forty-eight hours later, Pompidou had received no other messenger than the prefect, Pierre Somveille, who had been his direct colleague and had become Marcellin's *directeur de cabinet*. Matignon's "discretion" and the Elysée's apparent neutrality, which had exposed him and his wife to the mercy of a police investigation, left Georges Pompidou with a profound sense of bitterness that was to deepen the gulf between the General and himself, not to mention all those – he cites some of them in his book and, according to Michel Jobert,[23] kept a list of them on his person to his death – who, near or far, police, magistrates, politicians, journalists, had lent a hand to that sinister campaign. Pompidou gave his own version of the two discreet meetings that, at his request, he had with General de Gaulle on the Markovitch affair. The first may be summed up in this protest:

> "*Mon Général*, I have three things to say: I know my wife sufficiently well to know that it is unthinkable that she could be mixed up in any way whatsoever in this affair. Perhaps they will try to let me know what's going on. They won't find me involved in it. I can't say as much for all your ministers. Neither at M. Capitant's establishment at the Place Vendôme, nor at M. Couve de Murville's at Matignon has there been the slightest reaction of a man of honour." The General listened to me, looked at me and did not seem to react very much: "But I never believed in all that. I gave instructions that you should be warned." Without exaggerating, I can say that, as I left him, the General did not seem very pleased with himself.[24]

At the second meeting, Georges Pompidou had asked Bernard Tricot to be present to witness facts revealed by the counter-investigation that he had had carried out.

> The General listened to me stupefied. In my presence, he asked Tricot to summon Capitant. I know that the meeting took place and that Capitant, for good or ill, invited the public prosecutor to direct the investigation to the search for the murderers, which was, one has to admit, their primary duty. As I left him, the General advised me to treat gossip with the contempt that it deserved, adding that calumny was the fate of statesmen. I replied that I would have taken the same line if the affair had concerned me alone, but, since it involved my wife, anger could not but take precedence over contempt.[25]

On 3 January 1969, Pompidou wrote a letter to de Gaulle: he spoke of his "contempt" for the attacks directed at him by such men as Roger Stéphane and Maurice Clavel and denounced the "shameful" attitude of certain ministers in the Markovitch affair.

Charles de Gaulle's response was immediate and warm. Having expressed for his former Prime Minister "and for Mme Pompidou" wishes for the new year that "are, to the highest degree, those of esteem and friendship" he went on: "What you tell me concerning your state of mind cannot leave me unmoved. But it is my heartfelt wish that you should not allow yourself to be affected by the gossip, however grotesque and infamous it may be, that is being directed against you. On a certain plane, nothing matters but what is essential, that is to say, what one has done and what one is aware of being."[26]

On 9 January, Pompidou was received at the Elysée – this time, very officially. De Gaulle told him, in such a way that it was heard by others, that he advised him to travel, to assert himself, to take stock of himself. What the General wanted to show by this was that there had never been a Markovitch affair. De Gaulle's behaviour meant that the "destiny" of the deputy for Cantal had, for him at least, in no way been affected by that sordid incident.

Travel? He went to Rome, where the General advised his former Prime Minister to meet Amintore Fanfani, "the man of the future". He did call on him, between a couple of museum visits and an audience at the Vatican. On 17 January, the third day of his Rome trip, Georges Pompidou received in a room of his hotel French journalists working in Rome. There was a representative of the Agence France-Presse, the *Combat* correspondent, Jacques Chapus, who was covering the Pompidou trip for Radio Luxembourg, and four of their colleagues. The inevitable question was asked: "Would you, if the opportunity arose, be a candidate for the presidency of the Republic?" "The question does not, for the moment, arise," Pompidou replied. "But if de Gaulle retired, it goes without saying that I would be a candidate."

In his account of the episode, Pompidou remarks that his words aroused no reaction on the part of the journalists who heard them. The chief of the AFP office in Rome, Robert Mengin,* reacted differently. He wrote a rather sensational despatch that turned Pompidou's apparently quite ordinary words into a declaration of candidacy. The next day the Paris press followed suit. It was an explosion.

We know what de Gaulle's first reaction was in the account given by his ADC, Jean d'Escrienne. He had no sooner placed the copy of *France-Soir* recounting Pompidou's words in Rome on the General's desk, than he was summoned: "What do you think of it?" The officer replied that, since Pompidou had been received only a few days earlier at the Elysée, people might think that the declaration had been made with the General's agreement.

"Not at all! So I now have to publish a statement setting things straight."

"M. Pompidou should not have trusted journalists."

"Don't you believe it. He knows journalists very well and he's too clever to be taken by surprise."

Two days later, d'Escrienne returned to the matter. He tried to argue that what Pompidou had said in Rome referred to a candidature that the head of State had himself accredited:

That's true... But there's a right and a wrong way of presenting things! It would have been quite different, don't you see, if, for example, he had said to the journalists, with sadness or resignation: "You know perfectly well, when,

*Who, ever since London, had hated de Gaulle.

by some misfortune or other, the General goes, I shall try to do my best, if I happen to find myself at the head of the State!" But that's not at all what he said, or probably what he thinks![27]

Three days later, after a meeting of the Council of Ministers, the General handed Joël Le Theule, the new Information Minister, a statement that sounded like a rifle-shot: "In the fulfilment of the national task incumbent upon me, I was, on 19 December 1965, re-elected President of the Republic for seven years. I have a duty to carry out my mandate to the end of that term and intend to do so."

If Pompidou wanted to create an event, he had succeeded. He did so again. Three weeks later, when the Markovitch affair came back into the headlines, the deputy for Cantal happened to be in Geneva. Asked for an interview by Swiss television, he accepted.

> I was asked, "How do you see your political future?" Instinctively, but this time consciously, to show that, if the succession were not a matter for the present, I should not regard myself as thrown into outer darkness by the General's thunderbolt, I replied: "I have no political future in the sense that you understand it. I shall have, perhaps, and God willing, a national destiny."

This time the heretic had relapsed. He persevered all the more diabolically in that, with that phrase "national destiny", borrowed from Malraux, he was paraphrasing a man whom de Gaulle could not reject. As Pompidou wrote in his book: "'When you say such things, you might warn us,' Jobert said to me, smiling, on my return."[28] From now on Pompidou had swapped the role of dauphin for that of pretender.

General de Gaulle was so aware of this that, when he invited the Pompidous to dinner at the Elysée (with the Debrés) on 12 March, it was obviously not to attempt a *rapprochement*. It was intended simply as the payment of a debt of honour. Faced with public opinion, he owed that man a gesture. But what a fiasco! The dinner, writes the former Prime Minister, was "gloomy". Did he fear an outburst on the part of his wife, who, not having "forgiven" the General for his trip to Baden, cared even less for his reserve over the past three months! "We left early," Pompidou concludes. "The bonds of friendship had not been retied."[29]

And so the time for the referendum came round. De Gaulle had wanted it to be like a new coronation. One could not speak so frequently of retirement or abandonment, one could not make the strange detour to Baden, without feeling deep scars, wide splits in the façade of his legitimacy. And what of those shouts of "Ten years, it's enough!", those crowds of young people giggling when the old man spoke?

On 2 January 1969, de Gaulle received a small number of journalists. At first they talked about literature. Then they got on to the political prospects. What were his plans for the referendum? It would concern, he told them, participation in enterprises and the reform of the Senate. And when would it take place? "I am awaiting the government's proposals. But it must take place some time this year."[30]

So de Gaulle had already abandoned his original plan. For ever since the

General had declared at Lyon, in March 1968, that "it is the activities of the regions that appear to be the mainsprings of the power of tomorrow", the operation had certainly seemed to be directed towards a regionalization that would itself involve a revision of the Senate.

Was the referendum really inevitable? Had the General made it a question of principle? By about mid-January, the theme of participation in enterprises had been abandoned. It appeared that the theme of the consultation would be a double one: the regions and the Senate. The first was popular enough. The second, was, from the outset, received with widespread disapproval.

When they realized that the General was not going to give up his plan for a referendum, many of his friends and faithful supporters set about trying to persuade him to postpone the consultation until later, or to separate the two questions that he planned to put to the electors. During a meeting of the Council of Ministers, in late January, Jean de Lipkowski bravely took up position against the plan. Sensing that the head of State was immovable, he tried to manoeuvre him: since the two themes, which are more or less dissociable, enjoyed such different degrees of support, why not separate the consultation into two questions? The first, at least, would get a majority.

In that gloomy atmosphere, de Gaulle groped his way towards that lost battle. It was almost as if his stubborn determination were sucking him inevitably to the heart of a whirlpool. The first step on the road of no return took place at Quimper, on 2 February. De Gaulle had just travelled through a discontented Brittany. That sacred land of historic Gaullism had given him a stormy, almost tempestuous reception at Rennes and Brest. There were shouts of "Nous sommes tous des Québecois!" and when he arrived at Brest, on 1 February, the *Internationale* drowned out the *Marseillaise*, while someone spat on the lapel of his coat. President de Gaulle's last journey through France was to be the bitterest.

Yet, at Quimper, the atmosphere was better. It was even warm. The local deputy, Edmond Michelet, had done everything possible for the visitor to be welcomed and listened to with deference. Michelet, like almost all the General's colleagues, had tried hard, if not to dissuade him from his plans to announce the date of the referendum, at least to persuade him to postpone them. On that day, de Gaulle only agreed not to specify the date. The referendum would take place, he said, "in the spring". It was his last public speech. Guichard recounts:

I was at the foot of the platform from which the General spoke. I was facing the crowd and I couldn't see him speaking over me. But I heard the ritual chant, interspersed with obvious truths, historical references, a few verses in Breton, a few decisions taken for dividing up the territory, and then that paragraph on the forthcoming reforms, to which that usually faithful people did not respond. And when the General concluded: "Finally, since we are opening up the way to a new hope, we shall do it in the spring" – yes, I felt sick at heart.[31]

Two weeks later, on 17 February, Charles de Gaulle summoned Roger Frey, one of the most "political" of his long-time followers. A former Secretary-

General of the UNR, six years Interior Minister, now entrusted with responsibility for relations with parliament, he was an expert on electoral matters. The other two "sages" in this domain, Foccart and Guichard, had already been sounded out by the General and their reservations were known. The first was involved in African affairs, the second with preparations for regionalization. Frey was more available.

"This referendum, can we win it?" the General asked.

"I don't think so, *mon Général*."

"Then can we postpone it?"

"Give me time to think about it."

"No. I must have your opinion at once, the opinion dictated by your Gaullist instinct and your national responsibilities."

"Give me a few minutes."

De Gaulle acquiesced and picked up a newspaper.

How could Roger Frey assume responsibility for sending the great man to certain defeat? The important thing was the image. There must be no turning back therefore: "*Mon Général*, I don't think we can postpone it. Your reputation as a democrat is at stake."[32]

Two days later, the Council of Ministers accepted the fateful date: 27 April. But the atmosphere surrounding that decision, the looks exchanged and the sighs emitted suddenly made the General doubt the correctness of the decision. The Prime Minister was not alone in warning him. Michel Debré and Raymond Marcellin each made a final attempt. Debré thought he had won. Had not the General sighed: "It will be said that de Gaulle is retreating! Well, is it so shameful to withdraw?"[33]

A trace of these hesitations is to be found in an article published in *La Nation*, an organ of the UDR, which had been cleared with the Elysée: "De Gaulle would in no way feel that his general policies were not supported if the majority of the electors answered 'no' or abstained." And the next day, M. Jeanneney went further: "It's a political question, but it is not a fundamental one for the regime."

As each day and each hour passed the "shame" of withdrawal increased. Colleague after colleague urged him to play for time, only to be met by a passionate plea in favour of the absolute necessity for a referendum in April. This, for instance, is what he said to Maurice Schumann, in late March:

It's quite impossible to go back on the referendum. I have found no way out. Indeed, have I really looked for one? So let's get on with it. There is a choice: either the French want reforms and they will give us a majority. In which case, having set in motion, thanks to the regional policy, the vital forces of the country, we shall base the referendum on participation, which would change French society in depth. Or the French don't want me any more, or the reforms. In which case I shall show that I am not the preserver of ancient privileges, the protector of those who are afraid. I shall go.[34]

That eminent decoder of Gaullian puzzles, André Malraux, formulated the idea of the referendum as suicide. In *Les Chênes qu'on abat*, he tells de Gaulle that the theme of the referendum has been chosen because it is "absurd". This does not at all mean that it was a suicide option, but that, since the aim was to demonstrate the alliance between de Gaulle and France, the demonstration would be all the more brilliant the more the pretext chosen was arid or silly. It is not very difficult to get people to say "yes" to de Gaulle if he is asking you to declare your attachment to liberty, or to abundance, or even to grandeur! But to acquiesce in that enormous thirty-page questionnaire that raises at least two quite distinct problems, that really would be a proof of love!

It is true that during those years several of those close to de Gaulle had heard him express the wish – expressed very discreetly – that there was someone who could warn him when the moment came when he was no longer in possession of all his faculties, obsessed as he was by the precedents of Pétain and Churchill, ending a triumphal life in a pathetic state of physical and mental decline. This is what his aide-de-camp, Jean d'Escrienne, writes:

It was at the Elysée. The General was then seventy-eight. At the end of the day, I went into his office. He was still sitting at his desk, holding in front of him a sheet of writing paper. As I was going up to him to salute him, he showed me the piece of paper, without handing it to me. I saw only a list of names, with a few figures against each one. Then he said: "Did you know that Sophocles wrote *Oedipus at Colonus* when he was ninety? At over eighty, Michelangelo was still doing admirable work in the Sistine Chapel and on the building of the dome of St Peter's. Titian was painting *The Battle of Lepanto* at ninety-five and the *Descent from the Cross* at ninety-seven. Goethe was finishing Part II of his *Faust*, which is quite the equal of his earlier works, at eighty-three. At eighty-two, Victor Hugo wrote *Torquemada* and, at eighty-three, the second *Légende des Siècles*! Then there was Voltaire and today we have Mauriac!"[35]

One cannot, of course, base a rule of life on an anecdote of this kind. But it is good to know that, when faced with the rise of that danger, de Gaulle armed himself with such references and examples. If, in 1969, he sought for a way out, it was not so much by sinking into the grave or by retiring, as in the hope of a dazzling finale.

The time had come for the last battle. Did he still have any lingering doubts? On 10 April, seventeen days before the vote, when asked, in front of the television cameras, whether, in present circumstances, the referendum was opportune or whether the head of State was linking his presidential mandate to the fate of the referendum, he replied: "There cannot be the slightest doubt on the matter. The response that the country makes to what I am asking it will obviously affect my decision to continue with my mandate or to depart immediately."

It was four days later, he was to say, that he lost his final illusions – the day when Valéry Giscard d'Estaing let it be known, "with regret, but with certainty", that he would not be able to vote "yes". Most of the specialists estimated that about 10 per cent of the electorate would follow his former Finance Minister: this was more than was needed to swing the majority. And on Sunday 20 April, a week before the vote, de Gaulle, entertaining his children in the private apartment of the Elysée, showed his pessimism quite clearly: "I know this referendum will be lost. I shan't have the votes of the Independents who will follow Giscard."[36]

Three days later, on 23 April, the head of State chaired a meeting of the Council of Ministers. Which of the men there did not have a lump in his throat? After the meeting he confided to one of the younger members of the Council, the Secretary of State, Jean de Lipkowski, who, as we have seen, had tried to dissuade him from his plan: "It's true, the French don't want de Gaulle any more. But the myth, you'll see the myth grow. Thirty years from now!"[37]

A final request was made by a group of Gaullists led by Alexandre Sanguinetti and assembled by Jean Charbonel,[38] to get Pompidou to make a statement that he would not present his candidature in the event of the General's withdrawal. Such a gesture would strengthen the old threat ritually brandished by de Gaulle: "Me or chaos!" If the robust Pompidou were no longer there to turn to, everything might change. But Georges Pompidou refused to be sacrificed.

Is the former Prime Minister to be blamed, then, for General de Gaulle's defeat? A man who has every reason not to be kind to the deputy from Cantal, Maurice Couve de Murville, refrains from attributing the defeat to his predecessor. Valéry Giscard d'Estaing does as much:

> The only, the real reason why the General found himself in a minority, on 27 April 1969, was, as he himself said, that the French people did not want him any more. A page in history had been turned. A certain lassitude had set in, best expressed by the May slogan: "Ten years, it's enough!" The manoeuvrings of various individuals, Giscard's withdrawal of support and the presence of Pompidou as an alternative played a part, but only in a marginal way. General de Gaulle's credit had been exhausted – that was the truth of the matter. One might have regretted it, one might do still, for the sake of France. And nobody more than I did so. But it was something that neither he nor we could do anything about.[39]

There was still that last appeal, scheduled for 8 p.m. on the Friday evening and recorded during the late morning at the Elysée. He read his speech as a good professional, with a steady voice:

> *Françaises, Français*, I have often spoken to you of France, so you know that your answer on Sunday will determine my fate. Whatever the number may be, the ardour and devotion of the army of those who support me and who, in any case, hold the future of the nation in their hands, my present task as head of State will obviously become impossible and I shall cease immediately to carry out my functions.

Pompidou's implacable reaction as he heard him at Lyon, in the company of Joxe, was: "If he had announced in a firm and convinced tone that he was asking the country to renew the confidence that it had placed in him, that he expected to remain in power for some time longer, but would, before the end of his term, organize his succession so as to avoid any crisis, he might have won."[40]

In the lift that brought him back to his apartment, after the recording, the General asked Flohic: "Do you think that will do, as an exit?" He then summoned his press secretary, Pierre-Louis Blanc, in order to insert into his published text a few words that he had forgotten during the recording. Then, taking leave of his colleagues before setting out for Colombey as if it were just any ordinary Friday, he handed Bernard Tricot the text of a statement to be issued on the Sunday evening and a letter for the Prime Minister. Those who were there at the time remember a moment of great tension.[41] On arriving at La Boisserie, about 4.30, General de Gaulle said to the cook: "We're back permanently. This time, Charlotte, it's for good!"[42]

He spent most of Saturday alone. On the Sunday, General and Mme de Gaulle heard mass in the drawing-room at La Boisserie, then went down into the village to vote, under a barrage of photographers. He spent the rest of that day alone too. At 10 p.m., the defeat was confirmed. (In mainland France, the "yes" votes had won a little under 47 per cent, the "no" votes just over 53 per cent.) The General instructed Tricot to issue at midnight the statement that he had given him on the Friday to be issued in the late morning of the following Monday. About 11 p.m., Bernard Tricot handed Maurice Couve de Murville the letter that the head of State had left with him:

> It is from the bottom of my heart that I wish to thank you and to acknowledge the quite outstanding and, in every respect, excellent assistance that you have given me as Prime Minister in the service of our country, after serving for ten years as Minister for Foreign Affairs. Furthermore, all the members of the government, who have, around you, carried responsibility for public affairs, with so much distinction and devotion, may be assured of my profound esteem and my cordial affection.
>
> I would ask you to tell them so.

Finally, on 28 April, at 12.10 a.m., the Agence France-Presse issued the statement by which General de Gaulle wanted to put an end to his public life: "I am ceasing to exercise my functions as President of the Republic. This decision takes effect at noon today."[43] On the Monday afternoon, with Flohic, General de Gaulle was rather less laconic:

> In fact, I'm not displeased that things should end like this. What prospects did I have before me? Difficulties that could only reduce the figure that History has made of me and wear me out without any benefit to France. I offered her a reform, which was crucial for the future, and she rejected it. I was under no illusions as to the outcome of the vote. Think of all those whom I have beaten and who had very good reasons to vote against me, in the full knowledge that in doing so they were acting against France's interests! To begin with, there are the Vichyites, who will never forgive me for being right. Then there's the OAS, the supporters of *Algérie française* – some of whom were not entirely negligible. Then there were all the notables, whom I have kept out of power for so long! But there is a question that goes

beyond my person and that is the question of legitimacy. Since 1940 I have embodied it and that will last until my death. There are quite obviously 47 to 48 per cent of the electorate that is Gaullist through and through. I always had them. As soon as I am no longer there, the question will be whether they stay together. But it is on them, in these circumstances, that a regime and a government must be built. It is possible that my successors will resort to manoeuvrings and reconstitute, with some Pompidou or other, the Fourth Republic without actually saying so.

A few moments later the first and only visitor allowed into La Boisserie, Jacques Vendroux, appeared. De Gaulle's serenity amazed the visitor, who nevertheless heard a few melancholy words on the French, who "when they wake up, will no doubt see that I was right". Learning that Vendroux had resigned from the chairmanship of the Foreign Affairs Committee in the Chamber, de Gaulle dissuaded him from resigning as a deputy.

Charles de Gaulle confided two things to his brother-in-law. First, there was his decision not to leave La Boisserie, to receive nobody apart from his family and two or three immediate colleagues, whom he needed to put his papers in order and to prepare the writing of the next stage of his *Mémoires*. Secondly, he told Jacques Vendroux that he planned to go to Ireland, "where he might find traces of certain of his ancestors", during the ensuing presidential campaign. That very day, Georges Pompidou had announced his candidature: alone (with Louis Vallon) of all the Gaullist deputies, Jacques Vendroux, on leaving La Boisserie, refused to give him his support.

Before Vendroux left, General de Gaulle said to him: "I've nothing more to do with them any more; they are quite foreign to me."[44]

CHAPTER THIRTY-NINE

The Master of La Boisserie

De Gaulle took his leave of a people who had rejected him. He had managed to transform a defeat into a withdrawal, the supreme art of strategy.

In early May 1969, de Gaulle was an unhappy man. He was a man in whom Churchill, in an intuition of genius, had detected at the first glance, in June 1940, "an aptitude for suffering". Eighteen months later, before the stricken body, Yvonne de Gaulle was to say: "He has suffered so much over the past two years." In early May, he said to one of his close colleagues: "I was wounded in May 1968. Now they've finished me off. And now I'm dead."[1]

Did he, despite everything, retain any hope? The detachment of a very professional kind that he had shown since the evening of 27 April, analysing phlegmatically the results of the vote and the motives of the electors, announcing sarcastically the return of the "Fourth", sending a few arrows in the direction of Pompidou, commenting on his "successful exit", congratulating himself on at last having time to finish his *Mémoires*, was obviously no more than an attempt to conceal his terrible disappointment.

His *directeur de cabinet*, Xavier de La Chevalerie, who was one of the first to see him again after he had shut himself up at La Boisserie, found him "wounded to the depths of his soul. May 1968 had shattered him. April 1969 gave him the *coup de grâce*. The pain that he experienced as a result was of the kind that one does not recover from."[2]

Returning from a visit to Colombey, in early July 1969, Maurice Couve de Murville, when asked how he had found General de Gaulle, replied: "I saw a happy man." "Happy?" "Yes, because he is doing what he likes best: writing." Shattered by the verdict of 27 April, Charles de Gaulle had, by the same token, been returned to that profession of writer that history had allowed him to practise only occasionally. The suffering of the sovereign was the happiness of the writer. In eighteen months, a life was thus re-invented and turned back to its source: words. Now familiar with death, he abandoned himself, meanwhile, to the sweet demon of writing.

His great devil of a body held firm. He was nearly seventy-nine. His father and mother had both lived longer. His sister Marie-Agnes, three years his senior, was still active. The figure was getting a little more thickset – an abdominal ptosis was increasing his waist measurement month by month. But he was still firm on his feet, covering three kilometres at one go, in the park, in the forest of Les Dhuits or, especially on Sundays, in the forest of Clairvaux – and before long on the peat bogs of Ireland.

Apart from moments of illness, he slept regularly. He could not bear insomnia –

of the kind that had afflicted him in May 1968, for example. He liked to get up late – he was not very military in this respect. But the most important thing for him now, the great quarrel that he had with his "carcass", the faculties at the disposal of a man to carry out his mission, was the state of his memory. How could he see the decline of that prodigious gift, with which, among others, he had been so plentifully endowed, without feeling struck to the quick?

The attentive and not very tyrannical father ("Not severe, demanding", according to his son) had become a very tender grandfather. Anne de Boissieu and Yves de Gaulle, Philippe's second son, were the ones he usually took with him on walks, together with the dog Rase-Mottes. When told that his grandsons, riding past the police guarding the gates of La Boisserie, let go of their handlebars and raised their arms, shouting, "Je vous ai compris!" he laughed quite uninhibitedly.

It was the sweet life of an old country writer, a regular, almost cloistered life, marked by the chapters that flowed, family visits, walks under the trees, and the bustle of people going about their business. He devoted five or six hours a day to his *Mémoires* and two or three hours to correspondence. He calculated that, in half a century, he had signed 35 000 letters. During those final months, there was no shortage of correspondents, from Lady Churchill to the Comte de Paris, from Franco to Nixon, from Bourguiba to Senghor, from Hassan II to Houari Boumedienne.

Was he a recluse? He himself said that he had "retired" – from affairs and from the world. To the small general staff* that continued to work for him he said once and for all: "I am no longer concerned."

On 29 April Bernard Tricot called on him for the first time since the announcement of his resignation. There were still so many urgent questions to settle. During lunch the discussion touched on, among other things, François Flohic recounts, "the various possibilities as candidates for the presidency".** As he was leaving, the former Secretary-General seemed so overcome that the General noticed and remarked to his ADC: "M. Tricot looked very moved."[3]

On 1 May, he saw Jacques Foccart, whose mission was more political: he had to take to Georges Pompidou the General's answer to the message sent him by the former Prime Minister when announcing his candidacy on 28 April.

> I approve of your candidacy. It would no doubt have been better if you had not announced it several weeks in advance, which lost us certain "yes" votes, will lose you yourself votes and, above all, will do some damage to your public standing, if you are elected. But, in present circumstances, it is entirely natural and appropriate that you should present yourself. I very much hope, therefore, that you will succeed and I believe you will. It goes without saying that during the "campaign" I shall take no part in it.[4]

*When Captain Flohic and Colonel d'Escrienne had to rejoin their respective services, he called on Colonel Desgrées du Loû. Xavier de Beaulaincourt, who had been his secretary for thirty years, stayed. Pierre-Louis Blanc, the last press secretary at the Elysée under de Gaulle, assisted the General in the documentation of his *Mémoires*.
**Pompidou, Poher and Duclos were now in the running.

But when, a few days later, Foccart tried to get the General to intervene to prevent the candidacy of a "left-wing Gaullist" (Capitant) from adversely affecting that of Georges Pompidou, he came up against a blank refusal: "I couldn't care less. I don't want to know anything about such things." Flohic speaks of the General's "irritation" at this "division of his spoils" and concludes that the urgency of his departure for Ireland increased in direct proportion to the rise in electoral fever.[5]

Why Ireland? Since he had decided to keep strictly outside the electoral debate, de Gaulle clearly had to go abroad. However protected La Boisserie might be, the din of a political campaign could hardly fail to echo there. But where, abroad, could he escape an invading press? In a place that would not give rise to political or ideological interpretations? Furthermore, the General was insistent that he should not be the guest of anybody. Countries with strong currency or excessively expensive accommodation were also out of the question. If his choice fell on Ireland it was for a number of different reasons. It was a country apparently on the edge of everything, neutral, whose spirit of independence had become symbolic.

But the General's choice was also dictated by reasons of sentiment, which he explained at length to Flohic: it is said that his mother's family were descended from an Irish clan, the MacCartans. His grandmother, Josephine de Gaulle, wrote, among other biographies, that of Daniel O'Connell, the symbol of Irish nationalism. His uncle Charles was the author of a history of the Celts and his sympathetic curiosity was aroused when he read of the expedition of one of his heroes, Hoche, to the coasts of Ireland in 1796.

He did not want to die before discovering that land from which his family may have derived that stubborn intractability that he carried within him. Between *Sinn Fein* and *France Libre*, a certain kinship could be detected. This was one aspect of the trip that did nothing to help the General's image in the British press. In April, in Northern Ireland, in Londonderry in particular, violent demonstrations took place that were severely crushed by the authorities. This inevitably created great tension between London and Dublin. General elections were to take place on 18 June in the Republic. So the presence of Charles de Gaulle did create political and diplomatic problems – no British politician could believe that it was purely coincidental or due solely to the General's attachment to the MacCartan clan.

In his respectful biography of de Gaulle, the British diplomat Bernard Ledwidge even went so far as to say that "the visit of a world statesman, best known to Irish public opinion for his habit of thwarting the British government, was a considerable complication".[6]

Xavier de La Chevalerie was given instructions by the General to find "on the west coast of Ireland, in some wild place, far from any built-up area, with easy access to a beach as deserted as possible, near a forest where one can go walking, a small comfortable hotel, or some suitably furnished villa".* He spent between 3 and 7 May combing that part of Ireland. On 8 May, he was back at La Boisserie to report on his discoveries. The hotel owners were told that he was acting on behalf of "very important people" – some concluded that they were being asked to lodge

*I would like to thank M. de La Chevalerie for this unpublished note.

Princess Grace of Monaco (née Kelly and therefore Irish), others the Pope. On 9 May, the General decided to leave the following day.

It was an even more mysterious departure than that of 29 May 1968. Mme de Gaulle took care to pack her own luggage so as not to alert the discreet staff at La Boisserie; the police were out trout fishing and the journalists were fast asleep when, at 8 a.m., the General and his wife reached the air base of Saint-Dizier – where, a year before, the decision to land at Baden had been taken. A Mystère 2D took them in under two hours to Cork airport. The Irish Prime Minister, Jack Lynch, his wife and the Foreign Minister Aiken were waiting to welcome them.

To the Prime Minister, who declared that "the whole of Ireland is honoured by his arrival", de Gaulle replied that he was happy to find himself "in the country of his maternal ancestors, the MacCartans". Turning to the French Ambassador, Emmanuel d'Harcourt, an old Free France veteran, who had had a leg amputated, the General, still obsessed by the vote of 27 April, asked point blank: "Did you expect it?"

They went at once to the first of the three residences that had been booked for them: a hotel at Sneem, a village in Heron's Cove, County Kerry. It was situated on Kenmare Bay, which, with Dingle Bay and Bantry Bay,* carries the warm waters of the Gulf Stream far into Kerry. The hotel itself was simple enough, but the surrounding grounds, situated on a rocky promontory pointing out into the bay, offered inviolable shelter. There the de Gaulles led a very quiet life – meals, walks, reading, games of patience. The General re-read the *Mémoires d'outre-tombe*, the *Mémorial de Sainte-Hélène* and began to make notes for the next part of his own *Mémoires*: Flohic had brought with him a suitcase full of documents.

Not far from Heron's Cove was the big tourist hotel at Parknasilla, where the special envoys of several newspapers soon took up residence. They positioned themselves at the summit of Derrynane Dunes: it was from there that the well-known photographs were taken of the man of storms wrapped up in a loose black coat blown about by the off-sea winds, striding along a coast dotted with wild plants. François Flohic noted it bitterly: many newspapers published photographs of those walks, but the *Daily Mail* won the prize for malevolence by publishing a photograph of the General stumbling over a pebble and about to lose his balance. It had to be said that the old man who had dared to defy London at Quebec – if not now in Ireland – was now gaga.[7]

As if to prove the reverse, General de Gaulle devoted more time each day to working on the first volume of the *Mémoires d'espoir*. The book began to take shape. Before leaving France, he had left an outline with Pierre-Louis Blanc, who had been entrusted with the task of gathering together the required documents. On 15 May, François Flohic notes, only five days after his arrival in Ireland, General de Gaulle began the writing proper of *Le Renouveau* – which was to be the title of the first volume. The first chapter, devoted to the events of May 1958, was completed shortly afterwards. The ADC notes that the General's behaviour had become "serene", which made it possible to carry out the various plans made by the Irish authorities for their guest's stay: visits to Connemara and Killarney, and a recep-

*Where Hoche had tried in vain to land the army.

tion by President de Valera, in Dublin. "But I like it here," the General objected. Nevertheless, they left Heron's Cove for Cashel House on Friday 23 May.

The hotel at Cashel Bay was more comfortable than Heron's Cove, and the surrounding countryside even more beautiful. The General was enchanted by the stark wildness of Connemara, which he paced like some old chieftain of Celtic legend. His health and colour were transformed. With each day that passed, the ADC found him stronger and more enthusiastic.

On 3 June, for the last fortnight of the Irish visit, the travellers returned to Kerry. This time, they stayed near Killarney, on the Kenmare Estate, owned by the Duke of Westminster's granddaughter, who appears to have received him with some reluctance. Near a very beautiful lake surrounded by flowers, Dairy Cottage, a converted dairy attached to the house of the Earls of Kenmare, was an exquisite spot: the de Gaulles went for long walks in the park.

On 14 June, the day before the second round of the French presidential elections, de Gaulle dictated to Xavier de La Chevalerie a congratulatory telegram to Georges Pompidou: "For every national and personal reason, I send you my cordial congratulations." But François Flohic noted "a slight irritation" at the fact that "the dauphin had succeeded at last". Drawing a contrast between the new President and Maurice Couve de Murville, which was favourable to the second, de Gaulle came back to the results of the first round. With 37 per cent of the votes cast, Pompidou had won far less than the 47 per cent that he had himself received at the referendum, and remarked that if the Communists had wanted him, Poher would have been President. "France's slide into mediocrity," de Gaulle concluded, "will continue."

With the presidential elections over, the Irish trip came to an end and the climate created by the Irish elections on 18 June made any further stay by de Gaulle in Ireland unpropitious. On 17 June, the visitors were the guests of the Irish head of State at Aras in Uachtarain, the residence of President Eamon de Valera, the founder of the Republic of Ireland, after being one of the leaders of the anti-British guerrillas. At eighty-five, de Valera was blind. He asked the visitor to plant a tree in the park. Many of those who were there stressed the resemblance between the two very tall, bony old men, making their way through Phoenix Park like twins.

On 18 June, the de Gaulles were guests at the French Embassy. At the end of the meal, the Ambassador asked the General to dedicate his copy of the *Mémoires de guerre*. On the flyleaf he copied out this quotation, which he attributed to Nietzsche:* "Nothing is worth anything. Nothing happens, and yet everything happens. But it does not matter." He then added this from St Augustine: "You who will have known me in this book, pray for me!" And then: "He who has known pain has learnt much."**

After the dinner to which the French visitors had been invited by President de Valera that same evening, de Gaulle was in confidential mood: "At this grave point

---

*In a letter to Jean Mauriac, Malraux challenges the attribution to Nietzsche. It is, he says, by Théophile Gautier.

**"Moult a appris qui a connu ahan." In fact, it comes from the *Chanson de Roland* and, in its original form, is written: "Mult ad apris ki bien conuist ahan".

in my long life, I have found here what I was looking for: to be face to face with myself. Ireland has given me this, in the most delicate, the most friendly way."[8]

In the morning, Charles de Gaulle had received, in the presence of Eamon de Valera, his MacCartan "cousins", whose clan originated in County Down, in Ulster,* but who had since settled near Killarney. There were about thirty of them, François Flohic recounts. One of them affirmed that the General did indeed descend from the ancestor of the MacCartans, killed at the Battle of the Boyne in 1690, and more specifically from the last of his sons, who took refuge in France at the time of the Irish immigration known as the "flight of the wild geese". They went on to Dublin Castle, where the *Taoiseach*** and all his cabinet were waiting for General and Mme de Gaulle: the earliest results of the elections that had taken place the day before suggested that the party in power, Fianna Fáil, would remain in power.*** Jack Lynch declared that the "meeting between General de Gaulle and President de Valera has been a historic moment for all Irish people".

Charles de Gaulle replied: "It was a sort of instinct that led me towards Ireland, perhaps because of the Irish blood that courses in my veins. One always goes back to one's source." Then, suddenly, he said: "I raise my glass to a united Ireland." This was as explosive a declaration as the one that he had made at Montreal. But, Bernard Ledwidge suggests, "it is possible that the Irish authorities had not forgotten the Quebec incident, for there was a technical fault in the microphone just at the moment when de Gaulle was proposing his toast, and those who were not close to him did not hear it". Ledwidge adds: "Had he gone so far the night before, in the privacy of the dinner offered him by de Valera, as to say: *Vive l'Irlande libre*"?[9]

The master of La Boisserie returned home and immediately set to work. Between the end of June 1969 and July 1970 he was to write the first volume of his *Mémoires d'espoir*, seeing and consulting some of those who, having worked at his side, were best qualified to supply documentation, jog his memory, even re-read what he had written: Maurice Couve de Murville, Pierre Messmer, André Malraux,† Jean-Marcel Jeanneney, Bernard Tricot, Xavier de la Chevalerie, Alan Prate, François Goguel, Michel Droit, Marcel Jullian (his publisher, at Plon), Léon Noël, Pierre Lefranc†† and a few others.

With Couve and Messmer, he did not at all refrain from discussing public affairs. He urged the man who had been his Prime Minister in 1968–69 "to remain intact, to spurn all compromises", while he did not dissuade the man who had been his Armed Forces Minister for nine years from setting up "Présence du Gaullisme", even going so far as to recommend it – to command it – to be "a ferment", a leaven, in the body politic.

---

*The local MP in the Northern Ireland parliament, James O'Reilly, had invited the General: but that visit would have run the risk of unpleasant repercussions.
**The Irish Prime Minister. (trs.)
***In fact, it did maintain its majority.
†The visit was the origin of Malraux's *Les Chênes qu'on abat*.
††Who, in April 1970, was to convince the General of the need to found the Institut Charles de Gaulle, the first President of which was to be André Malraux. It was to set up its headquarters at 5 Rue de Solférino, where so many episodes in the history of Gaullism had taken place.

Each Tuesday, the master of La Boisserie saw one of his colleagues, Colonel Desgrées du Loû, his ADC, Xavier de Beaulaincourt, his secretary, or Pierre-Louis Blanc, his research assistant, who also dealt with his publisher.

Like all writers, he had his own methods. The journalist Michel Droit, who, in August 1970, was one of his last visitors at La Boisserie, has reported what the old writer told him. "In the morning, I come down about nine and write until noon. And again, after lunch, between four and six.* I think that's a maximum if one is to produce decent work. Anyway, I write slowly. I go over my manuscripts a great deal. I try to rid myself of my writing tics. It isn't always easy." He paused for a moment, then, rising a tone, went on: "What I am doing here, writing my *Mémoires*, is much more important for France than anything I could be doing at the Elysée if I were still there."[10]

As a writer, Charles de Gaulle was his own enemy, the executioner of his own texts, which were defaced by innumerable crossings out and which only his daughter Elisabeth could read. It is said that, on a visit to the Bibliothèque Nationale, he remarked, when shown some lines of Corneille, which had no deletions or insertions, "Well, didn't Corneille rewrite what he had written?"[11]

He was a true professional. Jean Mauriac recounts how, in July 1970, his publisher, Marcel Jullian, saw before him "a nineteenth-century notary carefully discussing his contracts with the publishing house of Plon,** and a very modern writer in his views of the relations between a writer and his readers".

The *Mémoires d'espoir* do not quite have the stature of the *Mémoires de guerre*: not that the subjects are less suited to the memoir-writer, the subject-matter less rich, the dramatic tension less constant. The "resurrection" of May 1958, the emotionally charged emancipation of Algeria, the reconstruction of the State, the diplomatic redeployment of France – these are subjects worthy of a good writer and are treated worthily. But de Gaulle cannot be blamed for the fact that René Coty was not Churchill, Pierre Pflimlin Roosevelt, Jacques Duclos Stalin, Maurice Challe Eisenhower or Raoul Salan Jean Moulin. Only Khrushchev provided him with a comparable subject. But if, as we pass from one book to the other, the individual portrait painter suffers, the historian, or rather the landscape-painter of history, remains masterly. The accounts of his Algerian strategy, of his conversations with Nikita Khrushchev or of Franco-German relations are de Gaulle at his best as, too, is his incomparably subtle account of his relations with Pompidou. As Gorky said of Lenin, Charles de Gaulle "bristled with words like a fish with scales".

As a young man, he strove for silence, but got drunk on Rostand. As an officer, he wanted to be distant, but lost no opportunity of demonstrating his didactic genius. As a prisoner, he tirelessly commented on the news from the front for the benefit of his comrades. Then he became professor of military history at Saint-Cyr, a post that was dearest to his heart, for de Gaulle was a born teacher. If one has to isolate two features of his art one might say that it is both didactic and aristocratic. The didactic character of the writer is obvious enough. He is always behind a desk or in a pulpit, teaching us his double lesson: that, without France,

*This timetable covers only the time spent on the *Mémoires*, not that devoted to correspondence.
**All the royalties were given to the Fondation Anne-de-Gaulle.

the world is not worth living in, and that, without de Gaulle, France is not likely to survive.

The General wanted to mark the anniversary of 11 November by a visit to Verdun, to the fortress of Souilly. He succeeded in surrounding the visit with the greatest discretion. A month later, on 11 December 1969, Malraux turned up, his forehead still covered by the great forelock of hair, with his plasterlike face, his prophetic gestures, his uncertain step, his voice seeming to come from some prehistoric cave – the Confidant was not going to miss the final meeting.

Did Malraux really regard himself as the friend of Charles de Gaulle? When the *Mémoires d'espoir* appeared, in 1970, and he read the magnificent paragraph devoted to him – "On my right, then as always, was André Malraux, this inspired friend" – he was overcome: so much so that he dashed off at once to his friend Manès Sperber to read it out to him aloud. However exceptional the signs of friendship, trust and esteem lavished on him by the General may have been, he remained convinced that he was at his side only as a sort of representative of the intellectual class, an historical monument, a guarantee, too, of a certain populism, and that de Gaulle regarded him as an amateur who had written two or three masterpieces, but much preferred as writers Montherlant and Mauriac. *Les Chênes qu'on abat* is a sort of manifesto. "It was to me," Malraux declares, "that he confided the essential, his true intellectual testament. It was before me that he indulged in the finest despair. If he ever had a double, it was I. We carried off what no one before us had attempted: a dialogue between Power and the Poet." Malraux speaks of the "confused telepathy" aroused between those "two solitary men", shut up in that closed room "despite the immense white landscape". It is a telepathy not so much confused as recreated, but based on a profound truth.

What is described here is the nature of a bond, a certain viewpoint shared by two men now in their last years, fascinated by History, haunted by the limits of action and obsessed by death, two men who had moved from the "what is to be done?" that had occupied their lives to a "why do anything?", two men who shared that idea of History which is made of the dreams in which Chateaubriand saw the raw material of the government of the French nation.

But a certain verve – a double verve – still lights up that shared twilight. When Malraux suggests that de Gaulle's real predecessor was not so much Clemenceau, perhaps, as Victor Hugo, the General cuts him short: "You know, my only real international rival is Tintin! Nobody realizes, because of my height." And when the visitor reminds him how, speaking one day of Jacqueline Kennedy, the day after her husband's funeral, the General had said to him: "She's a star, she'll end up on some oil tycoon's yacht,"* he got this reply: "I said that? Well, well. I would have thought she would have married Sartre. Or you!"

They returned to a more recent incident. And de Gaulle insists on the distance between himself and the centre of things. "That is why now I have as ministers only clouds, trees and, in a different way, books." And the future? "They will erect a large *croix de Lorraine* on the hill that dominates the others. And since nobody is

*This was, of course, to be Aristotle Onassis.

there, nobody will see it." Before André Malraux left La Boisserie, the master of the house said to him:

"Remember what I have told you: I intend that there should be nothing in common between me and what happens."

"Before ten years are up, you will be turned into a fictional character, who will be lurking in all our lives. I don't know as what – a ghost of the 18 June, a ghost from the era of decolonization".

"A ghost of France?" he asked bitterly.[12]

What strikes one about that dizzy, rather over-written exchange, rather too much a "dialogue of the dead", but poignant all the same, is the General's terrible "what is the point?" "I am the character of Hemingway's *The Old Man and the Sea*: all I have brought back is a skeleton."

Three weeks later, on 30 December, a very different de Gaulle received Jean-Marcel Jeanneney, his wife Marie-Laure and their son Jean-Noël. Jeanneney remembers de Gaulle's sense of irony and pugnacity when the subject of his "successors" came up. During the luncheon, the former Czechoslovak president, Eduard Beneš, whom de Gaulle had known in London, was mentioned. "He was not a statesman, he was a professor," de Gaulle declared. Jean-Noël Jeanneney, who, like his father, is a teacher, asked: "Can't a professor ever be a statesman?" "He can become one," said the General. "But what is a statesman?" "He's a man capable of taking risks."[13]

Charles de Gaulle had long wanted to go to Spain. A devotee of Corneille, a fervent lover of Hugo, an attentive reader of Claudel, an admirer of Montherlant, and, although painting was only one element in his world, he felt in harmony with the Castilian genius. "Why wouldn't the Spanish like me?" he apparently asked Malraux in December. "They like Don Quixote!"[14] Moreover, the first letter that the head of State received, the day after his return to Colombey, was signed by General Franco. In such cases, such things count. In any case, his reservations with regard to Francoism had tended over the years to fade. A man who showed de Gaulle such feelings could not be entirely perverse. So he decided to go to Spain in 1970.

The General expressed only four wishes. The first was to visit Madrid; the second to see the Escorial; the third to be able to spend ten days in some "quiet" spot in the south; the fourth to pay for his own trip and hotel bill. Mme de Gaulle, for her part, added two stages on the journey: St James of Compostella and Roncevaux, the site of the medieval battle in which Roland, Charlemagne's nephew, died.

The General had expressed no view on the Spanish State. Franco let it be known that he would like to receive de Gaulle at El Pardo. And the greatest zeal was put into planning each stage of the journey, especially in the *paradores*, the state-run hotels, which were often situated in out of the way places – and which were immediately emptied of their occupants. They set out on 3 June 1970, and in such great secrecy that the press were unaware that they had crossed France, from Colombey to Béhobie, and were informed only after the General's arrival in Galicia. Meanwhile, the de Gaulles had visited St James of Compostella and Avila.

On 8 June, the visitors were in Madrid. During the morning, they visited the

Escorial. At 1 p.m., General de Gaulle, his wife and the French Ambassador were received at the palace at El Pardo by the Spanish head of State. De Gaulle has left a brief account of the conversation, which lasted close on an hour. After noting that, though he had practically retired from "affairs", Franco felt obliged to encumber his desk with huge piles of documents, "for appearances' sake", de Gaulle adds: "You have to be careful with it, he's a cunning devil. I had to say to him: 'After all, you have been good for Spain!' And I don't have to tell you all that was implied in that 'after all'. All the repression, all the crimes! Of course, Stalin, too, committed crimes, far more in fact."

In the late afternoon, after a visit to the Museum of the Prado, to which de Gaulle decided to devote only thirty minutes ("I want to see the Goyas and the Velázquezes, that will be enough!"), the de Gaulles arrived at Toledo, where they were the guests of the "Cigarral los Dolores", a former sixteenth-century monastery, then the home of Dr Marañon Moya, director of the Hispanic Institute and son of Gregorio Marañon, a great Spanish man of letters and science.

De Gaulle refused to visit the Alcázar at Toledo, one of the sacred sites of Francoism and the setting of one of the finest scenes in Malraux's *Espoir*, though his hosts had insisted that he should see "the Spanish Saint-Cyr". When Dr Marañon suggested that, despite his conduct in Spain, he admired Napoleon, de Gaulle cut him short: "Napoleon was a soldier of genius. But he despised men."

On 9 June, the travellers arrived at the Parador de Santa Catalina, near Jaen, in eastern Andalusia (from which they were to visit the *mezquita* at Cordova, on 11 June). They then spent about ten days in the hunting lodge of Juanar, at Ojen, in the Sierra Blanca (north of Marbella).

Seville Cathedral, Cáceres, filled with the shadows of the conquistadores, Placencia, Segovia, Burgos, Santo-Domingo de la Calzada: a rough return on the torrid roads of Estremadura and Old Castile. The old gentleman bore the trial light-heartedly, apparently at least, picnicking on the roadside at noon, delighted by those landscapes in which the history of the Most Catholic kingdom seemed to be inscribed. Jean Mauriac, who was with the party, notes: "In Spain the General loved the harshness of the climate, the austerity of the sites, the isolation of the villages that, over the centuries, had determined the national character."[15]

Ireland had given him back a little serenity, Spain moved him. Why not, now, China? What finer, more epic journey could there be for an old man half-retired from the century? And where, in so short a time, could he learn more new things about the world? In March 1970 he had received a letter from Etienne Manac'h, an old colleague from Free France days,* for a long time in charge of Asian affairs at the Quai d'Orsay and only recently (at his own initiative) titular Ambassador at Peking, suggesting that he should "come to China" and meet Mao Tse-tung.

A few weeks later, General de Gaulle's niece, Thérèse de Corbie, a diplomat and specialist in Asian affairs, was appointed to Peking at the Ambassador's request. Before leaving, she called at Colombey. Observing that his "old friend

---

*He had represented Free France in the Balkans.

Manac'h" had been "bothering him with the idea of a trip to China", the General admitted to his niece: "For me, to go to China would be a dream fulfilled." And he went on to ask questions about "the best season" for such a trip, about a possible programme – the only condition being that he would be received by Mao. Exactly two months later, on the announcement of the General's death, the flag flew at half-mast over the Forbidden City.

In early September 1970, Léon Noël, an old friend of de Gaulle's, former chairman of the Constitutional Council, was received at La Boisserie. He found the General "lively, alert, moving around nimbly". His memory was still "prodigious": in short, he was "in perfect health". And what of his morale? "A serenity touched with sadness. The overriding sense was of an acceptance of facts, an absence of any real rancour, an indulgence towards men. His conscience and soul were at peace." But, the visitor adds, he seemed to be possessed by a double obsession: to shut himself away in "total retreat", and, above all, to have time to finish his *Mémoires*.[16]

CHAPTER FORTY

Without Music or Fanfare

Time spurred him on; death lay hidden in the half-darkness. How many years were left, how many months or weeks? Autumn came round again and he reached his eightieth year.

Because, as he himself said, he returned to power ten years too late, Charles de Gaulle's political strategy had been marked by a sort of haste, a sort of breathless, feverish, permanent acceleration. Now he was hinting that death was coming too soon, five years too soon. "At eighty-four," he remarked one day in 1969 to his ADC, "I shall have finished my work and my life." He had calculated in effect that, given the rate at which he worked, going through innumerable documents, handling endless figures and rewriting a great deal, he needed five years to write the last two volumes of his *Mémoires d'espoir*. His nephew, Bernard de Gaulle, who accompanied him on one of his last walks in the forest, in pouring rain, heard what amounted to a begging appeal: "How I would like to finish the *Mémoires* before I die. I hurry, I hurry. I hope to write a second volume in under a year. That's my mission before I die."[1]

The fear that he might not fulfil it haunted him. Close friends received letters in which he asked them to pray God to give him the time to complete his task. And although he had always been fond of entertaining friends or relations at his table, he more and more insisted now that the meal should be short: otherwise, he reminded his wife, it would be so much time lost in the writing of his *Mémoires*. As soon as the visitor's back was turned, he would slip back to his desk, to the sheets of paper on which he spread his swan-neck handwriting.

He described very beautifully to Philippe de Gaulle that prowling presence of death: "Old Marshal Hindenburg, sensing that his end was near, said to his son: 'When the angel of Death – the one that is called Raphael in the Bible – comes, you will warn me.' Shortly afterwards, the Marshal took to his bed. When his son ran up to his bedside, he said: 'Is Raphael in the house?' And the son replied: 'No. He is in the garden, but he will be in the house soon.'" De Gaulle then turned to his son and said: "I shall ask you the same question."[2]

Life at La Boisserie pursued its usual course. His friends were subjected to only two strict rules: to be back five minutes before meals (12.30, 7.15) and not to go into the master's study without being invited. In that refuge the General spent a third of his day, facing the three windows that looked out over the valley of the Aube, from which, at this season of the year, the usual mist rose. Beyond were the forests, Les Dhuits, Clairvaux, and beyond them Champagne and Lorraine. Twice a day, he picked up his cane and walked around the garden, and beyond, to the Blinfeix or La Chapelle woods. The windier it was, the more he liked it. "Do you know how to do nothing?" one visitor asked him. "Ask the cat," he replied. "We are both quite good at it. It isn't easy for anyone to impose a discipline of idleness on himself, but it's indispensable."[3]

In late September, Admiral Philippe de Gaulle, his son, spent two days at La Boisserie. At the end of a long walk in the Forêt des Dhuits, the General read to him a few pages from the second volume of the *Mémoires d'espoir*. "Each time he said goodbye to us as if we were not to see each other again," Philippe de Gaulle has remarked. And this time, it was true. Indeed the General had struck his son as "even sadder and more melancholy than usual".[4]

But a moment of joy was not long in coming: in October 1970 the first volume of the *Mémoires d'espoir*, *Le Renouveau 1958–1962*, appeared – in conditions of unimaginable secrecy for those who know anything of publishing life, the rumours and exigencies of the media. Suddenly, on 23 October 1970, without any information leaking out, there blazed from bookshop windows, under the navy blue jacket with gold lettering that he himself had chosen, the 750 000 copies of this so-long-awaited book. Success was immediate and overwhelming. Although the press, as a whole, expressed regret that, in the picture painted by the master of La Boisserie, too much art concealed some of the harsher realities of history, his mail brought him praise upon praise. Who could doubt that he was moved by this?

He was working hard on the second volume, revising the second chapter that he had already read to his son. He planned to complete that volume, which would deal largely with his foreign policy, by a series of dialogues in which he would speak in turn with Clovis and Charlemagne, Philippe-Auguste and Colbert, Napoleon and Clemenceau on the theme of "What would you have done in my place?" It was a fearsome undertaking, both for the statesman and for the writer.

Another pleasant occasion occurred on 4 November, the Feast of St Charles. For many years the General had refused to celebrate his birthday, 22 November – especially that year, when he reached eighty, "the terrible birthday!" he remarked to his niece Geneviève Anthonioz. But for that very reason he agreed to celebrate his name-day, which fell on the day after All Saints', though he moved the celebrations forward by two days to take advantage of the presence of his grandchildren.

That year, neither Philippe de Gaulle, who was held up by naval duties at Brest, nor his wife was able to come. The Boissieus were there, with their daughter Anne (aged eleven) and Pierre de Gaulle (aged seven). Honorine Manzani, the cook, described that family celebration to a journalist from *Paris-Match*: "We found the General in the library. The children came to fetch us from the kitchen, in the evening, before the meal. Anne picked up the bouquet of flowers, Pierre followed, after came the family and then us. It was like Christmas."

On 2 November, All Souls' Day, Charles and Yvonne de Gaulle went to visit the grave of their daughter Anne. "That's where I want to be buried," the General repeated, once again, this time adding that the cemetery gate would have to be widened, because "there may be a few visitors".[5]

On Saturday 7 November, de Gaulle and his wife went on a long outing by car through the countryside around Colombey. The next day, a Sunday, they attended mass in their village church – where the cook, Honorine, noticed that the General looked "very pale, his features drawn, his neck very white", but added that "since the weather was bad, I put it down to that".[6]

On Monday 9 November, the weather was still bad. The General took only a short walk in the garden, just before lunching with his wife, and, it seems, with a good appetite. After another brief attempt at going out for a walk, interrupted by rain, which was so strong that Mme de Gaulle, for once, did not want to go with him, the General received a visitor, René Piot, to settle a matter involving enclosure and grazing rights, recent boundary changes having altered long-accepted practices.

At 3.30, he telephoned – something he hated so much that the apparatus was placed symbolically under the stairs, so that he could only use it doubled up, as if he had wanted in this way to stress the torturing character of the instrument – his secretary, Xavier Beaulaincourt, whose visit to Colombey was planned for the following day.

Then, for about an hour, Charles de Gaulle shut himself up in his study. Did he work at his book? We know that he autographed several volumes and wrote various letters, in particular to his son and daughter-in-law. We know what he wrote to Mme Vendroux (she read it the following day, on returning to Paris after paying her respects to Charles de Gaulle's body at La Boisserie):

My dear Cada,
    You know how much pleasure your name-day wishes give me, expressing as they do the affection that you and Jacques have for me. I thank you for them from the bottom of my heart.
    Please make some wishes, and even say some prayers, for the great work that I have undertaken and which I intend not so much for our contemporaries as for future generations, on behalf of those who have acted with me to the same end, in the first rank of whom you have been and remain, my dear sister, together with Jacques and all your family.
    Yvonne joins with me in sending you both our very best wishes.
    Your brother

                                            Charles de Gaulle.[7]

As far as we know, those were the last words written by the General.

Just before 5 o'clock, he took advantage of a clearer sky to go for another walk in the park – alone, according to Charlotte, the chambermaid, "for Honorine had set Madame's hair and she was under the drier".

When the General came back, Charlotte served him tea, as usual. Since Yvonne de Gaulle was still "under the drier", the General took a cup of tea and the plate of biscuits up to his wife's room. He then went downstairs again to his study, where, this time, he worked at his correspondence.

About 6.30, carrying a few letters, he sought out his wife to ask her for some addresses and found her in the kitchen, settling the details of the dinner. He then went to the library, where he sat in front of the small card table he used, before dinner and the television news, to play patience, his "discipline of idleness". Yvonne de Gaulle joined him at about 6.45.

It was a little later, at five or six minutes to seven, that the General, still sitting at his card table, suddenly let out a cry and put his hand to his back. "Ah! What a pain!" Charlotte Marchal heard him say as she was laying the table in the dining-room. In any case, it was just before 7 p.m. when Charles de Gaulle, struck by a rupture of the abdominal aorta (usually called "breaking of a blood-vessel"), lost consciousness and immediately went into a coma. It is believed that he survived for another half-hour. In any case, Mme de Gaulle told Jean Mauriac that her husband's heart was still beating at the moment that extreme unction was administered to him. Specialists do not deny that such an eventuality may allow someone to survive for anything up to an hour. In any case, the "official" time of Charles de Gaulle's death is 9.25 p.m., 9 November 1970.

As soon as she heard her husband's cry and saw him collapse in his chair, his head to the left, his body held in place by the chair arm, Yvonne instructed Charlotte, Honorine and the chauffeur Francis Marroux to get the parish priest of Colombey, the Abbé Jaugey, and the doctor from Bar-sur-Aube, Dr Lacheny.

Cutting short his consultation hours, the doctor jumped into his car and covered in a few minutes the eight miles to Colombey. He arrived at La Boisserie at the same time as the priest – who gave him precedence. The General was now laid out on the sofa of the library, uttering "the death rattle", according to the Abbé Jaugey, who heard it from the drawing-room. The physician told Mme de Gaulle at once that there was no hope. But he gave the dying man an injection of morphine, in case he was still suffering any pain.

After the Abbé Jaugey had administered the last sacrament, Dr Lacheny informed Mme de Gaulle that it was all over. Looking at him, she said: "He has suffered so much over the past two years."

"In the small silent room, where a wood fire was still burning in the fireplace," writes Jean Mauriac, "the only people present, all kneeling, were Mme de Gaulle and her two servant women, the chauffeur Marroux, the doctor and the priest. 'Nobody,' according to the priest, 'said a word. Mme de Gaulle was impassive. The two servants were weeping.'"[8]

The fact is that the wife of the former head of State showed impressive self-control – which is part of the code of a certain section of society and has nothing to do with intensity of suffering, but serves, for a time, to control it. But her self-control was so evident that it even struck her brother, Jacques Vendroux.

After informing her daughter and General de Boissieu, who were then in Paris, and asking them to inform in turn Admiral de Gaulle, in Brest, she supervised the dressing of her husband's body, which had been transported on a sofa from the drawing-room, wearing his uniform bearing only the two insignia of Free France, and half-covered by the flag that was erected, at La Boisserie, for the Quatorze Juillet. In his hands was placed a rosary given to the de Gaulles by Pope Paul VI.

A single principle governed everything that was done from then on: for the Christian, death is a matter between God, himself and his family. Any ceremonial should be no more than a concession to custom, and as modest as possible. Thus Mme de Gaulle refused to allow the body to remain exposed to visitors any longer than necessary – that is to say, until her children arrived. She opposed the idea of a death-mask being taken of Charles de Gaulle's face, regarding it as a "disrespectful" gesture to the dead man. She refused to allow a lock of his hair to be cut off. She also took care to have her husband's bed linen (even the bed itself), his clothes, shoes and various personal effects burned. "No relics, no relics!" she said, obviously echoing the dead man's wishes. Nevertheless, she took care to keep, for the Musée de la Libération, General de Gaulle's cap, greatcoat and decorations.

Elisabeth de Boissieu and her husband arrived at La Boisserie shortly after midnight with their daughter Anne. They had passed on the news to Philippe de Gaulle and to the General's sister, Mme Cailliau. Mme de Gaulle took the decision not to announce the news until the following day, so that family and close friends would not learn it by the radio and so that the telephone at Colombey would not be besieged and the village invaded.

Thus the French people and the world, some fifteen individuals apart, were kept in ignorance of Charles de Gaulle's death for fourteen hours (twelve hours in the case of the head of State!). It was the General's final victory over his century and over the "hacks" of the press.

Alerted in the early hours of the morning by Alain de Boissieu, Jacques Vendroux and his wife arrived at La Boisserie around 11 a.m. the following morning. "Charles was there, turned towards us, lying on a sober white sheet, in uniform; a tricolour flag covered him from the chest to the feet; his hands, joined over the blue, held the rosary that had been given him by the pope. To his right, on a low table, were two lighted candles and a small crucifix."[9]

Philippe de Gaulle, alerted by his brother-in-law half an hour after his father's death, refused to use a navy plane, that is to say, to benefit from a State privilege and thus arouse attention, to get to Paris. He took the night train. He arrived in the capital before 7 a.m. and immediately telephoned his mother. He then tried to contact the Elysée, where Georges Pompidou was informed at 7.20 a.m. by Alain de Boissieu. There was the question of carrying out the General's last wishes: Philippe de Gaulle knew that the head of State, together with his sister and himself, were executors.

It was Pierre Lefranc, whom he contacted on his arrival in Paris, who was entrusted with the task of settling with Georges Pompidou the implementation of the dead man's last wishes. Curiously enough, the President of the Republic, who knew that the General's son was in Paris, at his apartment in the Avenue Ingres, apparently did nothing to contact him directly and agreed to handle the affair through an intermediary.

Lefranc arrived at the Elysée at 8.40 a.m. The President received him immediately. The visitor had come, he said, "on behalf of the General's family", to remind the head of State that "the arrangements made in 1952 are still valid". Pompidou, who had kept one of the copies of the funeral arrangements in his safe, asked: "Has the news not been announced?" "No," Lefranc replied. The copy that Pompidou had been given eighteen years earlier was at his home, in the Quai de Béthune: it was sent for immediately. In the meantime, Georges Pompidou read with great care the admiral's copy, which Lefranc had shown him. It specified that Charles de Gaulle wanted to be buried at Colombey without any ceremony. Shortly afterwards, the visitor was shown the statement that the President had just written and proposed to read to the television cameras at 1 p.m.

When the copy arrived from the Quai de Béthune, Georges Pompidou broke the seal on the envelope that the General had given him in 1952, read the text and declared that there was no difference between it and the one that Lefranc had shown him.

It was about 9 a.m. when the Prime Minister, Jacques Chaban-Delmas, who still knew nothing, turned up. The unexpected presence of Lefranc alerted him immediately: "Pierre, the General?"

"Yes, he died yesterday evening."

The Prime Minister found it hard to control his emotions. "We're alone now." The three men agreed to await the decisions of the family before announcing the date and form that any arrangements in Paris might take. Meanwhile, would the head of State go to Colombey? Lefranc was shocked that he had not brought the matter up. With Chaban, he put the question. "It will be difficult," said the President. "Tomorrow? Or the day after?" At which point Pierre Lefranc withdrew. A little later, Pompidou changed his mind: he would like to go to La Boisserie that afternoon. However, Mme de Gaulle opposed the idea.[10]

Admiral de Gaulle expressed his point of view on this episode in an interview given to Michel Tauriac, of France-Inter, on 18 June 1972: "I was rather surprised by what happened that morning. I imagined that at least some responsible official would have tried to get in touch with me. I think there was a misunderstanding and that in the confusion following the General's death, people must quite simply have forgotten that he had a family and a son." When Philippe de Gaulle arrived at Colombey, about 5 p.m., his father's coffin was still open. The General's body was seen, after his death, only by relations and close friends and – alone of people in public life – by Michel Debré, then Armed Forces Minister.

The village joiner, Louis Mergé, was asked to describe the coffin that he had been asked to make: "The same as for anybody, in light oak, with aluminium handles – only it was 2.05 metres. You know, I didn't look at him very closely. In my job, you're so used to the dead you don't take any notice any more."[11]

At 9.40 a.m., on 10 November, the Agence France-Presse made the event public: "General de Gaulle is dead." The radio stations immediately interrupted their programmes to announce and comment on the news and on the various stages of the dead man's career. Flags were put at half-mast on public buildings. At 11 o'clock, through the Elysée, General de Gaulle's political testament was made public:

> I want my funeral to take place at Colombey-les-Deux-Eglises. If I die elsewhere, my body must be brought home, without any public ceremony.
>
> My grave will be the one in which my daughter Anne lies and where one day my wife too will lie. Inscription: "Charles de Gaulle, 1890–...". Nothing more.
>
> The ceremony will be arranged by my son, my daughter, my son-in-law, my daughter-in-law, assisted by my private office, in such a way that it is extremely simple. I want no national funeral. No president, no minister, no representatives from the Assembly or any other corporate body. Only the French army may participate officially, as such; but their participation must

be on a very modest scale, without music, fanfare or ringing of bells.

No speech must be delivered, either in the church or elsewhere. No funeral oration in Parliament. No seats must be reserved during the ceremony, except for my family, my close friends, members of the Order of the Liberation, and the municipal council of Colombey.

Men and women of France and of other countries may, if they so wish, pay my memory the homage of accompanying my body to its last resting place. But it is my wish that this should be carried out in silence.

I wish to refuse in advance any distinction, promotion, dignity, citation, decoration, whether French or foreign. And if any is accorded me, it will be in violation of my last wishes.

It was in January 1952 that Charles de Gaulle produced that testament in three copies: one for Georges Pompidou, who was then *chef de cabinet* of the chairman of the RPF,* one to his son Philippe and one to his daughter, Elisabeth, and son-in-law Alain de Boissieu. On a number of occasions since then, Philippe de Gaulle had asked his father if, given the circumstances, in particular his accession to the Presidency of the Republic, his intentions had not altered: each time General de Gaulle had confirmed quite clearly that the 1952 text remained in force. So all the General's mistrust and disdain for the men of the Fourth Republic also applied to those of the Fifth: no politician, however faithful he may have been, would be allowed to use Charles de Gaulle's corpse.

The Council of Ministers met in extraordinary session at 12.30 and declared Thursday 12 November a day of national mourning and decided that on that day a solemn requiem mass would be celebrated at Notre-Dame in the presence of the innumerable heads of State who had announced their imminent arrival. At 1 p.m., the President of the Republic appeared on the television screens. His address began: "*Françaises, Français*, General de Gaulle is dead. France is widowed."

The President of the United States, Richard Nixon, who, from the early afternoon, had let it be known that he would be coming to Paris to join in the homage to Charles de Gaulle, whatever form it would take, declared in a message to M. Pompidou: "I have been deeply upset by the death of General de Gaulle. My country regarded General de Gaulle as a faithful ally in time of war and a true friend in time of peace. Greatness knows no national boundaries and consequently the loss felt by France is a loss that is felt by mankind as a whole."

Golda Meir, the Israeli Prime Minister, said: "It is with heavy heart that I join the crowds that are gathering at the announcement of the death of France's great leader, who was one of the greatest statesmen of our time. Israel and her people will never forget the man who gave back honour and liberty to the French people and led them in the struggle against Nazi dictatorship."

Josef Luns, Dutch Foreign Minister, for a long time NATO Secretary-General and a particular adversary of General de Gaulle's European policy, declared: "I regret that General de Gaulle did not become the President of a nascent united

*It is interesting to note that, despite the differences that had arisen between them, the General maintained his confidence in Pompidou in this domain.

Europe that was moving towards political unity, because his prestige and renown were such that, although he had a quite different conception of the role of France, he would certainly have been elected and accepted by all countries, including Great Britain, as the first leader of that Europe moving towards unification."

In France few discordant voices were heard. One view from the opposition came from the first secretary of the Socialist Party, Alain Savary: "The emotion of those who, under his orders, have served France is very deep. General de Gaulle has a right to the homage and gratitude of all French people."

On Wednesday 11 November, a few people were received at La Boisserie: General Lazard, an old Resistance fighter, the Comte de Paris, Maurice Couve de Murville, Gaston Palewski, Geoffroy de Courcel, Jacques Foccart, Etienne Burin des Roziers, René Brouillet, Gilbert Grandval, Pierre Lefranc, Pierre-Louis Blanc, and Colonel d'Escrienne, his last but one ADC.*

In the early afternoon arrived Marie-Agnès Cailliau, the General's elder sister, who was handed by her sister-in-law, in front of the coffin, a letter written to her by the dead man two days before and which had not yet been posted. "Everything is very quiet here," he had written. "I'm getting on with my great work."[12] At 4 p.m., on that 11 November, the President of the Republic, Georges Pompidou, and the Prime Minister, Jacques Chaban-Delmas, arrived together. The two men stood in silence before the now closed coffin, then spent a few moments in the General's study, without saying a word. Just as they were going, Mme de Gaulle went up to Jacques Chaban-Delmas and took his hands most warmly: "You must know this: he was very fond of you."

The de Gaulle family, following the General's last wishes, had decided not to attend the ceremony that the government had decided to organize at Notre-Dame, at 11 a.m. on 12 November. In his interview on France-Inter, on 18 June 1972, Philippe de Gaulle commented on this refusal: "The government could hardly do other than hold a requiem mass at Notre-Dame, on the day of the funeral, given the fact that so many sovereigns and heads of State had taken the trouble to come to Paris on that day. But since the General had insisted that his funeral should be a private, family matter, we obviously could not go to Notre-Dame. Had we done so it would have been like taking part in an international funeral."

In the great cathedral, cleansed during his reign, under Malraux's instructions, of seven centuries of accumulated dirt, now restored to its original honeyed hues, thirty sovereigns and the representatives of almost every nation in the world had gathered on that Thursday, to salute the memory of a man who could not make his death like the death of others and who, in the eyes of the world, was to have two funerals. In that cohort there were only a few partners of the dead man, a few heroes of the *Mémoires de guerre* and of Charles de Gaulle's long march: Haile Selassie, the Shah of Iran, David Ben Gurion, Queen Juliana of the Netherlands, Anthony Eden and Harold Macmillan.

At the intersection of the transept, there was no coffin. It was a formidable absence. It was a strange ceremony, organized against a dead man's will and

*Colonel Desgrées du Loû and M. de Beaulaincourt had come the day before. Captain Flohic was at sea.

deserted by him. But it was filled with him: for few places in the world had been more strongly associated with the history of Charles de Gaulle, since 26 August 1944.

At Colombey, where, in the morning, huge wreaths bearing the names of Mao Tse-tung and Chou En-lai arrived, the crowd had been gathering since dawn under what at first was a clear sky, but which, throughout the day, grew darker and darker. Eight special trains brought 5000 passengers from the Gare de l'Est. It was a quiet crowd, which seemed to have come neither to see nor to be seen, just to bear witness. By the early afternoon there were 40 000 people there. Many slept in their cars.

Just after 2 p.m., the bells rang out, as they did in many of the churches of France. At 2.50 p.m., an armoured reconnaissance vehicle appeared in front of the gates of La Boisserie, on which, turret raised, was placed the coffin of Charles de Gaulle, covered by the flag. What stronger symbol of the dead man's long crusade in favour of tanks and other armoured vehicles could there have been?

Slowly, at walking pace, the great insect crossed the threshold of La Boisserie and noisily rolled down the Rue du General-de-Gaulle, towards the church. It was followed by four cars, containing Mme de Gaulle, her children and her grandchildren, Colonel Desgrées du Loû, Xavier de Beaulaincourt, Charlotte Marchal and Honorine Manzani. The bell continued to toll. Many in the crowd were weeping. Many made the victory sign invented by Winston Churchill. At the entrance to the church, a few dozen pupils from Saint-Cyr, soldiers of the 501st Tank Regiment (one of the oldest in the Free French forces) and marines presented arms.

In the squat village church in which the pale head of Charles de Gaulle had floated so often above the others, looking impressive and preoccupied, the family, the parishioners and some three hundred and fifty members of the Order of the Liberation were assembled, packed in closely together: the church had only four hundred seats.* There, behind Mme de Gaulle and her family, were the Chancellor of the Order, Hettier de Boislambert, Geoffroy de Courcel, President Cassim, Pierre Messmer, Alexandre Parodi, André Dewavrin, known as "Passy", Maurice Schumann, Pierre Clostermann, Alain Savary, Christian Pineau, Yvon Morandat, Claude Serreulles, Guillain de Bénouville, Claude Bourdet, Rol-Tanguy, Admiral Cabanier, Generals Béthouart, Fourquet, Massu and Buis, Robert Letant, the youngest of them, whom the General called *Moustique* (mosquito) – and many others.

Yet there was one famous absentee: Malraux! A few moments before the service began, a squeal of tyres was heard from the village square. People turned round, expecting to see the cortège entering. The doors opened, a ray of sunlight flooded the small church: emerging from the car that had just taken them to La Boisserie to see Mme de Gaulle (but missing her), there was André Malraux.

Malraux, his coat open, his arms hanging loose, haggard-looking, a ghost of uncertain step, his forelock at half-mast over his ravaged forehead, plunged into the small nave, thrown forwards as if for some sort of charge. Groping his way

*This account is based on the memories of Georges Buis, Alain Savary and Jean Mauriac.

down the central aisle like a blind prophet, he stumbled over the stand erected in front of the altar on which the coffin was to be placed and seemed frozen as if in a daze, face to face with the huge plaster Christ that dominated the choir. He had to squeeze in to make room for himself and he sat there, gaunt, absent-looking, biting his hand, as the gates of the church opened again to let in the body, carried by a dozen young men of the locality.

The light oak coffin was surrounded by four Saint-Cyriens – including one African. As if to add a few pathetic notes to this poignant rendezvous, one of those young men-caryatids collapsed at the foot of the catafalque.

The ceremony was conducted by Father François de Gaulle, the General's nephew, the Bishop of Langres and the Abbé Jaugey, the parish priest of Colombey.

All those who attended were given a modest blue leaflet that had been hastily photocopied. A Lorraine Cross, a sketch of the church, the words "Burial mass of General de Gaulle, Colombey-les-Deux-Eglises, Thursday 12 November 1970". Then an extract from the will, which had been made public three days before: "no speech, extremely simple . . . in silence . . ."

There followed a few musical items, Psalm 129, and, among others, a prayer to recite at the Offertory, containing the words "Never again, never more: the world is hungry for peace."

"It was the funeral of a knight," André Malraux was to say to Jean Mauriac. "There was just the family, the order and the parish. But the General's body should not have been in a coffin, but laid, like that of a knight, on a pile of logs."

In his description of that day, in *Les Chênes qu'on abat*, there is a fine stroke. The crowd is there jostling to get close to the church. An old peasant woman wants to get by. The police have been ordered to block the way. A marine stands in her path, his rifle in front of him. The woman struggles to get through, shouting: "He said everybody, everybody!" Malraux intervenes: "It would give the General pleasure." The marine swings back without a word and, as the good woman limps her way to the coffin, "seems, by letting her pass, to be presenting arms to the people of France".

Shortly before 4 p.m., the twelve young men of the village, almost all farmers, hoisted the coffin on to their shoulders and carried it to the small graveyard next to the church, preceded by the Bishop of Langres and two priests, followed by the fifteen members of the family. The coffin was lowered very quickly into the vault – and henceforth, beside those that demarcate the brief life of Anne de Gaulle, are inscribed in stone the dates that frame the life of "the most illustrious of Frenchmen": 1890–1970.

NOTES

CHAPTER ONE
1. Charles de Gaulle, *War Memoirs*, translated by Richard Howard (New York, Simon and Schuster and London, Weidenfeld and Nicolson, 1959).
2. A. Dansette, *Histoire de la libération de Paris* (Paris, Fayard, 1946), pp.332–6
3. *War Memoirs*, II, p.316
4. A. de Boissieu, *Pour combattre avec de Gaulle* (Paris, Plon, 1981), p.259
5. *Histoire de la libération de Paris*, p.431
6. *War Memoirs*, III, p.130
7. C. Mauriac, *Aimer de Gaulle* (Paris, Grasset, 1978), p.65
8. F. Mauriac, *De Gaulle* (Paris, Grasset), pp.15–18
9. Paul Valéry, *Oeuvres complètes*, Bibliothèque de la Pléiade, II, p.1544
10. *Lettres, Notes et Carnets* (Paris, Plon, 1983), p.352
11. *Pour combattre avec de Gaulle*, p.258
12. B. Ledwidge, *De Gaulle* (London, Weidenfeld and Nicolson, 1982), p.202
13. *Lettres, Notes ...*, V, p.300
14. *War Memoirs*, III, p.11
15. Interview with the author, March 1984
16. *Aimer de Gaulle*, p.42
17. P. Viannay, *Nous sommes les rebelles*, coll. "Defense de l'homme", Paris, 1945
18. *Ibid.*, pp.79, 82, 97
19. Interview with the author, February 1984

CHAPTER TWO
1. *War Memoirs*, II, p.321
2. *Ibid.*, III, p.22–23
3. F.-L. Closon, *Le Temps des passions* (Paris, Presses de la Cité, 1974), pp.193–4
4. P. Villon, *Résistant de la première heure* (Paris, Editions sociales, 1983), p.116
5. J. Debu-Bridel, *De Gaulle et le CNR* (Paris, France-Empire, 1978), p.192
6. Interview with the author, November 1964
7. *Aimer de Gaulle*, pp.47 and 62
8. P. Robrieux, *Histoire intérieure du parti communiste* (Paris, Fayard, 1981), II, p.26
9. Interview with the author, March 1984
10. *Histoire intérieure du parti communiste*, II, pp.24 and 30
11. *Victoires sur la nuit*, p.242
12. Interview with the author, October 1980
13. Interview with the author, April 1984
14. Interview with Pierre Mendès France, July 1981
15. *Victoires sur la nuit*, p.242
16. *War Memoirs*, III, p.2
17. Interview with the author, February 1984
18. Interview with the author, April–June 1984
19. *War Memoirs*, III, pp.10–11
20. *Ibid.*, p.12
21. *Ibid.*, pp.13–14
22. *Aimer de Gaulle*, p.84
23. *War Memoirs*, III, p.40
24. *Ibid.*, pp.40–1
25. *Ibid.*, p.342

CHAPTER THREE
1. *Aimer de Gaulle*, p.69
2. *Colloque sur la libération de la France* (Paris, 1974), p.588
3. *Aimer de Gaulle*, pp.28, 32, 64
4. Interview with the author, April 1984

5. *War Memoirs*, III, pp.32–3
6. Quoted by Colonel Goyet, in *Colloque sur la libération de la France*, p.565; ibid., p.578
7. *Ibid.*, p.580
8. P. Repiton-Preneuf, *La 2ᵉ DB en France: combats et combattants*
9. *Ibid.*
10. *Aimer de Gaulle*, p.103
11. *Pour combattre avec de Gaulle*, p.284
12. *War Memoirs*, III, p.143
13. D. Eisenhower, *Crusade in Europe* (London, Heinemann, 1948), p.385
14. See the remarkable account of the affair by Jean-Marie d'Hoop in *L'Entourage de De Gaulle* (Paris, Plon, 1979), pp.284–97.
15. J. de Lattre, *Ne pas subir* (Paris, Plon, 1984), p.300
16. G. Patton, *Carnets secrets* (Paris, Plon, 1975), p.396
17. Cited in J. Nobécourt, *Le Dernier Coup de dés de Hitler* (Paris, Laffont, 1962), p.378
18. *Ibid.*, p.379
19. *War Memoirs*, III, pp.148–9
20. A. Juin, *Mémoires* (Paris, Fayard, 1960), II, p.85
21. *War Memoirs*, III, p.149
22. A. Juin, *Mémoires*, p.86
23. *Ne pas subir*, p.318
24. *War Memoirs*, III, p.482
25. *Crusade in Europe*, p.396
26. Colloque sur la libération de la France, p.585

CHAPTER FOUR
1. *War Memoirs*, III, p.43
2. Archives du Quai d'Orsay, série Y, volume 121, "Conférence de Yalta"
3. *Lettres, Notes...*, V, p.349
4. F. Kersaudy, *Churchill and De Gaulle* (London, Collins, 1981), p.373
5. *Ibid.*, p.321
6. *Victoires sur la nuit*, p.246
7. *War Memoirs*, III, p.49
8. *Victoires sur la nuit*, p.247
9. *Ibid.*, p.247
10. *Aimer de Gaulle*, p.89
11. *War Memoirs*, III, p.51
12. *Ibid.*, p.57

13. *Ibid.*, p.60
14. J. Laloy, *Revue des études slaves*, p.140
15. *Ibid.*, p.141
16. A. Werth, *De Gaulle* (London, Penguin, 1965), p.182
17. Interview with the author, October 1984
18. *War Memoirs*, III, pp.61–3
19. According to the collection published in 1983 by the Soviet Foreign Ministry entitled *Soviet–French Relations during the Great Patriotic War 1941–1945*, pp.157–66.
20. *War Memoirs*, III, p.61
21. *Revue des études slaves*, p.143
22. *Ibid.*, p.142
23. *War Memoirs*, III, p.67
24. *Ibid.*
25. A. Werth, *De Gaulle*, p.184
26. Gaston Palewski, in an interview with the author, 1964
27. *War Memoirs*, III, p.72
28. *Ibid.*, p.76
29. *Sovietsko frantsuskie otnoshenyia* (Moscow, 1969), cited by A. Werth, *De Gaulle*, p.185
30. *Revue des études slaves*, p.147
31. *Ibid.*, pp.147–8
32. *War Memoirs*, III, p.75
33. *Revue des études slaves*, p.148
34. *Ibid.*, p.150
35. *Ibid.*, p.152
36. *War Memoirs*, III, p.81
37. *Revue des études slaves*, p.150
38. *Ibid.*, p.151
39. *Ibid.*, p.152
40. C. Fouchet, *Au service du général de Gaulle* (Paris, Plon, 1971), p.52
41. E. Stettinius, *Yalta* (Paris, Gallimard, 1951), p.100
42. R. Sherwood, *Roosevelt and Hopkins* (New York, Harper, 1948), II, p.394
43. Archives du Quai d'Orsay, série Y, volume 121, "Conférence de Yalta"
44. *Ibid.*
45. *Discours et Messages* (Paris, Plon, 1970), I, pp.502–3
46. Interview with René Massigli, June 1983
47. *War Memoirs*, III, p.82
48. *Roosevelt and Hopkins*
49. *War Memoirs*, III, p.87

50. *Ibid.*
51. *Roosevelt and Hopkins*
52. *War Memoirs*, III, p.88
53. *Ibid.*
54. *Aimer de Gaulle*, p.143
55. *War Memoirs*, III, p.176
56. *Discours et Messages*, I, p.545
57. *War Memoirs*, III, p.178
58. *Discours et Messages*, I, p.550
59. *War Memoirs*, III, pp.202–3
60. A. Funk, *De Yalta à Potsdam* (Paris, Editions Complexe, 1983), p.161
61. *War Memoirs*, III, p.204
62. Archives du Quai d'Orsay, série Y, volume 282, "Affaires allemandes"
63. *War Memoirs*, III, p.211
64. H. Alphand, *L'Etonnement d'être* (Paris, Fayard, 1977), p.197
65. Archives du Quai d'Orsay, série Y, volume 283, "Affaires allemandes"
66. R. Aron, *Mémoires* (Paris, Julliard, 1983), p.202

CHAPTER FIVE
1. Interview with the author, March 1984
2. F.-L. Closon, *Commissaire de la République du général de Gaulle* (Paris, Julliard, 1980), p.44
3. *War Memoirs*, III, pp.91–2
4. *Ibid.*, p.93
5. *La Voix du Nord*, 2 October 1944, quoted by F.-L. Closon, *Commissaire de la République...*, pp.41–2
6. Georgette Elgey, *La République des illusions (1945–1951)*, (Paris, Fayard, 1965), p.32
7. Interview with the author, March 1980
8. Pierre Mendès France in an interview with the author, March 1980
9. R. Aron, *Mémoires*, p.234
10. Quoted by J.-C. Asselain in *L'Histoire*, No. 37, June 1981, p.13
11. *War Memoirs*, III, p.97
12. J. Lacouture, *Pierre Mendès France* (Paris, Le Seuil, 1981), p.158
13. "La politique financière de la France libérée", Commissariat aux Finances, Algiers
14. Interview with the author, October 1983

15. *War Memoirs*, III, Documents, pp.426–36
16. Interview with the author, 1971
17. *War Memoirs*, III, p.122
18. *Ibid.*, p.97

CHAPTER SIX
1. *Discours et Messages*, I, pp.318–9
2. M. Bardèche, *Lettre à François Mauriac*, La Pensée libre, 1947, pp.70–71
3. J. Paulhan, *Lettre aux directeurs de la Résistance* (Paris, Editions de Minuit, 1952)
4. *Ibid.*, p.12
5. Letter shown to the author by Jean Mauriac
6. P. Novick, *The Resistance versus Vichy. The Purge of Collaborators in Liberated France* (New York, Columbia University Press, 1968)
7. *Lettres, Notes...*, V, p.176
8. Interview with the author, March 1984
9. Interview with the author, March 1984
10. *Aimer de Gaulle*, p.71
11. *Ibid.*,
12. *Ibid.*, p.137
13. Interview with the author, 1973
14. *Aimer de Gaulle*, p.35
15. Interview with René de Chambrun, who gives a very similar version of the episode in his *"Procès" de Pierre Laval* (Paris, Editions France-Empire, 1983).
16. *Les Procès de Vichy*, p.152

CHAPTER SEVEN
1. *War Memoirs*, II, p.243
2. *Ibid.*, I, p.137
3. "Carnets" of Admiral d'Argenlieu (in J.-M. Royer, *En ce temps-là de Gaulle*, No. 62)
4. *Ibid.*
5. Quoted in the "De Gaulle et l'Indochine" colloquium, p.201
6. *War Memoirs*, III, p.226
7. Interview with the author, April 1984
8. *War Memoirs*, III, p.227
9. Quoted in the "De Gaulle et l'Indochine" colloquium, p.170

10. Interview with Alain de Boissieu, May 1984
11. *Churchill and de Gaulle*, p.399
12. *War Memoirs*, III, p.189
13. Quoted by F. Kersaudy, *Churchill and de Gaulle*, p.350
14. *War Memoirs*, III, p.192
15. *Old Men Forget* (London, Davis, 1953), pp.354–5
16. *War Memoirs*, III, p.196.
17. Quoted in a report by the Algiers Deuxième Bureau on the 1945 disturbances
18. *War Memoirs*, III, pp.225–6
19. M. Harbi, *Aux origines du FLN* (Paris, C. Bourgois, 1975)
20. C.-A. Julien, *L'Afrique du Nord en marche* (Paris, Julliard, 1972), p.252
21. Letter to the author, May 1984
22. Letter to the author, July 1984
23. *War Memoirs*, III, p.220
24. Interview with the author, June 1983

CHAPTER EIGHT
1. Interview with the author, March 1984
2. *War Memoirs*, III, p.234
3. *Ibid.*, p.235
4. *Discours et messages*, I, p.572
5. *Aimer de Gaulle*, p.177
6. *Journal officiel*, 29 July 1945, pp.1613–14
7. J. Fauvet, *La IVᵉ République* (Paris, Fayard, 1959), p.52
8. *Mon Général*, p.181
9. R. Stéphane, *Fin d'une jeunesse* (Paris, La Table ronde, 1954), p.96
10. *War Memoirs*, III, p.620
11. *La IVᵉ République*, p.53

CHAPTER NINE
1. *Mon Général*, p.170
2. *Espoir*, No. 41, December 1982, p.71
3. *Aimer de Gaulle*, p.146
4. *Mémoires de guerre*, III, p.101
5. *Ibid.*, p.273
6. *La République des illusions*, p.66
7. *Aimer de Gaulle*, pp.217–18
8. *Ibid.*, p.222
9. *La République des illusions*, p.70
10. P. Tesson, *De Gaulle Iᵉʳ*, p.253

11. *Mémoires de guerre*, III, p.271
12. *Ibid.*, p.273

CHAPTER TEN
1. Jules Moch, *Une si longue vie* (Paris, Laffont, 1976), pp.206–7
2. *Mémoires de guerre*, III, pp.277–8
3. *La République des illusions*, p.80
4. *Pour combattre avec de Gaulle*, p.337
5. *Journal officiel*, 1 January 1946, p.732
6. *Ibid.*, p.732
7. *Mémoires de guerre*, III, p.279
8. *Cette chance que j'ai eue*, p.157
9. *Ibid.*, pp.160–1
10. J. Moch, *Une si longue vie*, pp.208–9
11. Interview with the author, June 1984
12. *War Memoirs*, III, p.285
13. *La République des illusions*, pp.86–7
14. *War Memoirs*, III, p.285
15. J. Charlot, *Le Gaullisme d'opposition* (Paris, Fayard, 1983), p.23
16. J. Barsalou, *La Mal-Aimée* (Paris, Plon, 1964), p.30
17. *War Memoirs*, III, p.285
18. *La République des illusions*, p.93
19. Interview with the author, June 1983
20. Interview with the author, June 1984
21. *Aimer de Gaulle*, p.227
22. *War Memoirs*, III, p.281

CHAPTER ELEVEN
1. *War Memoirs*, III, p.287
2. *Cette chance que j'ai eue*, p.163
3. *Aimer de Gaulle*, pp.230–1
4. *War Memoirs*, III, p.647
5. *Aimer de Gaulle*, p.273
6. *Aimer de Gaulle*, p.267
7. *Ibid.*, p.288
8. *Cette chance que j'ai eue*, p.186
9. *Discours et Messages*, II, pp.29–33
10. *Aimer de Gaulle*, p.365
11. *Ibid.*, p.428
12. Interview with the author, August 1984
13. Interview with René Pleven, March 1984
14. *Aimer de Gaulle*, p.398
15. Quoted by J. Charlot, *Le Gaullisme d'opposition*, p.80

CHAPTER TWELVE
1. *Dix Ans avec de Gaulle* (Paris, France-Empire, 1971). Also an unpublished

interview kindly shown me by
Georgette Elgey

2. *Aimer de Gaulle*, pp.431–4
3. *Le Gaullisme d'opposition*, pp.87–9
4. Interview with the author, June 1984
5. RPF archives
6. Interview with the author, September 1964
7. *L'Etincelle*, 1 November 1947
8. *Journal du septennat*, I, p.493
9. Interview with the author, September 1984
10. L. Terrenoire, *De Gaulle 1947–1954. Pourquoi l'échec?* (Paris, Plon, 1981), p.12
11. *Lettres, Notes...*, VI, p.247
12. *L'Etincelle*, 15 November 1947
13. *L'Etincelle*, 10 January 1948
14. Interview with the author, November 1984
15. Interview with the author, July 1984
16. *Discours et Messages*, II, p.186
17. *Pour rétablir une vérité*, pp.129–30
18. Interview with the author, September 1984
19. *L'Oubli*, p.125
20. Interview with Louis Vallon, 1967
21. *La IVe République*, p.172
22. Interview with the author, July 1972
23. *Vingt-huit ans de gaullisme*, p.63
24. Interview with the author, December 1984
25. *Vingt-huit ans de gaullisme*, p.65

CHAPTER THIRTEEN

1. *Pour rétablir une vérité*, p.133
2. Interview with the author, November 1984
3. *Mon Général*, pp.294–5
4. *De Gaulle 1947–1954*, p.241
5. *Discours et Messages*, II, p.582
6. *Mon Général*, p.298
7. Interview with the author, June 1984
8. *De Gaulle 1947–1954*, p.221
9. F. Mauriac, *De Gaulle* (Paris, Grasset, 1964), pp.198–202
10. *Memoirs of Hope*, translated by Terence Kilmartin (London, Weidenfeld and Nicolson, 1971), pp.15–16
11. Interview with the author, July 1984
12. *De Gaulle 1947–54*, p.217

13. *Ibid.*, p.273
14. Louis Terrenoire, in collaboration with Gaston Bonheur, *Le Général* (Paris, Presses de la Cité, 1970)
15. *Pour servir le Général*, pp.73–4
16. *Discours et Messages*, II, pp.637–8
17. Interview with the author, July 1984
18. *Discours et Messages*, II, p.654
19. *Edmond Michelet, mon père*, p.233
20. Interview with the author, November 1984
21. Interview with the author, January 1985
22. *Le Monde*, 11 February 1984
23. *Le Monde*, 11 February 1958
24. J.-R. Tournoux, *La Tragédie du Général* (Paris, Plon, 1967), p.284

CHAPTER FOURTEEN

1. Cf. R. Rémond, *Le Retour de De Gaulle* (Paris, Editions Complexe, 1984), pp.10–11
2. *Ibid.*, p.62
3. J. Ferniot, *De Gaulle et le 13 mai*, Paris, Plon, 1965, p.273
4. *Memoirs of Hope*, pp.18–19
5. *Le Retour de De Gaulle*, p.78
6. R. Triboulet, *Un gaulliste de la IVe* (Paris, Plon, 1985), pp.308–9
7. *Memoirs of Hope*, p.22
8. J. Massu, *Le Torrent et la Digue* (Paris, Plon, 1972), pp.120–5
9. E. Jouhaud, *Serons-nous enfin compris?* (Paris, Albin Michel, 1984), p.53
10. *Ibid.*, p.53
11. *Avec qui vous savez*, p.119
12. *Serons-nous enfin compris?*, p.55
13. A. Dulac, *Nos guerres perdues* (Paris, Fayard, 1969), p.88
14. *Memoirs of Hope*, p.26
15. *Serons-nous enfin compris?*, p.62
16. Interview with the author, January 1985
17. *Memoirs of Hope*, p.27
18. Interview with the author, August 1984
19. H. Guillemin, *Le Général clair-obscur* (Paris, Le Seuil, 1984), p.94
20. J. Chauvel, *Commentaire III* (Paris, Fayard, 1973), p.244
21. *Le Monde*, 4 June 1958

22. *New York Times*, 3 June 1958
23. *New York Herald Tribune*, 4 June 1958
24. *Memoirs of Hope*, p.30

CHAPTER FIFTEEN

1. *Memoirs of Hope*, p.46
2. Letter to the author, February 1985
3. *New York Herald Tribune*, 2 June 1958
4. R. Salan, *Mémoires*, III (Paris, Presses de la Cité, 1972), p.374
5. *Pour servir le Général*, pp.99–100
6. *Le Monde*, 6 June 1958
7. *L'Esperance trahie*, p.54
8. *Ibid.*, p.53
9. *Avec qui vous savez*, p.129
10. Interview with Simonne Servais, April 1955

CHAPTER SIXTEEN

1. *Memoirs of Hope*, p.30
2. Interview with the author, February 1985
3. Odile Rudelle, *Revue française de science politique*, October 1984, p.701
4. *Memoirs of Hope*, p.32
5. *Espoir*, October 1984, pp.5–24
6. Quoted by Marcel Merle, *Revue française de science politique*, March 1959, p.145
7. Marcel Merle, op. cit., p.145
8. *Le Nef*, September 1958
9. *Memoirs of Hope*, p.34
10. P. Williams and M. Harrison, *Elections Abroad* (London, Macmillan, 1959)
11. M. Dogan, *Le Référendum et les Elections de 1958* (Paris, A. Colin, 1960), p.29
12. *Discours et Messages*, III, pp.46–7
13. *Mémoires d'espoir*, IV, p.125 [not in the translated version]
14. *Nos guerres perdues*, p.139
15. *Mémoires*, IV, p.144
16. *Ibid.*, p.148
17. *Discours et Messages*, III, pp.55–6
18. Interview with the author, October 1958
19. *Le Monde*, 28 October 1958

CHAPTER SEVENTEEN

1. *Memoirs of Hope*, p.167
2. *Ibid.*, p.188

3. M. Couve de Murville, *Une politique étrangère 1958–1969* (Paris, Plon, 1971), p.25
4. *Antimemoirs*, translated by Terence Kilmartin (London, Penguin, 1967), p.153
5. Interview with the author, March 1985
6. B. Ledwidge, *De Gaulle et les Américains* (Paris, Flammarion, 1984), pp.14–33
7. *Une politique étrangère*, p.33
8. F. Seydoux, *Mémoires d'outre-Rhin* (Paris, Grasset, 1975), p.212
9. *Memoirs of Hope*, p.176
10. *Ibid.*, p.179
11. *Mémoires d'outre-Rhin*, p.212
12. K. Adenauer, *Mémoires* (Paris, Hachette, 1969), III, pp.181–91 [French translation]
13. Revue *Espoir*, June 1976
14. Interview with the author, February 1985
15. Revue *Espoir*, June 1976
16. *Une politique étrangère*, p.49

CHAPTER EIGHTEEN

1. *Mon Général*, p.366
2. *Le Référendum et les Elections de 1958*, pp.235–6
3. Interview with the author, November 1984
4. *Memoirs of Hope*, p.152
5. J. Rueff, *Combats pour l'ordre financier* (Paris, Plon, 1972), pp.140–63
6. Speech of 26 February 1985
7. *Memoirs of Hope*, p.144
8. *Ibid.*, p.143
9. Interview with the author, January 1985
10. *Memoirs of Hope*, p.146
11. *Ibid.*, p.35
12. *Discours et Messages*, III, p.64
13. R. Aron, *Mémoires*, p.380
14. Interview with the author, February 1985
15. *Le Monde*, 9 January 1959
16. *Discours et Messages*, III, p.72
17. *Histoire de la République gaullienne*, p.52
18. *Memoirs of Hope*, I, pp.35–6

CHAPTER NINETEEN

1. *Espoir*, No.14, March 1976, pp.17–21
2. Interview with the author, March 1986
3. *Avec qui vous savez...*, p.155
4. *Memoirs of Hope*, p.297
5. *La Vie quotidienne à l'Elysée...*, pp.70–1
6. Interview with the author, May 1985
7. *Memoirs of Hope*, pp.271–4
8. *Les Gaullistes, Rituel et annuaire*, p.41

CHAPTER TWENTY

1. A. de Boissieu, *Pour servir le Général* (Paris, Plon, 1982), p.99
2. *Memoirs of Hope*, p.62
3. On this point cf. Mohamed Lebjaoui, *Vérités sur la révolution algérienne* (Paris, Gallimard, 1972), pp.151–62.
4. J. Soustelle, *L'Espérance trahie* (Paris, Ed. Alma, 1962), pp.89–93
5. *Ibid.*, pp.94–5
6. Interview with the author, February 1985
7. E. Faure, *Mémoires*, II (Paris, Plon, 1984), p.688
8. Interview with the author, February 1985
9. Interview with the author, April 1985
10. Interview with the author, June 1984
11. *La Décadence...*, p.192
12. Bernard Tricot, *Les Sentiers de la paix* (Paris, Plon, 1972), pp.103–4
13. *L'Express*, 6 August 1959
14. *L'Esperance trahie*, pp.112–14
15. Interview with the author, February 1986
16. *La Décadence...*, p.193
17. *Memoirs of Hope*, p.75
18. *Discours et Messages*, III, pp.117–22
19. *De Gaulle entre deux mondes*, p.635

CHAPTER TWENTY-ONE

1. M. and S. Bromberger, G. Elgey, J. Chauvel, *Barricades et Colonels* (Paris, Fayard, 1960), p.55
2. Account based on J.-R. Tournoux, *La Tragédie du Général* (Paris, Plon, 1967), pp.315–20, and corroborated by various witnesses (MM. Sudreau, Chatenet...)
3. *Barricades et Colonels*, p.88

4. *Lettres, Notes et Carnets (1958–1960)* (Paris, Plon, 1985), VIII, p.317
5. *Ibid.*, p.318
6. J. Massu, *Le Torrent et la Digue* (Paris, Plon, 1972), p.311
7. *Souvenirs d'outre-Gaulle*, p.39
8. *Lettres, Notes...*, VIII, p.321
9. Interview between Jean-Marcel Jeanneney and the author, November 1985
10. Interview with the author, May 1985

CHAPTER TWENTY-TWO

1. Letter from René Brouillet to the author, April 1985
2. Letter from René Brouillet to the author, May 1985
3. *Le Monde*, 6 March 1960
4. *De Gaulle et l'Algérie*, p.189
5. Ferhât Abbâs, *Autopsie d'une guerre* (Paris, Garnier, 1981), p.265
6. P. Viansson-Ponté, *Histoire de la République gaullienne* (Paris, Fayard, 1976); Laffont, 1984, coll. "Bouquins", p.192
7. *De Gaulle et l'Algérie*, pp.205–12
8. *Le Dernier Quart d'heure*, p.154
9. *De Gaulle et l'Algérie*, p.215
10. *Ibid.*, p.217

CHAPTER TWENTY-THREE

1. *La Décadence...*, p.229
2. *De Gaulle et l'Algérie*, p.219
3. Interview with the author, June 1985
4. Unpublished notes taken by M. Masmoudi
5. Unpublished notes by Jean Mauriac
6. *De Gaulle et l'Algérie*, p.224
7. *Discours et Messages*, III, p.293
8. *Ibid.*, p.290
9. *De Gaulle et l'Algérie*, p.277
10. *La Décadence...*, p.253
11. *La Fronde des généraux*, p.155
12. *De Gaulle et l'Algérie*, p.228
13. *La Décadence ...*, p.282
14. Interview given by André Malraux to the author, 1972
15. Interview with the author, August 1984
16. *De Gaulle et l'Algérie*, p.231
17. *Discours et Messages*, III, pp.306–8
18. M. Vaisse, *Alger, le Putsch* (Paris,

Editions Complexe, 1984), p.99
19. Interview with the author, 1967
20. Interview with Roger Seydoux, June 1985
21. *Memoirs of Hope*, pp.110, 111

CHAPTER TWENTY-FOUR
1. Interview with Louis Joxe, May 1984
2. Interview with Claude Chayet, July 1984
3. Interview with Geoffroy de Courcel, July 1985
4. Interview with A. Mehri, June 1985
5. *Souvenirs d'outre-Gaulle*, pp.59–60
6. *Memoirs of Hope*, p.122
7. *L'Expiation*, p.222
8. *De Gaulle et l'Algérie*, p.241
9. J. Delarue, *L'OAS contre de Gaulle* (Paris, Fayard, 1981), pp.64–5
10. *Discours et Messages*, III, p.340
11. *Ibid.*, pp.367–71
12. *De Gaulle et l'Algérie*, pp.241–2
13. Letter to the author, 1984
14. Quoted in *Histoire de la République gaullienne*, p.270

CHAPTER TWENTY-FIVE
1. *Souvenirs d'outre-Gaulle*, p.66
2. *Carnets politiques de la guerre d'Algérie* (Paris, Plon, 1975), p.187
3. *Histoire de la République gaullienne*, p.278
4. Cf. Mohammed Harbi, *Le FLN, mirages et réalités*, pp.296–7
5. *Le Monde*, 16 March 1982
6. *Carnets politiques . . .*, p.247
7. Interview with the author, June 1984
8. *Le Figaro*, 19 March 1982
9. *Carnets politiques . . .*, p.249
10. *Ibid.*, p.258
11. *Discours et Messages*, III, pp.391–3
12. *L'Express*, 22 March 1962
13. *Discours et Messages*, III, p.399
14. *Histoire de la République gaullienne*, p.282

CHAPTER TWENTY-SIX
1. *Discours et Messages*, III, pp.138–9
2. *Ibid.*, p.312
3. J.-R. Tournoux, *La Tragédie du général*, pp.415–16

4. C. Fouchet, *Au service du général de Gaulle* (Paris, Plon, 1971), pp.175–7
5. *OAS parle* (Paris, Julliard, 1964, coll. "Archives"), p.269
6. *La Décadence . . .*, pp.313–14
7. *Objectif de Gaulle*, pp.255–6
8. *Au service du général de Gaulle*, p.159
9. A. de La Tocnaye, *Comment je n'ai pas tué de Gaulle*, p.215
10. *Au service du général de Gaulle*, p.165
11. *Comment je n'ai pas tué de Gaulle*, p.275
12. *La Tragédie du général*, p.448
13. *Pour servir le Général*, p.169
14. *La Tragédie du général*, p.454

CHAPTER TWENTY-SEVEN
1. *Memoirs of Hope*, pp.210–11
2. M. Couve de Murville, *Une politique étrangère (1958–1969)* (Paris, Plon, 1971), p.241
3. *Ibid.*, p.245
4. *Mémoires*, III, p.256
5. *Ibid.*, pp.303–4
6. *Une politique étrangère*, pp.253–54
7. *Mémoires*, III, p.337
8. *Ibid.*, p.335
9. *Une politique étrangère*, p.257
10. "Le preambule terrible", *Espoir*, No.23, p.29
11. *Ibid.*
12. *Une politique étrangère*, p.273
13. *Memoirs of Hope*, pp.163–6
14. H. Macmillan, *Memoirs*, V, *Pointing the Way* (London, Macmillan, 1972), p.427
15. Speech at University College, London, 24 November 1982
16. *Au service du général de Gaulle*, p.199
17. Interview with the author, April 1986
18. *Memoirs of Hope*, p.197
19. Speech at University College, London, 24 November 1982
20. *Memoirs of Hope*, pp.234–5
21. *Discours et Messages*, III, pp.179–81
22. *Memoirs of Hope*, p.188
23. *Ibid.*, p.218
24. Address at University College, London, 24 November 1982
25. N. Beloff, *The General Says No* (London, Penguin, 1963), pp.215–16

26. *Le Monde*, 24 January 1963
27. *Espoir*, No.12
28. H. Macmillan, *Memoirs*, VII, *At the End of the Year* (London, Macmillan, 1973), p.367
29. Interview with Geoffroy de Courcel, June 1985
30. Interview with E. Burin des Roziers, July 1985
31. P. H. Spaak, *Combats inachevés* (Brussels, Vokaer, 1979, II), p.406
32. A. Grosser, *La Politique extérieure de la Ve République* (Paris, Le Seuil, 1965), p.140
33. Letter to the author, December 1985

CHAPTER TWENTY-EIGHT

1. Interview with the author, February 1985
2. Quoted by J. Hess, *De Gaulle avait-il raison?* (Paris, Mame, 1969), p.10
3. C. Bohlen, *Witness to History* (New York, Norton, 1973), p.502
4. Interviews with H. Alphant and R. Seydoux
5. *De Gaulle avait-il raison?*, p.12
6. H. Kissinger, *The Troubled Partnership* (New York, McGraw-Hill, 1965), pp.16–18, 42–3
7. V. Walters, *Services discrets* (Paris, Plon, 1979), p.254
8. *Memoirs of Hope*, pp.201–2
9. A. Fontaine, *L'Alliance atlantique à l'heure du dégel* (Paris, Calmann-Lévy, 1967), p.120
10. *Memoirs of Hope*, p.210
11. *Services discrets*, p.254
12. *Ibid.*, p.257
13. *Memoirs of Hope*, pp.242–3
14. *Ibid.*, pp.243–4
15. *Ibid.*, p.244
16. *Ibid.*, p.247
17. *Ibid.*, p.253
18. *Ibid.*, p.254
19. Interviews with the author, September 1985
20. H. Alphand, *L'Etonnement d'être* (Paris, Fayard, 1977), p.351
21. *Memoirs of Hope*, pp.254–5
22. B. Ledgwidge, *De Gaulle et les Américains* (Paris, Flammarion, 1984), pp.101–5 [French translation]

23. *Ibid.*, p.115
24. *L'Etonnement d'être*, p.355
25. *Memoirs of Hope*, p.255
26. *De Gaulle and the Americans*, p.123
27. *Une politique étrangère*, p.100
28. Interview with Hervé Alphand and Roger Seydoux, then France's representative on the Security Council, March 1985
29. *Une politique étrangère*, p.105
30. *Ibid.*, p.106
31. Interview with the author, October 1985
32. *L'Etonnement d'être*, p.411
33. Interview with Edgard Pisani, October 1985
34. *L'Etonnement d'être*, p.414
35. *Une politique étrangère*, p.119
36. Interview with H. Alphand, March 1985
37. *Une politique étrangère*, p.122
38. *De Gaulle and the Americans*, p.144
39. *Discours et Messages*, IV, pp.331–2
40. *L'Etonnement d'être*, pp.452–3
41. Interview with the author, March 1985
42. G. Ball, *The Past Has Another Pattern* (New York, Norton, 1982), pp.332–4
43. Interview with the author, February 1986
44. *Discours et Messages*, V, p.19
45. Richard Nixon, *Leaders* (New York, Warner; London, Sidgwick and Jackson, 1982), pp.66–7
46. *Ibid.*, pp.75–6
47. *Ibid.*, pp.78–9

CHAPTER TWENTY-NINE

1. *Discours et Messages*, III, pp.129–31
2. *Memoirs of Hope*, p.225
3. *Ibid.*, p.232
4. *Ibid.*, p.233
5. Interview with General de Boissieu, February 1985
6. *Memoirs of Hope*, p.234
7. *Ibid.*, p.248
8. My own notes
9. *Discours et Messages*, IV, p.155
10. *Une politique étrangère*, pp.197–8
11. Interview by the author with Etienne Burin des Roziers
12. *Discours et Messages*, IV, p.355

13. *Ibid.*, IV, p.408
14. *L'Etonnement d'être*, p.445
15. *Ibid.*, p.477
16. *Discours et Messages*, V, p.41
17. Weit, *Dans l'ombre de Gomulka* (Paris, Laffont, 1971), p.188
18. *Witness to History*, p.542
19. *L'Etonnement d'être*, p.385

CHAPTER THIRTY
1. P. Devillers, *De Gaulle et le Tiers-Monde*, p.308
2. *Observer*, 2 February 1964
3. *Espoir*, No.1, p.42
4. *Discours et Messages*, V, p.23
5. Cited by P. Devillers, *De Gaulle et le Tiers-Monde*, p.314
6. Interview with Prince Sihanuk, November 1985
7. Interview with the author, September 1966
8. *L'Entourage et de Gaulle*, p.130
9. E. Faure, *Le Serpent et la Tortue* (Paris, Julliard, 1957)
10. E. Faure, *Mémoires*, II, p.674
11. *Espoir*, No.1, pp.20–5
12. *Ibid.*, p.25
13. *L'Entourage et de Gaulle*, p.137
14. *Discours et Messages*, IV, p.178
15. *De Gaulle et le Tiers-Monde*, p.271
16. Interview with the author, March 1985
17. Letter to the author, July 1985

CHAPTER THIRTY-ONE
1. Interview with Francis Perrin, November 1985
2. *L'Aventure de la bombe* (Arc-et-Senans, 1985), p.52
3. Letter from Francis Perrin to the author, November 1985
4. P. Gallois, *Stratégie à l'âge nucléaire* (Paris, Calmann-Lévy, 1959)
5. *Discours et Messages*, III, pp.127–8
6. *Ibid.*, p.134
7. Interview with the author, November 1985
8. *L'Aventure de la bombe*, p.64
9. *Ibid.*, p.66
10. *Ibid.*, pp.153–4
11. Interview with the author, November 1985

12. *L'Aventure de la bombe*, p.154
13. A. Peyrefitte, *Le Mal français* (Paris, Plon, 1976), pp.81–5
14. *Ibid.*, p.84
15. Interview with General de Boissieu, February 1986
16. *L'Aventure de la bombe*, p.53
17. Interview with the author, January 1986
18. A. Beaufre, *Dissuasion et Stratégie* (Paris, A. Colin, 1964)
19. R. Aron, *Le Grand Débat* (Paris, Calmann-Lévy, 1963), p.156
20. P. Gallois, *L'Adieu aux armées* (Paris, Albin Michel, 1976), p.319
21. Interview with the author, October 1985
22. W. Lippmann, *L'Unité occidentale et le Marché commun* (Paris, Julliard, 1962)
23. R. Aron, *Mémoires*, p.426
24. L. Ruehl, *La Politique militaire de la Ve République* (Presses de la Fondation nationale des Sciences politiques, cahier 193), p.415
25. *Une politique étrangère*, p.58
26. *La Politique extérieure de la Ve République*, p.133
27. *Ibid.*, p.134
28. L. Hamon, *La Stratégie contre la guerre* (Paris, Grasset, 1966), p.312
29. *Revue de défense nationale*, December 1967, pp.1930–1.
30. Interview with the author, December 1985
31. Interview with the author, December 1985
32. Interview with the author, December 1985
33. P. Messmer and A. Larcan, *Les Ecrits militaires de Charles de Gaulle* (Paris, PUF, 1985), p.172
34. *L'Aventure de la bombe*, p.35

CHAPTER THIRTY-TWO
1. Interview with the author, June 1985
2. S. Cohen, in *La Politique étrangère du général de Gaulle*, colloque de Tel-Aviv, p.195
3. *Memoirs of Hope*, pp.265–6
4. Abba Eban, *An Autobiography* (London, Weidenfeld and Nicolson, 1978), pp.339–40

5. J.-F. Held, *Israël et les Arabes, le troisième combat* (Paris, Le Seuil, 1967), p.39
6. *Une politique étrangère*, p.469
7. *An Autobiography*, p.341
8. *Discours et Messages*, V, p.234
9. *An Autobiography*, p.341
10. *Une politique étrangère*, p.469
11. Interview with the author, December 1985
12. Interview with Albin Chalandon, March 1985
13. *Histoire de la République gaullienne*, p.331
14. C. Yost, *Foreign Affairs*, January 1968, p.319
15. Interview with the author, October 1985
16. Interview with the author, October 1985
17. *Discours et Messages*, V, pp.232–4
18. R. Aron, *De Gaulle, Israël et les Juifs* (Tribune libre, Paris, Plon, 1968)
19. J.-R. Tournoux, *Le Tourment et la Fatalité* (Paris, Plon, 1974), p.206
20. Presented at the Sorbonne in October 1983

CHAPTER THIRTY-THREE
1. *Memoirs of Hope*, pp.239–42
2. *Une politique étrangère*, p.455
3. *Souvenirs d'outre-Gaulle*, p.84
4. Quoted in A. and P. Rouanet, *Les Trois Derniers Chagrins du Général de Gaulle* (Paris, Grasset, 1980), p.43
5. R. Lescop, *Le Pari québécois du général de Gaulle* (Montreal, Boréal Express, 1981), p.140
6. Interview with the author, April 1986
7. *Les Trois Derniers Chagrins...*, pp.61–3
8. G. Bergeron, *Le Canada français après deux siècles de patience* (Paris, Le Seuil, 1966)
9. Notably the *Globe and Mail* of 24 July 1967
10. *Espoir*, No.12, p.27
11. *Souvenirs d'outre-Gaulle*, p.89
12. *Espoir*, No.12, p.29
13. *Souvenirs d'outre-Gaulle*, p.90
14. Interview with the author, April 1983

15. Interview with the author in Quebec, 22 April 1983
16. Interview with the author, April 1983
17. *Les Trois Derniers Chagrins...*, p.146
18. Interview with the author, April 1983
19. P.-L. Mallen, in *Espoir*, No.12, p.33
20. *Les Trois Derniers Chagrins...*, p.154
21. *Le Soleil*, Quebec, 26 August 1967, p.16
22. *Le Figaro*, 27 July 1967
23. *L'Etonnement d'être*, p.493
24. Unpublished notes taken during the meeting. There are a number of "blanks". J.-R. Tournoux has published another version.
25. Jean d'Escrienne, *Le général m'a dit, 1966–1970* (Paris, Plon, 1973), p.109
26. *Discours et Messages*, V, p.239

CHAPTER THIRTY-FOUR
1. *L'Etonnement d'être*, p.493
2. *De Gaulle de loin et de près*, pp.111–12
3. Account reconstructed from memory by Jean d'Escrienne and published in *De Gaulle de loin et de près*, p.116.
4. *Souvenirs d'outre-Gaulle*, pp.195–7
5. *Discours et Messages*, V, p.279
6. Notes taken by one of the General's colleagues in early July 1968.
7. *Pour servir le Général*, p.208
8. *Ibid.*, p.209
9. Interview with the author, March 1985
10. E. Manac'h, *Mémoires d'Extrême-Asie* (Paris, Fayard, 1977), p.34
11. *Ibid.*, pp.35–55
12. *De Gaulle*, p.363
13. *Ibid.*, p.364
14. *Le Monde*, 13 March 1969
15. *L'Etonnement d'être*, p.518
16. *De Gaulle*, pp.366
17. *Ibid.*, p.396
18. Notes communicated to the author
19. *La Politique extérieure de la Ve République*, p.168
20. Interview with the author, October 1985
21. *Sunday Times*, December 1970

CHAPTER THIRTY-FIVE
1. *Memoirs of Hope*, p.340
2. *Histoire de la République gaullienne*, p.315

3. Interview with Gaston Monnerville, October 1985
4. Interview with the author, November 1985
5. *Le Populaire*, 21 June 1946
6. *Memoirs of Hope*, pp.306–7
7. Interview with the author, October 1985
8. *Pour servir le Général*, pp.170–1
9. George Vedel, *L'Année dans le monde* (Paris, Arthaud, 1963), p.43
10. Interview with the author, August 1985
11. *L'Année dans le monde*, pp.49–50
12. *Ibid.*, pp.49–50
13. Interview with the author, December 1985
14. *De Gaulle parle*, II, p.55
15. *Ibid.*, p.59
16. *Ibid.*, p.64
17. 27 November 1962
18. Quoted in *De Gaulle parle*, II, p.65
19. *Memoirs of Hope*, pp.349–50
20. *Ibid.*, p.374
21. *Ibid.*, p.375
22. *Ibid.*
23. A. Prate, lecture given on 25 January 1985
24. *Memoirs of Hope*, pp.374–5
25. Interview with the author, February 1986
26. A. Prate, *Les Batailles économiques du général de Gaulle*, p.175
27. *Ibid.*, p.190

CHAPTER THIRTY-SIX
1. *De Gaulle parle*, II, p.92
2. A. Hauriou, *Droit constitutionnel* (Paris, Montchrestien, 1970), p.761
3. *Le Monde*, 2–3 February 1964 (under the signature of Sirius)
4. Interview with the author, July 1985
5. A. Lancelot and M. Chapsal, *La Vie politique en France depuis 1940* (Paris, PUF, coll. "Thémis", 1969), p.562
6. J.-F. Kahn, J. Derogy, *Les Secrets du ballottage* (Paris, Fayard, 1966), pp.40–1
7. *Le Tourment et la Fatalité*, p.133
8. *Souvenirs d'outre-Gaulle*, p.160
9. Interview with André Malraux, December 1972

10. Interview with the author, January 1986
11. Interview with the author, January 1986
12. F. Mitterrand, *Ma part de vérité* (Paris, Fayard, 1969), p.47
13. R. Barrillon, *La Gauche française en mouvement* (Paris, Plon, 1967), p.29
14. Interview with Alain Peyrefitte, January 1986
15. *Discours et Messages*, IV, p.401
16. *Les Secrets du ballottage*, p.162
17. Interview with the author, January 1986
18. Interview with the author, January 1986
19. *Le Monde*, 7 December 1965
20. Based on *Les Secrets du ballottage*, pp.233–4 and A. Peyrefitte's reminiscences
21. Interview with Alain Peyrefitte, January 1986
22. M. Droit, *ibid.*, p.31
23. *Histoire*, No.2, p.197
24. Interview with Alain Peyrefitte, January 1986
25. *Souvenirs d'outre-Gaulle*, p.160
26. Interview with M. Jobert, January 1986
27. *Discours et Messages*, IV, p.445
28. *Le Figaro littéraire*, 28 January 1966
29. *Le Provençal*, 2 February 1966
30. *Le Monde*, 3 February 1966
31. *Discours et Messages*, V, pp.13–16
32. P. Alexandre, *Le Duel de Gaulle–Pompidou* (Paris, Grasset, 1970), p.186
33. *Le Table ronde de Combat* (Paris, 1967), pp.211–12
34. G. Martinet, *Le Système Pompidou* (Paris, Le Seuil, 1973)
35. J. Charbonnel, *L'Aventure de la fidélité* (Paris, Le Seuil, 1976), p.122
36. L. Vallon, *L'Anti de Gaulle* (Paris, Le Seuil, 1969)
37. Interview with the author, January 1986
38. Interview with the author, January 1986
39. M. Loichot, *La Réforme pancapitaliste* (Paris, Laffont, 1966)
40. Interview with the author, 1967

41. Author's interview with B. Tricot, January 1986
42. Colloque *L'Entourage et de Gaulle*, p.212
43. *Ibid.*, p.212
44. *Discours et Messages*, V, pp.143–4

CHAPTER THIRTY-SEVEN
1. *Souvenirs d'outre-Gaulle*, p.172
2. *Le Monde*, 15 March 1968
3. Interview with the author, January 1986
4. Interview with Jacques Narbonne, January 1986
5. Quoted by J.-R. Tournoux, *Le Mois de mai du général* (Paris, Plon, 1969), p.51
6. C. Fouchet, *Au service du général de Gaulle* (Paris, Plon, 1971), p.225
7. P. Alexandre, *L'Elysée en péril* (Paris, Fayard, 1968), p.67
8. C. Mauriac, *Les Espaces imaginaires* (Paris, Grasset, 1975), p.261
9. G. Pompidou, *Pour rétablir une vérité* (Paris, Flammarion, 1982), p.184
10. C. Fouchet, *Les lauriers sont coupés* (Paris, Plon, 1973), pp.36–44
11. *Pour rétablir une vérité*, p.218
12. *Le Monde*, 14 May 1978
13. *Au service du général de Gaulle*, p.255
14. *Pour rétablir une vérité*, p.185
15. *Mémoires d'avenir*, p.45
16. *L'Elysée en péril*, p.299
17. *Histoire de la République gaullienne*, p.613
18. *Ibid.*
19. *Ibid.*
20. *Pour rétablir une vérité*, p.187
21. *Discours et Messages*, V, pp.289–91
22. *L'Elysée en péril*, p.313
23. *Souvenirs d'outre-Gaulle*, p.184
24. Interview with J-M. Jeanneney, January 1986
25. *Pour rétablir une vérité*, p.190
26. *Ibid.*, p.191
27. *Le Mois de mai du général*, p.218
28. *L'Elysée en péril*, p.316
29. *Les Trois Derniers Chagrins...*, p.277
30. Letter from General Fourquet to the author, 29 January 1986
31. *Les Espaces imaginaires*, p.269
32. *Ibid.*, p.267

33. M. Debatisse, *Le Projet paysan* (Paris, Le Seuil, 1983)
34. *Pour rétablir une vérité*, pp.190–1
35. *Les lauriers sont coupés*, pp.20–6
36. *Les Trois Derniers Chagrins...*, p.287
37. *Pour servir le Général*, p.185
38. Unpublished diary, June 1983
39. Interview with X. de La Chevalerie, January 1986
40. *Pour servir le Général*, pp.174–94
41. *Ibid.*, p.188
42. *Les grandes années que j'ai vécues*, p.319
43. F. Goguel, *Espoir*, No.24
44. F. Flohic, unpublished memoir, June 1983
45. *Ibid.*
46. *Le Figaro Magazine*, 23 April 1983
47. *Le Point*, 10 January 1983
48. J. Massu, *Baden 68* (Paris, Plon, 1983), pp.87–92
49. *Pour rétablir une vérité*, p.201
50. *Ibid.*, p.201
51. *Baden 68*, p.81
52. Interview with the author, January 1986
53. Unpublished memoir and interview with the author, January 1986
54. Interview with the author, January 1986
55. *Baden 68*, p.106
56. *Pour rétablir une vérité*, p.201
57. *Souvenirs d'outre-Gaulle*, p.182
58. *Le Point*, 29 April 1983
59. Interview with the author, July 1985
60. Interview with the author, April 1986
61. *Mon Général*, p.430
62. *Les Trois Derniers Chagrins...*, p.330
63. *Pour rétablir une vérité*, p.196
64. *Souvenirs d'outre-Gaulle*, p.283
65. *Les grandes années que j'ai vécues*, p.319
66. *L'Arbre de mai*, p.336
67. *Ibid.*, p.197
68. *Pour rétablir une vérité*, p.199
69. M. Grimaud, *En mai, fais ce qu'il te plaît* (Paris, Stock, 1977), p.294
70. *Discours et Messages*, V, pp.292–3
71. *Mon Général*, p.432

CHAPTER THIRTY-EIGHT
1. *Baden 68*, p.132
2. *Discours et Messages*, V, pp.295–304
3. *Pour rétablir une vérité*, p.204

4. Interview with the author, February 1986
5. Interview with Bernard Tricot, January 1986
6. *Pour rétablir une vérité*, p.205
7. *Ibid.*, p.138
8. Interview with the author, January 1986
9. Interview with the author, January 1986
10. *Discours et Messages*, V, p.329
11. *Histoire de la République gaullienne*, p.589
12. *Les Batailles économiques...*, p.278
13. *Discours et Messages*, V, pp.327–8
14. *Ibid.*, pp.327–8
15. *Le Monde*, 22 November 1968
16. *L'Anti de Gaulle*, p.63
17. Interview with the author, February 1986
18. Interview with the author, February 1986
19. Interview with the author, January 1986
20. *Mémoires d'avenir*, p.89
21. *Ibid.*, p.90
22. *Ibid.*, p.42
23. Interview with the author, January 1986
24. *Pour rétablir une vérité*, p.260
25. *Ibid.*, p.263
26. *Ibid.*, p.283
27. *De Gaulle de loin et de près*, pp.129–30
28. *Pour rétablir une vérité*, p.270
29. *Ibid.*, p.272
30. Notes provided by Jean Mauriac
31. *Mon Général*, p.441
32. Interview with the author, March 1985
33. J. Mauriac, *Mort du général de Gaulle* (Paris, Grasset, 1972), p.14
34. Interview with the author, April 1986
35. *De Gaulle de loin et de près*, pp.225–6
36. *Mort du général de Gaulle*, p.13
37. Interview with the author, March 1964
38. *L'Aventure de la fidélité*, p.167
39. Interview with the author, January 1986
40. *Pour rétablir une vérité*, pp.273–4
41. *Mort du général de Gaulle*, p.28
42. *Ibid.*, p.29
43. *Discours et Messages*, V, p.407
44. *Mort du général de Gaulle*, pp.41–2

CHAPTER THIRTY-NINE
1. *Mort du général de Gaulle*, p.60
2. Interview with the author, January 1986
3. *Souvenirs d'outre-Gaulle*, p.197
4. *Pour rétablir une vérité*, p.287
5. *Souvenirs d'outre-Gaulle*, p.201
6. *De Gaulle*, p.374
7. *Souvenirs d'outre-Gaulle*, p.206
8. *Mort du général de Gaulle*, p.68
9. *De Gaulle*, p.374
10. *De Gaulle de près et de loin*, p.220
11. *Le Figaro littéraire*, No.1278, 22 November 1970
12. *Les chênes qu'on abat* (Paris, Gallimard, coll. "Folio", 1971), pp.37, 66, 79, 124–43
13. Interview with the author, February 1986
14. *Les chênes qu'on abat*, p.37
15. *Mort du général de Gaulle*, p.82
16. *Ibid.*, p.132–4

CHAPTER FORTY
1. *Mort du général de Gaulle*, p.139
2. Television interview with Jacqueline Baudrier, 9 November 1971
3. J. Mauriac, *Paris-Match*, October 1979
4. *Mort du général de Gaulle*, p.152
5. *Ibid.*, p.147
6. *Paris-Match*
7. *Ces grandes années que j'ai vécues*, pp.375–6
8. *Mort du général de Gaulle*, pp.162–3
9. *Ces grandes années que j'ai vécues*, p.374
10. This section is based on Pierre Lefranc's *Avec qui vous savez* (Paris, Plon, 1979), pp.298–303.
11. Report by Michel Legris in *Le Monde*, 12 November 1970
12. *Mort du général de Gaulle*, p.181

BIBLIOGRAPHY

I *Major works by Charles de Gaulle*

La Discorde chez l'ennemi, Paris, Berger-Levrault, 1924; Plon, 1972; Le Livre de poche.

Le Fil de l'épée, Paris, Berger-Levrault, 1932; Plon, 1971; Le Livre de poche.

Vers l'armée de métier, Paris, Berger-Levrault, 1938; Plon, 1971; Le Livre de poche.

La France et son armée, Paris, Plon, 1938 and 1969; Le Livre de poche, UGE 10/18.

Trois études, including *Rôle historique des places françaises* (1 December 1925), *Mobilisation économique à l'étranger* (1 January 1934), *Comment faire une armée de métier* (12 January 1935), *Mémorandum adressé par le colonel de Gaulle aux généraux Gamelin, Weygand, Georges, et à MM. Daladier et Paul Reynaud* (26 January 1940), Paris, Berger-Levrault, 1945; Plon, 1971; Le Livre de poche.

Mémoires de guerre, I *L'Appel, 1940–1942*; II *L'Unité, 1942–1944*; III *Le Salut, 1944–1946*, Paris, Plon, 1954, 1956 and 1959; Le Livre de poche, Presses Pocket.

Discours et Messages, I *Pendant la guerre, 1940–1964*; II *Dans l'attente, 1946–1958*; III *Avec le renouveau, 1958–1962*; IV *Pour l'effort, 1962–1965*; V *Vers le terme, 1966–1969*, Paris, Plon, 1970.

Mémoires d'espoir, I *Le Renouveau, 1958–1962*, II *L'Effort, 1962–…*, Paris, Plon, 1970 and 1971; Le Livre de poche, Presses Pocket.

The following books by Charles de Gaulle have been translated into English:

Vers l'armée de métier. *The Army of the Future* (Hutchinson, 1940).

L'Histoire de l'armée française: *France and her Army* (Hutchinson, 1945).

Mémoires de Guerre: *War Memoirs*; Volume I, *The Call to Honour, 1940–42* (Collins, 1955), Volume II, *Unity, 1942–44* (Weidenfeld and Nicolson, 1959), Volume III, *Salvation, 1944–46* (Weidenfeld and Nicolson, 1960)

Le Fil de l'épée: *The Edge of the Sword* (Faber and Faber, 1960).

Mémoires d'espoir: *Memoirs of Hope*; *Renewal 1958–62* and *Endeavour 1962–* (Weidenfeld and Nicolson, 1971).

II *Articles and other writings*

Une mauvaise rencontre (1906), *La Congrégation* (6 May 1908), *La Bataille de la Vistule* (1 November 1920), *Préparer la guerre, c'est préparer des chefs* (1921?), *Le Flambeau* (1 March 1927), *La Défaite, question morale* (1927 ou 1928), *Philosophie du recrutement* (1 April 1929), *La Condition des cadres dans l'armée*

(1930 or 1931), *Histoire des troupes du Levant* (17 August 1931), *Combats du "Temps de paix"* (1932), *Pour une politique de défense nationale* (4 February 1933), *Le Soldat de l'Antiquité* (1 April 1933), *Métier militaire* (5 December 1933), *Forgeons une armée de métier* (13 January 1934), *Le Problème belge* (1936). Texts collected by the Institut Charles-de-Gaulle, Paris, Plon, 1975.

Lettres, Notes et Carnets, I *1905–1918*; II *1918–juin 1940*; III *Juin 1940–juillet 1941*; IV *Juillet 1941–mai 1943*; V *Juin 1943–mai 1945*; VI *Mai 1945–juin 1951*; VII *1951–1958*; VIII *Juin 1958–décembre 1960*; IX *1961–1968*, Paris, Plon, 1980 to 1986. Texts chosen and introduced by Philippe de Gaulle.

GENERAL

FRANCE

Abbâs Ferhât, *La Nuit coloniale*, Paris, Julliard, 1962.
— *Autopsie d'une guerre*, Paris, Garnier, 1980.
Adenauer Konrad, *Mémoires*, (2 vols.), Paris, Hachette, 1967.
Aglion Raoul, *De Gaulle et Roosevelt*, Paris, Plon, 1984.
Agulhon Maurice and Nouschi André, *La France 1914–1940*, Paris, Nathan, 1971.
Aït-Ahmed Hocine, *Mémoires d'un combattant. L'espri: d'indépendance*, Paris, S. Messinger, 1983.
Alexandre Philippe, *Le Duel de Gaulle-Pompidou*, Paris, Grasset et Tallandier, 1970; Le Livre de poche, 1975.
Alexandre Philippe and Tubiana Raoul, *L'Elysée en péril. 2–30 mai 1968*, Paris, Fayard, 1969; Le Livre de poche, 1971.
Alphand Hervé, *L'Etonnement d'être. Journal 1939–1973*, Paris, Fayard, 1977.
Amouroux Henri, *Le 18 juin 1940*, Paris, Fayard, 1964; "J'ai lu" series, 1967.
— *La Grande Histoire des Français sous l'occupation*, six volumes published, Paris, Laffont, 1976 to 1986.
Argoud Antoine, *La Décadence, l'imposture et la tragédie*, Paris, Fayard, 1974.
Aron Raymond, *De Gaulle, Israël et les Juifs*, Paris, Plon, 1968.
— *Le Spectateur engagé*, Paris, Julliard, 1981.
— *Mémoires*, Paris, Julliard, 1983.
Aron Robert, *Charles de Gaulle*, Paris, Librairie académique Perrin, 1964.
— *Histoire de la libération de la France juin 1944–mai 1945*, Paris, Fayard, 1959; Le Livre de poche, 1967.
Astier de La Vigerie Emmanuel d', *Les Grands*, Paris, Gallimard, "L'air du temps" series, 1961.
— *De la chute à la libération de Paris 25 août 1944*, Paris, Gallimard, 1965.
Astoux André, *L'Oubli. 1946–1958*, Paris, Jean-Claude Lattès, 1974.
Auburtin Jean, *Charles de Gaulle, soldat et politique*, Paris, Les Editions universelles, 1945.
— *Le Colonel de Gaulle*, Paris, Plon, 1965.
Auriol Vincent, *Journal du septennat* (Pierre Nora), Paris, Armand Colin, 1970. One volume per year.
— *Mon septennat* (notes collected by Pierre Nora and Jacques Ozouf), Paris, Gallimard, 1970.

Avril Pierre, *Le Régime politique de la Ve République*, Paris, Editions LGDJ, 1967.

Azéma Jean-Pierre, *De Munich à la Libération*, Paris, Le Seuil, 1979.

Balladur Édouard, *L'Arbre de mai*, Paris, Atelier Marcel Jullian, 1979.

Baraduc Jacques, *Tout ce qu'on vous a caché* (the secret archives of the Reich), Preface by Josée Laval, Paris, L'Elan, 1949.

Barrès Philippe, *Charles de Gaulle*, Paris, Editions Plon-Cartier, 1945.

Bellescize Diane de, *Les Neuf Sages de la Résistance*, Paris, Institut Charles-de-Gaulle/Plon, 1979.

Beloff Nora, *Le général dit non*, Paris, Plon, 1964.

Beuve-Méry Hubert, *Onze Ans de règne (1958–1969)*, Paris, Flammarion, 1974.

Binoche Jacques, *L'Allemagne et le général de Gaulle (1924–1970)*, Paris, Plon, 1975.

Bloch-Morhange Jacques, *Le Gaullisme*, Paris, Plon, 1963.

Boisdeffre Pierre de, *De Gaulle malgré lui*, Paris, Albin Michel, 1978.

Boissieu Alain de, *Pour combattre avec de Gaulle. 1938–1946*, Paris, Plon, 1981.

— *Pour servir le Général. 1946–1970*, Paris, Plon, 1982.

Bonheur Gaston, *Charles de Gaulle*, Paris, Gallimard, 1958.

Bourget Pierre, *Paris 1944*, Paris, Plon, 1984.

Bouscat René, *De Gaulle-Giraud, dossier d'une mission*, Paris, Flammarion, 1967.

Bromberger Merry and Serge, *Les 13 complots du 13 mai*, Paris, Fayard, 1959.

Bruneau Jacques, *Tribulations d'un gaulliste en Gaule*, Paris, La Pensée universelle, 1983.

Buis Georges, *Les Fanfares perdues*, Paris, Le Seuil, 1975.

Burin des Roziers Étienne, *Retour aux sources*, Paris, Plon, 1985.

Buron Robert, *Carnets politiques de la guerre d'Algérie*, Paris, Plon, 1975.

Caillet Gérard, *De Gaulle, le journal du monde. 1890–1970*, Paris, Denoël, 1980.

Gapitant René, *De Gaulle dans la république*, Paris, Plon, 1958.

Cassin René, *Les Hommes partis de rien*, Paris, Plon, 1974.

Catroux Georges, *Dans la bataille de Méditerranée*, Paris, Julliard, 1949.

Cattaui Georges, *Charles de Gaulle, l'homme et son destin*, Paris, Fayard, 1960.

Caviglioli François and Pontaut Jean-Marie, *Les secrets de l'OAS*, Paris, Mercure de France, 1972.

Cerny Philippe G., *Une politique de grandeur*, Paris, Flammarion, 1980.

Chaban-Delmas Jacques, *L'Ardeur*, Paris, Stock, 1975; Le Livre de poche, 1976.

— *Charles de Gaulle*, Paris, Editions Paris-Match, 1980.

Chambrun René de, *Le procès Laval*, Paris, Editions France-Empire, 1984.

Charbonnel Jean, *L'Aventure de la fidélité*, Paris, Le Seuil, 1976.

Charlot Jean, *Le Phénomène gaulliste*, Paris, Le Seuil, 1970.

— *Les Français et de Gaulle*, Paris, Plon, 1971.

— *Le Gaullisme d'opposition (1946–1958)*, Paris, Fayard, 1983.

Closon Francis-Louis, *Commissaire de la République du général de Gaulle*, Paris, Julliard, 1980.

Cohen Samy, *De Gaulle, les gaullistes et Israël*, Paris, Alain Moreau, "Histoire et actualité" series, 1974.

Cointet Jean-Paul, *La France libre*, Paris, Presses universitaires de France, 1975.

Cotteret Jean-Marie and Moreau René, *Le Vocabulaire du général de Gaulle*, Paris, Armand Colin, 1969.

Coulet François, *Vertu des temps difficiles*, Paris, Plon, 1966.

Courrière Yves, *La Guerre d'Algérie* (4 vols.), Paris, Fayard, 1968 to 1971.

Courtois Stéphane, *Le PCF dans la guerre*, Paris, Ramsay, 1980.

Couve de Murville Maurice, *Une politique étrangère. 1958–1969*, Paris, Plon, 1971.

Danan Yves Max, *La Vie politique à Alger 1940–1944*, Paris, LGDJ, 1963.

Daniel Jean, *De Gaulle et l'Algérie*, Paris, Le Seuil, 1986.

Dansette Adrien, *Histoire de la libération de Paris*, Paris, Fayard, 1966.

Daridan Jean, *De la Gaule à de Gaulle, une histoire de France*, Paris, Le Seuil, 1977.

Debré Michel, *Mémoires* (I), Paris, Albin Michel, 1985.

Debré Michel et Debré Jean-Louis, *Le Gaullisme*, Paris, Plon, 1978.

Debû-Bridel Jacques, *Les Partis contre de Gaulle*, Paris, Editions Aimery Somogy, 1948.
— *De Gaulle contestataire*, Paris, Plon, "Tribune Libre" series, 1970.
— *De Gaulle et le CNR*, Paris, France-Empire, 1978.

Delarue Jacques, *L'OAS contre de Gaulle*, Paris, Fayard, 1981.

Démaret Pierre and Plume Christian, *Objectif de Gaulle*, Paris, Laffont, 1973.

Demey Evelyne, *Paul Reynaud, mon père*, Paris, Plon, 1980.

Derogy Jacques and Kahn Jean-François, *Les Secrets du ballottage*, Paris, Fayard, 1966.

Domenach Jean-Marie, *Barrès*, Paris, Le Seuil, "Ecrivains de toujours" series, 1954.
— *Le Retour du tragique*, Paris, Le Seuil, 1973.

Droit Michel, *Les Feux du crépuscule*, Paris, Plon, 1977.

Droz Bernard and Lever Évelyne, *Histoire de la guerre d'Algérie*, Paris, Le Seuil, 1982.

Dulac André, *Nos guerres perdues*, Paris, Fayard, 1969.

Dulong Claude, *La Vie quotidienne à l'Elysée au temps de Charles de Gaulle*, Paris, Hachette, 1974.

Dupérier Bernard, *La Vieille équipe*, Paris, Berger-Levrault, 1950.

Duroselle Jean-Baptiste, *La France et les Etats-Unis*, Paris, Le Seuil, 1976.
— *Histoire diplomatique de 1919 à nos jours*, Paris, Librairie Dalloz, 1978.
— *Politique étrangère de la France: l'abîme*, Paris, Imprimerie nationale, 1982.

Duverger Maurice, *La Cinquième République*, Paris, PUF, 1974.
— *La République des citoyens*, Paris, Ramsay, 1982.

Effel Jean, *L'Unique*, Textes et dessins de Jean Effel, Paris, Julliard, 1960.

Elgey Georgette, *Histoire de la Quatrième République*, I *La République des illusions. 1945–1957*; II *La République des contradictions. 1951–1954*, Paris, Fayard, 1968.

Escrienne Jean d', *Le général m'a dit*, Paris, Plon, 1973.
— *De Gaulle de loin et de près*, Paris, Plon, 1978.

Fabre-Luce Alfred, *Gaulle deux*, Paris, Julliard, 1958.
— *Le Plus Illustre des Français*, Paris, Julliard, 1960.
— *Haute Cour*, Paris, Julliard, 1962.
— *Le Couronnement du prince*, Paris, La Table ronde, 1964.
— *Le Général en Sorbonne*, Paris, La Table ronde, 1968.
— *L'Anniversaire*, Paris, Fayard, 1971.

— *Deux Crimes d'Alger*, Paris, Julliard, 1980.

Faure Edgar, *Mémoires I, Avoir toujours raison... c'est un grand tort*, Paris, Plon, 1982. *Mémoires II, Si tel doit être mon destin ce soir*, 1984.

Fauvet Jacques, *La IVᵉ République*, Paris, Fayard, 1959.

Ferniot Jean, *De Gaulle et le 13 mai*, Paris, Plon, 1965.

Ferro Maurice, *De Gaulle et l'Amérique. Une amitié tumultueuse*, Paris, Plon, 1973.

Flohic François, *Souvenirs d'outre-Gaulle*, Paris, Plon, 1979.

Fonde Jean-Julien, *Les Loups de Leclerc*, Paris, Plon, 1982.

Fontaine André, *Histoire de la guerre froide*, Paris, Le Seuil, "Points Histoire" series, 1983.

— *Histoire de la "détente". Un seul lit pour deux rêves*, Paris, Le Seuil, "Points Histoires" series, 1984.

Fouchet Christian, *Mémoires d'hier et de demain*, I *Au service du général de Gaulle*; II *Les lauriers sont coupés*, Paris, Plon, 1971, 1973.

Friang Brigitte, *Un autre Malraux*, Paris, Institut Charles-de-Gaulle/Plon, 1977.

Frossard André, *La France en général*, Paris, Plon, 1975.

Galante Pierre (with the assistance of Gaston Bonheur), *Le Général*, Paris, Presses de la Cité, "Cercle du Nouveau Livre d'Histoire", 1968, 1970.

Garas Félix, *Charles de Gaulle seul contre les pouvoirs*, Paris, Julliard, 1957.

Gaulmier Jean, *Les Ecrits du général de Gaulle*, Beirut, Société d'impression et d'édition, 1942.

— *Charles de Gaulle écrivain*, Paris-Alger, Editions Charlot, 1946.

Gillois André, *Histoire secrète des Français à Londres de 1940 à 1944*, Paris, Le Cercle du nouveau livre, 1973.

Gonnet Jean, *Les Origines bourguignonnes du général de Gaulle*, Chalon-sur-Saône, Éd. J. Renaux, 1945.

Gorce Paul-Marie de la, *La Republique et son armée*, Paris, Fayard, 1963.

— *De Gaulle entre deux mondes*, Paris, Fayard, 1964.

— *La France contre les empires*, Paris, Grasset, 1969.

Gozard Gilles, *De Gaulle face à l'Europe*, Paris, Institut Charles-de-Gaulle/Plon, "Espoir" series, 1976.

Granier Jacques, *De Gaulle et l'Alsace*, Strasbourg, Editions Dernières Nouvelles de Strasbourg, 1970.

Grenier Fernand, *C'était ainsi*, Paris, Editions sociales, 1959.

Grosser Alfred, *La Politique exterieure de la Vᵉ République*, Paris, Le Seuil, 1965.

Guichard Olivier, *Un chemin tranquille*, Paris, Flammarion, 1975.

— *Mon Général*, Paris, Grasset, 1980.

Guillemin Henri, *Le Général clair-obscur*, Paris, Le Seuil, 1984.

Gun Nerin E., *Pétain-Laval-De Gaulle*, Paris, Albin Michel, 1979.

Hamon Léo, *De Gaulle dans la République*, Paris, Plon, 1958.

Hess John L., *De Gaulle avait-il raison?* Tours, Mame, 1969.

Hettier de Boislambert Claude, *Les Fers de l'espoir*, Paris, Plon, 1978.

Hoffmann Stanley, *Essais sur la France. Déclin ou renouveau?*, Paris, Le Seuil, 1964.

Hoffmann Stanley and Inge, *De Gaulle artiste de la politique*, Paris, Le Seuil, 1973.

Hostache, René, *De Gaulle 1944. Victoire de la légitimité*, Paris, Institut Charles-de-Gaulle/Plon, "Espoir" series, 1978.

Huard Paul, *Le Colonel de Gaulle et ses blindés*, Paris, Plon, 1980.

Ibazizen Augustin, *Le Testament d'un Berbère*, Paris, Albatros, 1984.

Israël Gérard, *Le Dernier Jour de l'Algérie française*, Paris, Laffont, 1972.

Izard Georges, *Lettre affligée au général de Gaulle*, Paris, Laffont, 1964.

Jeanneney Jules, *Journal politique (1939–1942)*, introduced by J.-N. Jeanneney, Paris, Armand Colin, 1972.

Jobert Michel, *Mémoires d'avenir*, Paris, Grasset, 1974; Le Livre de poche, 1976.

Jouhaud Edmond, *La vie est un combat*, Paris, Fayard, 1975.
— *Serons-nous enfin compris?*, Paris, Albin Michel, 1984.

Jouve Edmond, *Le Général de Gaulle et la construction de l'Europe*, Paris, LGDJ, 1967.

Joxe Louis, *Victoires sur la nuit*, Paris, Flammarion, 1981.

Jullian Marcel, *L'Homme de 40*, Paris, Laffont, 1980.

Julliard Jacques, *La IVᵉ République*, Paris, Calmann-Lévy, 1968,

Kermoal Jacques, *Le Procès en canonisation de Charles de Gaulle*, Paris, Balland, 1970.

Kersaudy François, *De Gaulle et Churchill*, Paris, Plon, "Espoir" series, 1981.

Khellil Mohammed, *La Kabylie ou l'ancêtre sacrifié*, Paris, L'Harmattan, 1984.

Kissinger Henry, *Les Malentendus transatlantiques*, Paris, Denoël, 1965.
— *Mémoires*, I, *Les Années orageuses*, Paris, Fayard, 1982.

Lacouture Jean, *De Gaulle*, Paris, Le Seuil, 1965, 1969, 1970.
— *Citations du président de Gaulle*, Paris, Le Seuil, 1968.

Lapie Pierre-Olivier, *De Léon Blum à de Gaulle, le caractère et le pouvoir*, Paris, Fayard, 1971.

Laurent Jacques, *Mauriac sous de Gaulle*, Paris, La Table ronde, 1964.

Lebjaoui Mohammed, *Vérités sur la révolution algérienne*, Paris, Gallimard, 1970.

Ledwidge Bernard, *De Gaulle*, Paris, Flammarion, 1984.
— *De Gaulle et les Américains*, Paris, Flammarion, 1984.

Lefranc Pierre, *Voici tes fils*, Paris, Plon, 1974.
— *Avec qui vous savez*, Paris, Plon, 1979.

Lescop Renée, *Le Pari québécois du général*, Montréal, Boréal Express, 1981.

Limagne Pierre, *La Vᵉ République de Charles de Gaulle et Georges Pompidou*, Paris, France-Empire, 1978.

Longuechaud Henri, *"L'Abominable" Armistice*, Paris, Institut Charles-de-Gaulle/Plon, "Espoir" series, 1980.

Lottman Herbert, *Pétain*, Paris, Le Seuil, 1984.

Loubet Del Bayle Jean-Louis, *Les Non-Conformistes des années trente*, Paris, Le Seuil, 1969.

Loustaunau-Lacau Georges, *Mémoires d'un Français rebelle*, Paris, Laffont, 1948.

Maitrot Jean-Claude et Sicault Jean-Didier, *Les Conférences de presse du général de Gaulle*, Paris, Presses universitaires de France, 1969.

Mallen Pierre-Louis, *Vivre le Québec libre*, Paris, Plon, 1978.

Mallet Serge, *Le Gaullisme et la Gauche*, Paris, Le Seuil, 1965.

Malraux André, *Antimémoires 1*, Paris, Gallimard, 1967; revised and corrected edition, Gallimard, "Folio" series, 1972.
— *Les chênes qu'on abat...*, Paris, Gallimard, 1971.
— *La Corde et les Souris*, Paris, Gallimard, coll. "Folio" series, 1976.

Manac'h Étienne, *Mémoires d'extrême-Asie*, I, II, III, Paris, Fayard, 1977, 1980, 1982.

Mannoni Eugène, *Moi, général de Gaulle*, Paris, Le Seuil, 1964.

Martin Nicolas, *L'Héritage gaulliste*, Paris, Debresse, 1971.

Martin du Gard Maurice, *Les Mémorables*, III, Grasset, Paris, 1978.

Massip Roger, *De Gaulle et l'Europe*, Paris, Flammarion, 1963.

Massu, Jacques, *Le Torrent et la Digue*, Paris, Plon, 1972.

— *Baden 68*, Paris, Plon, 1983.

Mauriac Claude, *Aimer de Gaulle* (version recomposée et augmentée d'*Un autre de Gaulle*), Paris, Grasset, 1978.

— *Les Espaces imaginaires*, (*Le Temps immobile* no. 2), Paris, Grasset, 1975.

Mauriac François, *Le Bâillon dénoué*, Paris, Grasset, 1945.

— *Bloc-Notes 1952–1957*, Paris, Flammarion, 1958.

— *Le Nouveau Bloc-Notes 1958–1960*, Paris, Flammarion, 1961.

— *De Gaulle*, Paris, Grasset, 1964.

— *Le Nouveau Bloc-Notes 1961–1964*, Paris, Flammarion, 1968.

— *Le Nouveau Bloc-Notes 1965–1967*, Paris, Flammarion, 1970.

— *Le Dernier Bloc-Notes 1968–1970*, Paris, Flammarion, 1970.

Mauriac Jean, *Mort du général de Gaulle*, Paris, Grasset, 1972.

Mendès France Pierre, *La vérité guidait leurs pas*, Paris, Gallimard, 1976.

Mengin Robert, *De Gaulle à Londres vu par un Français libre*, Paris, La Table ronde, 1965.

Menthon Pierre de, *Je témoigne*, Paris, Editions du Cerf, 1979.

Mercadet Léon, *La Brigade Alsace-Lorraine*, Paris, Grasset, 1984.

Messmer Pierre and Larcan Alain, *Les Ecrits militaires de Charles de Gaulle*, Paris, Presses universitaires de France, 1985.

Michel Henri, *Histoire de la France libre*, Paris, PUF, "Que sais-je?" series, 1963.

— *Jean Moulin l'unificateur*, Paris, Hachette, 1971.

Michelet Claude, *Mon père Edmond Michelet*, Paris, Laffont, 1981.

Michelet Edmond, *Le Gaullisme, passionnante aventure*, Paris, Fayard, 1962.

— *La Querelle de la fidélité. Peut-on être gaulliste aujourd'hui?*, Preface by André Malraux, Paris, Fayard, 1971.

Miribel Elisabeth de, *La liberté souffre violence*, Paris, Plon, 1981.

Mitterrand François, *Le Coup d'État permanent*, Paris, Plon, 1964.

— *Ma part de vérité*, Paris, Fayard, 1969.

Moch Jules, *Rencontres avec Charles de Gaulle*, Paris, Plon, 1971.

— *Une si longue vie*, Paris, Laffont, 1976.

Monnet Jean, *Mémoires*, Paris, Fayard, 1976.

Montalais Jacques de, *Qu'est-ce que le gaullisme?*, Paris, Editions Mame, 1969.

Morazé Charles, *Le Général de Gaulle et la République*, Paris, Flammarion, 1972.

Mounier Monique, *De Gaulle vu par…*, Paris, Editions et Publications premières, 1969.

Muselier Émile, *De Gaulle contre le gaullisme*, Paris, Editions du Chêne, 1946.

Nachin Lucien, *Charles de Gaulle, général de France*, Paris, Plon, 1945.

Nobécourt Jacques, *Le Dernier coup de dés de Hitler*, Paris, Laffont, 1962.

— *Une histoire politique de l'armée*, I *De Pétain à Pétain (1919–1942)*, Paris, Le Seuil, 1967.

Noël Léon, *Comprendre de Gaulle*, Paris, Plon, 1972.
— *La Traversée du désert*, Paris, Plon, 1973.
— *L'Avenir du gaullisme. Le sort des institutions de la Ve République*, Paris, Plon, "Tribune libre" series, 1973.
— *De Gaulle et les Débuts de la Ve République*, Paris, Institut Charles-de-Gaulle/Plon, "Espoir" series, 1976.
Noguères Henri, *Histoire de la Résistance*, I–V, Paris, Laffont, 1967, 1969, 1972, 1976, 1981.
Ory Pascal, *Les Collaborateurs*, Paris, Le Seuil, 1976.
— *De Gaulle ou l'Ordre du discours*, Paris, Masson, "Leur vie" series, 1978.
Palewski Gaston, *Hier et Aujourd'hui*, Paris, Plon, 1974.
Parodi Jean-Luc, *Les Rapports entre le législatif et l'exécutif sous la Ve République*, Paris, Armand Colin, 1972.
Passeron André, *De Gaulle parle (1958–1962)*, Paris, Plon, 1962.
— *De Gaulle parle (1962–1966)*, Paris, Plon, 1966.
Passy (Colonel), *Souvenirs I et II*, Monaco, Editions Raoul Solar, 1947.
Pendar Kenneth, *Le Dilemme France–Etats-Unis, une aventure diplomatique*, Paris, Editions Self, 1948.
Pierre-Bloch Jean, *De Gaulle ou le Temps des méprises*, Paris, La Table ronde, 1960.
Pisani Edgard, *Le Général indivis*, Paris, Albin Michel 1974.
Planchais Jean, *Une histoire politique de l'armée*, II *De de Gaulle à de Gaulle (1940–1967)*, Paris, Le Seuil, 1967.
Plumyène Jean and Lasierra Raymond, *Le Dernier des Mérovingiens*, Paris, Balland, 1969.
Pognon Edmond, *De Gaulle et l'histoire de France: trente ans éclairés par vingt siècles*, Paris, Albin Michel, 1970.
— *De Gaulle et l'armée*, Paris, Institut Charles-de-Gaulle/Plon, "Espoir" series, 1976.
Poirier Lucien, *Essais de stratégie théorique*, Paris, Fondation Etudes Défense nationale, 1982.
Pompidou Georges, *Pour rétablir une vérité*, Paris, Flammarion, 1982.
Pouget Jean, *Le Manifeste du camp no. 1*, Paris, Fayard, 1970.
— *Un certain capitaine de Gaulle*, Paris, Fayard, 1973.
Prate Alain, *Les Batailles économiques du général de Gaulle*, Paris, Institut Charles-de-Gaulle/Plon, "Espoir" series, 1978.
Prigent Mireille, *Tanguy Prigent*, Paris, Club socialiste du livre, 1982.
Purtschet Christian, *Le Rassemblement du peuple français 1947–1953*, Paris, Editions Cujas, 1967.
Quermonne Jean-Louis, *Le Gouvernement de la France dans la Ve République*, Paris, Dalloz, 1980.
Raïssac Guy, *Un combat sans merci: l'affaire Pétain–de Gaulle*, Paris, Albin Michel, 1966.
Rebatet Lucien, *Les Décombres*, Paris, Denoël, 1942.
Rémond René, *La Droite en France, de la 1re Restauration à la Ve République*, II *1940–juin 1968*, Paris, Aubier/Montaigne, 1968.
— *Le retour de De Gaulle*, Paris, Editions Complexe, 1985.

Rémy (colonel, pseudonym of Renault Gilbert), *De Gaulle, cet inconnu*, Monaco, Editions Raoul Solar, 1947.
— *Dix ans avec de Gaulle, 1940–1950*, Paris, France-Empire, 1971.

Revel Jean-François, *Le Style du général. Mai 1958–juin 1959*, Paris, Julliard, 1959.

Rey-Herme Yves, *De Gaulle écrivain. Mémoires de guerre*, Paris, Hatier, coll. "Profil" series, 1978.

Reynaud Paul, *La Politique étrangère du gaullisme*, Paris, Julliard, 1964.

Ribaud André (pseudonym of Roger Fressoz), *La Cour – Chronique du royaume*, Paris, Julliard, 1961.
— *Le Roi – Chronique de la cour*, Paris, Julliard, 1962.

Rioux Jean-Pierre, *La France de la Quatrième République*, I *L'Ardeur et la Nécessité (1944–1952)*, Paris, Le Seuil, 1980; II *L'Expansion et l'Impuissance*, Paris, Le Seuil, 1983.

Robichon Jacques, *Le 8 décembre 1942, jour "J" en Afrique*, Paris, Laffont, 1964.

Rouanet Anne and Pierre, *Les Trois Derniers Chagrins du général de Gaulle*, Paris, 1980.

Roy Jules, *Une affaire d'honneur*, Paris, Plon, 1983.

Ruehl Lothar, *La Politique militaire de la Ve République*, Paris, Presses de la FNSP (Fondation nationale des sciences politiques), 1976.

Sadoun Marc, *Les Socialistes sous l'occupation. Résistance et collaboration*, Paris, FNSP, 1982.

Saint-Robert Philippe de, *Le Jeu de la France*, Paris, Julliard, 1967.
— *Les Septennats interrompus*, Paris, Laffont, 1975.

Salan Raoul, *Mémoires*, III *Algérie française*, Paris, Presses de la Cité, 1972; IV *Fin d'un Empire. L'Algérie, de Gaulle et moi*, Paris, Presses de la Cité, 1974.

Sandhal Pierre, *De Gaulle sans képi*, Paris, La Jeune Parque, 1948.

Sauvy Alfred, *De Paul Reynaud à Charles de Gaulle*, Paris, Casterman, 1972.

Schneider Bertrand, *La Ve République et l'Algérie*, Paris, Editions Témoignage chrétien, 1959.

Schlesinger Arthur, *Les 1000 jours de Kennedy*, Paris, Denoël, 1966.

Schoenbrunn David, *Les Trois Vies de Charles de Gaulle*, Paris, Julliard, 1965.

Schumann Maurice, *Honneur et Patrie* (préface du général de Gaulle), Paris, Editions du Livre français, 1945.
— *L'Homme des tempêtes*, Paris, Éd. du Mail, 1946.
— *Un certain 18 juin*, Paris, Plon, 1980.

Serigny Alain de, *La Révolution du 13 mai*, Paris, Plon, 1958.

Seydoux de Clausonne François, *Mémoires d'outre-Rhin*, Paris, Grasset, 1975.

Simoen Jean-Claude, *De Gaulle à travers la caricature internationale*, Paris, Albin Michel, 1969; Le Livre de poche, 1973.

Sorensen Théodore, *Kennedy*, Paris, Gallimard, 1966.

Soustelle Jacques, *Envers et contre tout, de Londres à Alger 1940–1942*, Paris, Laffont, 1947.
— *Envers et contre tout, d'Alger à Paris 1942–1944*, Paris, Laffont, 1950.
— *28 ans de gaullisme*, Paris, La Table ronde, 1968; "J'ai lu" series, 1972.
— *L'Espérance Trahie*, Paris, Éd. Alma, 1962.

Suffert Georges, *Charles de Gaulle* (illustrated by André Gobert), Paris, Editions Groupes Express, 1970.

Sulzberger Cyrus L., *En observant de Gaulle*, Paris, Plon, 1962.
— *Dans le tourbillon de l'histoire*, Paris, Albin Michel, 1971.
Terrenoire Louis, *De Gaulle et l'Algérie*, Paris, Fayard, 1964.
— *De Gaulle vivant*, Paris, Plon, 1971.
— *De Gaulle 1947–1954: pourquoi l'échec*, Paris, Plon, 1981.
Tesson Philippe, *De Gaulle Ier*, Paris, Albin Michel, 1965.
Tillon Charles, *On chantait rouge*, Paris, Laffont, 1977.
Tocnaye Alain de la, *Comment je n'ai pas tué de Gaulle*, Paris, Editions Edmond
    Nalis, 1969.
Torrès Tereska, *Les Années anglaises – Journal intime de guerre (1939–1945)*,
    Paris, Le Seuil, 1981.
Touchard Jean, *Le Gaullisme, 1940–1969*, Paris, Le Seuil, "Points Histoire"
    series, 1978.
Tournoux Jean-Raymond, *Secrets d'État*, Paris, Plon, 1960; Presses Pocket,
    1972.
— *Pétain et de Gaulle*, Paris, Plon, 1964; Presses Pocket (abridged edition),
    1968.
— *L'Histoire secrète*, Paris, Union générale d'éditions, 1965.
— *La Tragédie du général*, Paris, Plon and Paris-Match, 1967.
— *Le Mois de mai du général*, Paris, Plon, 1969; Presses Pocket, 1970.
— *Jamais dit*, Paris, Plon, 1971.
— *Le Tourment et la Fatalité*, Paris, Plon, 1974.
Tricot Bernard, *Les Sentiers de la paix. Algérie 1958–1962*, Paris, Plon, 1972.
Trinquier Roger, *Le Coup d'État du 13 mai*, Paris, Editions L'Esprit nouveau,
    1958.
Vaisse Maurice, *Alger 1961: le putsch*, Paris, Editions Complexe, 1985.
Vallon Louis, *L'Anti de Gaulle*, Paris, Le Seuil, 1969.
— *De Gaulle et la démocratie*, Paris, La Table ronde, 1972.
Vendroux Jacques, *Cette chance que j'ai eue*, Paris, Plon, 1974.
— *Ces grandes années que j'ai vécues*, Paris, Plon, 1975.
— *Yvonne de Gaulle, ma sœur*, Paris, Plon, 1980.
Viansson-Ponté Pierre, *Risques et Chances de la Ve République*, Paris, Plon, 1959.
— *Les Gaullistes, rituel et annuaire*, Paris, Le Seuil, 1963.
— *Après de Gaulle, qui?*, Paris, Le Seuil, 1966.
— *Histoire de la République gaullienne*, I *La Fin d'une époque. Mai 1958–juillet
    1962; II Le Temps des orphelins 1962–1969*, Paris, Fayard, 1970, 1971
    (reprinted in the "Bouquins" Series, Paris, Laffont, 1984).
Viorst Milton, *Les Alliés ennemis: de Gaulle et Roosevelt*, Paris, Denoël, 1967.
Walters Vernon A., *Services discrets*, Paris, Plon, 1979.
Weygand Maxime, *En lisant les Mémoires de guerre du général de Gaulle*, Paris,
    Flammarion, 1955.
White Dorothy S., *Les Origines de la discorde: de Gaulle, la France libre et les Alliés
    1940–1942*, Paris, Editions de Trévise, 1967.
Winock Michel, *La République se meurt: chronique 1956–1968*, Paris, Le Seuil,
    1978.

UNITED STATES

Bohlen Charles, *Witness to History*, New York, W.W. Norton & Co., 1973.
Eisenhower Dwight D., *Crusade in Europe*, London, William Heinemann, 1949.
Kissinger Henry, *The Troubled Partnership*, New York, McGraw Hill, 1965.
 — *Years of Upheaval*, 1973–77, London, Michael Joseph, 1982.
Leahy Admiral W., *I Was There*, London, Victor Gollancz, 1950.
Patton, Jr. George S., *War as I Knew it*, London, W.H. Allen, 1948.
Sherwood Robert, *Roosevelt and Hopkins*, New York, Harper, 1948.
Sulzberger Cyrus L., *De Gaulle and Algeria*,
Sulzberger Cyrus L., *A Long Row of Candles*,

GREAT BRITAIN

Beloff, Nora, *The General Says No*, London, Penguin Books, 1963.
Borden, Mary, *Journey down a Blind Alley*, London, Hutchinson, 1946.
Churchill, Sir Winston, *The Second World War* (6 vols.), London, Cassell, 1948–53.
Eban, A., *An Autobiography*, London, Weidenfeld & Nicolson, 1978.
Eden A., *The Reckoning*, London, Cassell, 1965.
Horne, A., *A Savage War*, London, Macmillan, 1977.
Kersaudy, François, *De Gaulle*, London, William Collins, 1981.
Ledwidge, Bernard, *De Gaulle*, London, Weidenfeld & Nicolson, 1982.
Macmillan, Harold, *Pointing the Way* 1959–1961, Vol. 5, London, Macmillan, 1972.
Murphy, R., *Diplomat among Warriors*, New York, Doubleday, 1964.
Pickles, Dorothy, *The Uneasy Entente: French Foreign Policy and Franco-British Misunderstanding*, London, Oxford University Press, 1966.
Spears, Sir Edward, *Assignment to Catastrophe* (2 vols.), London, William Heinemann, 1954.
 — *The Fall of France*, London, William Heinemann, 1954.
Werth, Alexander, *France 1940–1944*, Ed. Robert Hale, London, 1956.
 — *De Gaulle, a Political Biography*, London, Penguin Books, 1965.

COLLECTIONS

Burnier Marc-Antoine et l'équipe d'Édition spéciale, *La Chute du général*, Paris, Éditions et Publications premières, 1969.
Cazenave Michel and Germain-Thomas Olivier, *Charles de Gaulle*, Paris, Editions de l'Herne, cahier No. 21, *Recueil de témoignages et d'études*, 1973.
Duhamel Olivier, Parodi Jean-Luc and others: *La Constitution de la Ve République*, colloque de l'AFSP, Paris, Fondation nationale des sciences politiques, 1984.
Druon Maurice, Marin Jean and others, *Charles de Gaulle*, Paris, Editions Réalités-Hachette, "Génies et Realités" series, 1973.
Friedlander Saül and others, *La Politique étrangère du général de Gaulle*, Paris, Presses universitaires de France, 1985.

Hoffmann Stanley, Kindleberger Charles, Wylie Lawrence, Pitts Jesse, Duroselle Jean-Baptiste, Goguel François, *A la recherche de la France*, Paris, Le Seuil, 1963.

Isoart Paul and others, *L'Indochine française 1940–1945*, Paris, Presses universitaires de France, 1982.

Meyer Jacques and others, *Vie et Mort des Français 1939–1945*, Paris, Hachette, 1971.

Paris-Match, *De Gaulle 1890–1970*, Paris, Editions Paris-Match, 1970.

Pilleul Gilbert and others, *L'Entourage et de Gaulle*, Paris, Institut Charles-de-Gaulle/Plon, "Espoir" series, 1979.

RPF, *La France sera la France, ce que veut Charles de Gaulle*, Paris, Editions RPF, imprimerie F. Bouchy, 1950–.

De Gaulle et le service de l'État, des collaborateurs du général de Gaulle témoignent, Paris, Institut Charles-de-Gaulle/Plon, "Espoir" series, 1977.

OAS parle, Paris, Julliard, "Archives" series, 1964.

ALBUMS

De Gaulle par l'affiche, Paris, Plon, 1980.

Tim, *Une certaine idée de la France*, Paris, Tchou, 1969.

JOURNALS

Espoir, Institut Charles-de-Gaulle, quarterly.

En ce temps-là, a Hennin publication, weekly, 71 issues since April 1971 edited by Henri Gautrelet and Guy Schoeller, André Frossard, A. M. Gérard and André Lacaze.

FILMS

Olivier Guichard, P. A. Boutang, *Mon Général*.

Pierre Lefranc, Pierre Cardinal, *Les Mémoires de Guerre*.

André Harris and Alain de Sédouy, *Français, si vous saviez...*

Marcel Ophuls, Harris and Sédouy, *Le Chagrin et la Pitié*.

Archives du Quai d'Orsay, 1944–1946.

Archives du Rassemblement du peuple français.

Archives de l'armée de terre, Vincennes.

Private archives of Georgette Elgey and Jean Mauriac (both of whom I wish particularly to thank).